world development report 2011

Conflict, Security, and Development

world development report 2011

Conflict, Security, and Development

THE WORLD BANK
Washington, DC

1818 H Street NW
Washington DC 20433
Telephone: 202-473-1000
Internet: www.worldbank.org

1 2 3 4 13 12 11 10

Softcover

ISBN: 978-0-8213-8439-8
ISSN: 0163-5085
eISBN: 978-0-8213-8440-4
DOI: 10.1596/978-0-8213-8439-8

Hardcover

ISBN: 978-0-8213-8500-5
ISSN: 0163-5085
DOI: 10.1596/978-0-8213-8500-5

Cover design: Heads of State

Photo credits: Overview Picasso/Corbis Images; **Chapter 1** Thomas Dworzak/Magnum Photos; **Chapter 2** Christopher Anderson/Magnum Photos; **Chapter 3** Jonas Bendiksen/Magnum Photos; **Chapter 4** Graeme Williams/Panos; **Chapter 5** Christopher Furlong/Getty Images; **Chapter 6** Gulbuddin Elham/Aina Photo; **Chapter** 7 Marco Vernaschi/Pulitzer Center; **Chapter 8** Ron Haviv/VII/Corbis; **Chapter 9** Werner Bischof/Magnum Photos

Contents

Boxes

Features

Overview

Chapters

Figures

Maps

Tables

Foreword

In 1944, delegates from 45 countries gathered at Bretton Woods to consider the economic causes of the World War that was then still raging, and how to secure the peace. They agreed to create the International Bank for Reconstruction and Development (IBRD), the original institution of what has become the World Bank Group. As the delegates noted, "Programs of reconstruction and development will speed economic progress everywhere, will aid political stability and foster peace." The IBRD approved its first loan to France in 1947 to aid in the rebuilding of that country.

Over 60 years later, the "R" in IBRD has a new meaning: reconstructing Afghanistan, Bosnia, Haiti, Liberia, Rwanda, Sierra Leone, Southern Sudan, and other lands of conflict or broken states. Paul Collier's book, *The Bottom Billion,* highlighted the recurrent cycles of weak governance, poverty, and violence that have plagued these lands. Not one low-income country coping with these problems has yet achieved a single Millennium Development Goal. And the problems of fragile states spread easily: They drag down neighbors with violence that overflows borders, because conflicts feed on narcotics, piracy, and gender violence, and leave refugees and broken infrastructure in their wake. Their territories can become breeding grounds for far-reaching networks of violent radicals and organized crime.

In 2008, I gave a speech on "Securing Development" to the International Institute for Strategic Studies. I chose the forum to emphasize the interconnections among security, governance, and development, and to make the point that the separate disciplines are not well integrated to address the inter-related problems. I outlined the challenge: bringing security and development together to put down roots deep enough to break the cycles of fragility and conflict.

As we are now seeing again in the Middle East and North Africa, violence in the 21st century differs from 20th-century patterns of interstate conflict and methods of addressing them. Stove-piped government agencies have been ill-suited to cope, even when national interests or values prompt political leaders to act. Low incomes, poverty, unemployment, income shocks such as those sparked by volatility in food prices, rapid urbanization, and inequality between groups all increase the risks of violence. External stresses, such as trafficking and illicit financial flows, can add to these risks.

The *2011 World Development Report* looks across disciplines and experiences drawn from around the world to offer some ideas and practical recommendations on how to move beyond conflict and fragility and secure development. The key messages are important for all countries—low, middle, and high income—as well as for regional and global institutions:

First, *institutional legitimacy is the key to stability.* When state institutions do not adequately protect citizens, guard against corruption, or provide access to justice; when markets do not provide job opportunities; or when communities have lost social cohesion—the likelihood of violent conflict increases. At the earliest stages, countries often need to restore public confidence in basic collective action even before rudimentary institutions can be transformed. Early wins—actions that can generate quick, tangible results—are critical.

Second, *investing in citizen security, justice, and jobs is essential to reducing violence.* But there are major structural gaps in our collective capabilities to support these areas. There are places where fragile states can seek help to build an army, but we do not yet have similar resources for building police forces or corrections systems. We need to put greater emphasis on early projects to create jobs, especially through the private sector. The Report provides insight into the importance of the involvement of women in political coalitions, security and justice reform, and economic empowerment.

Third, *confronting this challenge effectively means that institutions need to change.* International agencies and partners from other countries must adapt procedures so they can respond with agility and speed, a longer-term perspective, and greater staying power. Assistance needs to be integrated and coordinated; multi-donor trust funds have proven useful in accomplishing these aims while lessening the burdens of new governments with thin capacity. We need a better handoff between humanitarian and development agencies. And we need to accept a higher level of risk: If legislatures and inspectors expect only the upside, and just pillory the failures, institutions will steer away from the most difficult problems and strangle themselves with procedures and committees to avoid responsibility. This Report suggests some specific actions and ways of measuring results.

Fourth, we need to adopt *a layered approach.* Some problems can be addressed at the country level, but others need to be addressed at a regional level, such as developing markets that integrate insecure areas and pooling resources for building capacity. Some actions are needed at a global level, such as building new capacities to support justice reform and the creation of jobs; forging partnerships between producer and consumer countries to stem illegal trafficking; and acting to reduce the stresses caused by food price volatility.

Fifth, in adopting these approaches, we need to be aware that *the global landscape is changing.* Regional institutions and middle income countries are playing a larger role. This means we should pay more attention to south-south and south-north exchanges, and to the recent transition experiences of middle income countries.

The stakes are high. A civil conflict costs the average developing country roughly 30 years of GDP growth, and countries in protracted crisis can fall over 20 percentage points behind in overcoming poverty. Finding effective ways to help societies escape new outbursts or repeated cycles of violence is critical for global security and global development—but doing so requires a fundamental rethinking, including how we assess and manage risk.

Any such changes must be based on a clear roadmap, and on strong incentives. I hope this Report will help others and ourselves in sketching such a roadmap.

Robert B. Zoellick
President
The World Bank Group

Acknowledgments

This Report has been prepared by a core team led by Sarah Cliffe and Nigel Roberts and comprising Erik Alda, David Andersson, Kenneth Anye, Holly Benner, Natalia Cieslik, Ivan Crouzel, Markus Kostner, Daniel Maree, Nicholas Marwell, Gary Milante, Stephen Ndegwa, Kyle Peters, Nadia Selim, Pia Simonsen, Nicholas van Praag, Suranjan Weeraratne, and Nikolas Win Myint. Bruce Jones served as a Senior External Advisor to the team and made major contributions as did James Fearon, Jack Goldstone, and Lant Pritchett. Markus Kostner acted as Co-Director during part of the Report's preparation.

Bruce Ross-Larson was the principal editor.

World Development Report 2011 is co-sponsored by Development Economics (DEC) and the Operations Policy and Country Services (OPC). The work was conducted under the general guidance of Justin Yifu Lin in DEC and Jeffrey Gutman and Joachim von Amsberg in OPC. Caroline Anstey, Paul Birmingham, Hassan Cisse, Shahrokh Fardoust, Varun Gauri, Faris Hadad-Zervos, Ann Harrison, Karla Hoff, Phillip Keefer, Anne-Marie Leroy, Rui Manuel De Almeida Coutinho, Alastair McKechnie, Vikram Raghavan, and Deborah Wetzel also provided valuable guidance. The WDR team extends a special thank you to the World Bank's Fragile and Conflict-Affected Countries Group (OPCFC) and the Global Expert Team on Fragile and Conflict-Affected Countries (FCS GET) for their extensive inputs and feedback throughout the WDR development process.

An Advisory Council comprised of Madeleine Albright, Louise Arbour, Lakhdar Brahimi, Mohamed Ibn Chambas, Paul Collier, Nitin Desai, Carlos Alberto dos Santos Cruz, Martin Griffiths, Mohamed "Mo" Ibrahim, H.E. Paul Kagame, Ramtane Lamamra, Shivshankar Menon, Louis Michel, Jorge Montaño, Jay Naidoo, Kenzo Oshima, Surin Pitsuwan, Zeid Ra'ad Al-Hussein, Marta Lucía Ramírez de Rincón, H.E. Ellen Johnson Sirleaf, Dmitri Trenin, Wu Jianmin, and George Yeo provided extensive and excellent advice.

World Bank President Robert B. Zoellick provided guidance and comments.

Many others inside and outside the World Bank contributed with comments and inputs. The Development Data Group contributed to the data appendix and was responsible for the Selected World Development Indicators.

The team benefitted greatly from a wide range of consultations. Meetings were held in Afghanistan, Austria, Australia, Belgium, Canada, China, Colombia, the Democratic Republic of the Congo, Denmark, Egypt, Ethiopia, France, Germany, Haiti, India, Indonesia, Iraq, Italy, Japan, Kenya, Lebanon, Mali, Mexico, Nepal, the Netherlands, Norway, Pakistan, Rwanda, Saudi Arabia, South Africa, Spain, Sudan, Sweden, Switzerland, Timor-Leste, the United Kingdom, the United States, West Bank and Gaza, and Yemen. The team wishes to thank participants in these workshops, videoconferences, and online discussions, which included policy makers, government officials, and representatives of nongovernmental, civil society and private sector organizations.

The team would like to acknowledge the generous support of the African Union, the Association of Southeast Asian Nations, the European Union, the Government of Australia, the

Government of Canada, the Government of China, the Government of Denmark, the Government of Finland, the Government of Germany, the Government of Japan, the Government of Mexico, the Government of the Netherlands, the Government of Norway, the Government of Sweden, the Government of Switzerland, the Government of the United Kingdom, the Organization for Economic Cooperation and Development, and the United Nations.

The team also wishes to acknowledge the tireless support of the WDR Production Team: Jessica Ardinoto, Nga (Ty) Lopez, Bertha Medina, Brónagh Murphy, and Jason Victor. The resource management support of Irina Sergeeva and Sonia Joseph is also much appreciated as well as the excellent production, publishing, translation, and dissemination support provided by the Office of the Publisher and GSD Translation Services, with special thanks to Mary Fisk, Stephen McGroarty, Nancy Lammers, Santiago Pombo-Bejarano, Denise Bergeron, Janet Sasser, Jose de Buerba, Mario Trubiano, Alison Reeves, Mayya Revzina, Cecile Jannotin, and Hector Hernaez for their contributions. Debra Naylor and Gerry Quinn provided design and graphics expertise. We also thank Ivar Cederholm, Jean-Pierre Djomalieu, Sharon Faulkner, Vivian Hon, Gytis Kanchas, Rajvinder (Dolly) Kaur, Alexander Kent, Esabel Khoury, Nacer Megherbi, Thyra Nast, Jimmy Olazo, Nadia Piffaretti, Carol Pineau, Jean Gray Ponchamni, Swati Priyadarshini, Janice Rowe-Barnwell, Merrell Tuck-Primdahl, and Constance Wilhel for their kind support to the team. Many thanks as well to Jeffrey Lecksell for expert production of map graphics. We appreciate the efforts of the World Bank's New York Office, including Dominique Bichara and Tania Meyer, as well as colleagues who assisted with WDR consultations worldwide—including those in the World Bank offices in Afghanistan, Belgium, China, Colombia, the Democratic Republic of the Congo, Egypt, Ethiopia, Haiti, India, Indonesia, Iraq, Italy, Japan, Kenya, Lebanon, Mali, Mexico, Nepal, Pakistan, Rwanda, Saudi Arabia, South Africa, Sudan, Timor-Leste, West Bank and Gaza, and Yemen.

Glossary

Organized violence—the use or threat of physical force by groups. Includes state actions against other states or against civilians, civil wars, electoral violence between opposing sides, communal conflicts based on regional, ethnic, religious or other group identities or competing economic interests, gang-based violence and organized crime and international nonstate armed movements with ideological aims. While an important topic for development, we do not cover domestic or interpersonal violence. At times we refer to *violence* or *conflict* as a short-hand for *organized violence*, understood in these terms. Many countries address certain forms of violence, such as terrorist attacks by nonstate armed movements, as matters that are subject to their criminal laws.

Repeated cycles of violence—Countries or subnational areas that have seen more than one episode of organized violence for 20–30 years.

Stresses—The political, social, security, or economic risks that correlate with organized violence. Violence is more likely when a combination of stresses operate in an environment characterized by weak institutions. Stresses can be internal—within the potential capacity of an individual state to control—or external, emanating from regional or global dynamics.

Confidence—Trust between groups of citizens who have been divided by violence, between citizens and the state, and between the state and other stakeholders (neighbors, international partners, investors).

Expectations—The way people make judgments about the future and how it will affect them, their families, and their communities. In situations where a track record of violence has created low trust, both excessively low and excessively high expectations can create problems for government policy.

Elite pacts—Formal or informal agreements by the holders of political, military, or economic power. These agreements, often enforced through coercion and patronage, are typically "personalized," based on individual agreements. Throughout history the key motivating factor in forming an elite pact has been the wish to contain violence and to secure the property and economic interests and opportunities of pact members. The Report argues that elite pacts can provide short term security but that violence often recurs unless the pact broadens and is accompanied by institutional transformation.

Institutions—The formal and informal "rules of the game." They include formal rules, written laws, organizations, informal norms of behavior and shared beliefs—and the organizational forms that exist to implement and enforce these norms (both state and nonstate organizations). Institutions shape the interests, incentives, and behaviors that can facilitate violence. Unlike elite pacts, institutions are impersonal—they continue to function irrespective of the presence of particular leaders, and thus provide greater guarantees of sustained resilience to violence. Institutions operate at all levels of society—local, national, regional, and global.

Fragility and fragile situations—Periods when states or institutions lack the capacity, accountability, or legitimacy to mediate relations between citizen groups and between citizens and the state, making them vulnerable to violence. Research for the Report reinforces the close link between institutional fragility and the risk of conflict.

Legitimacy—Normatively, this term denotes a broad-based belief that social, economic, or political arrangements and outcomes are proper and just. The concept is typically applied to institutions. Legitimacy is acquired by building trust and confidence among various parties. Forms of legitimacy include process legitimacy (which relates to the way in which decisions are made), performance legitimacy (which relates to action, including the delivery of public goods), and international legitimacy (which relates to the discharge of values and responsibilities that international law view as the responsibility of states).

Capacity—The ability of institutions to carry out their core functions efficiently and effectively. When states lack this capacity, they cannot mitigate stresses that might induce organized violence.

Accountability—The ability of institutions to be responsive to citizens, including abiding by their aggregated preferences, disclosing necessary information, permitting citizen participation in decision-making, and allowing for citizen sanction of public officials on the basis of publicly recognized norms and procedures.

Citizen security—Both freedom from physical violence and freedom from fear of violence. Applied to the lives of *all* members of a society (whether nationals of the country or otherwise), it encompasses security at home, in the workplace, and in political, social, and economic interactions with the state and other members of society. Similar to human security, "citizen security" places people at the center of efforts to prevent and recover from violence.

Justice and inclusion—The Report uses justice in two ways. The first use refers to the broadly held notion of *fairness.* While this varies in different societies, it is a universally identifiable concept and carries the notion of fair process and due outcomes in the distribution of political power, resources, opportunities, and sanctions. The second use is more specific: the institutions that are central to resolving conflicts arising over alleged violations or different interpretations of the rules that societies create to govern members' behavior; and that, as a consequence, are central to strengthening the normative framework (laws and rules) that shapes public and private actions. This includes the elements of the justice system most critical to preventing or transitioning out of violence: core criminal justice functions—the ability of the police, courts, and penal system to fairly investigate, prosecute and punish acts linked to organized violence—and institutions required to address underlying disputes that contribute to violence (for example, institutions that deal with land and property dispute resolution).

Transition moments—Events that make new efforts to prevent or recover from violence possible. These can involve space for deep and wide-ranging change (for example, the end of a war, a deep national crisis, a change in government after one party has been in power many years) or more limited change (a new governmental reform plan or shift in key appointments, negotiations or coalition-building between different actors in society, events that spur reflection in society such as riots, military defeats, natural disasters, or key political anniversaries).

Collaborative, inclusive-enough coalitions—Unlike elite pacts, these coalitions involve broader segments of society—local governments, business, labor, civil society movements, in some cases opposition parties. Coalitions are "inclusive enough" when they involve the parties necessary to restore confidence and transform institutions and help create continued momentum for positive change; and when there is local legitimacy for excluding some groups—for example because of electoral gains, or because groups or individuals have been involved in abuses.

Signaling—Demonstrating an intention to break with past policies—in the context of this Report, policies that have increased violent risks. Signals are designed to mobilize coalitions of support, and can be made through announcements or through actions—for example, appointments and redeployments of security forces.

Commitment mechanisms—Ways to persuade stakeholders that intentions to break with past policies will not be reversed, including creating independent functions for implementing or monitoring agreements.

Early results—Visible improvements to security, justice, and inclusion, economic opportunities, and services, delivered in the first 100 days and the first 12 months following an announced change in policy prevent or recover from violent crises.

Sequencing and prioritizing reforms—Deciding on the type and scope of changes societies will make first, those that will be addressed later, and the timeframes for achieving change.

Pragmatic, best-fit approaches—Programs, institutions and reforms that are not technically the lowest-cost option for achieving outcomes, but are adapted to local political, security, and institutional realities.

Transforming institutions—Developing over time "rules of the game" that increase resilience to risks of violence, including laws, organizations, norms of behavior, and shared beliefs that ensure that the benefits from individuals choosing to act peacefully and lawfully exceed the costs.

Methodological Note

One of the greatest challenges in researching lessons on violence prevention and recovery is the lack of available quantitative and qualitative data, due to challenges of security and access, along with low statistical capacity. Even in the World Bank's comprehensive data sets, countries most affected by violence often register empty data columns. Polling, household surveys, and evaluations of the impacts of policies and project interventions are also limited in violence-affected countries and regions.

A growing body of literature on civil war focuses more on the causes of war than on the policies to prevent or recover from violence, and less analysis is available on organized criminal violence. Over the past decade, however, this Report has benefited from a growing body of multi-disciplinary research (political science, economics, sociology, psychology, security studies) and policy papers on peacebuilding, statebuilding, conflict prevention, reconstruction and stabilization operations, peacekeeping, and conflict recovery, complemented by a large data set from multiple sources (the Uppsala Conflict Data Program, the International Peace Research Institute of Oslo, and Human Security Report Project, homicide data from national sources, United Nations Office on Drugs and Crime (UNODC), the World Health Organization (WHO), geospatial coding of conflict events and data from the Armed Conflict Location and Event Database and polling from regional barometers as well as surveys conducted by Fafo).

As the topics of violence and development transcend academic and policy disciplines, it has been crucial that a common understanding of key terms be developed and used for the report (see the glossary). For this project, background papers by respected academic researchers have produced significant new econometric work on the relationship between institutions and violence, further complemented by country and regional case study research and consultations.

Learning from experience: Generating a global conversation

The WDR team sought to complement research by generating a global conversation with national reformers, civil society and private sector leaders, as well as regional and international policymakers, grappling with violence in diverse regions worldwide. The team focused explicitly on moving this conversation beyond the 'traditional' Organisation for Economic Co-operation and Development (OECD) donors and multilateral partners for the World Bank, to engage with national reformers, middle income country policy makers, regional institutions and diplomatic and security partners, including:

- Consultations and multi-stakeholder round-tables with government leadership, civil society, private sectors, media and international actors in some twenty low- and middle-income countries and regions that are presently affected by violent conflict, or have managed to escape from it in recent years. Countries and regions visited included Afghanistan, Austria, Australia, Belgium, Canada, China, Colombia, the Democratic Republic of the Congo, Denmark, Egypt, Ethiopia, France, Germany, Haiti, India, Indonesia, Iraq, Italy, Japan, Kenya, Lebanon, Mali, Mexico, Nepal, the Netherlands, Norway, Pakistan, Rwanda,

Saudi Arabia, South Africa, Spain, Sudan, Sweden, Switzerland, Timor-Leste, the United Kingdom, the United States, West Bank and Gaza, and Yemen.

- Regional discussions with policymakers and experts to explore diverse experiences and perspectives and the importance of regional action, including in two workshops in cooperation with the African Union and the UN Economic Commission for Africa in Addis Ababa, a session hosted by ASEAN in Jakarta, a regional workshop in Mexico City, a Middle East/North African regional workshop in Beirut, and sessions in Brussels in cooperation with the European Union.
- Cooperation and exchanges with the United Nations system on the political, security, development, and humanitarian dynamics of the challenge. A number of exchanges have been held with the UN General Assembly, the UN Security Council, the UN Economic and Social Council (ECOSOC), the UN Secretariat and UN agencies, funds and programs. The team has also engaged with the International Dialogue for Peacebuilding and Statebuilding, the OECD International Network on Conflict and Fragility, North Atlantic Treaty Organization (NATO), the African, Asian and Inter-American Development Banks.
- Consultations in capitals to generate lessons from policymakers, experts, nongovernmental organization (NGOs) and private sector representatives, including Berlin, Beijing, Berne, Cairo, Copenhagen, Delhi, the Hague, Helsinki, Jakarta, Jeddah, London, Mexico City, Oslo, Ottawa, Paris, Rome, Stockholm and Tokyo.
- The 2011WDR brought together an Advisory Council of high-level leaders and practitioners as a sounding board for emerging thinking, and to offer practical advice on the realities of policy-making in countries affected by conflict (box 1).
- WDR brainstorming sessions have also been held to tap the knowledge and experience of academics, policymakers and NGO Representatives, in partnership with other multilateral, think tank, academic, and regional institutions.

BOX 1 ***The 2011 WDR Advisory Council***

The 2011 WDR Advisory Council was convened at the beginning of the WDR process to exchange with the team on the Report's emerging messages and recommendations. Membership includes a diverse cross-section of national, regional, multilateral, and civil society leaders with deep experience in conflict prevention and recovery. The Advisory Council met three times during the Report development process: September 2009 in Washington DC; February 2010 in Addis Ababa, Ethiopia; and September 2010 in Beijing, China. AC Members also used their convening power to support WDR capital visits in regional consultations worldwide. Based on their reflections on WDR themes, the Report includes individual contributions from Advisory Council Members, which reflect their personal views. These boxes include lessons from AC Members' own involvement in conflict settings or topical discussions based on their expertise.

Advisory Council Members

Madeleine Albright, Chair, Albright Stonebridge Group; former U.S. Secretary of State

Louise Arbour, President, International Crisis Group; former UN High Commissioner for Human Rights

Lakhdar Brahimi, Former United Nations Special Representative to the Secretary General for Afghanistan and Iraq

Mohamed Ibn Chambas, Secretary-General of the African, Caribbean and Pacific Group of Sates

Paul Collier, Professor of Economics, Oxford University

Nitin Desai, Former UN Under Secretary General for Social and Economic Affairs

Carlos Alberto dos Santos Cruz, Former Force Commander of the United Nations Peacekeeping Mission in Haiti

Martin Griffiths, Former Director, Centre for Humanitarian Dialogue

Mohamed "Mo" Ibrahim, Founder, Mo Ibrahim Foundation and Founder, Celtel

H.E. Paul Kagame, President of Rwanda

Ramtane Lamamra, Commissioner, Peace and Security Council, African Union

Louis Michel, Member of the European Parliament

Jorge Montano, Director General, Asesoría y Análisis; former Ambassador of Mexico to the U.S.

Jay Naidoo, Chairman, Global Alliance for Improved Nutrition; former Chair, Development Bank of Southern Africa

Kenzo Oshima, Senior Vice President of Japan International Cooperation Agency

Surin Pitsuwan, Secretary-General of the Association of Southeast Asian Nations

Zeid Ra'ad Al-Hussein, Ambassador of the Hashemite Kingdom of Jordan to the United Nations

Marta Lucía Ramirez de Rincón, Fundación Ciudadanía en Acción; former Minister of Defense—Colombia

H.E. Ellen Johnson Sirleaf, President of Liberia

Dmitri Trenin, Director, Moscow Center, Carnegie Endowment for International Peace

Wu Jianmin, Chairman of the Shanghai Center for International Studies

H.E. George Yeo, Minister of Foreign Affairs, Singapore

Fostering a continuing conversation

This WDR has laid a major emphasis on communication because, from the start, the aim was not just to inform but to reach out across multiple policy communities, to enhance understanding of trends in conflict, and to promote practical changes in the way we address conflict. This implied a longer term strategy than for previous reports to build momentum over time with the aim of clarifying the challenges, testing policy prescriptions and advocating concrete proposals. The extensive outreach program has both contributed to the substance of the report and initiated the communication process much earlier than previous WDRs. This WDR is also making extensive use of video, the web and social media to broaden the public discussion on fragility and conflict. An interactive website has been launched featuring data used in the report, thematic background papers, WDR conflict case studies, video material, blogs, and twitter feeds (the WDR blog at http://blogs.worldbank.org/conflict and our twitter site at http://twitter.com/wbConflict).

Abbreviations and Data Notes

Abbreviations

AC	Advisory Council, *Word Development Report 2011*
ACLED	Armed Conflict Location and Event Database
ADB	Asian Development Bank
AfDB	African Development Bank
AFSIS	ASEAN Food Security Information System
AKDN	Aga Khan Development Network
ANC	African National Congress
ASEAN	Association of Southeast Asian Nations
AU	African Union
AUC	Autodefensas Unidas de Colombia (United Self-Defense Forces of Colombia)
AUPSC	African Union Peace and Security Council
AusAID	Australian Government Overseas Aid Program
Austrac	Australian Transaction Reports and Analysis Center
AZAPO	Azanian People's Organisation, South Africa
BRA	Badan Reintegrasi-Damai Aceh (Aceh Peace-Reintegration Board)
BRAVO	Birth Registration for All Versus Oblivion
CDC	Centers for Disease Control and Prevention
CCAI	Centro de Coordinación de Acción Integral (Colombia)
CDD	community driven development
CICIG	Comisión Internacional Contra la Impunidad en Guatemala (International Commission Against Impunity in Guatemala)
CODESA	Convention for a Democratic South Africa
CPA	Comprehensive Peace Agreement
CPA	Coalition Provisional Authority (Iraq)
CPIA	Country Policy and Institutional Assessment
CV	coefficient of variance
DAC	Development Assistance Committee
DDR	Disarmament, Demobilization, and Reintegration
DESEPAZ	Desarrollo, Seguridad y Paz
DfID	Department for International Development, UK
ECOSOC	United Nations Economic and Social Council
ECOWAS	Economic Community of West African States
ECSC	European Coal and Steel Community
EFCC	Economic and Financial Crimes Commission
EGSC	Economic Governance Steering Committee
EITI	Extractive Industries Transparency Initiative
ELN	National Liberation Army (Colombia)

ETA	Euskadi Ta Askatasuna (Spain)
EU	European Union
Fafo	Institutt for Anvendte Internasjonale Studier (Institute for Labor and Social Research, Norway)
FAO	Food and Agriculture Organization (United Nations)
FARC	Fuerzas Armadas Revolucionarias de Colombia (Revolutionary Armed Forces of Colombia)
FATA	Federally Administered Tribal Areas (Pakistan)
FATF	Financial Action Task Force
FDI	foreign direct investment
FINCEN	Financial Crimes Enforcement Network, U.S.
FINTRAC	Financial Transactions and Reports Analysis Center, Canada
FIU	financial intelligence unit
FMLN	Frente Farabundo Martí para la Liberación Nacional (Farabundo Martí National Liberation Front) El Salvador
FRELIMO	Frente de Libertação de Moçambique (Liberation Front)
GAM	Gerakan Aceh Merdeka (Free Aceh Movement)
GDP	gross domestic product
GEMAP	Governance and Economic Management Assistance Program
GMS	Greater Mekong Sub-region
GIS	geographic information system
GNI	gross national income
HNP	Haitian National Police (Police Nationale d'Haïti)
IADB	Inter-American Development Bank
ICRC	International Committee of the Red Cross
ICRG	International Country Risk Guide
IDA	International Development Association
IDP	internally displaced persons
IFAD	International Fund for Agricultural Development
IFC	International Finance Corporation
IFI	International Financial Institutions
IMF	International Monetary Fund
INCAF	International Network on Conflict and Fragility
IRA	Irish Republican Army
ISAF	International Security Assistance Force in Afghanistan
KDP	Kecamatan Development Program (Indonesia)
KP	Khyber Pakhtunkhwa (province in Pakistan)
MDG	Millennium Development Goal
MDRP	Multi-country Demobilization and Reintegration Program (Africa)
MDTF	Multi-donor Trust Fund
MINUSTAH	United Nations Stabilization Mission in Haiti
MONUC	Mission de l'Organisation des Nations Unies en République Démocratique du Congo (United Nations Mission in the Democratic Republic of Congo)
MOU	memorandum of understanding
NATO	North Atlantic Treaty Organization
NCP	National Conciliation Party (El Salvador)
NGO	nongovernmental organization
NSP	National Solidarity Program (Afghanistan)
NTGL	National Transitional Government of Liberia
ODA	official development assistance
OECD	Organisation for Economic Co-operation and Development

ONUMOZ	United Nations Operation in Mozambique
PAC	Pan Africanist Congress (South Africa)
PCNA	Post Conflict Needs Assessment
PFM	Public Financial Management Review
PRIO	Peace Research Institute (Oslo)
RAMSI	Regional Assistance Mission to the Solomon Islands
RENAMO	Resistência Nacional Moçambicana (Mozambique)
SADC	Southern African Development Community
SALW	small arms and light weapons
SOCA	Serious Organized Crime Agency, U.K.
SMS	short message service
STAR	Stolen Asset Recovery Initiative
START	Stabilization and Reconstruction Task Force (Canada)
SPF	Statebuilding and Peacebuilding Fund (World Bank)
UN	United Nations
UNCTAD	United Nations Conference on Trade and Development
UNDP	United Nations Development Programme
UNDPA	United Nations Department of Political Affairs
UNDPKO	United Nations Department of Peacekeeping Operations
UNHCR	United Nations Office of the High Commissioner for Refugees
UNICEF	United Nations Children's Fund
UNIFEM	United Nations Development Fund for Women
UNOHCHR	United Nations Office of the High Commissioner for Human Rights
UNMIL	United Nations Mission in Liberia
UNODC	United Nations Office on Drugs and Crime
UNOGBIS	United Nations Peacebuilding Support Office in Guinea Bissau
UNPBC	United Nations Peacebuilding Commission
UNPBF	United Nations Peacebuilding Fund
UNSC	United Nations Security Council
UNSCR	United Nations Security Council Resolution
USAID	United States Agency for International Development
WDR	World Development Report
WFP	World Food Programme
WGI	Worldwide Governance Indicators
WHO	World Health Organization

Definitions and data notes

The countries included in regional and income groupings in this Report are listed in the Classification of Economies table at the end of the Selected World Development Indicators. Income classifications are based on GNP per capita; thresholds for income classifications in this edition may be found in the Introduction to Selected World Development Indicators. Group averages reported in the figures and tables are unweighted averages of the countries in the group, unless noted to the contrary.

The use of the *countries* to refer to economies implies no judgment by the World Bank about the legal or other status of territory. The term *developing countries* includes low- and middle-income economies and thus may include economies in transition from central planning, as a matter of convenience.

Dollar figures are current U.S. dollars, unless otherwise specified. *Billion* means 1,000 million; trillion means 1,000 billion.

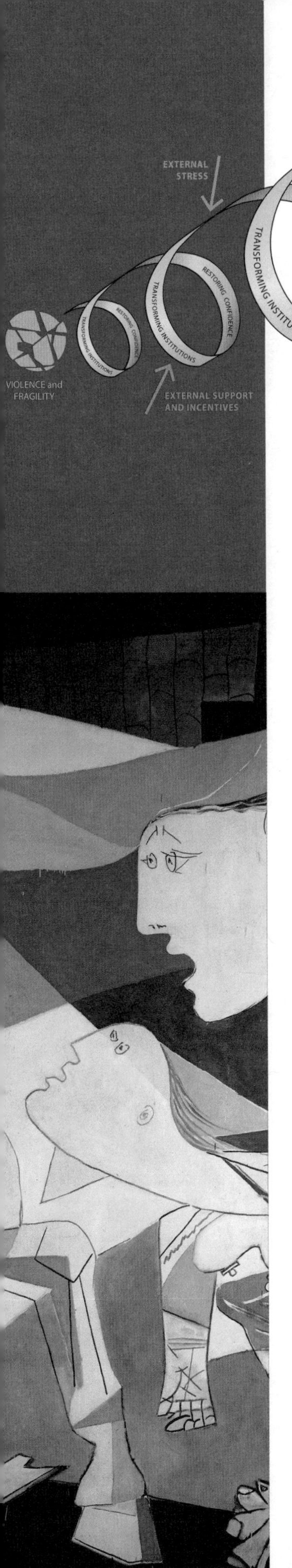

Overview

Preamble

Efforts to maintain collective security are at the heart of human history: from the earliest times, the recognition that human safety depends on collaboration has been a motivating factor for the formation of village communities, cities, and nation-states. The 20th century was dominated by the legacy of devastating global wars, colonial struggles, and ideological conflicts, and by efforts to establish international systems that would foster global peace and prosperity. To some extent these systems were successful—wars between states are far less common than they were in the past, and civil wars are declining in number.

Yet, insecurity not only remains, it has become a primary development challenge of our time. One-and-a-half billion people live in areas affected by fragility, conflict, or large-scale, organized criminal violence, and no low-income fragile or conflict-affected country has yet to achieve a single United Nations Millennium Development Goal (UN MDG). New threats—organized crime and trafficking, civil unrest due to global economic shocks, terrorism—have supplemented continued preoccupations with conventional war between and within countries. While much of the world has made rapid progress in reducing poverty in the past 60 years, areas characterized by repeated cycles of political and criminal violence are being left far behind, their economic growth compromised and their human indicators stagnant.

For those who now live in more stable neighborhoods, it may seem incomprehensible how prosperity in high-income countries and a sophisticated global economy can coexist with extreme violence and misery in other parts of the globe. The pirates operating off the coast of Somalia who prey on the shipping through the Gulf of Aden illustrate the paradox of the existing global system. How is it that the combined prosperity and capability of the world's modern nation-states cannot prevent a problem from antiquity? How is it that, almost a decade after renewed international engagement with Afghanistan, the prospects of peace seem distant? How is it that entire urban communities can be terrorized by drug traffickers? How is it that countries in the Middle East and North Africa could face explosions of popular grievances despite, in some cases, sustained high growth and improvement in social indicators?

This *World Development Report* (WDR) asks what spurs risks of violence, why conflict prevention and recovery have proven so difficult to address, and what can be done by national leaders and their development, security, and diplomatic partners to help restore a stable development path in the world's most fragile and violence-torn areas. **The central message of the Report is that strengthening legitimate institutions and governance to provide citizen security, justice, and jobs is crucial to break cycles of violence.** Restoring confidence and transforming security, justice, and economic institutions is possible within a generation, even in countries that have experienced severe conflict. But that requires determined national leadership and an international system "refitted" to address 21st-century risks: refocusing assistance on preventing criminal and political violence, reforming the procedures of international agencies, responding at a regional level, and renewing cooperative efforts among lower-, middle-, and higher-income countries. The Report envisages a layered approach to effective global action, with local, national, regional, and international roles.

Because of the nature of the topic, this Report has been developed in an unusual way—drawing from the beginning on the knowledge of national reformers and working closely with the United Nations and regional institutions with expertise in political and security issues, building on the concept of human security. The hope is that this partnership will spark an ongoing effort to jointly deepen our understanding of the links between security and development, and will foster practical action on the Report's findings.

PART 1: THE CHALLENGE OF REPEATED CYCLES OF VIOLENCE

21st-century conflict and violence are a development problem that does not fit the 20th-century mold

Global systems in the 20th century were designed to address interstate tensions and one-off episodes of civil war. War between nation-states and civil war have a given logic and sequence. The actors, sovereign states or clearly defined rebel movements, are known. If a dispute escalates and full-scale hostilities ensue, an eventual end to hostilities (either through victory and defeat or through a negotiated settlement) is followed by a short "post-conflict" phase leading back to peace. The global system is largely built around this paradigm of conflict, with clear roles for national and international actors in *development* in promoting the prosperity and capability of the nation-state (but stepping out during active conflict), in *diplomacy* in preventing and mediating disputes between states and between government and rebel movements, in *peacekeeping* in the aftermath of conflict, and in *humanitarianism* in providing relief.

21st-century violence[1] does not fit the 20th-century mold. Interstate war and civil war are still threats in some regions, but they have declined over the last 25 years. Deaths from civil war, while still exacting an unacceptable toll, are one-quarter of what they were in the 1980s (Feature 1, figure F1.1).[2] Violence and conflict have not been banished: one in four people on the planet, more than 1.5 billion, live in fragile and conflict-affected states or in countries with very high levels of criminal violence.[3] But because of the successes in reducing interstate war, the remaining forms of conflict and violence do not fit neatly either into "war" or "peace," or into "criminal violence" or "political violence" (see Feature 1, F1.1–1.2 and table F1.1).

Many countries and subnational areas now face cycles of *repeated* violence, weak governance, and instability. First, conflicts often are not one-off events, but are ongoing and repeated: 90 percent of the last decade's civil wars occurred in countries that had already had a civil war in the last 30 years.[4] Second, new forms of conflict and violence threaten development: many countries that have successfully negotiated political and peace agreements after violent political conflicts, such as El Salvador, Guatemala, and South Africa, now face high levels of violent crime, constraining their development. Third, different forms of violence are linked to each other. Political movements can obtain financing

FEATURE 1 *How violence is changing*

FIGURE F1.1 *Deaths from civil wars are declining*

As the number of civil wars declined, the total annual deaths from these conflicts (battle deaths) fell from more than 200,000 in 1988 to fewer than 50,000 in 2008.

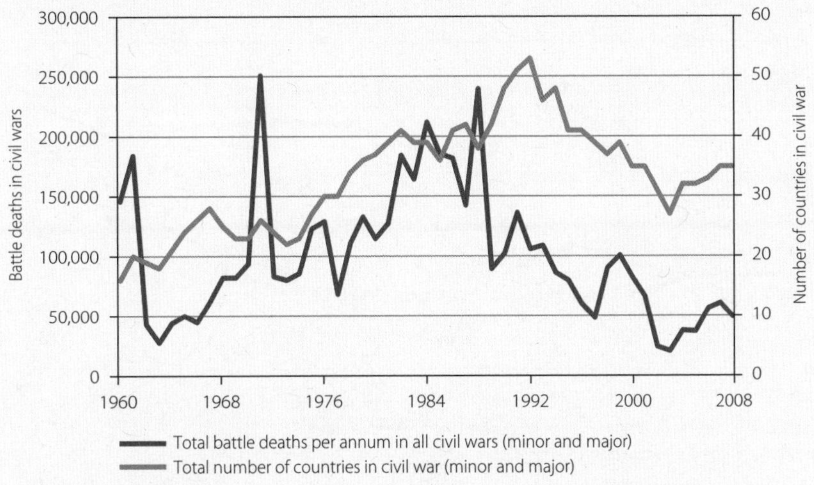

Sources: Uppsala/PRIO Armed Conflict dataset (Harbom and Wallensteen 2010; Lacina and Gleditsch 2005); Gleditsch and others 2002; Sundberg 2008; Gleditsch and Ward 1999; Human Security Report Project, forthcoming.

Note: Civil wars are classified by scale and type in the Uppsala/PRIO Armed Conflict dataset (Harbom and Wallensteen 2010; Lacina and Gleditsch 2005). The minimum threshold for monitoring is a minor civil war with 25 or more battle deaths a year. Low, high, and best estimates of annual battle deaths per conflict are in Lacina and Gleditsch (2005, updated in 2009). Throughout this Report, best estimates are used, except when they are not available, in which case averages of the low and high estimates are used.

TABLE F1.1 *Violence often recurs*

Few countries are truly "post-conflict." The rate of violence onset in countries with a previous conflict has been increasing since the 1960s, and every civil war that began since 2003 was in a country that had a previous civil war.

Decade	Violence onsets in countries with no previous conflict (%)	Violence onsets in countries with a previous conflict (%)	Number of onsets
1960s	57	43	35
1970s	43	57	44
1980s	38	62	39
1990s	33	67	81
2000s	10	90	39

Sources: Walter 2010; WDR team calculations.
Note: Previous conflict includes any major conflict since 1945.

(Feature continued on next page)

FEATURE 1 *How violence is changing (continued)*

FIGURE F1.2 *Organized criminal violence threatens peace processes*

Homicides have increased in every country in Central America since 1999, including those that had made great progress in addressing political conflict—and this is not unique; countries such as South Africa face similar second generation challenges.

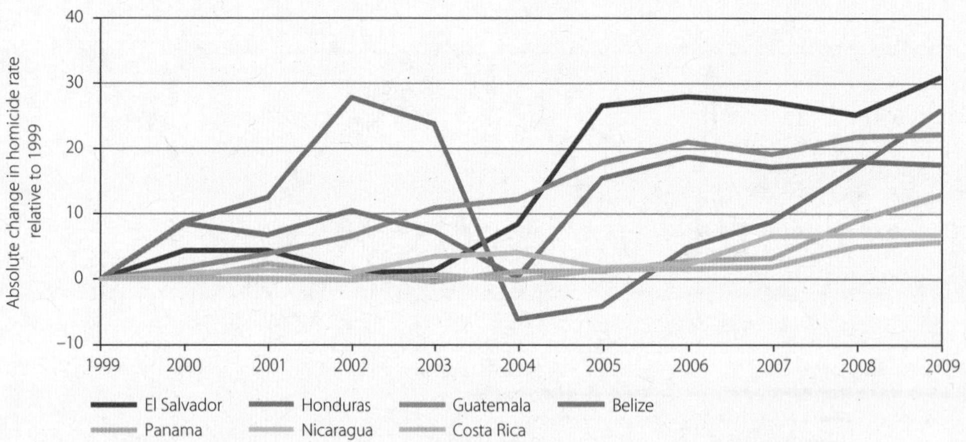

Sources: WDR team calculations based on UNODC 2007; UNODC and World Bank 2007; and national sources.

Note: Base year for homicide rate is 1999 = 0.

How violence disrupts development

FIGURE F1.3 *The gap in poverty is widening between countries affected by violence and others*

New poverty data reveal that poverty is declining for much of the world, but countries affected by violence are lagging behind. For every three years a country is affected by major violence (battle deaths or excess deaths from homicides equivalent to a major war), poverty reduction lags behind by 2.7 percentage points.

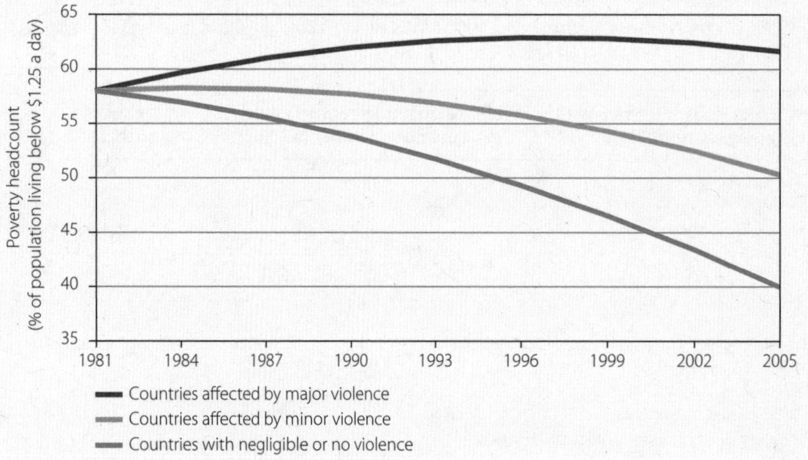

Sources: WDR team calculations based on Chen, Ravallion, and Sangraula 2008 poverty data (available on POVCALNET (http://iresearch.worldbank.org)).

Note: Poverty is % of population living at less than US$1.25 per day.

from criminal activities, as in the Democratic Republic of Congo and Northern Ireland.[5] Criminal gangs can support political violence during electoral periods, as in Jamaica and Kenya.[6] International ideological movements make common cause with local grievances, as in Afghanistan and Pakistan. Thus, the large majority of countries currently facing violence face it in multiple forms. Fourth, grievances can escalate into acute demands for change—and the risks of violent conflict—in countries where political, social, or economic change lags behind expectations, as in the Middle East and North Africa.

Repeated and interlinked, these conflicts have regional and global repercussions. The death, destruction, and delayed development due to conflict are bad for the conflict-affected countries, and their impacts spill over both regionally and globally. A country making development advances, such as Tanzania, loses an estimated 0.7 percent of GDP every year for each neighbor in conflict.[7] Refugees and internally displaced persons have increased threefold in the last 30 years.[8] Nearly 75 percent of the world's refugees are hosted by neighboring countries.[9]

The new forms of violence interlinking local political conflicts, organized crime, and internationalized disputes mean that violence is a problem for both the rich and the poor: more than 80 percent of fatalities from terrorist attacks over the last decade were in nonwestern targets,[10] but a study of 18 Western European countries revealed that each additional transnational terrorist incident reduced their economic growth by 0.4 of a percentage point a year.[11] Attacks in one region can impose costs all through global markets—one attack in the Niger Delta can cost global consumers of oil billions in increased prices.[12] In the four weeks following the beginning of the uprising in Libya, oil prices increased by 15 percent.[13] The interdiction of cocaine shipments to Europe has increased fourfold since 2003,[14] with even areas such as West Africa now seriously affected by drug-related violence.[15]

Attempts to contain violence are also extremely costly. For example, the naval operation to counter piracy in the Horn of Africa and the Indian Ocean is estimated to cost US$1.3–$2 billion annually, plus additional costs incurred by rerouting ships and increasing insurance premiums.[16] Efforts by households and firms to protect themselves against long-duration violence impose heavy economic burdens: 35 percent of firms in Latin America, 30 percent in Africa, and 27 percent in Eastern Europe and Central Asia identify crime as the major problem for their business activities. The burden is highest on those least able to bear the cost: firms in Sub-Saharan Africa lose a higher percentage of sales to crime and spend a higher percentage of sales on security than any other region.[17]

No low-income fragile or conflict-affected country has yet achieved a single MDG. People in fragile and conflict-affected states are more than twice as likely to be undernourished as those in other developing countries, more than three times as likely to be unable to send their children to school, twice as likely to see their children die before age five, and more than twice as likely to lack clean water. On average, a country that experienced major violence over the period from 1981 to 2005 has a poverty rate 21 percentage points higher than a country that saw no violence (Feature 1, figure F1.3).[18] A similar picture emerges for subnational areas affected by violence in richer and more stable countries—areas where development lags behind.[19]

These repeated cycles of conflict and violence exact other human, social, and economic costs that last for generations. High levels of organized criminal violence hold back economic development. In Guatemala, violence cost the country more than 7 percent of GDP in 2005, more than twice the damage by Hurricane Stan in the same year—and more than twice the combined budget for agriculture, health, and education.[20] The average cost of civil war is equivalent to more than 30 years of GDP growth for a medium-size developing country.[21] Trade levels after major episodes of violence take 20 years to recover.[22] In other words, a major episode of violence, unlike natural disasters or economic cycles, can wipe out an entire generation of economic progress.

These numbers have human consequences. In highly violent societies, many people experience the death of a son or daughter before their time: when children are late coming home, a parent has good reason to fear for their lives and physical safety. Everyday experiences, such as going to school, to work, or to market, become occasions for fear. People hesitate to build houses or invest in small businesses because these can be destroyed in a moment. The direct impact of violence falls primarily on young males—the majority of fighting forces and gang members—but women and children often suffer disproportionately from the indirect effects.[23] Men make up 96 percent of detainees and 90 percent of the missing; women and children are close to 80 percent of refugees and those internally displaced.[24] And violence begets violence: male children who witness abuses have a higher tendency to perpetrate violence later in life.[25]

Yet when security is reestablished and sustained, these areas of the world can make the greatest development gains. Several countries emerging from long legacies of both political and criminal violence have been among the fastest making progress on the MDGs:[26]

- Ethiopia more than quadrupled access to improved water, from 13 percent of the population in 1990 to 66 percent in 2009–10.
- Mozambique more than tripled its primary completion rate in just eight years, from 14 percent in 1999 to 46 percent in 2007.
- Rwanda cut the prevalence of undernutrition from 56 percent of the population in 1997 to 40 percent in 2005.
- Bosnia and Herzegovina, between 1995 and 2007, increased measles immunizations from 53 percent to 96 percent for children aged 12–23 months.

Vicious cycles of conflict: When security, justice, and employment stresses meet weak institutions

Internal causes of conflict arise from political, security, and economic dynamics.[27] Yet it is difficult to disentangle causes and effects of violence. Lower GDP per capita is robustly associated with both large-scale political conflict and high rates of homicide.[28] Youth unemployment is consistently cited in citizen perception surveys as a motive for joining both rebel movements and urban gangs (Feature 2, figure F2.2).[29] Feeling more secure and powerful is also cited as an important motivator across countries, confirming existing research that shows that employment dynamics have to do not only with income but also with respect and status, involving social cohesion as well as economic opportunity. Political exclusion and inequality affecting regional, religious, or ethnic groups are associated with higher risks of civil war,[30] (and are also cited in citizen surveys as a key driver of conflict alongside poverty—see figure F2.1) while inequality between richer and poorer households is closely associated with higher risks of violent crime (table 1.1).

External factors can heighten the risks of violence. Major external security pressures, as with new patterns of drug trafficking, can overwhelm institutional capacities (see Feature 2). Income shocks can also increase risks of violence. Work on rainfall shocks in Sub-Saharan Africa concludes that civil conflict is more likely following years of poor rainfall. Using rainfall variation as a proxy for income shocks in 41 African countries between 1981 and 1999, Satyanath, Miguel, and Sergenti found that a decline in economic growth of 5 percent increased the likelihood of conflict by half the following year.[31] Corruption—which generally has international links through illicit trafficking, money laundering, and the extraction of rents from sales of national resources or international contracts and concessions—has doubly pernicious impacts on the risks of violence, by fueling grievances and by undermining the effectiveness of national institutions and so-

TABLE 1.1 ***Security, economic, and political stresses***

Stresses	Internal	External
Security	• Legacies of violence and trauma	• Invasion, occupation • External support for domestic rebels • Cross-border conflict spillovers • Transnational terrorism • International criminal networks
Economic	• Low income levels, low opportunity cost of rebellion • Youth unemployment • Natural resource wealth • Severe corruption • Rapid urbanization	• Price shocks • Climate change
Justice	• Ethnic, religious, or regional competition • Real or perceived discrimination • Human rights abuses	• Perceived global inequity and injustice in the treatment of ethnic or religious groups

Source: WDR team.
Note: This table, although not exhaustive, captures major factors in the academic literature on the causes and correlates of conflict and raised in the WDR consultations and surveys.[33]

cial norms.[32] New external pressures from climate change and natural resource competition could heighten all these risks.[34]

However, many countries face high unemployment, economic inequality, or pressure from organized crime networks but do not repeatedly succumb to widespread violence, and instead contain it. The WDR approach emphasizes that risk of conflict and violence in any society (national or regional) is the *combination* of the exposure to *internal and external stresses* and the strength of the "immune system," or the social capability for coping with stress embodied in *legitimate institutions*.[35] Both state and nonstate institutions are important. Institutions include social norms and behaviors—such as the ability of leaders to transcend sectarian and political differences and develop bargains, and of civil society to advocate for greater national and political cohesion—as well as rules, laws, and organizations.[36] Where states, markets, and social institutions fail to provide basic security, justice, and economic opportunities for citizens, conflict can escalate.

In short, countries and subnational areas with the weakest institutional legitimacy and governance are the most vulnerable to violence and instability and the least able to respond to internal and external stresses. Institutional capacity and accountability are important for both political and criminal violence (see Feature 2).[37]

- In some areas—as in the peripheral regions of Colombia before the turn of the 21st century[38] or the Democratic Republic of the Congo[39] today—the state is all but absent from many parts of the country, and violent armed groups dominate local contests over power and resources.
- Most areas affected by violence face deficits in their collaborative capacities[40] to mediate conflict peacefully. In some countries, institutions do not span ethnic, regional, or religious divides, and state institutions have been viewed as partisan—just as they were for decades prior to the peace agreement in Northern Ireland.[41] In some communities, social divisions have constrained effective collaboration between elite dominated states and poor communities to address sources of violence.
- Rapid urbanization, as occurred earlier in Latin America and today in Asia and Africa, weakens social cohesion.[42] Unemployment, structural inequalities, and greater access to markets for firearms and illicit drugs break down social cohesion and increase the vulnerability to criminal networks and gangs.

- Countries with weak institutional capacity were more likely to suffer violent social unrest during the food shocks of 2008–09.[43]
- Some states have tried to maintain stability through coercion and patronage networks, but those with high levels of corruption and human rights abuses increase their risks of violence breaking out in the future (see Feature 2).

Weak institutions are particularly important in explaining why violence repeats in different forms in the same countries or subnational regions. Even societies with the weakest institutions have periodic outbreaks of peace. South-central Somalia has had interludes of low conflict over the last 30 years based on agreements by small numbers of elites.[44] But temporary elite pacts, in Somalia and elsewhere, do not provide the grounds for sustained security and development unless they are followed by the development of legitimate state and society institutions.[45] They are generally short-lived because they are too personalized and narrow to accommodate stresses and adjust to change. New internal and external stresses arise—a leader's death, economic shocks, the entry of organized criminal trafficking networks, new opportunities or rents, or external security interference—and there is no sustained ability to respond.[46] So the violence recurs.

A focus on legitimate institutions does not mean converging on Western institutions. History provides many examples of foreign institutional models that have proven less than useful to national development, particularly through colonial legacies,[47] because they focused on form rather than function. The same is true today. In Iraq, the Coalition Provisional Authority established commissions on every subject from tourism to the environment in parallel with struggling line ministries, and model laws were passed that had little relationship to national social and political realities.[48] Even transfers of organizational forms between countries in the South can be unproductive if not adapted to local conditions—the truth and reconciliation, anti-corruption, and human rights commissions that delivered so marvelously in some countries have not always worked in others. There are gains from sharing knowledge, as the Report makes clear—but only if adapted to local conditions. "Best-fit" institutions are central to the Report.

PART 2: A ROADMAP FOR BREAKING CYCLES OF VIOLENCE AT THE COUNTRY LEVEL

Restoring confidence and transforming the institutions that provide citizen security, justice, and jobs

To break cycles of insecurity and reduce the risk of their recurrence, national reformers and their international partners need to build the legitimate institutions that can provide a sustained level of citizen security, justice, and jobs—offering a stake in society to groups that may otherwise receive more respect and recognition from engaging in armed violence than in lawful activities, and punishing infractions capably and fairly.

But transforming institutions—always tough—is particularly difficult in fragile situations. First, in countries with a track record of violence and mistrust, expectations are either too low, so that no government promises are believed, making cooperative action impossible—or too high, so that transitional moments produce expectations of rapid change that cannot be delivered by existing institutions.[49] Second, many institutional changes that could produce greater long-term resilience against violence frequently carry short-term risks. Any important shift—holding elections, dismantling patronage networks, giving new roles to security services, decentralizing decision-making, empowering disadvantaged groups—creates both winners and losers. Losers are often well organized

FEATURE 2 *High stresses and weak institutions = risks of violence*

Justice, jobs, and violence

FIGURE F2.1 *What are citizens' views on the drivers of conflict?*

In surveys conducted in six countries and territories affected by violence, involving a mix of nationally representative samples and subregions, citizens raised issues linked to individual economic welfare (poverty, unemployment) and injustice (including inequality and corruption) as the primary drivers of conflict.

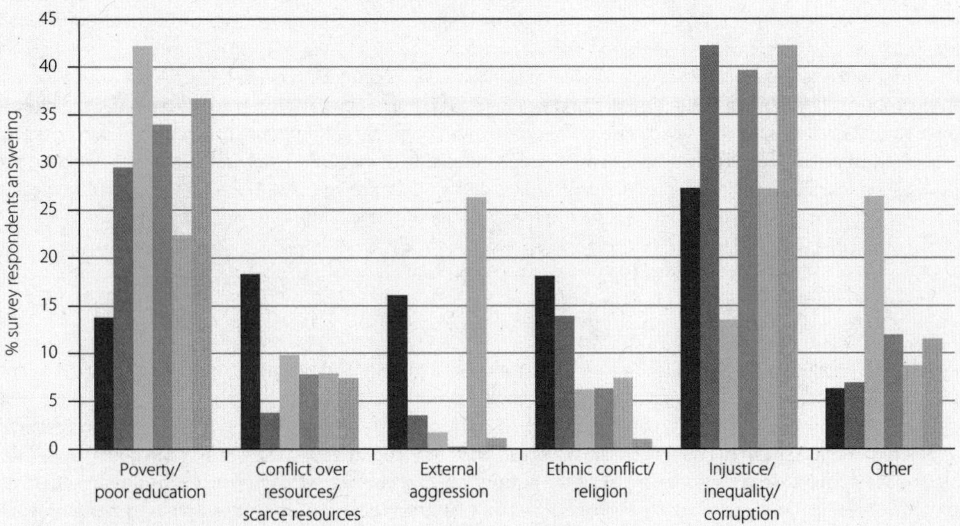

Source: Bøås, Tiltnes, and Flatø 2010.

FIGURE F2.2 *What drives people to join rebel movement and gangs?*

The same surveys found that the main reasons cited for why young people become rebels or gang members are very similar—unemployment predominates for both. This is not necessarily the case for militant ideological recruitment (chapter 2).

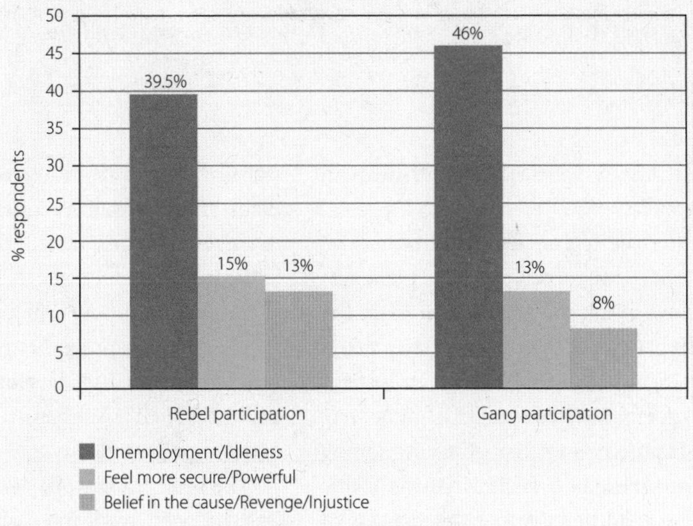

Source: Bøås, Tiltnes, and Flatø 2010.

REFLECTIONS FROM ADVISORY COUNCIL MEMBERS: *2011 WORLD DEVELOPMENT REPORT*

Jorge Montaño, Member, International Narcotics Control Board; former Ambassador of Mexico to the United States; *WDR Advisory Council Member*

The role of external stresses

Drug and human trafficking, money laundering, illegal exploitation of natural resources and wildlife, counterfeiting, and violations of intellectual property rights are lucrative criminal activities, which facilitate the penetration by organized crime of the already vulnerable sociopolitical, judicial, and security structures in developing countries.

In Central America, for example, several countries that regained political stability two decades ago are now facing the decay of the state, whose institutions lack the strength to face this onslaught. Transnational organized crime has converted some Caribbean countries into corridors for the movement of illegal drugs and persons toward Europe and North America. Bolivia, Colombia, and Peru, continue to be the main global cocaine producers, while Mexico is facing an unprecedented wave of violence given its border with the largest immigrant, drug consumption, and arms producing market. West Africa has become the newest passage of drugs coming from South America and destined for Europe. Several African countries suffer the illegal exploitation of their natural resources, while Asia is a hub for tons of opiates originating from Afghanistan. The unprecedented progression of organized crime could spell the collapse of many weak states as their institutions fall prey to the associated violence. The precarious economic development observed in many regions of the world provides a stimulus for consolidating these illegal activities, which will continue to thrive as a consequence of the impunity they encounter in developing countries.

WDR Note: Weak institutions are a common factor in explaining repeated cycles of violence

Building on previous work by Collier, Fearon, Goldstone, North, Wallis, and Weingast, and others, political scientists Jim Fearon and Barbara Walter used econometric techniques for the WDR to test whether general rule of law and government effectiveness, low corruption, and strong protection of human rights correlate with a lower risk of the onset and recurrence of civil war and of high homicides from criminal violence. Fearon finds that countries with above average governance indicators for their income level have a significantly lower risk of the outbreak of civil conflict within the next 5 to 10 years—between 30 to 45 percent lower—and that the relationship also holds true for countries with high homicides. This work confirms earlier directions in the policy community, such as the International Network on Conflict and Fragility's emphasis on the links between peacebuilding and state-building.

Measures of accountability are as important as measures of capacity in this calculation. Fearon finds that high levels of political terror in past periods increase the chances of current conflict. Walter finds that significant reductions in the number of political prisoners and extrajudicial killings make the renewal of civil war between two and three times less likely than in countries with higher levels of human rights abuses. She notes, "A reasonable interpretation of these results is that greater repression and abuse by a government creates both grievances and signals that those governments (sic) are not dependable negotiating partners; suggesting that less coercive and more accountable approaches significantly decrease the risk of civil conflict." Other measures of accountability also matter: measures of rule of law and corruption are as or more important than measures of bureaucratic quality.

and resist change. Third, external stresses can derail progress.

Creating the legitimate institutions that can prevent repeated violence is, in plain language, slow. It takes a generation. Even the fastest-transforming countries have taken between 15 and 30 years to raise their institutional performance from that of a fragile state today—Haiti, say—to that of a functioning institutionalized state, such as Ghana (table 2.1).[50] The good news is that this process of transforming institutions accelerated considerably in the late 20th century, with increases in citizen demands for good governance and in the technologies that can help supply it. Indeed, making progress in a generation is actually quite fast: progress at this speed would represent immense development gains for countries such as Afghanistan, Haiti, Liberia, and Timor-Leste today.

The basic framework of the WDR focuses on what we have learned about the dynam-

TABLE 2.1 ***Fastest progress in institutional transformation—An estimate of realistic ranges***

The table shows the historical range of timings that the fastest reformers in the 20th century took to achieve basic governance transformations.

Indicator	Years to threshold at pace of:	
	Fastest 20	Fastest over the threshold
Bureaucratic quality (0–4)	20	12
Corruption (0–6)	27	14
Military in politics (0–6)	17	10
Government effectiveness	36	13
Control of corruption	27	16
Rule of law	41	17

Source: Pritchett and de Weijer 2010.

ics of action to prevent repeated cycles of violence—both in the short term and over the time needed to reach a sustained level of resilience. Our knowledge of how to break these cycles is partial: the Report lays out lessons drawn from existing research, country studies, and consultations with national reformers. Experiences from Bosnia and Herzegovina, Chile, Colombia, Ghana, Indonesia, Liberia, Mozambique, Northern Ireland, Sierra Leone, South Africa, and Timor-Leste amongst others, are drawn on frequently in the Report because, while all of these areas still face challenges and risks, these societies have achieved considerable successes in preventing violence from escalating or recovering from its aftermath. These and the other experiences in the Report also span a range of high-income, middle-income and lower-income countries, a range of threats of political and criminal violence, and differing institutional contexts, ranging from situations where strong institutions faced legitimacy challenges due to problems of inclusion and accountability to situations where weak capacity was a major constraint.

There are some fundamental differences between fragile and violent situations and stable developing environments. First is the need to **restore confidence** in collective action before embarking on wider institutional transformation. Second is the priority of **transforming institutions that provide citizen security, justice, and jobs**. Third is the role of regional and international action to contain **external stresses**. Fourth is the specialized nature of **external support** needed.

Institutional transformation and good governance, central to these processes, work differently in fragile situations. The goal is more focused—transforming institutions that deliver citizen security, justice, and jobs. When facing the risk of conflict and violence, citizen security, justice and jobs are the key elements of protection to achieve human security.[51] The dynamics of institutional change are also different. A good analogy is a financial crisis caused by a combination of external stresses and weaknesses in institutional checks and balances. In such a situation, exceptional efforts are needed to restore confidence in national leaders' ability to manage the crisis—through actions that signal a real break with the past and through locking in these actions and showing that they will not be reversed.

Confidence-building—a concept used in political mediation and financial crises but rarely in development circles[52]—is a prelude to more permanent institutional change in the face of violence. Why? Because low trust means that stakeholders who need to con-

FIGURE 2.1 *Moving from fragility and violence to institutional resilience in citizen security, justice, and jobs*

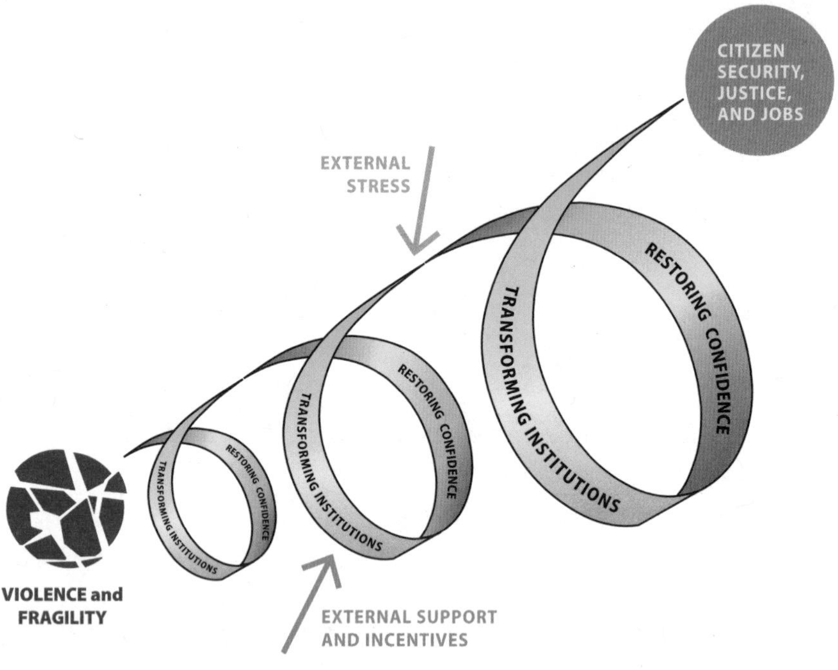

Source: WDR team.

tribute political, financial, or technical support will not collaborate until they believe that a positive outcome is possible.[53] But confidence-building is not an end in itself. Just as in a financial crisis, progress will not be sustained unless the institutions that provide citizen security, justice, and an economic stake in society are transformed to prevent a recurrence of violence.

Just as violence repeats, efforts to build confidence and transform institutions typically follow a repeated spiral. Countries that moved away from fragility and conflict often do so not through one decisive "make or break" moment—but through many transition moments, as the spiral path in figure 2.1 illustrates. National leaders had to build confidence in the state and to transform institutions over time, as with the Republic of Korea's transitions in the security, political, and economic spheres after the Korean War, or Ghana, Chile and Argentina's transitions from military rule, which included repeated internal contests over the norms and governance of society.[54] A repeated process enables space for collaborative norms and capacities to develop, and for success to build on successes in a virtuous cycle. For each loop of the spiral, the same two phases recur: building confidence that positive chance is possible, prior to deepening the institutional transformation and strengthening governance outcomes.

Confidence-building—Inclusive-enough coalitions and early results

The state cannot restore confidence alone. Confidence-building in situations of violence and fragility requires deliberate effort to build *inclusive-enough coalitions*, as Indonesia did in addressing violence in Aceh or Timor-Leste in its recovery after the renewed violence in 2006 or Chile in its political transition. Coalitions are "inclusive-enough" when they include the parties necessary for implementing the initial stages of confidence-building and institutional transformation. They need not be "all-inclusive."[55] Inclusive-enough coalitions work in two ways: (1) at a broad level, by building national support for change and bringing in the relevant stakeholders, through collaboration between the government and other sectors of society—as well as with regional neighbors, donors, or investors, and (2) at a local level, by promoting outreach to community leaders to identify priorities and deliver programs. Inclusive-enough coalitions apply just as much to criminal as to political violence, through collaboration with community leaders, business, and civil society in areas affected by criminal violence. Civil society—including women's organizations—often plays important roles in restoring confidence and sustaining the momentum for recovery and transformation, as demonstrated by the role of the Liberian Women's Initiative in pressing for continued progress in the peace agreement.[56]

Persuading stakeholders to work collaboratively requires signals of a real break with the past—for example, ending the political or economic exclusion of marginalized groups, corruption, or human rights abuses—as well as mechanisms to "lock-in" these changes and show that they will not be reversed. In moments of opportunity or crisis, fast and visible results also help restore confidence in the government's ability to deal with violent threats and implement institutional and social change. State-community, state-nongovernmental organization (NGO), state-international, and state-private-sector partnerships can extend the state's capacity to deliver. Actions in one domain can support results in another. Security operations can facilitate safe trade and transit, and the economic activity that creates jobs. Services delivered to marginalized groups can support perceptions of justice. More detailed approaches to support inclusive-enough coalitions are described in the section on practical policies and programs for country actors below.

Transforming institutions that deliver citizen security, justice, and jobs

There is a limit to the amount of change societies can absorb at any one time, and in fragile situations, many reforms need a build-up of trust and capacity before they can be successfully implemented. Getting the balance right between "too fast" and "too slow" transformative action is crucial, and some basic lessons emerge from successful country transitions.

First, prioritizing early action to reform the institutions responsible for citizen security, justice, and jobs is crucial, as in Singapore's post-independence development (see Feature 3). Stemming illegal financial flows from the public purse or from natural resource trafficking is important to underpin these initiatives. Pragmatic, "best-fit" approaches adapted to local conditions will be needed. For example, Lebanon restored the electricity needed for economic recovery during the civil war through small private-sector networks of providers, albeit at high unit costs.[57] Haiti's successful police reforms in 2004 to 2009 focused on ousting abusers from the force and restoring very basic work discipline.[58]

Second, focusing on citizen security, justice, and jobs means that most other reforms will need to be sequenced and paced over time, including political reform, decentralization, privatization, and shifting attitudes toward marginalized groups. Systematically implementing these reforms requires a web of institutions (democratization, for example, requires many institutional checks and balances beyond elections) and changes in social attitudes. Several successful political transitions, such as the devolution that underpins peace in Northern Ireland and democratic transitions in Chile, Indonesia, or Portugal, have taken place through a series of steps over a decade or more.

There are exceptions—where the exclusion of groups from democratic participation has been a clear overriding source of grievance, rapid action on elections makes sense; and where interests that previously blocked reform have diminished, as with post-war Japanese or Republic of Korea land reform,[59] fast action can take advantage of a window of opportunity. But in most situations, systematic and gradual action appears to work best.

REFLECTIONS FROM ADVISORY COUNCIL MEMBERS: *2011 WORLD DEVELOPMENT REPORT*

FEATURE 3 *Country experiences of confidence-building and transforming institutions for citizen security, justice, and jobs*

Confidence building in South Africa

Jay Naidoo, Chairman of Global Alliance for Improved Nutrition; Former General Secretary, Congress of South African Trade Unions; Former Minister of Reconstruction and Development, South Africa; and Former Chairman of the Development Bank of Southern Africa; *WDR Advisory Council Member*

(Abbreviated from WDR 2011, chapter 3)

In South Africa, the "moment" of transition in 1994 was preceded by multiple transition points which required efforts from the protagonists to shift the debate and that gave credibility to the process. On the African National Congress (ANC) Alliance side, this included the shift to a broader, more inclusive approach, and the realization of the need to ensure incentives for the National Party and the white population. On the National Party side, this included the shift from thinking in terms of group rights and protection of minorities to thinking in terms of individual rights and majority rule. Certain signals which were perceived as irreversible (notably the unconditional release of Nelson Mandela and the suspension of the ANC's armed struggle) were critical in maintaining trust between parties. After the 1994 elections, delivering a few early results—including maternal and infant healthcare and using community structures to improve water supply—were important to maintain confidence in our new government.

In addition to successes, there were opportunities missed which may be of use when other countries consider South Africa's experiences. This included too little attention to job creation for youth and risks of criminal violence. It meant that we did not fully address the critical need to ensure that the new generation who had not lived through the apartheid struggle as adults were provided with a strong stake—and economic opportunities—in the new democratic state.

There was also too much of an assumption that 1994 marked the culmination of a process of democratization and reconciliation. Relatively little attention was given to what was meant by the transformation to a constitutional state; the continued role of civil society in deepening not just democratization and accountability but also delivery. And there was a need for a deeper and more thorough ongoing debate on racism, inequality, and social exclusion.

All politics is local and early attention to security, justice, and jobs

George Yeo, Minister of Foreign Affairs for Singapore; *WDR Advisory Council Member*

(Abbreviated from WDR 2011, chapters 4 and 5)

Successful efforts must begin at the local level. Without emphasis on local results, citizens lose confidence in their government's ability to provide a better life. Actions to restore security, create trust, generate employment, and provide services in local communities lay the foundation for national progress. It is not enough to deliver results in big cities. In cases of ethnic and religious strife, where mutual insecurity can feed on itself, a local authority that is seen to be fair and impartial by all groups is absolutely essential before the process of healing and recovery can take place. This was Singapore's experience when we had race riots in the 1960s. A trusted leader can make a decisive difference.

It takes time to build institutions. Getting the urgent things done first, especially improving security and providing jobs, helps people to feel more hopeful about the future. Success then creates the condition for further success. Without a practical approach, new institutions cannot take root in the hearts and minds of ordinary people. For Singapore in the early years, the priority was on security, law and order, and creating favorable conditions for investment and economic growth. Confidence was everything. National Service was introduced within a year. Secret societies and other criminal activities were suppressed. Corruption was progressively rooted out. To promote investment and job creation, labor and land acquisition laws were reformed early. Against conventional wisdom in many developing countries at that time, we eschewed protectionism and encouraged multinationals to invest. Managing the politics of change was always a challenge.

The key was winning the trust of the people. Institutions which endure are sustained by the respect and affection of the population. It is a process which takes at least a generation.

REFLECTIONS FROM ADVISORY COUNCIL MEMBERS: *2011 WORLD DEVELOPMENT REPORT*

FEATURE 3 *Country experiences of confidence-building and transforming institutions for citizen security, justice, and jobs* **(continued)**

Colombia's restoration of confidence in safe transit

Marta Lucía Ramirez de Rincón, Director, Fundación Ciudadanía en Acción; former Senator and Chair of Security Commission, Colombia; former Defense Minister and former Foreign Trade Minister, Colombia; *WDR Advisory Council Member*

(Abbreviated from WDR 2011, chapter 5)

The challenge we faced in 2002 was preventing Colombia from becoming a failed state. This meant shielding our citizens from kidnapping and terrorism. It also meant protecting our infrastructure, roads, and democratic institutions against attacks by the guerrillas, the paramilitaries, and drug traffickers. These groups hijacked cars and kidnapped people as they travelled across the country. Since this problem had worsened in the years ahead of the 2002 elections, the government set the restoration of security in roads and highways as a key priority on their agenda. It devised the Meteoro program widely known as, "Live Colombia, travel across it" (*"Vive Colombia, Viaja por ella"*).

Meteoro aimed at restoring control of the roads and highways across the country back from the illegitimate hand of armed groups that inflicted fear in the population. The government invited the Colombian population to drive their cars and travel across the country without intimidation, while at the same time launching a major military, intelligence, and police operation to protect the roads and ensure the safety of the population. Through this plan, the government sought to give people back their country and to reactivate trade and tourism. Above all, this plan, implemented at the very early stage of the new government, brought about a breakthrough in the restoration of trust and hope in the Colombian society.

Do not confuse speed with haste in political processes

Lakhdar Brahimi, former UN Special Representative of the Secretary General to Iraq and Afghanistan; *WDR Advisory Council Member*

(Abbreviated from WDR 2011, chapter 5)

It is important not to confuse speed with haste in political processes: too hasty approaches can precipitate the opposite effect from the one we seek to support. The international community's high hopes for Iraq's 2005 experiment in proportional electoral democracy produced a contest for power which increased rather than allayed sectarian violence and the constitution hastily produced later is proving difficult to implement. Similarly, the 2009 election in Afghanistan proved to challenge rather than bolster perceptions of institutional legitimacy in the immediate aftermath.

The options are not mutually exclusive—there is great worldwide demand for more inclusive and responsive governance, and elections can be a crucial means to provide this. But their timing requires careful attention. Democratic traditions have developed in most countries over a considerable period. Democratization efforts today, similarly, require attention to historical heritages and existing political cleavages, and must be seen as an ongoing process of social transformation and the development of a broad range of institutions that provide checks and balances rather than an identifiable "event." Democratization does not start or end with elections.

Addressing external stresses and mobilizing international support

External stresses, such as the infiltration of organized crime and trafficking networks, spillovers from neighboring conflicts, and economic shocks, are important factors in increasing the risk of violence. In fragile situations, many of these external pressures will already be present and the institutions to respond to them are generally weak. If they are not addressed, or if they increase, they can derail efforts at violence prevention and recovery. Far more so than in stable development environments, addressing external stresses therefore needs to be a core part of national strategies and international supporting efforts for violence prevention and recovery.

International assistance needs also differ in fragile situations. The requirement to generate rapid confidence-building results puts a particular premium on speed. The focus on building collaborative, inclusive-enough coalitions and on citizen security, justice, and jobs draws together a wider range of international capacities that need to work in concert—for example, for mediation, human rights, and security assistance, as well as humanitarian and development aid. Where the political situation is fragile and the capacity of local systems to ensure accountability is weak, international incentives—such as recognition and sanction mechanisms—also play a significant role. Take one of the smaller West African countries that have recently had coups d'état. Local mechanisms to resolve the situation peacefully are limited, and African Union (AU) and Economic Community of West African States (ECOWAS) pressure to return to a constitutional path is critical. So regional and global recognition for responsible leadership can play a role in strengthening incentives and accountability systems at a national level.

Practical policy and program tools for country actors

The WDR lays out a different way of thinking about approaches to violence prevention and recovery in fragile situations. It does not aim to be a "cookbook" that prescribes recipes—each country's political context differs, and there are no one-size-fits-all solutions. While the choice of confidence-building measures and institution-building approaches needs to be adapted to each country, a set of basic tools emerging from experience can be the basis for that adaptation. These core tools include the options for signals and commitment mechanisms to build collaborative coalitions, demonstrating a break from the past and building confidence in positive outcomes. They also include a description of the programs that can deliver quick results and longer-term institutional provision of citizen security, justice, and jobs. The Report first presents the basic tools and then looks at how to differentiate strategies and programming to different country circumstances, using country-specific assessments of risks and opportunities.

Political and policy signals to build collaborative, inclusive-enough coalitions

There is a surprising commonality across countries in the signals that most frequently build confidence and collaborative coalitions (see Feature 4). They can include immediate actions in credible national or local appointments, in transparency, and in some cases, the removal of factors seen as negative, such as discriminatory laws. Security forces can be redeployed as a positive signal of attention to insecure areas, but also as a sign that the government recognizes where particular units have a record of distrust or abuse with communities and replaces them. Measures to improve transparency of information and decision-making processes can be important in building confidence, as well as laying the basis for sustained institutional transformation.

Signals can also be announcements of future actions—the selection of two or three key early results; the focus of military and police planning on citizen security goals; or setting approaches and timelines toward political reform, decentralization, or transitional justice. Ensuring that political and policy signals are realistic in scope and timing and can be delivered is important in managing expectations—by anchoring them in national planning and budget processes and discussing any external support needed in advance with international partners.

When signals relate to future action, their credibility will be increased by commitment mechanisms that persuade stakeholders that they will actually be implemented and not reversed. Examples are Colombia's and Indonesia's independent, multisectoral executing agencies and third-party monitors, such as

Feature 4 Core Tools

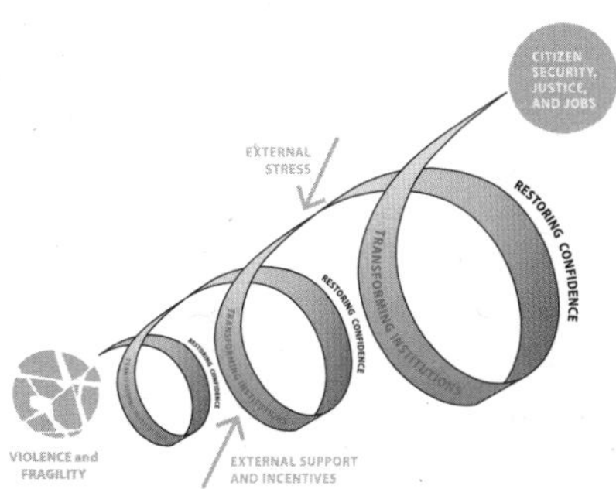

RESTORING CONFIDENCE

Signals: Future policy and priorities	Signals: Immediate actions	Commitment mechanisms	Supporting actions
• Citizen security goals • Key principles and realistic timelines for political reform, decentralization, corruption, transitional justice • Mix of state, community, NGO, and international capacity	• Participatory processes • Local security, justice, and development results • Credible appointments • Transparency in expenditures • Redeployment of security forces • Removal of discriminatory policies	• Independence of executing agencies • Independent third-party monitoring • Dual-key national-international systems • International execution of one or more key functions	• Risk and priority assessments • Communicating costs of inaction • Simple plans and progress measures on 2–3 early results • Strategic communication

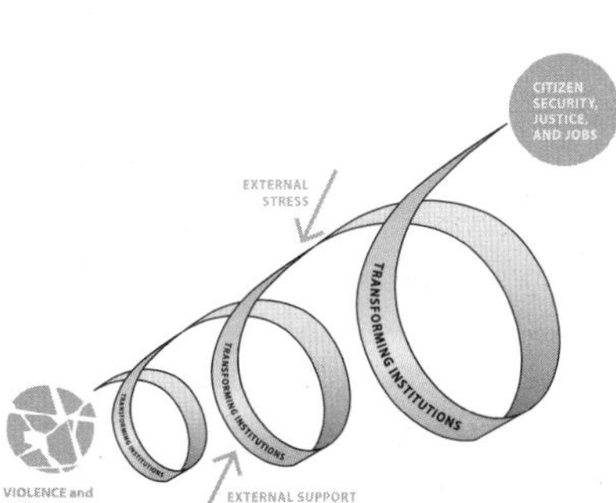

TRANSFORMING INSTITUTIONS

Citizen security	Justice	Jobs and associated services
Foundational reforms and "best-fit" approaches		
Security sector reform: • Designed to deliver citizen security benefits • Capacity increases linked to repeated realistic performance outcomes and justice functions • Dismantling criminal networks through civilian oversight, vetting and budget expenditure transparency • Use of low-capital systems for rural and community policing	***Justice sector reform:*** independence and link to security reforms; strengthening basic caseload processing; extending justice services, drawing on traditional/community mechanisms ***Phasing anti-corruption measures:*** demonstrate national resources can be used for public good before dismantling rent systems; control capture of rents and use social accountability mechanisms	***Multisectoral community empowerment programs:*** combining citizen security, employment, justice, education, and infrastructure ***Employment programs:*** regulatory simplification and infrastructure recovery for private-sector job creation, long-term public programs, asset expansion, value chain programs, informal sector support, labor migration, women's economic empowerment, and asset expansion ***Humanitarian delivery and social protection:*** with planned transition from international provision ***Macroeconomic policy:*** focus on consumer price volatility and employment
Gradual, systematic programs		
• Phased capacity and accountability in specialized security functions	• Political and electoral reform • Decentralization • Transitional justice • Comprehensive anti-corruption reforms	• Structural economic reforms such as privatization • Education and health reforms • Inclusion of marginalized groups

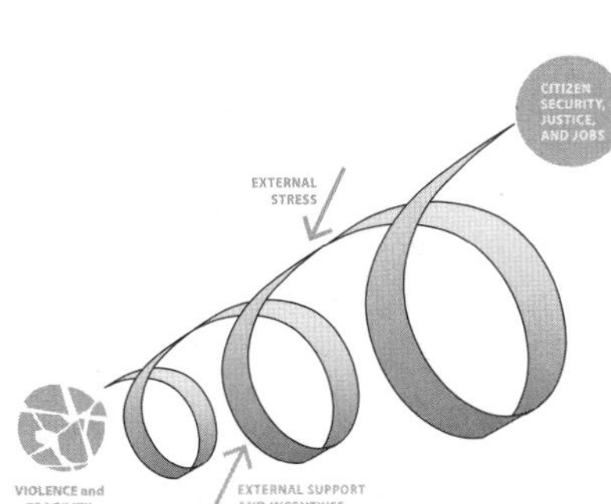

NATIONAL ACTION TO ADDRESS EXTERNAL STRESS

Citizen security	Justice	Jobs and associated services
• Border cooperation • Military, police, and financial intelligence	• Coordinate supply and demand-side responses • Joint investigations and prosecutions across jurisdictions • Building links between formal/informal systems	• Pooled supplementary administrative capacity • Cross-border development programming

FEASIBLE RESULTS INDICATORS TO DEMONSTRATE OVERALL PROGRESS

	Citizen security	Justice	Jobs and associated services
Short term	• Violent deaths • Perception survey data on increases/decreases in security	• Perception surveys by groups (ethnic, geographical, religious, class) on whether their welfare is increasing over time and in relation to others • Perception survey on trust in national institutions and on corruption	• Perceptions of whether employment opportunities are increasing • Price surveys (for real income implications)
Longer term	• Victim surveys	• Governance indicators refocused on outcomes and degree of progress within historically realistic timeframes • Household survey data on vertical and horizontal inequalities and access to justice services	• Household data on employment and labor force participation

the joint ASEAN-EU (Association of Southeast Asian Nations–European Union) Aceh monitoring mission.[60] Sole or "dual-key" authority over one or more functions involving international agencies—as with the jointly run Governance and Economic Management Assistance Program in Liberia,[61] the International Commission Against Impunity (CICIG) in Guatemala,[62] or when UN peacekeeping missions have executive responsibility for policing—is also a commitment mechanism when institutional capacity and accountability are low.

Strong strategic communication on these signals of change are always important—actions and policy changes cannot influence behaviors unless people know they have taken place and how they fit into a broader vision. Where the risks of crisis escalation are not fully recognized by all national leaders, providing an accurate and compelling message on the consequences of inaction can help galvanize momentum for progress. Economic and social analyses can support this narrative—by showing how rising violence and failing institutions are causing national or subnational areas to lag far behind their neighbors in development progress; or by showing how other countries that have failed to address rising threats have faced severe and long-lasting development consequences. The WDR analysis provides some clear messages:

- No country or region can afford to ignore areas where repeated cycles of violence flourish and citizens are disengaged from the state.
- Unemployment, corruption, and exclusion increase the risks of violence—and legitimate institutions and governance that give everyone a stake in national prosperity are the immune system that protects from different types of violence.
- Citizen security is a preeminent goal in fragile situations, underpinned by justice and jobs.
- Leaders need to seize opportunities before violence escalates or recurs.

National program design to restore confidence and transform institutions

The core program tools that emerge from different country experiences are deliberately kept small in number to reflect country lessons on focus and priorities. They are all designed to be delivered at scale, in large national or subnational programs rather than small projects. They include multisectoral programs linking community structures with the state; security sector reform; justice reform; national employment policy and programs; associated services that support citizen security, justice, and job creation, such as electricity and social protection; and phased approaches to corruption. They also include programs that can be crucial for sustained violence prevention: political reform, decentralization, transitional justice, and education reform where systematic attention is needed once early reforms in citizen security, justice, and jobs have started to make progress.

The top five lessons of what works in program design are:

- Programs that support bottom-up state-society relations in insecure areas. These include community-based programs for violence prevention, employment, and associated service delivery, and access to local justice and dispute resolution. Examples are community policing in a wide range of higher-, middle-, and lower-income countries, the Afghanistan National Solidarity Program, and Latin American multisectoral violence prevention programs.[63]
- Complementary programs for institutional transformation in the priority areas of security and justice. Early reform programs should focus on simple basic functions (such as criminal caseload processing, adequate basic investigation, and arrest procedures); include civilian oversight, vetting, and budget and expenditure transparency to dismantle covert or criminal networks; and link the pace of reform between the police and civilian justice systems to avoid situations where increasing

police capacity results in prolonged detentions or the release of offenders back into the community without due process.

- "Back to basics" job creation programs. These programs include large-scale community-based public works, such as those India and Indonesia use throughout the country, including in marginalized and violence-affected communities; private-sector regulatory simplification and addressing of infrastructure bottlenecks (in particular, electricity, which is the number one constraint for businesses in fragile and violent areas); and access to finance and investments to bring producers and markets together, as in Kosovo's and Rwanda's coffee, dairy, and tourism initiatives.[64]
- The involvement of women in security, justice, and economic empowerment programs, such as the Nicaragua, Liberia, and Sierra Leone reforms to introduce female staffing and gender-specific service in the police force; and economic empowerment initiatives in Nepal, which addressed issues of gender roles that had previously been divisive in insecure areas through the provision of finance and business training to women's groups.[65]
- Focused anticorruption initiatives that demonstrate that new initiatives can be well governed. Tools have included the use of private-sector capacity to monitor functions vulnerable to grand corruption, as with Liberia's forestry inspection and Mozambique's customs collection, combined with social accountability mechanisms that use transparent publication of expenditure and community/civil-society monitoring to ensure funds reach their intended targets.[66]

Some of the early confidence-building results that can be targeted through these programs include freedom of movement along transit routes, electricity coverage, number of businesses registered and employment days created, processing of judicial caseloads, and reduction of impunity through vetting or prosecutions. What is crucial here is that early results generate improvements in the morale of national institutions and set the right incentives for later institution-building.

For example, if security forces are set targets based on the number of rebel combatants killed or captured or criminals arrested, they may rely primarily on coercive approaches, with no incentive to build the longer-term trust with communities that will prevent violence from recurring. Targets based on citizen security (freedom of movement and so on), in contrast, create longer-term incentives for the role of the security forces in underpinning national unity and effective state-society relations. Similarly, if services and public works are delivered only through top-down national programs, there will be few incentives for communities to take responsibility for violence prevention or for national institutions to undertake responsibility to protect all vulnerable citizens, men and women. A mixture of state and nonstate, bottom-up and top-down approaches is a better underpinning for longer-term institutional transformation.

Phasing transitions from humanitarian aid is also an important part of transforming institutions. In countries where current stresses overwhelm national institutional capacity by a large margin, national reformers often draw on international humanitarian capacity to deliver early results. These programs can be effective in saving lives, building confidence, and extending national capacity. But a difficult trade-off occurs in deciding on the time needed to shift these functions to national institutions. For food programs, this generally means phasing down deliveries before local harvests and moving from general distribution to targeted programs, in coordination with government social protection agencies where possible. For health, education, water, and sanitation, it means reducing international roles step-by-step over time as the capacity of national or local institutions increases—as in the transition from international to national health provision in Timor-Leste, which moved from international execution to government contracting of international NGOs and then to government management.[67]

Regional and cross-border initiatives

Societies do not have the luxury of transforming their institutions in isolation—they need at the same time to manage external pressures, whether from economic shocks or trafficking and international corruption. Many of these issues are beyond the control of each nation-state to address, and the last section of the Report considers international policy to diminish external stresses. National leaders may play a significant role in galvanizing broad regional or global cooperation on issues such as trafficking, as well as bilateral cooperation. Possible initiatives include:

- Openness to discuss both security and development cooperation across insecure border regions, based on shared goals of citizen security, justice, and jobs rather than purely on military operations. Cross-border development programming could simply involve special arrangements to share lessons. But it could also move toward formal joint arrangements to design and monitor development programs in insecure border areas and move toward specific provisions to help insecure landlocked areas gain access to markets.
- Joint processes to investigate and prosecute incidents of corruption that can fuel violence, as Haiti and Nigeria have done (with the United States and the United Kingdom) to combat corruption and money-laundering.[68] These can build capacity in weaker jurisdictions and deliver results that could not be achieved by one jurisdiction alone.

Mobilizing international support

Some constraints in international support come from policies and systems established in the headquarters of multilateral agencies and donor countries. Actions on these issues are discussed in Part 3 under Directions for International Policy. National leaders and their partners on the ground cannot individually determine these broader changes to the international system, but they can maximize the benefits of existing support.

It helps when national leaders and their international partners in the field lay out clear program priorities across the security, justice, and development domains. Country experiences indicate that efforts need to focus on only two or three rapid results to build confidence, and on narrowly and realistically defined institution-building. Priorities are better laid out in a very limited number of clear programs—such as community-based interventions in insecure areas, security and freedom of movement on key roads—as in Liberia[69] after the civil war and in Colombia[70] in the face of criminal violence in 2002. Using the national budget process to decide on priority programs coordinates messages and develops cooperation in implementation between the security and development ministries.

National leaders can also produce better results from external assistance by being alert to the needs of international partners to show results and manage risks. International partners have their own domestic pressures—to demonstrate that assistance is not misused and to attribute results to their endeavors. A frank exchange on risks and results helps to find ways to bridge differences. In Indonesia in the aftermath of the Tsunami and Aceh peace agreement, for example, the government agreed with donors that incoming assistance would be "jointly branded" by the Indonesian Reconstruction Agency and donors, with special transparency measures in place to enable both sides to show visible results and manage risks while bolstering the legitimacy of state-society relations in the aftermath of crisis. A "double compact" between governments and their citizens and between states and their international partners, first proposed by Ashraf Ghani and

Clare Lockhart, is another way of managing different perspectives on risk, the speed of response, and long-term engagement with national institutions—by making dual accountability of donor funds explicit.[71]

Monitoring results

To evaluate the success of programs and adapt them when problems arise, national reformers and their international partners in country also need information on overall results in reducing violence, and on citizen confidence in security, justice, and employment goals at regular intervals. For most developing countries, the MDGs and their associated targets and indicators are the dominant international framework. The MDGs have raised the profile of broad-based human development and remain important long-term goals for countries facing fragility and violence. But they have drawbacks in their direct relevance to progress in violence prevention and recovery. They do not cover citizen security and justice. They move slowly, so they do not provide national reformers or their international partners with rapid feedback loops that can demonstrate areas of progress and identify new or remaining risks.

A useful supplement to the MDGs would be indicators that more directly measure violence reduction, confidence-building and citizen security and justice (Feature 4). Citizen polling data, glaringly absent in many fragile and conflict-affected countries, could help fill this role.[72] Middle- and higher-income countries use polling all the time to provide governments with feedback on progress and risks, but it is little used in low-income, fragile countries. Direct measurement of security improvements can also show rapid progress, but while data on violent deaths are fairly easy to collect, they are not available for the countries that would benefit most from them: low-income, fragile states. Employment data also need to be upgraded.

Differentiating strategy and programs to country context

While there is a basic set of tools emerging from experience, each country needs to assess its circumstances and adapt lessons from others to the local political context. Each country faces different stresses, different institutional challenges, different stakeholders who need to be involved to make a difference, and different types of transition opportunities. The differences are not black and white but occur across a spectrum—each country will have different manifestations of violence, different combinations of internal or external stresses, and different institutional challenges—and these factors will change over time. But all countries face some aspects of this mix. The Report covers some of the most important differences in country circumstances through the simple differentiation shown below.

National reformers and their country counterparts need to take two types of decisions in each phase of confidence-building and institutional reform, taking into account the local political context. First is to decide the types of signals—both immediate actions and announcements on early results and longer-term policies—that can help build "inclusive-enough" collaborative coalitions for change. Second is to decide on the design

Spectra of situation-specific challenges and opportunities	
Types of violence: Civil and/or criminal and/or cross-border and/or sub-national and/or ideological	
Transition opportunity: Gradual/limited to immediate/major space for change	**Key stakeholders:** Internal versus external stakeholders; state versus nonstate stakeholders; low-income versus middle-high income stakeholders
Key stresses: Internal versus external stresses; high versus low level of divisions among groups	**Institutional challenges:** Degree of capacity, accountability, and inclusion

of priority programs to launch for institutional transformation.

In differentiating political and policy signals, the type of stresses faced and the stakeholders whose support is most needed for effective action make a difference. Where ethnic, geographical, or religious divides have been associated with conflict, and the cooperation of these groups is critical to progress, the credibility of appointments may rest on whether individuals command respect across group divides. Where corruption has been a severe stress, the credibility of key appointments may rest on individuals' reputation for integrity.

The type of transition moment also makes a difference. At the end of the wars in Japan and the Republic of Korea, the birth of the new nation of Timor-Leste, Liberia's first post-war election, military victory in Nicaragua, and in the aftermath of the Rwandan genocide, there was greater space for rapid announcements of long-term political, social, and institutional change than exists today for the coalition government in Kenya or other situations of negotiated reform.

Institutional capacity, accountability, and trust among groups also affect the choices and timetable of early policy announcements. In countries with institutions that are strong but have been viewed as illegitimate because they are exclusive, abusive, or unaccountable (as in some transitions from authoritarian rule), action on transparency, participation, and justice may be more important for short-term confidence-building than delivering goods and services. Where social cohesion is factionalized, time may be needed to build trust between groups before wider reform is attempted. In South Africa, for example, leaders wisely allowed time for constitutional reform and the development of trust between groups before the first post-Apartheid election.[73] And in Northern Ireland the devolution of security and justice functions were delayed until trust and accountability increased.[74]

A core message is that the particular manifestation of violence at any one time is less important than the underlying institutional deficits that permit repeated cycles of violence—and that successful approaches to address political, communal, and criminal violence have much in common. But the mix of different types of violence does affect strategy. Inequality among ethnic, religious, or geographical groups is important as a risk for civil conflict—employment programs and services would thus target equity and bridging opportunities among these groups. But for organized criminal violence, inequality between rich and poor matters more (irrespective of ethnic or religious identities). Violence with strong international links—organized crime, international recruitment into ideological movements—requires greater international cooperation.

Country circumstances also make a difference for program design, requiring the "best-fit" to local political conditions. For example, multisectoral community approaches can be effective in contexts as different as Côte d'Ivoire, Guatemala, and Northern Ireland—but more care would be needed in Côte d'Ivoire and Northern Ireland to ensure that these approaches were not seen as targeted to one ethnic or religious group but, instead, as building bonds among groups. Both Colombia and Haiti are considering reform in the justice sector, but accountability and capacity problems are a bigger challenge in Haiti, and reforms would have to be designed accordingly.[75] For middle-income countries with strong institutions facing challenges of exclusion and accountability, lessons on program design, successes, and missed opportunities will come primarily from countries that have faced similar circumstances, such as the democratic transitions in Latin America, Indonesia, Eastern Europe, or South Africa. So national reformers and their international partners need to think through the political economy for interventions and adapt program design to that context (Feature 5).

Each country needs its own assessment of risks and priorities to design the best-fit strategy and programs for its political context. International assessment tools, such as post-conflict/post-crisis needs assessments, can identify the risks and priorities. These assessments could be strengthened by:

- Adapting assessments regularly and frequently at different transition moments, including when risks are increasing, not only after a crisis.
- Identifying the specific characteristics of transition opportunities, stresses, institutional challenges, stakeholders, and the institutions that provide citizen security, justice, and jobs.
- Identifying priorities from a citizen and stakeholder perspective through focus groups or polling surveys, as South Africa did in developing its reconstruction priorities or as Pakistan did in assessing the sources of violence in the border regions.[76]
- Considering explicitly the history of past efforts, as Colombia did in reviewing the strengths and weaknesses of previous efforts to address violence in the early 2000s.[77]
- Being more realistic about the number of priorities identified and the timelines, as with the changes recommended to the joint United Nations–World Bank–European Union post-crisis needs assessment.

PART 3: REDUCING THE RISKS OF VIOLENCE—DIRECTIONS FOR INTERNATIONAL POLICY

International action has delivered great benefits in improved security and prosperity. It is difficult to imagine how committed leaders in post–World War II Europe, Indonesia, the Republic of Korea, Liberia, Mozambique, Northern Ireland, or Timor-Leste would have stabilized their countries or regions without help from abroad. Many individuals working on fragile and conflict-affected states are dedicated professionals attempting to support national efforts. But they are held back by structures, tools, and processes designed for different contexts and purposes. Specifically, while processes exist to provide the kind of post-war assistance typical of 20th-century paradigms, there is little attention to helping countries that struggle with prevention of repeated cycles of political and criminal violence (Feature 6, figure 6.1) and with the challenges involved in transforming institutions to provide citizen security, justice, and jobs. Internal international agency processes are too slow, too fragmented, too reliant on parallel systems, and too quick to exit, and there are significant divisions among international actors.

The range of preventive tools in the international system has improved, with increases in global and regional mediation capacity[78] and in programs that support both local and national collaborative efforts to mediate violence. Examples include the Ghana peace committees supported by the UN Development Programme (UNDP) and the UN Department of Political Affairs (UNDPA)[79] and the Inter-American Development Bank (IADB) community projects for citizen security. Such programs do often support activities relating to citizen security, justice, and jobs, but they are not in the mainstream of diplomatic, security, or development thinking. UN, regional, and NGO-sponsored mediation has played a significant role in a range of cases—from AU-UN-ECOWAS mediation in West Africa to UN facilitation of Afghanistan's Bonn Agreement to nongovernmental efforts such as the Centre for Humanitarian Dialogue and the Crisis Management Initiative in Aceh.[80]

But these programs are still not delivered to scale. It is much harder for countries to get international assistance to support development of their police forces and judiciaries than their militaries. International economic development assistance is easier to obtain for macroeconomic policy, health, or education capacities than for job creation. UN police capacity, doctrinal development, and training have increased, but are not fully linked to justice capacities. While some bilateral agencies

FEATURE 5 *Adapting community-level program design to country context*

Countries: Afghanistan, Burundi, Cambodia, Colombia, Indonesia, Nepal, Rwanda

The basic elements of a post-conflict community development program are simple and can be adapted to a broad range of country contexts. All community programs under state auspices consist, essentially, of a community decision-making mechanisms to determine priorities and the provision of funds and technical help to implement them. Within this model is a great deal of variance that can be adapted to different types of stresses and institutional capacities as well as to different opportunities for transition. Three important sources of variance are in how community decision-making is done, who controls the funds, and where programs reside within the government.

Different stresses and institutional capacity and accountability affect community decision-making. In many violent areas, preexisting community councils either have been destroyed or were already discredited. A critical first step is to reestablish credible participatory forms of representation. In Burundi, for example, a local NGO organized elections for representative community development committees in the participating communes that cut across ethnic divides. Similarly, Afghanistan's National Solidarity Program began with village-wide elections for a community development council. But Indonesia's programs for the conflict-affected areas of Aceh, Maluku, Sulawesi, and Kalimantan did not hold new community elections. Community councils were largely intact, and national laws already provided for local, democratic, village elections. Indonesia also experimented with separating grants to Muslim and Christian villages to minimize intercommunal tensions, but eventually used common funds and councils to bridge divides between these communities.

Different institutional challenges also affect who holds the funds. Programs must weigh the trade-offs between a first objective of building trust with the risks of money going missing or the elite capture of resources, as shown in the following examples:

- In Indonesia, where local capacity was fairly strong, subdistrict councils established financial management units that are routinely audited but have full responsibility for all aspects of financial performance.
- In Burundi, a lack of progress in overall decentralization and difficulties in monitoring funds through community structures meant responsibility for managing the funds remained with NGO partners.
- In Afghanistan's National Solidarity Program, NGOs also took on the initial responsibility for managing the funds while councils were trained in bookkeeping, but within a year block grants were being transferred directly to the councils.
- In Colombia, where the primary institutional challenges were to bring the state closer to communities and overcome distrust between security and civilian government agencies, funds are held by individual government ministries but approvals for activities are made by multisectoral teams in field offices.
- In Nepal, community programs show the full range: some programs give primary responsibility for fund oversight to partner NGOs; in other programs, such as the country's large-scale village school program, community school committees are the legal owners of school facilities and can use government funds to hire and train their staff.

The type of transition moment affects how community decision-making structures align with the formal government administration. Many countries emerging from conflict will also undergo major constitutional and administrative reforms just as the early response community programs are being launched. Aligning community councils with the emergent structures of government can be difficult. In Afghanistan's National Solidarity Program, for example, the Community Development Councils, though constituted under a 2007 vice-presidential bylaw, are still under review for formal integration into the national administrative structure. In Cambodia's Seila Program, councils were launched under United Nations Development Programme (UNDP) auspices and then moved into the government's newly formed commune structure. In Rwanda, greater space for change after the genocide meant the councils could be integrated into the government's decentralization plans from the start.

Source: Guggenheim 2011.

provide specialized assistance for security and justice reform, their capacities are relatively new and underdeveloped in comparison with other areas. International financial institutions and bilateral economic assistance tends to focus primarily on growth rather than employment. Citizen security and justice are not mentioned in the MDGs.

The programs described above all require linked action by diplomatic, security, and development—and sometimes humanitarian—actors. Yet these actors generally assess priorities and develop their programs separately, with efforts to help national reformers build unified programs the exception rather than the rule. UN "integrated missions" and various bilateral and regional "whole-of-government" and "whole-of-systems" initiatives have emerged to address the challenge of merging development, diplomatic, and security strategies and operations.[81] But different disciplines bring with them different goals, planning timeframes, decision-making processes, funding streams and types of risk calculus.[82]

Assistance is often slow to arrive despite efforts of the UN, the international financial institutions, and bilateral donors to establish quick-disbursing and rapid deployment facilities. Aid is fragmented into small projects, making it difficult for governments to concentrate efforts on a few key results. In 11 fragile countries the Organisation for Economic Co-operation and Development (OECD) surveyed in 2004, there was an average of 38 activities per donor, with each project an average size of just US$1.1 million—too small for the most part to have an impact on the challenges of institutional transformation.[83] Aid donors often operate in fragile countries through systems parallel to national institutions—with separate project units for development aid and with humanitarian programs implemented through international NGOs. Despite progress in extending the time horizons of peacekeeping missions and some types of donor assistance, the system is constrained by a short-term focus on post-conflict opportunities and high volatility in assistance.[84] In a recent European Commission survey of assistance to Cambodia, more than 35 percent of all projects were less than one year in duration, and 66 percent were less than three years. Despite the need for more consistent and sustained assistance, aid to fragile states is much more volatile than that to nonfragile states—indeed, more than twice as volatile, with an estimated loss in efficiency of 2.5 percent of GDP for recipient states (Feature 6, figures F6.2 and F6.3).[85]

Regional and global action on external stresses is a key part of risk reduction, but assistance is still focused primarily at the individual country level. Some innovative processes against trafficking combine demand-side and supply-side incentives and the efforts of multiple stakeholders in developed and developing countries[86]—one is the Kimberley Process Certification Scheme to stem the sale of conflict diamonds.[87] Yet a general principle of co-responsibility, combining demand-side and supply-side actions and cooperation between developed and developing regions, is lacking. Existing efforts suffer from weakness and fragmentation in the financial systems used to "follow the money" flowing from corrupt transactions. And they are constrained by a multiplication of weak and overlapping multicountry endeavors rather than strong and well-resourced regional approaches. Despite some exceptions—the Asian Development Bank and European Union long-standing regional programs, the UN Department of Political Affairs regional offices, and recent increases in regional lending by the World Bank—most development donors focus primarily on national rather than regional support.

The international landscape is becoming more complex. The end of the Cold War had the potential to usher in a new age of consensus in international support to violence and conflict-affected areas. In fact, the last decade has seen an increase in complexity and continued coordination problems. The political, security, humanitarian, and development actors present in each country situation have become more numerous. Legal agreements that set standards for responsible national leadership have become more complicated over time: the 1948 UN Convention Against Genocide has 17 operative paragraphs; the 2003 Convention Against Corruption has 455. Within OECD countries, there are divided views over the relative role of security and development assistance and over aid through national institutions. The increase in assistance from middle-income countries, with a history of solidarity support, not only brings valuable new energy, resources, and ideas, but also new challenges in the differing views of international partners. WDR consultations frequently revealed divided views among national actors, regional bodies, middle-income countries, and OECD donors over what is realistic to expect from national leadership in improving governance, over what time period, and over the "forms" versus the "functions" of good governance (elections versus broader democratic practices and processes; minimizing corruption in practice versus establishing procurement laws and anticorruption commissions).

Dual accountability is at the heart of international behavior. International actors know that faster, smarter, longer-term engagement through national and regional institutions is needed to help societies exit fragility. But as highlighted by the OECD International Network on Conflict and Fragility,[88] they are also acutely sensitive to the risks of domestic criticism of waste, abuse, corruption, and a lack of results in donor programs. International actors need to be accountable to their citizens and taxpayers as well as to partner country needs, and these expectations can be at odds (figure 3.1).

The slow progress in changing donor behavior comes from these underlying incentives. For example, undertaking small projects through parallel systems, focusing on the "form rather than function" of change (with an emphasis on elections, model procurement laws, and anti-corruption and human rights commissions), and avoiding engagements in riskier institution-building—all help donors to manage domestic expectations of results and criticism of failure. In today's tight fiscal environment for many donors, the dilemma is becoming more prominent, not less. Domestic pressures also contribute to divisions among donors, since some donors face far more domestic pressure than others on corruption, gender equity, or the need to show economic benefits at home from aid overseas. Accountability to taxpayers is a desirable facet of donor aid—but the challenge is to make domestic expectations fit with the needs and realities of assistance on the ground.

Multilateral responses are also constrained by historical arrangements suited to more stable environments. For example, the international financial institutions' procurement procedures were based on the assumption of

FIGURE 3.1 ***The dual accountability dilemma for donors engaged in fragile and conflict environments***

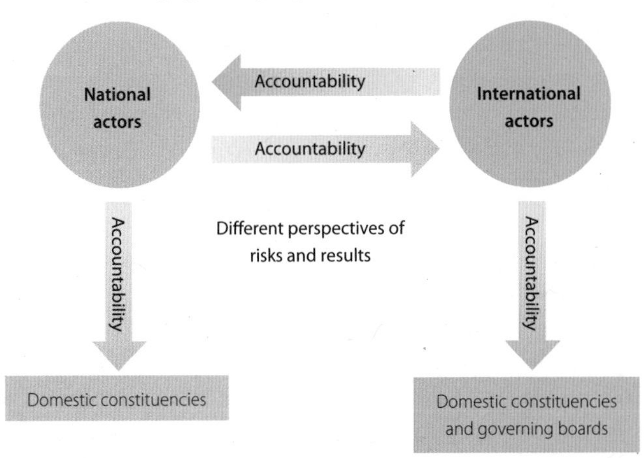

Source: WDR team.

FEATURE 6 *Patterns of international assistance to violence-affected countries*

FIGURE F6.1 *Uneven international support in West Africa—Post-conflict trumps prevention*

A one-off concept of progress and the difficulties of prevention have led to an excessive focus on post-conflict transitions. The amount of aid and peacekeeping assistance going to countries after civil war has ended greatly exceeds what is provided to countries struggling to prevent an escalation of conflict.

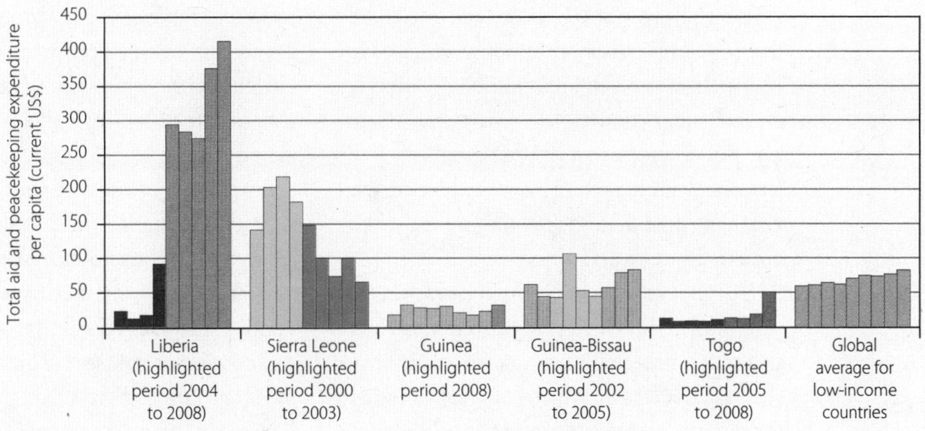

Source: WDR team calculations based on OECD 2010d.

FIGURE F6.2 *Aid volatility increases with duration of violence*

Over the last 20 years, countries that experienced longer periods of fragility, violence, or conflict experienced more volatility in their aid. Figure 6.2 shows that the coefficient of variance of net official development assistance (ODA), excluding debt relief, is higher for countries that have experienced prolonged violence since 1990. This relationship, reflected by the upward trend line, is statistically significant and suggests that, on average, a country that experienced 20 years of violence experienced twice the volatility in aid of a country that did not experience violence. Volatility of revenues has considerable costs for all governments, but particularly so in fragile situations where it may derail reform efforts and disrupt institution-building.

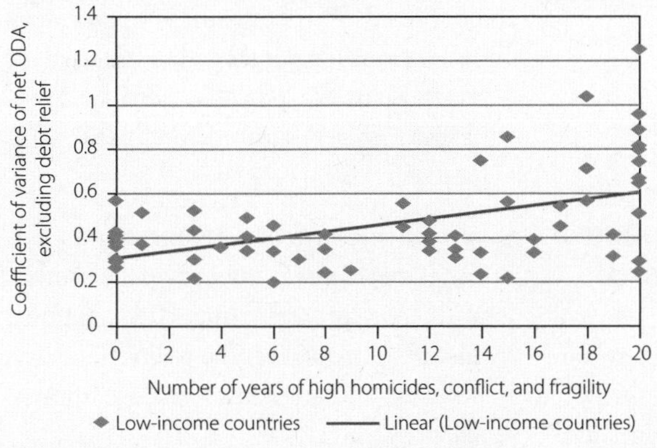

Source: WDR team calculations based on OECD 2010d.

FIGURE F6.3 *Stop-go aid: Volatility in selected fragile states*

The four countries below provide an illustration. It was not uncommon for total aid to Burundi, the Central African Republic, Guinea-Bissau, and Haiti to drop by 20 or 30 percent in one year and increase by up to 50 percent the following year (humanitarian aid and debt relief, excluded from these statistics, would further increase the volatility).

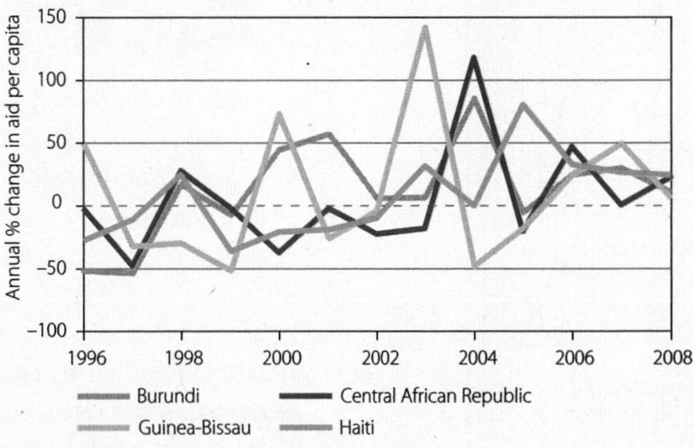

Source: WDR team calculations based on OECD 2010d.

ongoing security, a reasonable level of state institutional capacity, and competitive markets. They thus have difficulty adapting to situations where security conditions change between the design and tendering of a project, where a small number of qualified government counterparts struggle to manage complex procurement documentation, and where the number of qualified contractors prepared to compete and mobilize is very limited. Similarly, the UN Secretariat originally developed procurement systems designed for its function as a headquarters-based advisory service and secretariat to the General Assembly. But when peacekeeping operations were launched, these systems were extended with relatively little adaptation, despite the difference in contexts and objectives.

To achieve real change in approaches that can restore confidence and prevent risks from recurring, international actors could consider four tracks to improve global responses for security and development as follows:

- **Track 1:** Provide more, and more integrated, specialized assistance for citizen security, justice, and jobs—targeting prevention in both immediate post-conflict and rising risk situations.
- **Track 2:** Reform internal agency systems to provide rapid action to restore confidence and promote long-term institution-building, in support of national efforts.
- **Track 3:** Act regionally and globally on external stresses.
- **Track 4:** Marshal support from lower-, middle-, and higher-income countries, and global and regional institutions, to reflect the changing landscape of international policy and assistance.

Track 1: Providing specialized assistance for prevention through citizen security, justice, and jobs

Security-development linkages apply in all areas struggling to prevent large-scale political or criminal violence. Both political and criminal violence require "outside the box" thinking, outside the traditional development paradigm. Issues of citizen security and of grievances over justice and jobs are not peripheral to "mainstream" development. They are in varying forms a problem for larger and more prosperous countries facing subnational urban or rural violence, for countries emerging from conflict and fragility that need to prevent recurrence, and for areas facing new or resurgent threats of social protest and instability. Strengthening the institutions that provide citizen security, justice, and jobs is crucial to prevention of violence and instability—such action is not a "magic bullet" that can prevent every episode of violence with certainty, but it is crucial to changing the probabilities of violence, and to continuous risk reduction.

A key lesson of successful violence prevention and recovery is that security, justice, and economic stresses are linked: approaches that try to solve them through military-only, justice-only, or development-only solutions will falter. A specialized suite of programs is needed in fragile environments, combining elements of security, justice, and economic transformation. But because these areas are covered by different international agencies, both bilaterally and multilaterally, combined action under one overall program framework is rare. A specialized suite of combined security-justice-development programs needs to aim at a catalytic effect, supporting national collaborative efforts to address these challenges. Changes in international agency approaches to support such programs would include (figure 3.2).

- Moving from sporadic early warning to continued risk assessment wherever weak institutional legitimacy, and internal or external stresses indicate a need for attention to prevention and to capacities for peaceful reform processes.
- Simplifying current assessment and planning mechanisms to provide countries with *one* process supporting national planning that covers the political, justice, security, humanitarian, and developmental areas.

FIGURE 3.2 *Combined action across the security, development, and humanitarian spheres for external actors to support national institutional transformations*

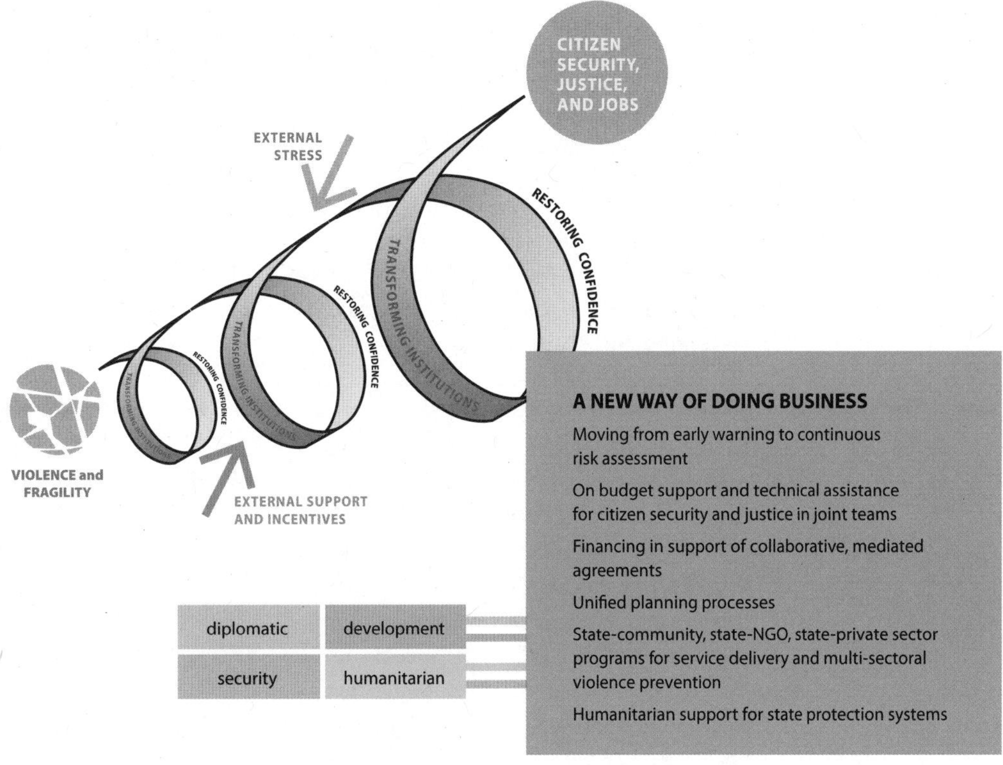

Source: WDR team.

- Shifting from the rhetoric of coordination to supporting combined programs for security, justice, and local jobs and associated services, each within their respective mandates and expertise. Two priorities for combined programs are—
  - ➢ Technical assistance and financing for security and justice reforms supported by combined teams. Development agencies, for example, can support measures to address budget and expenditure processes in security and justice functions, while partners with security and justice expertise can contribute to technical capacity-building, as was done in Timor-Leste in the run-up to independence.[89]
  - ➢ Multisectoral community programs that involve policing and justice as well as development activities, such as the initiatives in Latin America to provide local dispute resolution and justice services, community policing, employment and training, safe public and trading spaces, and social and cultural programs that promote tolerance.
- Establishing facilities for mediators and special envoys (internal and international) to draw on greater seconded expertise from international agencies, both to inform transition arrangements and to galvanize resources for integrated activities identified collaboratively by the different parties to a conflict situation. This should include specific efforts to support the growing role of regional and subregional institutions, such as AU and ECOWAS, by providing them with specific links to development expertise.
- Considering when humanitarian aid can be integrated into national systems without compromising humanitarian

principles—building on existing good practice by UNDP, UN Children's Fund (UNICEF), World Health Organization (WHO), World Food Programme (WFP), and others in combining humanitarian delivery with capacity-building, using local personnel and community structures, and purchasing food locally.

Implementing these programs would require systemic changes in international capacity. Citizen security and justice require new and interlinked capacities to address repeated waves of political and criminal violence. The starting point for deeper capacity in this area is government investment in standby, pretrained personnel for a range of executive and advisory police, corrections, and justice functions. States will need police and justice reserves to respond effectively to contemporary violence, drawing on retired personnel, active service volunteers, and formed police units in some countries. Second, these capacities must be trained, and able to deploy, under shared doctrine to address the challenges of coherence presented by different national policing models. Increased investment through the UN and regional centers in the development of joint doctrine and pretraining of government capacities would increase effectiveness and reduce incoherence.

Third, linking military and policing assistance with justice assistance is crucial, since disconnects have been a pervasive source of problems in fragile situations. So is linking criminal justice assistance with help for local justice services such as land and property disputes.[90] Fourth, it is important that new capacities provide a full range of services to countries facing challenges—from co-responsibility for policing or justice functions authorized by the UN Security Council or regional institutions, to police units and judicial personnel provided at the request of governments but without a corresponding intrusive mandate from global or regional institutions, to advisory, financing, and training services.

Last, ownership for justice reform work should be clarified in the international structure to enable multilateral and bilateral agencies to invest in developing the requisite capacity and expertise. There are areas where, at the request of government, the World Bank and other institutional financial institutions (IFIs) could consider playing a greater role in supporting the developmental underpinnings of violence prevention within their mandates—such as the links between public financial management and security sector reform and institution-building, legal administration, justice systems development and multisectoral approaches at the community level that combine community policing and justice services with social cohesion, developmental and employment creation programs. But the IFIs are not equipped to lead specialized international support in these areas. A clear lead within the UN system would help this effort.

Agencies with economic expertise need to pay more attention to jobs. National community-based public works programs should receive greater and longer-term support in fragile situations, in recognition of the time required for the private sector to absorb youth unemployment. Other priority programs for job creation include investments in supporting infrastructure, in particular, electricity and transit. A third program cluster is those that invest in skills and work experience; develop links between producers, traders, and consumers; and expand access to finance and assets, for example, through low-income housing. Current international financial institutions and UN initiatives focused on employment creation should explicitly address the specific needs of areas affected by fragility, conflict, and violence, recognizing that job creation in these situations may go beyond material benefits by providing a productive role and occupation for youth, and evaluating and expanding the examples of best-fit employment policies in fragile situations presented in this Report. Global employment work should include re-focusing on the risks posed by youth employment.

These approaches would help. But there is likely to be continued pressure from large youth unemployed populations unless a more significant international effort is launched.

A bolder approach could draw together capacities from development agencies, the private sector, foundations, and NGOs in a new global partnership to galvanize investments in countries and communities where high unemployment and social disengagement contribute to the risks of conflict. Focusing primarily on job creation through project finance, advisory support to small and medium businesses, training and work placement, and guarantees, the initiative could also support social and cultural initiatives that promote good governance, collaborative capacities in communities, social tolerance, and recognition of young people's social and economic roles. Private-sector capacities to draw on would include large companies that trade and invest in insecure areas (creating links with local entrepreneurs), as well as technology companies that can assist with connectivity and training in remote insecure areas.

Track 2: Transforming procedures and risk and results management in international agencies

To implement rapid, sustained, and integrated programs for citizen security, justice, and jobs, international agencies need internal reforms. For the g7+ group of leaders of conflict-affected and fragile states who have begun to meet regularly as part of the International Dialogue on Peacebuilding and Statebuilding, reforming internal agency procedures, particularly procurement procedures, was the number one suggestion for international reform.[91] International agencies cannot respond quickly to restore confidence or provide deep institutional support if their budget, staffing, approval, and contracting procedures take months and set unrealistic prerequisites for recipient institutional capacity. International agency systems would require fundamental changes to implement these programs effectively, based on the following four principles (how to approach implementing these is covered in Feature 7):

- Accept the links between security and development outcomes.
- Base fiduciary processes on the real world in fragile and violence-affected situations: insecurity, lack of competitive markets, and weak institutions.
- Balance the risks of action with the risks of inaction.
- Expect a degree of failure in programs that require innovation and engagement with weak institutions in risky environments, and adapt accordingly.

Donor risk management also relies primarily on headquarters controls rather than "best-fit" delivery mechanisms adapted to local conditions. This approach may manage donor risk, but it constrains real progress in institution-building on the ground. An alternative is to embrace faster engagement through national institutions, but vary the ways aid is delivered to manage risks and results. Some donors have a higher risk tolerance and will be able to choose modes that go more directly through national budgets and institutions; others will need greater oversight or nonstate involvement in delivery. Three complementary options:

- Vary the oversight and delivery mechanisms when engaging through national institutions. Oversight mechanisms to adapt to risk include shifting from budget support to "tracked" expenditure through government systems,[92] and from regular reporting and internal control mechanisms to independent financial monitoring agents, independent monitoring of complaints, and independent technical agents. Variations in delivery mechanisms include community structures, civil society, the private sector, the UN, and other international executing agencies in delivering programs jointly with state institutions.
- In situations of more extreme risk, where donors would normally disengage, have executive capacity supplement national control systems, as with "dual key" mechanisms, where international line manage-

REFLECTIONS FROM ADVISORY COUNCIL MEMBERS: *2011 WORLD DEVELOPMENT REPORT*

FEATURE 7 *Internal agency reform*

Quick action? Ghana helps restore electricity in Liberia

Ellen Johnson Sirleaf, President of Liberia; *WDR Advisory Council Member*

After the 2005 election in Liberia, the new government announced a 100-day plan that included the restoration of electricity to certain areas of the capital to help restore confidence in the state and jumpstart recovery in economic activities and basic services. With ECOWAS support, the Liberian government approached various donors to help, since the new government lacked resources and institutional capacity for implementation. None of the traditional donors, which included the United Nations, the World Bank, the African Development Bank, the European Union, and USAID, were able to provide the generators needed for this endeavor within the desired timeframe under their regular systems. The Liberian government was eventually successful in securing help from the Government of Ghana, which provided two generators that helped restore electricity in some urban areas.

The Liberian experience points to two key lessons. First is the need for early consultation between national governments and international partners on realism in delivering quick results and demonstrating progress to local populations. Second is the challenge of rigidities in donor systems unable to provide particular types of assistance fast. In fact, the EU, USAID, and the World Bank were able to provide other types of support (fuel, transmission line restoration) for the electricity system within the 100 days, but none of the donors were able to cover the specific need for generators. Indeed, there is a need to rethink existing policies and processes, to modify what I call procedural conformism for countries in crisis situations.

WDR Note: Options for applying the WDR principles for internal agency reform in different contexts

Accepting the links between security and development outcomes	Economic and social interventions in situations of insecurity can justifiably be designed to contribute to citizen security and justice outcomes (in the Liberia electricity program above, an increase in citizen trust in government would have been an appropriate measure of program success, rather than the sustainability of the electricity provision). Security programs can also be designed to contribute to development outcomes (an increase in trade, for example). This would require agencies to use outcome measure outside their traditional "technical" domains and work together within the combined program frameworks described above.
Base budget and fiduciary processes on the real world: insecurity, lack of perfectly competitive markets, and weak institutions	When insecurity is high, both the costs and benefits of interventions may change dramatically over a short period. This argues for greater flexibility in administrative budget and staff planning. In program budgets, it implies careful sequencing wherein some programs will be more beneficial at a later date, but also placing high weight on speed (over some cost-efficiency and quality concerns) in contracting where benefits to fast action are high. Where competitive markets are very thin and not transparent, different procurement controls—such as pre-tendering internationally under variable quantity contracts, or contracting processes that allow direct negotiations with knowledge of regional markets—can be appropriate. Where institutional capacity is insufficient, procedures need to be distilled to the simplest level of due process, together with flexible mechanisms to execute some activities on behalf of recipient institutions.
Balance risks of action with risks of inaction	Outside the realm of natural disasters, international actors often tend to be more sensitive to the risk that their support will backfire into criticisms of wastage or abuses than to the risk that delays in their support will increase the potential for violence or derail promising reform efforts. Decentralizing greater responsibility and accountability to international staff on the ground can increase responsiveness to the risks of inaction. Transparent publication of achievements against target timelines for donor funds release and activities—and reasons for delays—would also help.
Expect a degree of failure in programs in risky environments, and adapt accordingly	Because returns to successful programs are high, international assistance can afford a higher failure rate in violent situations. This is not how most assistance works, however: donors expect the same degree of success in risky environments as in secure ones. A better approach is to adapt private-sector principles for venture capital investment to support for fragile and violence-affected situations: pilot many different types of approaches to see which work best; accept a higher failure rate; evaluate rigorously and adapt quickly; and scale up approaches that are working.

ment capacity works alongside national actors and agency processes governed by joint national and international boards. Not all governments will wish to take up these options. Where they do not, using local personnel and community structures for delivering humanitarian, economic, and social programs still maintains some focus on local institutional capacity, mitigating the brain-drain of local skills overseas.

- Increase the contingencies in budgets, under transparent planning assumptions. Where governance is volatile, development program budgets, as well as the budgets for political and peacekeeping missions, would benefit from greater contingency measures so that activities and delivery mechanisms can be adjusted when new risks and opportunities emerge without disrupting overall support. The planning assumptions for such contingencies—for example, that additional oversight mechanisms will be adopted if certain agreed measures of governance deteriorate—should be transparent to both recipient governments and the governing bodies of international agencies.

To achieve results at scale, pooling funds in multidonor trust funds is also an effective option, since it provides recipient governments with larger single programs and international partners with a way to support programs that greatly exceed their own national contribution. It can also be an effective way to pool risks, shifting the burden of responsibility for risks of waste, abuse, or corruption from the shoulders of each individual donor to the multilateral system. Multidonor trust funds have delivered excellent results in some situations—funding, for example, a range of high-impact programs in Afghanistan through the Afghanistan Reconstruction Trust Fund (ARTF) and the Law and Order Trust Fund for Afghanistan (LOTFA), supporting essential start-up and system maintenance costs for the nascent Palestinian Authority under the Holst Fund in the mid-1990s in West Bank Gaza, or serving as catalytic funding in Nepal under the auspices of the Peacebuilding Commission.[93] But the performance of multidonor trust funds is mixed, with criticisms ranging from slowness to a lack of expectation management and mixed success in working through national systems.[94] The combined security-justice-development programs and internal agency reforms described above would help to mitigate this risk.

International agencies need to think carefully about how to lengthen the duration of assistance to meet the realities of institutional transformation over a generation without raising costs. For humanitarian programs in prolonged crises, building on existing initiatives to support local staffing, local purchases, and community-based delivery can increase the impact on institution-building and lower unit costs. For peacekeeping, there is potential for greater use of more flexible arrangements, including over-the-horizon security guarantees, where external forces outside the country either supplement forces on the ground during tense periods or extend the leverage of external peacekeeping after missions are drawn down—as suggested in inputs to this Report from the AU and the UN Department of Peacekeeping Operations. Better resourcing for mediation and diplomatic facilitation is also an easy win, since it is low cost and can reduce the probabilities of conflict.

For development agencies, reducing the volatility of flows to programs delivering results in citizen security, justice, and jobs—or simply preserving social cohesion and human and institutional capacity—can increase impact without increasing the overall cost. As already described, volatility greatly reduces aid effectiveness, and it is twice as high for fragile and conflict-affected countries as for other developing countries, despite their greater need for persistence in building social and state institutions. There are options for reducing volatility, including providing threshold amounts of aid based on appropriate modalities (as described by Advisory Council member Paul Collier in chapter 9), topping up aid allocations to the most fragile states when specific types of programs have demonstrated the ability to deliver effectively and at scale (as proposed in a recent working paper by the Centre for Global Development),[95] and dedicating a target percentage of assistance to larger and longer-term programs in fragile and conflict-affected states under the Development Assistance Committee framework.

To close the loop on internal agency reforms, results indicators should be more closely geared to priorities in fragile and violence-affected situations. The core tools for national actors and their international counterparts include proposed indicators to better capture both short- and longer-term progress, supplementing the MDGs (see Feature 4). The use of these indicators by international agencies—across the diplomatic, security, and aid divides—would increase the incentives for more integrated responses.

Track 3: Acting regionally and globally to reduce external stresses on fragile states

Effective action against illegal trafficking requires co-responsibility by producing and consuming countries. To stem the far-reaching impact of illegal trafficking, it must be recognized that effective action by one country alone will simply push the problem to other countries, and that regional and global approaches are needed. For trafficking where the supply, processing, or retail markets are concentrated and easily monitored—such as diamond trafficking—interdiction efforts combined with multistakeholder producer and consumer campaigns can be effective. In addition to the Kimberley Process for diamonds and the Extractive Industries Transparency Initiative, the new Natural Resource Charter and a recent World Bank/UN Conference on Trade and Development (UNCTAD)/Food and Agriculture Organization (FAO) initiative on standards for international land purchases have similar potential. For drug trafficking, the situation is complicated by highly fragmented illegal production sites and processing facilities. Supply-side and interdiction actions alone are constrained in these circumstances, and competition between gangs and cartels produces high levels of violence in production and transit countries. Exploring the costs and benefits of different combinations of demand- and supply-side measures would be a first step to underpinning more decisive demand-side actions.

Following the money—tracking illicit financial flows—is at the heart of action against the illegal trafficking of drugs and natural resources. For areas seriously affected by illegal trafficking and corruption, such as Central America and West Africa, most countries have nothing approaching the national capacity needed to gather and process information on sophisticated financial transactions, or to investigate and prosecute offenders. Along with initiatives that help to support a global community to address corruption issues, such as the International Corruption Hunters Alliance and the Stolen Asset Recovery Initiative (StAR), the following two key measures could help in this effort:

- Strengthen the capacity to conduct strategic analysis of these flows in a critical mass of countries with the majority of global financial transfers. About 15 major financial markets and hubs play this role. Concerted efforts to strengthen the openness of financial centers and financial intelligence unit capacities, as well as to proactively analyze suspicious flows, and exchange information could greatly increase the global ability to detect illicit financial flows and to recover stolen assets. Global financial institutions could also perform strategic analysis and make it available to affected countries. To respect privacy, this could be based on shifts in aggregate flows rather than individual account information.
- Expand commitments from developed states and financial centers to joint investigations with law enforcement authorities in fragile and violence-affected countries. As part of this commitment, they could also undertake capacity-building programs with law enforcement authorities in fragile

states—as with the U.K.-Nigeria and U.S.-Haiti examples above.[96]

Regional action can also target positive opportunities. Donors could increase their financial and technical support for cross-border and regional infrastructure—and various forms of regional administrative and economic cooperation—giving priority to violence-affected regions. Such support could take the following forms:

- ***Cross-border development programming.*** International actors could support more closely opportunities for cross-border activities that integrate action on citizen security, justice, and jobs. Even where regional or cross-border political collaboration is less well established, international support for cross-border programming may still be able to support and respond to bilateral government efforts, using development issues such as trade and transit infrastructure or cross-border health programs to support a gradual increase in trust. Special financial provision for access of fragile landlocked regions to markets, as has recently been agreed upon by the World Bank's governing structures, is another way to encourage developmental cooperation across borders.
- ***Shared regional administrative capacity.*** Pooling subregional administrative capacities can allow states to develop institutional capabilities they could not manage on their own. There are already good examples of shared courts in the Caribbean and shared central banking capacity in West Africa.[97] While these initiatives take time to establish, they supplement difficult national institutional transformations and merit assistance from regional and international development institutions.

Rather than these somewhat incremental approaches to specific cross-border initiatives, international donors could take a larger step to finance regional approaches. The principle of such an initiative would be to build on the local political knowledge and legitimacy of regional institutions, in combination with the technical and financial capacity of global agencies. Delivered through regional institutions in collaboration with global agencies, such an effort could adapt lessons from those initiatives that have already successfully pooled regional capacity. It could also draw lessons from existing cross-border cooperation, such as the Greater Mekong subregion,[98] West Africa's initiatives on trafficking and economic integration,[99] and the European Union's programs[100] for previously conflict-affected border regions. It would support political initiatives of regional institutions (such as the African Union's Border Program[101] and ASEAN's subregional initiatives),[102] with financial and technical expertise from global partners.

Further research is also needed to track the impacts of climate change on weather, land availability and food prices, each of which can impact in turn on conflict risk. Current research does not suggest that climate change itself will drive conflict, except perhaps where rapidly deteriorating water availability cuts across existing tensions and weak institutions. But a series of inter-linked problems—changing global patterns of consumption of energy and scarce resources, increasing demand for food imports (which draw on land, water and energy inputs), and the repurposing of land for climate adaptation—are increasing pressures on fragile states. These warrant further research and policy attention.

Track 4: Marshaling support from lower-, middle-, and higher-income countries and global and regional institutions, to reflect the changing landscape of international policy and assistance

The landscape of international assistance in fragile and violence-affected countries has changed in the last 20 years, with more aid and policy input from middle-income countries with a history of solidarity support. Several regional institutions are also playing a greater role in security and development issues. Yet, discussions of global conflict and violence, the norms of responsible leadership to respond to it, and the shape of international assistance have been driven more by northern than southern actors. The International Dialogue on Peacebuilding and Statebuilding has been created to help address this deficit.

The WDR team conducted wide-ranging consultations with violence-affected countries, regional policy makers, and regional institutions, as well as with traditional donor partners. It found many areas of agreement—such as the focus on institution-building and governance and on citizen security, justice, and jobs—but also some areas of difference. As described earlier, these differences included what it is realistic to expect in terms of responsible national leadership in improving governance, and over what time period, and over the "forms" versus the "functions" of good governance. Perceived double standards were also criticized by WDR interlocutors, who reflected a sentiment that donor countries and organizations that have faced their own internal governance challenges could approach shortcomings in fragile developing states with more humility. Developed countries are not immune to corruption, bribery, human rights abuses, or failures to account adequately for public finances. So effective implementation of standards of good governance is also a challenge in advanced countries, even more so when the international community has played an executive government or security role in violence-affected areas.

Lack of concerted support for the norms of responsible leadership is a concern, because progress in global norms is crucial for reducing the risk of violence. Regional and global standards, as well as recognition and sanction mechanisms in constitutionality, human rights, and corruption, have provided support and incentives for national reformers, particularly where the capacity of the domestic system to provide rewards and accountability is weak. For example, the Lomé Declaration in 2000, which established African standards and a regional response mechanism to unconstitutional changes in government, has been associated with a reduction in coups d'état from 15 in the 1990s to 5 in the 2000s;[103] and, despite an increase in coups in the last five years, continental action to restore constitutional government has been consistently strong.

Some modest actions could strengthen collaboration among higher-, middle-, and lower-income countries on shared problems of violence and development, both global and local, as follows:

- ***Increase both South-South and South-North exchanges.*** South-South exchanges have enormous potential to provide relevant capacity and lessons in current fragile and violence-affected situations.[104] Low- and middle-income countries that have gone through their own recent experiences of transition have much to offer to their counterparts—as demonstrated in this Report, where Latin American countries offered perspectives on urban violence prevention and security and justice reforms, China on job creation, India on local public works and democratic practices, and Southeast Asian and African countries on community driven development in conflict areas. Yet South-North exchanges are also important. While institutional capacities differ, many northern and southern countries, provinces, and cities face some similar stresses. Program approaches—such as addressing trafficking, reintegrating ex-gang members and disengaged young people, and fostering tolerance and social bonds among communities that are ethnically or religiously divided—will have lessons relevant for others. Such exchanges would increase understanding that the challenges of violence are not unique to developing countries and that developing countries are not alone in struggling to find solutions.
- ***Better align international assistance behind regional governance efforts.*** When

regional institutions take the initiative, as with the AU on constitutionality or ASEAN in certain conflict and natural disaster situations (Feature 8), they have great comparative advantage in traction with their member states. The potential convening role of regional institutions was also widely recognized in WDR consultations by higher-, middle-, and lower-income country interlocutors alike. Supporting regional platforms to discuss the application of governance norms is an effective way to increase ownership. Adopting clearer structures to discuss responses to major improvements or deteriorations in governance (such as coups d'états) among bilateral and multilateral actors would also improve information-sharing and the potential for coordinated responses, without creating unacceptable binding obligations on international actors.[105]

- ***Expand initiatives to recognize responsible leadership.*** While there is always a role for frank and transparent criticism, approaches from the North that are seen as disproportionately focused on criticism in fragile situations can be divisive. Initiatives such as the Ibrahim Prize for African leadership could be emulated to recognize leaders in different roles (for example, ministers who have a lasting impact on corruption or military leaders who implement successful security sector reform). Multistakeholder initiatives such as the Extractive Industries Transparency Initiative could consider provisions to recognize individual leaders or leadership teams who have improved the transparency of resource revenues and expenditures, whether in governments, civil society, or companies.

More focused and realistic expectations of the timetables for governance improvements would also help bridge gaps in perspectives among countries receiving international assistance, their middle- and higher-income international partners, and global and regional institutions. This is particularly crucial in light of recent social protests that demonstrate strong grievances and expectations over governance change—that were not picked up by standard analyses of security and of development progress. Indicators are needed that focus on whether countries are on track to make institutional and governance improvements within the realistic generational timeframes that the faster reformers have achieved, and how citizens perceive trends in the legitimacy and performance of national institutions across the political security and development domains. The indicators presented in Feature 4 would be a simple way, as Louise Arbour suggests (Feature 8), to compare progress, stagnation or deterioration. Ensuring that such indicators measure outcomes rather than just the form of institutions (laws passed, anti-corruption commissions formed) is also important to ensure that they encourage rather than suppress innovative national action and that they foster learning among low-, middle-, and high-income country institutions. The UN Peacebuilding Commission, which brings together fragile states, donors, troop-contributing countries, and regional bodies, has unexploited potential to advise on better tracking of progress and risks, and realistic timelines for governance transformation.

At the beginning of this overview, we asked how piracy in Somalia, continuing violence in Afghanistan, new threats from drug trafficking in the Americas, or conflict arising from social protests in North Africa can happen in today's world. The short answer is that such violence cannot be contained by short-term solutions that fail to generate the institutions capable of providing people with a stake in security, in justice, and in economic prospects. Societies cannot be transformed from the outside, and they cannot be transformed overnight. But progress is possible with consistent and concerted effort by national leaders and their international partners to strengthen the local, national, and global institutions that support citizen security, justice, and jobs.

REFLECTIONS FROM ADVISORY COUNCIL MEMBERS: *2011 WORLD DEVELOPMENT REPORT*

FEATURE 8 *Regional initiatives and norms and standards*

ASEAN experience in crisis prevention and recovery

Surin Pitsuwan, Secretary-General ASEAN; *WDR Advisory Council Member*

There are many conflicts simmering in the ASEAN landscape. But the region is not totally without its own experiences in mediation and conflict resolution. ASEAN has played an important role in endeavors. The ASEAN Troika in the Cambodian conflict of 1997–99, the Timor-Leste peace-keeping operation of 1999 onward, the Aceh Reconciliation of 2005, and the Myanmese Cyclone Nargis catastrophe of May 2008 were cases of mediation and eventual resolution where the regions and some ASEAN member states have made valuable contributions and learned lessons from the process. It has always been like putting pieces of a diplomatic jigsaw together, weaving tapestry of peace, improvising the best modality and pattern from the available and suitable materials at hand.

One important lesson for us is that our ASEAN structures can play an important political convening role when there are sensitivities with member states. There was a higher level of mutual confidence between Indonesia and of the ASEAN states participating in the Timor-Leste operation. We got around the rigid principle of "non-interference" by offering troops under a joint-command with an "ASEAN" military leader taking an active leadership role. And Indonesia made it easier for all ASEAN Partners by issuing an invitation to come and assist. In Myanmar, ASEAN played a central role in the dialogue with the Government after Cyclone Nargis, helping to open up the affected areas, where over 130,000 men, women and children had died and many more faced traumatic conditions, to international aid.

A second lesson is that we can find useful combinations of capacity between our local knowledge and political convening role, and the technical capacities of other partners. Our work in support of recovery after Cyclone Narghis was supported by technical teams from the World Bank, and performed in conjunction with the United Nations. In the Aceh Monitoring Mission, we worked jointly with colleagues from the European Union who brought valuable technical knowledge.

The third is that the more operations of this type that we undertake, the more our capacity builds. In Timor-Leste, long years of joint-military training and exercises between the Philippines, the Republic of Korea, and Thailand, and supported by partners outside the region such as the US, paid off. The troops on the ground could communicate, cooperate, and conduct joint operations without any delay—but their experiences in Timor-Leste also added to their capacity. In Myanmar, ASEAN's role meant drawing on personnel from many of our member states, such as Indonesia, Singapore, and Thailand, who have extensive experience of managing post-disaster recovery, and also building capacity within our Secretariat. Linked to long-term programs of capacity-building with some of our donor partners, these experiences make us more ready to face new challenges in future. The cumulative results of these efforts in managing political conflicts and natural disaster relief have helped ASEAN in enhancing its capacity to coordinate our development cooperation strategies. We have learned to contain sporadic violence and tension in the region and would not allow them to derail our community development efforts aiming at common security and sustainable prosperity for our people.

All the recommendations of this Report have at their heart the concept of shared global risk. Risks are evolving, with new threats to stability arising from international organized crime and global economic instability. The landscape of international power relations is also changing, as low- and middle-income countries increase their share of global economic influence and their contributions to global policy thinking. This shift requires a fundamental rethink of the approaches of international actors to manage global risks collectively—and as equal partners. Real change requires a strong rationale. But a dual rationale exists: fragility and violence are major obstacles to development and are no longer confined to poor and remote areas or cityscapes. This past decade has seen the increasing penetration of instability in global life—in terrorism, an expanding drug trade, impact on commodity prices, and the rising numbers of internationally mobile refugees. Breaking cycles of repeated violence is thus a shared challenge demanding urgent action.

REFLECTIONS FROM ADVISORY COUNCIL MEMBERS: *2011 WORLD DEVELOPMENT REPORT*

Reaffirming consensus on international norms and standards—the role of regional organizations

Louise Arbour, President, International Crisis Group; former UN High Commissioner for Human Rights; *WDR Advisory Council Member*

Whether based on universal values, such as the sanctity of human life, or on international legal rules, there are some universally accepted norms—reflected in the Charter of the United Nations and other international instruments.

These norms are not self-implementing, and, because they include the right to cultural diversity, their interpretation must reflect local, national, and regional diversity. The resistance to the exportation of "Western values" might be no more than the rejection of a foreign way of expressing a particular norm, rather than a rejection of the norm itself.

Regional institutions can bridge the distance between universal norms and local customs. Those customs or practices must conform, in substance, to the core international principles from which the international community derives its cohesion. Otherwise cultural diversity can simply override, and undermine, the international framework.

In the justice sector, for instance, uniformity of institutional models and procedures may obscure radical differences in the actual delivery of justice. But the adjudication of disputes based on principles of fairness, impartiality, transparency, integrity, compassion, and, ultimately, accountability can take many forms.

In their assistance to development, international actors must resist the exportation of form over substance and accept the regionalization of norms that enhance, rather than impede, their true universal character. In the same spirit, regional actors must translate, in a culturally relevant way, international norms and repudiate nonconforming practices.

And all must concede that the standards set by universal norms are aspirations. Measures of performance should reflect either progress, stagnation or regression, in a given country, toward a common, universal ideal.

Notes

1. The *World Development Report 2011* defines organized violence as the use or threat of physical force by groups, including state actions against other states or against civilians, civil wars, electoral violence between opposing sides, communal conflicts based on regional, ethnic, religious, or other group identities or competing economic interests, gang-based violence and organized crime, and international, nonstate, armed movements with ideological aims. Although these are also important topics for development, the WDR does not cover domestic or interpersonal violence. At times, violence or conflict are used as shorthand for organized violence, understood in these terms. Many countries address certain forms of violence, such as terrorist attacks by nonstate armed movements, as matters that are subject to their criminal laws.
2. Uppsala/PRIO Armed Conflict Database (Harbom and Wallensteen 2010; Lacina and Gleditsch 2005); Sundberg 2008; Gleditsch and Ward 1999; Human Security Report Project, forthcoming; Gleditsch and others 2002.
3. Countries affected by fragility, conflict, and violence include those countries with: (1) homicide rates greater than 10 per 100,000 population per year; (2) major civil conflict (battle deaths greater than 1,000 per year (as defined in the from 2006 to 2009), (3) UN or regionally mandated peacebuilding or peacekeeping missions; and (4) low-income countries with institutional levels in 2006–09 (World Bank's CPIA less than 3.2), correlated with high risks of violence and conflict. See Uppsala/PRIO Armed Conflict Database (Lacina and Gleditsch 2005; Harbom and Wallensteen 2010); UNDPKO 2010b; UNDP 2010c; World Bank 2010e.
4. For discussions of the trends in civil war onset and termination see Hewitt, Wilkenfeld, and Gurr 2010; Sambanis 2004; Elbadawi, Hegre, and Milante 2008; Collier and others 2003.
5. Demombynes 2010; UNODC 2010a.

6. Leslie 2010; Harriott 2004, 2008; International Crisis Group 2008b; Ashforth 2009.
7. Bayer and Rupert 2004. While Baker and others 2002 found that the effect of conflict is equivalent to a 33 percent tariff barrier. For an updated discussion of the methodology for determining growth effects of conflict and theory and new analysis based on primary and secondary neighbors, see De Groot 2010; Murdoch and Sandler 2002.
8. U.S. Committee for Refugees and Immigrants 2009; Internal Displacement Monitoring Centre 2008.
9. Gomez and Christensen 2010; Harild and Christensen 2010.
10. Global Terrorism Database 2010; National Counter Terrorism Center 2010; WDR team calculations.
11. Gaibulloev and Sandler 2008.
12. Davies, von Kemedi, and Drennan 2005.
13. WDR team calculations based on Europe Brent spot price FOB (dollars per barrel) reported by the U.S. Energy Information Administration 2011.
14. UNODC 2010b.
15. UNODC 2010b.
16. Hanson 2010; Bowden 2010.
17. World Bank 2010d.
18. WDR staff calculations based on Chen, Ravallion, and Sangraula 2008 poverty data (available on POVCALNET, http://iresearch.worldbank.org).
19. Narayan and Petesch 2010.
20. UNDP 2006.
21. For an overview of costs of conflict and violence, see Skaperdas and others 2009. Specific estimates of the economic costs associated with conflict are found in Hoeffler, von Billerbeck, and Ijaz 2010; Collier and Hoeffler 1998; Cerra and Saxena 2008; Collier, Chauvet, and Hegre 2007; Riascos and Vargas 2004; UNDP 2006.
22. Martin, Mayer, and Thoenig 2008.
23. UNICEF 2004; UNFPA 2002; Anderlini 2010a.
24. Beijing Declaration and Platform for Action 1995; Women's Refugee Commission 2009; UNICEF 2004.
25. American Psychological Association 1996; Dahlberg 1998; Verdú and others 2008.
26. WDR team calculations.
27. Theories of the causes of conflict are explored in chapter 2 of the main text. Of the literature discussed there, selected recommended readings include: Gurr 1970; Hirshleifer 1995; Skaperdas 1996; Grossman 1991; Fearon 1995; Collier and Hoeffler 2004; Satyanath, Miguel, and Sergenti 2004; Blattman and Miguel 2010; Keefer 2008; Besley and Persson 2009, 2010; Toft 2003; Murshed and Tadjoeddin 2007; Arnson and Zartman 2005. The linkages among political, security, and economic dynamics are also recognized in the policy circle. See Zoellick 2010b.
28. For relationship between income inequality and the risk of civil conflict see Fearon 2010a. For relationship between income inequality and criminal violence see Loayza, Fajnzylber, and Lederman 2002a, 2002b; Messner, Raffalovich, and Shrock 2002.
29. Fearon 2010b; Bøås, Tiltnes, and Flatø 2010; Neumayer 2003; Loayza, Fajnzylber, and Lederman 2002a, 2002b; Messner, Raffalovich, and Shrock 2002; WDR team calculations.
30. Stewart 2010.
31. Satyanath, Miguel, and Sergenti 2004.
32. For the relationship between institutional weakness and violence conflict, see Fearon 2010a, 2010b; Johnston 2010; Walter 2010.
33. In addition, there are structural and incremental factors that increase conflict risk. Among these are features of the physical terrain that make rebellion easier. These features do not cause war in the common sense of the word, they simply make it more possible. Mountainous terrain has been shown to increase risks, by increasing the feasibility of rebellion. Neighborhood matters too: there are both negative effects from proximity to other wars or countries with high rates of violent crime and illicit trafficking and positive effects from being in a neighborhood largely at peace. See Buhaug and Gleditsch 2008; Gleditsch and Ward 2000; Salehyan and Gleditsch 2006;

Goldstone 2010. On the effects of neighborhood on civil wars, see Hegre and Sambanis 2006 and Gleditsch 2007.

34. McNeish 2010; Ross 2003.
35. This follows recent literature on statebuilding, notably North, Wallis, and Weingast 2009; Dobbins and others 2007; Fukuyama 2004; Acemoglu, Johnson, and Robinson 2001, 2005, 2006. This learning is reflected in recent policy documents as well: OECD 2010a, 2010g, 2011.
36. Institutions are defined in the WDR as the formal and informal "rules of the game," which include formal rules, written laws, organizations, informal norms of behavior, and shared beliefs—as well as the organizational forms that exist to implement and enforce these norms (both state and non-state organizations). Institutions shape the interests, incentives, and behaviors that can facilitate violence. Unlike elite pacts, institutions are impersonal—they continue to function irrespective of the presence of particular leaders, and therefore provide greater guarantees of sustained resilience to violence. Institutions operate at all levels of society—local, national, regional, and global.
37. Fearon 2010a, 2010b; Walter 2010.
38. Arboleda 2010; WDR team consultations with government officials, civil society representatives and security personnel in Colombia, 2010.
39. Gambino 2010.
40. A 2010 meeting of Anglophone and Francophone delegates in Kenya, convened by UNDP, coined the phrase "collaborative capacities" and further defined the institutions relevant to prevention and recovery from violence as "dynamic networks of interdependent structures, mechanisms, resources, values, and skills which, through dialogue and consultation, contribute to conflict prevention and peace-building in a society." UN Interagency Framework for Coordination on Preventive Action 2010, 1.
41. Barron and others 2010.
42. World Bank 2010m; Buhaug and Urdal 2010.
43. See Schneider, Buehn, and Montenegro 2010. Food protests data are from news reports; governance effectiveness data are from Kaufmann, Kraay, and Mastruzzi 2010a.
44. Menkhaus 2006, 2010.
45. For the role of institutions in economic growth and development, see Acemoglu, Johnson, and Robinson 2005. Also see Zoellick 2010b.
46. North, Wallis, and Weingast 2009.
47. For the impact of colonialism on the development of modern-day institutions in former colonized countries, see Acemoglu, Johnson, and Robinson 2001.
48. Special Inspector General for Iraq Reconstruction 2009.
49. According to Margaret Levi, "Trust is, in fact, a holding word for a variety of phenomena that enable individuals to take risks in dealing with others, solve collective action problems, or act in ways that seem contrary to standard definitions of self-interest." Furthermore, Levi notes that "At issue is a *cooperative venture*, which implies that the truster possesses a reasonable belief that well-placed trust will yield positive returns and is willing to act upon that belief." Braithwaite and Levi 1998, 78.
50. Pritchett and de Weijer 2010.
51. The interlink between security and development has been debated under the notion of human security, which encompasses freedom from fear, freedom from want and freedom to live in dignity. By putting the security and prosperity of human beings at the center, human security addresses wide range of threats, both from poverty and from violence, and their interactions. While acknowledging the importance of human security and its emphasis on placing people at the center of focus, this Report uses the term "citizen security" more often to sharpen our focus more on freedom from physical violence and freedom from fear of violence. The hope is to complement the discussion on the aspect of freedom from fear in the human security concept. Building on the Commission on Human Security 2003 report, the importance of human security has been recognized in the UN General Assembly 2005 resolution adopted at the 2005 World Summit, the UN General Assembly 2009 report, and UN General Assembly 2010 Resolution, as well as in other fora such as Asia-Pacific Economic Cooperation, G8, and World Economic Forum. See Commission on Human Security 2003; UN General Assembly 2005b, 2009b, 2010.
52. "Confidence-building" in mediation terminology means building trust between adversaries; in a financial context, the term "confidence" denotes trust by market actors that governments are adopt-

ing sound policies and will be capable of implementing them. The WDR defines the term as building trust between groups of citizens who have been divided by violence, between citizens and the state, and between the state and other key stakeholders (neighbors, international partners, investors) whose political, behavioral, or financial support is needed to deliver a positive outcome.

53. On building trust and changing expectations, see Hoff and Stiglitz 2008.
54. Bedeski 1994; Cumings 2005; Kang 2002; Chang and Lee 2006.
55. See Stedman 1996; Nilsson and Jarstad 2008. On elite bargains, political settlements and inclusion, see Di John and Putzel 2009.
56. Anderlini 2000.
57. World Bank 2008f, 2009d; Republic of Lebanon Ministry of Environment 1999.
58. UNDPKO 2010a.
59. For Japanese land reforms, see Kawagoe 1999; Tsunekawa and Yoshida 2010; For broader statebuilding experience in Japan, see Tsunekawa and Yoshida 2010; For Korean land reforms, see Shin 2006.
60. Braud and Grevi 2005.
61. The Governance and Economic Management Assistance Program (GEMAP), introduced in the run-up to the 2005 elections in Liberia, provides "dual key" authority in the areas of revenue earning and expenditure. Jointly managed by the government and the international community, it was designed specifically to reassure a skeptical population and donors that years of official looting and corruption were over and that services would be reliably delivered. Dwan and Bailey 2006; Government of the Republic of Liberia Executive Mansion 2009.
62. To combat corruption and crime, Guatemala created the International Commission Against Impunity, known by its Spanish acronym, CICIG, through an agreement with the UN in 2007. Its mandate is to "support, strengthen, and assist institutions of the State of Guatemala responsible for investigating and prosecuting crimes allegedly committed in connection with the activities of illegal security forces and clandestine security organizations." See UN 2006a.
63. For Afghanistan National Solidarity Program, see Beath and others 2010; Ashe and Parrott 2001; UN Assistance Mission in Afghanistan and UNOHCHR 2010. For Latin American multi-sectoral violence prevention programs, see Alvarado and Abizanda 2010; Beato 2005; Fabio 2007; International Centre for the Prevention of Crime 2005; Duailibi and others 2007; Peixoto, Andrade, and Azevedo 2007; Guerrero 2006; Llorente and Rivas 2005; Formisano 2002.
64. For India, see India Ministry of Rural Development 2005, 2010. For Indonesia, see Barron 2010; Guggenheim 2011. For Kosovo, see Grygiel 2007; Institute for State Effectiveness 2007. For Rwanda, see Boudreaux 2010.
65. For Nicaragua, see Bastick, Grimm, and Kunz 2007. For Nepal, see Ashe and Parrott 2001.
66. For Liberia, see Blundell 2010. For Mozambique, see Crown Agents 2007.
67. For the Timor-Leste health programs, see Rohland and Cliffe 2002; Baird 2010.
68. Messick 2011.
69. Giovine and others 2010;
70. Guerrero 2006; Mason 2003; Presidencia República de Colombia 2010.
71. Ashraf Ghani and Clare Lockhart, in *Fixing Failed States*, analyze the issue of establishing legitimacy and closing the sovereignty gap in fragile and conflict-affected states through the lens of "double compact." The double compact focuses on the "network of rights and obligations underpinning the state's claim to sovereignty . . ." and refers first to the "compact . . . between a state and its citizens . . . embedded in a coherent set of rules, and second, "between a state and the international community to ensure adherence to international norms and standards of accountability and transparency." Ghani and Lockhart 2008, 8.
72. Agoglia, Dziedzic, and Sotirin 2008.
73. WDR consultation with former key negotiators from the ANC Alliance and the National Party in South Africa 2010.
74. Barron and others 2010.
75. WDR team consultation in Haiti, 2010; UNDPKO 2010a.
76. For South Africa, see Kambuwa and Wallis 2002; WDR consultation with former key negotiators from the ANC Alliance and the National Party in South Africa 2010. For Pakistan: World Bank and ADB 2010.

77. WDR team consultations with government officials, civil society representatives and security personnel in Colombia 2010.
78. These tools include UNDPA's mediation unit; AU and other regional mediation capacity; "track II mediation," such as the Centre for Humanitarian Dialogue.
79. Ojielo 2007; Odendaal 2010; UNDPA 2010a.
80. Crisis Management Initiative (CMI), a Finnish independent nonprofit organization, works to resolve conflict and to build sustainable peace. In 2005, CMI Chairman, former Finnish President Ahtisaari facilitated a peace agreement between the Government of the Republic of Indonesia and the Free Aceh Movement in Aceh, Indonesia. See Crisis Management Initiative 2011.
81. For UN "integrated missions," see Eide and others 2005. For "whole-of-government" approaches, see OECD-DAC 2006; DFID 2009, 2010. For "whole-of systems" approaches, see OECD-DAC 2007a. For regional tools, see African Union 2006, 2007b.
82. Stewart and Brown 2007.
83. OECD-DAC 2008.
84. OECD-DAC 2010a.
85. A recent study examined the cost to countries of aid volatility, which induces volatility into government revenues and development programs. The loss in efficiency from volatility of net ODA was more than twice as high for weak states than strong states, at 2.5 versus 1.2 percent of GDP (see Kharas 2008).
86. Trafficking is intrinsically regional and global in nature, with knock-on impacts between producing, transit, and consuming countries. Colombia's actions against drug cartels affect Central America, Mexico, and even West Africa; California's recent policy debate on legalizing drugs potentially impacts producing countries. Similar effects happen with other commodities: restraints on logging in one country can increase demand in other countries that do not have similar policies, bringing with it increased vulnerability to corruption and violence.
87. The Kimberley Process is jointly undertaken by civil society groups, industry, and governments to stem the flow of "conflict diamonds" used to fuel rebellions in countries like the Democratic Republic of Congo. The process has its own diamond certification scheme imposing extensive requirements on its 49 members (representing 75 countries) to ensure that the rough diamonds shipped have not funded violence. See Kimberley Process Certification Scheme 2010.
88. OECD-DAC 2010a.
89. WDR team consultation with country team in Timor-Leste in 2010.
90. UNOHCHR 2006.
91. The g7+ is an "independent and autonomous forum of fragile and conflict affected countries and regions that have united to form one collective voice on the global stage." The g7+ was established in 2008 and includes: Afghanistan, Burundi, Central African Republic, Chad, Côte d'Ivoire, the Democratic Republic of Congo, Haiti, Liberia, Nepal, the Solomon Islands, Sierra Leone, South Sudan, and Timor-Leste. See International Dialogue on Peacebuilding and Statebuilding 2010.
92. A practical example of this type of shift is Ethiopia in 2005, when government and donors agreed to move from regular budget support to a program of transfers to local and municipal governments. The program included measures to ensure that all regions of the country, irrespective of how they had voted in elections, received continuing central government support.
93. See Garassi 2010. For Afghanistan, see Atos Consulting 2009. For West Bank and Gaza, see World Bank 1999a. For Nepal, see UNOHCHR 2010; Government of Nepal, UNDP, and UNDG 2010.
94. See OECD 2010i; Scanteam 2010.
95. Gelb 2010.
96. Messick 2011.
97. See Favaro 2008, 2010.
98. The Greater Mekong Subregion (GMS) countries (Cambodia, China, Lao People's Democratic Republic, Myanmar, Thailand, and Vietnam) have implemented a wide-ranging series of regional projects covering transport, power, telecommunications, environmental management, human resource development, tourism, trade, private sector investment, and agriculture. The GMS is recognized as having enhanced cross-border trade while reducing poverty levels and creating shared interests in economic stability and peace.

99. West Africa Coast Initiative (WACI) is a joint program among the UNODC, UN Office for West Africa, UN Department of Political Affairs, and INTERPOL to combat problems of illicit drug trafficking, organized crime, and drug abuse in West Africa. The initiative comprises a comprehensive set of activities targeting capacity-building, at both national and regional level, in the areas of law enforcement, forensics, border management, anti-money-laundering, and the strengthening of criminal justice institutions, contributing to peacebuilding initiatives and security sector reforms.
100. The "Euroregion" began as an innovative form of transborder cooperation (between two or more states that share a common bordering region) in the late 1950s. With the purpose of stimulating cross border economic, sociocultural and leisure cooperation, the Euroregion model grew, and was boosted through the creation of a common European market and recent democratic transitions. There are currently more than one hundred Euroregions spread across Europe, and the model has in recent times been replicated in eastern and central European territories. Cooperation has not been without problems in areas previously affected by conflict, but there are good examples of cross-border developmental, social and security programs that involve areas where ethnic minorities reside across several states or in areas that have suffered the trauma of interstate and civil war in the past. See Greta and Lewandowski 2010; Otocan 2010; Council of Europe 1995; Council of Europe and Institute of International Sociology of Gorizia 2003; Bilcik and others 2000.
101. Recognizing that insecure borders have been recurrent hosts to conflict, the African Union established the African Union Border Program in 2007 to delimit and demarcate sensitive border areas and promote cross-border cooperation and trade as a conflict prevention tool. The program consists of four components. First, it pursues both land and maritime border demarcation since less than a quarter of Africa's borders have been formally marked and agreed, and disputes are likely to continue with future discoveries of oil. Second, it promotes cross-border cooperation to deal with itinerant criminal activities. Third, it supports cross-border peacebuilding programs. Fourth, it consolidates gains in the economic integration through the regional economic communities. Its first pilot project was launched in the Sikasso region in Mali and in Bobo Dioualasso in Burkina Faso—bringing together local, private, and public actors to strengthen cooperation. See African Union 2007a.
102. ASEAN has played an important role in mediation and conflict resolution in the Southeast Asia region. Examples include its assistance in the Cambodian conflict of 1997–99, the Timor-Leste peacekeeping operation of 1999 onward, the Aceh Reconciliation of 2005, and the Myanmese Cyclone Nargis catastrophe of May 2008.
103. WDR team calculations based on dataset in Powell and Thyne 2011.
104. Of the different forms that South-South cooperation has taken, technical assistance has been the most common. Although many technical assistance projects focus on economic and social development, countries in the Global South have also developed specialized capacities in post-conflict peacebuilding. Examples include South Africa's support to build structural capacities for public service through peer learning with Burundi, Rwanda, and Southern Sudan. Cooperation among 45 municipalities in El Salvador, Guatemala, and Honduras helps to manage regional public goods such as water in the Trifinio region. The African Development Bank also has a specific facility for South-South cooperation in fragile states. See also OECD 2010e.
105. In the West African countries that have recently experienced coups d'état, for example, the view of the African Union was that donor support to social and poverty reduction programs should continue in these countries, but that larger-scale support should be paced to support the return to a constitutional path. In practice, donors were divided between those that suspended assistance completely and those that continued assistance with no change. WDR team consultation with officials from African Union in Addis Ababa, 2010.

WDR Framework and Structure

The Report argues that the risk of violence increases when stresses—both internal and external—combine with weak institutions. Given this challenge, how have countries prevented or escaped violence? The WDR framework (figure 1) suggests that there is a need to first restore confidence and then to transform institutions that provide citizen security, justice, and jobs.

The interlink between security and development has been debated under the notion of human security, which encompasses freedom from fear, freedom from want, and freedom to live in dignity.[1] By putting the security and prosperity of human beings at the center, human security addresses wide range of threats, both from poverty and from violence, and their interactions. Building on the report by the Commission on Human Security in 2003, the importance of human security has been recognized in the United Nations General Asembly and other international fora. While acknowledging the importance of human security and its emphasis on placing people at the center of focus, this Report uses the term "citizen security" more often to sharpen our focus more on freedom from physical violence and freedom from fear of violence. Our hope is to complement the discussion on the aspect of freedom from fear in the human security concept.

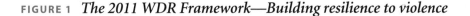

FIGURE 1 *The 2011 WDR Framework—Building resilience to violence*

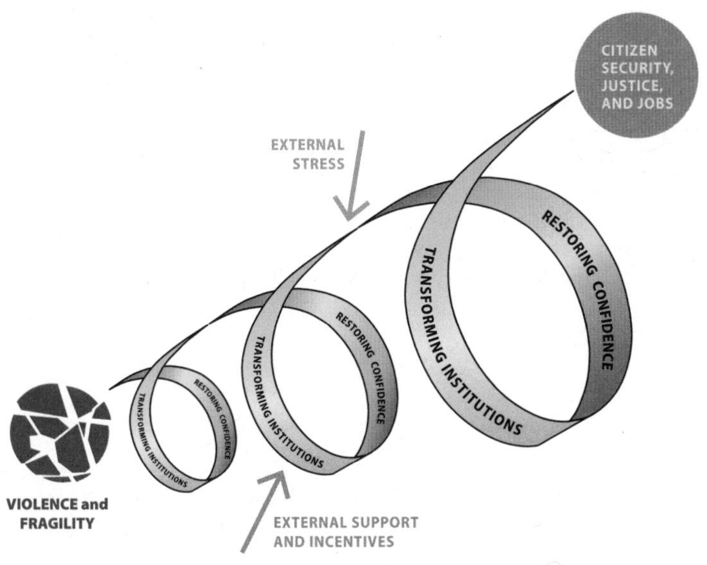

[1] The importance of human security has been recognized in the UN General Assembly 2005 resolution adopted at the 2005 World Summit, the UN General Assembly 2009 report, and UN General Assembly 2010 resolution, as well as in other fora such as the Asia-Pacific Economic Cooperation, G8, and World Economic Forum. See the Commission on Human Security 2003; UN General Assembly 2005b, 2009b, 2010.

This framework is graphically represented as a spiral, because these processes repeat over time as countries go through successive transition moments. Even as one set of immediate priorities is resolved, other risks and transition moments emerge and require a repeated cycle of action to bolster institutional resilience to stress. There is no "one path", institutions do not need to converge on Western models to create sustained security—in fact, local adaptation is best. Additionally, progress can be made within a generation, but areas that have already seen repeated cycles of organized violence cannot create sustained security overnight. The arrow below the spiral shows that external support and incentives can help this nationally led process, and the arrow above it shows that external stresses can derail it.

The WDR framework provides a roadmap for the nine chapters of the WDR, summarized in table 1.

TABLE 1 *Chapter structure*

PART 1: THE CHALLENGE	
VIOLENCE and FRAGILITY	Chapter 1, ***Repeated violence threatens development***, explores the challenge: repeated cycles of organized criminal violence and civil conflict that threaten development locally and regionally and are responsible for much of the global deficit in meeting the Millennium Development Goals.
Weak institutions not transforming Elite pact New stresses Violence	Chapter 2, ***Vulnerability to violence***, reviews the combination of internal and external stresses and institutional factors that lead to violence. It argues that capable, accountable, and legitimate institutions are the common "missing factor" explaining why some societies are more resilient to violence than others. Without attention to institutional transformation, countries are susceptible to a vicious cycle of repeated violence.
PART 2: LESSONS FROM NATIONAL AND INTERNATIONAL RESPONSES	
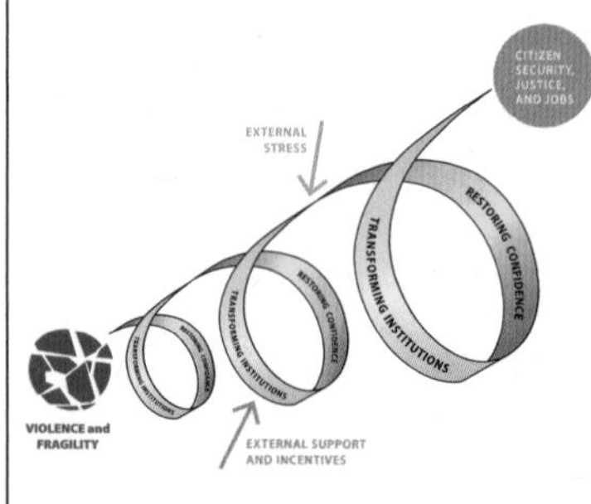	Chapter 3, ***From violence to resilience: Restoring confidence and transforming institutions***, presents the WDR framework, or "virtuous cycle." It compiles research and case study experience to show how countries have successfully moved away from fragility and violence: by mobilizing coalitions in support of citizen security, justice, and jobs to restore confidence in the short term and by transforming national institutions over time. This is a repeated process that seizes multiple transition moments and builds cumulative progress. It takes a generation.
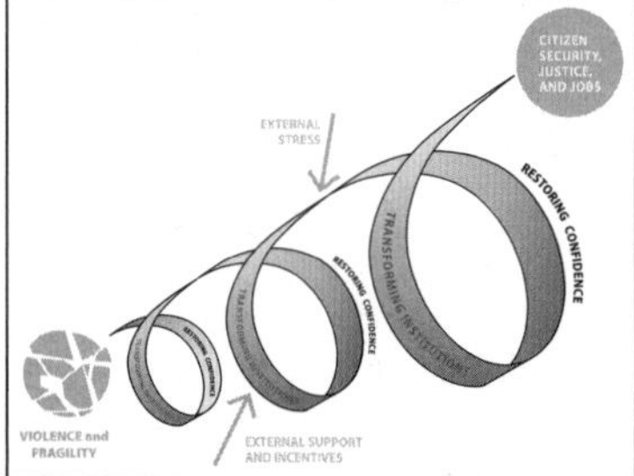	Chapter 4, ***Restoring confidence: Moving away from the brink***, reviews lessons from national experience in restoring confidence by mobilizing 'inclusive-enough' coalitions of stakeholders and by delivering results. Collaborative coalitions often combine government and nongovernmental leadership to build national support for change and signal an irreversible break with the past. Restoring confidence in situations of low trust means delivering some fast results, since government announcements of change will not be credible without tangible action.

<table>
<tr><td>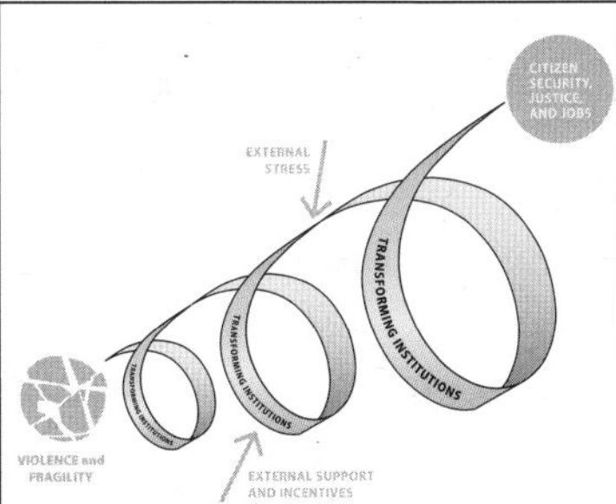
</td><td>Chapter 5, Transforming institutions to deliver security, justice, and jobs, reviews national experience in prioritizing foundational reforms that provide citizen security, justice, and jobs—and stem the illegal financing of armed groups. In moving forward institutional transformation in complex conflict settings, case studies emphasize that perfection should not be the enemy of progress—pragmatic, "best-fit" approaches should be used to address immediate challenges.</td></tr>
<tr><td>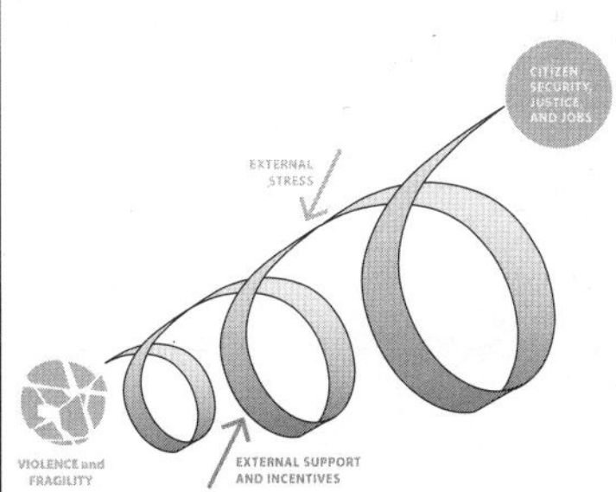
</td><td>Chapter 6, International support to building confidence and transforming institutions, turns to lessons from international support to national processes. While registering some notable successes, it argues that international interventions are often fragmented, slow to enter, quick to exit, reliant on international technical assistance, and delivered through parallel systems. The chapter considers why international action has been slow to change. International actors have to respond to their own domestic pressures to avoid risk and deliver fast results. Different parts of the international system—middle-income versus OECD actors, for example—face different domestic pressures, undermining cohesive support.</td></tr>
<tr><td>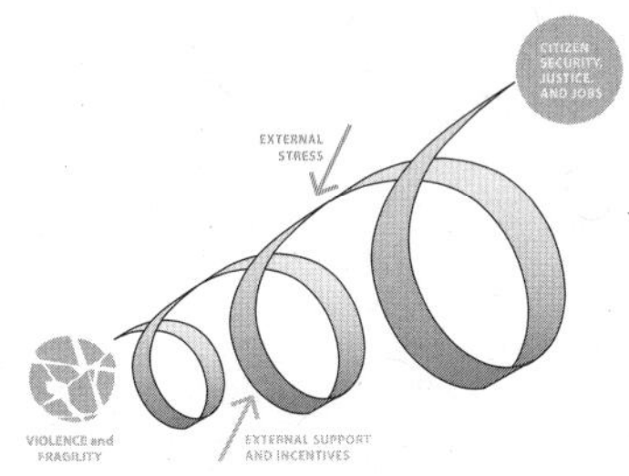
</td><td>Chapter 7, International action to mitigate external stresses, provides lessons from international action to combat external security, economic, and resource stresses that increase conflict risk. The stresses range from trafficking in drugs and natural resources to food insecurity and other economic shocks. The chapter also addresses lessons from regional and cross-border initiatives to manage these threats.</td></tr>
<tr><td colspan="2">PART 3: PRACTICAL OPTIONS AND RECOMMENDATION</td></tr>
<tr><td>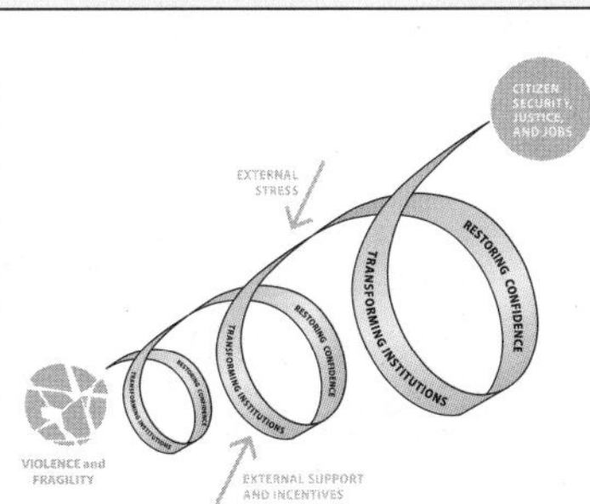
</td><td>Chapter 8, Practical country directions and options, provides practical options for national and international reformers to take advantage of multiple transition opportunities, restore confidence, and transform institutions in countries facing a range of institutional challenges, stresses, and forms of violence.</td></tr>
<tr><td>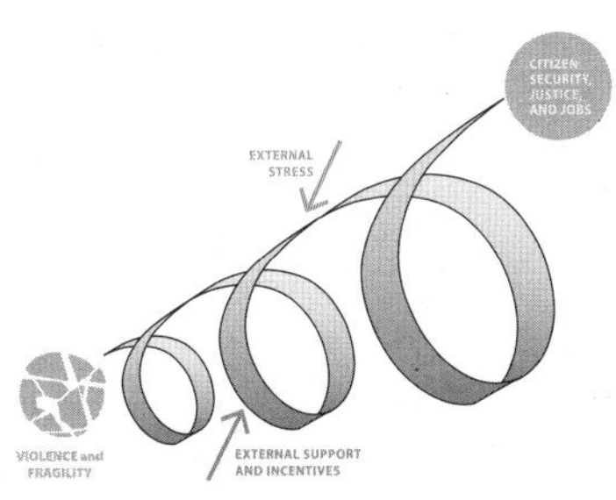
</td><td>Chapter 9, New directions for international support, identifies four tracks for international action. First, to invest in prevention through citizen security, justice and jobs. Second, internal agency reforms to provide faster assistance for confidence-building and longer term institutional engagement. Third, acting at the regional level on external stresses. Fourth, marshalling the knowledge and resources of low-, middle-, and high-income countries.</td></tr>
</table>

The dynamics of change are similar in countries facing violence of purely criminal origins and those facing political and civil conflict; in countries with different combinations of stresses and institutional characteristics; and in those at different incomes, including middle and high income countries facing subnational violence. This said, the Report's framework must be applied contextually, taking into account the specific features of the case in question. This differentiation is explored throughout the Report. Lessons from country case studies in chapters 4 to 8 include, for example, brief "differentiation tables" that summarize the relevant types of violence, transition opportunities, key stakeholders, key stresses, and institutional challenges faced (table 2). These tables provide a brief assessment of the critical dynamics that, based on experience, must be taken into account when designing an appropriate strategy to prevent, mitigate, or recover from violence.

TABLE 2 ***Sample differentiation table***

Types of violence: Legacy of civil conflict, political, criminal and gang related violence, trafficking	
Transition opportunities: Moderate space for change, presidential elections, strong international support	**Key stakeholders:** Government, investors, opposition parties, ex-combatants, victims, peacekeepers
Key stresses: Legacy of violence and trauma, grievances and mistrust, deep-rooted corruption, unemployment	**Institutional challenges:** Accountability and capacity constraints in economic, security, political spheres

PART I

The Challenge

This chapter presents the development challenge of political and criminal violence. The effects can be devastating. Violence kills and displaces people, destroys human and physical capital, stunts growth, and all too often spills across borders. More than 1.5 billion people live in countries affected by fragility, violence, or conflict. A child living in a conflict-affected or fragile developing country is twice as likely to be undernourished as a child living in another developing country and nearly three times as likely to be out of school. No low-income fragile or conflict-affected state has yet achieved a single Millennium Development Goal (MDG). There is hope, however. Countries that have managed to reduce violence have also produced some of the fastest development gains.

CHAPTER 1

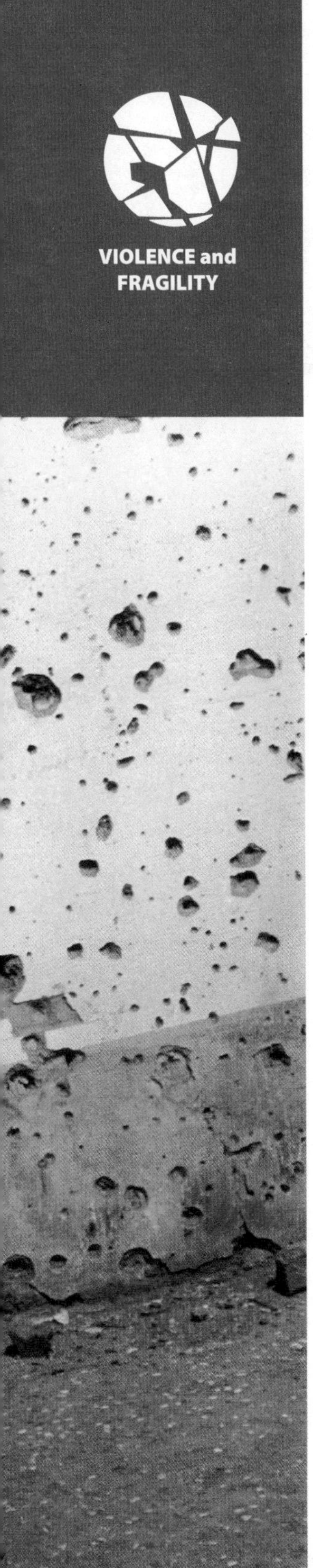

Repeated Violence Threatens Development

Interstate and civil wars have declined since peaking in the early 1990s

Wars between states are now relatively rare (compared with the large wars of the 20th century). Major civil wars, after peaking in the early 1990s, have since declined (see box 1.1). The annual number of battle deaths from civil war fell from more than 160,000 a year in the 1980s to less than 50,000 a year in the 2000s.[1] Homicide rates in most regions have also been declining, except in Latin America and the Caribbean and possibly Sub-Saharan Africa.[2]

The last two decades have also seen progress in developing global and regional standards to check the violent or coercive exercise of power. In Africa, the Lomé Declaration in 2000, which established standards and a regional response mechanism to unconstitutional changes in government, has been associated with a reduction in coups d'état from 15 in the 1990s to 5 from 2000 to mid-2010.[3] And, despite an increase in coups in the last five years, continental action to restore constitutionality has been consistently strong. In 1991, the Organization of American States adopted provisions supporting democratic and constitutional changes of government and laying out action in the event of a coup; a decision reinforced in the Democratic Charter of 2001.[4] The number of coups in Latin America fell from 30 between 1970 and 1989 to 3 since 1990.[5] New norms and associated sanctions to protect human rights have also made it possible to prosecute leaders for using extreme violence and coercion against their citizens: since 1990, 67 former heads of state have been prosecuted for serious human rights violations or economic crimes during their tenures.[6]

Countries emerging from severe violence have made striking development gains, often with strong assistance from the international community. Conflict-affected states often begin their recovery from lower development levels than is "natural," given their human and physical capital. This makes rapid strides in development possible, as shown in the following examples:[7]

- Ethiopia more than quadrupled access to improved water, from 13 percent of the population in 1990 to 66 percent in 2009–10.
- Mozambique more than tripled its primary school completion rate in just eight years, from 14 percent in 1999 to 46 percent in 2007.
- Rwanda cut the prevalence of undernourishment from 53 percent of the population in 1997 to 34 percent in 2007.

BOX 1.1 *Interstate and civil war—1900 to the present*

Interstate war has declined dramatically since the two world wars of the first half of the 20th century. Major civil conflicts (those with more than 1,000 battle deaths a year) increased during the postcolonial and Cold War era, peaking in the late 1980s and early 1990s (figure a). Since 1991–92, when there were 21 active major civil wars, the number has steadily fallen to less than 10 each year since 2002.[8]

FIGURE A Civil wars peaked in the early 1990s and then declined

Major civil wars increased from 1960 through the late 1980s and have decreased since the early-1990s.

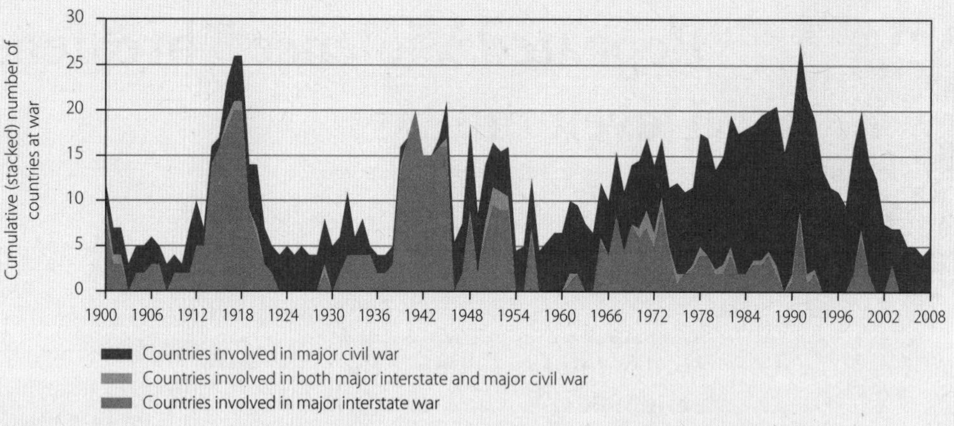

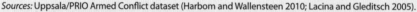

Sources: Uppsala/PRIO Armed Conflict dataset (Harbom and Wallensteen 2010; Lacina and Gleditsch 2005).

The declines are all the more remarkable given the rising number of sovereign states—from around 50 in 1900 to more than 170 in 2008. Despite a tripling in the number of states and a doubling of population in the last 60 years, the percentage of countries involved in major conflicts (interstate or civil) has not increased, and there has been a decline since 1992.

In addition, civil wars have become less violent. Battle deaths have dropped from an average of 164,000 a year in the 1980s and 92,000 a year in the 1990s to 42,000 a year in the 2000s (figure b). This is consistent with recent evidence of declines in the number of wars, human rights abuses, and fatalities in war—and in the indirect deaths associated with wars.[9]

FIGURE B Deaths from civil wars are also on the decline

As the number of civil wars declined, the total annual deaths from these conflicts (battle deaths) fell from more than 200,000 in 1988 to less than 50,000 in 2008.

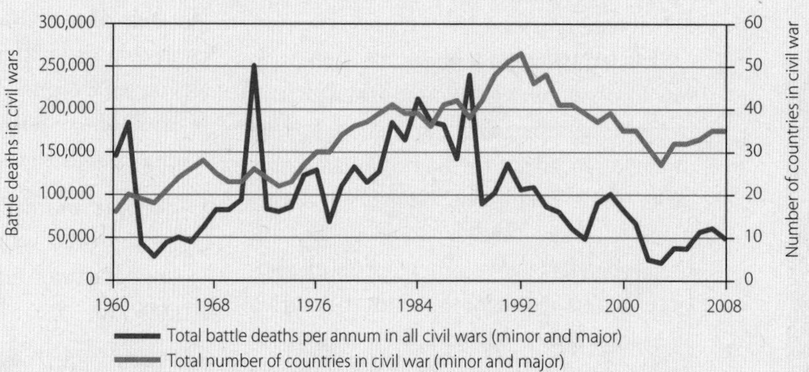

Sources: Uppsala/PRIO Armed Conflict dataset (Harbom and Wallenstein 2010; Lacina and Gleditsch 2005); Gleditsch and others 2002; Sundberg 2008; Gleditsch and Ward 1999; Human Security Report Project, forthcoming.

Note: Civil wars are classified by scale and type in the Uppsala/PRIO Armed Conflict database (Harbom and Wallensteen 2010; Lacina and Gleditsch 2005). The minimum threshold for monitoring is a minor civil war with 25 or more battle deaths a year. Low, high, and best estimates of annual battle deaths per conflict are in Lacina and Gleditsch (2005, updated in 2009). Throughout this Report, best estimates are used, except when they are not available, in which case averages of the low and high estimates are used.

FIGURE 1.1 *Gangs and trafficking are global concerns*

Following September 11, 2001, there was an exponential rise in media coverage of terrorism. Meanwhile, media coverage of gangs and trafficking has also been increasing. Recently, the coverage of gangs and trafficking approached that of civil war.

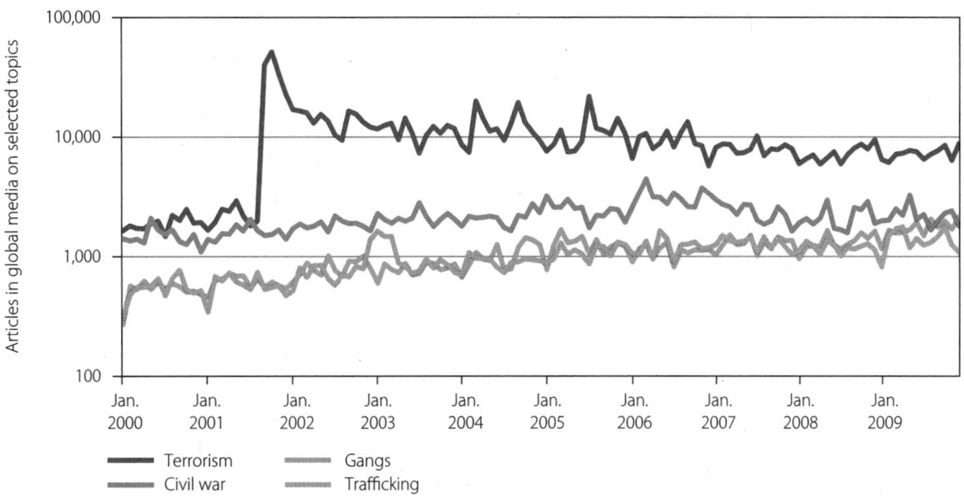

Source: Factiva.

Note: Data in the figure were compiled by using all available news sources from the Factiva search engine from January 2000 to December 2009 and using the following four search terms: "terrorism," "trafficking," "gangs," and "civil war" in multiple languages. Only articles where the search terms appeared in the headline and lead paragraph were counted.

- Bosnia and Herzegovina, between 1995 and 2007, increased measles immunizations from 53 to 96 percent for children aged 12–23 months, and reduced infant mortality from 16 to 12.6 per 1,000 live births. Telephone lines per 100 people increased fourfold, from 7 to 28.

But global apprehension remains. Media references to terrorism peaked after 9/11 and then gradually declined, but references to gangs and trafficking steadily increased over the last decade (figure 1.1). The Middle East and North Africa has experienced a series of dramatic social protests and political turbulence, escalating into outright conflict in some countries. Violence in Afghanistan and Pakistan is consuming the attention of global policy makers. As this report goes to print, a new nation is emerging in Southern Sudan, with all the opportunities and risks involved in that endeavor. Drug-based violence appears to be on the increase in Central America, threatening both local and national governance. Global terrorism remains a serious threat. And new and unpredictable risks are likely to emerge from a combination of demographic pressure, climate change, and resource scarcity.

Modern violence comes in various forms and repeated cycles

The tendency to see violence as interstate warfare and major civil war obscures the variety and prevalence of organized violence—and underestimates its impact on people's lives. The organized violence that disrupts governance and compromises development also includes local violence involving militias or between ethnic groups, gang violence, local resource-related violence and violence linked to trafficking (particularly drug trafficking), and violence associated with global ideological struggles (table 1.1). This violence is often recurrent, with many countries now experiencing repeated cycles of civil conflict and criminal violence.

TABLE 1.1 *Country case examples of multiple forms of violence*

Country	Local intergroup conflict	"Conventional" political conflict (contests for state power or for autonomy or independence)	Widespread gang-related violence	Organized crime or trafficking with accompanying violence	Local conflicts with transnational ideological connections
Afghanistan	Multiple incidents involving militias including Amanullah Khan and Abdul Rashid Dostum (2002–08)	Taliban, other actors (2002–present)	Warlordism (2002–present)	Opium production and trafficking	Al-Qaeda links with Taliban
Pakistan	Intratribal conflict (2004–09)	Pakistani Taliban (2007–present); Balochistan separatists (2004–present)		Drug production and trafficking	Cross-border ideological militant links
Mali	Rebel infighting (1994); ethnic violence in Gao, Kayes, and Kindal regions (1998–99)	Rebel groups in Northern Mali (1990–present)		Transnational trafficking of illicit goods, principally drugs and weapons	Al-Qaeda in the Islamic Maghreb
Papua New Guinea	Ethnic and tribal conflicts in the Highlands (2001–present)	Secessionist movement (Bougainville Revolutionary Army, 1989–2001)	Urban crime and gang violence	Human trafficking; source and transit point for illicit timber trade	
El Salvador		Rebel groups (1979–92)	La Mara Salva Trucha, La 18, La Mao Mao, and La Máquina	Drug trafficking	
Kenya	Clan and ethnic group violence (2005–08)	Election violence	Widespread gang activity (1980s–present)	Drug trafficking hub, particularly for heroin	
Tajikistan		Democratic and Islamist opposition groups (1992–96); Movement for Peace in Tajikistan (1998)		Major transit country for Afghan narcotics; human trafficking	Islamic Movement of Uzbekistan
Philippines	Local clan conflicts	Muslim separatist groups in Mindanao (Moro Islamic Liberation Front and Moro National Liberation Front)		Kidnap for ransom; human trafficking; methamphetamine source for East and Southeast Asia	Al-Qaeda and Jemaah Islamiyah links with Abu Sayyaf (Mindanao)
Northern Ireland (United Kingdom)	Local tensions over religion and economic disparities underlie much of the escalated violence	Irish Republican Army (IRA) (1971–98)	Splinter groups of IRA and Protestant paramilitaries	Drug trafficking (amphetamines)	

Sources: Lockhart and Glencorse 2010; Straus 2010; Demombynes 2010; Barron and others 2010; Dinnen, Porter, and Sage 2010; Europa Publications 2001; Economist Intelligence Unit 2010; Oxford Reference Online 2001; Uppsala University 2009b, 2009a; UNODC 2010b.

Violence is often interlinked

As table 1.1 suggests, many types of violence have direct links to each other, as illustrated in the following examples:

- Countries rich in oil and other minerals that can be illegally trafficked are much more likely to have a civil war,[10] and a longer one, with rebels financing their activity through the sale of lootable resources, such as diamonds in Sierra Leone and coltan (the mineral columbite-tantalite) in the Democratic Republic of Congo.[11] Illegal trafficking has been a source of finance for armed groups in Afghanistan, Mindanao, and Northern Ireland.[12]
- In countries as diverse as Côte d'Ivoire, Jamaica, Kenya, and the Solomon Islands, militant groups or criminal gangs have been mobilized during past political contests and elections.[13]
- In Melanesia, the ritualized community conflicts of previous generations have escalated into urban gang violence associated with particular ethnic groups.[14]

- In Central America, combatants on both sides of political conflicts between the state and rebel movements have migrated into organized crime.[15]

In other cases, violence may be linked through underlying institutional weaknesses. Yemen now faces four separate conflicts: the Houthi rebellion in the North, the presence of Al-Qaeda in the Arabian Peninsula, grievances in the south, and the popular protests for change that have swept through the Arab world. There is little direct evidence of links between these conflicts, other than through the weakness of national institutions to address them.[16] Similarly, in Nepal, following a decade-long insurrection (1996–2006) a Comprehensive Peace Agreement was signed between the Maoist rebels and the government. But violence between political rivals, quasi-political extortion, and criminal gang activity have increased markedly since the civil war.[17]

The modern landscape of violence also includes terrorist attacks by movements that claim ideological motives and recruit internationally. Terrorism—commonly, though not universally, defined as the use of force by nonstate actors against civilians[18]—stretches back at least to the Middle Ages. In modern times, the tactics and organizations have mutated. The dominant forms and groups from the 1960s to the early 1990s were leftist or nationalist groups based in OECD (Organisation for Economic Co-operation and Development) countries (the Baader-Meinhof Group, Red Brigades, the IRA, the Euskadi Ta Askatasuna (ETA), and groups associated with the Israeli-Palestinian struggle). In contrast, the 1990s saw a surge in right-wing nationalism and anti-government libertarian terrorism in the West,[19] until the center of gravity shifted with 9/11 and the later attacks in, among other places, Jakarta, London, Madrid, and Mumbai. This Report does not enter the debate on what terrorism is or is not. Instead, the concern with terrorism is about the elements of movements that pose particular threats to governance and development, along with their ability to recruit and to operate across national boundaries and the diverse motivations of those who join (chapter 2). While the preoccupation with terrorism is high in Western countries, some perspective on the global phenomenon is necessary—fatalities have been overwhelmingly concentrated on nonwestern targets in every year except 2001 (figure 1.2).

Organized crime and trafficking are an important part of current violent threats

Trafficking of drugs, people, and commodities has been an international concern for

FIGURE 1.2 *Victims of terrorism*

Over the last decade, 86 percent of nearly 50,000 fatalities from terrorism occurred in attacks aimed at non-Western targets. The attacks of September 11, 2001, are the exception rather than the rule, and the phenomenon of terrorism has long affected all regions of the world.

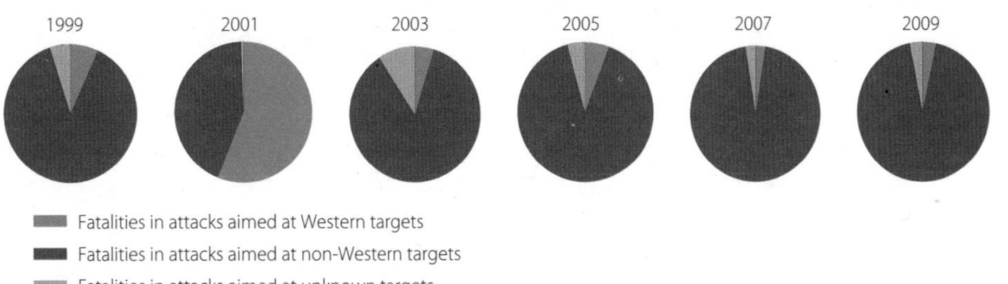

Fatalities in attacks aimed at Western targets
Fatalities in attacks aimed at non-Western targets
Fatalities in attacks aimed at unknown targets

Sources: National Counter Terrorism Center 2010; Global Terrorism Database 2010; WDR team calculations. The Global Terrorism Database (GTD) contains data from 1998 to 2008 and the National Counter Terrorism Center (NCTC) from 2004 to 2009. Pie charts from 1999 to 2003 are thus based on GTD data; from 2005 to 2007 on average shares from the two datasets; and for 2009 on NCTC data.

Note: From 1998 to 2009, 41,753 fatalities occurred in attacks on nonwestern targets, of a global total of 48,828. These statistics are based on the nationality of the principal target of each attack; "Western" targets are defined as all targets from OECD countries, targets in all other countries are defined as "non-Western." So attacks on non-Western targets may occasionally include Western fatalities, and vice versa.

BOX 1.2 *Instability, political violence, and drug trafficking in West Africa*

West Africa is one of the poorest and least stable regions in the world. All but 3 of its 16 countries are on the United Nations (UN) list of "least developed countries." Since independence, countries in the region have experienced at least 58 coups and attempted coups and many civil wars—and rebel groups remain active.

Where conflict has ended, recovery and the creation of resilient institutions take time; and the weakness of governance in post-conflict environments attracts transnational criminal networks. International drug traffickers began in 2004 to use the region as a base for shipping cocaine from South America to Europe.

In 2008 an estimated 25 tons of cocaine passed through West Africa, with a transit value of about US$1 billion by the time it reached West Africa, and an ultimate value of some US$6.8 billion at its destinations in Western Europe.[20] Drug traffickers use some of the profits to bribe government officials. As the UNODC (UN Office on Drugs and Crime) notes in its Transnational Organized Crime Threat Assessment for West Africa, "Law enforcement officials can be offered more than they could earn in a lifetime simply to look the other way."[21]

Trafficking and violence during conflicts in West Africa, 1990–2009

West Africa has experienced political, communal, and criminal violence since 1990. During conflicts, diamonds, timber, and oil were trafficked. Recently the region has become a transit route for cocaine trafficked from South America to Europe.

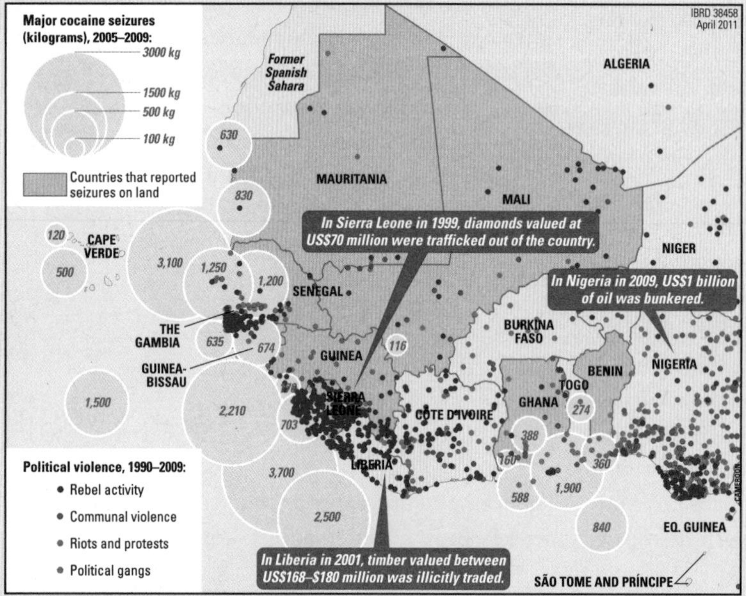

Sources: Conflict data are from Raleigh and others 2010 ACLED database (Armed Conflict Location and Event Database), seizure and trafficking data are from UNODC 2010a; WDR team calculations.

Note: The map above depicts West African political violence 1990–2009 overlaid trafficking and seizure data. Violence data for Sierra Leone and Liberia are for 1990–2010, while violence data for all other states are for 1997–2009.

decades. Criminal networks take advantage of communications, transport, and financial services—and overwhelm enforcement mechanisms that are either rooted in national jurisdictions or hampered by low cooperation and weak capacity. Drugs connect some of the wealthiest and poorest areas of the world in mutual violence, showing that many solutions to violence require a global perspective. The annual value of the global trade in cocaine and heroin today is estimated at US$153 billion (heroin US$65 billion and cocaine US$88 billion). Europe and North America consume 53 percent of the heroin and 67 percent of the cocaine; however, the high retail prices in these markets mean that economic share of consumption in Europe and North America is even higher: cocaine consumption in the two regions accounted for an estimated US$72 billion of the US$88 billion in global trade.[22] Drugs provide the money that enables organized criminals to corrupt and manipulate even the most powerful societies—to the ultimate detriment of the urban poor, who provide most of the criminals' foot-soldiers and who find themselves trapped in environments traumatized by criminal violence.[23]

Drug trafficking organizations thus have resources that can dwarf those of the governments attempting to combat them.[24] The value-added of cocaine traveling the length of Central America is equivalent to 5 percent of the region's GDP—and more than 100 times the US$65 million the United States allocates under the Mérida Initiative to assist interdiction efforts by Mexico and Central American nations.[25] Conservative estimates suggest there are 70,000 gang members in Central America, outnumbering military personnel there.[26] In many countries, drug cartels exert a heavy influence over provincial governance and, occasionally, national governance (box 1.2).

Organized crime networks engage in a wide variety of illicit activities, including trafficking drugs, people, and small arms and light weapons; financial crimes; and money laundering. These illicit activities require the absence of rule of law and, therefore, often thrive in countries affected by other forms of violence. According to various studies, organized crime generates annual revenues ranging from US$120 billion to as high as US$330 billion,[27] with drug trafficking the most profitable. Other estimates suggest that the world's shadow economy, including organized crime, could be as high as 10 percent of GDP globally.[28]

Countries affected by political violence that have weak institutions are also susceptible to trafficking. Since 2003, drug trafficking organizations have taken advantage of institutional weaknesses in West Africa to establish their operations there, resulting in a fourfold increase in cocaine seizures heading to Europe since 2003. Box 1.2 shows how trafficking and violence coexist in the region.[29] Armed groups in Central Africa secure their funding from mining and smuggling precious minerals such as gold. In the Democratic Republic of Congo, an estimated 40 tons of gold, worth US$1.24 billion, are smuggled out every year.[30] The link between criminal trafficking and violence is not unique to Africa. For example, Myanmar is still a major source of opium, accounting for 10 percent of global production, and continues to be a major trade hub to East and Southeast Asia. Illegal logging remains a major challenge in Myanmar; although trade in timber from Myanmar fell by 70 percent from 2005 to 2008, illegal trade into countries in the region continues. Myanmar also serves as a major conduit of wildlife trade coming from Africa and South Asia.[31]

Today's violence occurs in repeated cycles

There has been a tendency in the development community to assume that the progression from violence to sustained security is fairly linear—and that repeated violence is the exception. But recurring civil wars have become a dominant form of armed conflict in the world today. Every civil war that began since 2003 was a resumption of a previous civil war.[32] Of all conflicts initiated in the 1960s, 57 percent were the first conflict in their country (many countries having been newly created after the colonial era).[33] First conflicts fell significantly in each subsequent decade, to the point where 90 percent of conflicts initiated in the 21st century were in countries that had already had a civil war (table 1.2). Fighting has also continued after several recent political settlements, as in Afghanistan and the Democratic Republic of Congo. As the previous section showed, successful peace agreements can be followed by high levels of criminal violence.

Several Central American countries that ended civil wars are now experiencing more violent deaths from criminal activity than

TABLE 1.2 ***Countries often relapse into conflict***

Repeated violence is common in the world today, suggesting that few countries are ever truly "post-conflict." The rate of onset in countries with a previous conflict has been increasing since the 1960s, and every civil war that began since 2003 was in a country that had had a previous civil war.

Decade	Onsets in countries with no previous conflict (%)	Onsets in countries with a previous conflict (%)	Number of onsets
1960s	57	43	35
1970s	43	57	44
1980s	38	62	39
1990s	33	67	81
2000s	10	90	39

Sources: Walter 2010; WDR team calculations.
Note: Previous conflict includes any major conflict since 1945.

during their civil wars. Since 1999, homicide rates have increased in El Salvador (+101 percent), Guatemala (+91 percent), and Honduras (+63 percent) as criminal networks linked to drug trafficking have become more active (figure 1.3). All these countries suffered civil wars or political instability in the 1980s and 1990s. While El Salvador and Guatemala signed peace accords in the 1990s that avoided a return to civil war, both now face levels of violent organized crime equally disruptive to development.

The developmental consequences of violence are severe

The costs of violence for citizens, communities, countries, and the world are enormous, both in terms of human suffering and social

FIGURE 1.3 ***Criminal violence in Central America is on the rise despite political peace***

Homicides have increased in every country in Central America since 1999: in El Salvador from 30 to 61 homicides per 100,000 people and in Guatemala from 24 to 46 per 100,000.

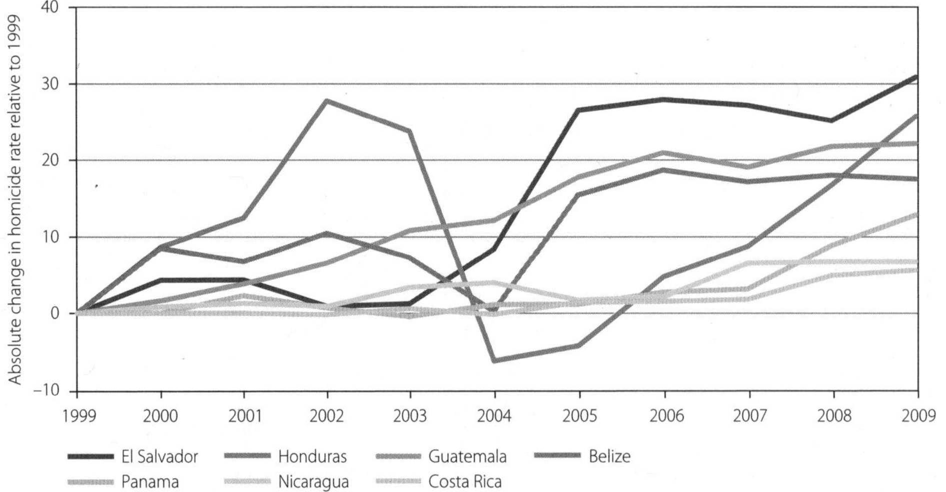

Sources: WDR team calculations based on UNODC 2007; UNODC and the World Bank 2007; and national sources.
Note: Base year for homicide rate is 1999 = 0.

and economic consequences. The costs are both direct (loss of life, disability, and destruction) and indirect (prevention, instability, and displacement). While some of these losses can be directly measured and quantified in economic terms, others are not easily measured (trauma, loss of social capital and trust, prevention cost, and forgone investment and trade).[34]

Human costs of violence

Most fundamentally, violence compromises human security and dignity—and for this reason, freedom from violence and fear is a basic human right. The 2008 Geneva Declaration on Armed Violence and Development, endorsed by more than 90 states, argues that "living free from the threat of armed violence is a basic human need."[35] To better understand the impact of violence on lives and livelihoods, the WDR team asked the Norwegian research institute Fafo to conduct surveys in seven countries and territories, involving a mix of nationally representative samples as well as subregions affected by violence.[36] In the past three years, up to 26 percent of respondents report that their immediate family's home had been looted, up to 32 percent had been displaced, and up to 19 percent had a family member who had been tortured (figure 1.4).

The most vulnerable groups in society are frequently most affected by violence. Tied to their homes or places of work, the vulnerable have little of the protection that money or well-placed contacts afford. Poor child nutrition for those displaced or unable to earn incomes due to violence has lasting effects, impairing physical and cognitive functioning. Violence destroys school infrastructure, displaces teachers, and interrupts schooling, often for an entire generation of poor children. War, looting, and crime destroy the household assets of the poor, and fear of violent attacks prevents them from tilling their fields or traveling to schools, clinics, workplaces, and markets. For poor people in poor

FIGURE 1.4 ***Violence creates suffering for families in myriad ways: Responses to survey on experiences of violence on immediate family member in last three years***

People in conflict-affected countries experience displacement, loss of contact, imprisonment, and humiliation, which affect entire families, disrupting life and destroying social capital. In Gaza, a third of respondents reported that someone in their immediate family had been displaced in the last three years. In the West Bank, a third had experienced someone being imprisoned. In Sierra Leone, 35 percent of the respondents reported that they lost contact with a member of their immediate family in the last three years.

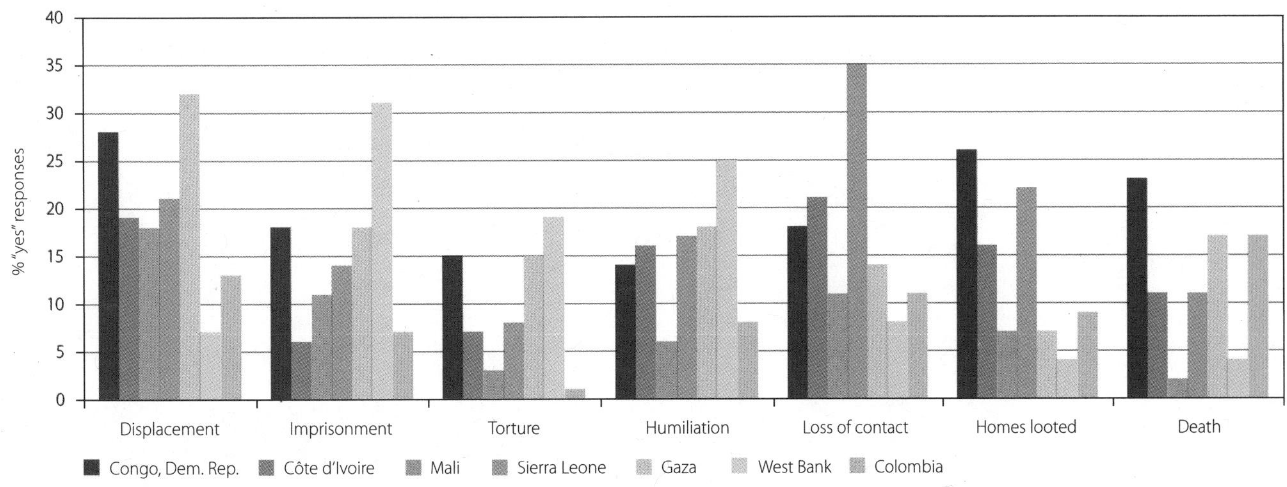

Source: Bøås, Tiltnes, and Flatø 2010.

Note: Surveys were undertaken in early 2010 for seven countries, territories, or subnational areas. The samples were selected from multiple regions to cover countries varying geographically, at different stages of development and facing or recovering from differing types of violence. Country representative samples were used for Côte d'Ivoire, Sierra Leone, and Colombia. The surveys were undertaken in selected regions of Democratic Republic of Congo and Mali. Independent representative samples were used in Gaza and the West Bank.

countries, extended families are often their only insurance, and deaths in the family often leave them alone and unprotected.[37]

Development impacts of violence

Poverty reduction in countries affected by major violence is on average nearly a percentage point slower per year than in countries not affected by violence.[38] After a few years of major violence, the contrast can be quite stark: countries affected by violence throughout the 1980s lagged in poverty reduction by 8 percentage points, and those that had experienced major violence throughout the 1980s and 1990s lagged by 16 percentage points. On average, a country experiencing major violence over the entire period (1981–2005) had a poverty rate 21 percentage points higher than a country that saw no violence (figure 1.5). The disruptive effect of violence on development and the widening gap between countries affected by violence and those not affected are deeply troubling.

The direct impact of violence falls primarily on young males, the majority of fighting forces, but women and children often suffer disproportionately from indirect effects (see table 1.3).[39] Men make up 96 percent of the detainee population and 90 percent of the missing,[40] women and children comprise close to 80 percent of refugees and those internally displaced.[41] And violence begets violence: children who witness abuses have a higher tendency to perpetrate violence later in life.[42]

Sexual and gender-based violence remains a major problem, particularly in fragile and conflict-affected countries.[43] Most contemporary armed conflicts are "low-intensity" civil wars fought by small, poorly trained, and lightly armed forces that avoid major military engagements—but that frequently target civilians with great brutality.[44] A global review of 50 countries finds significant increases in gender-based violence following a major war.[45] In some cases, it occurs due to a breakdown of social and moral order and to increased impunity, but the threat and perpetration of sexual and physical violence against women and children can also be a systematic weapon of war—to dominate, to terrorize, to humiliate. Mass rapes have occurred in Bosnia and Herzegovina, Liberia, Peru, and Uganda.[46] In Rwanda's 1994 genocide alone, an estimated 250,000 rapes took place.[47] Although those suffering rape and sexual abuse are overwhelmingly young

FIGURE 1.5 ***Widening gap in poverty between countries affected by violence and those not experiencing violence***

Poverty is on the decline for much of the world, but countries affected by violence are lagging behind. For every three years that a country is affected by major violence (battle deaths or excess deaths from homicides equivalent to a major war), poverty reduction lags behind by 2.7 percentage points. For some countries affected by violence, poverty has actually increased.

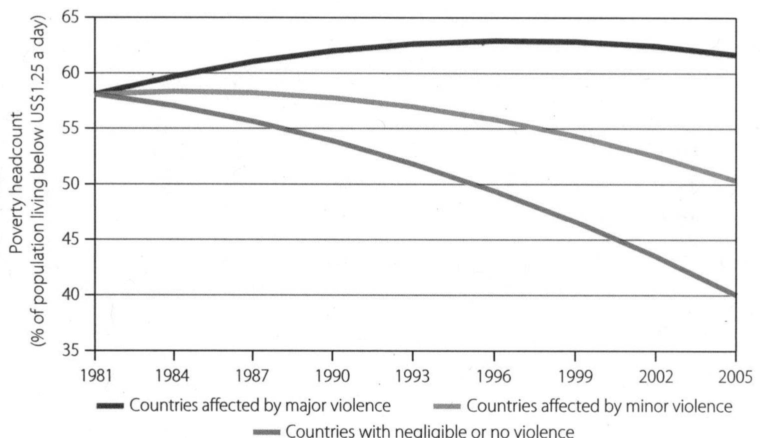

Source: WDR team calculations based on Chen, Ravallion, and Sangraula 2008 poverty data (available at POVCALNET, HTTP://iresearch.worldbank.org.)

TABLE 1.3 ***The gender-disaggregated impacts of violent conflict***

	Direct impacts	Indirect impacts
Men	Higher rates of morbidity and mortality from battle deaths Higher likelihood to be detained or missing Sexual and gender-based violence: sex-selective massacres; forcibly conscripted or recruited; subjected to torture, rape, and mutilation; forced to commit sexual violence upon others Higher rates of disability from injury	Risk of ex-combatants' involvement in criminal or illegal activities and difficulties in finding livelihoods Increased prevalence of other forms of violence—particularly domestic violence
Women	Higher likelihood to be internally displaced persons and refugees Sexual and gender-based violence: being subjected to rape, trafficking, and prostitution; forced pregnancies and marriages	Reproductive health problems Women's reproductive and care-giving roles under stress Changed labor market participation from death of family members and "added worker effect" Higher incidence of domestic violence Possibility for greater political participation Women's increased economic participation due to changing gender roles during conflict
Common	Depression, trauma, and emotional distress	Asset and income loss Tendency toward increased migration Disrupted patterns of marriage and fertility Loss of family and social networks, including insurance mechanisms Interrupted education Eroded well-being, particularly poor health and disability from poverty and malnutrition

Sources: Anderlini 2010a; multiple sources described in endnote.[48]

women,[49] men can also be subject to sexual victimization and violence, or be forced to perpetrate sexual violence against others, even their family members.[50]

A major human consequence of violence is the displacement of people from their homes. At the end of 2009 some 42 million people around the world had been forced to leave or flee their homes due to conflict, violence, and human rights violations—15 million refugees outside their country of nationality and habitual residence, and 27 million internally displaced persons (IDPs). And developing countries are also hosts to the vast majority of refugees, putting additional strains on their local and national capacities. In 2009 developing countries hosted 10.2 million refugees, or nearly 70 percent of the global total. The rising numbers of IDP populations, which include substantial new displacements in 2009 and 2010 in countries such as Pakistan, the Democratic Republic of Congo, and Sudan, undermine recovery from violence and interrupt human development.[51]

The suffering of displaced populations is often protracted. Camps in Chad, Jordan, Lebanon, and Sudan have become homes for many IDPs, not just for months or years, but often for decades. Most forced displacements in the 2000s were caused by internal armed conflicts rather than international conflicts. Population movements into urban centers have increased the potential for crime, social tension, communal violence, and political instability.[52] Meanwhile, the large-scale repatriation movements of the past have diminished, with return figures dropping since 2004.[53]

For all these reasons, areas affected by violence pose a major challenge to meeting MDGs. The arrested social development in countries affected by violence is evident in the poor showing in human development indicators (figure 1.6). Development in these

FIGURE 1.6 ***Violence is the main constraint to meeting the MDGs***

a. Incidence ratio of undernourishment, poverty and other ills for fragile, recovering, and non-fragile developing countries (non-FCS)

A child in a fragile or conflict-affected state is twice as likely to be undernourished as a child in another developing country—and nearly three times as likely to be out of primary school.

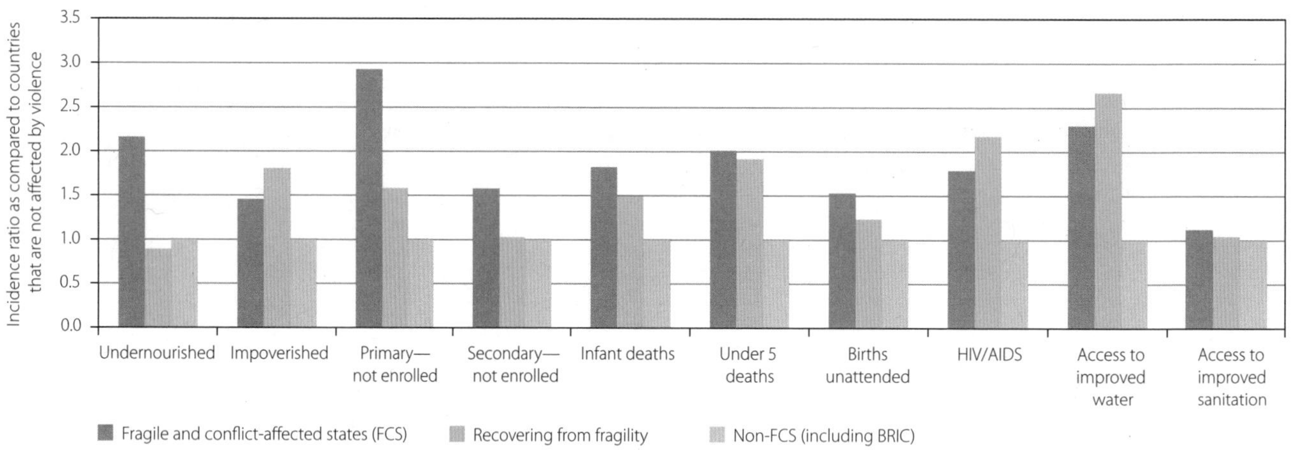

Sources: World Bank 2010n; WDR team calculations based on Gates and others 2010.

Note: Figure 1.6a shows the incidence of each of the ills associated with unmet MDGs for fragile, conflict-affected, and recovering countries in relation to the incidence for all other developing countries. The ratio is weighted by the affected population, so each bar can be read as the odds-ratio of a person being affected relative to a person in a non-fragile or conflict-affected state: for example, children of primary school age are three times as likely to be out of school in fragile and conflict-affected states as those in other developing countries.

b. Countries affected by violence account for:

Fragile and conflict-affected states and those recovering from conflict and fragility, account for 47 percent of the population considered here, but they account for 70 percent of infant deaths, 65 percent of people without access to safe water, and 77 of percent of children missing from primary school.

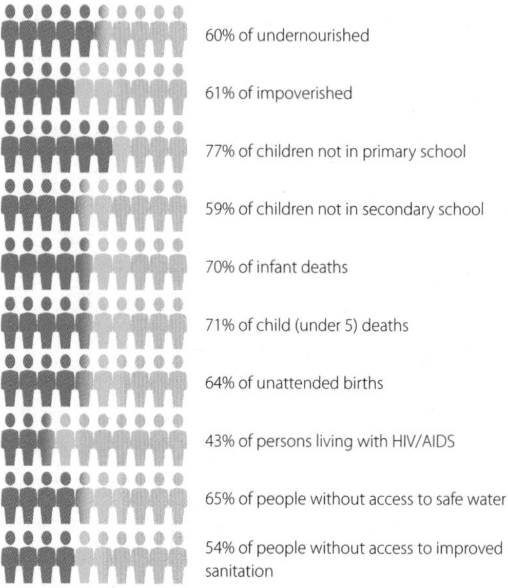

Sources: World Bank 2010n; WDR team calculations based on Gates and others 2010.

Note: Current fragile and conflict-affected states account for 33 percent of the population of the countries considered here. States recovering from fragility and conflict account for an additional 14 percent of the population. So, if the MDG deficit were borne evenly, these countries would account for 47 percent of each of the ills described. The red to orange people-figures represent the percentage of the deficit for each MDG in fragile, conflict-affected, and recovering countries. The blue figures represent the persons afflicted in other developing countries. Excluded here are Brazil, China, India, and Russian Federation, all significantly ahead of or on par with other developing countries on the MDGs (see panel a). Due to their size, including them in the calculations would skew any discussion involving the global population.

countries is lagging on nearly every indicator associated with the MDGs. The development deficit is concentrated in fragile and conflict-affected and recovering states,[54] which account for 77 percent of school-age children not enrolled in primary school, 61 percent of the poverty, and 70 percent of infant mortality.[55]

People in fragile and conflict-affected states are more likely to be impoverished, to miss out on schooling, and to lack access to basic health services. Children born in a fragile or conflict-affected state are twice as likely to be undernourished and nearly twice as likely to lack access to improved water; those of primary-school age are three times as likely not to be enrolled in school; and they are nearly twice as likely to die before their fifth birthday. As the world takes stock of progress on the MDGs, it is apparent that the gap between violence-prone countries and other developing countries is widening.[56] No low-income, fragile state has achieved a single MDG, and few are expected to meet targets by 2015.[57] Because most fragile and conflict-affected states have made slower progress in the last 10 years, the gap is widening. For example, over the last two decades, infant mortality has been falling in nearly all countries,[58] but the reduction in infant mortality in fragile and conflict-affected countries has lagged behind (figure 1.7). Of the countries with infant mortality greater than 100 per 1,000 in 1990, those not affected by conflict have reduced infant mortality by 31 percent—while fragile and conflict-affected states reduced it by only 19 percent. If these fragile and conflict-affected states had made the same rate of progress on infant mortality as other developing countries, almost a million more children in these countries each year would survive their first year of life.

FIGURE 1.7 ***The widening gap in infant mortality rates between countries affected by violence and others***

Of countries where more than 1 in 10 infants died in the first year of life in 1990, those affected by violence are lagging behind in reducing infant mortality. The gap between these two sets of countries has doubled since 1990.

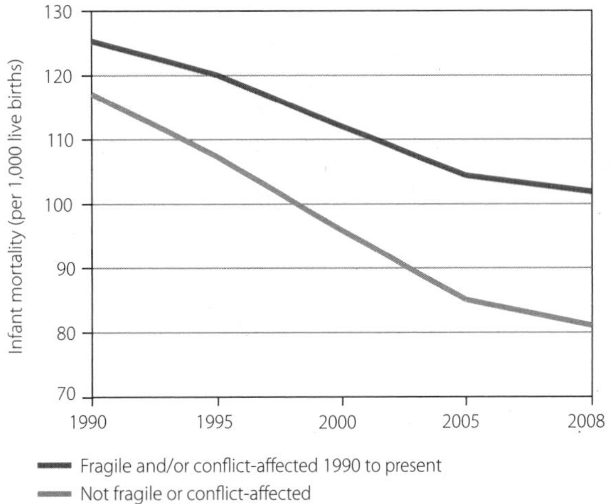

Sources: World Bank 2010n; WDR team calculations.

Note: Due to limited data, the most recent available data in the preceding five-year period were used for the point estimates. The sample consists of all countries with infant mortality higher than 100 per 1,000 live births. Low-income countries that were never fragile or conflict-affected from 1990 to 2008 are in the "non-fragile" cohort, and countries affected by conflict or fragile throughout the period are in the "fragile and/or conflict-affected" cohort.

Subnational violence can have severe socioeconomic consequences in middle-income countries. In countries with stronger economies and institutions, impacts tend to be relatively localized, but they still hold back key segments of human development and reduce the flow of foreign direct investment (FDI) into affected areas.[59] In the Indonesian province of Aceh, the economic cost of the conflict was estimated at US$10.7 billion, more than 60 percent of it through the damage and destruction of agriculture, livestock, enterprises, and fisheries. And during conflict, Aceh's infant mortality and poverty were 50 percent higher than the national average.[60]

The effects of violence are long-lasting. For countries that have gone through civil war, recovering to original growth paths takes an average of 14 years of peace.[61] Until 1990, Burkina Faso and Burundi had similar incomes and growth paths. With the onset of civil war in Burundi, real incomes declined to 1970 levels.[62] With no major conflicts, Burkina Faso now has an income more than two-and-a-half times that of Burundi (figure 1.8). This effect was confirmed locally in the Moving Out of Poverty study, which found that conflict-affected villages that feared renewed violence for two to three years out

FIGURE 1.8 ***Effects of violence on growth are dramatic and long-lasting***

Until the early 1990s, per capita incomes and growth in Burkina Faso and Burundi were similar. Following massive violence in Burundi, their growth paths diverged. In real terms, Burundi has lost nearly two decades of income growth, with incomes set back to 1970 levels.

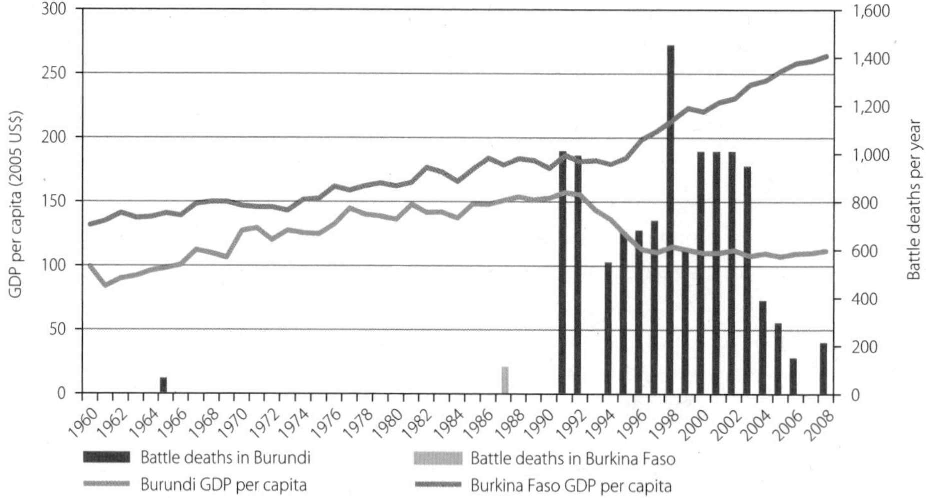

Sources: World Bank 2010n; Gleditsch and others 2002; Gates and others 2010; Uppsala/PRIO Armed Conflict dataset (Harbom and Wallensteen 2010; Lacina and Gleditsch 2005); WDR team calculations.

of the past decade stalled economically, while non-conflict-affected communities experienced only two to four weeks of apprehension over renewed violence and did not experience economic slowdown.[63]

One reason for the persistence of low growth in conflict-affected countries may be the difficulty of reassuring investors, both domestic and foreign. A civil war reduces a country's average rating on the International Country Risk Guide by about 7.7 points (on a 100-point scale); the effect is similar for criminal violence.[64] For the first three years after conflict subsides, countries have a rating 3.5 points below similar non-conflict countries. Although there is often a postviolence surge of economic activity, it is unlikely to be investment-based activity that reflects renewed investor confidence. Trade can take many years to recover as a result of investor perceptions of risk. It can drop between 12 and 25 percent in the first year of a civil war, and for the most severe civil wars (those with a cumulative death toll greater than 50,000) the loss of trade is around 40 percent.[65] And the interruption in trade can persist even 25 years after the onset of conflict. While effects are smaller for less severe conflicts, it still takes on average 20 years for trade to recover to pre-conflict levels.

Violence also has a lasting effect on human rights. The Physical Rights Integrity Index,[66] a measure of respect for human rights, drops on average by 3.6 points over the course of a major civil war (on a scale of 0–8, with a score of 0 indicating no government respect for human rights). That human rights abuses increase sharply during episodes of violence is to be expected. Less expected, however, is that after a conflict ends, the average society takes more than 10 years to return to the level of human rights observance before the conflict.[67] The unraveling of trust citizens have in one another and in the state due to violence is discussed in chapter 2.[68]

In addition to the human suffering, organized violence poses social and economic costs that can dwarf the impact of other events of concern to development practitioners, such as economic shocks and natural disasters. While all the costs cannot be quantified, conservative estimates of the economic costs of lost production range from 2 to 3 percent of GDP both for civil war and for very high levels of violent crime (box 1.3).[69] This does not include the destruction or loss of assets, which can also be considerable. For example, the material costs of crime in Latin America and the Caribbean are estimated to be nearly twice those of the United States, as a percentage of GDP.[70] Other indirect costs may not always be reflected by measures of productivity, as when military spending increases and commensurately reduces investments in development and human capital. Military spending typically increases by 2.2 percent during civil war and remains 1.7 percent higher than prewar levels after conflict.[71] As noted at the beginning of this chapter, these estimates do not include the human costs of conflict, including deaths, injury, trauma, and stress.

BOX 1.3 *Violent crime and insecurity exact high economic costs*

Indirect costs—associated with stress and trauma, time off work due to violent incidents, and lower productivity from injury or mental illness—far overshadow direct costs. In Brazil in 2004, the direct medical costs of all interpersonal violence were estimated at US$235 million and the indirect medical costs at US$9.2 billion. Comparable figures, respectively, for Jamaica are US$29.5 million and US$385 million, and for Thailand US$40.3 million and US$432 million. Emerging findings from Kenya estimate total costs of violence at 1.2 percent of GDP. In the United Kingdom, the direct costs of domestic violence are estimated at £5.7 billion annually.

When other indirect costs are added, such as those for policing, health care, private security, and reduced investment, the figures are even more staggering. In Guatemala, criminal violence cost an estimated US$2.4 billion, or 7.3 percent of GDP, in 2005—more than twice the damage caused by Hurricane Stan the same year, and more than twice the budget for the ministries of agriculture, health, and education for 2006. In El Salvador, criminal violence in 2003 cost about US$1.7 billion, or 11.5 percent of GDP. The Mexican government estimates that crime and violence cost the country 1 percent of GDP from lost sales, jobs, and investment in 2007 alone. Estimates suggest that if Haiti and Jamaica reduced their crime levels to those of Costa Rica, they could increase annual GDP growth by 5.4 percentage points. These costs are comparable to estimates of the cost of civil war. Based on growth base lines for cross-country panel date in the last 50 years, researchers estimate the costs of civil wars to range from 1.6 percentage to 2.3 percentage of GDP per year of violence. For the average country affected by violence, these effects, compounded over time, can cost the equivalent of up to 30 years of missing GDP growth.

Insecurity takes a significant toll on the private sector, in direct costs of criminal acts (theft, arson, or other victimization) and in investments in security systems. Cross-country surveys found that these costs represented 1–3 percent of sales in Senegal, South Africa, Tanzania, and Uganda, and 6 percent in Kenya. In nearly all cases, the bulk of these costs were for security technology and services. These estimates are conservative: other studies estimate the costs of crime to range from 3.1 percent to 7.8 percent of GDP.

Sources: Collier and Hoeffler 2004; Butchart and others 2008; Walby 2004; Geneva Declaration 2008; UNDP 2005c, 2006; UNODC and World Bank 2007; Skaperdas and others 2009; Willman and Makisaka 2010; Farrell and Clark 2004; Altbeker 2005; Alda and Cuesta 2010; Kenya Ministry of Public Health and Sanitation 2007; World Bank 2010d.

Spillover effects of violence

The development consequences of violence, like its origins, spill across borders, with implications for neighbors, for the region, and globally. Violence in one country can create a "bad neighborhood." For example, the manifestations of conflict in Liberia under President Charles Taylor during the late 1990s (people trained in violence, proliferation of small arms, and illicit trade in timber and diamonds) hurt Côte d'Ivoire, Guinea, and Sierra Leone.[72] Bad neighborhoods affect economic prospects: estimates suggest that countries lose 0.7 percent of their annual GDP for each neighbor involved in civil war.[73] And a doubling of terrorist incidents in a country is estimated to reduce bilateral trade with each trading partner by some 4 percent.[74] As terrorism taps into illicit global markets, violent extremists can finance their activities through smuggling, evading taxes, trafficking drugs and counterfeit money, and trading foreign currency on illegal exchanges in Europe.[75]

Piracy also reduces regional trade and economic activity, as, for example, Somali pirates operating in the Gulf of Aden.[76] To counter piracy in the Horn of Africa and the Indian Ocean, more than 27 countries deployed naval forces in anti-piracy missions, with a range of costs estimated at US$1.3–2.0 billion annually.[77] At a global level, efforts aimed at containing and deterring maritime piracy are estimated to range between US$1.7 and US$4.5 billion in 2010.[78] All told, maritime piracy is estimated to have direct economic costs of between US$5.7 billion and US$11.2 billion, once ransoms, insurance, and rerouting of ships are included.[79]

The spillover effects of violence are not just economic. As described above, nearly 75 percent of the world's refugees are hosted by neighboring countries.[80] Refugees from Liberia and Togo have sought shelter in Ghana for extended periods, straining the state's ability to deliver services and opening tensions with the local population.[81] The massive influx of Kosovo Albanians into Macedonia in 1999 during the Kosovo conflict heightened tensions between the Slavic majority and the Albanian minority.[82] Infectious disease can also be traced to disrupted health care associated with violence or areas without public services. For every 1,000 refugees entering an African country, for example, the host state acquires 1,400 new malaria cases.[83]

Spillovers of violence and instability are felt globally. Even for parts of the world fairly immune to insecurity, thanks to wealth and distance, the costs of global insecurity are both psychological (in the preoccupation with threats of gangs, trafficking, and terrorism) and very practical, through the increased costs of security measures. A study of 18 Western European countries from 1971 to 2004 revealed that each additional transnational terrorist incident per million people reduced economic growth by 0.4 percentage points, and each additional domestic terrorist incident reduced it by 0.2.[84] And after insurgents struck an export terminal owned by Royal Dutch Shell in the oil-rich Niger Delta in June 2009, oil prices rose US$2.33 a barrel (3.4 percent) on the New York Mercantile Exchange.[85] In the four weeks following the beginning of the uprising in Libya, oil prices increased by 15 percent.[86]

Repeated violence is a shared challenge

Political and criminal violence both disrupt development—and occur in repeated cycles. It is essential to look across that spectrum and to consider local conflicts, social protest, gang violence, organized crime, and transnational terrorism alongside the major civil wars that have been the focus of most academic research. This interlocking landscape raises questions about the coherence of the approaches to deal with these various forms of violence—approaches often divorced from one another—as well as the treatment of "post-conflict" reconstruction and "prevention" as separate problems. The risks of violence and the responses to it are shared by countries across divides of income, national identity, religion, and ideology. One of the key messages of this Report is the shared interest in global and regional peace and prosperity—and the potential for greater exchanges between countries on how to address the common challenges.

FEATURE 1 *The interlinked and evolving nature of modern organized violence*

The Caribbean has known political and criminal violence for decades. Except for Cuba, every large island country and many smaller ones—the Bahamas, the Cayman Islands, the Dominican Republic, Haiti, Jamaica, St. Kitts and Nevis, St. Vincent and the Grenadines, and Trinidad and Tobago—have homicide levels above 10 per 100,000. In some of them, criminal gang activity has spilled over into political violence, with mutually reinforcing dynamics. Since 1970, most of Haiti's elections have been marked by violence—with 34 deaths in 1987 and 89 in 2004—and the country experienced political violence in 2010. The relationship can be reversed as well; in some countries, drug trafficking has exacerbated local organized violence.[87]

The Western Balkans are known for the civil wars that dissolved Yugoslavia in the 1990s. In the chaotic aftermath of the wars, many turned to trafficking in drugs, people, human organs, and weapons, such that organized crime perpetrated the most widespread and destabilizing violence.[88] Crime has gradually declined in recent years, but organized crime remains formidable.[89] Some 32 percent of human trafficking victims come from or through the Balkans, and the Balkan route is the main trafficking corridor for more than US$20 billion in heroin from Afghanistan to Western Europe a year.[90] Gang-related violence targeted political figures. The Zemun gang, with close connections to heroin trafficking, assassinated Serbian Prime Minister Zoran Djindjic in 2003.[91]

In West Africa, the conventional political conflict that began in Liberia and spread to Sierra Leone and Côte d'Ivoire, later gave way to more organized crime across the region, as warring factions pillaged natural resources, drug trafficking networks entered the region, and the rule of law weakened. What had begun as a means of financing war became a successful business model for trafficking diamonds, timber, arms, and humans.[92] Charles Taylor, the leader of one of the factions and later president of Liberia, is accused in his indictment by the Special Court of Sierra Leone of "a joint criminal enterprise . . . [to exercise] control over the territory of Sierra Leone . . . and the population . . . [through] unlawful killings, abductions, forced labor, physical and sexual violence, use of child soldiers . . . ."[93] It is estimated that Taylor amassed US$105–450 million through this criminal enterprise.[94] At the height of the conflict in Sierra Leone, illegal exports accounted for more than 90 percent of its diamond trade,[95] or more than US$200 million in 2002.[96]

In Nigeria, a largely subnational struggle in the oil-rich Niger Delta has given way to organized criminal syndicates that deal in oil, arms, and kidnapped foreign workers. An estimated 250,000–300,000 barrels, valued at more than US$3.8 billion, are stolen each year through "oil bunkering" (the theft of oil from pipelines or storage facilities).[97] Local gangs and political groups can also be drawn into ethnic violence; in the 2007 election aftermath in Kenya, gangs and politically motivated groups engaged in ethnically aligned violence.[98]

In Afghanistan, Pakistan, and the tribal areas on their borders, violence from the headline conflict in the region—between the government and international forces and the Taliban and other armed groups—is linked to drug trafficking and criminal violence, as well as kidnapping, extortion, and smuggling of a range of natural resources. New tensions and the presence of foreign fighters exacerbate long-standing conflicts between capitals and peripheral regions over power, governance, and resources.

Tensions and violence between ethnic groups can quickly transform into political violence where elections and other political contests affect the distribution of power and resources. In the Solomon Islands in the late 1990s, skirmishes between armed militias from the two main islands of Guadalcanal and Malaita, which displaced some 35,000 Malaitan settlers, culminated in the emergence of a Malaitan militia group, which—in response to the government's failure to curb Guadalcanal militancy—forced the resignation of the prime minister. In Papua New Guinea, longstanding ethnic and tribal conflicts in the Highlands—caused by a mix of traditional animosities, competition for resources, and land disputes—morphed into "raskol" gang activities in Port Moresby and other urban areas.[99] The advent of international operations to exploit timber and minerals has added fuel to preexisting ethnic contests over natural resources.

Cross-border violence goes beyond the destabilization from sanctuaries in neighboring countries, as in West Africa and the Afghanistan-Pakistan border areas. Uganda's Lord's Resistance Army has spread far beyond its original geographical origins to operate across a wide number of countries and borders—again drawing on criminal trafficking for its financing. And Somali pirates hijacked more than 125 merchant ships passing through the Gulf of Aden in 2009.

Many religious and ideological grievances in one part of the world are grafted onto a local conflict in some faraway place.

At the height of the war in Bosnia and Herzegovina in the 1990s, Islamic groups from outside the region joined the fight alongside Bosnian Muslims.[100] Likewise, foreign fighters and ideological links between armed groups dominate international press coverage of Afghanistan and Iraq, though spillovers of international ideological groups into the Sahel, affecting countries as isolated and historically peaceful as Mali, get less attention.

In other cases, violence may be linked through underlying institutional weaknesses. Yemen now faces four separate conflicts: the Houthi rebellion in the North, the presence of Al-Qaeda in the Arabian Peninsula, grievances in the south, and the popular protests for change that have swept through the Arab world. There is little direct evidence of links between these conflicts, other than through the weakness of national institutions to address them.[101]

Sources: Harriott 2004; Curtis and Karacan 2002; Shanty and Mishra 2008; Andreas 2004; International Crisis Group 2003; UNODC 2008, 2010a; Anastasijevic 2006; Special Court for Sierra Leone Office of the Prosecutor 2007; Lipman 2009; Coalition for International Justice 2005; Duffield 2000; Gberie 2003a; Even-Zohar 2003; Davies, von Kemedi, and Drennan 2005; International Crisis Group 2008b; Ashforth 2009; Porter, Andrews, and Wescott 2010; Kohlmann 2004.

Notes

1. These numbers include best estimates of battle deaths from Uppsala/PRIO Armed Conflict Dataset (Lacina and Gleditsch 2005; Harbom and Wallensteen 2010).
2. For details on regional trends in homicide, see the background paper on homicides prepared for this Report by Fearon 2010b and the 2008 Global Burden of Armed Violence report (Geneva Declaration 2008). Homicide rates decreased for nearly every region of the world, except Latin America and the Caribbean; however, insufficient data are available on current and past homicide rates in Sub-Saharan Africa to establish a regional trend.
3. WDR team calculations based on Powell and Thyne 2011.
4. OAS 2001.
5. The number of coup attempts also decreased, from 22 in the 1990s to 12 from 2000 through 2009. The average success rate of a coup attempt in the 1990s was 40 percent, compared to 29 percent in the period 2000–09 (see Powell and Thyne 2011).
6. Lutz and Reiger 2009.
7. WDR team calculation based on World Bank 2010n.
8. Throughout this Report, countries affected by fragility, violence, and conflict include (1) countries affected by high levels of criminal violence—countries with homicide rates greater than 10 per 100,000 population, (2) conflict-affected countries—countries with major civil conflict (battle deaths greater than 1,000 per annum as defined in the Uppsala/PRIO Armed Conflict Database (Harbom and Wallensteen 2010; Lacina and Gleditsch 2005) from 2006 to 2009, (3) countries with UN or regionally mandated peacebuilding or peacekeeping, non-border missions, (4) fragile countries—low-income countries with institutional levels (World Bank's CPIA less than 3.2) in 2006–09 (see World Bank 2010e). "Low income fragile and conflict-affected countries" are low-income countries that meet any of the last three criteria (homicide data are not consistently available for many low-income countries). Following World Bank definitions, "developing countries" includes both low- and middle-income countries.
9. Human Security Report Project, forthcoming.
10. Ross 2003; McNeish 2010.
11. Ross 2003.
12. Demombynes 2010; UNODC 2010a.
13. Harriott 2004; Shanty and Mishra 2008; UNODC 2010a; Duffield 2000; Gberie 2003a; International Crisis Group 2008b; Ashforth 2009; Porter, Andrews, and Wescott 2010.
14. Constraints tended to operate in ritualized warfare in Melanesia that, for example, served to limit the number of people killed or restrict the parties against whom violence could be used. The Interna-

tional Committee of the Red Cross compares these "traditional" constraints on the use of violence to those pertaining in modern international humanitarian law. See Dinnen, Porter, and Sage 2010.

15. Brands 2009; Parson 2010.
16. International Crisis Group 2009c.
17. Thapa 2010.
18. The UN Secretary-General's High-level Panel on Threats, Challenges, and Change defined terrorism as "any action, in addition to actions already specified by the existing conventions on aspects of terrorism, that is intended to cause death or serious bodily harm to civilians or noncombatants, when the purpose of such an act, by its nature or context, is to intimidate a population, or to compel a government or an international organization to do or to abstain from doing any act" (UN 2004a, 52). Earlier debates focused on whether definitions should be based only on nonstate actors; the High-level Panel pointed out that issues of state use of force against civilians are covered in the international laws of war, international criminal law, and international humanitarian law. See also Geneva Conventions 1949; UN 1998.
19. Most notably, the 1995 Oklahoma City bombing of the Alfred P. Murrah Federal Building by terrorists affiliated with the U.S. Militia Movement, in which 168 people died: the most destructive attack on U.S. soil prior to September 11, 2001. See Foxnews.com 2001.
20. UNODC 2010a.
21. UNODC 2010a, 235–36.
22. UNODC 2010b.
23. Jordan 1999; Lupsha 1991.
24. See Demombynes 2010.
25. Demombynes 2010.
26. Estimate of number of gang members from Comisión de Jefes y Jefas de Policía de Centroamérica y El Caribe in World Bank 2010c. In terms of military forces, Nicaragua and Honduras have armies of about 12,000 soldiers each, El Salvador has 13,000 soldiers, and Guatemala has 27,000 (see Rodgers, Muggah, and Stevenson 2009).
27. UNODC 2010a. This figure only accounts for illicit flows of criminal activities, namely drug, arms, trafficking people, smuggling, counterfeit currency and goods, and racketeering. Including corruption and fraudulent commercial activities, the value of illicit flows increase to as high as US$1.1 trillion annually. See also Baker 2005.
28. Van der Elst and Davis 2011; Glenny 2008; Garzón 2008; Naim 2006; Schneider, Buehn, and Montenegro 2010.
29. UNODC 2010b.
30. UNODC 2010b.
31. UNODC 2010b.
32. See Uppsala/PRIO Armed Conflict Database (Harbom and Wallensteen 2010; Lacina and Gleditsch 2005). For discussions of the trends in civil war onset and termination see Hewitt, Wilkenfeld, and Gurr 2010; Sambanis 2004; Elbadawi, Hegre, and Milante 2008; Collier and others 2003.
33. The statistics in table 1.2 are based on the incidence of civil war after World War II, thus countries with previous conflicts in the 1960s are those that had conflicts between 1945 and 1959, and those with conflicts in the 1970s had conflict between 1945 and 1969, and so on.
34. See Skaperdas and others 2009 and Geneva Declaration 2008 for a deeper exploration of these costs and of the methods for measuring them. See also Human Security Report Project, forthcoming, for a discussion of measuring direct and indirect deaths associated with civil wars and other conflict.
35. Geneva Declaration 2008, 1.
36. Country representative samples were used for Côte d'Ivoire, Sierra Leone, and Colombia. The surveys were undertaken in regions of the Democratic Republic of Congo and Mali. Independent representative samples were used in Gaza and the West Bank. The original country sample included Haiti; however, the survey could not be undertaken following the earthquake of January 2010.
37. See Justino and Verwimp 2008; Blattman, forthcoming. See also papers published through the Households in Conflict Network (http://www.hicn.org) for broader analysis of micro-level conflict effects on households and individuals.
38. These results are based on country year fixed effect Generalized Least Squares regressions for a panel of developing countries from 1981 to 2005, based on poverty data from Chen, Ravallion, and Sangraula 2008 (available on POVCALNET (http://iresearch.worldbank.org)) and the WDR database. Countries with three years of major violence (major civil war or violent deaths above 10 per

100,000, equivalent to a major civil war) lagged behind other countries by 2.7 percentage points on poverty headcount. Those with minor civil war (or equivalent homicides) lagged behind countries without violence by 1.29 percentage points. These results were statistically significant at the $p < 0.10$ level and robust to period effects and time trends.

39. Anderlini 2010a.
40. Beijing Declaration and Platform for Action 1995; Women's Refugee Commission 2009; UNICEF 2004.
41. UNFPA 2002; Plümper and Neumayer 2006; Murray and others 2002; Bastick, Grimm, and Kunz 2007; El Jack 2003.
42. American Psychological Association 1996; Dahlberg 1998; Verdú and others 2008.
43. UN 2000, 2011.
44. Human Security Centre 2005.
45. Bastick, Grimm, and Kunz 2007.
46. See UNDP 2005b; Peruvian Truth and Reconciliation Commission 2003.
47. Bijleveld, Morssinkhof, and Smeulers 2009.
48. Effects in this table drawn from multiple sources: Amnesty International 2005; Brück and Schindler 2008; Carpenter 2006; Chamarbagwala and Morán 2011; Bijleveld, Morssinkhof, and Smeulers 2009; Chun and Skjelsbæk 2010; El Jack 2003; Falch 2010; Finegan and Margo 1994; Guerrero-Serdán 2009; Heuveline and Poch 2007; Ibáñez and Moya 2006; ICRC 2001; Internal Displacement Monitoring Centre 2007; International Alert and Eastern Africa Sub-Regional Support Initiative for the Advancement of Women 2007; ILO 2009; Jayaraman, Gebreselassie, and Chandrasekhar 2009; Kelly 2010; Lamb and Dye 2009; Lewis 2009; Menon and Rodgers 2010; Peltz 2006; Murray and others 2002; Ndulo 2009; Plümper and Neumayer 2006; Prieto-Rodríguez and Rodríguez-Gutiérrez 2003; Li and Wen 2005; Rehn and Johnson Sirleaf 2002; Shemyakina 2006; Torres 2002; UNFPA 2007; UN 2002, 2006b; Verwimp and Van Bavel 2005; Verpoorten 2003; Ward and Marsh 2006; Willman and Makisaka 2010; Women's Refugee Commission 2008; Verdú and others 2008; WHO 2010.
49. Ward and Marsh 2006.
50. Lewis 2009; Willman and Makisaka 2010; Anderlini 2010a; Carpenter 2006.
51. Internal Displacement Monitoring Centre 2010.
52. UNHCR 2009.
53. Gomez and Christensen 2010; Harild and Christensen 2010.
54. "Recovering countries" are those affected by fragility, conflict, or violence in the previous 10 years.
55. Similar effects are found in Bowman and others 2008.
56. See also Geneva Declaration 2010.
57. In 2010, after 10 years, fragile and conflict-affected states had closed only 20 percent of the gap in reaching the MDGs, while low-income countries not affected by violence had closed 40–70 percent of their MDG gap (see World Bank 2010e). Current data compiled for the MDG Summit in 2010 show that no low-income fragile or conflict-affected state has met the targets for a single MDG. Some countries are close and have made dramatic gains in recent years and it is possible that they could meet targets. For more information, see World Bank 2010n; UNSTAT 2010; UN 2007.
58. Progress in basic health services has advanced even in war zones; see the Human Security Report Project, forthcoming, for a description of global trends.
59. Lacina, Gleditsch, and Russett 2006.
60. RAND Corporation 2009.
61. Hoeffler, von Billerbeck, and Ijaz 2010.
62. Note that civil war coding in the Armed Conflict Database does not include all political violence. As evidenced by the experience of Burundi, while the onset of political violence resulted in battle deaths coded as civil war in Burundi in 1991, there was one-sided violence in the 1960s through 1980s in Burundi. See the Uppsala/PRIO Armed Conflict Database (Harbom and Wallensteen 2010; Lacina and Gleditsch 2005).
63. Narayan and Petesch 2010, 12.
64. Hoeffler, von Billerbeck, and Ijaz 2010.
65. Martin, Mayer, and Thoenig 2008.
66. For more details on the Index see Cingranelli and Richards 1999.
67. Hoeffler, von Billerbeck, and Ijaz 2010.
68. Hoeffler, von Billerbeck, and Ijaz 2010.

69. For an overview of costs of conflict and violence, see Skaperdas and others 2009. Specific estimates of the economic costs associated with conflict are found in Hoeffler, von Billerbeck, and Ijaz 2010; Imai and Weinstein 2000; Collier and Hoeffler 1998; Stewart, Huang, and Wang 2001; Cerra and Saxena 2008; Collier, Chauvet, and Hegre 2007. An overview for the estimates of the cost of crime is found in Skaperdas and others 2009, with specific estimates in Riascos and Vargas 2004; UNDP 2006.
70. Skaperdas and others 2009 survey the recent literature on costs of crime. Material costs of crime, including injuries, property damage, and theft, were estimated as 3.6 percent of GDP for the Latin American and Caribbean countries and 2.1 percent of GDP for the United States.
71. Hoeffler, von Billerbeck, and Ijaz 2010.
72. Patrick 2006.
73. Bayer and Rupert 2004, while Baker and others 2002 found that the effect of conflict is equivalent to a 33 percent tariff barrier. For an updated discussion of the methodology for determining growth effects of conflict and theory and new analysis based on primary and secondary neighbors, see De Groot 2010; Murdoch and Sandler 2002; Bayer and Rupert 2004. The effects of conflict on trade are reviewed in Glick and Taylor 2005.
74. The study investigated bilateral trade flows in more than 200 countries from 1960–93 (see Nitsch and Schumacher 2004).
75. Europol 2007.
76. See Gilpin 2009.
77. For methodology, see Bowden 2010; for cost to the U.S. Navy, see U.S. Government Accountability Office 2010a. For additional information, see European Affairs 2010 and Hanson 2010.
78. This figure includes ranges for the costs of deterrent security equipment, cost of naval forces, cost of piracy prosecutions, and operating cost of anti-piracy organizations (see Bowden 2010).
79. Included in this figure are the costs of ransoms, insurance premium, rerouting, deterrent security equipment, naval forces, piracy prosecutions, and anti-piracy organizations (see Bowden 2010; Chalk 2008).
80. Gomez and Christensen 2010; Harild and Christensen 2010.
81. Out of 13,658 refugees in Ghana at the end of 2009, nearly 11,500 were from Liberia (84 percent) with a further 1,600 from Togo (12 percent) (UNHCR 2010).
82. See International Crisis Group 1999; Salehyan and Gleditsch 2006.
83. See Patrick 2006. Also see Collier and others 2003; Garrett 2005; National Intelligence Council 2000, 37.
84. Gaibulloev and Sandler 2008.
85. Mufson 2009.
86. WDR team calculations based on Europe Brent Spot Price FOB (dollars per barrel) reported by the U.S. Energy Information Administration 2011.
87. Harriott 2004.
88. See Curtis and Karacan 2002; Shanty and Mishra 2008; Andreas 2004; International Crisis Group 2003.
89. UNODC 2008.
90. UNODC 2010a.
91. Anastasijevic 2006.
92. UNODC 2010a; Harwell 2010.
93. Special Court for Sierra Leone Office of the Prosecutor 2007, 5.
94. Lipman 2009; Coalition for International Justice 2005; Duffield 2000.
95. Gberie 2003a.
96. Even-Zohar 2003.
97. Davies, von Kemedi, and Drennan 2005.
98. International Crisis Group 2008b; Ashforth 2009.
99. Porter, Andrews, and Wescott 2010.
100. Kohlmann 2004.
101. International Crisis Group 2009c.

Throughout history, agreement between powerful leaders has been the most common strategy to prevent large-scale violence. This type of agreement, which we call an "elite pact," does impose security for periods, but violence generally recurs. The immediate cause of the violence varies greatly by country, with many countries experiencing a combination of security, economic, and political stresses. These stresses may be internal (including low income or high inequality between groups) or they may be external (including global economic shocks, international drug trafficking, or the infiltration of foreign forces). This Report argues that in these environments, institutions and governance serve as an "immune system" and defense against stresses. When these stresses occur in societies with weak institutions and governance, violence often occurs. Reform is often difficult or impossible where violence is present. As a result, countries that fail to build legitimate institutions risk entering a vicious cycle of repeated violence and weak institutions. This chapter spells out what we know about this vicious cycle and why some countries are more vulnerable to violence than others.

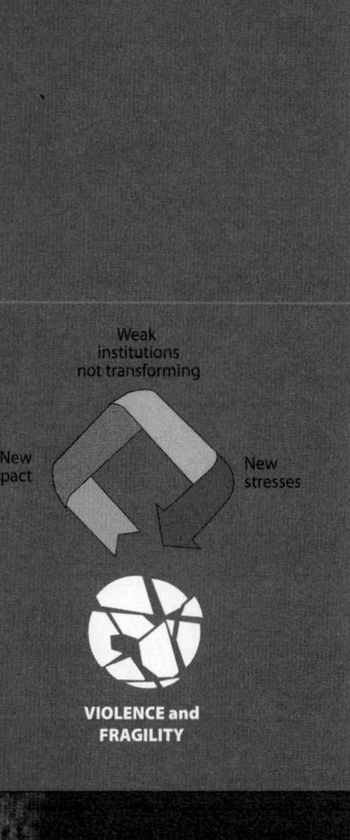

CHAPTER 2

Vulnerability to Violence

Multiple stresses raise the risks of violence

Economic, political, and security factors can all exacerbate the risks of violence. Some of these factors are domestic, such as low incomes, high unemployment, and inequality of different sorts. Some factors may originate outside the state, such as external economic shocks or the infiltration of international drug cartels or foreign fighters. This Report refers to these triggers of violence as "security, economic, and justice stresses" (see table 2.1). Often related, they rarely exist in isolation.

This Report summarizes what is known about the factors associated with organized violence and development. It draws on research from a variety of fields, particularly research on the risk of civil war, largely because it is further advanced than research on violent organized crime, trafficking, gang activity, or terrorism (box 2.1).

Our approach is multidisciplinary and draws on both quantitative and qualitative evidence. Box 2.1 reviews the literature from various disciplines on causes of conflict. Often this debate has been characterized as "greed versus grievance."[1] This chapter describes how the stresses in table 2.1 can precipitate organized violence through a vicious cycle of vulnerability to violence. Later, in chapter 3, the framework demonstrates how countries can build institutions that are resilient to these stresses to prevent organized violence, moving the discussion beyond the base causes of "greed and grievance" and showing how justice and jobs can work together to promote confidence and help to deliver citizen security.

Where possible, quantitative and econometric work has been used to assess the importance of the stress factors listed, but there are data constraints. Data on civil wars at the national level are fairly comprehensive, but data on extreme criminal violence, normally measured by homicides, are incomplete for many developing countries, let alone parts of these countries. Cross-country data are fairly good for economic factors, such as incomes and growth rates, but the comparability of data on unemployment is poor. Data are reasonably reliable for income inequality within countries, but less so for inequality among geographical areas and among ethnic or religious groups, and for political exclusion or injustice. Therefore, new survey data, country case studies, and country consultations complement the analysis here.

Security stresses

Internal security stresses can arise when particular elites or groups feel threatened—

TABLE 2.1 ***Security, economic, and political stresses***

This table is not exhaustive, but reflects major factors identified in the academic literature and raised in WDR consultations on the causes of violence.[2] The complex relationship between factors that can trigger violence and the onset of violence is similar to the relationship between health threats and risk factors at individual, relationship, community, and societal levels found in the public health/ecological framework developed by the World Health Organization.[3]

Stresses	Internal	External
Security	• Legacies of violence and trauma	• Invasion, occupation • External support for domestic rebels • Cross-border conflict spillovers • Transnational terrorism • International criminal networks
Economic	• Low income levels, low opportunity cost of rebellion • Youth unemployment • Natural resource wealth • Severe corruption • Rapid urbanization	• Price shocks • Climate change
Justice	• Ethnic, religious, or regional competition • Real or perceived discrimination • Human rights abuses	• Perceived global inequity and injustice in the treatment of ethnic or religious groups

Source: Compiled by the WDR team from the literature cited in box 2.1 and from WDR team consultations.

often as a result of past oppression—and organize to defend themselves. In interstate war, a preemptive move based on perceptions of the other state's intentions is called a "security dilemma." If one state believes another is preparing to attack, it may decide to strike first to give itself a decisive advantage. Understood as a trigger for war from the time of the Greeks, preemption featured strongly in Cold War strategic thinking and follows from the realist approaches to international relations, though opinions are mixed about its validity under international law.[4] In the late 1990s, researchers asked whether security dilemmas were causing civil wars as well.[5] If one group believes that another clan, ethnic, or religious group is preparing to attack, it may choose to make the first move. How often this occurs is debatable, but this risk is now accepted.[6]

Manipulating fears of oppression has been a factor causing civil conflicts as distinct as the Rwandese genocide and the Balkan wars of the 1990s. And it can be an obstacle to ending violence—once conflicts break out, perceptions of the enemy harden and societies tend to portray their opponents in distorted and fearsome terms.[7] Security dilemmas and defensive arming are also prevalent among criminal groups. The illicit nature of drug markets means that traffickers often resort to violence to settle disputes both within and between trafficking organizations, since they do not have access to the formal legal system to adjudicate disputes and constrain the misuse of group funds or property. For these groups, violence becomes the first recourse for enforcing contracts.[8]

External threats to security can heighten internal pressures. Many states face pressure or incursions from outside state and nonstate actors. That external actors could at any time intervene in a country makes it particularly difficult for internal actors to make credible commitments with each other—as in the "internationalized" civil conflicts in Afghanistan or the Democratic Republic of Congo. International trafficking networks can also place heavy pressures on local institutions (see box 2.2). Outside resources and armed intervention may tip the scales in favor of one actor, allowing it to renege on agreements with other actors. This can come in the form of attacks from "safe havens" in

BOX 2.1 *Economic and political theories of violence and this Report*

Violent conflict has been the subject of large and long-standing literatures in many academic disciplines, and this report draws from many strands of that literature.

Rapid change and rising expectations

One common perspective has been the importance of drivers such as rapid economic and social change. Drawing on research by psychologists and sociologists, Gurr argued that social and political conflict arises when groups experience feelings of "relative deprivation" and the frustration of expectations for deserved or anticipated economic or social status. Huntington agreed that economic modernization raises expectations and mobilizes members of traditional societies toward national politics, contending that conflict occurs when political institutions lack the capacity to accommodate and manage rapidly rising demands.

Failing to credibly agree to abstain from violence

Many economists and political scientists see violence as originating from "commitment problems"—situations where organized groups have opposing interests but cannot credibly agree to abstain from violence for a variety of reasons. The focus in these theories is on the difficulty of groups or individuals in some settings to commit themselves to not using force when it would be advantageous to do so. This thinking can be traced back as far as Hobbes, who contended that violent civil conflict is a consequence of low state capacity to deter challengers and manage conflict among groups in society. Recent theories on opportunistic arming and consequent violence can be found in Hirshleifer, Skaperdas, Grossman, and Fearon. Becker developed a rational actor model of crime. Thinking on the "security dilemma"—that arming for defense can also be used to attack, leading to violence—can be traced to Schelling, Posen, Snyder and Jervis, and de Figueiredo and Weingast.

Greed or grievance

These contending theories have led to debates over the relative importance of normative and economic motives for violence, which has recently led to debates on whether economic incentives or broader social and political motives drive societies to violence. This question was formulated as "Greed and Grievance" by Collier and Hoeffler, who suggested that primary commodities, diasporas, low earnings, human capital, and dispersed populations were positively correlated to the outbreak of civil conflict, suggesting support for the "greed" hypothesis. Further exploration, review and critique of these issues can be found in Nathan and Sambanis, as well as Satyanath, Miguel, and Sergenti and Blattman and Miguel.[9]

Horizontal inequality and identity

Significant contributions to this debate include recent theories of polarization and horizontal inequality and analysis of violence based solely on identity, such as nationalism and ethnicity. Theories of horizontal inequality as developed by Stewart, and polarization proposed by Esteban and Ray argue that inequality alone does not predict civil war—violence may be driven by relationships between inequality and identity that contribute to the onset of civil violence.[10] In addition, national or ethnic identity may lead to a violent response to oppression or marginalization and need not include any equity concerns, but may be motivated instead by a disposition for self-government.[11]

Ethnic divides and commitment problems

Bridging the arguments on grievance and rational choice motives for conflict, Fearon contends that ethnic polarization is most likely to precipitate conflict when ethnic groups cannot make credible commitments to abstain from violence. This is consistent with the philosophy in this Report: both political and economic dynamics are often at play, and neither greed nor grievance alone is sufficient to explain the incidence of violence.

Avenues for peaceful contests

The question remains: why do some societies avoid violence when others do not? To answer this question, we build on the hypotheses put forward by North, Wallis, and Weingast, who focus on impersonal institutions with open access to political and economic opportunities, creating avenues for peaceful and credible contestation.[12] Besley and Persson contend that investments in legal systems and state capacity can reduce the incidence of violence. Keefer argues that violence occurs when societies cannot collectively punish leaders who engage in predatory behavior or collectively build a capable counterinsurgency force, suggesting that institutionalized political parties serve as a bulwark against conflict by resolving these problems of collective action and credibility. Recent empirical quantitative evidence supports these hypotheses—Goldstone and others find that the quality of political institutions is an order of magnitude more important than other factors in determining risks of political crises and civil wars, while Brückner and Ciccone suggest that institutions are necessary to accommodate shocks in prices to avoid violence. More work is needed to confirm these findings thus to better understand the channels through which institutions contribute to resilience to violence.

(box continues on next page)

BOX 2.1 *Economic and political theories of violence and this Report (continued)*

Institutions matter in preventing violence

This chapter draws on existing research on the risk factors of violence across the political science, social science, and economic disciplines and extends understanding of violent conflict in two ways:

- It presents the risk factors associated with violence, organized into security, economic, and political factors. This adds to existing work on drivers of conflict, with an emphasis on the role of external stresses—those outside a country's control. Examples are international organized crime and trafficking, infiltration of foreign fighters, and economic shocks.
- It then presents empirical findings that support arguments by theorists (such as North, Wallis, and Weingast) that institutions matter for violence prevention. It concludes by hypothesizing why and how the failure to develop legitimate, capable, and accountable institutions causes repeated cycles of violence.

Sources: Gurr 1970; Hobbes 1651; Hirshleifer 1995; Skaperdas 1996; Grossman 1991; Fearon 1995, 2004; Schelling 1960; Posen 1993; Snyder and Jervis 1999; de Figueiredo and Weingast 1999; Collier and Hoeffler 2004; Nathan 2005; Sambanis 2004; Satyanath, Miguel, and Sergenti 2004; Blattman and Miguel 2010; Esteban and Ray 2008; Stewart 2005, 2010; Keefer 2008, forthcoming; North, Wallis, and Weingast 2009; Besley and Persson 2009, 2010; Huntington 1968; Goldstone and others 2010; Becker 1968; Brückner and Ciccone 2010.

REFLECTIONS FROM ADVISORY COUNCIL MEMBERS: *2011 WORLD DEVELOPMENT REPORT*

BOX 2.2 *The stress posed by transnational organized crime and drug trafficking*

Jorge Montaño, Member, International Narcotics Control Board; former Ambassador of Mexico to the United States; *WDR Advisory Council Member*

The diversification and sophistication that characterizes the challenge of transnational organized crime demands coordinated global action. Drug and human trafficking, money laundering, illegal exploitation of natural resources and wildlife, counterfeiting and violations of intellectual property rights are lucrative criminal activities which facilitate the penetration by organized crime of the already vulnerable sociopolitical, judicial, and security structures in developing countries.

In Central America, for example, several countries that regained political stability two decades ago are now facing the decay of the state, whose institutions lack the strength to face this onslaught. Transnational organized crime has converted some Caribbean countries into corridors for the movement of illegal drugs and persons to Europe and North America. Bolivia, Colombia, and Peru continue to be the main global cocaine producers, while Mexico is presently facing an unprecedented wave of violence given its border with the largest immigrant, drug consumption, and arms producing market. West Africa has become the newest passageway for drugs coming from South America destined for Europe. Several African countries suffer the illegal exploitation of their natural resources, while Asia is a hub for tons of opiates originating from Afghanistan. It is evident that there is a lack of a coordinated multilateral strategy against a phenomenon that cannot be dealt with in a fragmented way.

In industrialized countries, organized crime syndicates operate with minimal use of violence, thus assuring that the heavy hand of the law does not interfere in their activities, both in the banking system as well as satisfying the insatiable market for illegal drugs. In developing countries, on the other hand, organized criminal groups take advantage of apparent impunity to acquire access to a limitless supply of arms, with which they destabilize national and local institutions.

The unprecedented progression of organized crime could spell the collapse of many weak states as their institutions fall prey to the associated violence. The precarious economic development observed in many regions of the world provides a stimulus for consolidating these illegal activities, which will continue to thrive as a consequence of the impunity they encounter in developing countries.

neighboring countries (for example, Hutu rebels crossing into Rwanda from the Democratic Republic of Congo).[13] It can also come from the activities of drug traffickers (much of Central America today) or transnational terrorists (such as "Al-Qaeda in the Maghreb" activity in northern Mali).[14] Some countries—Afghanistan and Somalia—have had the misfortune of experiencing all these forms of external security stress, in addition

BOX 2.3 *Spillover of conflicts in Central Africa*

The countries of Central Africa have been engaged for decades in a variety of conflicts that often spill across borders. The maps here show the locations of major conflict events involving rebel groups that operate across borders for two periods: 1997 to 2000 and 2006 to 2009. Each colored circle indicates a geospatial information system-coded conflict event involving groups originating from a given country, identified in the legend (usually a battle, though establishing a headquarters and recruitment campaigns are also included). Many conflict events involve groups active across borders.

Highlighting the spillover of conflict across borders in Burundi, the Democratic Republic of Congo, Rwanda, Sudan, and Uganda, and increasingly in the later period, in the Central African Republic and Chad, these maps show how violent groups can disperse and commingle in areas of weak governance. These groups make common cause when it suits them to do so and shift their bases of operations to conform to local political opportunities. Much of their *raison d'être* has become profit, plunder, or simple subsistence, with political goals at times stronger, at times weaker. Such groups as the Lord's Resistance Army no longer have a strong domestic base, so they continue moving opportunistically among areas of instability.

MAP A Cross-border political violence spreads across Central Africa

Violence is not easily contained. The colored circles represent conflict events by those militant and rebel groups that are active across borders. Recent violence has spilled across many borders in Central Africa, most notably those of the Central African Republic, Chad, the Democratic Republic of Congo, and Sudan.

a. January 1997–March 2000

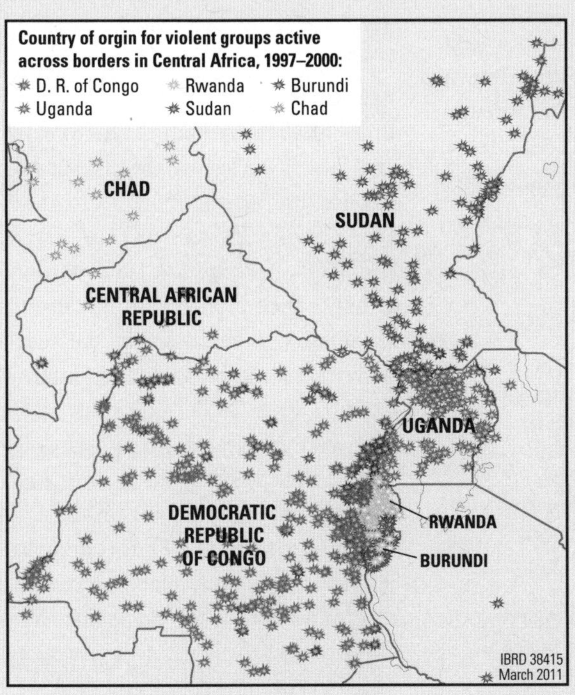

b. October 2006–December 2009

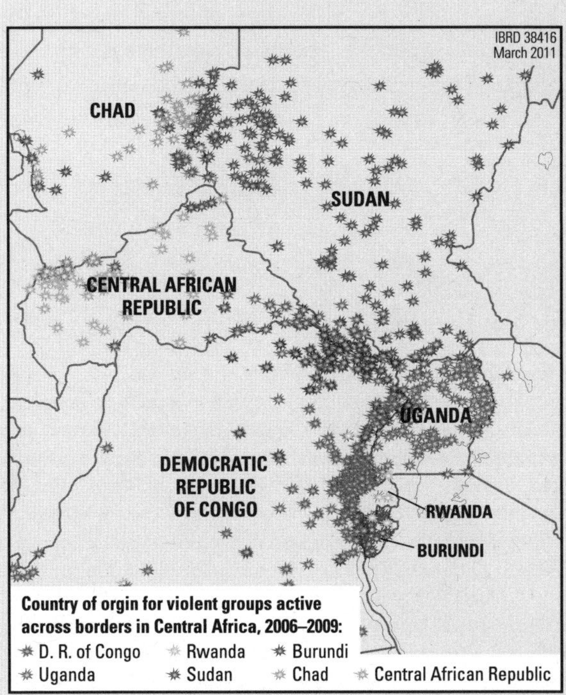

Source: Raleigh and others 2010; Raleigh 2010.

to internal stresses.[15] Areas with cross-border ethnic links and low civilian government presence have long been subject to insecurity—and remain so today (box 2.3).

External security threats can also develop out of violence in neighboring countries. As described in chapter 1, the "neighborhood effect" can both increase the risk of civil war in countries with neighbors at war and have detrimental development effects over borders.[16] The movement of persons trained in violence, the displacement of persons who may cross borders and become refugees, the disruption of trade, the expansion of criminal networks through globalization or trafficking, and the safe haven that rebels often seek by crossing borders suggest that violence cannot be easily contained, especially when institutions in neighboring countries are weak (box 2.4).[17]

These spillovers effects can also derive from interstate conflicts in a region. The invasion of Kuwait in 1990, the occupation of Iraq in 2003, and the military operations in the West Bank and Gaza are, in historical terms, less common than invasion and occupation were earlier in the 20th century—but had profound effects on neighbors.

External movements that have common cause with local groups and internal poltical movements can act as stresses. While motives for individuals to join ideology-based groups may be linked to beliefs in larger causes, the ability of these groups to garner local support depends on relating these larger narratives to local claims of injustice. A more material ethos prevails in the business alliances between local gangs and transnational drug cartels in Latin America.

BOX 2.4 *External stresses: The deportation of the maras*

One notable external stress for Central America was the U.S. deportation of maras in the 1990s. One of the main gangs (maras) to be deported, La Mara Salvatrucha, was established in Los Angeles in the late 1970s and early 1980s by mainly Salvadoran and Guatemalan refugees and immigrants to the United States. In 1996, the U.S. Congress passed the Illegal Immigration Reform and Immigrant Responsibility Act, whereby non-U.S. citizens sentenced to one year or more in prison were to be repatriated to their countries of origin. Between 1998 and 2005, the United States deported nearly 46,000 convicted felons to Central America, in addition to another 160,000 illegal immigrants.

El Salvador, Guatemala, and Honduras received more than 90 percent of the deportees, many of them members of the maras who had arrived in the United States as children. On being sent back to countries they barely knew, they reproduced the structures and behaviors that had given them support and security in the United States, founding gangs that quickly attracted local youth.

This deportation did not affect all countries in Central America equally. Nicaragua, for example, has a comparatively low deportation rate from the United States—with fewer than 3 percent of all Central American deportees. The difference in settlement and deportation may be one factor explaining why gangs in El Salvador, Guatemala, and Honduras are more violent than those in Nicaragua.

Sources: Rodgers, Muggah, and Stevenson 2009; WDR regional consultation in Mexico City with government officials, academics, and development practitioners from Latin America.

Economic stresses

Low incomes reduce the opportunity cost of engaging in violence. From an economic perspective, it is important to understand the cost-benefit calculus for decisions by those who become involved in violence, as the literature on criminal motives has traditionally highlighted.[18] Much recent research on civil war has focused on economic motives, with rebellion perceived to offer economic rents to rebel leaders and a viable living to followers who have no other source of livelihood. Capturing this perspective, the leader of the Sudan People's Liberation Movement, John Garang, said, "Under these circumstances the marginal cost of rebellion in the South became very small, zero, or negative; that is, in the South it pays to rebel."[19] In a low-income environment the opportunity costs of engaging in violence may be small.

Slow-developing low-income economies largely dependent on natural resources are 10 times more likely than others to experience civil war.[20] Reviewing these results for this Report, Fearon again finds a strong relationship between income and the risk of civil conflict.[21] Of course, low per capita income is also highly correlated with low institutional capabilities, as evidenced by the Worldwide Governance Indicators and International Country Risk Guide indicators.[22] More recent work by Keefer and by Fearon for this Report indicates that the income links with violence may be the joint product of other underlying factors.[23] Thus, countries have political and institutional characteristics that determine *both* their capability to address violence and the level of governance necessary for economic growth.

High unemployment, particularly youth unemployment, appears to increase the risk of violence. The *World Development Report 2007: Development and the Next Generation* points to how young people's initial failures in finding a job can lead to persistent joblessness, a loss of interest in further schooling, delayed family formation, mental distress, and "negative manifestations of citizenship."[24] Findings from the Voices of the Poor Project affirm this: presence of unemployed and frustrated young men in post-conflict situations is often linked to higher levels of violence, substance abuse, and gang activities.[25] In surveys for this Report in areas affected by violence, unemployment and idleness was cited as the most important factor motivating young people to join rebel movements. The issue was also raised as important in every WDR consultation: Liberia's President Ellen Johnson Sirleaf summarizes, "[Without] jobs for our very young population, we run the risk of having their vulnerabilities exposed and the risk of them once again being recruited into conflict, undermining all the progress we have made."[26] But econometric work has consistently failed to find any correlation between unemployment and violence, perhaps because data are poor or because the link is indirect rather than direct (box 2.5).[27]

Exploitative employment is also a risk factor in violence. The relationship between unemployment and violence often involves social identity and exclusion. Several qualitative studies on Latin America and African gangs and rebel movement recruitment point to links between employment, respect, and identity (box 2.5). This mirrors a larger literature on unemployment and domestic violence, showing how power relations and perceptions of "dignity" can be more important than simple pecuniary motives as drivers of violence.[28] This is consistent with employment being more than a purely financial transaction. It is also a social interaction carrying aspects of personal status and expectations of how one should be treated.[29] In other words, the nature of work relationships on offer matters a great deal. As with the causes of rebel movements, unemployment and a sense of low status also emerge as risk factors for recruitment into gangs (box 2.6).

Research has found a strong relationship between income inequality and criminal violence, measured by homicide rates.[30] Many scholars have investigated whether income inequality and civil war are related and found no statistically significant relationship.[31] However, there is evidence that *horizontal* inequalities (between regional, ethnic, or reli-

BOX 2.5 *Does unemployment cause violence? Arguments for and against*

The proposition that unemployment can lead to involvement in violence is often traced to Becker, who applied an "economic calculus" to criminology, with the aim of improving policies toward crime. In such an opportunity-cost argument, scholars like Cincotta, Engelman, and Anastasion and Grossman consider unemployment a cause of violence and conflict. Urdal argues that the risk of violent conflict can be correlated with a high population proportion of young adults and poor economic performance.

More recently, simplistic cost-benefit approaches have been questioned by Berman and others on the motives of groups claiming ideological inspiration:

> Most aid spending by governments seeking to rebuild social and political order is based on an opportunity-cost theory of distracting potential recruits. The logic is that gainfully employed young men are less likely to participate in political violence, implying a positive correlation between unemployment and violence in places with active insurgencies. We test that prediction on insurgencies in Iraq and the Philippines, using survey data on unemployment and two newly available measures of insurgency: attacks against government and allied forces and violence that kills civilians. Contrary to the opportunity-cost theory, we find a robust negative correlation between unemployment and attacks against government and allied forces and no significant relationship between unemployment and the rate of insurgent attacks that kill civilians.[32]

Other research suggests that unemployment and violence may be related through respect, social justice, and social identity dynamics rather than pure cost-benefit motives. Contemporary case studies emphasize how employment, identity, and perceptions of social justice are intertwined. Padilla's work on Puerto Rican drug gangs in Chicago stresses the insecure and demeaning nature of legal work opportunities compared with gang membership—which offered not only income but social respect and a sense of belonging. Similar motives are echoed by those joining gangs in Guatemala, who "did so because they were searching for the support, trust, and cohesion—social capital—that they maintained their families did not provide, as well as because of the lack of opportunities in the local context."[33]

Evidence on recruitment into the FARC (Revolutionary Armed Forces of Colombia) suggests that many recruits, employed before joining, were motivated by status and the excitement of the rebel life in comparison with the drudgery of agricultural wage labor. Gutierréz Sanín quotes a rancher kidnapped by the FARC: "The *guerrilleros* say: we, work with a *machete?* Never! Then they say: Peasants speak with us because of this. And they kiss their weapon! And they say that women love arms [sic]: the police, the army, the guerrilla." Ethnographic work on militias in rural Sierra Leone and insurgents in El Salvador[34] suggests that oppressive work relations can be a key motive for rebellion.

Another understudied element of these dynamics is the time necessary for such interventions to be effective. A WDR study in southern China tests how long it takes migrant workers to develop social networks, finding that broad social networks are developed only after five years of secure employment.

Further research is needed to test the links between unemployment, idleness, the temporal effects of unemployment, the differing forms of employment, and recruitment into violence.

Sources: Urdal 2004; Berman and others 2009; Padilla 1992; Moser 2009; Gutiérrez Sanín 2008; Becker 1968; Cincotta, Engelman, and Anastasion 2003; Grossman 1991; Wood 2003; Richards 1996; Chauveau and Richards 2008; Cramer 2010; Huang 2010.

BOX 2.6 *Do similar economic factors create risks for political conflict and extreme levels of violent organized crime?*

The most reliable indicator to compare violence across countries is the homicide rate, which has risen markedly in Latin American and Caribbean countries since the early 1990s—from 12.6 homicides per 100,000 inhabitants to almost 20 homicides in recent years.

Analysis of global data confirms earlier work by Loayza, Fajnzylber, and Lederman on homicide rates in Latin America, revealing that:

- Institutional capacity and accountability is associated with lower risks of civil war and homicide rates.
- Higher country GDP, like civil wars, is associated with lower homicide rates, even comparing periods within countries.
- Democratic collapses, as with civil wars, are associated with increasing homicides.
- Oil production, associated with civil war risk, does not predict higher homicide rates.
- Countries with higher income inequality tend to have more homicides, a pattern that holds when comparing countries in the same region. These findings are the principal factor that distinguishes criminal violence from civil wars, which are not found to be correlated with income inequality, but exhibit some relation to horizontal inequalities across ethnicity or other identity groups.

In qualitative studies, unemployment and idleness also feature as risk factors that spur recruitment into both rebel movements and gangs. Surveys showed remarkably similar perceptions about motives for participation in gangs and in rebel movements (see figure). In both cases, unemployment and idleness were cited as the primary reasons for young people to join gangs or rebel movements, reinforcing the links between social inequality and violence.

Rebel movements and gangs attract people with similar motives

Surveys found that the main motivations young people cited for becoming rebels or gang members are very similar—unemployment, idleness, respect, and self-protection, all well ahead of revenge, injustice, or belief in the cause.

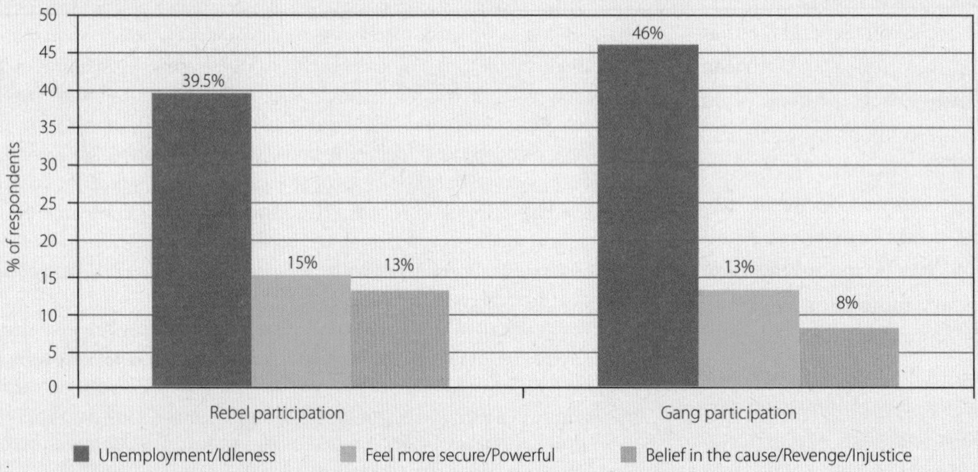

Sources: Fearon 2010b; Bøås, Tiltnes, and Flatø 2010; Neumayer 2003; Loayza, Fajnzylber, and Lederman 2002a, 2002b; Messner, Raffalovich, and Shrock 2002; WDR team calculations.

Notes: Figure shows aggregates of the most common responses for the questions, "What is the main reason why young people join rebel groups?" and "What is the main reason why young people join gangs?" for surveys conducted in Colombia; the Democratic Republic of Congo; Côte d'Ivoire; Gaza; Mali; Sierra Leone; and West Bank. Survey methodology described in Bøås, Tiltnes, and Flatø 2010.

gious identity groups) lead to political violence (discussed further in the section on political stresses below). The structure of the inequality and the manifestation of violence may be linked, but the results are hardly conclusive; more research on this is needed. It is also possible that demographic shifts create stresses on societies that are not prepared for change—rapid urbanization, as earlier in Latin America and today in Asia and Africa, is associated with weakened social cohesion and increased risks of violence.[35]

Countries with significant natural resource wealth may face armed attempts to capture the benefits. Because control of the state or specific areas is needed to benefit from revenues from the sale of oil, timber, or minerals, countries with significant natural wealth are particularly vulnerable to conflict.[36] This is demonstrated by the prolonged struggles between rival militias in the Democratic Republic of Congo, from the civil war period of the 1990s[37] to present-day rebel "taxation" of artisanal mining of coltan, tin, and gold deposits in the eastern part of the country. Subnational contests over resources are important in country cases, although cross-country data are not available. Once again, the key is the cost-benefit calculus associated with engaging in trafficking and the violence that can accompany it. In addition, leaders of countries with significant natural resources may be reluctant to invest in the institutions to mediate or suppress violence, since these same institutions can challenge their regime and reduce their share of the rents.[38] For example, a strong military in a country with weak civilian oversight is associated with the capture of natural resource rents by military leaders.[39]

Economic shocks can also arise from factors beyond the control of the state—and food and energy price shocks can increase the risk of conflict. Work on rainfall shocks in Sub-Saharan Africa concludes that civil conflict is more likely to occur following years of poor rainfall. Using rainfall variation as a proxy for income shocks in 41 African countries between 1981 and 1999, Satyanath, Miguel, and Sergenti found that a 5 percent decline in economic growth increased the likelihood of conflict by half in the following year.[40] A majority of fragile states are food importers—and average household expenditure on food is higher in fragile developing countries (57.5 percent) than in other developing countries (49.4 percent).[41] Sharp food price increases, in particular, have a long association with urban instability. But there is less risk of violence where institutions protect exporters and consumers against these economic shocks.[42]

Economic factors are important—but do not tell the full story. Many developing countries face multiple economic challenges, with low or stagnant growth, high exposure to global commodity price trends, and rapid population growth. Potent as these factors are, explanations for conflict based purely on economic motives are inadequate—to avoid violence, societies must do more than just create growth. The attention in recent years to quantitative correlations between economic factors and conflict has led some to argue that economics is *all* that counts. Not only is this facile—it misrepresents the state of the research. It is much more difficult to test the importance of identity, ideology, injustice, and political motivations using statistical methods, but current research suggests that these are very important in explaining violence and conflict.[43]

Justice

Humans value justice and fairness, the most obvious example being political inclusion of all citizens. When fairness is absent, injustice and exclusion can act as stresses. Justice and fairness are difficult concepts to measure, though psychological experiments show that they can have value beyond pure material self-interest (see box 2.7).

One aspect of injustice and unfairness is pure political exclusion of particular groups based on race, ethnicity, religion, or geographical location and origin. Political exclusion was clearly an important motive for armed resistance in the anti-colonial wars and the anti-apartheid struggle. Today, few areas of the world have systems of political representation so obviously inequitable. But recent research by Cederman, Wimmer, and Min and Goldstone and others suggests that countries with high political exclusion or ethnic exclusion are more likely to experience violent upheaval.[44]

Economic and social inequality and perceived injustice matter. Security and economic stresses may be amplified by the way people perceive their identity—and their treatment by others may be based on that identity. Data are incomplete on horizontal

BOX 2.7 *People expect fairness and punish inequity*

Using the Ultimatum Game, a two-player experimental psychology game conducted under laboratory conditions, economists have demonstrated that many people from a wide variety of cultures are willing to punish others at a cost to themselves in order to sanction unfair behavior. In this game, one bargainer makes a proposal on how to divide a sum of money with another bargainer—who has the opportunity to accept or reject the proposed division.

The first bargainer is called the *proposer*, the second the *responder*. If the responder accepts the proposed division, each bargainer earns the amount proposed; but if the responder rejects it, each bargainer earns nothing. If the only consideration is material interest, responders could be expected to accept quite a low percentage of the "pie" since this will still result in a net gain to them.

The Ultimatum Game has been run hundreds of times in diverse cultures around the world and the results have been surprisingly consistent, which suggests widespread consensus on interpretations of fairness and equity. From semisedentary Dolgan/Nganasan hunters, to wage laborers of Siberia, to sedentary Sanquianga fishermen of the Colombian Pacific coast, to Hadzan nomads in Tanzania—and from sedentary laborers in rural Missouri to urban wage workers in Accra—the offer from the proposer consistently averages 26 to 48 percent, while the responder is willing to punish if the offer is less than 12 to 17 percent.[45]

The responders would rather have both players get nothing than accept a small share while the proposer gets a much larger one. The results suggest that many individuals react strongly to what they perceive to be unjust—and are willing to forgo material benefit to punish behavior they perceive as unfair.

Sources: Hoff 2010; Henrich and others 2010.

inequalities (for example, inequalities between identity groups based on religion, caste, ethnicity, or region).[46] But analysis across 55 countries for 1986–2003 reveals a significant rise in the probability of conflict in countries with severe horizontal inequalities, both economic and social.[47] Côte d'Ivoire illustrates the connection, where decades of socioeconomic inequalities persisted between north and south. After President Houphouët-Boigny's death in December 1993, a confluence of economic and political factors eventually led to civil war.[48] The rebels' *Charte du Nord* clearly expressed the economic grievances of northerners as well as their resentment over insufficient state recognition of the Muslim religion. To portray identity as driven by economic considerations alone is to ignore the consistency with which the qualitative literature identifies such features as humiliation, pride, and desire for affiliation as motivators for action.[49]

State oppression and human rights abuses often accompany authoritarian approaches to prevent violence fueled by injustice. Are such tactics sustainable? Surprisingly little quantitative research has been done on the links between human rights abuses and political violence. A review of evidence suggests a strong correlation between past human rights abuses and current risks of conflict (box 2.8). Additional quantitative work is needed to determine the direction of causality and control for possibly omitted variables, while further qualitative work would be needed to understand the links between abuses and risks of violence. It is not clear whether human rights abuses affect the motives of those who engage in armed opposi-

BOX 2.8 *Human rights abuses and future conflict risk*

Are improvements in human rights correlated with lower risks of conflict? Countries with recent human rights abuses are far more likely to experience conflict than countries with a strong history of respect for human rights. Each one-step deterioration on the Political Terror Scale—which measures arbitrary detention for nonviolent political activity, torture, disappearances, and extrajudicial killings—resulted in a more than twofold increase in the risk of civil war in the subsequent year.

Holding large numbers of political prisoners makes a renewal of civil war twice as likely, while significant numbers of extrajudicial killings make it three times more likely.[50] This is best summed up by Walter: "A reasonable interpretation of these results is that greater repression and abuse by a government creates both grievances and signals that those governments are not dependable negotiating partners; suggesting that less coercive and more accountable approaches significantly decrease the risk of civil conflict."[51]

Sources: Fearon 2010a; Walter 2010.

tion, whether there is a wider effect in spurring indirect popular support for armed opposition movements, or whether oppressive state tactics can under certain circumstances cause disaffection among groups within the military or political and economic circles of power. Whatever the specific mechanisms at work, the results suggest that improvements in human rights often accompany a reduced risk of violence.[52]

The combination of political and socioeconomic exclusion, especially when perceived to be government policy, can be used to support narratives of social injustice. In Côte d'Ivoire an explosive mixture of socioeconomic and political inequalities appears to have contributed to the outbreak of civil war.[53] In Sri Lanka, some historians have argued that political and social exclusion of the Tamil minority through the 1956 Official Languages Act (which declared Sinhalese the only official language of Sri Lanka) and the 1972 constitution (which gave Buddhism "foremost status" in the country) contributed to early Tamil demands for greater autonomy and to later support for Tamil militancy.[54] Perceived injustice in access to political power and economic opportunities between Protestants and Catholics played a role in the Northern Ireland secessionist conflict.[55] Actual or perceived exclusion can be a powerful motivator of violence, creating pools of hostility for rebel leaders to draw on.[56] For extreme levels of violent crime, inequality between classes—which may also carry aspects of exclusion and perceived injustice—appears to matter more that inequality between ethnic, geographical, or religious groups.[57]

Injustice and inequity are often cited as motivations for terrorism. Invasion, occupation, political repression, and the curtailment of human rights and civil liberties form much of the rationale that terrorist organizations give for their attacks. Much of the empirical literature validates the relevance of these factors.[58] Some scholars posit a relationship between poverty and terrorism,[59] but many others find no direct evidence that poverty (or a lack of education) leads to terrorism.[60]

FIGURE 2.1 ***What drives people to join ideological militant movements?***

Respondents in Mali and the West Bank cited revenge, injustice, and belief in a cause as reasons for participating in ideologically based militant movements. These results contrast with the results for gang and rebel group participation (box 2.5), which showed unemployment and idleness as leading reasons for participation.

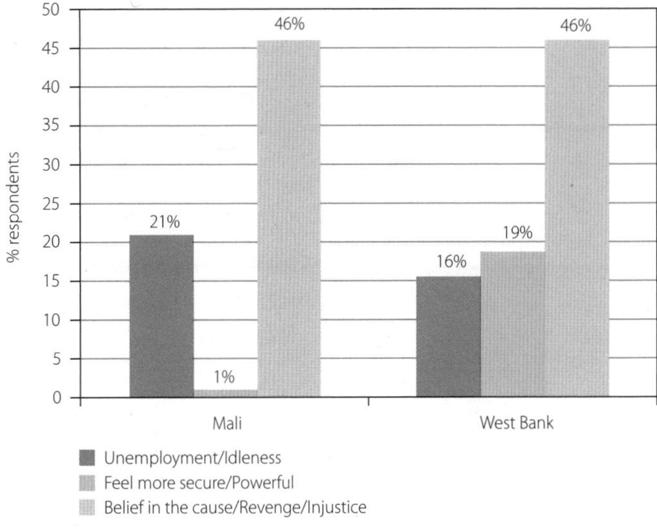

Source: Bøås, Tiltnes, and Flatø 2010.

Notes: Figure shows percentage of responses for the question, "What drives people to join ideological movements?" for surveys conducted in Mali and West Bank. Survey methodology described in Bøås, Tiltnes, and Flatø 2010.

On the contrary, some research finds that perpetrators of terrorist attacks are more likely to be well-off, with advanced education.[61]

While the motives for individuals to join ideology-based groups may be linked to beliefs in larger causes, the ability of these groups to garner local support also depends on relating these larger narratives to local claims of injustice.[62] The Taliban gained support in Pakistan's Swat valley in part by building on a variety of local grievances, including weaknesses in local law enforcement and justice institutions.[63] Leaders of militant ideological groups often espouse narratives of injustice or exclusion, and this appears to have popular resonance. Mali and the West Bank cited "belief in the cause and injustice" as far more important for recruitment into militant religious groups than for recruitment into gangs or rebel movements (figure 2.1).

Thus, stresses related to security, economics, and politics can increase the risk of violence, and they tend to combine and precipitate actual violence. But the actual combinations of stresses and the pathways to violent conflict are highly specific to country circumstances. As discussed earlier, recent research, while in its infancy, points to the importance of institutions in mediating disputes and reducing violence. Where societies fail to reform institutions and insulate themselves from stresses associated with violence, they risk repeated cycles of violence.

The vicious cycle of weak institutional legitimacy and violence

Much good work has been done on conceptualizing the relationship between institutions and violence, both historically (North, Wallis, and Weingast and many others); in contemporary analysis of the coercive capacities of the state (Fearon and Laitin); and in relation to processes of democratization (Goldstone and others).[64] The policy world has also focused on the relationship between state-building and peacebuilding, including work by the Organisation for Economic Co-operation and Development (OECD) International Network on Conflict and Fragility, as well as other bilateral, regional, and multilateral institutions. New research for this Report from Fearon, Walter, and Hoeffler, von Billerbeck, and Ijaz explores how the characteristics of state-society institutions and governance outcomes are associated with risk of violence (box 2.9).[65] Meanwhile, recent research supports the finding that states with weak institutions run the greatest risk of the onset and recurrence of civil war, and of extreme levels of criminal violence.[66] These studies should be further expanded and tested, but, taken together, they provide compelling early evidence that institutions are indeed critical for avoiding violence.

The capacity and accountability of institutions both matter. The accountability of institutions—expressed, for example, in the results described above on human rights, corruption, and the presence of a written constitution—appear to matter as much as their capacity. Both capacity and accountability are applicable to security, political, and economic systems: political scientists typically use the term "accountability" to refer to processes or political representation, for example, while economists more often use the term to refer to responsible use of public funds and responsiveness to citizen needs and complaints. For this Report, "legitimacy" refers to the responsiveness of institutions and is used as shorthand for capacity, inclusion, and accountability. Several sources of legitimacy have been identified in the state-building literature.[67] The most important are as follows:

- ***Political legitimacy (accountability) and inclusion***, or the use of credible political processes to make decisions that reflect shared values and preferences, provide the voice for all citizens equally and account for these decisions. This includes providing information to citizens and mechanisms for legal recourse to resolve disputes and complaints, including complaints against the state. This can also be considered to include international legitimacy: the state's exercise of responsible sovereignty as laid out under international law.

- ***Performance legitimacy (capacity)***, earned by the effective discharge by the state of its agreed duties, particularly the provision of security, economic oversight and services, and justice.

Recent events demonstrate how different aspects of institutional legitimacy can relate to conflict and violence. The Middle East and North African countries generally possess relatively strong institutional capacity, but their systems have historically scored low on indicators of accountability. In some countries, such as Libya, institutions have remained more personalized than in neighboring states such as Egypt and Tunisia, and perceived tensions between regional, ethnic, or tribal groups are

BOX 2.9 *Quantitative research on institutions and violence risk*

For this Report, Fearon and Walter tested whether the rule of law, government effectiveness, low corruption, and strong protection of human rights, as measured by the Worldwide Governance Indicators (WGI), correlate with a lower risk of onset and recurrence of civil conflict. This test involved a more detailed statistical examination of these governance indicators than undertaken before.

Because countries with high incomes generally have stronger governance indicators, it has been difficult for previous researchers to distinguish the effect of institutional weakness from the effect of low income. Fearon approached this problem by controlling the sample for national incomes, and then identifying "surprisingly good" governance—when a country has higher governance ratings than other countries at the same per capita income. The attempt to identify the impact of governance on the risk of violence then comes from seeing whether surprisingly good or bad governance in one period is associated with the onset or recurrence of conflict later.

Fearon finds that a country with "surprisingly good" governance indicators has a 30–45 percent lower risk of civil war in the next 5–10 years than its peers with more modestly rated governance. Once institutions are added to the analysis, they become a more important factor than income as a correlate of civil war. Similarly, he finds that institutions are highly related to the risk of extreme levels of criminal violence, proxied by homicides, with countries that had measures of better governance in 1996–98 experiencing lower homicide rates in 2000–05, even when controlling for income.

Walter finds a similar governance impact on the risk of recurring civil war. A formal constitution—a simple measure of the rule of law and the expression of societal values through formal institutions—reduces the odds of renewed conflict by 64 percent. Measures of accountability are as important as measures of capacity in this calculation: as described earlier, past human rights abuses have a particularly strong impact on the risk of future conflict, and measures of rule of law and corruption are as important as, or more important than, those of bureaucratic efficiency.

Sources: Fearon 2010a, 2010b; Walter 2010.

higher. This may help explain why initial demands for change in Egypt and Tunisia were managed largely peacefully, whereas protests in Libya escalated into civil conflict.

Fragile institutions and poor governance help explain why similar external shocks can produce violence in one country but not in another. Consider external economic stress and the long association of sharp food price increases with urban instability. In mapping food protests during the 2006–08 period of price spikes against government effectiveness data, the occurrence of violence was much higher in developing countries with less capable governance (figure 2.2).

The essential links between institutional weakness, governance, and violence are captured in the concept of "fragility" (box 2.10). Weak capacity, accountability, and legitimacy of institutions are the basis of many definitions of state fragility. The World Bank, for example, uses indicators of institutional strength to identify fragile situations. And the last decade has seen a sharper international focus on the developmental and security implications of "fragile situations," and a focus on the links between state-building and peacebuilding.[68]

Why does the lack of legitimate institutions open the risk of recurring violence?

All societies face stresses, but only some succumb to repeated violence. Unemployment, income shocks, rising inequalities between social groups, external security threats, and international organized crime—all of these have plausible causal relationships with violence. The analytical problem in identifying

FIGURE 2.2 ***Food price protests and associated violence are concentrated in fragile states***

Developing countries with low government effectiveness experienced more food price protests during the food crisis (2007–08) than countries with high government effectiveness. More than half of those protests turned violent. In states in the bottom half of the governance spectrum, the incidence of violent protests was three times higher than in the top half.

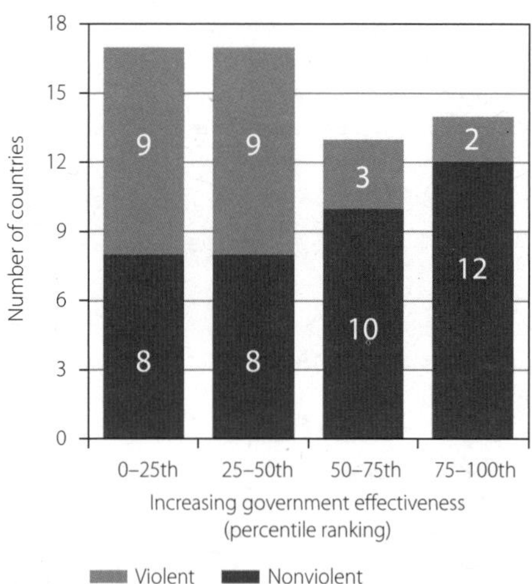

Sources: Compiled by Schneider, Buehn, and Montenegro 2010; food protest data are from news reports; government effectiveness data are from Kaufmann, Kraay, and Mastruzzi 2010a.

Notes: Food protests are defined as strikes, protests, or riots on food- or agriculture-related issues in 2007 and 2008. A violent food protest is defined as one that involves the use of physical force, results in casualties, or both.

the causes of violence is that many countries face these stresses, but not all of them actually experience outright violence, while others contain it to small geographical areas or short periods of time. As described earlier, a common, underexplored condition across countries facing violence, particularly repeated violence, is their weak institutions and governance.

The causal relationship between weak institutional legitimacy and violence may be compared to the relationship between the human body's immune system and disease. Weak institutions make a country vulnerable to violence, just as a weak immune system makes a body vulnerable to disease. To restore a body to health means not only treating the disease but also restoring the body's ability to fight off disease. Similarly with weak institutional legitimacy and governance. The cause of each outbreak of violence may vary, but the underlying reason for societies' inability to resist stresses is that their institutions are too weak to mediate them peacefully. Durable solutions to violence, therefore, require more than addressing each individual stress—they require action to address the underlying weaknesses in institutional legitimacy.

Solutions that do not involve transforming institutions may postpone rather than solve problems. Throughout history, agreements between powerful leaders have been the most common strategy to prevent large-scale violence—"I'll prevent my armed men from attacking your territory if you prevent yours from attacking mine, so that we can all profit from trade or selling natural resources." As North, Wallis, and Weingast suggest, if these arrangements create sufficient incentives for powerful leaders and organizations, they can contain violence.[69]

Such arrangements, however, lead to a political system that manipulates the economy, so that economic rents are an essential component of the stability. Unfortunately, such arrangements are personal and rarely lead to the development of impersonal institutions that can act irrespective of whether a particular leader is still in power, or to wider governance improvements that protect citizens' interests. These "elite pacts" can establish limits on violence, but this type of agreement is subject to constant renegotiation as circumstances change, and the threat of violence remains.

Does violence recur because, without impersonal institutions, elite pacts have difficulty in adapting to change? This Report's work on institutional correlations is new, and more research is needed on why countries with weak formal institutions experience repeated bouts of violence. One hypothesis is that these systems have difficulty in adapting to change—because agreements are personal and need to be renegotiated when leaders die or lose power, or when new internal and external pressures force a change in the division of economic or political benefits. A further consideration is that these systems may lead

BOX 2.10 *Fragility, weak institutions, governance, and violence*

To capture state fragility, the World Bank and other multilateral development banks have used measures of institutional weakness, such as their Country Policy and Institutional Assessment (CPIA) frameworks. The CPIA indicators attempt to measure, however imperfectly, the quality and influence of key state and society institutions and the policies they implement. Low-income countries with scores below a composite 3.2 in the CPIA are coded as fragile. Nothing in the indicators themselves directly measures the levels of political or criminal violence. The figure illustrates that countries lacking the institutional capacity and accountability to absorb systemic stress are more likely to experience violence—and less able to extract themselves from it or to contain its effects.

Of 17 countries that remained fragile between 1990 and 2008, 14 experienced major civil war violence in the same period and 2 experienced minor civil wars, as shown in the figure.[70] In other words, nearly every country with prolonged periods of weak institutional capacity experienced organized political violence. Of course, this violence is in turn likely to compromise development and further erode institutional capacity (similarly to the "conflict trap" identified by Collier and others (2003)). Even though the CPIA indicators do not include direct measurement of political and security institutions and policies, there is a striking correlation between "fragility" as defined in the CPIA scores, and the incidence of major episodes of organized violence. By measuring institutional fragility, the CPIA is in effect measuring the presence or risk of organized violence.[71]

Source: Mata and Ziaja 2009.

Countries that remained fragile were very likely to experience civil war

Of 17 countries that were fragile five or more years between 1977 and 1989 and remained fragile until 2009

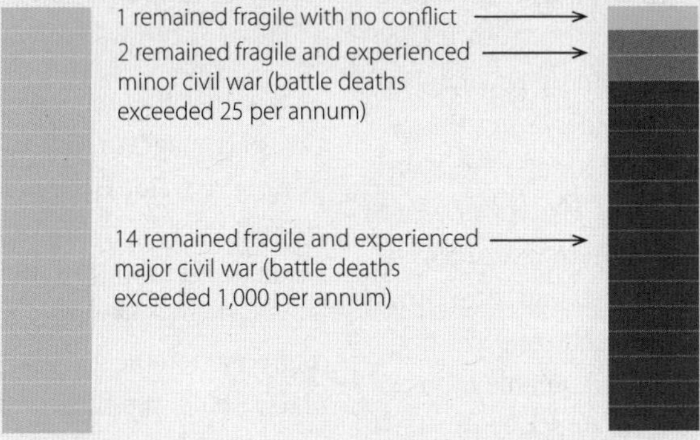
1 remained fragile with no conflict
2 remained fragile and experienced minor civil war (battle deaths exceeded 25 per annum)
14 remained fragile and experienced major civil war (battle deaths exceeded 1,000 per annum)

Source: WDR team calculations.

Note: Throughout this report, major civil war includes conflicts with more than 1,000 battle deaths per annum and minor civil war includes conflicts with more than 25 battle deaths per annum. A fragile country has a CPIA of less than 3.2.

*Correlation statistically significant at $p < 0.01$.

to the buildup of grievances over time—possibly because corruption and coercion attract external condemnation and domestic protests. These factors are surely becoming more important as the global pace of change quickens, the vulnerability to external shocks increases, and the tolerance of corruption and coercion diminishes.

Institutional economics offers a wide body of theory and evidence on how institutions (formal and informal rules) facilitate and constrain the behavior of economic and political actors (individuals, groups, and firms).[72] In relation to violence, this Report offers three key hypotheses for institutions to matter in shaping the incentives for violence:

- ***Institutional capacity.*** Strong policing and defense capacities give states the power to overcome armed threats from rebel or organized criminal groups. If an individual is contemplating political or criminal violence, the knowledge that the country's security forces have weak intelligence and coercive capacity will make that person more likely to pursue violent options. Conversely, if the country's formal institutions do not deliver local justice, education, or employment, an individual has a greater incentive to turn toward nonstate groups that can deliver, even if the groups are violent. Social and family cohesion can also be a critical national capacity: if an individual feels no sense of national pride, or if the family and community place no value on abiding by national laws, there is less to constrain that person from taking up arms against the state or engaging in criminal activities. But increasing the capacity of the state is fraught with risks: particularly when some leaders perceive a threat to their own interests from well-organized security forces and economic institutions, and where citizens are fragmented and unorganized, unable to insist that economic, justice, and security services be provided equitably to all citizens.
- ***Inclusion.*** Government capacity alone is not enough, however: many of the stresses described in this chapter relate to the failure of institutions to make all ethnic, religious, or social groups feel equally served by the actions of the state. If the geographic, ethnic, or religious community an individual belongs to is excluded from political or economic opportunities (for example, from taking part in political decision making, civil service appointments, education, health care, social protection, access to infrastructure, or business opportunities), that person will have less to lose by resorting to rebellion or crime. Accountable and inclusive political, social, and economic institutions can mediate contests between different classes or ethnic, religious, or regional groups peacefully—ensuring that each party feels adequately represented in decision making, that demands are heard, and that rights are protected. But inclusion is less likely for groups that are fragmented and unorganized—indeed, their very fragmentation could explain the ease with which the political system abuses them.
- ***Active abuse and institutional accountability.*** If a person or a family member is tortured or arbitrarily imprisoned or preyed upon by corrupt officials, that person may have little to lose by risking injury or further imprisonment by taking up a life of crime or rebellion. Accountable security forces and government agencies avoid the human rights abuses and corruption that can fuel grievances and create incentives for violent opposition.

Societies that rely on elite pacts, coercion, and patronage to control violence risk repeating a vicious cycle. Where agreements among elites to end fighting do not result in a transformation in state-society institutions and better governance outcomes, they remain vulnerable to the same stresses that precipitated fighting in the first place. In these circumstances, any stresses that shift the balance of power—such as the death of a leader, external security threats, or economic and demographic pressures—risk further violence. At some point this violence will be ended through another elite pact, but without broader and deeper institutional transformation, the cycle will repeat (figure 2.3). The vicious cycle can become more difficult to escape over time, as each successive bout of violence further weakens institutions and destroys social capital. In countries where children have been brutalized as victims or witnesses of violence, or, worse yet, as perpe-

FIGURE 2.3 ***The vicious cycle of violence, elite pacts, weak institutions—and vulnerability to repeated violence***

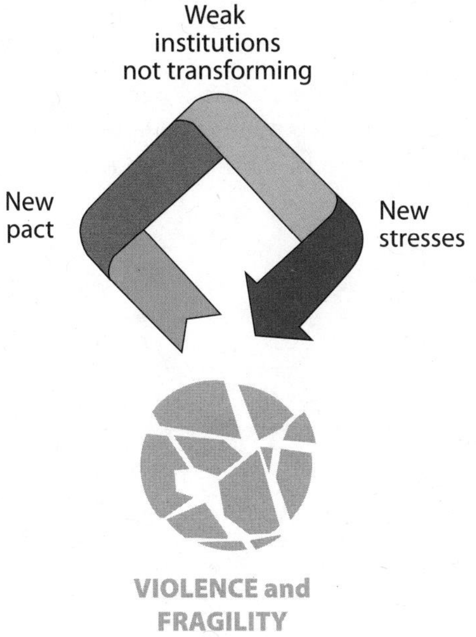

Source: WDR team.

trators by being coerced to be child combatants, the lasting trauma and lost human and social capital become an impediment to future social progress.[73]

The challenge for these societies is escaping this vicious cycle of repeated violence. Historically, large-scale episodes of violence have been a feature of all human societies. This cycle is doomed to repeat until societies find collective institutions to mediate and control violence. Escaping this vicious cycle is the focus of the rest of this Report.

FEATURE 2 *Nepal: Stresses, institutions, violence, and legitimacy*

Chapter 2 argued that organized violence is likely to occur when internal and external stresses are not countered by capable, legitimate institutions. Despite an evolution in the nature of violence and the intensity and variety of stresses faced, the weaknesses and exclusion in Nepal's institutions leave the country continually vulnerable to renewed risk of conflict, as shown in table 1.

TABLE 1 *Interlinked stresses in Nepal*

Stresses	Internal	External
Security	• Mistrust of security forces • Culture of impunity • Legacy of violence and trauma • Lack of legitimate security presence and public security crisis	• Cross-border criminality in the Tarai region • Refugees
Economic	• Low incomes, joblessness • Electricity, food, and fuel shortages • Corruption and extortion	• Floods and other natural disasters • Price shocks • Illegal trade in natural resources
Political	• Ethnic, gender, caste-based, regional exclusion • Discrimination in access to opportunity and in representation in institutions • Human rights abuses	• Regional or international involvement in internal affairs

Sources: Thapa 2010; Sharma 2008; Jha 2010.

Political stresses and the continuation of elite politics

Feudalism is a system of governance designed to restrict power and wealth to a very small minority. Conflict in Nepal is rooted in struggles to depart from the country's feudal past and move to a more inclusive and open society. Nepal is home to more than 100 ethnic groups, speaking 92 languages, and a caste system dictating group-based opportunity and achievement. The groups most marginalized constitute the majority of Nepal's population—nearly 70 percent.[74]

Nepal's recent history can be described as a protracted struggle between the country's elites and the groups, classes, and ethnicities that believe they have been excluded from the national patrimony and institutions. The modern era in Nepal began in 1950, with the overthrow of the autocratic Rana regime by a coalition of political parties supported by newly independent India. This action restored the authority of the Nepalese monarchy within a constitutional framework, and ushered in a period of democratic politics. The distribution of power between Parliament and the Palace remained contested, however, and in 1960, King Mahendra dismissed the parliament, assumed full executive powers, and instituted the "party-less" Panchayat system. Nepali nationalism was modeled after the ruling elite—one religion (Hinduism), one language (Nepali), and the authoritarian Panchayat system kept dissent in check.

This political settlement withstood pressures for democratization until 1990. In that year, the first *Jana Andolan* (People's Movement), led by a coalition of leftist and democratic parties and endorsed by the international community, forced King Birendra to reinstitute open national elections and to accept a severe curtailment of royal power. A series of governments led by the Congress Party and coalitions of leftist parties followed, all committed to modernization, equitable economic growth, and broader social justice. Yet the political parties that came to power in the wake of this movement failed to sustain public confidence—instead relying on a small group of political party elites to draft the new constitution and retain the preeminence of the Hindu religion and an army under the continued control of the king (see table 2).

As the high expectations for meaningful change turned to disenchantment, the Communist Party of Nepal Maoist[75] launched its People's War in February 1996 to bring about the country's "social and economic transformation." The Maoists drew their supporters from marginalized groups in the countryside, long left out of Nepal's political structures and lacking socioeconomic opportunity. In 2006, the Maoist movement joined with political parties to overthrow the king and create a

TABLE 2 ***Officer-level entry into Nepal government service by caste/ethnic group (percentages)***

Caste/ethnicity	1984–85	1988–89	1992–93	1996–97
Bahun-Chhetri	69.3	69.9	80.5	83.1
Newar	18.6	18.8	10.7	9.4
Non-Newar *Janajati* [a]	3.0	1.6	2.5	1.7
Madhesi	8.5	9.0	5.3	5.5
Muslim	0.6	0.2	0.6	0.2
Dalit	0	0.5	0.4	0.1

Source: Thapa 2010.
a. Pre-Hindu conquest ethnic groupings.

"New Nepal." With the signing of the Comprehensive Peace Agreement in November 2006, the Maoists and the political parties committed themselves to a democratic transition and the reform of Nepal's traditional structures. Yet, in the years since the signing, the elected Constituent Assembly made little progress, and minority groups became increasingly frustrated with the continuation of Kathmandu's elite-driven politics.

In 2007, Madhesi groups across the southern Tarai belt of Nepal began calling for regional autonomy through a federal Nepal, a notion that has since then gained traction. But questions remain about the impact of ethnic federalism on national unity, minority protection, and administrative functioning.

Security stresses and weaknesses in security and justice institutions

The Maoist movement raised a new consciousness in Nepal. But the movement's tactics—coercion, intimidation, extortion—left Nepali society deeply bruised. Across the countryside, Maoists set up parallel security and judicial structures, such as people's courts and the People's Liberation Army. The failure to address the crimes and human rights abuses by both sides during Nepal's 10-year civil war (1996–2006) has resulted in citizen distrust of the police, armed police, and army by significant groups in society, compounded by a lack of representation of marginalized groups in leadership positions in the security forces. Nepal's political establishment has also had to manage its external relations very delicately, given its strategic location. The multitude of actors, competing interests, and demands, as well as the long, porous borders between Nepal and its neighbors, add to the complexity.

Against this backdrop, insecurity in Nepal has evolved from a Maoist insurgency to opportunistic violence and criminality. This sense of lawlessness is most clearly manifest in the southern Tarai region, where the government has identified more than 100 violent groups and criminal gangs (the map shows how the epicenter of violence shifted from the middle hills during the Maoist insurgency to criminality in the southern Tarai).

MAP A The shifting epicenter of political violence in Nepal

a. Violent events, 1996–99

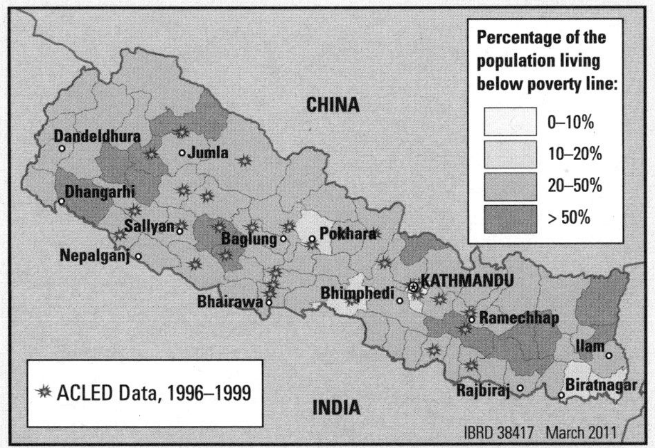

b. Violent events, 2006–07

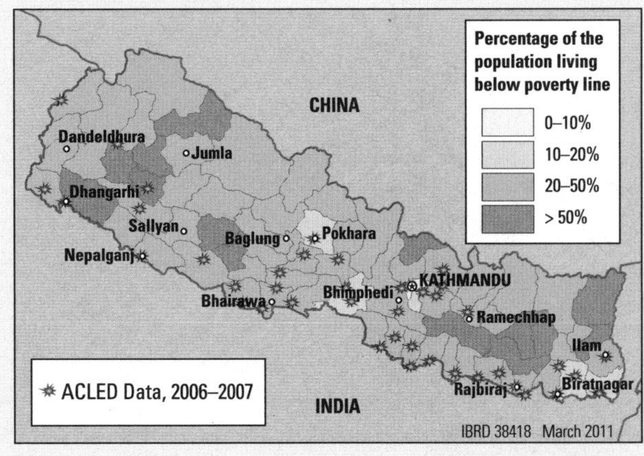

Source: Raleigh and others 2010.
Note: ACLED = Armed Conflict Location and Event Database.

FEATURE 2 *Nepal: Stresses, institutions, violence, and legitimacy (continued)*

Economic hardship and exclusion

Nepal remains the poorest country in South Asia, with the exception of Afghanistan. In the mid-1990s, after decades of "development," 42 percent of Nepal's population still lived below the internationally established absolute poverty line. But this figure declined to 31 percent by 2003–04. The main driver: remittances from young men working in the Gulf, India, and Malaysia, which account for about a half of Nepal's strong recent GNI growth (5.3 percent in fiscal year 2008 and 4.7 percent in fiscal year 2009). Ironically, this increase was spurred in part by flight from the violence of the civil war.

More recently, political insecurity and extortion have caused disinvestment in the Tarai and investor hesitancy elsewhere. Kathmandu, with an influx of rural migrants and rising energy demands, also has frequent rolling blackouts, disrupting economic activity. In 2008, the government had to declare a nationwide power crisis, with blackouts lasting up to 16 hours a day.[76]

Continuing vulnerability to violence

Despite some progress in institutional development and peacebuilding, Nepal remains vulnerable to different manifestations of violence and fragility. Table 1.1 in chapter 1 showed how multiple forms of violence co-exist in many fragile states. Reproducing it for Nepal reveals the following (table 3).

TABLE 3 *Nepal's multiple forms of violence, 1960–present*

Localized or subnational intergroup violence	"Conventional" political violence (contests for state power or for autonomy or independence)	Localized criminal or gang-related violence	Transnational crime or trafficking with accompanying violence	Local conflicts with transnational ideological connections
"Repressed" intergroup conflicts over land, access to political power Caste and ethnic exclusion underpinning People's War (civil war) of 1996–2006 Regionalism and *Tarai Andolan* of 2007	Clandestine opposition to the Panchayat regime; reactive imprisonment, denial of human and political rights *Jana Andolan I* 1990 People's War of 1996–2006 *Jana Andolan II* 2006 Party-related extortion, intimidation post-2006 (activities of the Young Communist League)	Gang-based extortion, theft, smuggling in Tarai, major increase in levels of violence after 2006	Human trafficking (prostitution) from the 1960s Heroin transshipment from the 1960s Illegal trade in timber, opium cultivation post-2006	Revolutionary left cross-fertilization with "Maoists" from the 1960s

Source: Compiled by the WDR team.

Exiting the vicious cycle

Following the Comprehensive Peace Agreement, a broad-based constitutional assembly was created, which has been trying to create a new settlement that will divide political and economic power more equitably between Nepal's many ethnic and caste groups. This process represents a major attempt to broaden the nature of Nepal's polity and move it beyond the high-caste elite competition that has dominated the country's history. While there has been undeniable progress from a series of more-or-less exclusive elite pacts toward a more permeable and inclusive approach to statehood, curtailing today's lawlessness and preventing further episodes of political violence requires the creation of broader based coalitions, transformation of national institutions, and a process that delivers improved political, security, and economic outcomes to all citizens.

Sources: Thapa 2010; Sharma 2008; Jha 2010.

Notes

1. Ballentine and Nitzschke 2006; Murshed and Tadjoeddin 2007.
2. In addition, for example, there are structural factors that increase conflict risk, which include features of the physical terrain that make rebellion easier. These features do not cause war in the common sense of that word, but simply make it more possible. Mountainous terrain has been shown to increase risks by increasing the feasibility of rebellion. See Buhaug and Gleditsch 2008; Gleditsch and Ward 2000; Salehyan and Gleditsch 2006. See also Murdoch and Sandler 2004. On terrain and neighborhood effects, see Fearon 2010a; Fearon and Laitin 2003; Goldstone and others 2010. On the effects of neighborhood on civil wars, see Hegre and Sambanis 2006; Gleditsch 2007.
3. See Dahlberg and Krug 2002.
4. See Strassler 1996; Herz 1950; Jervis 1978.
5. Posen 1993; Snyder and Jervis 1999; Walter 1999; de Figueiredo and Weingast 1999.
6. Stedman 1996; Jones 1999; Posen 1993.
7. Brown 1996; Stedman 1996; Fearon and Laitin 2003; Horowitz 2000. On the shifting nature of national identity, see Laitin 1998.
8. Kumar and Skaperdas 2009.
9. Much of this response has taken the form of critical discussion; see, for example, Nathan 2005. A particularly useful "study of studies" is Sambanis 2004, which finds that GDP per capita and political instability are the only variables that consistently predict civil war onset. Researchers looking at natural resources have found mixed results—oil being most consistently associated with civil war outbreak. Recent work by Satyanath, Miguel, and Sergenti 2004 tied rainfall and agricultural shocks to the onset of civil war, while Besley and Persson 2009 explore the effect of international price shocks on the onset of conflict. Arnson and Zartman 2005 cover much of the core arguments in the greed versus grievance debate.
10. On horizontal inequality, see Stewart 2005; Østby 2008; and Stewart 2010. On polarization, see Esteban and Ray 2008; Montalvo and Reynal-Querol 2005.
11. Thinking on this topic can be traced back to Gellner 1983; recent responses to the debate include Toft 2003; Laitin 2007.
12. Brückner and Ciccone 2010 are also noteworthy in highlighting that institutions help societies to weather natural resource price shocks to avoid violence.
13. Clark and Kaufman 2011; IRIN 2010; Gettleman 2009.
14. Rubin 2002; Straus 2010.
15. See, for example, Menkhaus 2007; Lockhart and Glencorse 2010.
16. Buhaug and Gleditsch 2008; Gleditsch and Ward 2000; Salehyan and Gleditsch 2006. See also Murdoch and Sandler 2004; Fearon 2010a; Hegre and Sambanis 2006; Gleditsch 2007.
17. The presence of weak neighbors, rival neighbors, and refugee diasporas can play a crucial role in the emergence of transnational rebel (TNR) organizations, bargaining failure, and civil conflict; see Salehyan 2007.
18. See Becker 1968.
19. See Collier and Sambanis 2005, 193. Also see Garang 1987.
20. See Collier and others 2003.
21. Fearon 2010a.
22. Fearon 2010a.
23. Keefer 2008; Fearon 2010a.
24. World Bank 2006f, 10.
25. Narayan and Petesch 2010.
26. Sirleaf 2007a, 4.
27. Labor market data in developing countries are irregular and unreliable. For example, very few Sub-Saharan African countries have carried out labor force surveys. Population censuses (an important source for claims about labor force participation and unemployment rates) are commonly out of date, and often unreliable even when recent. Further, wage employment in agriculture in poor countries is "invisible" in most conventional databases. See Cramer 2010.
28. Macmillan and Gartner 1999; Panda and Agarwal 2005; Jeyaseelan and others 2007; Krishnan and others 2010; Silberschmidt 1999, 2001; see Cramer 2010.
29. This is consistent with Relative Deprivation theory; see also Solow 1990; Argandoña 2001.
30. See Loayza, Fajnzylber, and Lederman 2002a, 2002b; Messner, Raffalovich, and Shrock 2002.
31. Fearon and Laitin 2003; Collier and Hoeffler 2002, 2004; Anyanwu 2004.

32. Berman and others 2009, 1.
33. Moser 2009, 240.
34. Gutiérrez-Sanín 2008, 22.
35. World Bank 2010m; Willmann 2010.
36. Collier and Hoeffler 1998, 2002; Anyanwu 2004; Fearon and Laitin 2003; de Soysa 2002; Bannon and Collier 2003; McNeish 2010.
37. Ross 2003.
38. See Keefer, forthcoming.
39. Fearon 2005 argues that oil predicts civil war risk not because of its role as a source of start-up finance for rebels but, instead, because producers demonstrate relatively low state capabilities given the level of per capita income.
40. Satyanath, Miguel, and Sergenti 2004.
41. Brinkman and Hendrix 2010.
42. See Besley and Persson 2010.
43. Furthermore, there is a complex relationship between motivations for and incidence of violence, as noted in Fearon and Laitin 2003.
44. Cederman, Wimmer, and Min 2010; Goldstone and others 2010.
45. These results are from the second comparison study collected by Henrich and others 2010.
46. The difficulty of studying this phenomenon is compounded by the fact that our understanding of and data sets on identity are weak; as Hegre and Sambanis have shown, slight changes in how different features of ethnicity—language groupings, affiliation measures, and so on—are operationalized in studies have major effects on findings about causality and the direction of causality (Hegre and Sambanis 2006). On how identity affiliations form, see Fearon 2006; Berman and Iannaccone 2006.
47. See Østby 2008 who defines groups alternatively by ethnicity, religion, and region, and finds a significant relation between horizontal inequalities (HIs) and the onset of violent conflict for each definition. Economic HIs are measured by average household assets and social HIs by average years of education. The effect of HIs is quite high: the probability of conflict increases threefold when comparing the expected conflict onset when all variables have average values, compared to a situation where the extent of horizontal inequality of assets among ethnic groups is at the 95th percentile. In the case of inter-regional HIs, the probability of conflict increases 2.5 times as HIs rise from the mean value to the 95th percentile value. See also Stewart 2010.
48. Stewart 2010.
49. Gurr 1968; Herbst 2000; Stewart 2010; Strom and MacDonald 2007.
50. The data on political prisoners and extra-judicial killings were obtained from the Cignarelli and Richards Human Rights data set (Cingranelli and Richards 2010). Each indicator is coded from 0 to 2, with 0 denoting large/significant degrees of human rights abuses and 2 denoting no abuses.
51. Walter 2010, 21.
52. See Gurr 1968; Herbst 2000; Stewart 2010; Strom and MacDonald 2007; Brown 1996; Stedman 1996. On recent quantitative literature on this topic, see Bhavnani and Miodownik 2009. See also Abbink and Herrmann 2009; Kalyvas 2006; Sambanis 2001.
53. Langer 2005; Stewart 2010.
54. De Silva 2005.
55. Barron and others 2010.
56. Qualitative and case study literature as well as WDR input from national officials and leaders consistently highlight political injustice, social exclusion, and inequity between social groups as key correlates of conflict. Among the many qualitative and case-based studies, see, for example, Heraclides 1990; Murshed and Gates 2006; Salehyan and Gleditsch 2006. On measurement difficulties, see Laitin 2000; Cramer 2002; Posner 2004.
57. See Loayza, Fajnzylber, and Lederman 2002a, 2002b; Messner, Raffalovich, and Shrock 2002.
58. Pape 2003; Krueger and Laitin 2008; Abadie 2006.
59. Stern 2003.
60. Atran 2003; Berrebi 2007.
61. Krueger and Maleckova 2003; Hassan 2001; Kimhi and Even 2004.
62. Smith 2004; Wright-Neville 2004.
63. World Bank and ADB 2010; also WDR team consultations with government officials and representatives from donor community, multilateral organizations, and civil society in Pakistan, 2010. See also Abbas 2008, 2010.
64. North, Wallis, and Weingast 2009; Fearon and Laitin 2003; Goldstone and others 2010.

65. See Fearon 2010a; Walter 2010; Hoeffler, von Billerbeck, and Ijaz 2010. A range of indicators can be used to measure governance and institutional capacity. The *Users' Guide on Measuring Fragility* provides an excellent contemporary stocktaking of the literature and concepts (Mata and Ziaja 2009). The World Bank Country Policy and Institutional Assessment (CPIA) scores are prepared internally and are publicly available for International Development Association (IDA) countries for the years 2005 to present. The World Bank has recently undertaken an annual harmonizing exercise to align the definitions of fragility with regional development banks (the Asian Development Bank and the African Development Bank). Other well-known measures of governance and quality of institutions include the Worldwide Governance Indicators measures of government and the International Country Risk Guide (ICRG) measures compiled by the PRS Group. The Worldwide Governance Indicators are an index comprising multiple sources, whereas the ICRG measures are expert assessments on multiple dimensions of political, economic, and financial risk. It locates three common attributes of states, "legitimacy, authority, and effectiveness," among a variety of indexes and definitions of fragility and compares the results across indices. See Kaufmann, Kraay, and Mastruzzi 2010b. There is a blurred line in the indicators between the measurement of governance outcomes (actual levels of representation and participation, accountability for decisions and for illegal actions, and corruption and human rights abuses) and institutional characteristics (whether there are systems and capacities that regulate state-society relations within the rule of law, provide for prosecution of abuses, and so forth). Most governance indicators actually measure both: whether a system is in place (for example, a constitution or anti-corruption law, government policy on equitable service provision) as well as some measurement, often imperfect, of whether these systems deliver good governance outcomes in practice (low corruption levels, free and fair elections, avoidance of impunity for human rights abuses, and so on).
66. See Stedman 1996; Brown 1996; Posen 1993; Snyder 2000; Goldstone and Ulfelder 2004; Goldstone and others 2010; Besley and Persson 2009, 2010.
67. State legitimacy is tied to agreed rules and processes that promote accountability to its citizens, whether through participation or through patronage. Patronage is particularly pervasive in fragile situations where state capacity is weak; yet, it can also weaken state legitimacy if seen as unfair and reinforcing horizontal inequalities (OECD 2010g, 2011). Shared beliefs are essential to link the state and its society in constructive ways (Bellina and others 2009); for example, elections only become more than a formal tool to collect opinion when there is a common and entrenched belief that they express the "will of the people." Together with collective identities and religion, "tradition" is a very important way to "ground" state legitimacy (Clements 2010). These sources of legitimacy do not exist in isolation: improving service delivery does not necessarily increase state legitimacy if the other elements are missing. State legitimacy results from a combination of these sources and may take various forms, depending on context.
68. The development community's focus on fragility is related to pioneering work undertaken by Paul Collier and Ngozi Okonjo-Iweala under the Low Income Countries Under Stress initiative. The policy implications of this original work were extensively elaborated by INCAF, an organization within the Development Assistance Committee (DAC) of OECD, as well as by the UN and various bilaterals, most notably the U.K.'s DFID (Department for International Development). INCAF has produced innovative thinking on security system reform, service delivery in fragile situations, the legitimacy of the state, and the role of donors. The United Nations identified the need for institution-building for a more secure and developed world at an early stage, particularly in the fields of conflict prevention and peacebuilding. New thinking on fragility and state-building has received significant support from research funded by DFID over the past 10 years; for a synthesis, see Garassi 2010.
69. North, Wallis, and Weingast 2009.
70. The current CPIA cutoff was normalized by year to account for the changing methodology in CPIA over time.
71. For further discussion on measurements of governance, institutions, and fragility, see Mata and Ziaja 2009.
72. See North 1990; Williamson 1985; Rodrik, Subramanian, and Trebbi 2004.
73. Maynard 1997.
74. The high-class group of Bahun-Chhetri constitutes 28 percent of Nepal's population.
75. The Communist Party of Nepal (Maoist) was renamed Unified Communist Party of Nepal (Maoist), or UCPN (Maoist), following its merger in January 2009 with the Communist Party of Nepal–Unity Centre (Masal).
76. Sharma 2008.

PART 2

Lessons from National and International Responses

This chapter sets out the Report's framework for how countries escape the vicious cycle of fragility and move toward a virtuous cycle of confidence-building and institutional transformation, especially in the areas of citizen security, justice, and jobs. The framework is presented as an expanding spiral because these processes repeat over time as countries enter and exit multiple transition moments. Even as one set of immediate priorities is resolved, other risks emerge and require a repeated cycle of action to bolster institutional resilience. This process takes at least a generation. Societies undertaking this endeavor face a legacy of pervasive and enduring mistrust, which makes collective action to address challenges or provide public goods so difficult. Outsiders cannot restore confidence and transform institutions for countries because these processes are domestic and must be nationally led. But to help countries restore peace and reduce regional and global instability, international actors can provide external support and incentives and help reduce external stresses.

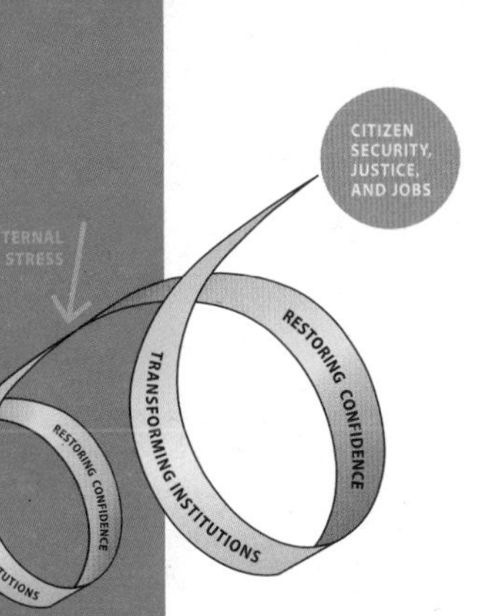

CHAPTER 3

From violence to resilience: Restoring confidence and transforming institutions

Why transforming institutions is so difficult

Changes in power relations and contests around them are a constant feature of all societies. There is nothing unusual about intense social confrontation during the transformation of institutions, which normally involves changes in the distribution of power and wealth. Such contests do not end at some point in a society's development. U.S. government support for private banks and greater state involvement in health care provision have stirred fierce controversy, as have the recent transformations in public sector functions caused by the impact of the financial crisis in Europe. In other words, change is contested and painful in all circumstances. But some societies can accomplish change in the national interest, even when this involves temporary losses for some groups. Other societies find this more difficult.

What makes institutional transformation particularly difficult for states affected by violence? Many countries that recovered from war in the mid-20th century, including most of Europe and Japan, transformed their institutions quickly and smoothly. But they had a long history of national institutional development and high levels of physical and human capital—and they had faced an external war, not internal violence. Today's middle- and low-income countries affected by internal violence face greater challenges—for three key reasons. First, launching an initial agreement on change is hard because elites do not trust each other and few people trust the state. Second, maintaining an agreement is difficult because institutional change can increase the risks of violence in the short term, due to political backlash from groups that lose power or economic benefits. Third, countries do not exist in isolation: during fragile periods of institutional transformation, they may face external security threats or economic shocks that can overwhelm progress. These challenges are difficult to overcome when physical, institutional, and human capital is relatively low.

The challenge of low trust and rising expectations

Launching an initial transition in fragile situations is difficult because of low trust and low capacity to deliver on promises.[1] Mistrust is much more pervasive in violence-affected countries than in those with a long history of a reasonably stable social compact between state and citizen. This makes many forms of cooperation difficult, including measures to address the stresses triggering violence in the first place. When there is

BOX 3.1 *Unrealistic expectations in fragile states are hurdles to progress*

The impact of a legacy of mistrust in violence-affected countries

A legacy of mistrust can mean that key actors do not respond as hoped to new political signals or new public programs. Consider Afghanistan, where citizens need to calculate the risks of siding either with the Taliban or with the government and NATO (North Atlantic Treaty Organization)—or with neither.

In making these decisions, individuals consider what they think others are likely to do. The thinking process might go like this: "The consequences of my decision to provide the authorities with information on the Taliban depend on what others around me are going to do. If my neighbors won't cooperate, the authorities are going to lose control, and I'd be crazy to help them. So, even though I do not support the Taliban, I'm better off helping them." The same could apply to providing information on drug traffickers.[2]

All institutional change requires the coordinated actions of many people. That is why small events that change the beliefs about what others will do can evoke big changes in the choices each individual makes. A single, but widely publicized, government humiliation in combat operations, for example, can translate into a major loss of popular support. A single, but widely publicized, incident of corruption can evoke big changes in expectations and in political and economic behavior.

Expectations and trust in fragile states and in non-fragile states

Analysis of 280 country surveys in Latin America and Africa shows a significant difference in citizen trust in fragile and non-fragile states. The results reveal that countries that are not fragile or affected by conflict have significantly higher levels of trust in the police, the justice system, and the parliament. This is consistent with recent research that explores cross-country differences in trusting neighbors and governments.

In simple terms, people's expectations are often wrong about the future in fragile states. A simple cross-country regression using data on expectations of economic improvements and actual economic growth suggests that, in non-fragile states, peoples' expectations of the direction the economy will take in the next 12 months has a significant correlation with actual outcomes.[3] But in fragile states, there is no such correlation: responses to the survey question, "will economic prospects improve in the next 12 months?" bear no relationship to what subsequently happens in the economy. This is important, because all rational expectations theory in economics and political science—and the policy decisions linked to it—assume that people have a reasonably informed ability to make judgments about the future.

The low trust in government institutions in fragile and conflict-affected countries poses a formidable constraint to leaders trying to launch positive change. To further complicate the situation, operational experience and input from national policymakers highlight a second, quite different version of the expectations problem, that is, the excessively *high* popular expectations that arise in moments of political hope and transition. Governments repeatedly encounter this: signing a peace agreement or a donor pledge conference can create a wave of enthusiasm and the expectation that rapid change will follow. When the bubble bursts, as it usually does, governments can experience a rapid loss of credibility.

If policy makers understand these dynamics, they can harness public enthusiasm for change to their advantage by crafting signals in ways that conform to expectations (chapter 4). Where mistrust is high, they have to take actions that send very strong signals—signals that are self-evidently costly, such as integrating former rebels into the national army structure, as in Burundi, or guaranteeing long-term employment to former adversaries, as in South Africa through the "sunset clause" offered to white civil servants. They also have to find ways to make promises binding, often using third parties as guarantors.

Sources: Braithwaite and Levi 1998; Hoff and Stiglitz 2004a, 2004b, 2008; Schelling 1971, 1978; Axelrod 1984; Nunn 2008; Nunn and Wantchekon, forthcoming.

Note: Differences in trust and expectations between fragile and non-fragile states reported here were statistically significant at the 5 percent level. These differences were significant whether non-fragile was defined as CPIA (Country Policy and Institutional Assessment) greater than 3.2 or CPIA greater than 3.8.

no convincing track record of progress and information is poor, individuals can easily have expectations that are either too low (they are unresponsive to positive signals of change)—or too high (they hold unrealistic expectations and are easily disappointed) (see box 3.1).

Low institutional capacity to deliver further reduces trust. Low-trust environments require strong signals of real change. Yet the capacity to deliver change is weak in most societies that score low on governance indicators.[4] A further reason for failure in reform is the "premature load-bearing" of institutions: too many demands and expectations are placed on them in a short period. When they do not deliver, there is a loss of confidence and legitimacy (see box 3.2).

The process of reform itself may carry short-term security risks. Research suggests that a shift from authoritarian rule toward democracy is associated with a higher risk of civil war and an increase in criminal violence.[5] Taking on too many reforms too fast—such as decentralizing services and combating insurgents or traffickers—can risk backlash and institutional loss of credibility. Rapid reforms make it difficult for actors in the post-conflict society to make credible commitments with each other, since they do not know how the reforms will affect the "balance of power." Elections, often seen as "winner takes all" events in fragile states, can evoke powerful reactions from those who lose.[6] And if disadvantaged groups or regions are empowered by reform, existing power-holders must lose some power as a result. Economic restructuring changes the balance of economic access and opportunity. Anti-corruption efforts attack entrenched interests, sometimes very powerful ones. The point here is not that it is wrong to attempt such reform: instead it is to be aware of the risks—and to adapt the design of reforms accordingly, to ensure that the state can deliver on promises.[7]

A history of recent violence sharpens this dilemma. In societies that lack effective security and rule of law, potential reformers may well perceive that reforms will put their lives at risk and cause them to postpone or avoid change. In the 1983–93 "narco-terrorist" period in Colombia, the Cali and Medellín drug cartels ordered an estimated 3,500 assassinations of presidential candidates, politicians, judicial officers, and government officials seen to oppose them.[8] For those who need protection, legacies of violence can undermine their belief in the efficacy of the state and weaken their willingness to support reform. For those considering violence, the possibility of impunity can reinforce their willingness to use violent means.[9] A potent illustration of how reforms can evoke violence is the transitional experience of the former Soviet Union, where homicide rates soared as the state undertook wide-ranging reforms (see box 3.3).

BOX 3.2 *Premature load-bearing*

Public policy (or program) implementation involves agents taking action with a particular set of standards. Tax implementation, for example, involves the collection of taxes (sales, income, dutiable import, property valuation, and so on) according to rules for assessing the amount due. Procurement involves assessing bids according to stipulated procedures, followed by contract awards. Premature load-bearing can occur during a reform process when there is a large divergence between what is in the agents' best interest and what they are supposed to do.

For example, in implementing a revised customs code, if the tariff is very high, the importer may offer the customs officer a side payment to avoid (or reduce) what is owed. Higher tariffs entail greater pressure on the system: but so do complex tariff codes with exemptions based on intended use. In Kenya and Pakistan the collected tariff rate increased with the official tariff (not one for one, but it did increase) up to around 60 percent, after which the collected rate stopped increasing. After that point, further increases in the tariff just increased the discrepancy between the official rate and the collected rate. As the tariff rate increases, the amount importers would pay to evade the tariff increases too, so the temptation for customs officers to deviate also increases. In other words, complexity and its ambiguity make collusion with importers easier. In this case a low and uniform tax would create less organizational stress.

These same considerations apply across the range of state activities, from policing to justice and to public financial management and education. Different tasks create different organizational load-bearing pressures and different inducements to deviate from organizational standards. When those pressures overwhelm capacity and incentives are not aligned, systems fail.

Systems often fail when stress is placed on individual components. Pressure can sometimes cause a nonlinear degradation in performance. In many organizational situations where one agent's performance depends on many other agents around them, modest amounts of stress can bring about total collapse. An example is the Chad College, established to enhance government accountability in the use of proceeds from newly discovered oil. The mechanism relied heavily on local civil society to secure, evaluate, and provide opinions on government funding allocations out of the oil revenues—a formula that works well in environments where civil society has high capacity, and where a tradition of government openness and accountability to citizens has been established. Under stress, however, the civil society groups could not hold government to account, and the mechanism collapsed.

Sources: Pritchett and de Weijer 2010; Kaplan 2008; Lund 2010.

The challenge of vulnerability to external stress

Countries with weak institutions are disproportionately vulnerable to external shocks. Severe external shocks can overwhelm even fairly strong institutions: witness the incipient social unrest in 2010 in many parts of Europe as a result of austerity measures to contain the global financial crisis, or the assaults on governance from shifting patterns in global drug trafficking. When institutions are both well-developed and reasonably static—

BOX 3.3 *Violence can increase during fast institutional transformations*

The late 1980s witnessed major economic reform in the Soviet Union under Mikhail Gorbachev's *glasnost* and *perestroika* initiatives. Among the consequences were severe unemployment, the virtual collapse of a previously comprehensive social welfare regime, and a sharp contraction of many public services. This was followed by the breakup of the Soviet Union into independent republics and the introduction of multiparty politics. A rise in homicides accompanied this period of turbulence, peaking in 1993 at 18 per 100,000 population and again in 2001 at 20 per 100,000 (see figure). With reforms beginning to pay dividends by the 2000s, social instability subsided and homicides began to fall.

Homicides in turbulent times: The Soviet Union

Homicide rates increased in Russia following the dissolution of the Soviet Union and the rapid reforms during the 1990s. This phenomenon was not unique to Russia: nearly every former Soviet country had homicides increase in the early 1990s.

a. Homicide rates in Russia, 1986–2008

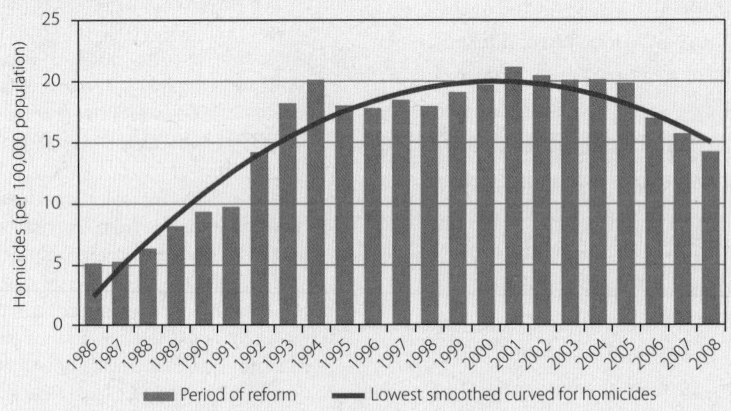

b. Homicide rates in former Soviet republics, 1990–2000

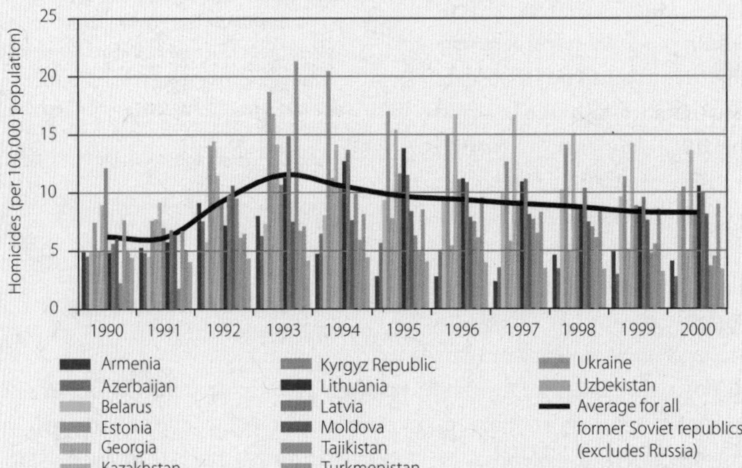

Most former Soviet republics experienced a spike in homicides following the dissolution of the Soviet Union, with notable peaks in Estonia (20 in 1994), Georgia (17 in 1993), Kazakhstan (17 in 1996), and Tajikistan (21 in 1993). In every country except Turkmenistan and Uzbekistan, homicides increased between 1990 and 1994, followed by a decline, though the average homicide rate in 2000 remained above the level of 1990, and only a few countries had lower homicide rates at the end of the decade.

Sources: The PRS Group 2010; World Bank 2010n; WDR team calculations.

as in the OECD (Oranisation for Economic Co-operation and Development) countries—external shocks can be absorbed, but even then, they will affect reform plans. Chapter 2 showed that fragile countries experienced more food protests, and more violence during food protests, than non-fragile countries during recent food price crises. Likewise, recent research suggests that the impact of natural disasters is more pronounced in fragile states.[10] Not only are fragile countries more vulnerable to the effects of disasters, but disasters and external shocks can interrupt institutional transformation, as was the case in promising sectors after Haiti's devastating earthquake in early 2010.[11]

Escaping violence, developing resilience

Given the difficulties, how have countries escaped from violence and achieved institutional resilience? These pathways are under-researched, and this Report has only some of the answers. The framework below suggests some fundamental differences between fragile and violent situations and stable developing environments.[12] The first is the need to **restore confidence** in collective action before embarking on wider institutional transformation. Second is the priority of **transforming institutions that provide citizen security,**[13] **justice, and jobs.** Third is the role of regional and international action to **reduce external stresses.** Fourth is the **specialized nature of external support needed** (figure 3.1).

The framework is not meant to be a "grand theory" of violence, nor is it the only way to understand violence prevention. It builds, however, from the research described in chapters 1 and 2 and a review of country experience, and provides a useful organizing framework for action. First, it provides a systematic way of thinking about what can be done to prevent violence—and the recurrence of violence over time. Indeed, the question of most relevance to national reformers

FIGURE 3.1 ***WDR Framework: Repeated cycles of action to bolster institutional resilience***

The WDR framework is presented as an ever-expanding spiral because these processes repeat over time as countries go through multiple transitions. Even as one set of immediate priorities is resolved, other risks and transition moments emerge and require a repeated cycle of action to bolster institutional resiliency. The arrow below the spiral illustrates that external support and incentives *can help this nationally led process, and the arrow above it illustrates how* external stresses *can derail it.*

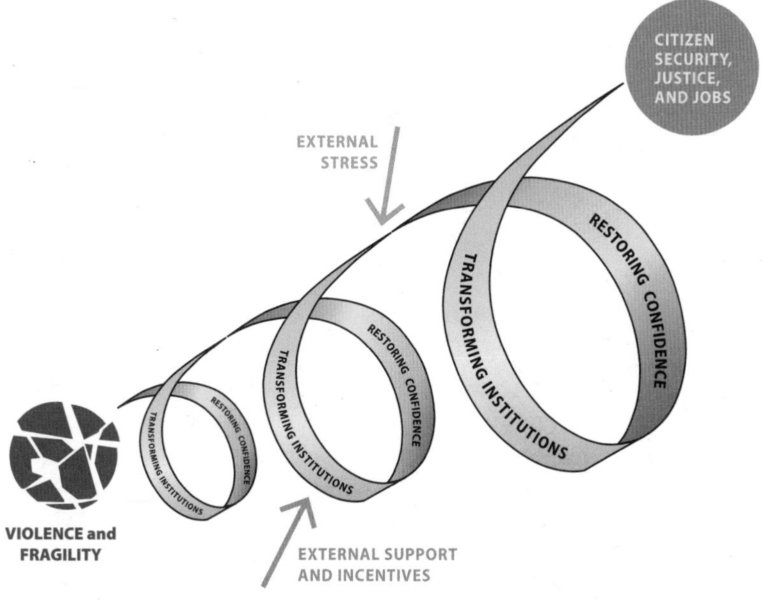

Source: WDR team.

and international agencies—and the one that an institutional emphasis puts front and center—is in practical terms, "what can we do to prevent violence?" Second, the framework is compatible with the theories of violence in different disciplines (box 3.4). Third, by focusing on the challenges in moving from crisis management to security, justice, and economic institutional transformation, it brings together the thinking of local, national, and international actors as well as political, security, and development agencies.

The framework suggests that institutional transformation and good governance, which are important in development generally, work differently in fragile situations. The goal is more focused—transforming institutions that are directly important to the prevention of repeated cycles of violence. The dynamics of institutional change are also different. A good analogy is a financial crisis caused by a combination of external stresses and historic weaknesses in institutional checks and balances. In such a situation, exceptional efforts are needed to restore confidence in national leaders' ability to manage the crisis—through actions that signal a real break with the past, and through locking in these actions and showing that they will not be reversed. To prevent the crisis recurring, concerted action will also be needed to address the underlying institutional and governance weaknesses that precipitated it—but without a restoration of confidence among both national and international stakeholders, these reforms will not be possible.

Restoring confidence and transforming institutions

The framework therefore argues that confidence-building—a concept used in political mediation and financial crises but rarely in development circles[14]—is a prelude to more permanent institutional change in the face of violence. Why apply this to the challenges of fragility and violence? Because the low trust caused by repeated cycles of violence means that stakeholders who need to contribute political, financial, or technical support will not collaborate until they believe that a positive outcome is possible. Chapter 4 examines country-level experiences of three mechanisms to restore the confidence of key stakeholders in fragile and violent situations:

- ***Developing collaborative, "inclusive enough" coalitions.*** To bridge problems of low trust between societal groups and between the state and society, we examine the role that coalitions involving a broad range of stakeholders have played in successful exits from violence—whether government-led alliances in support of security and development actions or negotiated agreements between parties to a conflict. Inclusion can embed strong political economy incentives. It brings benefits to leaders—by providing support and resources from key stakeholder groups and ensuring that individual leaders or parties do not take all the blame for unpopular decisions.[15] It can also signal change and provide incentives for reform if parties responsible for abuses are excluded. An inclusive approach can also carry longer-term political economy benefits, by creating pressure for continuing change, avoiding narrow and persistent elite captures of the state.
- ***Using signals and commitment mechanisms to build support.*** Without strong signals of a break with the past and ways to reassure stakeholders that the new direction will be sustained, developing coalitions of support for change can be difficult. Leaders need ways to find the right signals to galvanize support—signals that have been successful in different country contexts are examined. When trust in announcements on future policy is low, leaders also need mechanisms to lock promises in and persuade people that they will not be reversed—called "commitment mechanisms" by economists and political scientists. We consider the type of commitment mechanisms that have been useful in the face of risks of repeated cycles of violence.
- ***Delivering early results.*** Expectations from government policy announcements alone will likely be insufficient to persuade

BOX 3.4 The WDR framework and theories of violence prevention

Paul Collier in *Breaking the Conflict Trap* and *The Bottom Billion,* and Douglass North, John Wallis, and Barry Weingast in *Violence and Social Orders* have been among the most influential theorists of the links among conflict, violence, and development.

North, Wallis, and Weingast describe three "doorstep conditions" for fragile countries to move toward long-term institutional violence prevention:

- Ensuring the rule of law, particularly over property issues, for elites
- Creating a "perpetual state" in the constitutionality of transfer of power and the ability of state commitments to bind successor leaders
- Consolidating control over the military.

Their framework provides a perceptive analysis of national development dynamics but does not explicitly address international stresses on states, international assistance, or the influence of international norms and standards.

Collier's work, by contrast, focuses less on domestic political dynamics and more on low income, corruption, and natural resource rents. He explicitly considers external security guarantees and international standards for resource extraction.

This Report brings together these strands of thinking and adds analysis that both supports earlier hypotheses and provides new questions for further research. It uses quantitative techniques to confirm that institutions matter for violence prevention. It brings this together with other work from economics, political, and social science on how institutional transformations take place. And it adds some concepts and examples from country case studies and regional and country consultations to flesh out understanding of these transitions.

Chapter 2 provided empirical analysis of the importance of institutions for long-term violence prevention. It supports the theories of economists and political scientists who have focused on institutions, such as Collier; Fearon and Laitin; and North, Wallis, and Weingast. Interestingly, it provides some initial evidence not only that very highly developed countries defined by North and colleagues as "open access orders" have lower rates of violence, but also that institutions and good governance outcomes matter at much lower levels of development. Institutions matter for preventing criminal violence and organized crime as well as for preventing political conflict.

This chapter focuses on practical lessons that can be applied in extreme conditions of insecurity and weak institutions. It expands on existing work in three ways:

- ***Why institutional reforms are so difficult.*** The chapter draws upon scholars such as Acemoglu and Robinson, Fearon, and Laitin; Keefer, Weingast and others who have studied early transition periods to describe why the political economy of institutional reform in insecure environments is so difficult, and why so many reform efforts therefore fail.
- ***What it takes to make institutional reforms happen.*** The chapter uses country case studies and inputs from national reformers to look at how countries in outright crises have restored confidence, and how countries with ongoing insecurity and weak legitimacy, capacity, and accountability have transformed their institutions in the longer term. This work builds on North and colleagues' analysis of the pathways to move to broader institutional transformation, prevent violence from recurring, and lay the basis for longer-term development—but it focuses on earlier periods of transition in very insecure environments. In so doing, it moves beyond most existing theories by explicitly considering how external stresses and external assistance can affect these processes.
- ***Understanding that transformations take time and adopting appropriate institutional models is critical.*** The chapter adds empirical measures of how long these transformations take, even for the countries that made the fastest transitions in the late 20th century, and considers what can accelerate them. It also adds an important qualifier to "institutions matter for violence prevention" by arguing that this does not mean convergence toward Western institutional models. Societies that prevent violence from recurring have designed solutions based on their own history and context—and have created or adapted rather than simply copied institutions from other countries.

The rest of this chapter elaborates the arguments in each of these areas. Chapters 4–9 then show how countries can restore confidence and transform institutions—and how international support can help them do so.

Sources: Collier and others 2003; Collier 2007; North, Wallis, and Weingast 2009; Weingast 1997; Fearon and Laitin 2003; Acemoglu and Robinson 2006; Keefer 2008.

stakeholders that a positive outcome is possible due to credibility issues described above. Delivering early tangible results in areas that reflect the priorities of key stakeholder groups and the broader citizenry is vital. We look at the mechanisms countries have used to deliver early, confidence-building results, including results that span the security, justice, and economic domains, and the use of combined state, community, private sector, and civil society capacities to deliver.

Confidence-building is not an end in itself. Institutional reforms to deliver security and check the power of those in government are necessary to prevent a reversion to the vicious cycle of narrow elite pacts and recurring violence (chapter 2). For this to happen, personalized leadership has to shift toward more permanent, depersonalized institutional capacity and accountability. Unless confidence-building signals and early results are linked to the development of more legitimate, accountable, and capable institutions, countries remain acutely vulnerable to violence. In chapter 5, we explore two mechanisms for sustained institutional transformation:

- ***Devoting early attention to the reform of institutions that provide citizen security, justice, and jobs.*** The interlink between security and development has been debated under the notion of human security, which encompasses freedom from fear, freedom from want, and freedom to live in dignity. By putting the security and prosperity of human beings at the center, human security addresses a wide range of threats, both from poverty and from violence, and their interactions. While acknowledging the importance of human security and its emphasis on placing people at the center of focus, this Report uses the term "citizen security" more often to sharpen our focus more on freedom from physical violence and freedom from fear of violence. The hope is to complement the discussion on the aspect of freedom from fear in the human security concept.[16] In institutional reform efforts, there is a tendency to tackle everything at once, and immediately. We explore early efforts that have proven successful in reforming institutions that directly address the correlates of violence—security, justice, and economic stresses—and which reform areas have generally been addressed more gradually.
- ***Using and exiting "best-fit" reform approaches.*** The record of backlash against change described above argues that reforms of institutions in fragile contexts need to be adapted to the political context rather than be technically perfect. We explore the extent to which countries that have become resilient to violence have often used unorthodox, "best-fit" reform approaches that allow for flexibility and innovation—public support for employment; non-electoral consultative mechanisms; combinations of state, private sector, faith-based, traditional, and community structures for service delivery, for example (see box 3.5).

Marshaling external support and resisting external stresses

Building resilience to violence and fragility is a nationally owned process, but external support and incentives and external stresses can contribute to progress or to backsliding. Outsiders cannot restore confidence and transform institutions—these processes are domestic and have to be nationally led. But to help countries restore normalcy and reduce regional and global instability, international actors can offer the following:

- ***Providing effective external support and incentives.*** Some countries have restored confidence and transformed institutions using only their own financial and technical resources, but most have drawn on diplomatic, security, and development assistance from outside. External action can help by building trust through external commitment mechanisms; delivering quick results that reinforce government

BOX 3.5 *"Best-fit" reforms*

What do we mean by "best-fit" reforms? Because of the risks of political backlash and premature overloading described earlier, in conditions of imperfect security and weak institutions, "best-practice" technocratic reform options may not work. Less orthodox approaches that are best-fit in the context of imperfect security, institutional capacity, and competitive markets can work better—but may have "second best" implications that need to be managed.[17] Consider the following five examples:

- A country wants to legitimize the formation of a government and a new reform direction through an election, but insecurity still rages over most of the territory, many voters cannot get to the polls, and polling and vote-counting cannot be monitored. Non-electoral representative mechanisms, where perceived by citizens to provide genuine voice and accountability, can be used in the short term, but in the medium term, they will require renewed legitimization.
- A country has 20–30 percent unemployment, criminal gangs recruiting from its youth population, and an economy structurally underinvested in areas of its comparative advantage. In the short term, publicly subsidized employment may be the best-fit option, but in the longer term, an exit pathway to formal employment in the private sector will be needed.
- A country needs electricity for the economy to recover, but insurgents have the capability to attack large generation and distribution facilities. Medium-size generators may cost more but may be the best-fit option in the short term. In the longer term, the country may need to exit to a lower-cost solution.
- A country wants to divert public spending to education and infrastructure, but has a large standing army and a rebel army in place. In the short term, integrating these forces and paying their salary costs may be the best-fit option, but in the longer term, the force may need to be downsized and professionalized.
- A country has tens of thousands of people accused of past human rights violations, but its formal justice system can process only 200 cases a year. A community-based process may be the best-fit option, but the formal justice system will still need to be built, with redress for families inadequately dealt with in the initial process.

Source: WDR team.

legitimacy; supporting institutional transformation with flexible approaches that respect best-fit reform options; applying realistic timelines for institutional progress; and providing incentives to reward responsible governance and to sanction failing leadership.

- ***Diminishing external stresses on fragile states.*** Reducing external stress includes action to contain the adverse impact of illegal trafficking, international corruption, and money laundering—and protecting countries against economic shocks. Some of these challenges are beyond the control of individual states. Analyzing the strengths and weakness of regional and global initiatives can ensure that national reform efforts are not overwhelmed by new pressures and that successful action in one country does not simply push problems to neighboring countries.

Doing it again—and again, and in different types of transition

Just as violence repeats, efforts to build confidence and transform institutions typically follow a repeated spiral. Countries that moved away from fragility and conflict often did so not through one decisive "make or break" moment—but through many transition moments, as the spiral path in figure 3.1 illustrates. National leaders had to build confidence in the state and to transform institutions over time, as with the Republic of Korea's transitions in the security, political, and economic spheres, which included repeated internal contests over the norms and governance of postwar society.[18] A repeated process enables space for collaborative norms and capacities to develop, and for success to build on successes in a virtuous cycle. For each loop of the spiral the same two phases recur: building confidence that positive chance is possible, prior to deepening the institutional transformation and strengthening governance outcomes.

Transitions out of fragility and repeated cycles of violence occur through preventive actions as well as post-conflict recovery. The South African transition was not a classic post–civil war transition: while low-level civil and political violence existed, leaders took preventive action before the country succumbed to outright civil war (feature 3). This is not unusual: two-thirds of the societies exiting fragility in the last 20 years did so without a major civil war.[19] Some opportunities arose when incumbent leaders recognized the need for change and created the conditions to make change happen—as in Ghana in 2003, where a potential conflict over succession rights between two clans in the north was avoided.[20] Other opportunities arose from mass protests or social action, as in Benin in 1990, where a popular movement precipitated a national conference that led to a new constitution, multiparty elections, and the end of 17 years of autocratic rule.[21] Multiple transitions have also been the general pattern in middle-income countries emerging from authoritarian rule, such as Argentina and Chile.

Even the worst natural disasters can provide opportunities for transitions from conflict and fragility: although movements to negotiate a settlement between the Indonesian government and the Free Aceh Movement (Gerakan Aceh Merdeka) began just before the devastating 2004 Indian Ocean tsunami, the resulting humanitarian crisis and massive reconstruction effort created common ground, as both sides turned to helping survivors and rebuilding Aceh. While countries can remain in a vicious cycle of severe violence for long periods, there are many opportunities for key participants to recognize that change is in their self-interest.

Do not expect too much, too soon

The passage of time permits the development of an institution's identity and the shared values that support it. And repeated successes in delivery by an institution both reinforce internal morale and build credibility in the eyes of the public. To make reasoned judgments about time frames, it is important to have historical reference points. One approach is to ask how long it took today's high- or middle-income societies to achieve current institutional attainment levels. A comparison between the most and the least developed societies is unhelpful: in 1700, for example, the Netherlands already had a real per capita GDP higher than that of the poorest 45 countries today.[22] A more useful approach is to compare current rates of institutional development among today's fragile states against rates of more recent "transformers."

Historically, the fastest transformations have taken a generation. Well-known institutional indices are relevant to reducing the risk of violence—the rule of law, corruption, human rights, democratic governance, bureaucratic quality, oversight of the security sectors, and equity for the disadvantaged.[23] How much time has it taken to move from current average levels in fragile states around the world to a threshold of "good enough governance"? The results are striking. It took the 20 fastest-moving countries an average of 17 years to get the military out of politics, 20 years to achieve functioning bureaucratic quality, and 27 years to bring corruption under reasonable control (box 3.6). This did not mean perfection, but rather adequacy. Nor should these targets be considered easy benchmarks for most of today's fragile and violence-affected countries, since the "fastest transformers" described above often had more favorable starting conditions than today's fragile states. Portugal and the Republic of Korea are among the fastest institutional transformers of the 20th century, but both started their transformations with a foundation of extensive state institutional experience, and with literacy rates far higher than

BOX 3.6 *Fastest progress in institutional transformation—An estimate of realistic ranges*

The table shows the historical range of timings that the fastest reformers in the 20th century took to achieve basic governance transformations.

Scenarios for dimensions of "state capability"

Indicator	Years to threshold at pace of:	
	Fastest 20	Fastest over the threshold
Bureaucratic quality (0–4)	20	12
Corruption (0–6)	27	14
Military in politics (0–6)	17	10
Government effectiveness	36	13
Control of corruption	27	16
Rule of law	41	17

Source: Pritchett and de Weijer 2010.

Note: Calculations are based on International Country Risk Guide indicators that ranked countries on a 0–4 scale over the period 1985–2009. The column "fastest 20" shows the average number of years the fastest 20 performers have taken to reach the threshold, and the second column shows the time it took the fastest ever country to achieve a threshold indicator score.

those in, say, the Democratic Republic of Congo or Haiti today.[24]

The track record of institutional transformations indicates that they have been getting faster over time: modern transformations can be contrasted with the 100+ years common in previous centuries. Three international trends may plausibly support a "virtuous spiral" for faster transformations:

- First, states do not operate in isolation from each other or the global system. Modern states are part of an international system that confers certain benefits and requires specific behaviors. Today these behaviors include helping to maintain interstate security (by not threatening other states, for example, and by observing "rules of warfare"), upholding international law, and abiding by treaty obligations—and behaving at home in ways consistent with international norms (by protecting human rights and eschewing corruption or unconstitutional changes in government, for instance). Global and regional norms are dealt with in more detail in chapter 6.[25]
- Second, new technologies support growing demands for good governance. People today have much easier access to information on what others think (including others across the world), and this makes it far harder for governments to ignore the interests of their broad masses.[26] Videos of events at the end of the Soviet era showed citizen movements from Nepal to Romania what could be achieved through mass protest, while recent revolutions[27] have exploited the newer personal communication technologies, such as the so-called Twitter revolution in Moldova, and the role of social media in the Middle East and North Africa.[28] States do sometimes reject citizen demands, but the price they pay today tends to be higher, measured in repression, economic stagnation, and international isolation. The spread of new technologies reinforces the circulation of international principles

and the benchmarking of government performance by citizens and civil society organizations. This, and the organizational capabilities embodied in new technology, has a huge impact on people's ability to put pressure on their state institutions (as in the Islamic Republic of Iran in 2009).[29] But the expansion of communications channels can cut either way. For example, in early 2008 in Kenya, following the contested December 2007 elections, mobile phones played a dual role of encouraging violence and preventing its spread.[30]

- Third, new technologies also create possibilities for improving service delivery, even in the most fragile situations. Technologies that enable communication between citizen groups within and across countries can help governments accelerate the type of institutional transformation that improves performance and process legitimacy. In the Democratic Republic of Congo, transitional payments were made to over 100,000 ex-combatants via cell phone since 2004, and citizen surveys have been conducted using SMS (short message service).[31] Such services would have been costly and inefficient across a vast territory with little infrastructure before the advent of technological change.

Wishful thinking on timing pervades development assistance when it comes to governance and institution building. In part it derives from the desire to meet international norms quickly, which is understandable: human rights abuses and gross corruption are abhorrent. But goals are then set that require state capability, sometimes without considering whether the capability exists, and sometimes under the presumption that it can be created quickly (given resources and "political will"). This is mistaken. Even the Republic of Korea, which had the resources and political will (and a higher level of human capital than many fragile states today), took a generation to make these changes.[32] No country today is likely to be able to make it in three to five years, the typical timeline of national leadership and the international community (box 3.7).

Adapt to different contexts

The process necessary to restore confidence and transform institutions are similar in countries that have different combinations of stresses and institutional characteristics; between low- and middle-income countries, and even high-income countries facing subnational violence; and between countries facing violence of purely criminal origins and those facing political and civil conflict. While the dynamics of change may be similar, the framework must be applied differentially, depending on the specific features of the case in question.

In some countries, stresses from international trafficking in natural resources or infiltration of armed groups from abroad are important, while in others, trafficking of drugs

BOX 3.7 *Optimism or wishful thinking?*

Haiti at the end of 2009 had made considerable advances in restoring security and better governance in the wake of the 2004 crisis following the removal of President Jean-Bertrand Aristide. Security had been restored in urban areas. Trust in government institutions, including the police, had risen. Basic public finance functions were functioning. And considerable humanitarian and community services and small reconstruction projects had been launched.

Before the earthquake struck Haiti in 2010, the government was in discussions with various parts of the international community—diplomatic, peacekeeping, and development—on pressing institutional transformations. These included fundamental economic restructuring needed to create jobs in agriculture and textiles; the appointment of personnel in both the Supreme Court and the lower courts to restore better basic functioning to the justice sector; constitutional changes to, among other things, reduce the frequency of elections; increased decentralization in the administration; rapid expansion of the police force; anti-corruption measures to avoid diversions of aid funds; revenue reform to increase the tax base; and action against drug traffickers to address shifts in transit patterns into the Caribbean. All these actions were to take place over 18 months when Haiti also had two elections scheduled.

The tragedy that overtook the country in January 2010 makes it impossible to know whether these reforms would have been completed. The link between violence and institutions, and of historical state-building experiences elsewhere, does show that these changes would make Haitian society more resilient to renewed violence—but that no country has ever successfully completed this level of change in 18 months.

Sources: WDR consultation with government officials, United Nations and donor representatives, local nongovernmental organizations (NGOs), and community-based organization representatives in Haiti, 2010.

BOX 3.8 *Spectrum of situation-specific challenges and opportunities*

<table>
<tr><td colspan="2">Types of violence: Civil, criminal, cross-border, subnational, ideological, or any combination of these</td></tr>
<tr><td>Transition opportunity: Gradual/limited to immediate/major space for change</td><td>Key stakeholders: Internal vs. external stakeholders; state vs. nonstate stakeholders; low-income vs. middle-high-income stakeholders</td></tr>
<tr><td>Key stresses: Internal vs. external stresses; economic vs. political stresses; high vs. low level of divisions among groups</td><td>Institutional challenges: Low capacity constraints vs. high capacity; low accountability vs. high accountability; exclusion vs. inclusion</td></tr>
</table>

Source: WDR team.

may be the principal external stress. Internal stresses stemming from actual or perceived inequalities between groups may take the form of urban-rural divides in some countries, ethnic or geographical in others, or religious in still others. Economic shocks or high unemployment may be important in some countries but not in others.

Institutional challenges in dealing with these stresses also vary (box 3.8). Some countries have to deal with weak capacity in both state and civil society institutions, combined with weak accountability; others may possess reasonably strong capacity and resources, but face challenges in state legitimacy because the state is perceived to lack accountability in political representation, in its management of public resources, or in its respect for human rights—or is perceived to represent the interests of only one section of the population, to the exclusion of others. In some countries, the challenge is national: all areas of the country are affected. In others, it is contained but still significant: subnational areas exhibit characteristics of fragility, with risks of actual or potential violence.

Stresses and institutional characteristics also change over time, with new stresses arising and new capabilities being developed. In addition, the trajectory of change is important. In some countries, events may provide an opportunity for major political, social, and economic change. In others, a history of recent deterioration may mean that upcoming transition moments present an opportunity to reverse deterioration in the situation, but may not yet present a real opportunity to deliver decisive improvements. The types of transition moment that offer an opportunity for change of course vary enormously—from elections to external crises to new government reform plans to anniversaries that are important in the country's national psyche.

Thus, differentiated application of the framework is essential. In applying the framework, the choice of different types of "inclusive-enough" coalitions and priorities for early results, the sequencing of institutional transformation efforts, and the development of politically innovative institutions all depend on country-specific circumstances. Equally, external support and incentives and international actions to address external stresses need to be designed to fit the specifics of each country situation. Throughout this Report, a differentiated political economy framework is used to ask the following questions:

- What stresses does the country face that increase the risks of violence occurring or reoccurring? Areas to explore include the infiltration of external armed groups and trafficking networks; potential corruption pressures from natural resources or other forms of trafficking; political, social, or economic inequalities and tensions between groups; high or rising unemployment and income shocks; and stresses that arise in terms of ex-combatant or gang-member activity and circulation of arms.

- What institutional characteristics are paramount: capacity, including in different state and nonstate institutions; accountability, including for different aspects—political representation, corruption, respect for human rights; inclusion of different groups, ethnic, religious, class, geographical? What risks do these institutional characteristics present for national actors and international actors?
- Which stakeholder groups are crucial to building confidence and transforming institutions, and what signals, commitment mechanisms, and results are most important to these groups? This may include different groupings among political actors, security force leadership, excluded citizens, business, labor, faith-based institutions, or other influential civil society groups, and external actors such as neighboring governments, donors, and investors.
- What types of transition moments are coming up, and what opportunities do they present? This needs to include not only a creative assessment of opportunities for change, but also a realistic assessment of what these opportunities can and cannot achieve—for example, some upcoming transition moments may offer an opportunity to reverse deteriorations, but not yet consolidate all the dimensions of change needed for long-term resilience to violence.

* * *

Institutions matter, doubly so for countries affected by violence. It is well known in the economic literature that institutions matter for economic development.[33] The emerging econometric evidence suggests that countries are doubly affected by very weak institutions—because the lack of institutions slows development, but also because weak institutions make them more vulnerable to violence, which, itself, reverses development. They find themselves in a trap: the institutional reforms they need to exit the vicious cycle of violence and temporary elite pacts are difficult to achieve, precisely because the threat of violence remains very real.[34] As a result, the virtuous spiral of restoring confidence and transforming institutions cannot expand—since credibility is missing where violence (including the legacy of violence or the threat of violence) is present, leaders must first engage in confidence-building through inclusive enough pacts and early results for their commitments to be credible.

Only after actors have built trust and established their commitment to peaceful development through confidence-building can they then credibly undertake the institutional reforms necessary to escape the vicious cycle. The repeated expansion of the WDR framework spiral is important because transformation takes time. Leaders, stakeholders, and the international community must remember that societies will go through multiple cycles of confidence-building and institutional reform before they can achieve the resilience to violence necessary for "development as usual."

FEATURE 3 *Restoring security in Colombia*

Types of violence: Trafficking, criminal and gang violence, civil conflict	
Transition opportunity: Preventive action in the face of rising criminality and failed peace talks	**Key stakeholders:** Government, armed groups, citizens, civil society, regional, international partners, criminal networks
Key stresses: Legacies of violence, presence of international trafficking and criminal networks, social and economic inequity	**Institutional challenges:** Absence in parts of the country of state institutions; legacy of capacity, inclusion, and accountability challenges

Colombia, a middle-income country, has experienced peace for only 47 of its first 200 years of independence. Until the turn of the 21st century, large parts of the territory were marked by the absence of state institutions, and a long sequence of amnesties and negotiations with armed groups merely recycled, but did not resolve, incentives for violence.

Over the past two decades, a number of new initiatives were taken to restore confidence and security. These have been led by both local and national governments and have had a significant impact in recent years.

DESEPAZ—an acronym for Desarrollo, Seguridad y Paz, or development, security, and peace—started in Cali in 1992, based on epidemiological studies of the violence that afflicted the city (murder rates had climbed from 23 per 100,000 inhabitants to 93 from 1983 to 1992). Contributing to significant reductions in violence, its programs included mulitsectoral coordination of arms control, policing and justice, education, housing, and recreation activities.

With homicide rates very high, Bogotá, like Cali, implemented a multisectoral approach in the 1990s that included cooperation between community police and local residents, and initiatives to stimulate the local economy. These and other interventions reduced homicide rates in Bogotá from 80 per 100,000 people to 28 between 1993 and 2004, and increased arrest rates by a factor of four.

More recently, Medellín also experienced a dramatic reduction in levels of criminal violence. As a city directly affected by rebel groups and the violence of the drug cartels, Medellín became in 1991 the most violent city in the world, with a homicide rate of 381 per 100,000. The impact of national and local security policies combined with social development strategies helped reduce this to 29 per 100,000 people in 2007.

Serious efforts to negotiate with rebel groups began in the 1990s and included the creation in 1998 of a neutral zone under the control of the Revolutionary Armed Forces of Colombia (FARC). The failure of these efforts was blamed by many on the FARC, and this helped build popular support for a shift in strategy that branded the FARC as a criminal group. Beginning in 2002, the new administration decided not to continue with the previous government's four-year negotiation with the FARC and the National Liberation Army (ELN). It focused instead on consolidating state control throughout Colombia, protecting the population and fighting the illicit drug trade—aims subsequently formalized in the government's "democratic security" policy. Based on an integrated approach to restoring confidence through security, private-sector job creation, and social cohesion, the new policy aimed at "institucionalidad," or building and transforming institutions.

From 2002 to 2008, this approach had considerable success: the armed forces were expanded from about 300,000 in 2002 to more than 400,000 in 2007,[35] and state presence throughout the country reduced violence, particularly in rural areas. National homicide rates were halved, from 70 per 100,000 people to 36,[36] households forcefully displaced fell by 60 percent, and kidnappings fell by 83 percent.[37] To increase the transparent functioning of government, Colombia improved on measures of corruption (from -0.44 to 0.24), the rule of law (from -0.92 to -0.50), government effectiveness (from -0.40 to 0.13), and accountability (from -0.50 to -0.26).[38] The reduction in violence helped sustain rapid economic growth—at an average of 4.9 percent a year between 2002 and 2008, almost three times the rate in the previous seven years.[39] These impressive security achievements did not come without costs, however: more than 300,000 people were newly displaced in 2008. Crime and insecurity have also begun to rise again in some urban areas, such as Medellín (an increase in the homicide rate from 33.8 to 94.5 per 100,000 in 2007–09),[40] as new forms of organized crime have emerged. Nor has the FARC insurgency been decisively ended.

Several key lessons follow:

- The government used an "inclusive-enough" approach, building broad national support for security goals when ceasing negotiations with the FARC. After an in-depth dialogue with business groups, a "wealth tax" paid by the country's richest taxpayers was introduced in 2002, earmarked for the security effort. Social network campaigns were

FEATURE 3 *Restoring security in Colombia (continued)*

mounted against kidnapping and later against FARC's use of violence.

- Early confidence-building measures were crucial. The government deployed military resources to protect the main road network, sponsoring convoys of private vehicles that allowed many Colombians to travel between major cities in safety for the first time in years. Mobility increased markedly: the number of vehicles passing through toll stations rose from about 60,000 vehicles in 2003 to close to 150,000 vehicles in 2009.
- Combining political, security, and economic development measures was central to the approach. The government established a national agency, reporting to the presidency, to coordinate military, police, and civilian developmental efforts in the least secure areas. The multidisciplinary teams of the Centro de Coordinación de Acción Integral (CCAI), worked in the same offices and developed joint plans to guide their actions. Common concepts—"democratic security" and the restoration of "institutionality" to areas where the state had been absent—were important for close collaboration between military and civilian actors.

WDR consultations underlined two big challenges going forward. The first is to match the success in restoring confidence and security with longer-term institutional transformation. Surveys of popular perceptions show an enormous increase in confidence in both the security situation and in the delivery of education services, as well as in overall trust in the

a. Popular confidence dramatically improved in services and security

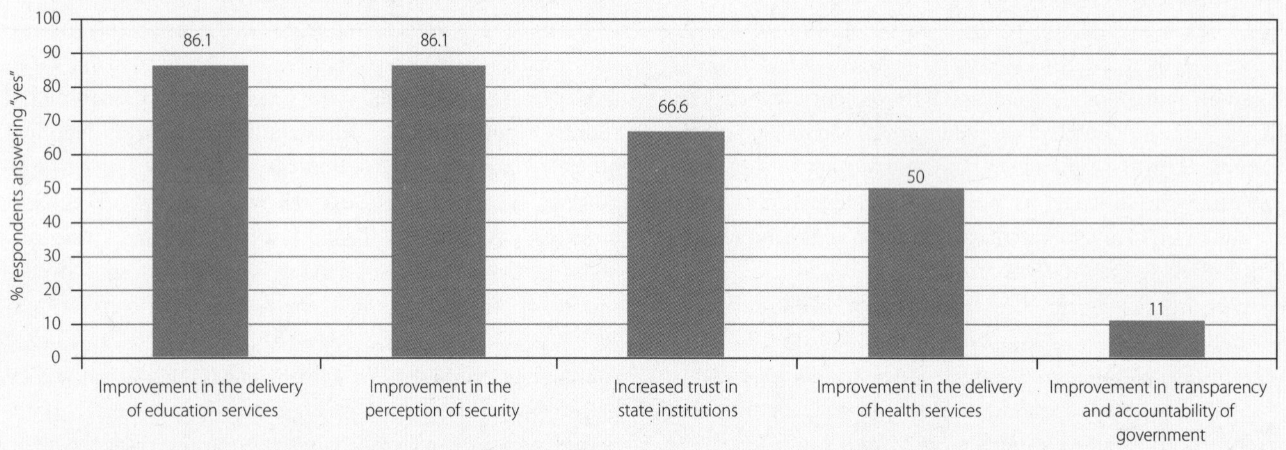

Source: WDR team calculations based on results from Bøås, Tiltnes, and Flatø 2010 for representative surveys conducted in early 2010.

state (see figure a). However, Amnesty International gave Colombia its lowest rating in 2008, and Freedom House maintained a rating of 4 (on a scale of 7) between 2002 and 2008.

A second challenge relates to security and justice institutions. The justice system, while preserving its independence, was not reformed at the same pace as the military and police, and had difficulty keeping pace with the caseloads emerging from more effective policing. A culture of impunity persisted, and threatened progress made in security sector reform. National institutions also faced a credibility test in relation to so-called false-positive deaths: ongoing investigations and prosecutions are looking into evidence that innocent poor young men were killed and falsely portrayed as rebels killed in military operations.

Colombia's success in attacking the larger drug cartels also had unintended effects on its neighbors. The area under coca cultivation has increased in Bolivia and Peru. Along with increases in productivity, this boosted South America's potential cocaine production to 865 metric tons in 2008, up from 800 metric tons in 2002.

Sources: Arboleda 2010; UNODC 2010b; World Bank 2010n; Guerrero 1999; Centro de Coordinación de Acción Integral 2010; WDR team consultations with government officials, civil society representatives, and security personnel in Colombia, 2010; WDR interview with former President Álvaro Uribe, 2010; WDR team calculations.

REFLECTIONS FROM ADVISORY COUNCIL MEMBERS: *2011 WORLD DEVELOPMENT REPORT*

BOX 3.9 *Lessons of the South African transition: Restoring confidence and transforming institutions*

Jay Naidoo, Chairman of Global Alliance for Improved Nutrition; Former General Secretary, Congress of South African Trade Unions; Minister of Reconstruction and Development, South Africa; and Former Chairman of the Development Bank of Southern Africa; *WDR Advisory Council Member*

Based on discussions with Mac Maharaj, Sydney Mufamadi, Roelf Meyer, Leon Wessels, Fanie van der Merwe, and Jayendra Naidoo.

In May 2010, as part of the *World Development Report 2011* process, I was part of a discussion with key negotiators from the ANC Alliance and National Party in which we reflected on the lessons that could be learnt from the political transition to democracy in 1994. We were all agreed that a prerequisite for successful political transitions had to be strong national ownership and that the peace process underpinning it had to be embedded at a local level and deliver a peace dividend that benefitted local communities. The following points are what I extracted from South Africa's experiences:

There were ***multiple transition*** points which required efforts from the protagonists to shift the debate, rather than only one "moment" of transition in 1994. These included citizen protests and strikes; legalization of unionism for black workers; the start of undercover contacts in the late 1980s; the release of Nelson Mandela and the unbanning of the ANC and political parties in February 1990; the National Peace Accord in 1991; CODESA in 1992; the Transitional Executive Council and associated bodies in 1993–94; the Reconstruction and Development Program in 1993–94; the Growth, Employment and Redistribution Program in 1996; and the local government democratic transition which only culminated in 2000.

Restoring confidence

South Africa's transition steps in the early 1990s were preceded by a much longer period of change in mentality, or paradigm shift, amongst the protagonists that gave credibility to the process:

- On the ANC Alliance side, this included the shift to a *broader, more inclusive approach*, and the realization of the need to ensure incentives for the National Party and the white population.
- On the National Party side, this included the shift from thinking in terms of group rights and protection of minorities to thinking in terms of individual rights and majority rule.
- Certain signals which were perceived as irreversible (notably the unconditional release of Nelson Mandela and the suspension of the ANC's armed struggle) were critical in maintaining trust between parties.
- Leaders on both sides had to move quickly to avoid getting bogged down by narrow interests in their own constituencies, in particular in periods of devastating crisis such as the political assassination of Chris Hani.

After the 1994 elections, *delivering a few early results*—including maternal and infant healthcare and using community structures to improve water supply—were important to maintain confidence in our new government.

Transforming institutions

Unorthodox, locally adapted reforms. Participants agreed that much of the global communication on South Africa's transition has been on the specific organizational form of the institutions used (for example, Truth and Reconciliation Committees, national peace committees); and that in fact it may be more useful to consider the underlying principles and approaches (including those described above), on the basis that each country needs to design their own institutional forms if they are to have full ownership of political processes.

Challenges in prioritizing and sequencing. In addition to some of the key principles emerging from South Africa's successful transition, participants reflected on mistakes made or opportunities missed which may be of use when other countries consider these experiences. Four elements were highlighted as particularly important:

- Very little of the discussions leading up to 1994 considered preparation for delivery through the civil service. Problems which later emerged as a result include lack of preparation in setting up the provinces and defining local government delivery responsibilities. We should have anticipated the capacity constraints as we increased the number of provinces and set up new institutions.
- Too little attention to job creation for youth and risks of criminal violence meant that we did not fully address the critical need to ensure that the new generation who had not lived through the apartheid struggle as adults were provided with a strong stake—and economic opportunities—in the new democratic state.
- There was a need for tradeoffs on timing and the maintenance of social consensus to manage the mismatch between the aspirational goals of the Reconstruction and Development Program, the macro and fiscal framework to pay for them, and the institutional capacity to implement them.
- There was too much of an assumption that 1994 marked the culmination of a process of democratization and reconciliation. Relatively little attention was given to what was meant by the transformation to a constitutional state; the continued role of civil society in deepening not just democratization and accountability, but also delivery; and there was a need for a deeper and more thorough ongoing debate on racism, inequality, and social exclusion.

Notes

1. According to Margaret Levi, "Trust is, in fact, a holding word for a variety of phenomena that enable individuals to take risks in dealing with others, solve collective action problems, or act in ways that seem contrary to standard definitions of self-interest." Furthermore, Levi notes that "At issue is a *cooperative venture*, which implies that the truster possesses a reasonable belief that well-placed trust will yield positive returns and is willing to act upon that belief" (Braithwaite and Levi 1998, 78).
2. Similar problems arise in the transition from communism to a rule-of-law state. The thought process might be as follows: "If I build value in a new firm rather than stripping the assets of the state, I will gain only if rule of law is established. That will happen only if others demand rule of law, too. If others don't believe rule of law will be established, they will prefer to strip assets rather than build value, so they will be unlikely to demand rule of law, and in that case, I'd be crazy to build value in a new firm. Thus, even though most people would be better off building value under rule of law than stripping assets in a lawless state, given my expectations of political development, I'm better off stripping assets."
3. A 30 percent increase in people who believe that growth will improve in the next 12 months is associated with a 1 percent increase in actual growth rates in the subsequent year, significant at the 5 percent level.
4. A few societies have very strong state capacity, but score low on governance indicators because they are highly exclusionary—South Africa under apartheid is an example. These countries will have less difficulty in implementing promises because their military and civilian organizations are capable. But it is possible that, even in these cases, institutional weaknesses in shared values and cohesion make it difficult to deliver on change. Indeed, in South Africa change has not been a simple process.
5. Collier, Hoeffler, and Söderbom 2008; Fearon 2010a; Acemoglu and Robinson 2006.
6. Goldstone 2010.
7. de Figueiredo and Weingast 1999; Acemoglu, Johnson, and Robinson 2005.
8. Rich 2010.
9. Economic theory helps us understand the consequences of a perception of impunity that increases willingness to use violent means. Chapter 2 referred to the way in which insecurity dynamics produce "prisoner's dilemmas," where lack of trust between two actors undermines their ability to cooperate to produce mutually beneficial outcomes. Economic theory shows that if the actors in question believe they will encounter the same dilemma again in the future, their calculation may differ—they might recognize that taking a risk by trusting their counterpart in the present can produce important payoffs in the future. So-called iterated prisoner's dilemmas make cooperation possible, though not guaranteed. If a society is confronted by a situation where many actors believe that others within society may use violence to resist change, their willingness to bet on future cooperation is diminished. Where insecurity is not an immediate issue, betting on future payoffs makes sense; where the future is highly uncertain, logic dictates placing an excessive premium on protecting existing privileges and resources, not risking them for collective gains. See Axelrod 1984.
10. See Keefer, Neumayer, and Plümper 2010.
11. See UN Security Council 2010a, WDR consultation with government officials, UN donor representatives, local nongovernmental organizations, and community-based organizations in Haiti, 2010.
12. An alternative perspective to the intertwined relationship between institutions and violence can be found in Cramer 2006.
13. The WDR defines "citizen security" as both freedom from physical violence and freedom from fear of violence. Applied to the lives of *all* members of a society (whether nationals of the country or otherwise), it encompasses security at home; in the workplace; and in political, social, and economic interactions with the state and other members of society. Similar to human security, "citizen security" places people at the center of efforts to prevent and recover from violence. Also see Frühling, Tulchin, and Golding 2003.
14. Confidence-building in mediation means building trust between adversaries; in financial crises, trust in markets means that governments are adopting sound policies and will be capable of implementing them. The WDR defines the term as building trust between groups of citizens who have been divided by violence, between citizens and the state, and between the state and other key stakeholders (neighbors, international partners, investors) whose political, behavioral, or financial support is needed to deliver a positive outcome.
15. These incentives are not always enough. Chapter 4 discusses cases where leaders are unwilling to recognize an impending crisis or take action, and the approaches used to resolve these situations.
16. Building on the Commission on Human Security 2003 report, the importance of human security has

been recognized in the UN General Assembly 2005b resolution adopted at the 2005 World Summit, the UN General Assembly 2009b report, and UN General Assembly 2010 Resolution, as well as in other fora, such as Asia-Pacific Economic Cooperation, G8, and World Economic Forum.

17. Throughout this report, the term "best-fit" describes solutions that are fitted to context of the society at the moment and may not be the first best solutions by other metrics. Thus, these solutions invoke the concept of the "second best" as used in economic theory—reforms may only be optimal once all distortions and considerations are taken into account. In this way, best-fit solutions may be optimal given all of the economic, political, physical, and institutional constraints and conditions.
18. Bedeski 1994; Cumings 2005; Chang and Lee 2006.
19. Based on historic CPIA scores, 40 countries would have been classified as fragile for five or more years between 1977 and 1989. Box 2.10 showed that 17 of these countries remained fragile until 2009 and that 16 of those experienced minor or major civil war. Of the 23 that "escaped" fragility, 15 had no war, 4 had minor civil war and 4 had major civil war between 1990 and 2009. WDR team calculation. Also see Mata and Ziaja 2009.
20. Odendaal 2010; Ojielo 2007; UNDPA 2010a.
21. Encyclopedia of the Nations 2010.
22. Pritchett and de Weijer 2010.
23. The indices are the Quality of Government Institute's "quality of government" indicator (derived from International Country Risk Guide data; the Kaufmann, Kraay and Mastruzzi indicator of "government effectiveness"; the Failed State Index's "progressive deterioration of public services" indicator, and the Bertelsmann Transformation Index's "resource efficiency" indicator). See Pritchett and de Weijer 2010.
24. Pritchett and de Weijer 2010.
25. Global and regional norms play an essential part in preventing violence by constraining leadership abuses of power, and in supporting local institutional transformations by helping maintain a focus on goals and functions rather than particular institutional forms. These norms can take the form of formal international agreements and can also manifest as social movements, such as the Otpor movement.
26. For example, while both Myanmar and the Democratic People's Republic of Korea have—to varying degrees of success—used communication and travel bans to limit access to information and maintain control domestically, their ability to restrict information has declined dramatically in recent years, as Internet access in Myanmar, and satellite television in both countries, convey images of the world outside. See Horsey and Win Myint 2010.
27. Color revolutions refer to a series of spontaneous movements that arose in succession in several former Soviet republics and one Balkan state during the early 2000s. These were mainly nonviolent protests advocating for democracy against governments seen as corrupt and/or authoritarian. Starting as small spontaneous actions, they evolved within days or weeks into mass movements that toppled governments and instituted new democratic regimes. Each movement adopted a specific color or flower as its symbol, and at the center of these movements were nongovernmental organizations (NGOs) and particularly student activists. These movements were successful in Serbia (2000), Georgia (Rose Revolution 2003), Ukraine (Orange Revolution 2004), and the Kyrgyz Republic (Tulip Revolution 2005). See Kuzio 2006; D'Anieri 2006; Michalcik and Riggs 2007.
28. See Mungiu-Pippidi and Munteanu 2009.
29. See, for example, Afshari and Underwood 2009.
30. Goldstein and Rotich 2008.
31. MDRP 2006.
32. Bedeski 1994; Cumings 2005; Chang and Lee 2006.
33. North 1989, 1995; Rodrik 2000; Acemoglu, Johnson, and Robinson 2005.
34. There is an important difference between what this report argues and the "conflict trap" described by Collier and others 2003. In a "conflict trap," low incomes lead to conflict, and conflict leads to low incomes, creating a low-level equilibrium. The WDR focuses on the institutional deficit: the institutions that enable the peaceful resolution of contests are missing from fragile environments. With actors lacking the means to make credible commitments to reform, societies are unable to break free from the threat of violence. A low-level equilibrium of dysfunctional institutions and recurrent violence is thereby created.
35. See Arboleda 2010.
36. WDR team calculations.
37. See Arboleda 2010.
38. Kaufmann, Kraay, and Mastruzzi 2010a.
39. WDR team calculations, based on World Bank 2010n.
40. Municipio de Medellín 2010.

Chapter 4 analyzes country lessons on building confidence through coalitions and early results. Most states moving back from the brink of violence have developed "inclusive-enough" coalitions for action, with different forms suiting their circumstances. In forming such coalitions, leaders took action to build trust by signaling that new policies would be different from the past and would not be reversed. They built confidence by achieving a few concrete results as a prelude to wider institutional transformation. States that have succeeded in early confidence-building measures have often done so through a pragmatic blending of policy tools and by calling on non-state capacity, both civic and international.

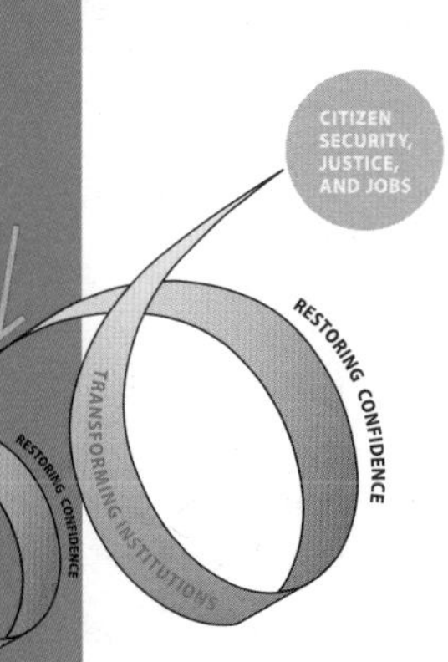

CHAPTER 4

Restoring confidence: Moving away from the brink

Drawing on lessons from national reformers

Leadership actions to restore confidence of stakeholders and citizens in collective capacities for change are a crucial first step in moving away from the brink of violence. As chapters 2 and 3 described, the trust that the population and stakeholders have in state institutions to deal with violence can become shaky when insecurity is rising, or in the aftermath of repeated bouts of conflict. Knowledge about effective ways to restore confidence in countries affected by violence is limited. This chapter thus expands ideas explored in the policy and academic worlds, with lessons drawn from the WDR background papers and country consultations, including the views of national reformers involved in efforts to lead their countries away from the brink.[1]

Analysis of country cases reveals a variety of pathways away from the brink—but also suggests two common elements. The first lesson is the importance of building inclusive-enough coalitions and identifying the signals and commitment mechanisms[2] that can galvanize support for change. Second, national reformers have delivered results on the ground to build confidence in citizen security, justice, and economic prospects. In both elements, successful transitions made astute use of supplemental capacity beyond government: from the private sector, from traditional institutions, and from nongovernmental organizations (NGOs). This chapter considers what makes coalitions "inclusive-enough" and the signals, commitment mechanisms, and early results that can help achieve momentum for later institutional transformation.[3]

These pathways away from violence have been analyzed in the literature. Stedman and Nilsson suggest that pacts to end violence need not be all-inclusive—they can promote peace if they are minimally inclusive at the beginning.[4] Fearon, Keefer, Azam and Mesnard examine why some conflicts may be more intractable because of distrust and how commitment mechanisms (ways to ensure that promises will be difficult to reverse) can be designed to solve those problems; examples include peace agreements, power-sharing arrangements, and security sector reform.[5]

Societies use these and other commitment mechanisms to suit conditions on the ground. More important than the form of these mechanisms is their adaptability to changing conditions over the course of multiple transitions. The lessons explored in this chapter build on this research through practical country examples and cross-country lessons.

Inclusive-enough coalitions

This section looks at country experiences in building "inclusive-enough" pacts for change; different approaches to coalition-building at national, subnational, and local levels; and the guiding principles that emerge on what is "inclusive-enough." It considers the type of immediate actions and signals on future policy that have built support for change.

How inclusive is inclusive enough?

Action by national leaders during transitional moments can be decisive in preventing violence. Two contrasting cases illustrate this point. In Kenya, warnings of election-related violence in 2007 led Kenyan groups and several foreign governments to offer support to peace committees and other forms of mediation or violence prevention; leaders of the various political factions refused them.[6] The predicted violence following the announcement of the election results led to nearly 1,000 deaths and the displacement of 300,000 people. By contrast, the Ghanaian government took decisive action in 2003 to forestall a potentially serious dispute over succession rights between rival Dagomba clans in the north. After national efforts failed to find compromise between the feuding groups, the government requested United Nations (UN) assistance in designing confidence-building interventions, including the facilitation of government and civil society dialogue and negotiations.[7] That action defused the potential for violence, and the country avoided a major conflict that could have undermined the 2004 national elections.

Leadership is sometimes shared, and sometimes dominated by individuals. That was the case with Mali's General Amadou Toumani Touré, whose willingness to deal differently with the Tuareg rebellion launched a sustained tradition of democratic resolution.[8] South Africa benefited both from the exceptional personal leadership of President Nelson Mandela and the depth of collective leadership developed during decades of resistance in the African National Congress, the Communist Party, and the civil society organizations of the United Democratic Front.

Transition opportunities have led to more decisive action where leaders have built coalitions for change.[9] Inclusive-enough approaches may be formal power-sharing arrangements, as with the government of the Democratic Unionist Party and Sinn Féin in Northern Ireland.[10] Most frequently, the coalitions are informal, as with the Colombia and Timor-Leste approaches described below. Some successful experiences and challenges in coalition-building in situations of political and civil conflict include the following:

- Inclusive rather than exclusive approaches can be important in preventing a recurrence of violence. Timor-Leste leadership reached out in 2007 to other political parties and to entrepreneurs to help in reconstruction, involving independent figures and those from other parties in government, and providing for local business involvement. This approach contrasted with that taken in the period between independence in 2002 and renewed violence in 2006, when the ruling party engaged relatively little with civil society, the church, or other domestic actors to build support for its program.[11]
- In some situations, specific focus on building national and provincial support for change simultaneously can be important. In Aceh, Indonesia, which had experienced a long and costly civil conflict, a careful process of mediation involving the Free Aceh Movement (Gerakan Aceh Merdeka or GAM)—a rebel movement—and leadership and government leaders from the province and from Jakarta secured a peace agreement in 2005 that mobilized a broad range of stakeholder support, as well as international engagement (feature 4).
- Inclusion strategies can change over time. In Sierra Leone, the initial inclusion of the Revolutionary United Front (RUF) in the

1999 Lomé Agreement was subsequently repudiated in 2000 as conditions changed and following repeated abuses. Although initial arrangements did not succeed, they were nonetheless necessary to encourage the RUF leaders to cease fighting. Having the leaders in the capital also helped in monitoring their activities once the arrangements collapsed.[12]

- Conversely, in Sudan, peace talks between 2000 and 2005 were held between a narrow group of leaders on both sides, with both North and South continuing to face internal divisions that were not managed through a broadening of the coalition after the peace agreement was signed in January 2005.[13]

Inclusive-enough coalition-building has also been important in successful non-post-conflict political transitions, as the following examples demonstrate:

- The political transition in Chile in 1990 and onward involved heavily institutionalized political mechanisms to reach agreement in policy among the five political parties of the "concertación democratica"; outreach to labor and civil society; and clear signals to business that responsible economic management would be part of the new direction. In Chile, as in other middle-income country political transitions such as Indonesia, a delicate balancing approach was used to undertake security and justice reforms while maintaining support from the military for change.[14]
- In South Africa, inclusive-enough coalition-building in the run-up to the 1994 election meant involving all political parties and civil society in discussions over the country's future, although the African National Congress (ANC) maintained a hierarchy where it led decision-making among other ANC Alliance and Democratic Front members.
- The Colombian government mobilized the military, civil service, business groups, and civil society actors in 2003 to support its democratic security policy. This process excluded the FARC (Revolutionary Armed Forces of Colombia), whose breaches of the peace talk provisions from the late 1990s to 2002 created nationwide demand for action against the kidnappings and violence. Government communication and outreach bolstered popular confidence for difficult military and police actions and civil service reforms.[15]
- The Consultative Assembly (CA), established to draft a new constitution, was the basis of Ghana's inclusive-enough coalition-building process during the transition to multiparty democracy. The 260-member Consultative Assembly was made up of 117 representatives from the District and Metropolitan Assemblies, 121 representatives of various "established organizations" (that is, corporate groups) and associations, and 22 government appointees. The Assembly, which contained many opposition sympathizers, displayed independence and drafted a constitution that was approved in a referendum that set the stage for an orderly nonviolent transition.[16]

In diverse circumstances of negotiated peace settlements, military victories, and political crises, leaders have often used broad-based governments to send a positive signal on inclusion—but it is no simple matter. Cabinets in developed countries not affected by violence, where efficiency is a primary concern, generally range from 15 to 20 appointments in each administration. But when stability, rather than efficiency, drives the composition, cabinets are often larger, as in Kenya and Zimbabwe.[17] When fragmented decision-making is exacerbated by internal divisions, the efficiency costs can be considerable.

The stresses that spur violence can be rooted in provincial or local as well as national dynamics, and local coalitions can be crucial in preventing violence. The links made between central and provincial govern-

REFLECTIONS FROM ADVISORY COUNCIL MEMBERS: *2011 WORLD DEVELOPMENT REPORT*

BOX 4.1 *"All politics is local."*

George Yeo, Minister of Foreign Affairs, Singapore; *WDR Advisory Council Member*

Successful efforts must begin at the local level. Without emphasis on local results, citizens lose confidence in their government's ability to provide a better life. Actions to restore security, create trust, generate employment, and provide services in local communities lay the foundation for national progress. It is not enough to deliver results in big cities. In cases of ethnic and religious strife, where mutual insecurity can feed on itself, a local authority that is seen to be fair and impartial by all groups is absolutely essential before the process of healing and recovery can take place. This was Singapore's experience when we had racial riots in the 1960s. A trusted leader can make a decisive difference.

ments in Aceh (see feature 4) are one example, as are the conflict prevention approaches in Ghana described above and attention to the impartiality of local administration in Singapore (box 4.1). Country lessons also raise two developmental mechanisms to support local coalition building and strengthen relations between the state and citizens at the local level: first, where government provides resources directly to communities to carry out development activities (through community-driven development, or CDD), and second, where communities do not necessarily control funds, but are active partners in actions undertaken by others (local administrations, nongovernmental organizations (NGOs), international partners) that are implemented for their benefit.

Building coalitions at the local level—where the state works with community leaders to combat violence—can be an important part of responses to criminal violence as well as political violence. Across Latin America, approaches that work with local community leaders and combine security and development initiatives have replaced the older, security-only "mano duro" (iron fist) approaches. Higher-income countries have used similar approaches, from community policing in the United Kingdom or France to building local alliances to combat drug-trafficking and gang activity in Los Angeles (see box 4.2).

The private sector is also crucial for countries coping with and emerging from violence. While in the short run, recovery from violence can be supported by external assistance or natural resource revenues, the path to longer-term development is dependent on a healthy private sector. Private sector activity often cuts across ethnic and religious lines, where rules-based competition is the cornerstone. Violence shortens the time horizons of consumers, producers, traders, and policy makers. Outreach to the private sector can help build a sense of the long term, which is critical for planning, investment in the future, and sustainable growth.[18] In the Colombia, Chile, and Timor-Leste examples above, reaching out to the private sector was a crucial part of coalition building.[19]

The ability of leaders to govern and to effect change also depends on a network of civil society and informal institutions and actors—and the interaction between the state and informal institutions takes on even greater significance in societies ravaged by violence.[20] Many nongovernment initiatives have helped contain or stop violence.[21] The inclusion of civil society, informal, and traditional institutions in inclusive-enough coalitions helps in acquiring broader societal legitimacy and in ensuring that citizen security, justice, and jobs reach all segments of society. Community, traditional, and civil society structures can also be crucial partners for the delivery of early results where state reach and trust with violence-affected communities is low. By drawing on nonstate capacity, governments can "stretch" their

BOX 4.2 *Gang-related homicides in Los Angeles*

In Los Angeles, gang and drug-related violence accounts for a large percentage of crime (nearly 50 percent of homicides) and negatively affects education, health, business and jobs, housing prices, and the ability for families to enjoy parks and other leisure activities. While gangs are not new to Los Angeles County, gang membership ballooned from negligible in 1970 to 70,000 to 100,000 30 years later. Almost 6,000 people died from gang violence between 1995 and 2006, comparable to the civil war in Uganda over the same period, where estimates of battle deaths between 1995 to 2006 range from 3,300 to 16,000, with a best estimate of 7,500 (Uganda has more than twice the population of the Los Angeles metropolitan area).[22]

After years of struggling to deal with gang-related violence, a team of experts recently wrote, "In short, Los Angeles needs a Marshall Plan to end gang violence" (Advancement Project 2007, 1). New initiatives aim to prevent violence before it escalates by funding and training outreach workers who can mediate disputes, stop rumors, and engage with those who cause violence ("shotcallers"). The strategy involves regular confidence-building initiatives through frequent consultations among key stakeholders, which can include reformed gang members and community leaders. This outreach approach also involves multisectoral coordination (law enforcement officers conduct community visits accompanied by parole officers, educators, child services, and representatives from other city departments as well as civil society) to develop relationships and trust between the community and law enforcement.

Sources: WDR team consultations with law enforcement and civil society and Brian Center (Executive Director, A Better LA) in Los Angeles, August 2010; Advancement Project 2009; Uppsala/PRIO Armed Conflict dataset (Lacina and Gleditsch 2005; Harbom and Wallensteen 2010); Los Angeles Almanac (Thornton and others 2011).

Note: The challenges of measuring progress in these environments and scaling up successes are not dissimilar from those discussed in the rest of this Report. So-called outreach models are in their early stages of implementation in Los Angeles and have not been fully integrated into Los Angeles Police Department or County Sheriff practice.

ability to deliver public goods and signal an inclusive partnership between the state and other parts of society.

Informal patronage networks also mediate the effects of attempts to prevent violence in many fragile situations: these networks can undermine the institutional change needed to develop resilience to violence in the long run, but in the short term there is often little to replace them. Country lessons indicate a balance between the credibility of initial coalition-building efforts—which the involvement of individuals and groups known to be corrupt can undermine—and the need to dismantle patronage systems over time as institutional strength builds. Chapter 5 discusses lessons on sequencing anti-corruption efforts in fragile situations.

The participation of women in political reform can help to broaden initial coalitions to serve wider groups of citizens. As peace negotiations between the Liberian government of Charles Taylor and rebel groups in 2003 were under way, the Liberian Women's Mass Action for Peace movement mobilized thousands of supporters in Liberia and Ghana, where the talks were being held, and barricaded delegates in meeting rooms, prompting international mediators to set deadlines and secure agreements.[23] In Papua New Guinea/Bougainville, women's delegations consulted with the Bougainville Revolutionary Army to end the war, held initiatives to create peace areas, and convened and led peace talks.[24] Southern Sudanese women in the New Sudan Council of Churches organized the Wunlit tribal summit in 1999 to bring an end to hostilities between the Dinka and Nuer peoples. The Wunlit Covenant resulted in an agreement to share rights to water, fishing, and grazing land, which had been key points of disagreement.[25] In Latin America, women's groups have been active on human rights abuses; one of the most well known is Las

Madres de la Plaza—a group of mothers who began nonviolent demonstrations in 1977, demanding information from the Argentinean government on the whereabouts of their "disappeared" children during the years known as the Dirty War (1976–83).[26]

An essential, yet often underrated, ingredient in successful transitions from violence is proactive communication by the government to build public understanding and support. Successful coalitions have usually managed to "capture the narrative"—that is, to articulate a compelling vision of hope, develop a sense of shared identity, generate broad popular buy-in, and mobilize citizens even when the vision entails some short-term sacrifices for their supporters. Common to successful leadership, whether individual or collective, is this ability to redefine citizen and elite expectations, to move them beyond negative frames of reference, and to transform public policies and institutions in ways that will enable the state to address immediate and long-term sources of discord.

Citizens who lack credible information about progress made and challenges ahead will likely attribute the lack of visible improvements to a lack of political will, and they can lose trust in—and even turn against—those they believed or elected.[27] An inclusive public dialogue requires capacity and resources, not just of state institutions or of civil society, but also of the media, which can play an important role in ensuring public accountability and act as a citizen voice. Experience indicates this capacity needs to be developed in a coordinated manner—media development should focus not only on basic skills and journalistic training but also on establishing of professional standards and an enabling regulatory environment for the media. Governments, meanwhile, need to be endowed with appropriate outreach and communication capacity.

How inclusive is inclusive-enough? It may seem that conflict can only be prevented when all parts of society work together to set the country on a new path. This is correct in one sense: successful efforts to prevent and recover from violence have built alliances. But as illustrated above, they have not necessarily included all groups within society.

Four key lessons on what makes for inclusive-enough coalitions are as follows:

- Groups may legitimately be excluded where there is an evolving belief among the population that they have sacrificed their right to participate due to past abuses.
- Including groups that bring political legitimacy and financial and technical resources and will continue to press for deeper institutional transformation—such as business, labor, women's, or other civil society groups—is valuable, but there may be a hierarchy of decision making at the beginning, with parties present at the table but deferring on some decisions to political leadership.
- There can be trade-offs between wide inclusiveness and the efficiency of subsequent state decision-making, as when governments with very large numbers of ministries are created.
- Inclusion strategies can change over time as it becomes possible to marginalize consistently abusive groups.

Signals and commitment mechanisms

In the early stages of transition, gaining the confidence of these stakeholder groups often requires policies that signal a break from the past and instill trust that the new directions will not be reversed. Signaling a break from the past can include immediate actions or announcement of future actions. Committing to the future requires assuring stakeholders—who may be skeptical on the basis of broken promises in the past—that changes will be difficult to reverse. The signals used by countries that successfully made the initial transition away from the brink involved combined actions across the security-economic or political-economic domains.

The most powerful signals show that leaders are not prisoners of anti-reform, anticompromise forces among their own supporters. Strategic appointments can be a vital signal of future intent. The first president elected after the Nicaraguan peace agreement retained the chief of staff of the army in his position. That sent a strong reassuring signal to the defeated opposition that she would not use an electoral victory to resume military campaigns.[28] In Mozambique, the former RENAMO (Mozambican National Resistance, the former rebel movement that is now an opposition party) supreme commander was appointed deputy chief-of-staff of the Mozambican Defense Force, and seven RENAMO members were appointed to the national electoral commission (alongside 10 government representatives).[29]

In the security sector, signals from governments or opposition armed movements have demonstrated what the security forces will not do—as much as what they will do. The Mozambique government unilaterally announced the start of troop confinement as part of the demobilization. This created enough trust for RENAMO to announce its own steps toward demobilization.[30]

In Iraq, the "surge" to restore order in 2006–07 was preceded by a decision to withdraw the police, who were accused of taking factional sides in the violence, from insecure urban areas and to deploy the army instead. While this created longer-term challenges of returning the army to its typical role and building up the civilian police, it did restore civilian confidence.[31] Strong signals can also be sent by rebel movements: the decision by Xanana Gusmão in 1999 to confine to barracks the Timorese resistance troops, Falintil, even in the face of widespread destruction in the country, avoided a repeat of the 1975 descent into civil war.[32]

Signals on political reform are crucial where political exclusion was a central factor in motivating violence or civil protests. These may include rapid action toward elections or lay out a series of preparatory steps—as with the transitional executive bodies and constitutional reform processes in South Africa, supported by civic education and national and local action to maintain security during the political process through the National Peace Accords (box 3.9). Where elections will take place quickly, indicating that these are not an end but a step toward institutional transformation (as described in the inputs by Lakhdar Brahimi and Nitin Desai in box 5.11) is important. The creation of commitment mechanisms to ensure that announcements on political reforms will be honored in their implementation—such as robustly independent electoral commissions, supplemented where useful by regional or international technical and monitoring capacity—can help to build trust.

Signaling early intent to redress human rights violations is also possible even when the processes take time. Countries emerging from severe violence often carry legacies of human rights violations and trauma that shatter social norms or break the social contract between state and citizen.[33] Often poor and marginalized communities bear the brunt of predatory actions by state and nonstate actors, and tackling such evident injustices can be a high priority in a government attempt to break with the past, while starting to rebuild the institutions of the formal justice system.

With trust so important for stabilization and recovery, some societies have signaled early commitments to transitional justice. These efforts include steps leading to truth commissions, reparations programs for victims, and counter-impunity initiatives that may involve prosecuting the worst abusers and vetting security forces.[34] Such initiatives send powerful signals about the commitment of the new government to the rule of law. Even if institutional or political factors do not allow for full redress, early gathering of evidence of human rights violations and assisting victims can signal serious intent to overcome legacies of impunity and rights violations at both the community and national level. These approaches have also been tried with some success in middle-income countries making a transition from military rule. The state governments in Brazil provided early economic compensation to some victims of political violence during the country's military dictatorship, prompting a process of truth-telling and public discussion of past crimes.[35]

Given the link between corruption and violence, judicious, rapid transparency and anti-corruption measures can help to restore stakeholder and citizen confidence. In some countries, legacies of corruption leave heavy resentment and mistrust, which must be addressed for the new political arrangements to have credibility. In Liberia, government corruption was widely viewed as a major motivator for the rebellion of 1980, launching Liberia's long-running sequence of internal wars, temporary transitional governments, coups, and further wars. One of President Ellen Johnson Sirleaf's first and most popular actions was to fire two prominent figures on corruption charges and maintain tight controls over corruption (box 4.3). The power

BOX 4.3 *Signals and commitments for economic management: GEMAP in Liberia*

Types of violence: Civil conflict, political violence, criminal and gang-related violence, trafficking	
Transition opportunity: Moderate space for change, presidential elections, strong international support	**Key stakeholders:** Government needed to restore confidence of opposition parties and civil society, neighboring countries and regional institutions, donors and investors
Key stresses: Long history of violence, trauma, grievances and mistrust, corruption, youth unemployment	**Institutional challenges:** Extreme corruption and low domestic revenues, undermining political governance and constraining efforts to increase government capacity

Following the end of the 14-year Liberian civil war in 2003, the international community became increasingly concerned about the mismanagement and corruption under the National Transitional Government of Liberia (NTGL). Corruption was not just an economic concern: political and army reactions to the extensive corruption of the Tolbert government have been widely cited as a trigger for the coup that sparked Liberia's first civil war in 1989, and the theft of national resources continued to finance violent groups. The extreme corruption prevented improvements in government capacity by constraining national revenues and diverting external resources.

After intense negotiations, diplomatic pressure, and the threat of an embargo on external assistance, the NTGL and Liberia's international partners agreed to the Governance and Economic Management Assistance Program (GEMAP). The AU (African Union) and ECOWAS (Economic Community of West African States) led discussions with the NTGL, and the UN Security Council welcomed GEMAP in Resolution 1626 of September 19, 2005. GEMAP's aim was to improve revenue collection, budgeting, and expenditure management; upgrade procurement practices; strengthen transparency over concessions of national resources; control corruption; and build government capacity.

A defining feature of GEMAP is the use of international experts with co-signatory authority in the operations of ministries and state-owned enterprises, the review of concessions and contracts (including timber and diamonds), and the establishment of an oversight mechanism, the Economic Governance Steering Committee (EGSC), to guide and monitor GEMAP implementation. The EGSC is a mechanism of shared accountability, chaired by President Johnson Sirleaf and the American Ambassador as the deputy chair.

GEMAP has helped bring some rapid improvements and was an appropriate response to Liberia's particular mix of stresses, stakeholders, and institutional challenges at the time. Revenues increased from US$84.5 million in 2005–06 to a projected US$347 million in 2010–11, and Liberia's ranking on the Transparency International Corruption Perceptions Index climbed from 150 to 97 between 2007 and 2009.

GEMAP, however, has also ignited debate over the management role of expatriates. President Johnson Sirleaf told the UN Security Council that "a major deficiency still exists as with other technical assistance programs—the lack of capacity development for sustainability. This fault has contributed to tensions between foreign and local experts, thereby raising issues of ownership and sovereignty."[36] A lesson from GEMAP is to look closely at phasing the handover of responsibilities over time and manage local understanding and support.

Sources: AllAfrica 2009; Andersen 2010; Atkinson 2008; Bøås 2009; Dwan and Bailey 2006; Jahr 2010; Government of the Republic of Liberia Executive Mansion 2009.

and enduring effect of such a signal rests on informing citizens that the leader can reject supporters who might prefer to renege on commitments to citizens or the opposition. (Chapters 6 addresses temporary external support to justice systems, especially for redressing crimes committed during episodes of violence.)

Successful early stabilization efforts have often featured greater transparency in decision-making and budgeting to improve trust between citizens and the state. The new government of Timor-Leste broke with tradition in 2008 when it broadcast the budget debate in its entirety on radio and television.[37] Open consultations over policy in Chile and public inputs to appointment confirmation processes in Argentina created confidence that new directions would not be reversed.

Other governments have pursued greater transparency at the grassroots. In the early 1990s in Uganda, concerns arose over the apparent disparity between budget allocations and actual spending on education. This served as an impetus for the first Public Expenditure Tracking Survey. The initial survey of 250 government-run primary schools in 1991–95 revealed that only 13 percent of the education funds from the central government went to the schools, with the remaining 87 percent used for personal gain or non-education purposes. Later surveys, implemented after the first was made public, showed that the flow of funds to schools increased to around 80–90 percent in 1999–2000. The expenditure tracking system boosted citizen and donor confidence in the aftermath of the civil war. However, the system has since weakened.[38]

Wealth-sharing can generate support and confidence in stable situations and in transitions. Most countries rich in natural resources share smaller or larger amounts of the revenues from extraction with subnational governments (as in Brazil, Mexico, and Nigeria). Such wealth-sharing arrangements are often vital when civil wars have been fueled by natural resources or have featured disputes over natural resource control. The arrangements for sharing oil revenues in Sudan are an essential aspect of the Comprehensive Peace Agreement of 2005 (an Agreement on Wealth Sharing, Chapter III of the CPA, was signed in early 2004). In Pakistan the government used a budgetary provision to signal greater attention to areas of growing insecurity (box 4.4). Commitments were built into these agreements by passing them into law—and, in Sudan, through limited third-party monitoring.

Social cohesion policies are another strong signal that helps create a sense of fairness and social justice across population groups. Such policies foster the participation of hitherto excluded groups or areas in economic and political decision-making, enabling them to benefit from development assistance and ensuring that civil service recruitment is nondiscriminatory. To signify the state's concern for the victims of violence or those previously excluded from state services, Rwanda provided housing support and Timor-Leste cash transfer payments for internally displaced persons.

Signals can involve removing or amending laws perceived as unjust and discriminatory—such as abolishing apartheid laws in South Africa and, in Pakistan, the discussion over the Frontier Crimes Regulation, which applies a legal regime to the federally administered tribal areas differing from the rest of Pakistan.

In pursuing social cohesion policies, another signal is restoring public services to the middle class, who may be crucial for political support for change. For example, increasing social investments in Chile in the 1990s was balanced by restitution of civil service pensions and appointments;[39] sunset clauses for white civil servants in South Africa balanced fast action on maternal and child health care for the poorest communities.[40] Policies aimed at tangible results for these groups are often not pro-poor, and hence are often difficult for development practitioners to agree on as priorities. But they can be part of the political economy of successful change.[41]

BOX 4.4 ***Pakistan: Using the budget to signal change***

Types of violence: Subnational, political, cross-border, trafficking, ideological including transnational	
Transition opportunity: Limited space for change following accession of new government in 2008 and military campaign of 2009 in Swat valley	**Key stakeholders:** Federal, regional, and local government (including tribal areas); excluded groups; neighboring countries; international partners; national and transnational militant groups
Key stresses: Cross-border conflict spillovers; transnational terrorism; regional competition; corruption; political and social inequality; income and asset inequality; regional inequities; youth unemployment; tensions over natural resource wealth-sharing in peripheral regions	**Institutional challenges:** Accountability and capacity constraints in public administration; security, judicial, and political institutions

Late in 2009, the agreement by Pakistan's federal and provincial government leaders to the Seventh National Finance Commission Award was hailed as a "major achievement and a positive event for those who believe that the future of a vibrant Pakistan lies in a democratic federation."[42]

In Pakistan, grievances over inequity in revenue-sharing go back a long time and have been part of a broader set of tensions between regions within Pakistan. They have been exacerbated by debates over the distribution of political power and, more recently, over the independence of institutions of accountability, notably the judiciary. All this in a context where Pakistan faces terrorist threats, subnational tensions, separatist movements, regional insecurity, and severe economic inequality.

Attempts to set in place a new agreement had failed for 17 years. As part of the 2009 five-year public finance award, the federal government sacrificed part of its share of the national divisible pool of resources in favor of the provinces. While all provinces will receive an increase in resources, two of them also accepted a reduction in their shares to provide more resources to Balochistan and Khyber Pakhtunkhwa Provinces—which were both affected by internal conflict and the war in Afghanistan. The award was also an important part of efforts to assuage separatist sentiments in Balochistan and to settle more than 30 years of disputes between Sindh and Punjab about the distribution of water. On its own, however, the award does not address local governance and institutional challenges. The decline of public revenues and the impact of the floods of 2010 have also constrained the overall potential for the allocation and transfer of funds, and legal and resource challenges remain constraints to implementation.

Source: Porter, Andrews, and Wescott 2010.

Delivering early results

Country lessons show that inclusive-enough coalitions have to be complemented by tangible results to restore confidence in national institutions. Results on the ground build confidence for three reasons. First, they are concrete indicators of a government's good intentions toward citizens. Second, they demonstrate the government's ability to deliver on its promises. Third, they build confidence by indicating that leaders are able to withstand pressure from their own supporters to play a "winner take all" game and that they instead provide benefits to all citizens. This confidence-building requires listening to popular expectations, setting realistic priorities for what can be delivered, drawing on nongovernment capacity to deliver, and communicating results to the population. This section identifies various practical ways to deliver results to violence-affected populations. (Chapter 5 then presents examples of possible interventions across the security, justice, and jobs spectrum for both the immediate and longer term.)

Perception surveys in Africa and Latin America indicate that employment and security are people's most pressing problems.[43] Electricity, literally the most "visible" of all results, can be critical for progress in security and job creation. In many countries, a perception of increased justice for excluded populations may come about not only through action in the justice sector per se but also through broader social justice that includes greater provision of health, education, or social protection. The specific short-term results most important for restoring confidence will depend on an assessment of the priorities of the population and the preferences of key stakeholder groups (box 4.5).

REFLECTIONS FROM ADVISORY COUNCIL MEMBERS: *2011 WORLD DEVELOPMENT REPORT*

BOX 4.5 *Building early confidence in Haiti—Challenges and reflections*

Carlos Alberto Dos Santos Cruz, Lt General, Brazilian Army; former Force Commander of the United Nations Peacekeeping Mission in Haiti; *WDR Advisory Council Member*

During my time as UN force commander in Haiti, the mission faced many challenges. In the very beginning, the biggest one was how to balance demands for security and development.

From the start, it was made clear that the primary goal of the UN force was to protect and serve the interests of the citizens. At the same time, troops were encouraged to act with determination against individuals and groups responsible for violence. This meant good intelligence work followed, when necessary, by robust operations using force if necessary. At the same time, troops tried to show that they were respectful and supportive of the population.

Institutions and individuals are not alone in such circumstances, and they must work with others in the international and nongovernment communities and encourage them to set aside parochial mindsets and behaviors. If there is not success in this, there is risk of wasting lots of time talking on coordination and cooperation without improving performance.

Once the environment is safe, it is important to focus on delivering basic services, creating jobs, and improving infrastructure. At that time, as soon as the mission defeated the street gangs, the peacekeeping forces began to deliver potable water each day and, working with local leaders, to help with small-scale projects like renovating community centers and cleaning schools. Military troops also worked with NGOs to clear canals and distribute food, mattresses and stoves.

In all this, there was careful concern to not waste scarce funds on projects ill-suited to local conditions. Indeed, making the most of financial resources was always uppermost in the mind of the military contingent. It was important to guard against the very human desire to not act quickly unless it is sustainable in the longer term. For instance, a generator was provided to a small fishing community to use in the fish market. It seemed like a good idea at the time, but the locals were not used to sharing the costs for fuel or maintenance, and very soon the generator was broken.

The performance of local institutions is fundamental. Without strong political leadership, reasonable laws, and a judicial system that works, efforts will be in vain. Indeed, many actions may actually make matters worse. In Cité Soleil, after many years without either a courthouse or police headquarters, one of the aid agencies rebuilt the courthouse and military troops started patrolling jointly with the national police. Pretty soon things started to improve as the police gradually won the trust of the local people.

It was amazing to watch long lines of citizens in front of the courthouse waiting to resolve their problems through the law and to see the growing numbers who went to the commissariat to ask for help from the police. People know when someone is trying to help and they respond positively. In Haiti, after just a few months, they began to bring to the UN troops valuable intelligence, to hand in weapons, and to deal with criminals and the perpetrators of violence. They also began to participate in community efforts and start businesses. People moved back into their homes, rebuilt the markets, and thronged previously abandoned streets. The experience in Haiti convinced me that if national leaders, with the right kind of support from the international institutions, focus on a few basic building blocks, citizens themselves will fix the problems and rebuild their countries.

WDR note: Haiti is often referred to as a "post-conflict" country, but this is inaccurate. Haiti did experience civil uprisings against the autocratic Duvalier regime; Jean-Claude ("Baby Doc") Duvalier fled the country in 1986. Since that time, Haiti has experienced a succession of military rule, flawed elections, coups, democratic elections, militia activity, and gang violence.

What is the right balance of quick, visible results and longer-term institution-building?

Although tangible results are needed in the short term, these will be insufficient to prevent violence recurring without simultaneous steps toward transforming institutions (see chapter 5). Striking a balance requires an astute reading of available capacity and tradeoffs. WDR consultations in several countries highlighted the need for governments to demonstrate at least two to three visible results locally in the first year following a new pact for change, and ideally one or two in the first months (box 4.6). Results need to be repeated at regular intervals, however, to maintain momentum and citizen confidence.

Combined political, security, and developmental capacities are often needed to deliver confidence-building results quickly

BOX 4.6 *Only a few visible results are needed to restore confidence: Examples from civil war, organized criminal, and subnational violence*

Liberia

Types of violence: Civil conflict, political violence, criminal and gang-related violence, trafficking	
Transition opportunity: Moderate space for change, presidential elections, strong international support	**Key stakeholders:** Government needed to restore confidence of opposition parties and civil society, neighboring countries and regional institutions, donors and investors
Key stresses: Long history of violence, trauma, grievances and mistrust, corruption, youth unemployment	**Institutional challenges:** Corruption and low domestic revenues, undermining political governance and constraining efforts to increase government capacity

The Liberian government capitalized on a well-managed donor program and a long-standing dearth of public-spirited government to visibly deliver public goods, restoring confidence in government. The key was to be specific about what was promised—restoring electricity in Monrovia in a year, for example—and to make sure that the government actually delivered what it had promised. Tornorlah Varpilah, Liberian Deputy Minister of Health, told the WDR team that Liberia took some immediate actions to satisfy public opinion. The first was to guarantee peace and security using UN forces. Then the President took action to provide free primary education, free primary health care, and electricity in the capital city. Those interventions helped build confidence in the government.[44] Simultaneously, the government worked to improve capacity in the public finance and justice systems for the longer term.

Colombia

Types of violence: Civil conflict, trafficking, criminal and gang-related violence	
Transition opportunity: Preventive action in the face of rising criminality and failed peace talks	**Key stakeholders:** Government, armed groups, citizens, civil society, regional, international partners
Key stresses: Legacies of violence, presence of criminal networks and drug production/trafficking, perceived social and economic deprivation, natural resource wealth	**Institutional challenges:** Lack of reach of state; accountability challenges

In 2002, the government made restoring security a top priority and defined a set of fairly narrow targets for violence-affected areas: restoring safe transit by deploying military resources to protect the main road network and sponsoring convoys of private vehicles that allowed many Colombians to travel between major cities in safety for the first time in years; reducing homicides and kidnappings; restoring social services to the national average; and improving trust in the state. Meetings around the country during the electoral campaign and a review of the strengths and weaknesses of past efforts informed selection of these targets. A review of the previous Politica Nacional de Rehabilitación (PNR)[45] program, for example, indicated that it had spread its efforts too thinly across different regions, so the new government chose a smaller number of violence-affected areas. It also drew on wider capacities to execute the program, including U.S. support for security-sector capacity-building and the engagement of Colombian NGOs and other donors in social programs in violence-affected rural areas. Frequent perception surveys of citizens kept the government up-to-date on progress.

Pakistan

Types of violence: Subnational, political, cross-border, trafficking, ideological, including transnational	
Transition opportunity: Limited space for change following accession of new government in 2008 and 2009 military campaign in Swat valley	**Key stakeholders:** National, regional, and local government (including tribal areas), excluded groups; neighboring countries; international partners; national and transnational militant groups
Key stresses: Cross-border conflict spillovers, transnational terrorism, regional competition, corruption; political, social, income, and asset inequality; regional inequities; youth unemployment; tensions over natural resource wealth sharing in peripheral regions	**Institutional challenges:** Accountability and capacity constraints in public administration, security, judicial, and political institutions

BOX 4.6 *(continued)*

Following the Pakistan government's 2009 military offensive to drive militants from the Federally Administered Tribal Areas (FATA) and the Khyber Pakhtunkhwa Province (KP; formerly the Northwest-Frontier Province), the government—with the World Bank, Asian Development Bank, UN, and European Union—undertook an assessment to address needs and understand the factors underlying violence. In addition to traditional analyses of economic and social data, the assessment involved a crisis analysis and consultations with more than 1,000 representatives of communities from FATA and KP. Focus group discussions were also held by local NGOs and women's groups. The primary issues were jobs and justice system reform, including the country's overall legal framework (different in FATA from the rest of Pakistan) and the resolution of land and family disputes. The exercise highlighted the danger of overpromising: initial plans did not take capacity into account, resulting in unrealistic timelines. Since the assessment, Pakistan has faced the even more immediate challenges of the devastating humanitarian disaster caused by the floods in August 2010. But the assessment still gives a detailed picture of citizen priorities.

Sources: Baily and Hoskins 2007; McCandless 2008; World Bank and ADB 2010; WDR team consultation with national leaders from fragile and conflict-affected countries in Berlin, 2009; WDR team consultation with government officials, representatives from civil society organizations, and security personnel in Colombia and Pakistan, 2010; Arboleda 2010; Centro de Coordinación de Acción Integral 2010.

and initiate cross-sectoral institutional transformations. Governments have used tools associated with one domain of action (security, justice, economic) to achieve goals in another. Navigating transitions has involved a clear focus on the stresses that drive violence and on designing programs to mitigate them. This implies an interdisciplinary approach to strategy based not on sectoral programs and outcomes but on balancing security, justice, and economic opportunity (box 4.7).

How can results be delivered when states face a legacy of weak capacity and legitimacy?

Governments that have restored confidence of stakeholders and citizens have typically mobilized nonstate actors to deliver results rather than doing everything themselves.[46] Drawing on "supplementary capacity" has meant tapping into both local nonstate structures (communities and community organizations, traditional institutions of justice, the domestic private sector, NGOs) and external assistance (regional organizations, international donors, the international private sector; see chapter 6).

Governments are often concerned that drawing in NGO, private sector, or community capacity will take the credit away from the government, or that it will be difficult to transform these modes of delivery farther down the line when state institutional capacity has increased. It is indeed critical that nongovernmental programs, particularly international programs, give appropriate, visible attributions of credit to national institutions. Development programs stamped with the logo of international institutions do not build trust in national institutions. Yet nongovernmental mechanisms can be used to boost confidence in government responsiveness to its citizens, as box 4.8 on Afghanistan's National Solidarity Program indicates. Similarly, the involvement of NGOs under government coordination in Afghanistan and Timor-Leste (see chapter 8) increased the perception of government effectiveness in the health sector.

Community-driven development (CDD) approaches have been applied in varied contexts. While such programs alone cannot transform the security, justice, or economic dynamics in violent settings, their use is a good indicator of the range of purposes they can serve and the relative ease of adapting their design to different needs.[47] Attributes such as participatory planning and decision-making, cooperation between local authorities and the committees selected by community members for the purpose of a CDD program, and community control of funds

BOX 4.7 *Different sectors, core goals*

National programs (sometimes with international support) have used tools from one "sector" to meet goals in another. These approaches can be effective in a variety of situations—in countries recovering from civil war and in societies affected by drug-related violence, ranging from low to middle income.

Justice and inclusion goal—Security intervention. In Burundi, a key part in the Arusha peace process that stabilized the long-running civil war was the creation in 2004 of a new national army, the *Force de Défense Nationale*, in which the Hutu ethnic group represented 40 percent of the officer corps. This was important for the Hutu, who account for more than 80 percent of the population but had long been excluded from the military and had suffered from military actions against them as far back as 1972.

Justice and inclusion goal—Economic intervention. Jamaica's inner cities have been at the center of the country's crime and violence problem, which, coupled with growing poverty, has further exacerbated social fragmentation and the weakness of civic organizing in inner-city communities. With donor support, the government launched a program to provide inner-city community infrastructure and services for the poor in 2006, which includes measures to promote short-term conflict mitigation and resolution, as well as medium-term social prevention and capacity enhancement interventions.

Security goal—Economic intervention. In Mozambique, the civilian population was caught up in successive military offensives. During Mozambique's transition, joint international-national efforts to provide assistance and sustainable resettlement to both former combatants and the internally displaced eased the potential tension that postwar population shifts and a lack of livelihood opportunities might otherwise have caused.

Security goal—Multisectoral intervention. To address rising urban violence in Cali, Colombia, the DESEPAZ program (a Spanish acronym for development, security, and peace) integrated employment and microenterprise programs for youth, urban upgrading, and primary education alongside security interventions. The program was also noteworthy for its organizers' understanding of crime: because most homicides occurred on weekends, holidays, and at night, selling alcohol and carrying guns at those times were banned. A 30 percent decline in homicides in 1994–97 is attributed directly to the program.

Economic goal—Justice and inclusion intervention. After early efforts to implement the Dayton Accords in Bosnia and Herzegovina, international monitors found through interviews with business persons that trade between Bosnian, Croat, and Serb majority regions was substantially affected by ethnically denominated license plates. The Office of the High Representative mandated that nonethnic license plates be issued to all cars in Bosnia and Herzegovina, and within weeks of this initiative, traffic and trade had surged.

Economic goal—Security intervention. After the establishment of the UN Interim Mission in Kosovo in June 1999, UN administrators observed that trade between Kosovo and its neighbors was depressed. Insecurity on the major highways from Pristina to border crossings was identified as an obstacle, so NATO's KFOR troops were deployed to provide security along major highways and transit points. Exports rose from €27.6 million in 2002 to €297 million in 2010, and imports from €854.8 million to €2.1 billion.

Economic goal—Security intervention. In Liberia, partnership between the UN peacekeeping mission, the United Nations Development Programme, and the World Bank maintained the country's degraded roads, so that parts of the country were no longer cut off from the capital during the rainy season, with a consequent boost in confidence.

Sources: Roque and others 2010; Economist Intelligence Unit 2008a; International Crisis Group 2007; Igreja and Dias-Lambranca 2008; Villaveces and others 2000; World Bank 1999b, 2006e; Cousens and Harland 2006; Statistical Office of Kosovo 2010; Chesterman 2004; Giovine and others 2010.

mean the programs can signal a change in the attitude of the state to communities, even before physical projects are completed. They can thereby enhance state-society relations, increase citizen trust in institutions, and contribute to longer-term institution building (box 4.8). Experience from a range of applications[48] suggests that CDD programs can extend the state's reach, especially in areas from which it has been absent during a conflict; reconstruct social capital and strengthen social cohesion;[49] signal inclusion of marginalized groups (such as women and youth); and contribute to decentralization, either by design or through adaptations over time.

The importance of community engagement in local-level interventions can be illustrated by psychosocial support programs. Political and criminal violence alike can cause significant psychological and social

BOX 4.8 *Community-driven development strengthens state-society relations in Afghanistan*

Types of violence: Intergroup, ethnic, and political violence; organized crime and trafficking; cross-border; transnational ideological	
Transition opportunity: Initial large space for change: Bonn Accord, loya jirga, presidential, parliamentary and provincial elections, national development budget	**Key stakeholders:** National and local government, security forces, community leaders, civil society groups, citizens, international partners, transnational militant groups
Key stresses: Legacies of violence and trauma, transnational terrorism, criminal networks, low incomes, youth unemployment, corruption, gender discrimination	**Institutional challenges:** Severe accountability and capacity constraints in public administration, security, judicial, and political institutions

Afghanistan, one of the world's poorest countries, has experienced a near continuous period of invasion and occupation, civil war, and oppression since the late 1970s. Between the overthrow of President Daoud before the Soviet invasion in 1979 and the Bonn Accord in 2002, the central government never had authority across the entire country. In addition to a long legacy of violence and poverty, the country faces the daunting stresses of internal conflict, terrorism, ethnic tension, regional and global security stresses, and extensive corruption.

Development under these conditions obviously is particularly challenging. However, the largest development program in Afghanistan, the National Solidarity Program (NSP), has registered some important successes. Since its inauguration in 2003, it has established more than 22,500 community development councils across 361 districts in all 34 provinces and financed more than 50,000 development projects. Through the democratically elected, gender-balanced councils, the program builds representative institutions for village governance. Typical projects construct or improve critical infrastructure, such as communal drinking water facilities, irrigation canals, local roads and bridges, and electrical generators, and offer vocational training or literacy courses to villagers.

Economic evaluations show consistently high rates of return across all sectors (above 12 percent). A midterm evaluation by the University of York in the United Kingdom in 2005–06 found significant evidence of greater public faith in the national government, along with better community relations. The independently conducted Randomized Impact Evaluation of Phase-II of Afghanistan's National Solidarity Program in 2010[50] reinforced this finding through a large-sample quantitative assessment using randomized controlled trials to compare outcomes in 250 villages covered by the NSP, with 250 villages not yet participating in the program. As part of the independent evaluation indicated above, a survey was conducted between October 2007 and May 2008 that showed that the simple process of electing councils and planning local investments increased villagers' trust in all levels of government. Across the board, those in villages participating in the NSP had more trust in government officials, showing that it is possible to markedly change perceptions of state institutions through effective local interventions.

Furthermore, a separate study by the Center for Strategic and International Studies, in Washington, DC, found that "the CDCs and tribal *shuras*[51] are seen as more responsive to Afghan needs than provincial governments and provincial councils, and in many cases are the only sign of improvement villagers have seen in the past five years."[52]

Sources: Beath and others 2010; Patel and Ross 2007; Selvarajan 2008; Brick 2008; Barakat 2006.

(box continues on next page)

suffering. Activities aimed at improving mental health and well-being of at-risk populations through psychosocial support have proven to be more effective if communities are involved. For example, evaluations of two psychosocial programs in conflict-affected regions of Indonesia from 1999 to 2001 found that the program that used a more holistic approach, engaging the wider community, had a greater impact than the one that focused solely on trauma and used a medical model.[53] Similarly, engaging the community in traditional healing and cleansing rituals for child soldiers in Angola, Liberia, and northern Uganda was found to be mutually empowering and more effective in reintegration than traditional psychological efforts—the child soldiers felt "decontaminated" psychologically and the community was more willing to accept them back socially.[54]

Traditional and community structures for dispute resolution are also potential partners in delivering early results—and it may be unwise to ignore them. In many fragile settings, formal systems for the provision of justice are weak or broken down. At the local level, this breakdown opens gaps not only in the core criminal justice system, but also in the

BOX 4.8 *Community-driven development strengthens state-society relations in Afghanistan (continued)*

Do officials work for the benefits of all the villagers?

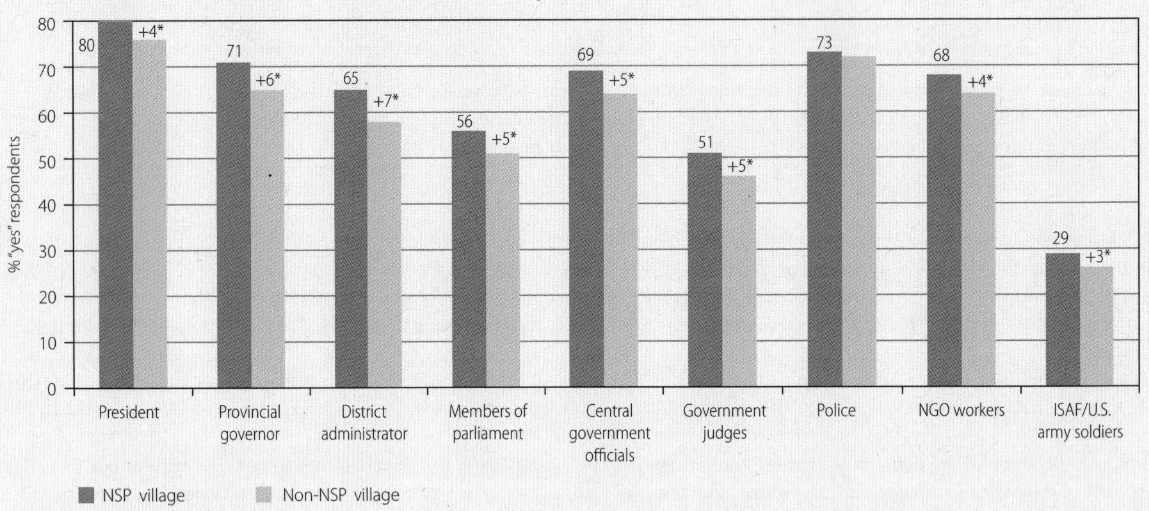

Source: Beath and others 2010.

Note: Villages that participated in the NSP program exhibit more trust in national and local governments. Participants responded that they believed that national and local government officials worked for the benefit of all villagers significantly more often in NSP villages than in other villages. Statistically significant differences are shown with asterisked percentages above the Non-NSP Village bars. In the x-axis, the label ISAF is referring to the International Security Assistance Force in Afghanistan.

regulation of land and family disputes. Such gaps have led to popular frustration and have opened opportunities to violent opposition movements such as the Taliban in both Afghanistan and Pakistan, which have in some areas of the country established a shadow presence offering an alternative local dispute resolution system.[55] Gangs can play a similar role in urban communities. The WDR Fafo perception surveys in countries affected by violence found that most respondents saw traditional authorities as best placed to resolve land disputes, even though they also believed that national or local state structures should deliver other key governance functions.[56] (Chapter 5 explores complementarities between traditional and formal systems in justice reform.)

Civil society and faith-based actors can also play an important role in service delivery in many violent contexts when government capacity and reach are limited. Many successful initial transitions have drawn heavily on nongovernmental capacity associated with the credibility of national institutions. For instance, religious organizations run 81 percent of public primary schools and 77 percent of public secondary schools in the Democratic Republic of Congo, through a protocol-based school management system,[57] which was what kept the schools running through the turbulent 1990s.[58]

Communities can also play a central role in service provision (box 4.9). In many fragile environments, NGOs often ensure that basic social services, such as health care, education, water, and sanitation, continue to be provided to the population. Delivery modes can include government agencies contracting out some social services to local NGOs,[59] international NGOs working closely with local NGOs and community groups, and local NGOs collaborating with community groups in the absence of the government.

One area that does not lend itself well to partnership with nonstate actors to deliver fast results is security. Nonstate actors can be effective in *supporting* security efforts, for instance in community policing aiming to reduce crime through community partnership; joint programs against crime between municipalities, civil society, and the private sector; and community engagement to prevent and respond to gender-based violence (see chapter 5). Going further and implicitly ceding to others the state monopoly on security should be avoided. New research shows that preexisting social networks, when used by the state and competing elites, can stir up conflict or perpetuate its damaging social effects—as in the evolution of vigilantism in Nigeria (box 4.10).[60] While circumstances clearly vary, the risks of such groups becoming predatory or difficult to demobilize are considerable—not least because their methods of recruitment are not generally based on merit, while their armed status can make their social accountability tenuous. A similar tradeoff exists with private security companies in internationally supported operations. For instance, Coalition Forces in Iraq faced problems in addressing abuses by private security companies entrusted with core state security tasks.[61]

A related issue is the proliferation of private security companies around the globe. They provide an array of functions, including monitoring, investigation services, and bodyguards. Their growth is often attributed to a widespread sense of insecurity and a lack of trust in the police and the judiciary. In Central America, the private security industry expanded dramatically in the 1990s following the signing of peace agreements. In El Salvador and Guatemala, private security firms sometimes incorporated ex-combatants from civil wars, and throughout the region, many working for private security firms are former government security personnel. By 2008, legal and illegal private security companies in Guatemala and Honduras employed around 120,000 and 60,000 guards, respectively, with five to six private security personnel for each police officer.[62] A worrisome development, as noted by the president of the Guatemala Chamber of Security, is the severe shortage of trained security personnel, so the typical marginal company ends up recruiting farmers from the interior of the country and sending them to work with little or no training.

BOX 4.9 Nepal: Bringing others in—supplementing government capacity in education

Types of violence: Civil conflict, interethnic and political violence, criminal violence, and trafficking	
Transition opportunities: Modest space for change: "palace killings" and stepped-up Maoist campaign in 2001	**Key stakeholders:** National and local governments, civil society groups, marginalized ethnic groups, international partners, regional neighbors
Key stresses: Legacies of violence and trauma; social, political, and economic inequality; youth unemployment; corruption; human rights abuses; rising expectations of formerly unrepresented	**Institutional challenges:** Feudal structures and associated exclusion; accountability and capacity constraints in public administration, security, judicial, and political institutions; lack of inclusion of different groups

In 2001, recognizing that extensive local capacity to provide education already on the ground had better success than the nationalized education system, the government devolved responsibility for primary schooling back to school management committees through amendments to the Education Act. (The government relied exclusively on communities for the delivery of basic education until 1971.) The responsibilities of these committees included generating resources; formulating budgets (using a combination of government incentive grants, international aid, and local resources); and hiring teachers. Significant local resources were unlocked, with every rupee of government grants leveraging 1.5 rupees in community financing.

Decentralizing teacher hiring also spurred accountability, as the government froze the number of government-appointed teaching slots and introduced salary grants to allow communities to recruit teachers locally and hold them accountable for classroom performance. Better school governance reduced teacher absenteeism, improved learning achievements, increased community donations, and boosted primary completion rates (from 42 percent in 1998 to 60 percent in 2003).

Even though the country was in active conflict, net enrollment rates in primary education increased from 69 to 92 percent between 1998 and 2008. Gender parity improved from 83 to 98 percent from 2003 to 2008. The impact on girls, dalits, and janajati (Nepal's lower-caste groups) children was also significant: the rate of out-of-school children dropped from 50 percent in 2004 to 15 percent in 2008 for dalits, from 42 percent to 11 percent for girls, and from 44 percent to 11 percent for janajatis.

Sources: World Bank 2009e.

BOX 4.10 *Nigeria: Strengths and risks of nongovernment capacity in the security sector—the Bakassi Boys*

Types of violence: Widespread criminal and gang violence, vigilantism	
Transition opportunity (missed): Rising insecurity and criminality	**Key stakeholders:** Government, vigilante groups, perpetrators of crime and their victims, citizens
Key stresses: Criminal networks, youth unemployment, corruption	**Institutional challenges:** Low capacity and accountability in police and judicial institutions

Vigilantism has often provided security in the absence of effective state performance. While it may be seen initially as legitimate, it presents tremendous risks to both the state and citizens, especially in protecting universal standards of due process (often the justice is summary) or in separating petitioner, prosecutor, and judge (often a mob dynamic prevails).

Although Nigeria has had significant income from oil revenue, the country remained stuck in low per capita income and saw little by way of the development of effective institutions. Throughout the 1990s and the early part of the 2000s, corruption and non-accountable institutions remained defining features of the Nigerian political landscape. Earlier episodes of separatist conflict (in Biafra) had not resurfaced, but oil-rich areas in the south had seen civil violence, and Nigeria had also experienced sectarian violence in its eastern provinces.

In the late 1990s and early 2000s, vigilantism was rampant in eastern Nigeria. In response to a rash of robberies and home invasions, residents formed vigilante groups that patrolled and guarded entire neighborhoods at night. One such group was the Bakassi Boys, who initially earned the support of politicians and the public because they reduced crime. In the words of one newspaper columnist: "I am a living witness to the fact that for three years before the year 2000, in my part of Imo State, life was made unbearable by the callous activities of armed bandits. They suddenly seemed to have so multiplied that anybody found outside his front door after dusk was risking his or her life. Then suddenly things began to happen. Well-known hoodlums who were friends of the police gradually took notice and either fled or stayed at their peril. Home was becoming haven again, and evening parties and outside engagements returned to the community. It was such a great relief. Asked thereafter to choose between the Bakassi Boys and the police, the village folks preferred the former."[63]

Vigilante groups are celebrated in Nigerian popular culture—pictured in movies and on calendars—as appropriate defenders of the public against criminals. Even mainstream observers of Nigerian society, including eminent political scientists like Peter Ekeh, saw the Bakassi Boys as qualitatively different from other vigilante groups. Yet, as noted by Human Rights Watch in 2002, the Bakassi Boys came to be viewed as an uncontrollable and illegal band, which, though filling a void left by a weak state, had become ruthless mercenaries who could be hired to eliminate political or commercial opponents. Beyond these accusations, the celebrated operations of the Bakassi Boys were problematic because of the lack of due process accorded presumed criminals. As one anthropologist notes: "The Bakassi Boys originated in acts of necessity undertaken in the face of terror. Noble intentions, however, have a tenuous existence in the midst of the endemic corruption, political factionalism, and electoral machinations that characterize the Nigerian political landscape. Thus Nigerians remain suspicious of the power ceded to vigilantes."[64]

Sources: Ekeh 2002; Nwana 2000; McCall 2004.

Early results need to be compatible with, rather than undermine, long-term institution-building. The choice of results and the manner in which they are to be achieved is important because it can set directions for later institution-building. For instance, if communities are passive recipients of aid, they have fewer incentives to take responsibility for violence prevention; and if social protection is provided by external actors alone, national institutions have fewer incentives to undertake responsibilities to protect vulnerable citizens. Hence, there is a need for building coalitions for delivery that include a mixture of state and nonstate, bottom-up and top-down approaches. Such coalitions are a better underpinning for longer-term institutional transformation; in fact, some early results actively build momentum for institutional transformation, as has been the case with the National Solidarity Program in Afghanistan. As countries end one episode of violence or go through an initial political transition, they remain at high risk of recurring violence. The need at this point is to create legitimate social and governmental institutions and improve prospects of economic prosperity. Chapter 5 will discuss these issues.

FEATURE 4 Indonesia: Restoring confidence in Aceh

Types of violence: Civil conflict, gang-related violence, vigilantism	
Transition moment: Significant space for change: 2004 Indian Ocean tsunami, 2005 peace agreement	**Key stakeholders:** National and provincial governments; GAM (political and military wings); conflict victims; Association of Southeast Asian Nations (ASEAN), European Union (EU), and wider international community
Key stresses: Distribution of natural resource wealth, legacies of conflict, reintegration of ex-combatants, loss of life and devastation due to tsunami	**Institutional challenges:** Weak capacity and accountability of provincial political and administrative institutions, coordination of external inputs

In the choreography of peace negotiations—from efforts to build both national support and local inclusion to the judicious use of external support—the peace process in Indonesia's Aceh province exemplifies many of the attributes of effective conflict prevention and resolution after 30 years of suspicion and outright hostility.

Inclusive-enough coalition

Agreement on the parameters of the peace agreement—in the form of a memorandum of understanding (MOU) signed in Helsinki in August 2005—came at the end of six months of carefully mediated negotiations between the Indonesian government and the Free Aceh Movement (Gerakan Aceh Merdeka, or GAM). Both sides did their best to ensure things went smoothly. The team representing the Indonesian government was handpicked by President Susilo Bambang Yudhoyono and Vice President Jusuf Kalla. In a deliberate effort to assuage GAM's concerns about adequate representation for non-Javanese, the core team was drawn from other provinces. Learning from previous processes, the government was careful to manage communications in Jakarta and at a national level to demonstrate the benefits of the process, avoiding focusing on provincial buy-in at the expense of national support. The Finnish nongovernmental organization, Crisis Management Initiative, led by former Finland president Martti Ahtisaari, played a key role in facilitating the discussions.

The government mobilized support at the national level for peace talks by emphasizing the cost of the conflict to the national budget—in expenditures on security measures (estimated at US$2.3 billion or 21 percent of the total economic cost of the conflict) and forgone tax revenues from lower oil and gas exports—and the imperative of stability in Aceh to private investment in the country.[65]

Signals for confidence-building

The Helsinki MOU articulated the main elements of the peace settlement, signaling a genuine break with the past. Acehnese demands for greater political autonomy within a unitary Indonesian republic were clearly spelled out, along with provisions for this autonomy to be institutionalized in a new Law on the Governing of Aceh. This would give provincial and local government authority over a broad spectrum of public affairs, except in foreign affairs, external defense, national security, and monetary and fiscal matters, where the central government would retain jurisdiction. The MOU also allowed for greater Acehnese political participation, including a commitment to facilitate the establishment of Aceh-based political parties—a prerogative not granted to other provinces. Provisions were also made to hold local elections in Aceh as soon as possible.

Equally important, the MOU dealt with key security and justice concerns: reintegrating former combatants and assisting victims of conflict. Provisions included the release of political prisoners and detainees within 15 days of signing the MOU; amnesty to all who had engaged in GAM activities; and full political, economic, and social rights to all political prisoners and detainees. The Indonesian and Aceh authorities pledged reintegration support to ex-combatants in the form of farmland, employment opportunities, and social security (in the event of incapacity). GAM agreed to demobilize all 3,000 of its military troops and decommission their arms. In return, the Indonesian government agreed to withdraw "non-organic" forces, with the remaining permanent battalions composed mostly of ethnic Acehnese.[66]

Rights to natural resources had long been a bone of contention, and the MOU addressed them by stipulating that Aceh would retain 70 percent of revenue from all current and future hydrocarbon deposits and from other natural resources

FEATURE 4 *Indonesia: Restoring confidence in Aceh (continued)*

in the province. This was a better deal than that enjoyed by other hydrocarbon-producing regions.[67] Addressing deep-rooted fears about the rule of law and human rights, the MOU provided for the separation of powers between the executive, legislative, and judiciary branches of government.

Commitment mechanisms to lock in signals

A key commitment mechanism was the Law on the Governing of Aceh, passed by the Indonesian Parliament in August 2006. This institutionalized many of the provisions agreed in the Helsinki MOU and serves as a framework for relations between Aceh and the central government.

A special effort went into addressing the ongoing commitment to peace and economic integration. The Aceh Peace-Reintegration Board (Badan Reintegrasi-Damai Aceh, or BRA) was created by a governor's decree in 2006 as the principal local agency responsible for overseeing the peace process and the economic reintegration of ex-combatants, political prisoners, and conflict victims. BRA—a provincial agency reporting to the governor of Aceh—was given a broad mandate encompassing the design, funding, and implementation of various policies and procedures related to the reintegration process.

The Aceh Monitoring Mission, created after the Helsinki MOU, is a good example of external parties monitoring stakeholders' commitment to their promises. Comprising representatives from the EU, Norway, Switzerland, and five ASEAN countries, it was deployed to oversee the demobilization of GAM, the decommissioning of its weapons, the reintegration of GAM forces, and the removal of "non-organic" police forces and military battalions from the province. In addition, the European Commission funded the Aceh Peace Process Support Program to assist in implementing the peace agreement in four areas: election support, police reform, justice reform, and local governance reform.

Delivering early results

In Aceh, the government, working with external and local actors, delivered some crucial early results for peace-building. The total estimated amount of funds committed to reintegration and peace-building is Rp 9 trillion.[68] The distribution of funds across districts is evidence of effective geographic targeting of aid. The four most heavily conflict-affected districts—Aceh Utara, Bireuen, Aceh Timur, and Pidie—received more than 50 percent of all funds. GAM members (both combatants and noncombatants) and political prisoners received the largest share of direct assistance, collectively worth almost Rp 400 billion.[69]

These provisions helped get ex-combatants and other key target groups back into the workforce. The Aceh Reintegration and Livelihood Survey, commissioned by the World Bank, indicates that male ex-combatants are 7 percent more likely to be in full-time employment than their civilian counterparts. Most former combatants and ex-political prisoners have returned to the occupations they held prior to joining the insurgency—mainly farming and agricultural wage labor. The survey also finds that male victims of conflict are 14 percent more likely to be in full employment than male nonvictims.[70] Poverty has decreased in Aceh since the end of the conflict, more so in the conflict-affected areas than in the nonconflict-affected areas, but the province still lags behind the national average.

Aceh also shows how community-driven programs can kick-start local reconstruction and social protection. Soon after the peace agreement was signed, BRA initiated community-based reintegration assistance through the Kecamatan Development Program. Aimed exclusively at conflict victims, the program provided US$22.7 million of government money in one round of grants and operated in 1,724 villages in 2007.[71] It focused on conflict-affected communities to help them improve living conditions through small projects. Poverty declined by 11 percent more in villages participating in the program than in those that did not.[72] Given that almost 90 percent of funds went to purchase private goods, community-driven development (CDD) projects can be an effective mechanism for distributing one-off cash transfers in emergency situations.[73] Survey data show that 88 percent of recipients felt that both BRA-KDP and KDP funds were spent on the most important needs.[74]

Sources: Aspinall 2005; International Crisis Group 2005; Morfit 2007; MSR 2009; World Bank 2010a; Government of Republic of Indonesia and Free Aceh Movement 2005; Braud and Grevi 2005; Schulze 2007; World Bank 2008a; Barron 2010; Barron and others 2009; Morel, Watanabe, and Wrobel 2009; Government of Aceh, Syiah Kuala University, and World Bank 2008.

Notes

1. Background work for this Report included review of almost 30 low- and middle-income country cases—both successful efforts to transition away from violence and those less successful—that experienced a mix of forms of stress and types of violence as identified in chapters 1 and 2. The cases varied widely in their institutional characteristics, ranging from low-capacity countries with relatively accountable institutions to higher capacity countries with weak accountability mechanisms. This work was supplemented by national and regional consultations with politicians and analysts from government and nongovernment institutions.
2. As noted in the guide to the WDR, commitment mechanisms are means of persuading stakeholders that intentions will not be reversed. This follows the common economic definition of commitment mechanisms or commitment devices. See Dixit 1980; Schelling 1960; Spence 1977.
3. See Hartzell, Hoddie, and Rothchild 2001; Walter 2004; Nilsson and Jarstad 2008; Wennmann 2009.
4. See Stedman 1996; Adam and Mesnard 2003; Nilsson 2008.
5. Fearon 2004, Keefer 2008. Also, for peace agreements, see Suhrke, Wimpelmann, and Dawes 2007. For power-sharing arrangements, see Papagianni 2009; Gates and Strøm 2008; Spears 2002; Sawyer 2004. For security sector reforms, see Azam and Mesnard 2003. For consociationalism, see Lijphart 1969, 1977; and Andeweg 2000.
6. International Crisis Group 2008b; Friends Committee on National Legislation 2009.
7. Odendaal 2010; Ojielo 2007; UNDPA 2010a.
8. Seely 2001; Keita 1998; Straus 2010.
9. According to leadership development literature, the three qualities of effective leadership include the ability to set direction, including defining and vetting a vision among relevant individuals and groups; to create alignment, including coordinating the knowledge and work of a collective in service of this broader direction/vision; and to maintain commitment to this broader direction/vision, including through the expansion of the group's efforts to achieve collective goals, not just individual goals. For more information about leadership theories, see Northouse 2008; Hughes, Ginnett, and Curphy 2005; McCauley and Van Velsor 2004.
10. Knox 1996.
11. Timor-Leste Ministry of Finance 2010; WDR team consultation in Timor-Leste, 2010.
12. Dupuy and Binningsbø 2008.
13. de Waal and Flint 2008.
14. See Sapelli 2000. Other examples include Argentina, where under the Alfonsin administration, efforts to make more rapid progress in transitional justice within the security sectors were accompanied by four coup attempts, a political crisis, and the subsequent more cautious approach to reform adopted by the Menem administration. See Addison 2009; de Greiff 2010.
15. WDR team interview with former president Álvaro Uribe, 2010; WDR team consultation with government officials, representatives from civil society organizations, and security personnel in Colombia, 2010.
16. Jeffries and Thomas 1993.
17. Kimani 2008; International Crisis Group 2009d; Cheeseman and Tendi 2010.
18. Mack 2003.
19. WDR team consultation with government officials, representatives from civil society organizations, and security personnel in Colombia, 2010; WDR team consultation in Timor-Leste, 2010.
20. Walter 1997.
21. These include inter-clan pacts in Somaliland; traditional dispute resolution at a national level in Mali; the ceasefire agreement brokered by community action in Bougainville, Papua New Guinea; and the peace committees in South Africa. See also Menkhaus 2010; Bradbury 2008; Van der Graaf 2001; Dinnen, Porter, and Sage 2010; Carl and Garasu 2002.
22. Data on battle deaths in Uganda from the UCDP/PRIO Armed Conflict dataset (Lacina and Gleditsch 2005; Harborn and Wallensteen 2010). Data on homicides comes from statistics based on LA County Sheriff's Department, California Department of Justice and Los Angeles Police Department, and compiled by the Los Angeles Almanac (Thornton and others 2011).
23. Anderlini 2010b.
24. Sirivi and Havini 2004.
25. Hunt and Posa 2001.

26. Las Madres de la Plaza first appeared as a distinct group on April 30, 1977, when 14 women decided to gather near the pyramid of the Plaza de Mayo in downtown Buenos Aires and demand that the repressive military regime disclose the whereabouts of their children who were abducted by the military due to their political ideals and associations and subsequently disappeared. Initially dismissed, then ridiculed, and later brutally persecuted, the ranks of Las Madres continued to grow and received recognition internationally for their nonviolent demonstrations in a society cowed into silence where all the traditional means of public expression, dissent, and protest were forbidden. Over time, the group of mothers transformed into a political movement and became a symbol of resistance against the military dictatorship. See Navarro 2001.
27. For instance, shaping a positive and inclusive relationship between citizens and the state has been an important part of Timor-Leste's institutional and political agenda since 2007. The government has actively worked on improving its communication and engagement capacity; a relaxation of the country's language policy (though most young Timorese speak Bahasa and very little Portuguese, the official language policy since 2000 mandated that Portuguese would be the national language of instruction and administration. This resulted in poor functioning of the civil service, a lack of development of media, and weak communication between the state and its people) is indicative of a general shift in the government's approach. Simultaneously, the international community started to lend more consistent support to initiatives that promote dialogue (see Von Kaltenborn-Stachau 2008).
28. Hartzell 2006; Paris 2004.
29. Cadeado and Hamela 2009.
30. Cadeado and Hamela 2009.
31. U.S. Government Accountability Office 2007.
32. Agence France-Presse 1999.
33. See de Greiff 2010, 11: "How do transitional justice measures promote this sense of civic trust? Prosecutions can be thought to promote civic trust by reaffirming the relevance of the norms that perpetrators violated, norms that precisely turn natural persons into rights-bearers. Judicial institutions, particularly in contexts in which they have traditionally been essentially instruments of power, show their trustworthiness if they can establish that no one is above the law. An institutionalized effort to confront the past through truth-telling exercises might be seen by those who were formerly on the receiving end of violence as a good faith effort to come clean, to understand long-term patterns of socialization, and, in this sense, to initiate a new political project around norms and values that this time around are truly shared. Reparations can foster civic trust by demonstrating the seriousness with which institutions now take the violation of their rights . . . vetting can induce trust, and not just by 're-peopling' institutions with new faces, but by thereby demonstrating a commitment to systemic norms governing employee hiring and retention, disciplinary oversight, prevention of cronyism, and so on."
34. Transitional justice approaches are defined by the UN as the "full range of processes and mechanisms associated with a society's attempt to come to terms with a legacy of large-scale past abuses in order to ensure accountability, service justice and achieve reconciliation. These may include both judicial and non-judicial mechanisms and individual prosecution, reparations, truth seeking, institutional reform, vetting and dismissals, or a combination thereof" UN 2004b, 4. See also Orentlicher 2004, 2005; UN General Assembly 2005a.
35. Gonçalve 2008.
36. Sirleaf 2007b.
37. Porter and Rab 2010.
38. See Kanungo 2004.
39. Sapelli 2000.
40. WDR consultation with former key negotiators from the ANC Alliance and the National Party in South Africa 2010.
41. Successful social cohesion policies require recognition of language and/or cultural practice in cases where a group perceives itself systemically excluded and disrespected. In so doing, care must be taken to avoid creating further fissures or entrenching practices that curtail the civil rights of women, caste groups etc. See Easterly, Ritzen, and Woolcock 2006; Gupta 1970.
42. Pakistan Ministry of Information and Broadcasting 2010, 10.
43. WDR calculations based on data from the Latinobarómetro survey (1993–2008) and the Afrobarometer survey (1999–2009). See Afrobarometer 2009; Latinobarómetro 2009.

44. WDR team consultation with current and former leaders from conflict-affected countries and regions in Berlin, 2009.
45. The Politica Nacional de Rehabilitación (PNR) is a program of the Presidency of the Republic aimed at the establishment of peace; national reconciliation; and the normalization of areas affected by development imbalances, weakness in the institutional presence of the state, and social conflicts. See Presidencia República de Colombia 1993.
46. See Pavanello and Othieno 2008; Baird 2010.
47. Barron 2010.
48. The literature on community-driven development in situations of fragility and conflict is extensive; see, for example, Baird 2010; Cliffe, Guggenheim, and Kostner 2003.
49. Experimental evaluations of CDD programs are rare. One example is Fearon, Macartan, and Weinstein 2009, who carried out research on the impact of a community-driven reconstruction program in 42 communities in Liberia. "A field experiment in which villages in northern Liberia were randomly assigned to receive international development assistance provides evidence that the introduction of new local-level institutions can alter patterns of social cooperation in a way that persists after the program's conclusion. Villages exposed to a community-driven reconstruction program exhibit higher subsequent levels of social cooperation than those in the control group, as measured through a community-wide public goods game. These results are striking. They suggest that changes in community cohesion can take place over a short period of time; can occur in response to outside intervention; and can develop without fundamental changes either to the structure of economic relations or to more macro-level political processes. Random assignment of communities to treatment provides confidence in the causal nature of the relationship, and the use of behavioral outcome measures reinforces our sense that the effects are real. These findings suggest that post-conflict development aid can have a measureable impact on social cohesion" (Fearon, Macartan, and Weinstein 2009, 12). For a broader discussion of violent conflict and the transformation of social capital, see Colletta and Cullen 2000.
50. The randomized impact evaluation of the National Solidarity Programme (NSP) is a multiyear study designed to quantify changes—across indicators such as economic activity, agricultural production, access to infrastructure and services, and structures and perceptions of local governance—in 250 "treatment villages" compared to those villages not participating in the NSP. The evaluation is being led by Andrew Beath of Harvard University; Professor Fotini Christia of Massachusetts Institute of Technology (MIT), Shahim Kabuli of the World Bank, and Professor Ruben Enikolopov of the New Economic School, and is being implemented in conjunction with the Vulnerability Analysis Unit (VAU). It is being supported by the World Bank, the Food and Agriculture Organization of the United Nations (FAO), and the Ministry of Rural Rehabilitation and Development (MRRD) of the Government of Afghanistan. For more information, see the National Solidarity Programme website: http://www.nsp-ie.org/index.html.
51. Shura is an Arabic word for "consultation" or "council." The word itself can describe an assembly, an organized body of participants, or an administrative body or council, or may describe a decision-making process. In Afghanistan, tribal shuras have played an important role in community security and governance since the absence of a functioning government in 1978, and continue to play a pivotal role in the provision of justice.
52. Patel and Ross 2007, 43.
53. See Melville 2003.
54. Verhey 2001.
55. Carter and Clark 2010; Siddiqui 2011.
56. As noted in chapter 1, the WDR team asked the Norwegian research institute Fafo to conduct surveys in seven countries and territories, involving a mix of nationally representative samples as well as subregions affected by violence. One of the survey areas focused on the entity that should be responsible for providing public goods, such as reducing unemployment and protecting national security. The survey offered respondents a range of actors (the national government, private enterprises, traditional authorities, and so forth). In answering the question: "Who should be the main body/entity responsible for allocating land?" respondents as a whole (across the seven locations—Colombia, Côte d'Ivoire, the Democratic Republic of Congo (North and South Kivu provinces), Mali, Sierra Leone, and the West Bank and Gaza) chose traditional leaders as the second most important entity for land allocation following national governments. In some countries (for instance, Côte d'Ivoire), the percentage of respondents who identified traditional leaders (57 per-

cent) actually surpassed those who identified the national government (30 percent). Of all the responsibilities, land allocation (22 percent) was on average the most popularly identified area for traditional leaders, followed by protecting rivers and forests (6 percent). See Bøås, Tiltnes, and Flatø 2010.

57. Protocol-based school management system is a school management system in which control is decentralized. The government provides authorization for private entities (in most cases faith-based groups) to operate schools under specific government guidelines and regulations. These guidelines cover areas such as curricula, norms regarding class size, qualification and salaries of teachers, and system of assessment.
58. Baird 2010.
59. Contracting out is one mechanism for accountability between policy makers and service providers and tends to work better when both parties are focused on outcomes and keep the formal processes light. Effective monitoring and evaluation of results is essential to reward good performers and improve or replace those who are not doing a good job. See Baird 2010.
60. See, for example, Wood 2008, which shows how warring parties make use of networks at the substate level, and also how legacies of conflict are transmitted through these networks into political and military life, local identities and authority structures, gender roles, and political relationships. See also Peterson and Zuckerman 2010. Blattman charts the need for further micro-level research on the topic. See Blattman, forthcoming; Spear and Harborne 2010.
61. For a discussion about privatizing certain security functions in peacemaking, peacekeeping, and enforcement, see Gerson and Colletta 2002.
62. Gómez 2008; Meléndez 2007; Muñoz 2010; Arias 2009.
63. Nwana 2000, 1.
64. McCall 2004, 1.
65. World Bank 2010a.
66. Government of Republic of Indonesia and Free Aceh Movement 2005.
67. MSR 2009.
68. This amount represents only one-seventh of the amount provided for the tsunami reconstruction effort—even though the estimated economic cost of the conflict (Rp. 107.4 trillion) was almost twice the cost of damage and losses from the December 2004 tsunami (MSR 2009).
69. MSR 2009.
70. The MSR report hypothesizes that this could be because people who were employed during the conflict were more likely to be targeted or possibly that nonvictims are more likely to be students. Moreover, it is also likely that employment-generating projects that target conflict victims may miss non-victims who also need assistance (MSR 2009).
71. Barron 2010.
72. Barron and others 2009.
73. Morel, Watanabe, and Wrobel 2009.
74. Barron and others 2009.

Chapter 5 describes the dilemmas of institutional transformation for resilience to violence. The first of these is about timelines: delays in a "too slow" reform process prolong states' vulnerability to violence. But lessons from the history of institutional transformation provide cautionary evidence that going "too fast" creates other risks of backlash. Countries that have addressed violence have sequenced reforms, frequently over a generational time period, to develop social consensus, and to allow their societies to absorb change and to develop their institutional capacities. The second dilemma is about the prioritization of institutional reforms. This chapter provides lessons from country reform approaches to security, justice, and jobs, as well as from wider issues like elections and corruption, on how experimentation, adaptation, and pacing can result in "best-fit" reforms that are adapted to the local political context.

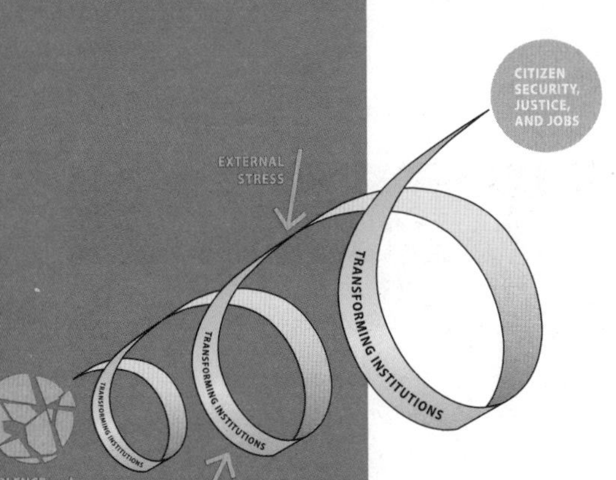

CHAPTER 5

Transforming institutions to deliver citizen security, justice, and jobs

Pacing and sequencing institutional transformation

Pent-up demands for change in fragile and transitional situations, and the importance of legitimate, capable, and accountable institutions for violence prevention, mean institutional transformation is central to effectively linking security and development approaches. This section of the Report describes lessons on the pacing, prioritization, and sequencing of reform.

Avoiding "too much, too soon," and finding the "best fit"

With deficits in the quality of governance in many sectors in most fragile situations, the best approach may seem to be rapid, across-the-board institutional transformation. But the *scope* and *speed* of reform are themselves risk factors—and attempting to do too much too soon may actually increase the risk of resumed conflict. The "too much, too soon" syndrome leads to many of the symptoms observed in difficult transitions such as the following:

- Overtaxing the existing political and social network capacity of national reformers (as in the Central African Republic and Haiti in the early 2000s).[1]
- Transplanting outside "best practice" models without putting sufficient time or effort into adapting to context (for instance, in Iraq).[2]
- Adopting an output orientation that defines success in the de jure space in the capital city (for example, by passing laws, writing sector plans and policies, or creating new commissions or organizational structures) and not an outcome orientation in the de facto world where people live (by improved services, even if basic, in insecure and marginalized rural and urban areas), such as in Timor-Leste from 2002 to 2005.[3]
- "Cocooning" efforts into parallel channels that facilitate short-run accomplishment by bypassing national organizations and institutions, and undermine national institution-building in the longer term, as, for example, in Afghanistan in 2001–03 and to some extent afterward.[4]

Once national and local reformers have set priorities and sequenced their goals for transforming institutions, the next steps might seem straightforward. Out there somewhere is the "state of the art," the "best practice," the "technically perfect" way. Common sense says not to "reinvent the wheel" but to adopt what works well. And so, national and international actors alike feel the temptation

REFLECTIONS FROM ADVISORY COUNCIL MEMBERS: *2011 WORLD DEVELOPMENT REPORT*

BOX 5.1 *China's approach to gradually piloting economic reform*

Ambassador Wu Jianmin, Chairman of the Shanghai Center for International Studies; *WDR Advisory Council Member*

China's economic reform and opening up to the outside world policy has led China in the last 32 years to a strong and steady growth. This policy generated a tremendous change in China. There are three key factors which made China's economic reform successful: bottom-up approach, gradualism, and a principle to pilot reforms and measure their impact before debating whether they should be national policy.

China's economic reform started first in the countryside. In 1978 China's urbanization rate was 17 percent. The overwhelming majority of the Chinese population was in the countryside. In 1978, 18 peasants from Anhui province, Xiaogang village, decided to break away from the centrally-planned economy and signed a secret contract. In accordance with this contract, they divided the land at their disposal into small pieces. Every peasant was responsible for his small piece of land and agricultural production. This contract provided a powerful incentive for them to produce more food, so that they could enjoy a better return. The provincial government was very much supportive of this 18 peasants' initiative. At the same time, in Guangdong province, some people started private business with the local government's tacit agreement. However, other provinces were very much skeptical about it. They believed that kind of reform was wrong, "capitalistic," and incompatible with a socialist China.

The central government of China did not ask other provinces to adopt the same reform. It wanted the good results of the reform to convince those hesitant provinces. The fact speaks louder than any argument. Three years later, Anhui province which practiced this reform enjoyed more food on their plate. Gradually, other provinces followed suit.

At the beginning of China's economic reform, people had very different views about it. Many people believed that the reform underway was not in compliance with Chairman Mao's teaching. The Chinese government under Deng Ziaoping adopted a principle to pilot reforms and measure their benefits before debating whether they should be national policy, building on the change in thinking that had taken place after the Cultural Revolution which aimed to "emancipate the mind" from divisive ideological debate.

To carry on successfully the reform, what we need most is people's support. We can get it only when reform brings tangible benefits to the people. Step by step, a unified narrative on development, based on results, was created. History proved Deng Xiaoping right, avoiding the division of the Chinese people into different camps, or engaging in an endless sterile debate and instead producing a real improvement in the people's welfare.

to apply off-the-shelf international best practices. But these practices are often designed for environments that are secure, have a high degree of capacity in state institutions, and have functioning competitive markets. Environments of repeated violence are insecure, have institutional deficits, and generally have only partially functioning markets. So the simple notion of "not reinventing the wheel" and just adopting best practice does not succeed nearly as often as one might hope.

An alternative is to focus on pragmatic, best-fit options adapted to political realities, institutional capacity, and levels of insecurity. Countries successfully moving away from fragility or violence have adapted solutions from abroad to suit their context. The fact that simply copying does not work does not negate the value in learning from other country experiences. By so doing, countries create their own practical and feasible solutions adapted to their particular set of available institutions and capabilities. An example is China's Township and Village Enterprises: These were not "private sector" firms at all. They were instead a transitional device that provided many of the functions of private sector firms (dynamism, innovation, investment) without all the legal and institutional accoutrements private sector firms need. So, rather than wait for the environment to be right for one institution (private firms), the Chinese government created a new form of enterprise (box 5.1).

Early attention to basic functions of citizen security, justice, and job creation

Chapter 2 underlined that the stresses associated with violence can occur in the security, justice, and economic arenas. The research

REFLECTIONS FROM ADVISORY COUNCIL MEMBERS: *2011 WORLD DEVELOPMENT REPORT*

BOX 5.2 *It takes time to build institutions. First things first—citizen security, justice, and jobs*

Minister George Yeo, Minister of Foreign Affairs, Singapore; *WDR Advisory Council Member*

It takes time to build institutions. Getting the urgent things done first, especially improving security, delivering basic justice, and providing jobs, helps people to feel more hopeful about the future. Success then creates the condition for further success. Without a practical approach, new institutions cannot take root in the hearts and minds of ordinary people. For Singapore in the early years, being pragmatic was not a choice but a necessity. Ideology was a luxury we could not afford. We had to do first things first and get our priorities right. Then, as the economy took off and life got better, we could be more refined and sensitive in public policy. We were fortunate to have many friends who wished us well and assisted us in ways big and small.

In the first few years of independence, the priority was on security, law and order, and creating favorable conditions for investment and economic growth. Confidence was everything. National Service was introduced within a year. Secret societies and other criminal activities were suppressed. Corruption was progressively rooted out. To promote investment, labor and land acquisition laws were reformed early. Against conventional wisdom in many developing countries at that time, we eschewed protectionism and encouraged multinationals to invest. We did not allow profit to become a dirty word. Opening wide the portals to the outside world was a sine qua non—the sea port, the airport, telecommunications. Managing the politics of change was always a challenge. At every step of the way, we had to give hope to the population that tomorrow would be better than today. A long-term massive public housing program was launched with home ownership a priority. This gave every household an equal stake in Singapore's development. The program was financed through a system of compulsory savings. A national focus was brought to the education system, helping us to overcome racial and religious divisions. Having to accommodate so many people on a small island, we had to develop skills in urban planning, including good public transportation, traffic management based on pricing of scarce road space, and provision of green space so important for public morale. We studied the experiences of other countries and adapted them to our own situation.

All this had to be done in a way that won majority support at every general election. The key was winning the trust of the people. Institutions which endure are sustained by the respect and affection of the population. It is a process which takes at least a generation. Institutions are not built by merely passing laws or engaging consultants.

on the stresses and institutional factors associated with risks of violence covered in chapter 2, country cases studies, and consultations with national reformers all point to the importance of prioritizing the institutions that provide citizen security, justice (including control of corruption), and jobs to prevent a recurrence of violence and lay the basis for future reform.[5] This prioritization is confirmed by findings of the Voices of the Poor project and the country-level surveys conducted for the WDR: people's top priority after basic security and law and order is their own economic survival.[6] Prioritizing security, justice, and jobs does not mean addressing all the wide-ranging functions that will be needed in these areas as societies develop—but simply focusing on basic progress in these areas early in transitions from violence (box 5.2)

This chapter presents a range of practical interventions across the domains of security, justice, and jobs. These interventions include those that deliver early results to build citizen confidence, which can either buy time for institutional reforms to take hold, or actively support such reforms. Emphasis is also placed on interventions that use best-fit institutional approaches that offer practical solutions to given problems; they may be context-specific, but they demonstrate the adaptability of a wide range of tools. Early actions and best-fit approaches are linked to priority reforms that can be undertaken with limited capacity, even in fragile contexts. These are set apart from reforms that would generally be applied more gradually as they require more fundamental social, economic, or political shifts.

Multisectoral approaches

The interventions in this chapter are presented for each domain—security, justice, and jobs and associated services—separately.

BOX 5.3 *Coordinated political, security, and development responses to violence—Lessons from urban, subnational, and organized criminal violence in Latin America*

Multisectoral violence prevention programs suggest a way of bringing different actors together to address the complexities of violence. In rapidly urbanizing areas—not only in the developing world, but also in high- and middle-income countries—violence is characterized by the convergence of a wide range of risk factors, including overcrowding, inequality, youth unemployment, and drug crime. While violence has traditionally been managed through the criminal justice sector and coercive responses, recent multisectoral approaches, particularly in Latin American cities, have demonstrated the benefits of a more integrated response. The approaches emphasize a balance between long-term structural prevention and control-oriented approaches and address a variety of stress factors simultaneously. The emphasis on local government and community engagement in design, implementation, and oversight has fostered better diagnoses of the drivers of violence and ensured stronger community ownership.

The city of Belo Horizonte, Brazil, had a steep rise in homicide rates from 1997 to 2001. The victims and perpetrators of violence were often young men under the age of 24 living in slums. Preventive actions were implemented by the state government of Minas Gerais, in partnership with the city and nongovernmental organizations, under the program *Fica Vivo*, which targeted youth for social support, education, and sports. Social interventions were accompanied by a new form of policing that first captured sought-after criminals and then installed a permanent community police element—gaining the trust and confidence of the population. An evaluation of the program in one of the targeted communities showed reductions of as much as 45 homicides per 100,000 inhabitants per semester compared with the rest of the city. *Fica Vivo* has a return on investment of 99–141 percent of the total cost of the program.

In Bogotá, Colombia, between 1993 and 2002, a multisector strategy was credited with progress in combating urban violence. The strategy included campaigns to promote citizen disarmament and control of alcohol consumption; neighborhood crime-monitoring committees; family police stations to control domestic violence and reduce assaults on women; police reform measures; urban renewal efforts, such as the *Transmilenio* urban transport program; and employment programs. Evaluations showed that some of these interventions resulted in sizable reductions in the levels of violent crime. For example, restrictions on gun carrying during weekends and holidays are credited with reducing the homicide rate by 14 percent. The urban renewal and transportation program, known as *Transmilenio,* was credited in some of the most violent areas of Bogotá with reducing overall levels of crime and violence dramatically by 86 percent. Interventions related to the strengthening of the police force and interventions to alleviate the backlog of cases in the judicial system and speed up trials also had notable reductions in the levels of violent crime, with a 76 percent reduction in the assault rate.[7]

Source: Alvarado and Abizanda 2010; Beato 2005; Fabio 2007; International Centre for the Prevention of Crime 2005; Duailibi and others 2007; Peixoto, Andrade, and Azevedo 2007; Guerrero 2006; Llorente and Rivas 2005; Formisano 2002; WDR team consultation with law enforcement, civil society, and Brian Center (Executive Director, A Better LA in Los Angeles), 2010.

However, their combination, both within and across the domains, is both feasible and, in fact, desirable in most instances, as highlighted in chapter 4. The interventions thus should not be viewed in isolation but as part of a comprehensive approach to delivering results and transforming institutions. Specific multisectoral approaches bridging these areas have generated promising results. For instance, in rapidly urbanizing areas in Latin America and the United States, where gang- and drug-related violence have resisted "hard" policing efforts,[8] there has been over time a gradual shift toward multisectoral programs of prevention at the community level. The programs combine short-term, quick-impact programs (targeted policing, urban upgrading, and social service provision) with longer-term preventive interventions (changing cultural norms, building alternative conflict resolution mechanisms). Brazil and Colombia have established some of the most intensive efforts to foster multiagency approaches, creating teams drawn from the military, police, and civilian service agencies that work together in combined national and local offices to address all aspects of local crime reduction and violence prevention (box 5.3). While programs of this kind are demanding for interagency coordination, their results suggest that their underlying principles are worth considering in violence-affected areas in other regions.

Citizen security

Consolidating and coordinating security services is a fundamental first step in institutional reforms to prevent violence. Former United Nations (UN) Under-Secretary-General for Peacekeeping Operations Jean-Marie Guéhenno points out that, "Re-establishing trust between the people and the state must therefore start with the core function of a state, the capacity to assert its monopoly on the legitimate use of force."[9]

A state may have lost the monopoly over the use of force because rebel forces or armed criminal groups operate in its territory with impunity—but also because fragmented security services within the state operate without overall coherence of command and control, contradicting each other. In the West Bank and Gaza, prior to security reforms enacted in 2005, the Palestinian security forces had 12 divisions under multiple chains of command and multiple authorities, employing 40,000 people. This lack of monopoly of force and clear lines of authority had the effect of increasing the potential for corruption and racketeering.[10] The need to consider a coordinated approach on police and military reform is also recognized in the 2007 security sector reform framework of the Organisation for Economic Co-operation and Development–Development Assistance Committee (OECD-DAC).[11]

Civilian oversight of the security forces is important early on if security forces are to be used in the national interest and prevent abuses. It involves links between political and security strategy and public finances. Three key elements in successful civilian oversight are as follows:

- Have political and military leaders discuss the mission of the security forces in supporting national objectives. This occurred in Colombia as part of the Democratic Security Policy (box 5.4). In contrast, little dialogue was held in Timor-Leste between 2000 and 2005 on the missions of the army and the police, which some argue culminated in renewed violence in 2006.[12]
- Use public finance systems to reinforce civilian control. Obviously, security sector personnel need to be paid and adequately equipped to perform effectively. They also need to be accountable for their finances: civilian oversight cannot work effectively where the security forces draw their sources of revenue off-budget. Equally important, ensuring that the security and justice sectors are funded adequately and transparently is critical to stem the diversion of illegal revenues from natural resources or trafficking to the security forces. Reforming budget systems in the security services was part of the Colombian Democratic Security Policy (box 5.4).[13] Reducing off-budget sources of finance (such as revenues from companies) was similarly important in Indonesia's transformation of the role of the military in political life. Palestinian leadership eventually addressed the fragmentation of the security forces by complementing political and security strategy with the use of budget and payment systems to increase accountability.[14]
- Commit the military to improvements in accountability and human rights. Underdeveloped security forces deployed into intensified operations may end up accused of preying on civilians, as in the Democratic Republic of Congo.[15] Such abuse is potentially disastrous for the legitimacy of the state because it cuts to the heart of the government's obligation to care for its citizens.

In post-conflict contexts, large security forces can be an unavoidable necessity in the short term, even if they are a drain on financial resources. The need to build trust between erstwhile enemies may call for the integration of the belligerent forces rather than their immediate disarmament, demobilization, and reintegration (DDR). For instance, following the end of the Ugandan civil war in 1986 and subsequent agreements between opposing forces, fighters were integrated into the National Resistance Army before the demobilization and reintegration program, the Uganda Veterans Assistance Program, was launched in 1992.[16] Similarly,

REFLECTIONS FROM ADVISORY COUNCIL MEMBERS: *2011 WORLD DEVELOPMENT REPORT*

BOX 5.4 *Colombia's establishment of civilian oversight and the Democratic Security Policy*

Marta Lucía Ramirez de Rincón, Director, Fundación Ciudadanía en Acción; former Senator and Chair of Security Commission, Colombia; former Defense Minister and former Foreign Trade Minister, Colombia; *WDR Advisory Council Member*

The challenge we faced in 2002 was preventing Colombia from becoming a failed state. This meant shielding our citizens from kidnapping and terrorism. It also meant protecting our infrastructure, roads, and democratic institutions against attacks by the guerrillas, the paramilitaries, and drug traffickers.

President Uribe's Democratic Security Policy called for the presence of the military and police over the entire territory of the nation within six months. This required not just more people in the armed forces, but also providing them with more equipment and better training in human rights and doctrine, so the police and military could operate successfully under a single command. It was also a result of American cooperation through Plan Colombia, a program initiated by the previous Colombian government, headed by Andrés Pastrana.

From the beginning, we stressed the importance of greater civilian control over defense. We brought civilians into the ministry to work with the military commanders on defense and security policy. This had the additional benefit of greater transparency in budget allocations and the management of other resources used by the military. Civilian engagement in budget planning with security force colleagues helped in the success of the Democratic Security Policy.

Having strengthened civilian control of the ministry, we embarked on an unprecedented exercise in developing a 10-year strategic plan with performance indicators against which we could chart progress in implementing the president's security policy. As Minister of Defense, I brought in representatives of the business community and academics of different ideological tendencies to provide input for the national security policy. The goal was both to increase the legitimacy of the policy and to build confidence in the armed forces. This was the first time such consultations had taken place. I also called on entrepreneurs to let us use their experience to help the government with procurement systems, logistics, and state-of-the-art technologies.

It is hard to put your finger on the precise reasons for our success. But over the past eight years we have won back control of the national territory. We have ended kidnapping on our roads—in the so-called "Pescas Milagrosas." And we have seen the number of terrorist organizations decline to the point where it would be hard to imagine their revival. Our focus now is on maintaining momentum. We must continue to pursue the policies that have brought success in recent years. And we must go further by strengthening our institutions and ensuring democratic civilian control of the armed forces whose monopoly over the use of force is recognized and respected.

WDR note: Why is it important to pay attention to the security and justice budgeting process?

Security and justice are essential public goods that benefit development and poverty reduction. It is both appropriate and necessary for the state to allocate resources for the maintenance of security and access to justice. Attention must therefore be paid to the financial management of the security and justice sectors so that resources are used effectively and efficiently against agreed priorities in a transparent and accountable manner.

Three crucial, inter-related components of managing security and justice expenditure are as follows:

- ***As in other parts of the public sector, security and justice budgets should be prepared against sectoral strategies.*** Governments must be able to identify the needs and key objectives of the security and justice sectors as a whole and the specific roles that the various security and justice actors will be asked to play.
- ***Resources must be allocated according to priorities both within the security and justice sectors and between security and justice and other sectors.*** Sectoral strategies and information on performance are critical components of the allocative process. The key financial and economic managers plus the legislature must have the capacity to be fully involved in this process, and the process must include all relevant actors. Security and justice must compete fully with other sectors for funding. Public expenditure analysis that covers the whole of government can help provide information to inform this process.
- ***Finally, resources appropriated must be used efficiently and effectively.*** This requires careful monitoring and evaluation of operational performance, both within the security and justice services and by civil servants. Basic well-functioning financial management information systems are critical in this regard. Additionally, it is extremely important that irregularities identified in the course of monitoring are addressed, lest a climate of noncompliance be created or reinforced. The transparency of procurement processes is as important in security and justice as in other areas. Internal audit units or inspector-general functions within the defense, justice, and interior ministries can play important roles in ensuring effective resource use.

Sources: Ball and Holmes 2002; Harbone and Sage 2010.

South Africa expanded the wage bill for security services as a transitional measure.[17] A lack of alternative livelihood opportunities also argues for a cautious approach to DDR. In Colombia, many former Autodefensas Unidas de Colombia (AUC) guerillas passed through a DDR process, only to reemerge as hired killers for the existing drug dealers or as leaders and operatives in new drug gangs.[18] The "least-bad answer" between fiscal costs and security risks may be tolerating an oversized security sector for a transitional period as a source of employment for combatants who would otherwise have little chance of finding work.[19]

Guéhenno also notes that "Trust depends on legitimacy, but legitimacy is also a function of effectiveness. A reformed security force needs to be perceived as professional. Recruitment and vetting [are] probably the single most important factor."[20] Dismantling covert, abusive, or corrupt networks within the security forces through recruitment or vetting has also been an important early reform in many countries that have sustained successful institutional transformations away from violence. In Bosnia and Herzegovina between 1999 and 2002, the United Nations Mission in Bosnia and Herzegovina (UNMIBH) vetted all law enforcement personnel in the country.[21]

The removal of abusers has often been achieved through indirect professionalization measures. For example, vetting in security services was not conducted in Argentina, but the requirement to accept nongovernmental organization (NGO) submissions on past abuses when confirming security appointments resulted in implicit "vetting out" of officers who did not want to face queries over their past records. Both Chile and Argentina made use of the recruitment of graduates into the security forces and increased emphasis on professional training to create an environment that furthered professional standards and made it difficult for abusers to prosper.[22]

Vetting programs can be strongly customized to context in three principal ways:

- Vetting programs differ in terms of their *targets.* No transitional society has reformed or vetted all institutions at the same time and, in fact, rarely even a single institution at all hierarchical levels. Choices have to be made about both the institutions where vetting will be applied and the positions within those institutions that will be subject to screening.
- Programs differ also in terms of the *screening criteria.* What kind of abuses, precisely, is the system designed to root out?
- Not all programs are the same in terms of the *sanctions* they impose; even firings can take place in many different ways (starting with a relatively mild one involving giving people the opportunity to resign without disclosing their participation in behavior considered abusive). Vetting sanctions can involve different degrees of publicity and also prospective limitations in seeking employment in various sectors in the future.[23]

Actions to reform the security services during transitions are often combined with deliberate decisions not to undertake actions that could threaten military support for change. In Indonesia, for example, the role of the military in civilian administration and in the economy was dramatically decreased, but little action was taken on past human rights abuses. In Chile, civilian oversight, elimination of abusive security units, and some prosecutions of past human rights abuses were undertaken quickly, but initial prosecutions were targeted and limited in scope and military revenues were protected under the "copper law."[24]

Attention to gender sensitivity and women's full participation in security-sector reform can contribute to success.[25] Women bring a more gender-specific value-added to broader security tasks, including enhanced access to services by women, fewer incidents of sexual misconduct, and greater trust of the civilian population in the security sector. Moreover, studies on policing have found that female police officers use less force, are better at defusing potentially violent situations, and facilitate community policing well.[26]

In Nicaragua, gender reforms of the police sector initiated in the 1990s resulted in the police being described as the most "women-friendly" force in the region, hailed for its success in addressing sexual violence.[27] In a similar vein, the UN Mission in Liberia's (UNMIL) all-female Formed Police Unit undertook joint crime prevention night patrols with local police in Liberia, helping them overcome lingering suspicions of citizens whose trust in the uniform had been eroded by civil war.[28] In Namibia, a Women and Child Protection Unit was created within the police force to address the problem of domestic violence.[29] In Sierra Leone, female victims had also been reluctant to come forward and seek help from police. The UN Mission in Sierra Leone helped create a Family Support Unit within the police department that included female police officers. This more compassionate environment for victims resulted in an increase in reports on sexual violence, 90 percent of which came from women and girls.[30]

Citizen security can be addressed at both local and national levels. At the local level, involving communities and the private sector can improve the relations between the state and its citizens and thereby help prevent violence and conflict. Effective interventions include the following:

- Community policing works by reducing crime through community partnership. Working with community members, it identifies, responds to, and solves crimes and other problems that affect the community.[31] Neighborhood policing is similar to community policing. It aims to provide a visible police force that is citizen focused and accountable to community members, expressing local solidarity, in order to meet a community's needs. For instance, community policing in Kosovo brought together residents, municipal governments, and security providers to agree upon specific "community safety plans." Easier and less sensitive security problems such as traffic violations were tackled first to allow for quick wins. Harder security concerns such as recovery and removal of illicit weapons were addressed once confidence was built in the process. Interviews with residents show tangible progress in reduction of minor security breaches, as well as improved community-police relations and perceptions of security.[32] Similarly, in the municipality of Hatillo in Costa Rica has applied community policing, involving community members in action plans for public safety. One year after implementation, the program's impact on delinquency was not significant, but the feeling of insecurity decreased from 36 percent of community members to 19 percent, and public perceptions of the police improved.[33]

- The private sector can support municipal governments and civil society in local crime and violence prevention initiatives. The police pacification units in Rio de Janeiro, Brazil, were started in late 2008 to replace coercive, short-term interventions in *favelas* with a long-term police presence and social services. The aim is to ensure the consolidation of territorial control and peace in the areas of intervention through the promotion of citizenship and development, fully integrating these areas into the larger city. The private sector helps finance the initiative, thus contributing to social and economic development in the pacified favelas.[34]

- Communities have prevented and responded to gender-based violence. The European Union (EU) military operation in the Democratic Republic of Congo collaborated with local women's organizations, which provided information on whom to contact regarding psychosocial, medical, and legal support whenever EU forces came across cases of sexual violence. The UN Mission there also organized villagers to establish a community alarm scheme to warn against intruding forces committing violent acts, often against women.[35]

It can be helpful to maintain long-established, functioning practices to help address policing and public security, even if these are not very "technical" solutions. In Haiti, Prime Minister Jean-Max Bellerive noted that the country needs a modernized force with advanced technical equipment for large urban areas, which face sophisticated and highly violent networks of gangs and organized crime. In rural areas, however, the traditional rural police force operated effectively in resolving small land and property disputes. Establishing a force with sophisticated technical equipment and a mission more suited to urban areas "should not make the police feel that it is no longer their job to walk up the hill and resolve a property or family dispute before it escalates into violence."[36]

Making security reform a top priority does not mean fully comprehensive reform and modernization across all aspects of these systems. Basic reforms that improve citizen security, and that prevent outright capture of the system, can enable reforms to move forward in other political and economic areas, allowing more gradual comprehensive reform and professionalization. Haiti's police force provides an example of progress in basic functions and state-society trust in the security institutions from a very fragile start (box 5.5).

BOX 5.5 ***Reform of the Haiti police force, even in difficult circumstances***

Types of violence: Widespread crime and gang-related violence, militia activity, organized crime, drug trafficking	
Transition moments: Major space for change, new national and police leadership, significant external support	**Key stakeholders:** Government, citizens, international partners, police
Key stresses: Legacy of violence and mistrust, drug trafficking and organized crime activities, low incomes, youth unemployment, corruption	**Institutional challenges:** Weak political, judicial, and security institutions; lack of accountability; low trust in security forces

The transformation of the Haiti National Police from the least to the most trusted institution of the state over five years can be attributed to a reform plan of internal and external actors. Reform was viewed not only as an internal technical activity, but first and foremost as a political process requiring the buy-in of Haiti's leaders. Their political support ensured that financial resources were allocated to pay salaries and support day-to-day police operations. Another external factor was that the UN Stabilization Mission in Haiti (MINUSTAH), through its military and police presence, contributed to internal security, allowing space for a thorough police training program.

With these critical external factors in place, the Haiti National Police (HNP), supported by MINUSTAH, professionalized the force, raised the morale of its officers, and boosted public confidence. It implemented procedures to vet existing officers and recruit new ones. Including women in the police force was given a priority by both the government and police leadership. A strengthened internal affairs unit acted decisively in cases of wrongdoing, reinforcing the value of and need for officer integrity. A seven-month initial recruit training program (rather than the typical two to three weeks often seen in post-conflict environments) was implemented alongside other specialized training programs. Each officer was properly equipped to undertake his or her policing functions and received regular salary payments. The police uniform, closely associated with the corruption and human rights abuses of the past, was changed—both to prevent former officers from using their uniforms for illegal activities and, more important, as a public symbol of the change in the police force. The HNP also strengthened its management, delegated more authority to the field, and enhanced its administrative and support functions.

Haiti's population has recognized the changes in the HNP: asked in 2009 whether they had seen a change in police work over the past year, 72 percent reported a positive change, and 83 percent reported that the security situation in the country was either "a lot" or at least "a little" better than in the year prior. Tested by floods, hurricanes, earthquakes, and nationwide food riots, the service on each occasion has performed credibly. Immediately after the earthquake and aftermath of January 12, 2010, the police was the only arm of government seen to be functioning in the streets of Haiti.

Source: UNDPKO 2010a.

Justice

Criminal justice functions and dispute resolution

Experience has shown that coordination across justice agencies is critical to reduce impunity, and that effective linkages must exist between the police and other justice institutions, including the judiciary, public prosecutors, and prisons, to address crime and violence.[37] While the police force in Haiti post-2004 made impressive strides (see box 5.5), advances in the courts and prison system did not match the police force's increase in capacity and legitimacy, so offenders were often released back into communities without due process and continued to engage in illegal activities. By contrast, the rule-of-law reforms introduced by the Regional Assistance Mission to the Solomon Islands (RAMSI) focused in parallel on police reforms, further developing a court system that once had a good reputation and refurbishing the country's prisons.[38] In middle-income country contexts such as the transitions from military rule in Chile and Argentina, where accountability posed greater constraints than capacity, reform of security and justice services proceeded at a more or less similar pace and were mutually reinforcing (some early changes, some more gradual).[39] Conversely, as noted in chapter 3, in Colombia capacity increases in the military and police were not matched by similar increases in resourcing and capacity within the courts, constraining overall progress.[40]

Vetting of personnel, discussed above in connection with the security forces, can also be crucial for judges and prosecutors. In Bosnia and Herzegovina, three High Judicial and Prosecutorial Councils (HJPC), made up of international and national personnel, restructured the court system and reappointed all judges and prosecutors between 2002 and 2004. Almost 1,000 posts were declared vacant, and there was open competition to fill them.[41] Indirect mechanisms have also been used to improve professionalism in the justice sectors. In Chile following the transition to military rule, rapid action on civilian oversight of the Carabinieri was combined with a reform to the promotion and confirmation processes of judges, which encouraged lower-level prosecutorial independence and merit-based promotion to higher courts.[42]

In terms of capacity-building, a focus on basic administrative functions, replacing of obsolete procedures, and targeting of improvements in caseload processing have tended to deliver better results than grand legal and judicial reform plans.[43] Governments and donors have often tended to sacrifice this pragmatism in approaches to reform justice systems, favoring redrafting legal codes over the administration of essential justice and basic institution-building (as in Afghanistan after 2001 and Iraq after 2003).[44] Provision of local-level justice services is important to maintain confidence in institutional reform efforts, and partnering with communities or civil society to do so can be an important link between early results and later institution-building. In Latin America, innovative local courts have been effective in bringing justice to the population (box 5.6).

Other approaches to increase access to justice that have shown positive results in areas underserved by the formal system are mobile courts and the use of paralegals. In Nicaragua in the early 2000s, mobile courts and community-based paralegals were credited with a 10 percent reduction in crime where the scheme operated.[45] The approach by Timap for Justice, a not-for-profit organization offering free justice services in sites across Sierra Leone, has also demonstrated important results. Paralegals backstopped by lawyers have assisted communities to address disputes and grievances since 2003. Qualitative research has shown that Timap's interventions have empowered clients (especially women) to claim their rights. Community perceptions of institutional fairness and accountability of the police, traditional leaders, and courts also improved as a result of Timap's work.[46] Building on Timap, donors and the government of Sierra Leone joined with nongovernmental organizations and community-based groups in 2010 to develop a national approach to justice services, including a front line of community paralegals and a smaller core of supporting lawyers.

Access to justice (and services) is often denied to those who are not registered, and registration initiatives can be an important form of recognition of citizenship and community identity for marginalized groups.[47] Organizations like the Community of Sant'Egidio, through its BRAVO (Birth Registration for All versus Oblivion) program,[48] the International Committee of the Red Cross, United Nations Children's Fund (UNICEF), and United Nations High Commissioner for Refugees (UNHCR), as well as nongovernmental organizations, have supported national authorities in registering births in difficult contexts. Effective tools include putting specific provisions in peace agreements for birth registration and proper identification, utilizing community "reporters" such as midwives through mobile registration programs, and combining birth regis-

BOX 5.6 Innovative court solutions in Latin America

Twenty-four-hour courts—arraignment courts that hear complaints and review fresh evidence—show how criminal cases can be expedited. One example is the 24-hour court that was established in 2005 by the Supreme Court of Guatemala. This is an interinstitutional effort, with not only the judiciary, but also the Public Ministry, the Ministry of Government, the National Civil Police, and Public Defense Institute participating. Apart from operating 24 hours a day, 365 days a year, the 24-hour court availability has facilitated compliance by the police with the due process requirement of presenting detainees to a court within a six-hour limit. Over the first three years of the court's operation, the number of cases it dismissed declined from 77 percent to under 15 percent. Nearly 50 percent of all arraignments ended in alternatives to detention, such as bail, house arrest, weekly presentations at the local court, or restrictions on travel. Drug consumption cases fell from over 30 percent to about 7 percent. And the courts made greater use of alternatives to trial.

In flagrante delicto courts were established in Costa Rica in 2008 on a pilot basis in San José to reduce criminal case disposition times. They were set up within the existing legal framework, with no need for further legal reforms. Their purpose is to ensure due process guarantees in simplified procedures to handle cases where the defendant is caught in the act of committing of a crime (that is, *in flagrante delicto*). These courts remain open 24 hours a day, 365 days a year and operate with several shifts of judges, prosecutors, and public defenders. The cases are turned over immediately to the prosecutors, who may request an immediate hearing with the judge to analyze alternative mechanisms, such as summary judgment or preventive detention. When the defendant and the public defender choose an expedited trial, it can take place immediately or be set in a few days.

In Colombia, ***Justice Houses***—integrated, multi-agency service centers—are used to solve conflicts. These Justice Houses, first designed and implemented by USAID (the United States Agency for International Development) in 1995, have assisted over 7.8 million citizens since inception, mainly from low-income communities. There are now 50 well-staffed facilities throughout the country in urban and rural areas, some of which are regional in nature. Given their success in reducing local conflict and preserving peace, plans include the construction of 10 new Regional Justice Houses in partnership with the Ministry of Interior and Justice. Other social services include *Peace Centers,* which are expanded versions of Justice Houses where the community has access to programs that promote citizenship values, peaceful coexistence, and amicable solution of conflicts. The first Peace Center opened in December 2002 in Barrancabermeja, one of the most violent areas in Colombia, and there are now 15 throughout Colombia.

Sources: World Bank 2010i; USAID Guatemala 2008; USAID 2009b.

tration with the provision of complementary services such as immunization.[49]

Supplementing formal justice with traditional community systems can be another best-fit. Deep and comprehensive judicial reforms can rarely be achieved in the short or medium term. One challenge of justice reform, then, is to create bridges between the formal and informal systems in the early stages of transitions. Traditional systems all over the world settle disputes over land, property, and family issues. As many as 80 percent of the people in today's fragile states relies on nonstate actors for various forms of security and justice.[50] For instance, in Kenya—where land is frequently a source of private and communal disputes, even when and sometimes because it is titled—traditional institutions are widely held to be more reliable in resolving conflict than the state.[51] In Mali in recent years, combinations of local traditional institutions and the state have settled land disputes, with community groups adjudicating between contestants, and all parties then recording the judgment at the local prefecture.[52] Informal women's courts can also supplement formal structures, generally convened by civil society to allow women to recount abuses. Women's courts have been used in Guatemala for abuses during the civil war, in Palestinian refugee camps in Lebanon for rapes during the 1982 Sabra and Shatila massacres, and in Japan around issues of World War II "comfort women."[53]

The lesson here appears to be to use a process of recognition and reform to draw on the capacities of traditional community structures and to "pull" them gradually in the direction of respect for equity and international norms. One such example is Timor-Leste's blending traditional customary law provisions into the formal legal system. In Timor-Leste after independence, a de facto hybrid system emerged, where local justice mechanisms continued to function in parallel to the formal legal system. The main reasons for confidence in the traditional system were that it resolved conflicts according to cultural norms and heritage (51 percent of survey respondents) and was less expensive and more effective than the formal justice system (38 percent of survey respondents).[54] As the formal justice system gained capacity, rather than attempting to entirely displace this informal system, the government in 2009 began a nationwide public consultation on the legal recognition of customary law processes, as envisioned under the constitution. Customary penalties, such as financial compensation, are being incorporated into the formal legal code. The process has also involved a debate on the tensions between formal and customary approaches applied to such crimes as rape.[55]

Corruption

Justice is also concerned with ensuring equitable access of citizens to the state's resources, that is, it is concerned with corruption. In Georgia, the Saakashvili government that was swept up to power by the Rose Revolution of 2003 cracked down on corruption in the public sector after 2003 by better disclosing public officials' assets, strengthening whistleblower protections, and improving public financial control and procurement measures. In addition, it criminalized active and passive bribery, enforced its criminal legislation and created the Anti-Corruption Interagency Council, tasked with developing and implementing a new national anti-corruption strategy. Three years later, Georgia ranked as a top anti-corruption reformer on several global actionable governance indicators, such that 78 percent of Georgians felt that corruption had decreased in the last three years, the best result among the 86 countries surveyed.[56]

Private and international capacity can supplement state systems in applying best-fit approaches to fight corruption in fragile situations. Liberia recognized it lacked the capacity to properly oversee its national forestry industry in the post-conflict period and turned to nonstate capacity to ensure revenue recovery from logging (under former president Charles Taylor, less than 15 percent of taxes owed from forestry revenue were collected) and to safeguard against money from sale of illegal wood being laundered through the legal supply chain. The government contracted a private inspection company to build and operate a system to track all timber from point of harvest through transport to sale, with an agreement to transfer the system back to the government after seven years. The system ensures the government collects all revenues because it will not issue an export permit until the Central Bank confirms that all taxes have been paid.[57] Similarly, both Indonesia and Mozambique have used private sector customs collection agencies to help increase efficiency in an area that is always highly vulnerable to corruption.[58]

Transparency of budget and expenditure information is an easy change to put in place early on, and can be crucial to stem illegal flows of funds into violent activities. For example, Timor-Leste's Petroleum Law, which came into effect in 2005, was established very early in the transition to independence. It establishes a high degree of transparency over funds and recommends that the government only withdraw amounts up to what is needed to maintain the capital value of the country's oil assets.[59] The framework for petroleum revenues has remained robust and protected national assets, even during a bout of renewed insecurity in 2005–06, and is supplemented by open reporting to parliament and the public on expenditures in each ministry, including the security sectors.

Local community and civil society organizations can also combat corruption. "Social accountability" approaches draw on the incentives for citizens and communities to monitor the expenditures most directly affecting their welfare. These tools include citizen report cards, community scorecards, participatory public budgeting, and public expenditure tracking surveys, as well as community-driven development approaches where expenditures are publicized transparently at the local level. In fragile situations, such social accountability tools can contribute to building citizens' trust in the state at the national and local levels.[60] The results can be significant. In the Kecamatan Development Program in Aceh, Indonesia, 88 percent of the population surveyed believed that the program funds had been properly administered and spent on what they considered most important.[61] In Madagascar, community monitoring in the health sector (via community scorecards) led to a 10 percentage point increase in consumer satisfaction with health services (from 39 percent to 49 percent) in as little as four months. Scorecards also helped improve the regularity of salary payments and interactions between users, health staff, and village administrators.[62]

Determined reformers, supported by equally determined international partners, can achieve important gains in public accountability and transparency, even in difficult circumstances (box 5.7). In 2002 the Palestinian Authority embarked on a reform of its public financial management system and in less than two years achieved several notable improvements. All revenue payments were centralized into the central treasury account, eliminating previous discretionary and non-transparent spending by line ministries. The Department of Supplies and Tenders in the Ministry of Finance assumed full jurisdiction over all purchases (above the threshold value of US$15,000) by ministries and agencies, including the Security Financial Administration. Salary payments to security personnel were made directly into their bank accounts instead of the previous cash handouts. And the previous large discretionary transfer appropriation for the president's office was virtually eliminated, with these funds instead transferred to service ministries (Health, Education, and Social Affairs).[63]

Private sector enterprises can also establish their own pragmatic, best-fit procedures to deal with the risk of corruption, even in weak institutional contexts (box 5.7).

Jobs

Private sector recovery

Alleviating key bottlenecks identified by the private sector can help to restore confidence by signaling to entrepreneurs a more business-friendly environment generating economic revival and setting the stage for broader reform. An early emphasis on simplification of business regulations—rather than expansion or refinement—has proved effective. In Bosnia and Herzegovina, the "Bulldozer Initiative" of 2002, and subsequent "guillotine" initiatives by the entity governments, mobilized the local business community to lobby for the elimination of significant bureaucratic impediments to private sector growth. The Bulldozer Initiative delivered 50 reforms aimed at eliminating excessive bureaucratic steps in 150 days, improving the investment climate.[64] Selective legal amendments that permitted freer trade and simplified inward investment have also produced early successes. Similarly, in 2001, as part of a strategy for private sector–led development, Rwanda overhauled its contract enforcement regime, long an impediment to investment. Domestic business registrations increased at 10 percent a year from 2001 to 2004, driving formal sector growth of 6 to 7 percent in 2003 and 2004.[65]

In violent situations, where business confidence is very low, however, creating the right environment for businesses is often not enough to attract investment; more direct intervention is needed for the private sector to play its catalytic role. One approach is to support value chains.[66] Links between producers, traders, and consumers can unravel with violence, eroding trust between social groups.

REFLECTIONS FROM ADVISORY COUNCIL MEMBERS: *2011 WORLD DEVELOPMENT REPORT*

BOX 5.7 *Experiences in countering corruption*

Flexible and robust mechanisms for combating corruption in the private sector

Mo Ibrahim, Founder, Mo Ibrahim Foundation; Founder, Celtel; *WDR Advisory Council Member*

When I founded Celtel in 1998 to build and operate mobile phone networks across Sub-Saharan Africa, well-meaning friends, shaking their heads in disbelief, told me two things: You will not succeed because there is no potential market for this new technology in this poor continent and you must be prepared to bribe every decision maker, at every level.

Well, Celtel was indeed a tremendous success. Africa proved to be the fastest growing continent for mobile phones. As for corruption, I did two simple things. First, I established a powerful and prominent company board. Then we decreed that any payment, initially above US$30,000, must be board approved.

This decision proved to be crucial to enforce the anti-bribery stand of the company and provided our managers on the ground with invaluable protection and cover. It indeed enhanced financial discipline throughout the operations. The wonderful support of our board members and their commitment to respond quickly to any unpredictable funding requirements was crucial. In fairness to African officials, the number of incidents where our people came under pressure to pay was far less than we had expected. On the three occasions we did resort to legal action in local courts, we won every single case. The valuable lesson I learnt was that corporate governance pays and it enhances your bottom line. It is not enough for company boards to make grand statements on corruption. Until and unless they put in place the policies that enforce and support their managers on the ground, their pronouncements will remain an empty attempt at discharging their fiduciary duties.

Making anti-corruption institutions effective in Rwanda after the genocide

H.E. Paul Kagame, President of Rwanda; *WDR Advisory Council Member*

In the early post-genocide period, Rwanda's recovery efforts were focused on stabilization, restoring security, fostering social trust, and rebuilding and reforming political institutions, as well as laying the foundations for economic recovery and growth. Three years after the genocide and civil war, work on institution-building to restore virtue and fight corruption began in earnest. Such efforts included the creation of the Rwanda Revenue Authority, Ombudsman's Office, Auditor General's Office, National Public Prosecution Authority, National Police and the Rwanda Public Procurement Authority, among others. These were complemented by legislative measures such as the Organic Law on the Leadership Code of Conduct, all of which were in place prior to the development of long-term economic strategies, thus ensuring that our fragile economic development was not wasted away through theft and greed.

A vital lesson drawn from our experience is that institution-building and appropriate laws are imperative. Nonetheless, making institutions and laws work effectively is often more difficult. In our context, the commitment to fight corruption was an important priority for the incoming Government in July 1994. A zero-tolerance policy resulted in the resignation or dismissal of holders of public office, among others, including some members of the Government of National Unity. Action was taken in this respect, by Parliament and the Executive, to enforce the notion of political accountability at a critical moment in our history and has nurtured increasingly effective governance institutions. This has been reinforced by a continued policy of consistently prosecuting corrupt officials. Upon reflection, it is clear that action against high-level officials, demonstrating that no one is untouchable, was critical. A continued strong public support for the anti-corruption effort was and is still of utmost importance, as this remains a work in progress.

Restoring these connections by bringing together market actors and providing information about market trends can create jobs and rebuild social cohesion.[67] It also provides local businesses with legitimate new market connections as an alternative to illegal activities, as with the Kosovo dairy and Rwandan coffee sectors (box 5.8). An approach that is promising for new market development, even in fragile environments, is matching grants for new market development that exploit the private sector's capacity to innovate and help entrepreneurs develop new product lines while sharing the risk of investment.[68]

Investment in basic infrastructure

Domestic and international investors need basic infrastructure. Electricity emerges as a key constraint to recovery efforts by the

BOX 5.8 *Value chain development in Kosovo and Rwanda*

Kosovo

Types of violence: Civil conflict; ethnic violence; political, criminal, and gang-related violence	
Transition moment: Large space for change, declaration of statehood, national and municipal elections, new constitution	**Key stakeholders:** Farmers, private sector, ethnic groups, municipal and national government, Serbian government, regional and international partners
Key stresses: Unemployment, legacies of violence and trauma, corruption, ethnic divisions, trafficking, unemployment, low incomes	**Institutional challenges:** Accountability and capacity constraints in public and private institutions, destroyed infrastructure, legacy of exclusion

Dairy is a traditional consumer product in Kosovo. In the 1990s, the command production system broke down and cooperatives dissolved. Many families became self-sufficient units, producing to meet their own consumption needs and trading surplus for other goods and services. The conflict of 1998–99 destroyed much of the production base, damaged infrastructure, displaced people, widened ethnic divisions, and eroded Kosovars' trust in each other and their government. Shortly after agricultural production and economic activity resumed in Kosovo, donors began working with value chain participants to upgrade the dairy industry. Value chain implementers worked first with individual farmers to make no- or low-cost changes to improve yields and quality, then expanded their reach by working with larger groups and associations. Thereafter, they steered farmers toward commercial channels, helping them further upgrade their processes to improve productivity and quality and to rebuild links with processors. In parallel, they worked with processors to orient them to end markets and, based on demand, to upgrade their processes and products to improve quality, expand production, and increase market share. By working from the micro to the macro as Kosovo moved from relief to development, donors and implementers supported upgrading and sustained growth in the dairy sector. In just over three years, for example, the Kosovo Dairy Value Chain project boosted domestic sales by €36 million and added 624 new jobs following an investment of €3.9 million. The impact on social cohesion is unclear. While a dairy board was set up that explicitly included both ethnic Albanians and Serbs, there was no evidence as to whether the board had a direct impact on participation of different ethnic groups or increased cooperation between ethnic groups.

Rwanda

Types of violence: Genocide; political, communal, and cross-border	
Transition opportunity: Large space for change post-genocide	**Key stakeholders:** Smallholder farmers, private sector, government, international partners
Key stresses: Intercommunal tension and ethnic divides, continuing security threat—mistrust/fear, trauma and legacy of abuse, return of refugees and IDPs (internally displaced persons)	**Institutional challenges:** Severe accountability and capacity constraints in judicial, security, and political institutions—public and private; legacies of communal suspicion and violence

Coffee, grown mostly by subsistence farmers, has long been an important source of income in rural areas and foreign exchange for the Rwandan economy. But the war and genocide of 1994 had a devastating effect on the coffee sector due to loss of life and the destruction or neglect of coffee trees. By 1996, coffee production was only about half the 1993 level. Between 2002 and 2006, the USAID (United States Agency for International Development)-funded US$5 million Agribusiness Development Assistance to Rwanda project boosted export-ready coffee production and created several thousand seasonal jobs.

Traditionally, farmers depulped and washed their cherries by hand before selling them to traditional exporters of semiwashed coffee. Modern stations now encourage farmers to sell them unwashed cherries, since they can process them more efficiently with modern equipment. By selling directly to the station rather than through intermediaries, the farmers are paid more per pound while avoiding the tedious hand labor.

The result has been tremendous. Between 2000 and 2006, the country went from producing 18 tons of fully washed coffee to 940 tons. There is also some evidence that greater economic security among participants in the coffee value chain is also linked to lower ethnic distance, lower distrust toward other ethnic groups, and a tendency toward conditional forgiveness.

Sources: USAID Rwanda 2006; Boudreaux 2010; Grygiel 2007; Parker 2008; Chuhan-Pole 2010.

private sector in fragile environments—but comprehensive reform of the electricity sector is made difficult by insecurity. Based on the World Bank Group's Enterprise Surveys, the number one business environment constraint faced by firms working in conflict areas is lack of electricity.[69] A state-of-the-art electrical grid typically has fewer generators (because of the economies of scale to generation, bigger is better) that are located far from consumers (since fuel sources—coal, natural gas, hydro—can be expensive to move). That design assumes away violent conflict: the technically perfect design is particularly susceptible to disruption, takes a long time to build, and is difficult to defend. Restoration of electricity in Lebanon demonstrates both the positives and the negatives of a best-fit approach to reform and institution-building in the electricity sector, which is also critical to private sector job creation. An alternative best-fit system gave nearly all households access to power, but at higher costs in the long term (box 5.9).

BOX 5.9 *Technically less than perfect, but robust to circumstances: Best-fit electricity provision in Lebanon*

Types of violence: Civil war, sectarian violence	
Transition opportunity: Space for rapid reconstruction and confidence building, but continued instability and threat of violence	**Key stakeholders:** Citizens, government, private sector, sectarian interests, governments of neighboring countries, international partners
Key stresses: Corruption, sectarian competition, legacies of violence, cross-border conflict spillovers, regional political involvement	**Institutional challenges:** Weak institutional capacity for public service provision, tenuous inclusion arrangements

By the time the Ta'if Accord (1989) put an end to civil war (1975–90), Lebanon was marked by widespread destruction of infrastructure and a climate of instability. At the time, little public confidence existed in the state and its institutions to deliver basic services. The electricity sector had suffered heavily during the war from extensive destruction and the significant reduction of payment collections. Despite this, most Lebanese people still benefited from some access to electricity during the war and in the initial stages of recovery—and continued to do so in subsequent periods of instability.

Already during the war, the bulk of electricity was provided by the private sector in the absence of a functioning public sector. A mix of individual and collectively owned electricity generators, run by a few formal and many informal private businesses, became an established part of the utility market. The ability of the private sector to fill the void left by a flawed public service owed much to an open and unregulated economy—and a strong culture of entrepreneurship.

Even after the end of the civil war, the private sector remained a critical energy supplier. Privately sold generators continued to supply electricity (primarily during blackouts) to both households and businesses and often covered whole neighborhoods. By 1994, for example, 98 percent of businesses and 95 percent of households were estimated to have received round-the-clock electricity, with a signification portion from private sources.

Although small-scale private capacity filled a void left by a lack of public sector engagement, the small, unregulated, and private provision of electricity has serious economic and environmental drawbacks as a long-term system. Private generation costs Lebanese households nearly twice as much as public generation. And the public electricity sector has yet to be reformed. State subsidies to the sector in 2007 were estimated to have reached 4 percent of the country's GDP. Lebanon's electricity sector thus illustrates the benefits of best-fit approaches during periods of crisis, but also the need to exit them over time to prevent long-term inefficiencies.

Given the electricity crisis during reconstruction efforts in Iraq, the question arises as to whether a best-fit, short-term solution could have been found. Iraq opted to rebuild its national electricity grid, but lack of progress in such a massive undertaking has left the proportion of unmet demand for electricity largely constant since 2003, at 40–50 percent. Did the political, economic, and security context in Iraq create an enabling environment for a private sector–led solution? In 2003–04, several Lebanese companies started establishing secondary neighborhood grids in Baghdad, supplied by small, private electricity generation. The Government of Iraq also considered policies to promote small, private generation in 2005, recognizing its own lack of capacity to meet demand in the short term. However, the deepening security crisis in Baghdad, including active campaigns to target small private power suppliers, preempted this approach. In comparison to Lebanon, Iraq's weaker tradition of private entrepreneurship and record of effective public service delivery into the 1990s may be additional reasons for the lack of emergence of privately generated electricity in the past decade.

Sources: World Bank 2008f, 2009d; Republic of Lebanon Ministry of Environment 1999; UN Inter-Agency Information and Analysis Unit 2010.

Road rehabilitation is another infrastructure investment critical to both private sector recovery and employment generation. It can aid both directly, by using local contractors and applying labor-intensive methods, and indirectly, by facilitating access to markets. For instance, in Afghanistan, the Salang tunnel—the only pass connecting Kabul to northern Afghanistan that is in use throughout the year—was reopened for traffic within weeks of the 2001 Bonn agreement after a four-year blockage, cutting travel time from 72 hours to 10.[70] In the Democratic Republic of Congo, the construction of a bridge linking two cities, Kikwit and Tshikapa, had similar effects. Travel time was cut to a few hours, as opposed to the previous five days, lowering the prices for food, fuel, and most other commodities imported to the diamond city of Tshikapa from the agricultural zones of Kikwit and surrounding cities.[71]

Public finance for employment and other "best-fit" approaches

Regulatory reform and infrastructure investments often take time to deliver jobs, however. Governments aiming to generate employment in insecure areas may need to provide an initial "bridge."[72] A 2009 World Bank review of labor-intensive programs in 43 low- and middle-income countries in the past 20 years finds that well-administered programs can have a substantial impact on the welfare and nutrition of poor beneficiaries, and that it is feasible to operate such programs on a large scale—as with Ethiopia's Productive Safety Net Programme (7 million beneficiaries in 2006) and India's National Rural Employment Guarantee Act.[73] Labor-intensive programs in fragile and violent settings can be a quick win for stabilizing a high-risk situation; examples include sporadic employment initiatives in the Gaza Strip since the 1990s and the Liberian Emergency Employment Plan, which created 90,000 jobs within two years.[74] Afghanistan's National Emergency Employment Program, now known as the National Rural Access Program, was expanded across the country after early successes and has generated 12.4 million labor days building or rehabilitating more than 10,000 kilometers of roads through 2010 in all of Afghanistan's 34 provinces.[75]

But labor-intensive public works are rarely sustained in fragile situations. These programs commonly are donor financed, and donors prefer short durations, between two and three years. Alternatives to short-term interventions could be labor-intensive public works programs in rural areas that are seasonal or vary in intensity between the seasons, to complement employment in agriculture (and that could be integrated into community-driven development programs; see chapter 4), or programs that are linked to a longer-term national strategy, such as the Feeder Roads Program in Mozambique, in operation since 1981, and India's long-term National Rural Employment Guarantee scheme.[76] For public works programs to be successful, evidence suggests that it is important to have clear objectives (for instance, aimed at addressing one-time shocks or poverty), to select projects that can create valuable public goods, and to ensure predictable funding.[77]

Providing (short-term) jobs needs to be complemented by enhancing skills and employability. Low skill levels—especially of young people like former gang members and combatants—constrain their opportunities for sustainable employment. International experience has shown that traditional vocational training programs without clear links to the labor market, though frequently implemented, are ineffective.[78] A more promising intervention is traditional apprenticeship programs and programs that include work placement opportunities.[79]

For those who did not complete primary education, second-chance programs (such as education equivalency or life skills training) are an important stepping stone to further education, training, and employment opportunities. Second-chance programs can have a positive impact on at-risk youth, both directly (which increases their chances of acquiring employment and receiving higher wages) and indirectly (by providing them with information and skills to make good decisions, giving them better prospects for a successful life, and consequently reducing their chances of engaging in risky behavior).[80] Conditional cash transfers could be linked to programs that focus on preparing both offenders and communities for offenders' reintegration, through technical and life skills training and links to employment opportunities,[81] such as YouthBuild International, which is active in over a dozen countries and supports youth for a period of up to 24 months.[82]

Support to agriculture in violence-affected countries is also essential. Together with the informal sector, agriculture is the most likely source of jobs in many conflict-affected situations.[83] Even in a relatively advanced economy, such as Bosnia and Herzegovina, informal employment is estimated to account for more than one-third of total employment,[84] and agriculture is an important income provider. There, for example, self-employment in agriculture was successfully supported for many demobilized soldiers who chose to reintegrate in rural areas and engage in small-scale farming. They received livestock and equipment (with a minimum holding period to ensure that they would not be sold on the market) and counseling, which enabled them to reestablish their livelihoods.[85] A wide range of activities can support this sector, including strengthening agricultural services, providing local extension programs that combine input supply with training on basic business skills, restoring rural roads, improving the agribusiness-enabling environment, improving land and water management, and organizing farmers into associations to connect them to commodity buyers and agricultural credit.

Supporting self-employment is another best-fit approach to creating jobs and generating incomes.[86] The main constraints to self-employment include the lack of market-creating infrastructure that brings trade into rural areas, lack of electricity that allows the use of higher productivity technology, lack of formal marketplaces and workplaces, high local taxes and fees, lack of access to informal savings and financial services (which could be alleviated by the use of mobile financial services such as M-Paisa in Afghanistan),[87] and lack of appropriate training (which needs to be designed for those with limited education and also stress basic skills such as literacy and numeracy). In order to be effective and avoid indebting poor households, self-employment assistance programs need to address all these constraints and not be limited to providing financial assistance.[88] Despite the popularity of self-employment programs in fragile and stable settings, evidence is scarce, however. The evidence (for middle-income countries) shows that self-employment programs can significantly increase the probability of young participants finding jobs, at least in the short term. But the cost-effectiveness and the longer-term effects still need to be proven.[89]

Asset expansion programs have also helped in some successful transitions from violence—such as land reform in the Republic of Korea and Japan,[90] and housing programs in Singapore (see box 5.2). Land reform contributed to post-conflict stability in those countries and, when combined with policies that favored agricultural growth and exports, set the stage for high rates of economic growth in succeeding decades. These positive experiences have proved difficult to replicate though, due to political resistance and institutional capacity weaknesses.[91] A different type of program to help violence-affected communities reestablish livelihoods and restore lost assets is, very simply, transferring funds directly to citizens to support their recovery. This may be done by government transfers, as with transitional payments to demobilized ex-combatants in Angola, Mozambique, and Rwanda—or Timor-Leste's cash payments to internally displaced people and veterans. Such programs can provide a sense of justice for populations previously excluded from state attention. There is a common perception that corruption or leakage is more likely in a cash transfer program, but years of practice have highlighted proven safeguards to reduce leakage.[92]

Temporary labor migration to neighboring countries or farther abroad can provide job opportunities for skilled and unskilled laborers from fragile or conflict-affected countries and requires few reform elements. Successful examples include the Russia Federation's aid for the post-conflict Tajik regime,[93] and the various migration streams for Pacific Islanders especially to Australia and New Zealand.[94] Such measures include fixed annual migration quotas, temporary seasonal employment, skilled and professional workers provisions, and education scholarships. Labor migration can diffuse some of the pressures on the labor market and generate remittances that can be used for social and economic expenditures like schooling or business start-up capital. Well-designed bilateral schemes can thus deliver important economic gains but also mitigate the economic and social costs for sending and receiving countries.[95]

Economic empowerment of women

Involving women in economic initiatives can generate jobs and income and lay the basis for longer-term empowerment, as well as enable them to contribute to the recovery of their communities. Women can be actors in violence; for instance, in El Salvador and Eritrea, nearly a third of the combatants were women.[96] But far more often, violence uproots women's lives and livelihoods, as chapter 1 described. Aiding women to recover socially and economically from violence not only benefits the women themselves, but also their families and communities. For example, in El Salvador, involving former women guerrillas in land reform led to the inclusion of both men and women as beneficiaries, ensuring that grievances on these issues would not later affect the post-conflict settlement.[97] A different example of economic empowerment, from Nepal, demonstrates how well thought out projects can produce small but significant social shifts within just a few years (box 5.10).

Engaging women in economic activities in fragile and post-conflict countries is not, however, without challenges. Women face limited mobility and physical access to markets, incomplete access to market information, and restricted access to credit and other

BOX 5.10 *Economic empowerment of women: Women's Empowerment Program in Nepal*

Types of violence: Civil conflict, interethnic and political violence, criminal violence, trafficking	
Transition opportunities: Modest space for change: "palace killings" and stepped-up Maoist campaign in 2001	**Key stakeholders:** Federal and local government, civil society groups, marginalized ethnic groups, international partners, regional neighbors
Key stresses: Legacies of violence and trauma: social, political, and economic inequality; youth unemployment; corruption; human rights abuses; rising expectations of formerly unrepresented groups	**Institutional challenges:** Feudal structures and associated exclusion; accountability and capacity constraints in public administration, security, judicial, and political institutions; lack of inclusion of women

Women in Nepal have suffered disproportionately from the decade-long civil war and the continued waves of political, criminal, and ethnically driven violence, including in the country's southern Tarai region. Women are among the poorest population groups; their traditional social and economic networks were severely affected and many became heads of households as a result of the conflict, and their educational attainment is significantly below that of men. In this context, empowerment of women is especially critical in engendering sustainable economic growth and human development, as well as signaling a break from the past.

The Women's Empowerment Program provided cost-effective training and support to 6,500 groups of 130,000 members in the Tarai from 1999 to 2001. Its impact on the lives of the participating women has been encouraging. Almost half of the women who participated in the program gained a level of literacy, and two-thirds of the women started a business since joining it, thus having an independent source of income for the first time. When 200 groups were asked how the program had changed their lives, they most frequently mentioned gaining self-confidence and an enlarged sphere of influence in the household, followed by learning to read and being accorded more rights.

Source: Ashe and Parrott 2001.

financial services, and they are also subject to restricting attitudes and systemic gender discrimination and exclusion through unfavorable legislation.[98] These obstacles are not insurmountable, however. Efforts as varied as promoting women's access to finance and helping financial institutions to bank on women entrepreneurs profitably (such as in Afghanistan), establishing baselines with a gender focus on helping the government formalize women's participation in national reconstruction efforts (for instance, in Liberia), promoting training and business mentoring opportunities that reach women entrepreneurs (in Iraq and Jordan), and using legal reform initiatives to ensure that existing gender-discriminatory legislation is revised and that new legislation provides a level playing field for women (as in the Democratic Republic of Congo) can be effective tools to make the gender balance less unfavorable to women.[99]

What to do systematically but gradually

Focusing on citizen security, justice, and jobs means that most other reforms will need to be sequenced and paced over time, including political reform, decentralization, privatization, and shifting attitudes toward marginalized groups. Systematically implementing these reforms requires a web of institutions (democratization, for example, requires many institutional checks and balances beyond elections) and changes in social attitudes. There are exceptions—where the exclusion of groups from democratic participation has been a clear, overriding source of grievance, as in South Africa, fairly rapid action on elections makes sense. But in most situations, systematic and gradual action appears to work best.

Elections are a means of institutional transformation, not its end

Elections without a substantial degree of cooperation among those wielding economic, political, or military influence at national and local levels are unlikely to succeed in their broader objectives. Initial transitions to multiparty elections have been shown to increase the short-term chances of conflict, even though countries with very robust democratic institutions lower their risks of violence in the long term.[100] Elite cooperation may require prior steps to build trust and confidence, such as those undertaken in South Africa.[101] In contrast, leaders lacking trust in "winner-take-all" scenarios may manipulate outcomes and protests, which can trigger serious violence—as in Iraq in 2005 and Kenya in 2007.[102] Holding elections before a reasonable degree of security has been achieved, and a non-coercive environment established for polling, makes little sense (box 5.11).

Where conditions of trust and security do not indicate that rapid elections will deliver increased legitimacy, other options exist. Approaches that build on traditional decision-making mechanisms (such as the Afghan Loya Jirga[103]) have been used to transition toward greater inclusiveness. National sovereign conferences in francophone Africa in the 1990s, which in most cases represented a cross-section of society, were effective for negotiating transitions from one-party autocratic rule to plural democratic regimes and provided a workable framework for a peaceful change of power.[104] Some nonelectoral structures, as in the case of the South African constitutional convention and transitional executive structures, have also provided for considerable accountability downward to the members of the groups represented, through debates within political parties and business and labor groupings. Using alternative options while the conditions are put in place for elections also allows time to build a culture of democratic practices (see box 5.11).

Devolution and decentralization can broaden power-sharing but are best approached step-by-step

Territorial devolution and decentralization of political, administrative, and economic pow-

REFLECTIONS FROM ADVISORY COUNCIL MEMBERS: *2011 WORLD DEVELOPMENT REPORT*

BOX 5.11 *Pacing institutional transformation*

Elections are not a panacea

Lakhdar Brahimi, former UN Special Representative of the Secretary General to Iraq and Afghanistan; *WDR Advisory Council Member*

It is ten years since the Report of the Panel on UN Peace Operations, which I had the great privilege to chair, was produced. The Report called for the exit of UN forces to be determined on the basis of a broad and carefully studied range of peacebuilding and institution-building requirements being met. We said that elections were not a panacea. I think there has been movement in the right direction over the past decade, but there still is some way to go to better understand how and when to conduct elections to the maximum benefit of a peace process.

Attention is needed to ensure that new democratic processes reinforce rather than undermine the fragile peace that has been achieved and promote institutional legitimacy and accountability. Institutions for political participation and checks and balances devised at the national and local level, by their very nature, can take many different forms, such as constituent assemblies, consultative conferences, and power sharing pacts. For example, the Afghan Loya Jirga drew its legitimacy from a traditional system of political exchange and decision making (although some Afghans and larger numbers of foreigners were critical of the participation of Members viewed by them as responsible for past abuses).

It is important not to confuse speed with haste in political processes: too hasty approaches can precipitate the opposite effect from the one we seek to support. The international community's high hopes for Iraq's 2005 experiment in proportional electoral democracy produced a contest for power that increased rather than allayed sectarian violence, and the constitution hastily produced later is proving almost impossible to implement. Similarly, the 2009 presidential election in Afghanistan proved to challenge rather than bolster perceptions of institutional legitimacy in the immediate aftermath.

The options are not mutually exclusive—there is great worldwide demand for more inclusive and responsive governance, and elections can be a crucial means to provide this. But their timing requires careful attention. Democratic traditions have developed in most countries over a considerable period. Democratization efforts today similarly require attention to historical heritages and existing political cleavages and must be seen as an ongoing process of social transformation and the development of a broad range of institutions that provide checks and balances rather than an identifiable "event." Democratization does not start or end with elections.

Building a culture of democracy

Nitin Desai, former UN Under Secretary General for Social and Economic Affairs; former Secretary and Chief Economic Adviser, Ministry of Finance, India; *WDR Advisory Council Member*

A constitution and elections are only the beginning of a functioning democracy. A lot depends on the emergence of working practices that respect the rights of the opposition and that set standards for political behavior that, in time become traditions. Even constitutional provisions like those for an independent election commission to supervise the electoral process require unwritten working practices for independence to become effective. That has been the experience of India, where the respect for parliamentary norms shown by Pandit Nehru and the early congress leaders set a standard that matters, not least when it is under threat. Thus, the leader of the opposition is treated with as much respect as the head of government and is entitled to public services that allow him or her to function effectively.

Traditions can be invented but are most effective when they are not codified, leaving some elasticity to accommodate changes in the balance of political power. These traditions come often from imitation of practices in old established democracies like the United Kingdom or the United States. How can one impart some knowledge of something that should remain unwritten? Perhaps by showing the parties to the post-conflict settlement the way in which democratic processes work in developing countries where they have stood the test of time, India being one big example. Maybe this is something that these young democracies can themselves contribute to the post-conflict effort.

ers also offer the potential to broaden power-sharing, but with caveats. Between 1946 and 2008, 49 countries experienced secessionist demands that resulted in violent conflict.[105] Fragile states that have resisted movements for autonomy or independence by force have often found themselves embroiled in costly wars, as Nigeria did with Biafra (1967–70); Sudan with its southern region (1955–1972,[106] 1983–2002); Pakistan with East Pakistan, which became Bangladesh (1971); and Myanmar with the Karen and Shan people and other ethnic groups (1948–today).[107] The argument in favor of greater decentralization of power (for example, through federalist structures that hand significant autonomy to local representatives) is that it can avert center-periphery ethnic conflict, or secession. For example, in Sierra Leone in 2010 the OECD reported that "decentralization and devolution are important peace-building and state building activities" and that "the decentralization process has gone a long way to redressing some of the fundamental flaws in Sierra Leone's original political structure."[108]

However, devolution and decentralization also carry risks. The OECD-DAC "Do No Harm" paper warns that donor support for devolution without sufficient analysis of political context or capacity constraints can cause serious problems if "political power at the center is highly fragmented, or constellations of local power are misunderstood."[109] Similarly, evidence shows that decentralization processes may make local democracy more vulnerable to political capture when restraints and accountability measures are absent.[110] Devolution can also lead to a lack of local accountability and significant opportunities for corruption[111] and reinforce or create elites who can use devolved power to pursue their own interests—to the detriment of both local and national interests.[112]

Successful devolution requires gradual preparation. Agreeing in detail on the degree of "subsidiarity" (pushing authority to the lowest capable level) in security, justice, and economic functions is essential to prevent further center-periphery friction. A second success factor is to ensure proper accountability of devolved structures to local citizens, offsetting the potential for local elite capture.[113] It is also important to ensure that new institutions are offered adequate technical support and the fiscal resources to deliver services.[114] Various decentralization experiences indicate that achieving success on all three fronts at once—political arrangements, technical capacity, and adequately accounted funding—is difficult, and that agreeing on a sequence is critical, as with the experience in Northern Ireland (box 5.12).[115]

Transitional justice to recognize past crimes

Some countries have addressed the sins of the past early through traditional justice measures to define a healthy new form of nationhood. Germany made a deliberate effort after World War II to address the past, including a focus on the dangers of totalitarianism and the atrocities of the holocaust in the high-school curriculum, and the establishment of sites of remembrance and education throughout the country, including former concentration camps.[116] Other countries that have instituted early transitional justice procedures include Argentina and Chile after their transitions from authoritarian rule. In Argentina, in addition to a truth commission[117] and various reparation programs for victims, junta leaders were tried and convicted for massive human rights violations. While initial processes faltered and were suspended for a 10-year period, prosecutions of human rights violators have resumed and currently comprise more than 600 cases.[118] Chile's experience is not radically different: truth-seeking[119] and reparations have been followed by more than 600 prosecutions, with more than 200 convictions thus far.[120]

Other countries have relied less on prosecutions and formal justice processes. A comparison of transitional justice approaches in five countries that have made promising transitions out of violence (Cambodia, Mozambique, Rwanda, South Africa, and Vietnam)[121] found that nonjudicial measures include truth commissions[122] and repara-

BOX 5.12 ***Devolution and decentralization can help manage conflict, but are better done gradually***

Types of violence: Political and sectarian violence	
Transition opportunity: Space for progress—Good Friday Accord, referendum that represented opportunity for power-sharing arrangements	**Key stakeholders:** British and Irish governments, political parties and armed forces/groups in Northern Ireland, citizens, diaspora
Key Stresses: Inequitable access to political and economic power, sectarian tensions, perceptions of discrimination	**Institutional challenges:** Low inclusion and accountability in security and justice institutions, low trust, legacies of extrajudicial dispute resolution

In many center-periphery conflicts—where groups are engaging in violence to gain autonomy or secede from the state—the devolution of political power has been proposed as a possible solution to resolve conflict, maintain or restore law and order, and rebalance relations between local and central governments.

But devolution is not an automatic answer to regional tensions and can at times amplify conflict. In Northern Ireland, it was not only the 1921 partition of Ireland that drove the conflict, but also the devolution of authority to a new Northern Ireland Assembly and the effects on center-periphery relations. Unionists found a need to reemphasize that they were British, while the Catholic minority lost faith in political structures that provided few safeguards for them.

In Northern Ireland, a new process of devolution was a centerpiece of the Good Friday Accord, introduced gradually to allow confidence to be built up. The Accord was signed in 1998, but decommissioning of the Irish Republican Army's weapons and the security reforms were not completed until 2005, and the devolution of policing and justice to the Northern Ireland Assembly was finally completed on March 8, 2010.

Source: Barron and others 2010.

tions programs for victims,[123] as well as administrative sanctions, such as vetting,[124] and traditional or local justice measures.[125] While the differences in the approaches were significant, there was no straightforward relationship between the approach and the attainment of stability.[126]

Where abuses are on such a huge scale that the formal justice system is unable to deal with them, special procedures may be justified. Rwanda faced this challenge following the genocide that left at least 800,000 people dead at the hands of their fellow citizens. In November 1994, the UN Security Council set up an international tribunal in Arusha, Tanzania, to prosecute people accused of violations of international law. Rwanda's own jails, meanwhile, were bursting with 120,000 people accused of genocide-related crimes—and there were only 15 judges to oversee their trials. The situation called for extraordinary measures. Rwanda's solution was to adopt a traditional community conflict resolution system, *gacaca*, and to train more than 250,000 community members to serve on panels in 12,000 community courts. Gacaca is based on an extended plea bargaining principle and has elements of both punishment and reconciliation; it is expected to draw to a close in 2011, having processed more than 1.5 million cases. It was a contentious approach, but with only 30 convictions to date at the international tribunal, a decimated national judicial system, and jails filled beyond capacity, there were few options other than a community process to deal with the enormous pressures.[127]

Economic reforms—in moderation

Economic reforms are needed to escape the cycle of violence, but they must not be victims of the "too slow-too fast" trade-off. Fragile and conflict-prone situations often share a raft of structural economic problems—low per capita GDP, fiscal imbalances, chaotic regulations, dependence on agriculture and natural resources, high illiteracy, rapidly growing populations, and a dearth of physical infrastructure. All raise the risk of violence, but addressing them too rapidly also raises the risk of reigniting violence or deepening societal cleavages. Major issues for investors are "significant downside risks," which implies that individual economic policies may be less important initially than conveying certainty about the overall trajectory—including security.[128] Most economic reforms create real or perceived "winners" and "losers." Reform areas particularly sensitive to social tensions include access to land and water. It is therefore important to pay attention to the distributive aspect of growth.

In macroeconomic policy, gradually introducing feasible and prioritized reforms will allow for an appropriate level of breathing space and enable foundational institutional reform without running the risk of political backlash. The benefits of adopting a gradualist approach are evident in Mozambique, where early macroeconomic reforms after the 1992 peace accord focused on overcoming fiscal crises, curbed hyperinflation, created a situation of stability, and built the confidence and trust needed to enact deeper reforms.[129] In order to be effective, early reform efforts must also reflect the specific political and economic contexts and macroeconomic problems in a given situation, instead of attempting to be one-size-fits-all solutions. For instance, while the government in the Democratic Republic of Congo in 2002 to 2004 undertook a decisive stabilization policy involving a major tightening of the fiscal stance to curb hyperinflation, Bosnia and Herzegovina adopted, in the early post-conflict period, a currency board, preventing the central bank from printing money.

Experience indicates that privatizing for the purpose of economic growth is better done gradually. Moving economic assets from public to private hands has two distinct motives: one is fiscal, to stem losses or gain revenue from the sale of assets, and the other is productivity, to spur economic growth. Clarity about motives helps avoid common mistakes. Shutting down inessential enterprises that drain revenues can be an early priority. But early or rapid privatization of essential or valuable state assets runs major risks. A review of privatization efforts in fragile settings suggests that such reforms need to be carefully prepared.[130] This can be a lengthy process, but it can assist both with transparency and with managing expectations about the gains and accommodating the losers.

Shifting attitudes toward excluded groups is crucial but takes time

Tackling horizontal inequalities[131] between social groups is particularly challenging because it demands behavioral change to reverse deeply ingrained habits, attitudes, and ways of doing business among the "excluders." Frances Stewart distinguishes direct approaches (to privilege groups), indirect approaches (to reduce group disparities), and integrationist approaches (to break down group boundaries).[132]

Histories of exclusion create pent-up demands for action in redressing the legacies of the past, such as preferential quotas for employment or education. The risk is that they can make existing differences more permanent and salient, actually slowing integration. Pratap Mehta argues that "the best way of conflict mitigation or prevention is the creation of political structures and identities where questions of rights and citizenship are progressively detached from questions of which particular communities people belong to."[133] The implementation of affirmative action programs is often associated with mounting opposition as well as perceptions of corruption.

Addressing gender equality beyond economic empowerment also takes time. Gender roles and relations change during periods of conflict, and appear to signal social progress. But such gains may not be sustained or may be counterbalanced by a reversion to traditional identities and norms when families and communities are threatened. In effect, economic realities can push in one direction while social traditions pull in the other. In many countries the economic situations of women widowed by violence may mean that they need to look for jobs and business opportunities, but social mores can make this difficult. The experience of the National Solidarity Program in Afghanistan indicates the significant potential benefits of programs that enable women to participate in the public sphere but also indicates that social and cultural change takes time (box 5.13).

Education and health reforms are crucial medium-term challenges

Education systems have the potential to mitigate conflict and contribute to peacebuilding in the long term, but also to exacerbate and perpetuate violent settings, depending on the nuances of policies, designs, and implementation efforts, as well as the different drivers of conflict and fragility. For instance, an internationally led education campaign in Afghanistan in 2002–03 failed to remove messages of hate and intolerance from curricula, and it is feared that this socialization of intolerance may exacerbate social tensions over time.[134] Conversely, in Bosnia and Herzegovina, the international community made deliberate efforts to exclude divisive messages from educational content, but has had unintended consequences of increasing suspicions of external politicization of education, in effect exacerbating local divisions.[135]

Education does not need to stop at the classroom door. Parental behavior, the family environment, and the extent to which young people feel connected to their parents (or to caregivers who play a parental role) have shown to be either one of the strongest protective factors in the lives of young people or one of the strongest risk factors. Evidence shows that investing in family-based parenting training that promotes positive, healthy, protective parent-child interactions can reduce domestic violence, the extent to which young people associate with delinquent peers, alcohol and substance abuse, school dropout, and arrests.[136] Therefore, parenting training is one of the most cost-effective ways to prevent risky behavior among young people.

Where reform of the health service and the training of national personnel would take years, delivering public services using international capacity for transitional periods can create the space to build national capacities in the longer run. Timor-Leste, after the 1999 referendum, faced serious health problems, a destroyed infrastructure, and virtually no trained personnel. Instead of pursuing a top-down reform of the health service immediately, the Interim Health Authority signed agreements with international NGOs for each district and focused its efforts on developing sensible plans, monitoring delivery, and training a new cadre of health staff. The Timor-Leste model fostered a learning environment by using 100-day planning cycles with clear targets and a strong focus on results, building confidence and capacity by meeting those targets. Over time, the government gradually phased out NGOs and took back responsibility for the health services. The program had drawbacks—among them, high unit costs—but it did provide a path toward institutional transformation while continuing to serve immediate needs.[137] A similar approach has been used in Afghanistan and has proven reasonably robust in insecure circumstances (see also chapter 8).

Institutional transformation as a continuous process

The risk of a moderately paced and flexible approach to reform is getting stuck, either moving too slowly or not making the next step when needed. Many best-fit solutions may indeed remain in place for the long term—for example, this may occur with traditional justice systems because they are more effective at maintaining social cohesion at the community level—while others are temporary stop-gap measures only. For the latter, realism about timelines is essential to avoid losing ground on hard-won results. There are a variety of ways to sustain impetus for improvement that we discuss here.

One way to build both internal esprit de corps and external legitimacy is to work up from small, more achievable targets to progressively more ambitious ones. Stress is carefully calibrated, and tasks are selected in ways that do not threaten to overwhelm

BOX 5.13 *Development approaches can empower women in the most fragile environments*

Afghanistan

Types of violence: Intergroup, ethnic, and political violence; organized crime and trafficking; cross-border; transnational ideological	
Transition opportunity: Initial large space for change: Bonn Accord; Loya Jirga; presidential, parliamentary, and provincial elections; national development budget	**Key stakeholders:** Federal and local government, security force, community leaders, civil society groups, citizens, women, international partners, transnational militant groups
Key stresses: Legacies of violence and trauma, transnational terrorism, criminal networks, low incomes, youth unemployment, corruption	**Institutional challenges:** Severe accountability and capacity constraints in public administration, security, judicial, and political institutions; lack of representation of women

Gender has been one of the most politicized issues in Afghanistan for a century. Afghan women and girls today still face suffering, humiliation, and marginalization from the discriminatory views of the role and position of women in society. Gender gaps are widespread in health, education, access to and control over resources, economic opportunities, and political power and voice. And yet, this role is not stagnant. The National Solidarity Program (NSP), the country's largest development program, operates in villages across the country through democratically elected community development councils (CDCs). Through mobilization by facilitating partners, women are involved in voting, while CDC modalities provide a variety of configurations enabling more balanced gender participation (mixed CDCs, parallel committees (one male, one female) that report to a mixed-gender CDC, or a women's committee that consults with a fully male CDC). Results of a comparison between NSP and non-NSP villages using a rigorous study design in an independent evaluation suggest that having women in charge of decisions in community projects improves the perceptions by both men and women of women in leadership roles (see figure). This is not being advocated as "the" solution, but it shows that incremental steps can lead to incremental progress, even for culturally difficult issues of inclusion.

FIGURE A Opinions on the role of women in community life: "Is there a woman in the village who is well respected by men and women?"

More men and women in villages that participated in the NSP believe that there is a woman who is well respected in their village than did respondents in villages that did not participate in the program. Statistically significant differences are shown with percentages above each bar.

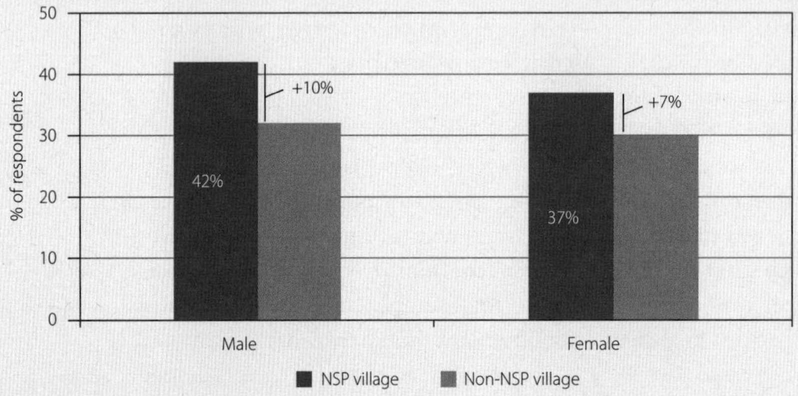

Source: Beath and others 2010.

Sources: Beath and others 2010; UN Assistance Mission in Afghanistan and UNOHCHR 2010.

the organization. In 2006, with support from the World Bank Institute, the government of Burundi introduced a rapid-results approach. This approach, now applied across 80 government projects, breaks up long-term development plans into manageable 100-day chunks. A pilot program in the Ministry of Education resulted in the distribution of 250,000 textbooks to primary schools in 60 days, a task that had previously taken an entire school year. In a health care pilot program, 482 pregnant women visited health centers and were provided with HIV/AIDS screening in one month—almost seven times the previous monthly average of 71.[138] A similar simplified approach was followed in Indonesia in the early years following the turbulence of the 1960s, where ministries undertook simple annual targets to improve service provision.

This chapter began by describing the "too fast-too slow" dilemma in institutional transformation. What are the principles of a middle way of progress that can produce success? An emerging literature on approaches to development across a variety of domains—from economic policy to social policy to institution building—promotes a flexible and pragmatic, and thus "experimental best-fit," approach to progress.[139] This includes the following:

- **Pressure for performance around meaningful goals.** Overall, this is a shift from measuring progress around "outputs" (whether budgets spent, items procured, legislation passed, or policies adopted) to assessing performance around "outcomes including citizen trust."
- **Pragmatism and flexibility in the ways goals are accomplished.** Pressure for performance must be accompanied by giving flexibility to the agents responsible for performance. Reformers need to be given the space for "disruptive" innovations that may look inferior but hold the seeds to progress.[140]
- **Monitoring, information, and evaluation systems for decision-cycle-oriented feedback loops and continuous learning.** Rigorous evaluation of results is one key element of evaluating alternative approaches, but not the only one.[141] Programs need built-in mechanisms of learning so that what is promising can be scaled up and what is not working can be changed—in shorter cycles of continuous feedback. Such evidence about what works and what does not work will in turn be useful for other countries as they strive to adapt experience from abroad to their own context.

This "middle way" requires capacity, which is scarce in fragile states. That is why the "best-fit" approach and careful prioritization and sequencing go hand in hand. If existing capacity is focused on prioritizing items in sequence (rather than trying to do everything all at once), some items can move ahead rapidly, and once they have enough momentum to sustain gradual progress, the country can move on to tackle the next items.

Delivering results and transforming institutions are primarily the responsibility of state and nonstate actors in countries affected by violence. However, the international community—bilateral donors, international organizations, nongovernmental organizations, businesses—can provide essential support for such processes, and it has done so on many occasions, including many of the initiatives described in this chapter. Yet, the international community is itself challenged by the evolution of violence since the Cold War era, and has its own transformation to adapt to new contexts. To this we turn in chapter 6.

FEATURE 5 *Violence in Central America—Depth of institutional transformation matters*

Types of violence: Civil conflict, trafficking (national and cross-border), criminal and gang violence	
Transition opportunities: Peace agreements, cease-fires, elections, rapidly rising insecurity and criminality	**Key stakeholders:** Governments, armed groups, refugees, ex-combatants, conflict victims, citizens, international partners
Key stresses: Legacies of violence and trauma: presence of international criminal networks, repatriation of suspected gang members, perceived social and economic deprivation, youth unemployment; human rights abuses	**Institutional challenges:** Severe accountability and capacity constraints in judicial and security institutions

Most countries in Central America experienced violent civil conflicts through the 1980s and into the 1990s. Although all of those that experienced war signed peace accords, the legacy of civil strife has had long-lasting and profound negative repercussions. Although civil war has ended, new forms of violence, such as trafficking and organized crime, have been on the rise. During the civil wars, around two million people are estimated to have been displaced or sought refuge in other countries. The trauma exacted by these conflicts created a culture of violence with a long legacy.

More recently, external stresses—specifically, increased transit of drugs through Central America—have contributed to violence. The dismantling of the Cali and Medellín drug cartels in Colombia, which had controlled the production and transport of drugs, led to dispersed competition for control of transit routes with a consequent impact on several countries in the region—particularly those in the Northern Triangle of El Salvador, Honduras, and Guatemala. Today, the majority of the drugs transiting from South America to the United States comes through Central America en route to Mexico or the Caribbean.

In the last 10 years, homicide rates have resurged significantly, and Central America now has an estimated 70,000–300,000 gang members. Not all countries are equally affected, however: according to official statistics, El Salvador, Guatemala, and Honduras exhibit significantly higher homicide rates than the rest of Central America. In 2009, Guatemala recorded 6,450 murders and only 231 convictions. In El Salva-

Repeated violence in Central America and rising homicide rates

a. Repeated violence in Central America, 1965–2009

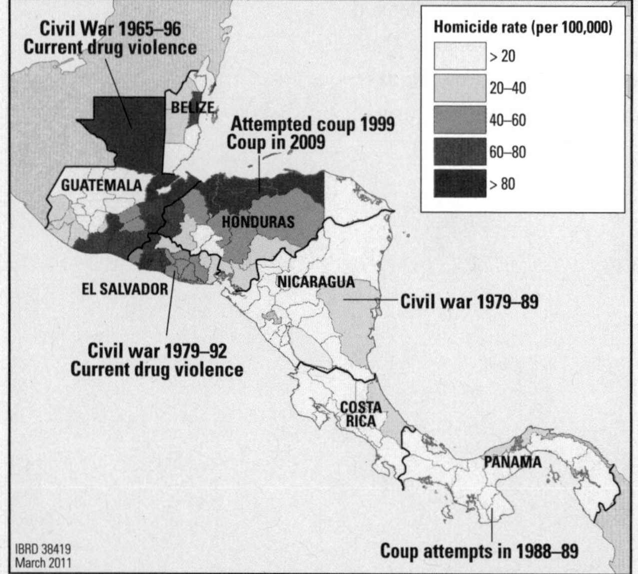

Source: WDR team.

b. Homicide rates in Central American countries

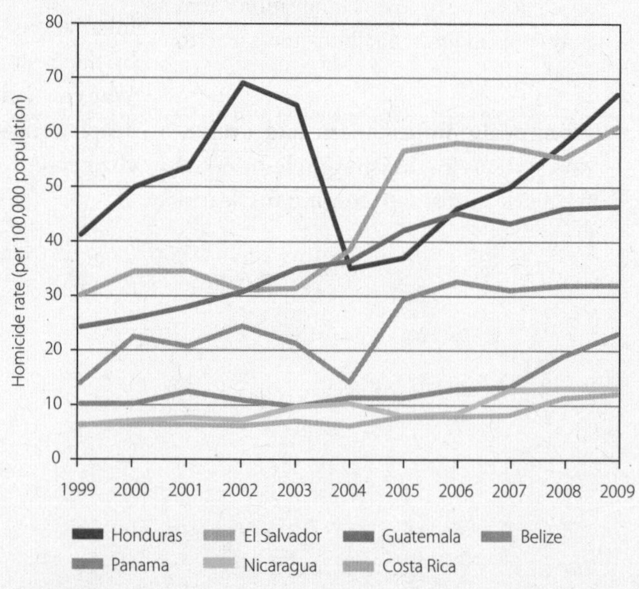

Source: WDR team calculations based on homicide data from WDR Database.
Note: Homicide rates are per 100,000 population.

dor, levels of impunity are also very high: in 2005, only 4 percent of homicides were resolved by legal convictions.

Both external stresses and differences in approaches to institutional transformation between the Central American countries may help explain the current differences in levels of violence.

External stresses

The deportation of suspected gang members from the United States back to Central America has influenced gang culture and membership. El Salvador, Guatemala, and Honduras suffered the effects of the massive repatriation of suspected gang members and illegal immigrants from the United States while Nicaragua was much less affected (box 2.4). Where drug trafficking is more intense, the levels of violence seem to be higher. Guatemala's Peten region, a corridor for transshipments into Mexico, suffered more than 100 homicides per 100,000 people in 2008 and 2009.[142]

Institutional capacity, inclusion, and accountability

After the end of the civil wars, each country undertook reforms—including reforming the security forces and, eventually, the judiciary. Both Guatemala and El Salvador included such reforms in their long-negotiated and comprehensive peace agreements, while in Nicaragua reforms were undertaken at the end of the war. In accordance with the peace agreement signed in January 1992, El Salvador reduced the size of the military (from 60,000 to 15,000), disbanded elite military groups and two police bodies, and over time created an entirely new National Civilian Police that integrated elements of the former guerrilla movement, former police officers, and new recruits (allowing a 20-20-60 percent proportion among these cohorts in its first promotion). The approach therefore was broad-ranging. The comprehensive peace accords in Guatemala signed on December 29, 1996, not surprisingly included some of the same elements: redefinition of the functions of the military and police, reduction of the military, disbandment of special elite units, and reform of civilian police.

The type of transition moment each country faced at the end of its internal conflicts affected the reach of otherwise similar measures. In Nicaragua, the Frente Sandinista won the conflict outright. Its ability to induce institutional reform therefore was significantly greater than in Guatemala or El Salvador. Both the Nicaraguan security forces and the judiciary were amply vetted. In addition, Nicaragua also undertook an extensive reform of its police forces, adopting legislation and national guidelines on arms control, piloting targeted community policing, and initiating public health projects focusing on the risks of armed violence. Notably, the modernization of the National Police Force of Nicaragua included a number of initiatives to mainstream gender and increase the participation of women, such as the addition of training modules on gender-based violence within police academies; the introduction of women's police stations (staffed by female police officers and focusing on cases of gender-based violence); the reform of recruitment criteria, including female-specific physical training and the adaptation of height and physical exercise requirements for women; introduction of transparent promotion requirements; introduction of family-friendly human resource policies; and establishment of a working group to evaluate and improve the working conditions of female officers.

The conflict in El Salvador, by contrast, ended in a military stalemate with no clear victor. This led to compromises: the Frente Farabundo Martí para la Liberación Nacional (FMLN) decided, for example, to abandon its demands for vetting the judiciary in exchange for deeper reforms of the military, although there were some subsequent reforms in the judiciary. On the other hand, the military had to accept, for the first time, having its officers vetted by civilians (the ad hoc commission established by the peace agreement, which recommended the dismissal or transfer of 103 officers), and the integration of former FMLN members into the new NCP (National Civilian Police).

The Comprehensive Peace Agreement that settled the Guatemalan conflict was negotiated with the Salvadoran experience as a backdrop and featured intense international pressure to obtain similar results—but in circumstances in which the state had essentially defeated the insurgency. The severity of the crimes committed by forces that belonged to or supported the state, in a context of international pressure, helps explain why the government appeared to make concessions. Yet while some units of the armed forces were eliminated and the police force was reformed, the changes were not significant enough to make a sustained difference in terms of security; with new pressures from drug trafficking networks, violence increased rapidly.[143]

Sources: Bateson 2010; CODEH 2008; CICIG 2010; Dudley 2010; Instituto Universitario en Democracia Paz y Seguridad 2010; STRATFOR 2009; UNODC 2007; UNDP 2008a; Zamora and Holiday 2007; Popkin 2000; WDR team calculations.

Notes

1. World Bank 2006c; WDR consultation with government officials, United Nations, donor representatives, local nongovernmental organizations, and community-based organization representatives in Haiti, 2010.
2. Special Inspector General for Iraq Reconstruction 2009.
3. Porter and Rab 2010.
4. Lockhart and Glencorse 2010.
5. Spear and Harborne 2010; Harbone and Sage 2010; de Greiff 2010; Guehenno 2010; Sherman 2010; Sage and Desai 2010; Roque and others 2010; Dobbins and others 2007; Collier and others 2003; Collier 2007; Johnston 2010.
6. Narayan and Petesch 2010.
7. Guerrero 2006; Llorente and Rivas 2005; Formisano 2002.
8. Crawford 1999; Sutton, Cherney, and White 2008; Willman and Makisaka 2010. *Mano dura* ("iron fist") policies may be effective in the short term but may have long-term negative consequences—they promote youth incarceration, reducing crime in the short term, but may ultimately lead to greater recidivism and more serious crime in the longer term (see Cunningham and others 2008).
9. Guehenno 2010, 2.
10. Pan 2005.
11. OECD-DAC 2007a.
12. UN Security Council 2006.
13. Ball and Holmes 2002; Transparency International 2011.
14. Public financial management (PFM) reviews are a useful tool to improve transparency and governance in the security sector. A PFM review in the Central African Republic found that 25 percent of the national budget was spent on the security sector, of which 21 percent was on the military and gendarmerie (law enforcement agency charged with police duties, but organized along military lines) and only 3 percent was on the police, and that 75 percent of the security sector expenditures were on salaries, which were relatively clearly controlled. A major drain on recurrent expenditure was an over-age component, comprising over one-third of the army. The main area of concern was about receipts and income, which remained off-budget, including taxation on flow of persons and commerce. As a result of this report, the European Commission has started financing the pensioning off of the over-age in the army, and the World Bank has provided training in public financial management practices to key staff in the security sector as part of its program on improving capacity and functioning of public financial systems in the government (World Bank 2009f).
15. Perry 2008; International Crisis Group 2009a; Human Rights Watch 2009; Reyntjens 2007; Kelly 2010.
16. Colletta, Kostner, and Wiederhofer 1996.
17. South Africa Ministry of Defence 1996; Williams 2005; Batchelor and Dunne 1998.
18. Rozema 2008.
19. Guehenno 2010.
20. Guehenno 2010, 5.
21. OECD-DAC 2007a.
22. International Center for Transitional Justice 2010; Mayer-Rieckh and de Greiff 2007; Patel, de Greiff, and Waldorf 2009; de Greiff 2006; Hayner 2010.
23. de Greiff 2010.
24. Addison 2009.
25. The general target for female representation in police formers and other security agencies in post-conflict countries has been 30 percent. However, this may take time and not be feasible, especially as most developed societies do not fulfill this target. For example, Finland has 10 percent, the United States 12–14 percent, and Canada 18 percent. Mobekk 2010.
26. Mobekk 2010.
27. Bastick, Grimm, and Kunz 2007.
28. UNIFEM, UN Action Against Sexual Violence in Conflict, and UNDPKO 2010.
29. OECD-DAC 2007a.
30. OECD-DAC 2007a.
31. Sherman 2010.
32. OECD-DAC 2007a.
33. Willman and Makisaka 2010; International Centre for the Prevention of Crime 2008.

34. O Dia Online 2010; Jornal O Globo 2010.
35. UNIFEM, UN Action Against Sexual Violence in Conflict, and UNDPKO 2010. Similarly, traditional dispute resolution systems can be adapted to address violence against women. For instance, 90 percent of women were satisfied with the *shalishi* process (a community dispute resolution system) when it was introduced by a rural women's group in West Bengal, two-thirds felt that they were better off, and nearly 90 percent said that physical violence by the husband had decreased or stopped. See International Center for Research on Women 2002; Bott, Morrison, and Ellsberg 2005. For more on Shalishi process, see Samity 2003.
36. WDR team interviews with Prime Minister Jean-Max Bellerine in Haiti, 2010.
37. For example, the *OECD Handbook on Security System Reform* underscores this approach when advocating that police reform be done as part of an integrated justice sector reform that includes the judiciary and prisons; see OECD-DAC 2007a; UNODC and the World Bank 2007.
38. Dinnen, Porter, and Sage 2010; Wainwright 2005.
39. International Center for Transitional Justice 2010; Mayer-Rieckh and de Greiff 2007; Patel, de Greiff, and Waldorf 2009; de Greiff 2006; Hayner 2010.
40. For more information, see feature 3 in chapter 3.
41. Guehenno 2010; OECD-DAC 2007a.
42. International Center for Transitional Justice 2010; Mayer-Rieckh and de Greiff 2007; Patel, de Greiff, and Waldorf 2009; de Greiff 2006; Hayner 2010.
43. World Bank 2010i.
44. Between 2001 and 2009, the Government of Afghanistan passed 244 laws, legislative decrees, regulations, and amendments, addition and repeal of laws and regulations. In addition, the government has entered into 19 charters, conventions, agreements, and protocols. See World Bank 2010g.
45. Another successful example of the use of Peace Justices and mobile courts to provide better access to justice, especially for the most disadvantaged groups, was in Honduras, as part of a project to modernize the judicial branch. Project results include (1) enhanced access to justice for vulnerable groups (30,000 annual users), first-instance courts in rural zones (1,000 annual users), and mobile courts in urban-marginal areas (7,000 annual users); (2) specialized service to 10,000 women in family courts; (3) improved protection to 15,000 women and children against domestic violence; (4) specialized service to 1,500 persons from vulnerable groups; (5) establishment of an integrated financial management system that promotes transparency and efficiency of the courts; (6) development of the judicial career with all the manuals for the selection, classification, and evaluation of personnel that will allow the transparent and competitive selection of 3,200 personnel; (7) adoption of a new management model for case management that will allow monitoring and evaluation of 1,200 judges; and (8) improved services to internal and external users of the courts through an IT (information technology) system and judiciary information kiosks. See Scheye 2009.
46. Dale 2009.
47. For example, in Angola, over 70 percent of children were unregistered in the mid-1990s. UNICEF 2007.
48. Comunità di Sant'Egidio 2010.
49. UNICEF 2007.
50. OECD 2007.
51. Berger 2003; Coldham 1984.
52. Straus 2010.
53. Bastick, Grimm, and Kunz 2007.
54. Everett 2009, 33.
55. Timor-Leste Independent Comprehensive Need Assessment Team 2009; WDR team consultation with Attorney General Ana Pessoa in Timor-Leste, 2010; Everett 2009, 33.
56. See OECD 2010e; World Bank 2006a.
57. Blundell 2010.
58. For Indonesia, see SUCOFINDO 2002. For Mozambique, see Crown Agents 2007.
59. Porter and Rab 2010.
60. Boko 2008.
61. Barron and Burke 2008. Another tool includes social audits involving communities in cross-verification of government records, such as the one used successfully under the National Rural Employment Guarantee Scheme in Andhra Pradesh, India (Centre for Good Governance 2009).

62. Agarwal, Heltberg, and Diachok 2009.
63. World Bank 2004.
64. Herzberg 2004.
65. BizCLIR 2007.
66. See Parker 2008 for a synthesis of practical lessons from value chain projects in conflict-affected environments; see also Bagwitz and others 2008; The SEEP Network 2009; Stramm and others 2006.
67. Evidence about the impact of value chain projects on social cohesion is mixed. For example, in Nepal, participants in a fresh vegetable value chain project pointed to improved community relations stemming from their expanded common interest. And joint efforts and research in Rwanda indicates that participation in a coffee value chain project was linked to low ethnic distance and distrust. In contrast, a groundnut value chain project in Guinea, while strengthening ties between two ethnic groups, did not include the local refugee population, a key party in local tensions. For Guinea and Nepal, see Parker 2008. For Rwanda, see Boudreaux and Tobias 2009.
68. In the West Bank and Gaza for instance, the Facility for New Market Development (FNMD), funded jointly by the U.K. Department for International Development and the World Bank, has been providing matching grants and technical support to private Palestinian companies seeking to expand their product lines and markets since 2008. In just over two years and with financial support amounting to US$2.4 million, companies enrolled in the project realized US$32.7 million in incremental export and local sales from market development plans the project supported; 42 companies entered 34 export markets in five continents; 48 products have been improved, including 15 products that are now certified by international and local standards bodies; 92 new products have been developed; more than 670 people have been hired to help with business expansion; and 85 business service providers offer their services through the FNMD Online Roster. Development Alternatives Incorporated 2010.
69. Twenty-two of the 181 countries included in the Enterprise Surveys are fragile and conflict-affected states. Ten of these countries have electricity as the most important environment constraint facing firms (and usually electricity is much higher than any of the other issues). It is also in the top three issues for 17 out of the 22 countries assessed. Only two countries, Côte d'Ivoire and Tonga, do not have electricity in their top six environmental constraints. Other constraints include obtaining finance, political instability, practices of the informal sector, and corruption. World Bank 2010d.
70. BBC News 2010.
71. World Bank 2011a.
72. A thorough review of job creation programs in post-conflict environments can also be found in ILO 2010.
73. The Productive Safety Net Programme launched in Ethiopia in 2005 is an important policy initiative by government and donors to shift millions of chronically food-insecure rural people from recurrent emergency food aid to a more secure, predictable, and largely cash-based form of social protection. See Sharp, Brown, and Teshome 2006. The National Rural Employment Guarantee Act in India was implemented on February 2006 in 200 of the poorest districts in its first phase. An additional 130 districts were covered by the Act during 2007–08 in its phase II. The remaining districts have been brought under subsequently. See del Ninno, Subbarao, and Milazzo 2009; India Ministry of Rural Development 2005, 2010; Blum and LeBleu 2010.
74. Giovine and others 2010; Arai, Cissé, and Sock 2010; Sayigh 2010.
75. Lockhart and Glencorse 2010; UNOPS 2009.
76. Wilson 2002; McLeod and Dávalos 2008; Centre for Good Governance 2009; India Ministry of Rural Development 2005, 2010.
77. del Ninno, Subbarao, and Milazzo 2009.
78. Lamb and Dye 2009; Tajima 2009.
79. Beasly 2006.
80. Cunningham and others 2008.
81. Mattero and Campbell-Patton 2008.
82. Cross 2010 discusses both opportunities and challenges of this approach.
83. Mills and Fan 2006.
84. Demirgüc-Kunt, Klapper, and Panos 2011; Cunningham and others 2008
85. Heinemann-Grüder, Pietz, and Duffy 2003.

86. See, for instance, ILO 2010 for a detailed analysis of self-employment and other local economic recovery activities in post-conflict settings.
87. M-Paisa builds on the experience of M-PESA in Kenya; see Mas and Radcliffe 2010.
88. See, for example, World Bank and others 2009. A successful management training program for small and medium enterprises is Business Edge of the International Finance Corporation (IFC), which makes locally adapted and translated adult-learning materials available, trains local trainers, builds capacity of local training companies (who tend to be small and medium enterprises themselves), and establishes quality assurance mechanisms so that local firms might in turn train the local population. Business Edge operates in several fragile and conflict-affected economies, including Iraq, Papua New Guinea, West Bank and Gaza, and Yemen. In Yemen, nearly 30,000 participants were trained from 2006 to 2010. An independent evaluation found that the program had a lasting impact on the country. Business Edge fostered a vibrant management training market that is active even after subsidies have been withdrawn. In Pakistan, an assessment of the program showed that the number of small and medium enterprises preparing cash flow statements after training increased by 20 percent and that 71 percent of participants with irregular credit histories had cleared or decreased their outstanding amounts six months after the training. See Peschka 2010.
89. Cunningham and others 2008.
90. For Japanese land reforms, see Kawagoe 1999; Tsunekawa and Yoshida 2010; For broader state-building experience in Japan, see Tsunekawa and Yoshida 2010; For Korean land reforms, see Shin 2006.
91. Lipton 2009; Rosset, Patel, and Courville 2006; IRIN 2009.
92. See World Bank 2008d on the design and implementation of cash transfer programs in emergency situations.
93. It is estimated that more than 650,000 Tajiks live and work in Russia—representing 18 percent of Tajikistan's adult population and as much as 80 percent of all Tajiks abroad. Remittances are estimated to account for around 50 percent of GDP—one of the highest figures in the world (Kireyev 2006, 3, 7).
94. *Economic Times* 2008.
95. Four elements are considered the backbone of successful schemes: (1) choice of workers to ensure that hiring is skill-appropriate rather than hiring overqualified workers who are likely to use the scheme as a stepping stone; (2) circular movement of workers to allow good employees to return in subsequent years rather than be offered a one-time-only chance at offshore employment thereby reducing the incentive to violate the agreement; (3) cost-sharing on travel-related costs with employers so that fixed costs borne by migrants are not so large that they make overstaying attractive; and (4) commercial viability so that the scheme remains private sector driven and reflects labor market conditions in host countries rather than by arbitrary quotas that become outdated if labor market conditions in destination countries change (World Bank 2006b).
96. Kingma 1997.
97. International Alert and Women Waging Peace 2004.
98. "For example, in the Democratic Republic of Congo, where women run only 18 percent of the small businesses, discriminatory provisions in the Family Code require married women to obtain marital authorization to go to court in a civil case, to buy and sell property, or to enter into any obligations, including starting a business. Banks generally require co-signature/approval of husbands if women are to obtain loans. The Family Code also affects the ability of all women to obtain employment, because proof of marital status is required, and this is difficult in a context in which identification papers are largely unavailable. Neighboring Rwanda, by contrast, has no such regulations, and women in that country run more than 41 percent of the small businesses." IFC 2008, 3.
99. IFC 2008.
100. Fearon 2010a.
101. Eades 1999; WDR consultation with former key negotiators from the ANC Alliance and the National Party in South Africa, 2010.
102. See, for example, Snyder 2000; Fearon and Laitin 2003; Epstein and others 2006; Goldstone and others 2010; Zakaria 2003; Mansfield and Snyder 2005. For Iraq, see Special Inspector General for Iraq Reconstruction 2009. For Kenya, see International Crisis Group 2008b.
103. The Loya Jirga is a forum unique to Afghanistan in which, traditionally, tribal groups have come together to settle affairs of the nation or rally behind a cause. Historically, it has been used to

settle intertribal disputes, discuss social reforms, and approve a new constitution. More recently, a Loya Jirga was convened in 2002 following the fall of the Taliban government and the Bonn Accord to choose the new transitional government for the country. See BBC News 2002.

104. Success was not universal, however, and some conferences failed to produce an institutional avenue for peaceful transition (Robinson 1994; Clark 1994; van de Walle and Bratton 1997).
105. Harbom and Wallensteen 2010.
106. Historically, the first civil war in Sudan started in 1955 and ended with the Addis Abba agreement of 1972 (see Gadir, Elbadawi, and El-Batahani 2005). However, rebels in the south (primarily Anya Nya) were not organized until the early 1960s, and battle deaths from violence did not reach major civil war thresholds until 1962, not falling till 1973 (Harbom and Wallensteen 2010).
107. See also Horowitz 2000; Barron and others 2010.
108. OECD 2010c, 24.
109. OECD 2010a.
110. Narayan and Petesch 2010.
111. Narayan and Petesch 2010.
112. Wilkinson and others argue that proportional representation may spur in-fighting among various ethnic groups over a small number of highly coveted political offices, limited economic resources, and positions of social status; it may also lead ethnic leaders to bargain harder with their rivals and overplay their hands (Wilkinson 2000; de Zwart 2000). Others argue that decentralization can reinforce ethnic identities, produce discriminatory legislation, provide resources for rebellion, and facilitate the collective action necessary for secession. Those that have recently found in favor of devolution as a way of maintaining national integrity have done so with caveats: Brancati argues that decentralization can reduce the likelihood of secession and ethnic conflict, but can have the opposite effect if regional parties are too strong. Lustick and others have run simulations that suggest that power-sharing in multicultural countries can lessen the likelihood of secession—but will in the process mobilize ethnic minorities (Brancati 2006; Lustick, Miodownik, and Eidelson 2004; OECD 2004.
113. Crook and Manor 1998.
114. Schelnberger 2005; Tukahebwa 2000.
115. Crook and Manor 1998; Ndegwa and Levy 2004.
116. Grimm 2010.
117. Truth commissions are non-judicial, independent panels of inquiry typically set up to establish the facts and context of serious violations of human rights or of international humanitarian law in a country's past. Commissions' members are usually empowered to conduct research, support victims, and propose policy recommendations to prevent recurrence of crimes. See International Center for Transitional Justice 2010.
118. See, for example, Filippini 2009.
119. Truth-seeking is a process through which societies attempt to make sense of the atrocities they have suffered during conflict or authoritarian regime and to prevent future injustices. Through the truth-seeking process, victims are able to find closure by learning more about the events they suffered, such as the fate of disappeared individuals, or why certain people were targeted for abuse. It involves the protection of evidence, the opening and maintenance of archives, the opening and publication of state information, and production of comprehensive reports. These efforts often come from official inquiry groups called *truth commissions*. See International Center for Transitional Justice 2010.
120. For recent numbers, see, for example, Estrada 2010.
121. Roque and others 2010.
122. See Hayner 2010; UNOHCHR 2006.
123. See de Greiff 2006.
124. See Mayer-Rieckh and de Greiff 2007.
125. See, for example, Huyse and Salter 2008.
126. Roque and others 2010.
127. Roque and others 2010.
128. Svensson 2000.
129. UNDP 2008b.
130. A World Bank study found: "There was a tendency in some post-conflict situations to give high priority to immediate and widespread privatization. While there is much in the histories of the countries studied to support the priority given to privatization of state enterprises, this does not

necessarily imply that sweeping and total privatization should be among the first reforms undertaken" (Kreimer and others 1998, 34).

131. Horizontal inequality is a measure of inequality among *individuals* or *households,* not *groups.* It differs from "vertical" inequality in that measurement of vertical inequality often is confined to income or consumption between groups. See Stewart 2010.
132. Stewart 2010.
133. Mehta 2010, 23.
134. INEE 2010.
135. INEE 2010.
136. Betancourt and Williams 2008; Melville 2003.
137. After the 1999 referendum, Timor-Leste faced serious health problems, a destroyed infrastructure, and virtually no trained personnel. The Interim Health Authority signed agreements with international NGOs for each district, and focused its efforts on developing sensible plans, monitoring delivery, and training a new cadre of health staff. The initial priority was to provide basic health care and services. In the first phase, international and national NGOs occupied a central role in providing emergency health services throughout Timor-Leste, independently funded through humanitarian assistance. In the second and third phase, Timor-Leste fostered a learning environment by using 100-day planning cycles to standardize the service packages provided in different parts of the territory, with clear targets and a strong focus on results, building confidence and capacity by meeting those targets. Over time, the Interim Health Authority was replaced by a new Ministry of Health, which assumed district management of the system and facilities. As a result of this framework, by late 2001 a fully Timorese Ministry of Health had recruited more than 800 health staff, given 60 percent of the population access to basic services within a two-hour walk from their homes, and boosted health facility use to 1.0 outpatient visits per capita. By 2004, an estimated 90 percent of the population had a facility within a two-hour walk, and health facility use rose from 0.75 outpatient visits per capita to 2.13. The health ministry and district operations were among the few state functions resilient to renewed violence in 2005–06, continuing to operate and indeed to provide assistance to the displaced population. World Bank 2002a, 2008h; Baird 2010; Rohland and Cliffe 2002; Tulloch and others 2003.
138. World Bank 2008c.
139. For economic policies, see Rodrik 2007; for social policy, see Grindle 2010; for institution building, see Andrews 2010.
140. Christensen 2003.
141. Banerjee and Duflo 2009; Demombynes and Clemens 2010.
142. The homicide rate in Peten region was 101 in 2008 and 96 in 2009 according to homicide statistics collected by the Guatemalan National Police. WDR team calculations.
143. The peace agreement stipulated a one-third reduction during 1997, down from a benchmark figure of 45,000 members to 31,000. Shortly after the signing of the accords, however, the army reported that its force level actually stood at 35,000, so it only needed a 4,000 troop reduction, which indeed took place (more systematically among rank and file than among the officer corps) (Stanley and Holiday 2002). See the report of the UN Verification Mission in Guatemala, as it was winding down its operations (UN Verification Mission in Guatemala 2003, 2004).

Chapter 6 examines the achievements and shortfalls of international support for violence prevention and recovery. Multilateral, bilateral, and nongovernmental agencies have helped committed national leaders deliver great accomplishments in reducing levels of civil wars. But the international system has not kept pace with the adaptation of violent actors themselves, and it is ill-equipped to navigate repeated cycles of violence or the blurred boundaries between political conflict and criminal violence. International agencies are geared to minimizing domestic reputational and fiduciary risk—increasingly so—rather than supporting "best-fit" institutional solutions that match political realities on the ground. And there are critical gaps: development agencies have long focused on building national capacity, but much less so in the spheres of security and criminal justice. Security agencies operate in those spheres, but with less long-term focus on building national institutions. "Support for job creation is a crucial gap across the international architecture."

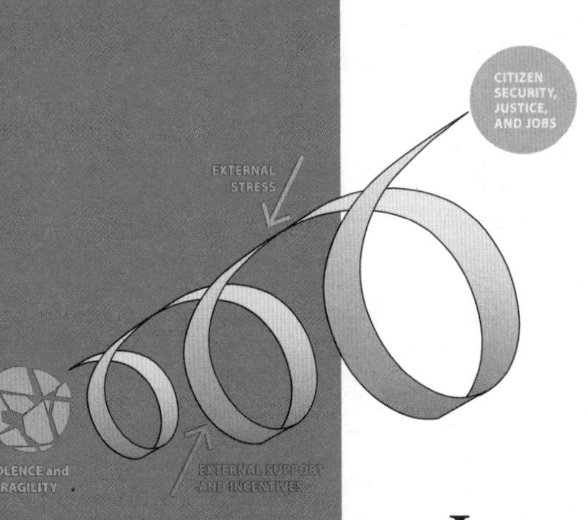

CHAPTER 6

International support to building confidence and transforming institutions

The promise and peril of outside support

Restoring confidence in societies struggling to prevent or recover from violence generally requires a combination of leadership and international support—normally, neither alone can suffice. The achievements of the global system in supporting such processes have been significant: societies facing diverse stresses—from organized crime and gang violence in Colombia to long-standing, brutal civil war in Mozambique (box 6.1)—used international support to help stop violence, save lives, and rebuild economies. Many of the measures in chapters 4 and 5 that helped restore confidence and transform institutions in situations of criminal and political violence have been supported, financially and technically, by international actors.

As important as these accomplishments are, they are incomplete: repeated and new forms of violence mean that hundreds of millions of people are still trapped in a vicious cycle of legacies of violence, low trust, weak institutions, and continuing risk. This chapter delineates patterns and trends in the international architecture that affect its ability to respond effectively in fragile and violence-prone settings. The analysis includes lessons from international efforts to prevent violence at multiple transition points, encourage inclusive-enough coalitions, support the delivery of early results, and provide sustained and predictable assistance to help with institutional transformation. This chapter also identifies measures to address the dual accountability dilemma faced by international actors—accountability pressures both from domestic constituencies and shareholders and from the leaders and citizens of recipient states—that often constrains effective international support.

The evolving international architecture

The international community has made important strides over recent decades in building international institutions and expertise to support a reduction in the incidence of civil war. However, the international system has not been adjusted to keep pace with the emerging analysis of conflict—in particular, recognition of the repetitive and interlinked nature of conflict, and the increasing challenge of organized crime and trafficking. At the same time, the expansion in international assistance efforts has led to overlaps and discontinuities between humanitarian, development, security, and political initiatives.

BOX 6.1 *The benefits of international support: Mozambique*

Type of violence: Civil conflict	
Transition opportunities: Ceasefire, peace agreement, elections	**Key stakeholders:** Governments, rebels, civil society, regional and international partners
Key stresses: Social and economic deprivation, human rights abuses, external political and security interference	**Institutional challenges:** Accountability, inclusion, capacity constraints

After 17 years of violence that killed an estimated 900,000 people and displaced a quarter of the country's people, a General Peace Agreement (GPA) was brokered from June 1990 to October 1992 by the Roman Catholic Community of Sant'Egidio. The final outcome was a full-fledged peace agreement owned by the two parties, the Mozambique Government led by FRELIMO (the Mozambique Liberation Front) and RENAMO (the Mozambique National Resistance). The result was a complex legal and political system that provided institutions and methods for the transition to the 1994 elections. The sustainability of the peace agreement itself was immediately proved by the absence of any fighting in the seven-month vacuum in which Mozambique was left, before the United Nations (UN) operation in Mozambique (ONUMOZ) strengthened its presence in the country to monitor the implementation of the peace agreement, support the resettlement of refugees, and help form a national army. The ONUMOZ mandate brought together for the first time the political, military, electoral, and humanitarian components of the UN intervention, with an emphasis on enhancing coordination.

ONUMOZ acted as a guarantor of the ceasefire, playing a stabilizing role on the basis of its perceived neutrality and helping create trust on both sides. Its role was facilitated by the content and quality of the peace agreement resulting from the 27 months of negotiations in Sant'Egidio, where a full set of guarantees was devised and proved a key element in facilitating a durable peace settlement after the end of fighting. Strong donor engagement and financial contributions also played a key role in demobilizing combatants from both sides, while humanitarian aid during the early years after the GPA helped lessen tensions among displaced populations. Since the GPA, Mozambique has grown rapidly—GDP increased an average of 8 percent a year between 1993 and 2007. Civil liberties and political rights have also increased,[1] reflected in elections held in 1994, 1999, 2004, and 2009.

The readiness of both bilateral and multilateral donors to support the implementation of the peace agreement through large-scale financial support for reconstruction was crucial in the transition process. Mozambique is calculated to have received about US$500 million a year (in both humanitarian and development aid) on average throughout the 1990s, which was equivalent to about two-thirds of imports and 60 percent of the government budget. This external aid has played a pivotal economic role in supporting private consumption at the outset, and subsequently in providing finance for investment and institutional strengthening that became the driving force behind Mozambique's economic growth.[2]

Sources: Quinn 2007; Dobbins and others 2005; Manning and Malbrough 2009; Moran and Pitcher 2004; Jones 2008; Cingranelli and Richards 2010; Brück, Fitzgerald, and Grigsby 2000; Cadeado and Hamela 2009; World Bank 2005b; Hume 1994; Morozzo Della Rocca 2003; Morozzo Della Rocca and Riccardi 2003; Edis 1995; Alden 2001; Bartoli 2005; Walter 1997.

The volume of assistance and the number of actors are increasing

Worldwide, international support to countries affected by violence has increased in the last 15 years. The international community has scaled up peacekeeping missions. More than 124,000 personnel are currently deployed in the UN peacekeeping missions, with troop contributions from 115 countries.[3] The African Union now has significant peacekeeping capacity. Support for mediation has increased at the United Nations, in regional institutions, and through civil society actors. Aid to fragile and conflict-affected states has also grown from 29 percent of total aid in 1996–98 to 41 percent in 2006–08. However, much of that shift is due to increases in humanitarian assistance and debt relief, which have become increasingly concentrated in fragile and conflict-affected states. In the period 1996–98, 34 percent of humanitarian assistance and debt relief was to fragile and conflict-affected states—that increased to 75 percent in 2006–08. Once humanitarian assistance and debt relief are taken out, aid to fragile and conflict-affected states was 28 percent of the total in 1996–98, and 30 percent in 2006–08.[4]

Increasing engagement by middle-income countries with a history of solidarity support is also changing the international landscape at a fundamental level in many regions. The past decade has brought with it new energy, resources, and influence from a wider set of players. Middle- and new higher-income countries have become important donors, investors, and diplomatic and trading partners for countries affected by fragility, violence, and conflict. They bring with them additional resources, lessons from their own economic and institutional transitions, and strong regional connections. Consider China's economic investment in and trade with Africa (investment is estimated to have at least tripled since 2002),[5] Brazil's peacekeeping role in Haiti, Indian development assistance to Afghanistan, Saudi Arabia's increased assistance to the World Food Program, and the evolving roles of South Africa, Qatar, and the United Arab Emirates in mediation.[6]

Alongside the increase in support has come a proliferation of humanitarian, development, security, and political actors and initiatives, bringing increased complexity. In 2009–10, there were 14 special envoys to Afghanistan alone.[7] Even security responses are complicated by multiple actors: of 54 peacekeeping or monitoring operations deployed in 2009, 40 involved two or more international or regional organizations—creating coordination, co-management, and accountability challenges.[8] International nongovernmental organizations (NGOs) have also proliferated. Haiti's Ministry of Planning placed the number of NGOs operating in Haiti following the January 2010 earthquake as high as 10,000. The number of international humanitarian workers has similarly increased at an average annual 6 percent globally over the past decade, with roughly 211,000 in the field in 2009, and humanitarian funding has tripled since the start of the decade.[9]

As a result, and despite continuous policy attention and recommendations for reform, aid management and broader strategic coordination are more daunting today than 20 years ago. In high-profile contexts like Afghanistan, Bosnia and Herzegovina, Haiti, and the West Bank and Gaza, strategic importance, significant funding, and limited local capacity have brought forward a dizzying array of international and bilateral aid and humanitarian agencies, NGOs, and contractors, each competing for a piece of the action—and often displacing local initiatives.

Current international assistance focuses on recovery rather than prevention

The international architecture for cooperation has evolved significantly over the last 60 years, attesting to the ability of the international system to adapt its support to changing circumstances and challenges. It is in need of adaptation again today: its focus on political rather than social protest and criminal violence, its linear view of the transition from violence to peace, its separation of actors across fields of engagement, and the preponderance of high-income Organization for Economic Co-operation and Development (OECD) countries in development policy discourse no longer reflect today's realities.

Since the end of the Cold War, international support has focused on ending civil conflict. There are good reasons for this: at the conclusion of the Cold War, civil war was the dominant form of violence, consuming millions of lives globally and retarding development in the South. Bilateral and multilateral agencies underwent major transformations to adapt their activities to helping end civil

FIGURE 6.1 ***Uneven international support in West Africa—Post-conflict trumps prevention***

Total aid and peacekeeping assistance per capita to five West African countries during their transition periods over the last decade. Assistance to "post-conflict" Liberia was over US$415 in 2008 and Sierra Leone's averaged US$186 between 2000 and 2003. In contrast, assistance to "fragile" Guinea, Guinea-Bissau, and Togo averaged just US$42 in each country.

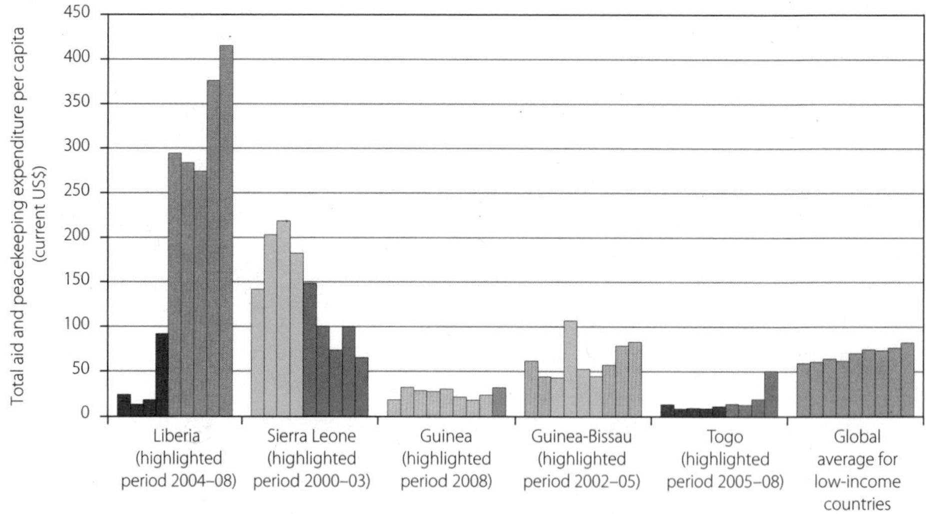

Source: WDR team calculations based on OECD 2010d.

Note: Total combined aid and peacekeeping assistance. This effect of greater assistance to "post-conflict" countries is not due to small state issues (small states typically receive higher per capita aid): Liberia is larger than Guinea-Bissau, and Sierra Leone is the same size as Togo. Peacekeeping expenditures accounted for roughly 55 percent of the aggregate in Liberia and 63 percent of the aggregate in Sierra Leone.

wars and supporting recovery efforts, with important successes. In the process, though, the international architecture for cooperation has paid less attention to other forms of conflict, including social protest, organized crime, trafficking, and cross-border violence.

This focus on civil war has led aid and security systems to give priority to post-conflict transitions. With some exceptions, countries affected by violence and fragility receive special attention only in post-conflict situations—as West Africa illustrates (figure 6.1). The aid and peacekeeping assistance going to countries after civil conflict ends greatly exceeds what is provided to countries struggling to prevent an escalation of conflict. Of course, countries that have experienced major conflict can have exceptional needs in costly areas such as infrastructure. But societies struggling to prevent violence also have particular needs. Some interventions, such as state-society consultations, are inexpensive. But tangible financial and security assistance to address rising violence can often make a vital difference, as in the institutional reforms and community programs supported by donors in Colombia. Moreover, assistance to post-conflict countries usually pays little attention to "second generation challenges" in countries that face risks of repeated violence, such as Guatemala and Yemen.

International actors do support violence prevention outside the "post-conflict" countries, but the degree and nature of this engagement varies substantially across types of violence and from state to state. International diplomats and security actors have been less involved in cases of criminal violence; the UN Peacebuilding Commission's role in Guinea-Bissau is an exception. Bilateral counter-terrorism and counter-crime programs provide operational support but rarely cross over into supporting political dialogue or development programs. No bilateral or multilateral agency known to the authors has a specific policy for assisting countries confronted by rising criminal violence or social protest.

The international tools to address violence—diplomacy, defense, and development—were not originally designed to work together. This weakness in the international architecture has long been recognized, and there is a growing international policy consensus that addressing violent conflict and promoting economic development both require deeper understanding of the close relationship among politics, security, and development.[10] UN "integrated missions"[11] and various bilateral and regional "whole-of-government"[12] and "whole-of-system"[13] initiatives have emerged to address the challenge of merging development, diplomatic, and security strategies and operations.[14]

But different disciplines bring with them different goals, planning time frames, decision-making processes, funding streams, and risk calculi. They can also create complexity when each agency in donor countries works through their own national counterparts, making it difficult to set national priorities.[15] Whole-of-system entities also often leave out those departments and ministries that address organized crime and trafficking. And most international actors do not have specific processes to ensure a whole-of-government approach in their representation in multilateral agencies, so that different signals on priority action within the same recipient country can be provided to the international financial institutions and to different parts of the UN system.

A number of governments have been making headway at integrating whole-of-government strategy design and resource allocation. Australia's experience with mounting a truly cross-governmental operation in the Solomon Islands (Regional Assistance Mission to Solomon Islands, RAMSI) is perhaps the most developed; notably, it relied on the personal involvement of the prime minister and his office to drive deep engagement by AusAID, and the Australian Defense, Treasury, Justice, Federal Police, Foreign Affairs, and other departments.[16] Canada's Stabilization and Reconstruction Task Force (START) recently finalized interdepartmental guidance that requires joint assessment by the Ministries of Defense, Foreign Affairs, and Development (and other departments where relevant) before a recommendation is made to ministers about whether Canada should engage in a given high-risk setting. The Dutch Ministry of Foreign Affairs approved an approach to its security sector reform work that keeps the question of resources separate from strategy design, so that programs are not hampered—as many are—by issues of ODA eligibility (official development assistance.) The U.K. Department for International Development's (DFID) Stabilization Unit and the U.S. Office of the Coordinator for Reconstruction and Stabilization have development interagency assessment and planning frameworks to encourage joint action, including for bilateral interventions in Afghanistan, Haiti, and Sudan,[17] and the U.K. Multilateral Agency Review assesses the support provided by multilaterals in fragile situations.

Building confidence

International actors have supported, or facilitated, "inclusive-enough" coalitions; helped develop leadership capacity across a wide range of responsibilities; undertaken third-party mediation and prevention activities; supported commitment mechanisms; and invoked sanctions when positive incentives did not bring national leaders together. They have also helped deliver early results (see international support for national action in chapter 4). But international interventions have not always been as fast, as flexible, or as responsive to local political conditions as was needed to support early confidence-building efforts.[18]

Support to building inclusive-enough coalitions

Across cases with different attributes and facing different stresses, international actors can use a range of tools to create incentives for coalitions to avoid violence. These include

- ***Providing evidence of a deteriorating situation.*** Communications from diplomatic and development actors in Togo and Zimbabwe in the early 2000s, for example, focused on the growing gap between countries that had once led their neighbors in social and economic outcomes but had fallen behind in periods of fragility.
- ***Highlighting the potential negative consequences of inaction.*** Following the resumption of Israeli-Palestinian violence in the fall of 2000, the World Bank, with assistance from the UN and other donors, prepared a series of reports that addressed the relationship between Israeli security measures and Palestinian socioeconomic development. The parties used this analysis as the basis for a resumption of bilateral negotiations in the context of Israel's disengagement from Gaza in 2005.
- ***Jointly signaling the need for governments to address crisis situations.*** When Cyclone Nargis hit Myanmar in 2008, the government initially resisted offers of international support. Association of Southeast Asian Nations (ASEAN) mediation and a visit by the UN Secretary-General—buttressed by technical support from the UN, the World Bank, and the Asian Development Bank—produced a policy shift that resulted in Myanmar opening its borders to large-scale humanitarian assistance. South-South exchanges with Indian and Indonesian political and technical leaders who had been involved after natural disasters helped to open dialogue.

The cost savings to the international community of avoiding or minimizing violence are potentially considerable—a 1997 Carnegie Commission Report on Preventing Deadly Conflict estimated that seven major international post-conflict interventions in the 1990s cost some US$200 billion, while prevention would have required only around US$70 billion.[19] More recent work on six cases concluded that conflict prevention would have been cost-effective in each instance, even allowing for large margins of error in estimating costs and benefits: every dollar of prevention would have saved the international community US$4.1.[20] And each time the *Fica Vivo* program in Brazil prevented a homicide, it saved up to US$82,000.[21] Yet since the probability of successful preventive action in a given case is not known, and since preventive action often requires diplomatic risk-taking, it is difficult to marshal political and financial support resources. For instance, the UN Department of Political Affairs often scrambles to find travel funds for its envoys despite the high return on investment in a successful preventive effort.

External mediation has helped build collaborative coalitions to promote prevention of or recovery from violence—and is economical. Mediation has played a significant role in a range of cases—ECOWAS (Economic Community of West African States) mediation in West Africa (see feature 6), UN facilitation of Afghanistan's Bonn Agreement, Norway's facilitation in Sudan, and NGO efforts such as those of the Crisis Management Initiative and the Centre for Humanitarian Dialogue in Aceh, Indonesia.

It is hard to attribute results conclusively to mediation, or to demonstrate what would have happened without it; but we do know that it is cheap. The UN Department of Political Affairs estimates[22] that the start-up budget for "light mediation support" is US$330,000 and for "heavy mediation" is US$1.1 million.[23] However, mediation to manage transitions tends to neglect economic factors and thus faces capacity and personnel constraints (box 6.2). Because mediation support is provided mainly by diplomatic mechanisms, there are few cases of integrated political mediation and economic diagnosis provided to governments grappling with transitions. Routinely lamented, this situation has rarely been addressed.[24] Some exceptions include the World Bank's support during the Dayton negotiations on Bosnia and Herzegovina, final status negotiations for Kosovo, and the Agreement on Movement and Access between Israel and the Palestinian Authority.[25]

REFLECTIONS FROM ADVISORY COUNCIL MEMBERS: *2011 WORLD DEVELOPMENT REPORT*

BOX 6.2 *Investing in long-term mediation as a cost-effective approach to preventing and responding to violence*

Martin Griffiths, Former Director of the Centre for Humanitarian Dialogue; *WDR Advisory Council Member*

As has often been observed, most armed conflicts today are internal to states, rather than between states. Mediation in these conflicts is rarely preventive. It is also often short-lived. This is partially because mediation is still often seen as interference in the internal affairs of a state, partially because there are few national mediators and there are limited numbers of international officials with the necessary stature and diplomatic skills. Mediation is seen as a last resort, only acceptable when it becomes evident that armed victory is unlikely and when non-state armed groups gain credibility and a degree of international acceptance.

The record, though, varies between regions. In Africa there is a robust tradition of mediation, typically led by former senior statesmen from the continent, assisted by the AU's Peace and Security Commission, which increasingly holds its member states to political account on the basis of a broad consensus. In Asia, the picture is very different. Mediation, especially by neighbors, is extremely rare, and it is no surprise that regional mechanisms are, by comparison with Africa, much less developed. Europe, by further contrast, has been quite open to third-party mediation, but usually by individuals or international NGOs.

The nature of mediators exacerbates the difficulties. Mediators are, on the whole, drawn from the ranks of serving or former senior politicians and officials. This is a limited pool, and those willing to take on the dubious rewards of mediation are likely to be very busy men. And they are mostly men: there are precious few women mediators, an imbalance which does nothing for the quality of the output.

A further factor that abbreviates mediation efforts is a simple human one: many mediators prefer to avoid involvement in the post-agreement implementation phase, which extends the time of their involvement and is usually messy and complicated. A striking contrary example comes from the AU panel that mediated in Kenya in 2008, where former Secretary-General Kofi Annan was a "prisoner of peace" for 41 straight days of talks. That 41 days of continuous effort is viewed as unprecedented says volumes about the nature of standard mediation efforts.

Agreements intended to initiate a durable peace must deal, if not immediately, with the whole range of issues relevant to social transformation. A political settlement is thus necessary but not sufficient. However, the flaws in today's approach to mediation make such a comprehensive and thoughtful inclusion in the negotiation rather unlikely. Typically, therefore, difficult issues are left for later resolution. It is not by chance, therefore, that peace settlements, aided by the brilliant but passing presence of mediators, often fail the more rigorous tests of implementation.

In peace negotiations, international mediators often pursue inclusive-enough coalitions by encouraging or pressuring for agreements that include key minority rights and human rights provisions, as well as early political participation. As third-party facilitation and mediation in internal conflict and violence have developed, there has been growing emphasis on including core human rights provisions in peace agreements, and in 1999 there was formal guidance for the UN against endorsing agreements that contained amnesties for war crimes.[26] Similarly, external actors have urged that democratic processes or other accountability and voice mechanisms be made a routine part of conflict settlements. The UN Security Council has included such provisions in most of the 54 operations it has authorized since the end of the Cold War.[27] Such provisions in an initial settlement can create incentives for inclusive social and economic strategies.

But international support often swings between "all-inclusive" and "not inclusive enough" options. In some processes there is pressure to treat all political groupings equally and to give everyone a seat at the table—in Timor-Leste in 1999, the National Council for Resistance in Timor was told by international counterparts that it was only one among many political groups, despite almost 80 percent of the Timorese population having voted for independence under its logo. International actors have also pressured national authorities not to engage in dialogue with groups listed as terrorist organizations by the UN, regional organizations, or bilateral donors, even when those groups command substantial domestic followings. Consequently, those actors have withdrawn support when national authorities have taken a different path.

International approaches to coalition building often exclude women, despite international efforts such as UN Security Council Resolution (UNSCR) 1325 and UNSCR 1960.[28] Women bring different issues to the negotiating table—not only gender-related topics but also different visions of how to share power, address security concerns, and promote human rights.[29] According to UNIFEM (United Nations Development Fund for Women), fewer than 7 percent of negotiators on official delegations in peace processes since 2000 have been women. Moreover, women make up just 2.3 percent of military peacekeeping personnel globally.[30] Similarly, in peace support operations, at the end of 2003, women represented only 25 percent of civilian professional staff and 4 percent of civilian police.[31]

Despite the challenges, both international political actors and international development actors have demonstrated their ability to support effective prevention activities in fragile transition moments. Donors have funded diverse interventions in fragile and conflict-affected countries to help support effective leadership and enhance collaborative capacities,[32] coalition-building, and national and local strategy development. In Guyana in 2006, after a period of rising political tension, the first-ever violence-free elections were conducted.[33] The Social Cohesion Program—a joint UNDP-UNDPA (UN Development Programme–UN Department of Political Affairs) national initiative that included a national dialogue, a network of local mediators to help ease tensions among communities, and agreements among political parties—contributed much to this result. In Burundi, the World Bank and others financed leadership support, which aided in developing a vision for economic recovery for the transitional period and led to an extension of the program for army and rebel commanders to prepare for the upcoming cease-fire.[34] Another type of program is international support to national efforts to build an institutional infrastructure for conflict prevention and prevention and risk reduction (box 6.3).

Commitment mechanisms

International actors have also helped in providing ongoing monitoring and implementation guarantees—the commitment mechanisms described in chapter 4.[35] In the post–Cold War era, their most significant role has been in helping to implement post-conflict settlements when trust is low. External forces can reassure parties and begin to restore confidence by monitoring and providing credible information about implementation, and thus intent. They can also deploy troops to provide physical security guarantees against a relapse.[36] Cross-country studies repeatedly show that peace settlements with third-party guarantees are more stable than those without.[37] Similarly, IMF (International Monetary Fund) and World Bank programs, including those that carry no financing but simply give an imprimatur of good financial practice, can help governments reassure investors and citizens of their commitment to fiscal responsibility and clean government. Among nongovernment actors, the Extractive Industries Transparency Initiative (EITI)[38] and the new Natural Resource Charter[39] have in effect set new standards for the responsible use of some natural resources in a partnership of civil society, the private sector, and governments. Adherence to these standards and their reporting requirements can also act as a commitment mechanism.

Commitment mechanisms that mix national and international capacity can help shepherd economic recovery and progress on justice. They are particularly appealing because they combine the strength of international guarantees with elements of national institution-building. Liberia's Governance

BOX 6.3 *Heading off escalation: Dialogue and compromise in Ghana in 2003–04*

Type of violence: Political, local, and intergroup conflict	
Transition opportunity: Preventive actions leading to peace negotiations before a critical national election	**Key stakeholders:** Local and national government, clans, police, civil society, opposition party, international organizations
Key stresses: Ethnic competition linked to a political contest	**Institutional challenges:** Capacity and legitimacy of formal and informal governance systems

Ghana, viewed as one of the most stable countries in Sub-Saharan Africa, has experienced its own bouts of local or community violence; a recent study identified more than 200 low-level conflicts between 1994 and 2002. The potential for serious violence threatened to emerge in 2002 over the succession to the Dagbon chieftaincy, after the Andani clan chief of the Dagbon ethnic group and 40 of his followers were murdered by the rival Abudu clan. This had national implications: Ghana's vice president was a Dagomba, and the main opposition party had chosen its vice presidential candidate from a faction contesting the succession. The central government therefore needed to defuse tension before the next national election. A state of emergency was declared in the Dagbon kingdom, and a commission of inquiry established. But the commission failed to bring a settlement: its report was rejected by both sides.

The government then sought UN help to broker a dialogue among youth, women, and labor leaders and state institutions, including the police. A compromise was devised that included a funeral with full state honors for the slain Andani leader and the nomination of an Andani regent. An agreed "roadmap" for succession gave both factions a future chance at providing a successor. The 2004 national elections were peaceful, with chiefs and police cooperating to avoid violence.

Building on this dialogue, the Ministry of the Interior, supported by UNDP and UNDPA, created a National Architecture for Peace, consisting of district, regional, and national councils, which brings together locally respected, politically neutral Ghanaians and provides a platform for community dialogue and consensus-building on divisive issues. The councils also serve as an early warning mechanism, used by state officials to identify problems. The national government now has a Peace Building Support Unit in the Ministry of the Interior to coordinate preventive efforts by national, regional, and district government agencies and to provide mentoring and capacity-building to government and nongovernment actors.

Sources: Ojielo 2007; GhanaWeb 2006; UNDPA 2010a.

and Economic Management Assistance Program[40] (chapter 4) shows the benefits of joint international-national mechanisms in the economic sphere, as does Guatemala's International Commission Against Impunity in the justice sphere (box 6.4).

In the extreme, international actors can threaten a range of sanctions when national actors seem reluctant to take meaningful steps to avoid new cycles of violence.[41] While sanctions are often cited as an important measure in forcing political change in the target state (for example, contributing to the fall of apartheid in South Africa), their causal effects remain disputed.[42] Critics cite negative humanitarian effects and the creation of illicit economies that can enrich regimes.[43] Efforts to mitigate such effects have emerged in the two decades through the use of "targeted" sanctions—financial and travel restrictions imposed on individual leaders or groups.[44] The European Union imposed travel restrictions, for example, on Zimbabwe's leaders when they failed to deal with a deteriorating economy and suppressed mounting political tensions.

BOX 6.4 *International-national institutional partnerships—CICIG in Guatemala*

Types of violence: Legacy of civil conflict, rising criminal and gang violence, trafficking	
Transition opportunity: Rising crisis, moderate space for change	**Key stakeholders:** Government, opposition parties, victims, gangs, international drug networks, citizens, regional partners, wider global partnership
Key stresses: Rising external pressures from drug trafficking, perceptions of injustice and impunity by victims of violence and marginalized groups	**Institutional challenges:** Low capacity in police and civilian justice system, past problems of accountability

To combat corruption and crime, Guatemala created the International Commission against Impunity, known by its Spanish acronym, CICIG, through an agreement with the UN in 2007. Its mandate is to "support, strengthen, and assist institutions of the State of Guatemala responsible for investigating and prosecuting crimes allegedly committed in connection with the activities of illegal security forces and clandestine security organizations."[45] It is one of the few instances of an international commitment mechanism deployed to help a state deal with gang-related and criminal violence.

CICIG responds to the reality that Guatemala, after a 36-year civil war, has experienced continuous and mounting stresses of gang-related violence and police and judicial corruption. Studies show that a legacy of failed reintegration of demobilized soldiers at the end of Guatemala's civil war has contributed to today's spike in criminal violence and gang activity.

CICIG draws on independent international and local investigative expertise and refers cases to Guatemalan prosecutors in the domestic judicial system. A Special Prosecutor's Office for CICIG has been established in the Public Prosecutor's office, and CICIG has also provided technical assistance and capacity-building support to the National Civilian Police, the Ministry of the Interior, and the Public Prosecutor.[46] As of March 2010, CICIG had mounted 1,544 judicial proceedings and arrested 135 individuals, including former President Alfonso Portillo, accused of embezzling funds.

CICIG has been an innovative response to the twin challenges of high external stress and low internal capacity. However, while CICIG has registered successes within Guatemala, larger regional challenges of organized crime and trafficking lie beyond its control.

Sources: CICIG 2009; Férnandez 2010; Donovan 2008; *The Economist* 2010; UN 2006a; UN General Assembly 2009a; Hudson 2010.

But international and regional norms—and mechanisms for recognition and sanctions—are not always fully aligned. Some regions have developed norms and principles that recognize responsible national leadership. The African Union (AU) and the Organization of American States have norms for dealing with extra-constitutional changes of government, notably *coups d'état*.[47] But even where a region has a strong principle-based standard, international mechanisms do not always reinforce it. For example, there are no structured discussions on international cooperation among non-regional bilateral partners, the UN, and international financial institutions following the imposition of sanctions by the AU on a member.[48]

Support to delivering early results

For the leaders of an initial pact to build confidence, they must deliver results quickly; when timely, international assistance can bolster these efforts. Rapid assistance for confidence-building can take many forms (chapter 4). Early results can be achieved when programs are appropriately designed, as the initiatives described in chapters 4 and 5 make clear. However, much of the assistance for priority development tasks remains slow, in particular when best-fit needs on the ground fall outside the regular donor processes (see box 6.5). A critical ingredient for bridging the gap is the mutual involvement of humanitarian and development actors in planning.

REFLECTIONS FROM ADVISORY COUNCIL MEMBERS: *2011 WORLD DEVELOPMENT REPORT*

BOX 6.5 *Quick action? Ghana helps restore electricity in Liberia*

H. E. Ellen Johnson Sirleaf, President of Liberia; *WDR Advisory Council Member*

After the 2005 election in Liberia, the new government announced a 100-day plan that included the restoration of electricity to certain areas of the capital to help restore confidence in the state and jumpstart recovery in economic activities and basic services. With ECOWAS' support, the Liberian government approached various donors to help, since the new government lacked resources and institutional capacity for implementation. None of the traditional donors, which included the United Nations, the World Bank, the African Development Bank, the European Union, and USAID, were able to provide the generators needed for this endeavor within the desired timeframe under their regular systems. The Liberian government was eventually successful in securing help from the Government of Ghana, which provided two generators that helped restore electricity in some urban areas.

The Liberian experience points to two key lessons. First is the need for early consultation between national governments and international partners on realism in delivering quick results and demonstrating progress to local populations. Second is the challenge of rigidities in donor systems unable to provide particular types of assistance fast. In fact, the EU, USAID, and the World Bank were able to provide other types of support (fuel, transmission line restoration) for the electricity system within the 100 days, but none of the donors were able to cover the specific need for generators.

Indeed, there is a need to rethink existing policies and processes, to modify what I call *procedural conformism* for countries in crisis situations. Another case in point is the rebuilding of two primary roads in Liberia. The World Bank, joined by other donors, made significant commitments to this project. However, a new procedure was to be adopted which calls for a multiyear construction and maintenance arrangement. This represented an innovative new process, but one which required a long gestation period for implementation. Liberia gained when the Bank agreed to proceed with one of the roads under more flexible procedures, but the other will likely experience a two-year delay under the new process. This case in point is a clear demonstration of both the problems of procedural conformism and the possibility of more flexible thinking.

Humanitarian assistance, the main tool the global system has for rapid relief, can provide vital life-saving and stabilizing assistance. There is evidence that "indirect deaths"—those caused by disease and malnutrition in violent environments—have declined faster than deaths caused directly by war. This is in part a testament to the increasing effectiveness of humanitarian aid—but humanitarian assistance alone cannot deliver on priority political, security, and development needs.[49]

As domestic pressure on donors to demonstrate results has increased, so has the appeal of branding as a communications tool. For example, the United States Agency for International Development's (USAID) policy is that all programs and commodities funded by USAID are marked with the USAID logo. However, there is some flexibility—where needed, a partner country symbol or ministry logo may be added, while branding may be avoided altogether if it can be shown to threaten the neutrality of a program.[50] Other donors, such as the European Commission, have similar practices.[51] Where the population sees all assistance marked with logos of international agencies, the opportunity to boost confidence in the ability of national reformers and institutions to lead the country out of violence may be lost. In some circumstances, "joint branding," as was adopted in Aceh, Indonesia, between the Indonesian Government and donors, can help maintain donor visibility while boosting the legitimacy of national institutions.

When protracted, humanitarian assistance confronts a dilemma: because it does not, for the most part, deliver through national institutions, it can undermine national institutional capacity. Yet international agencies and NGOs that have both humanitarian and development mandates can build bridges from relief to early results and institutional transformation. For instance, the United Nations Children's Fund (UNICEF) has been developing the capacity of national and local actors to protect the rights of disadvantaged groups. Most successful are activities that support individuals (such as teachers), improve organizational capacities (such as school management structures), and address state and civil society capacities simultaneously. In Sri Lanka, UNICEF has worked with the Ministry of Education and communities to adopt a child-friendly-schools approach, even in conflict-affected areas, increasing student and teacher attendance and reducing dropout rates. Similarly, the World Food Programme has increased its uses of local purchase of food to support domestic agricultural capacity.

The potential gap between humanitarian and development assistance has long been recognized.[52] As the examples above demonstrate, UN agencies and international NGOs with humanitarian and development mandates can do much in the critical early phase of transitions to provide quick support while paying attention to longer-term institution-building. Another example is recovery in the health sector in Timor-Leste: the government drew on the capacity of humanitarian NGOs for immediate service provision as an integral part of a program that gradually transferred management and service delivery to national institutions (see chapters 5 and 8).[53]

Even when citizen security is acknowledged as a priority, responses can still be slow. In 2005, the UN Mission in Sudan took more than nine months to deploy 3,600 troops, just 40 percent of its mandated level. The UN Department of Peacekeeping Operations took 12 months to achieve the authorized troop levels for MONUC, the UN Peacekeeping Force in the Democratic Republic of Congo.[54] Overcoming barriers to rapid contracting and recruitment would make a difference in the ability of the UN and regional institutions to deploy peacekeeping operations to confront violence in a timely manner. The adoption of the UN global support package in Spring 2010 is an important step in this direction.

Similar delays have affected bilateral security cooperation. Between 2008 and 2010, the United States pledged US$1.6 billion to the Mérida Initiative, which aims to provide law enforcement support to Mexico and Central American countries. By July 2010, only 9 percent of the funds had been spent.[55]

Global funds for peacebuilding and statebuilding have also increased in recent years to fill financing support gaps in transition settings. For example, the UN Peacebuilding Fund (PBF) plays a catalytic role bridging the humanitarian and the transitional and development phases, while the World Bank's Statebuilding and Peacebuilding Fund (SPF) is able to mobilize technical and financial resources and foster coherence with longer-term development planning.[56] In Nepal, for example, the PBF has provided US$2.2 million in catalytic funding to discharge and rehabilitate minors, post-cease-fire recruits, and discharged women back to civilian life. The discharge process was completed across the seven principle cantonments in some of the most inaccessible areas of the country over a four-week period; this initial funding was followed by investments by the Governments of Norway and the United Kingdom to finance the reintegration efforts that have followed.[57]

Collaborative tools for national-international strategy development have emerged in recent years to set goals, financing priorities, and progress indicators in conflict-affected countries. Commonly focusing on early results, they may also contain measures to aid institutional transformation. The tools range from Post Conflict Needs Assessments (PCNAs)[58] to international compacts and strategic peacebuilding frameworks.[59] Effectively implemented, they can galvanize national and international stakeholders in support of a jointly agreed-upon and well-coordinated program of priority actions sensitive to the underlying drivers of conflict.

In practice, however, joint planning and assessment tools have not generally been used to their full potential. Among the recognized shortcomings is a lack of real integration of economic, security, humanitarian, and political programs—and thus a focus on economic or technical development issues to the detriment of attention to political and security concerns, as well as a near complete neglect of transitional justice.[60] Some bilateral governments—such as the United Kingdom and the United States[61]—have integrated diplomatic, development, and security assessment tools, but these are rarely coordinated with other international or, more importantly, national assessment and planning processes. In only two PCNA cases, Georgia and Liberia, did humanitarian and development partners fully coordinate the humanitarian appeal and needs assessment processes to ensure consistency among the humanitarian and the transitional and development actions and promote the necessary continuum from humanitarian response to development.[62]

International assessment and planning processes have also registered mixed results in engaging national actors and linking strategy development processes. They are typically structured around discrete one-off transitions from conflict to post-conflict that ignore the multiple transitions required for progress. They often omit attention to the security and justice sectors. Although adaptable to a wide range of situations, they have rarely been used for prevention or for the analysis of interlinked and cross-border forms of violence (such as organized crime and trafficking)—nor do they generally focus on external stresses.[63]

International planning processes in the early stages of transition have proliferated.[64] Burundi has had, in addition to its own poverty reduction strategy, 13 international or joint national-international strategies and plans, on different timetables and with different priorities identified, between 2008 and 2010.[65] In some countries, this kind of risk has been minimized by strong support to government planning and a close dialogue with donors over results. Timor-Leste's transition benchmarks in 2001–02 and Liberia's results-focused transition framework in 2002 both used a simple matrix planning format to lay out expected results—from both government and donors.[66] These plans have the effect of a "double compact" (an idea first proposed by Ashraf Ghani and Clare Lockhart).[67] Double compacts describe in a simple form the results that governments are aiming to provide to their own citizens, and can be used to facilitate cross-government action in weak institutional environments. They can also be designed to make donor commitments explicit, and to monitor whether these commitments have been met. In practice, donor reporting inside recipient countries on how much of their own funds have been disbursed, and in what activities, has often been weak, complicating national reformers' efforts to report on public promises.[68]

Supporting institutional transformation

Essential building blocks of international support to successful institutional transformation are time and patience, best-fit approaches appropriate to the local political context, and supporting capacity for critical institutional reform in the areas of citizen security, justice, and jobs. The international community's track record in supporting these building blocks is mixed.

Time and patience

International assistance needs to be sustained for a minimum of 15 years to support most long-term institutional transformations. Longevity is something that some international NGOs have understood for some time (box 6.6), while bilateral and multilateral donors have started to adopt longer time frames. Witness the U.K. DFID's 10-year partnership agreements, the recent Dutch agreement with Burundi on a 10-year security-sector reform plan, and the 10-year exceptional assistance to post-conflict countries from the World Bank. But most strategic donor and financing frameworks cover from three to

BOX 6.6 The Aga Khan Development Network: Local knowledge, longevity, realistic expectations

For decades the Aga Khan has supported local initiatives in Northern Afghanistan, Northern Pakistan, and Eastern Tajikistan—areas geographically and economically isolated, environmentally marginal, and marked by interethnic tensions. The Aga Khan Development Network (AKDN) approach was forged in self-help traditions to "facilitate change that is . . . long-lasting in consequence and sustainable into the future."[69] In Afghanistan, Tajikistan, and Pakistan, the AKDN cements its commitment in protocols, agreements, and treaties with local, district, and national governments. It builds a diverse donor base, including local, national, and international contributions; invests heavily in local management and implementation capacity; develops approaches and services that can be sustained by local partners and institutions if donor interest declines; and adopts a cautious approach to area and program expansion unless driven by local demands, priorities, and readiness.[70] Typical engagements exceed 20 years.

Working closely with communities, local institutions, and government entities, the AKDN bases its development approach on trust earned through demonstrated long-term commitment to these regions and their peoples. That commitment is reflected in its staff: some 95 percent are nationals or regional expatriates who work in beneficiary communities for many years.

Sources: Aga Khan Development Network 2003, 2010; Agence Française de Développement and others 2005; Commission on Growth and Development 2008.

five years, with many projects having an even shorter life cycle. Foundational reforms can rarely be achieved within such time frames, and so are subject to renegotiation whenever a strategy or project ends.

Long-term security commitments are also rare. The majority of peacekeeping missions run from two to six years—for understandable reasons. A long-term presence on the ground would be both exceedingly costly and unwelcome by host communities and states. UN missions do exist that have been present for decades—such as the UN Military Observer Group in India and Pakistan (since 1949) and the UN Peacekeeping Force in Cyprus (since 1964)—but these are small in size and mandate. Over-the-horizon forces or longer-term security commitments are alternatives to too short or too long deployments. But the use of such devices to provide long-term security support has been rare. An exception is the European Union's Congo force, which provided MONUC with rapid and strategic support during the national elections of 2006.[71]

Despite the need for sustained support for institution building, volatility of aid flows is a major problem, especially in fragile states. Practitioners have long argued that fluctuations in donor aid destabilize the budget and fiscal deficit, and that predictable assistance is needed to enhance a government's capacity to plan expenditures rationally.[72] Insecure situations are in particular need of consistent support because of the high potential that interrupted reforms will be reversed. Yet aid to fragile and conflict-affected states is much more volatile than that to other developing countries—indeed, more than twice as volatile, with the efficiency costs of volatility much more profound in fragile states than in those with stronger institutions (see box 6.7). In a recent study, the economic losses associated with volatile net official development assistance were more than twice as high for weak states as for strong states (2.54 percent versus 1.19 percent of GDP).[73] These estimates suggest that from 30 to 50 percent of volatility is donor-driven, independent of events in or actions by the recipient country.

BOX 6.7 *Stop-go aid: Volatility in selected fragile states*

Over the last 20 years, countries that experienced longer periods of fragility, violence, or conflict experienced more volatility in their aid. Figure A shows that the coefficient of variance (CV) of net official development assistance (ODA), excluding debt relief, is higher for countries that have experienced more violence since 1990. This relationship, reflected by the upward trend line, is statistically significant and suggests that, on average, a country that experienced 20 years of violence experienced twice the volatility in aid of a country that did not experience violence. Volatility of revenues has considerable costs for all governments, but particularly so in fragile situations where it may derail reform efforts and disrupt institution-building.

FIGURE A Aid volatility higher for countries that have experienced violence

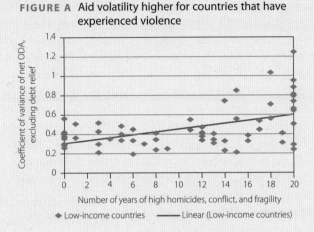

Coefficient of variance of net ODA, excluding debt relief

Number of years of high homicides, conflict, and fragility

◆ Low-income countries —— Linear (Low-income countries)

Source: WDR team calculations based on OECD 2010d.

This volatility is illustrated by figure B—it was not uncommon for total aid to Burundi, the Central African Republic, Guinea-Bissau, and Haiti to drop by 20 or 30 percent in one year and increase by up to 50 percent the following year (humanitarian aid and debt relief, excluded from these statistics, would further increase the volatility).

FIGURE B Annual percentage change in disbursed aid per capita, net of debt relief and humanitarian assistance

Aid to these four fragile countries has been extremely volatile over the past 15 years. Aid to Guinea-Bissau more than doubled in 2003, only to be cut in half the following year. Likewise, the Central African Republic experienced a doubling of aid in 2004 and a 25 percent cut in 2005. This applies in all fragile states, for which variance in aid is 0.7 compared to 0.3 in other developing contexts.

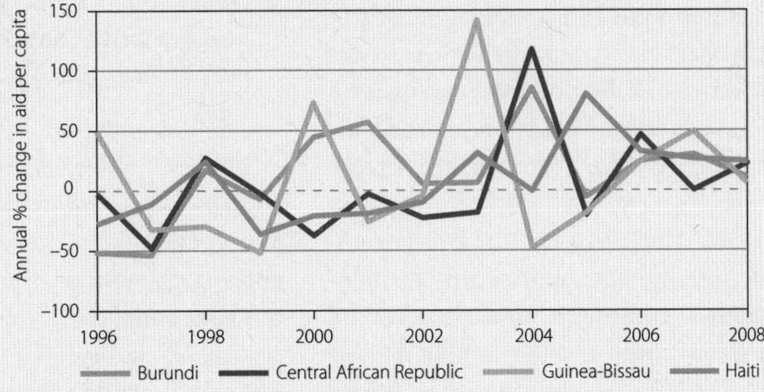

Source: WDR team calculations based on OECD 2010d.

Using methodology developed in Kharas and adopting conservative assumptions, a reduction in volatility of 30 percent by donors would deliver a value to each recipient fragile or conflict-affected country of US$27–39 million a year.[74]

Short project duration and small project size compound the problem. While the median IDA (International Development Association, the World Bank's "fund for the poorest") operation is US$22.7 million, it is as little as US$116,000 and US$65,000 for some bilateral donors.[75] According to a European Commission study, 63 percent of all donor projects in Cambodia have a duration of less than three years, and over one-third, a duration of less than a year.[76] A performance review of aid partners in Mozambique indicates that while the number of multiyear aid projects has increased, most of them are still only for two years.[77] Longer project life cycles is vital, given the timelines for institutional transformations, even under the most accelerated conditions.

Approaches adapted to the local context

The international community remains tempted to emphasize form rather than the function to be accomplished.[78] Within a year of its creation, for example, the Coalition Provisional Authority (CPA) in Iraq promulgated more than 100 separate regulations and orders covering a wide range of security, economic, and administrative matters. Although the international drafters tried to improvise in a complex and volatile setting, they were hampered by their lack of knowledge of Arabic, local sociopolitical realities, and Iraq's broader jurisprudential principles. As the United States Special Inspector-General for Iraq Reconstruction reported, "The CPA—and the U.S. government agencies that supported it—demonstrated an inadequate understanding of both Iraqi culture and the complicated internal political relationships that existed among and within various Iraqi groups."[79]

The general response of the international community to the pervasive capacity deficits in fragile situations is technical assistance. Because they are constrained by short contracts and under pressure to deliver reports, technical advisers often bring with them a focus on transplanted best practices from other country experiences, which can undermine the search for tailored and context-specific, best-fit approaches. In fragile states, technical assistance works best in the turnaround period, when leaders and reformers are looking for help in well-specified areas.[80] The attributes of effective technical assistance in fragile environments have long been established.[81] Yet, despite a general understanding of the elements of good design, much technical assistance has not been well prepared or effectively implemented. Some critiques include the following:

- A quarter of international aid to Afghanistan goes for technical assistance, intended to support government capacity-building, with minimal impact.[82]
- More than 80 cents of every dollar of aid Kosovo receives is delivered as technical assistance, but this has not produced lasting capacity within government institutions.[83]
- Despite there being only five donors involved in technical cooperation in Sierra Leone in 2007, a mere 22 percent of aid dollars was coordinated with country programs.[84]
- Donor technical assistance services have been between 11 and 30 percent more expensive than those available from other vendors.[85]

Bilateral and regional actors[86] have also created civilian surge capabilities with rosters of experts who can be deployed at short notice to countries affected by violence.[87] But large numbers of expatriate personnel, particularly if deployed for short periods without knowledge of the country context, are, as with "normal" technical assistance, unlikely to build sustainable capacity. The UN Independent Review of Civilian Capacities recently reached a similar conclusion, stressing national ownership and partnership as key principles for the UN's civilian response.[88] Providing capacity to deliver donor-designed projects is very different in both philosophy and approach to supporting national institutional capacities to deliver good-quality public services.[89]

South-South learning offers promise for effective capacity development and best-fit approaches because it can draw on knowledge from countries that have more recently experienced transitions or share regional political, economic, or sociocultural characteristics.[90] The African Development Bank (AfDB), UNDP, and the World Bank all now have specific South-South facilities, the AfDB's being notable for its size and focus on fragile states.[91]

Learning from recent transformations in middle-income countries can be particularly valuable. The Brazilian NGO Viva Rio works in Haiti's slum Bel Air to reduce armed violence, using its experience of working in Brazilian favelas.[92] Triangular cooperation to support South-South cooperation, involving a financing donor and a southern partner providing technical assistance, has also shown some success in peacebuilding.[93] The Republic of Ireland engaged in a triangular learning partnership with Liberia and Timor-Leste on the role of women in conflict prevention, management, and resolution.[94] South-South cooperation might prove particularly relevant in supporting executive management.[95] Another important area for South-South cooperation is peer learning for effective leadership and the successful management of conflict.[96]

Internal international agency systems

Responsiveness to the local context in fragile situations is also hampered by internal processes that were originally developed for more stable environments. For example, the international financial institutions' procurement procedures were based on the assumption of ongoing security, a reasonable level of state institutional capacity, and competitive markets. They thus have difficulty adapting to situations where security conditions change between the design and the tendering of a project, where a small number of qualified government counterparts struggle to manage complex procurement documentation, and where the number of qualified contractors prepared to compete and mobilize is very limited.

Similarly, the UN Secretariat originally developed procurement systems designed to support its function as a headquarters-based advisory service and secretariat to the General Assembly. When peacekeeping operations were launched, these systems were extended with relatively little adaptation to all the requirements of a peacekeeping operation, despite the difference in contexts and objectives. Most bilateral aid agencies do not have "risk policies" specific to fragile and conflict-affected situations—instead, they apply their normal criteria. Some donors have approaches or instruments that recognize the problem, but these have not yet been mainstreamed across country strategies or in the criteria for project funding decisions.[97]

When the environment is insecure, these standard procedures (*procedural conformism*, as Liberia's President Ellen Johnson Sirleaf calls them in box 6.4) often do not produce the results intended. Frequently complex and time-consuming, they can be difficult to manage for weak institutional counterparts and can cause delays. In environments such as Cambodia, Liberia, and Sudan, it has often been difficult to find qualified international contractors to bid on projects, and their mobilization has been slow.[98] Standard procedures can also undermine best-fit institutional approaches to develop capacity or they can have difficulties in meeting objectives of transparency and anti-corruption in environments with difficult political economy considerations (box 6.8). The g7+ group of

BOX 6.8 *Publishing cost estimates as best practice? Trade-offs between transparency and collusion*

Transition opportunity: Pressure for speed of action in fragile situations	**Key stakeholders:** Government agency tendering, domestic citizens, domestic companies, international donors and companies
Key stresses: Perceptions of cronyism toward contractors from particular political, ethnic, regional groupings in contracting that can exacerbate risks of violence	**Institutional challenges:** High insecurity, low institutional capacity, shallow competition, legacy of past corrupt practice
Dual accountability dilemma: Conducting processes acceptable to international donors and investors while achieving speed and legitimacy in local context	

In its loan agreements, the World Bank often requires the publication of partner countries' engineering estimates of the costs of building a road. When the market is competitive, publishing the estimates can produce lower bids. Such publication also ensures a procurement norm of transparency and equity—that all bidders are on equal footing and companies with close ties to the roads authority cannot obtain the estimates "under the table."

Set against these benefits is the risk that this procurement practice will facilitate the opposite of its intent—collusion. When firms are negotiating an agreement on a collusive price, the cost estimate provides a target or focal point for their agreement. This effect is dramatically illustrated in a World Bank Institutional Integrity comparison of the estimated price against the winning bid on 46 contracts for road construction and repair let during 2009 and 2010 under a Bank-financed project in an Eastern European country. The closeness of the two is inconceivable without collusion (see figure). As a result, a procurement norm has achieved neither the goal of quick support—delays are created in publishing the estimate, nor fostering a legitimate and transparent process—due to real or perceived collusion.

FIGURE A Closeness of bids inconceivable without collusion

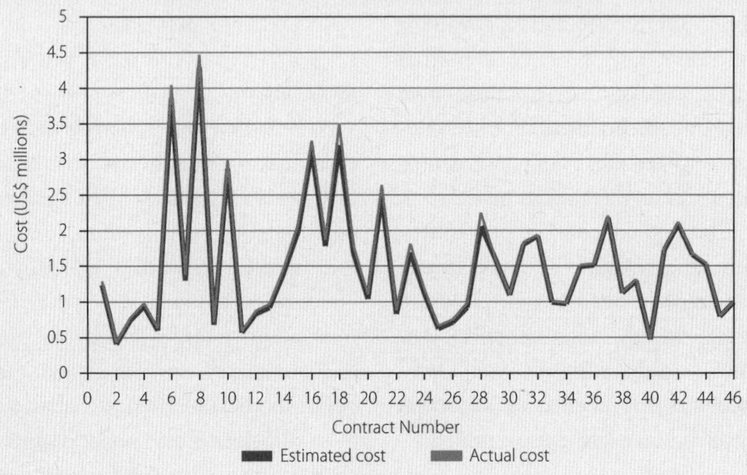

Source: Adapted from discussion with the World Bank Integrity Vice Presidency in 2010.

fragile states' Dili Declaration of May 2010 states: "Although we all accept international standards, the donor community must be aware of our conditions and needs. That is why we must give ourselves a transitional period to reinforce our capabilities and systems and not have complex and slow procedural requirements and conditions imposed upon us."[99] Responsible leaders appreciate the ability of well-functioning fiduciary systems to significantly reduce opportunistic rent-seeking and reinforce rule-based behavior—but they need processes adapted to the reality of local conditions.[100]

Suggestions for "best-fit" procurement arrangements are not hard to come by. Country experience points to the need for contracting processes that allow direct negotiations with knowledge of regional markets, a focus on speed of mobilization and track record in operating in insecure environments in contracting, better information to the local private sector about procurement procedures, subcontracting to local contractors to build their capacity, pre-tendering internationally under variable quantity contracts, civil society monitoring of procurement to build trust, simplifying processes and documentation consistent with existing donor guidelines, and decentralizing donor decision-making to the country office.[101] But the search for best-fit procurement practices has proceeded further in some donors than others, and multilateral systems have not caught up with innovations in bilateral procurement.

The fragmentation of international aid efforts also acts against the provision of institutional support at sufficient scale. Not only have the number of donors and vertical programs grown to more than the number of recipient countries,[102] but aid has itself also become more fragmented. In the Democratic Republic of Congo, 30 active donors are financing 362 projects in the health sector, 262 for less than US$1 million, and 305 projects in the justice sector, 199 for less than US$1 million.[103] A recent OECD study identified 32 countries receiving aid from 15 or more donors.[104] In contrast, studies on Botswana and the Republic of Korea argue that development successes in these cases can be at least partly attributed to the presence of a single or dominant donor.[105] Fragmented assistance places a huge administrative burden on weak capacities, draining rather than building them.

Focus on citizen security, justice, and jobs

Assistance to countries struggling to develop well-governed police, justice, and corrections systems in the face of fluid violent threats is much more limited than assistance available to build military capacity. The supply of personnel is constrained, since states do not have the kinds of reserve capacities in police or criminal justice that they do in their militaries. For justice, the UN's Independent Review on Civilian Capacities found that it was one of the largest lacunae in international civilian mechanisms, despite efforts to fill gaps.[106] The UN Department of Peacekeeping Operations (UNDPKO), bilateral donors, the Inter-American Development Bank (IADB), the UNDP, and others have each deepened their delivery capacity related to citizen security and justice, and the World Bank has expanded somewhat assistance for legal and judicial issues—but major gaps in personnel and delivery remain.

Support to the criminal justice system is frequently more challenging to provide than support to military reform and capacity building because of the great disparities in policies, legal frameworks, and organizational structures between different nation-state providers.[107] These disparities have historically caused tensions in international support to policing and civilian justice, from Bosnia to Timor-Leste.[108] Regional organizations like the European Union have focused on training to bridge differences in national practices. The UN's 50-person-strong Standing Police Capacity and its Office of Rule of Law and Security Institutions have also begun to make headway in developing standard doctrine and training packages for police units willing to deploy into UN operations, but this is still a small capacity to manage the current growth in police deployments, let alone support a broader international capacity.[109] There is no similar mechanism for joint training of national judicial personnel to expose them to different systems and practices, and less of a body of knowledge on approaching institution-building in fragile settings.

Structural constraints in the international architecture also limit international support to security and justice. The UN's peacekeeping budget can support the deployment of police forces, but only if a country is under a Security Council mandate. This poses a major political obstacle to countries that might seek international support for their police sector but are hesitant to agree to being on the Security Council's agenda. Without a peacekeeping operation, national authorities can seek civilian or advisory support from the UN and operational support from bilateral actors. But the former does not include the actual deployment of police units, while the latter lacks the legitimacy of support provided by a multilateral organization to which the national authority belongs.

Chapter 5 described the common problems arising at a country level from disconnects between support to the military and police and support to the civilian justice system. The lack of a clear focal point for criminal justice as a whole in the international system may underpin this problem—remarkably, there are international agencies for a wide range of functions, but no agency charged with taking the lead on criminal justice issues. Fragmentation of financial support for the security sectors and civilian justice functions, due to the current division in what can be counted as "Official Development Assistance under DAC rules" and to the differing financial rules applying under peacekeeping missions and voluntary support in these areas, also exacerbates disconnected approaches on the ground.

With regard to employment creation, understandable shifts by donors to focus support on the MDGs have led many to dedicate significant parts of their development assistance to health, education, and basic services like water and sanitation—with relatively little emphasis on job creation. International economic policy advisory services have generally focused on growth rather than jobs. This has included consideration of labor-intensive growth paths as central to poverty reduction, but has placed relatively little emphasis on the value of employment in terms of violence prevention, and the type and quality of employment that can strengthen social cohesion and promote a positive role for youth in the community. As a result, there is little consensus on the type of employment-related interventions that can systematically make a difference in fragile environments. An exception is the use of community-based public works: while having very different designs, programs supported by bilateral donors, UN agencies, and international financial institutions in Afghanistan, Indonesia, Nepal, Burundi, Rwanda, and various Latin American countries have generated considerable transitional employment. Some bilateral donors, such as the United States and India, have also dedicated a significant proportion of their assistance in fragile states to income-generating activities.

The role of the private sector in mitigating and recovering from the effects of violence at both the local and national level is now widely recognized,[110] especially if creating jobs and incomes is to outlast donor-funded, short-term emergency works. Various innovative schemes, including some supported by the International Finance Corporation and by several bilateral donors, have proven effective in building up private sector and entrepreneurship capacity; examples include linking local entrepreneurs to larger national or international businesses and linking education to entrepreneurship development.[111] Donors such as the Multilateral Development Banks, Japan, and China provide significant investments in infrastructure that supports private sector development.[112] However, the international community has not paid as much attention to labor-intensive private sector development as is warranted by the importance of equitable growth and job creation for violence prevention.[113]

Dual accountability and managing the risks of action

International actors know that fast engagement, long-term commitments, and support to national institutions are central to preventing repeated cycles of violence.[114] Why then is international practice slow to change? We argue that this is because of the "dual accountability dilemma"—international actors, whether bilateral or multilateral, are accountable first to their domestic constituencies and shareholders, and only second to their counterparts or to the citizens of recipient states. This leads them to emphasize one set of risks—the risks of action and of engagement with weak counterpart institutions—at the expense of the risks of inaction or lack of long-term institution-building outcomes, for which there is less accountability (figure 6.2). The consequences are twofold: privileging the reputational risks of action over the consequential risks of delay and hesitation to channel financing and assistance through the budget of fragile national institutions.

FIGURE 6.2 ***International support to nation-states—The dual accountability dilemma***

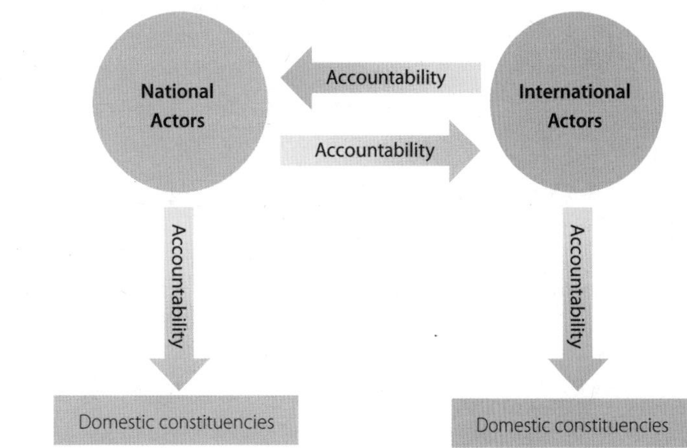

Source: WDR team.

Working in fragile states necessarily involves uncertainty, fluidity, and high risk—but there are risks of action and risks of inaction. A highly simplified example illustrates the problem: A community of 100,000 people faces a dire humanitarian threat. The external world is willing to help and has two broad options to do so. Both are estimated to cost US$50 million. Under option A, external donors can wait six months to ensure that all the funds will be used appropriately, but this will mean that only 20 percent of the people will be saved. Under option B, donors can be confident of saving all the people, but can only be confident that 80 percent of the funds can be properly accounted for. Which option to choose? Most people would say that option B *should* be chosen. Indeed, sensitivity to the risk of inaction and a tolerance for a certain degree of fiduciary risk underpins humanitarian interventions—and most humanitarian actors *would* adopt option B.

Now consider this for developmental or peacekeeping interventions: airlift support for troops; financing to pay salaries of police, education, and health workers and to keep the electricity system functioning; and a program to reopen schools are deemed highly likely to prevent the spread of violence. The same options are available—option A, wait six months to be confident that the funds will be used properly, but at the cost of averting an estimated 20 percent of the risk, or option B, act immediately with a high degree of confidence that violence can be averted, but with confidence that only 80 percent of the funds can be satisfactorily accounted. Again, most people would say option B should be chosen.

There is no certainty that development interventions will save lives and prevent the spread of violence—while hasty interventions often are less likely to succeed. But what if the risk is differentiated? One can probably judge that delays in the arrival of peacekeeping troops and the financing for salaries and the electricity system are likely to spur violence if no action is taken—80 percent likely, for the sake of illustration. For the schools program, however, one might judge this risk to be lower and that spending a few months working on the design of the program would deliver better results. Most people would then say pay for the airlift, the salaries, and the electricity—but wait for the schools program. Yet, in practice, the development community *would* likely treat the issues of electricity and schooling in the same manner; and while the UN Security Council sometimes takes decisions rapidly, the supporting infrastructure for peacekeeping deployments results in option A outcomes. The strategic challenge is to move from *should* to *would*—in other words, to rework risk-management systems to better align risk measurement and risk-taking to optimal outcomes.

A further example of the impact of dual accountability is donor reluctance to channel assistance through the national budget and national institutions in a violence-affected and fragile state despite its impact on transforming institutions. In addition to avoiding the negative effects of parallel systems, aid through the budget supports institutional mechanisms of political decision-making on priorities and trade-offs, leverages the development of public financial management and accountability systems, and creates a tool for coordinating international assistance.[115] However, donors confront a dilemma—assistance to weak institutions is needed if they are ever to become strong, but their weakness in itself poses political and fiduciary risks.[116] In these high-risk engagements, the international community is therefore prone to rely on bilateral and multilateral organizations to perform functions normally performed by the state,[117] in order to avoid being associated with the corrupt use of resources or the violence or human rights abuses by the parties being supported.

Available options for risk management

A range of approaches that deal with differing levels of fiduciary and reputational risk exist to engage with national institutions. They include greater independent oversight and monitoring of government-executed programs. For instance, in Afghanistan and the West Bank and Gaza under World Bank–administered multidonor trust funds, independent monitors have been employed to scrutinize procurement and expenditures by both national institutions and international contractors.[118] A related example is releasing donor funds only upon unqualified monthly or quarterly audits by a certified external auditing firm, as undertaken for the Uganda Veterans Assistance Program.[119] A third is in external financial management and procurement agencies, where international firms have overall responsibility for program financial management and procurement and maintain a program's consolidated budget and accounts, as was carried out in demobilization and reintegration in Angola, Guinea-Bissau, and Sierra Leone.[120] A fourth is "dual key" programs, where both national and international actors sign off on critical, high-risk transactions, such as the Liberia Governance and Economic Management Assistance Program described in chapter 4. And a fifth is in-kind support to items in the national budget, as in Zimbabwe, where a bilateral donor has directly financed, procured, and provided such items through contractors, as with the provision of medicines to state-run clinics.

These approaches can manage donor fiduciary risk and provide space to establish and strengthen national systems. But since they use international expertise, they are generally expensive. A range of more localized options is also available to engage with national institutions while dealing with differing levels of fiduciary and reputational risk. They include community-driven development programs (chapter 4) and contracting to NGOs using results-based financing and output-based aid in key sectors. Direct support to subnational administrations and assistance through nongovernment agencies that employ local staff are other ways of managing assistance outside government budget systems in situations of weak governance, maintaining a focus on local institutional capacity and skilled personnel.

Pooling funds also provides a way to manage risk. Multi-Donor Trust Funds (MDTFs) have increasingly been used in fragile and conflict-affected situations—for example, in Afghanistan and Southern Sudan (box 6.9), Iraq, Indonesia, West Bank and Gaza, and Haiti. MDTFs can help to bridge the dual accountability dilemma. For national actors, they improve the transparency of donor investments, ensure greater coherence with national planning, and provide a platform for resource mobilization. For donors, MDTFs

BOX 6.9 *Multidonor trust funds: Afghanistan and Southern Sudan*

Types of violence: Intergroup, ethnic, and political violence; organized crime and trafficking; cross-border; transnational; ideological	
Transition opportunity: Initial large space for change; Bonn Accord/Comprehensive Peace Agreement; elections; national development budget	**Key stakeholders:** Federal and local government, security forces, militias, community leaders, civil society groups, citizens, women, international partners, armed transnational groups
Key stresses: Legacies of violence and trauma, cross-border violence, criminal networks, low incomes, youth unemployment, corruption, gender discrimination	**Institutional challenges:** Severe accountability and capacity constraints in public administration, security, judicial, and political institutions; lack of representation of women
Dual accountability dilemma: Accountability and capacity constraints at the national level made multidonor trust funds an attractive solution; trust fund arrangements took advantage of the mandates and competencies of the UN and the World Bank.	

Afghanistan

UNDP established the Afghan Interim Authority Fund (AIAF), supported by 24 donors and valued at US$73 million for a limited period of six months, to pay for the most pressing needs of reestablishing the civil service: paying salaries, rehabilitating government buildings, and procuring equipment. This support bolstered government capability and legitimacy in the early phases of transition and bridged the gap until such time as a subsequent MDTF could provide long-term budget support and finance investment programs.

The Afghanistan Reconstruction Trust Fund (ARTF), supported by 32 donors, disburses funds through a "recurrent window" to finance the budget (salaries of civil servants and facility costs, particularly in education and health) and an "investment window" to support the government's National Priority Programmes. The ARTF is intended to coordinate funding and reduce the burden on the government, promote transparency and accountability, and reinforce the role of the national budget in promoting national objectives. Since its inception in 2002, donors have committed US$4 billion (as of December 2010), the largest contribution to the Afghan budget. The ARTF moved quickly, disbursing 99 percent of committed funds in 2003–04 and 75 percent in 2005–06, serving as the main vehicle for financing payment of government salaries, as well as key projects such as the Salang Tunnel and the National Solidarity Program. UNDP administers the complementary Law and Order Trust Fund for Afghanistan (LOTFA), which largely funds police salaries. The current phase of LOTFA was funded by 15 donors providing around US$306 million.

Southern Sudan

A US$545 million Southern Sudan Multidonor Trust Fund was established in 2005, with financing from 14 donors and with the World Bank appointed as trust fund administrator.

The government of Southern Sudan, donors, NGOs, and civil society have criticized the MDTF for slowness and inefficiency, lagging disbursements, and inflexibility. Reviews have pointed to the World Bank's underestimation of logistical difficulties, institutional deficiencies, and communication challenges—and to inconsistent managerial oversight, especially in the critical early phase. Part of the explanation for this was the dilemma faced by the World Bank in trying to balance the risk posed by swift action (possible misuse of the funds) with the risks of inaction (failing to disburse funds and not achieving goals).

The World Bank has taken steps to improve the fund's management—disbursements in 2010 amounted to US$188 million and reached a total of US$400 million by December 2010 (almost three-quarters of the funds committed).

Source: Scanteam 2007; Fenton and Phillips 2009; Randel 2010; Atos Consulting 2009; Scanteam 2010; OECD 2010c; Government of Afghanistan and UNDP 2010; World Bank 2005a, 2009a, 2010b, 2010j; Randel and Mowjee 2006.

can reduce transaction costs and provide a forum for donor collaboration and dialogue with national authorities, while MDTF secretariats can provide information to capitals that donors may not be able to generate on their own.[121] MDTFs can enable donors to adopt a collective approach to the risks inherent in transition situations.[122] In the humanitarian context, pooled mechanisms may increase funding levels because they enable donors to disburse larger sums than they can manage directly.

MDTFs, however, are rarely the most important financing instrument in conflict settings—total funding through some 18 operative MDTFs in 2007 amounted to US$1.2 billion, still a small fraction of international financing for fragile and conflict-affected states.[123] Moreover, MDTF performance has been uneven across country examples in speed and delivery of outputs, in quality of processes, and in stakeholder perceptions of success. Recent evaluations of MDTFs have pointed to inconsistency of MDTF management processes within and across agencies, the need for better management of expectations, more robust monitoring and impact evaluation, quicker delivery of funds to support national confidence building, and more emphasis on support through national systems for institution building.[124] Balancing the competing demands of providing short-term financing and building longer-term institutional capacity is illustrated in the experience of the Southern Sudan MDTF.

Because of their high-profile nature and complex governance system, MDTFs can also increase risk aversion within their hosting agency. Bilateral donors, in effect, transfer their risk to multilateral MDTF administrators.[125] There can also be micromanagement by donors of MDTF portfolios and earmarking of funds, undermining alignment with nationally driven strategy and budgeting.[126]

Monitoring progress out of fragility

Making the dual accountability dilemma even worse is a lack of systems to monitor progress out of fragility. The only agreed global framework for measuring the results of development assistance is the MDGs and their associated indicators. No global measures exist to assess progress in efforts to improve human and citizen security. So a simple agreed set of indicators to measure progress in reducing violence and creating better institutions would allow both the international community and national leaders to track progress on violence risk management alongside the MDGs.

Nor do reliable global data exist on levels or patterns of insecurity. Basic data on war battle deaths are poor—best estimates are missing in 36 percent of the cases, and low and high estimates are often separated by an order of magnitude.[127] The quality of data on indirect deaths due to war is significantly worse—estimates of casualties in Iraq for 2003 to 2006 range from 50,000 to 600,000.[128] Homicide data are similarly inadequate for monitoring violence. While every OECD country reports homicide statistics for every year of the past five, only 62 percent of developing countries have one or more observations for the past five years, and only 29 percent of fragile or conflict-affected states in Sub-Saharan Africa report a single homicide rate.

An innovative approach that tracks conflict and violence reported in the local press is being used in Aceh since the signing of the peace accord in August 2005.[129] Another source of information on attitudes toward domestic violence is UNICEF's periodic Multiple Indicator Cluster Surveys, which cover around 100 countries, many of them fragile and violence-affected. On the whole, however, there are few agreed baselines for measuring reductions in violence. Better data collection is an easy win for improving international responses (chapter 9).

Polling to measure citizen confidence and expectations over time is rarely used in fragile states. Perception-based polling could be an important part of measuring citizen priorities and citizen trust in government. Such data have rarely been collected consistently in fragile states,[130] for reasons that range from poor communications and underfunded organizations to fears of how the information will be used.[131] But technological advances make collecting survey data easier—this WDR, for example, carried out rapid SMS (short message service) surveys in the Democratic Republic of Congo.[132]

Lessons of international engagement

The paradox of dual accountability is well understood by actors on the ground—the question is how to do better. Any number of major reports on international assistance that have to do with conflict-affected countries in the last decade have underlined the limits to what international support can do to reduce conflict and bring about institutional transformation in fragile conditions. This chapter calls for the consistent application of best-fit practices that have already proved their usefulness, and reaches the following three conclusions:

- First, there are serious gaps in support for citizen security, justice, and jobs for countries struggling to prevent violence.
- Second, "procedural conformism" in international agencies is unsuited to the challenges of rapid confidence-building and best-fit approaches to institutional transformation. Better ways to manage accountability to domestic taxpayers and local counterparts are needed.
- Third, new challenges and the changing landscape of international assistance require new efforts to work together. Complex problems of political and criminal violence require the combined capacities of diplomatic, security, and development actors—and better understanding between OECD, low-income, middle-income, and regional partners.

FEATURE 6 *A tale of two assistance programs—Liberia and Guinea-Bissau*

Liberia: Strong leadership, critical recovery assistance

Types of violence: Civil conflict, political violence, criminal and gang-related violence, trafficking	
Transition opportunity: Significant space for change following the Comprehensive Peace Agreement in September 2003	**Key stakeholders:** Ex-combatants, victims, government, opposition parties, international partners and peacekeepers
Key stresses: Legacy of abuse, violence, trauma grievances and mistrust, corruption, unemployment, ethnic competition	**Institutional challenges:** Accountability and capacity constraints in economic, security, judicial, and political spheres
Dual accountability dilemma: Need to increase capacity in national institutions in an environment of extreme fiduciary risk	

The international community can provide critical assistance to fragile states during difficult transitions. When done well, this support can make a major difference to countries trying to avoid or recover from violent conflict, but only when domestic processes are headed in a positive direction. The recent history of international support to Liberia and Guinea-Bissau offer two starkly contrasting stories (see box 6.10).

The international community played a key role in supporting the Accra Comprehensive Peace Agreement (CPA), signed in Accra, Ghana, in September 2003, which brought an end to two civil wars that had devastated Liberia. The UN mobilized a peacekeeping mission of 25,000 troops. The highest troop-to-population ratio in the history of peacekeeping, it provided a credible deterrent against opponents of the peace process and third-party assurances that peace would be maintained.

Liberia's transition government, however, experienced serious governance and corruption problems (see below). Yet, with a peace agreement and international security guarantees in place, Liberia's GDP grew at a healthy 6.4 percent a year between 2004 and 2008 (having contracted by almost a third in 2003). In the same period, the international aid community provided US$2.6 billion to Liberia, an average of US$146 per capita per year (total international spending, including security, was considerably higher at US$415 per capita in 2008—the highest to date in Africa).

That was not all. International actors such as the UN and the World Bank worked with the government of Liberia to lift public confidence through an innovative program to provide jobs, restart the economy, and provide tangible evidence of the peace process. "Roads with UNMIL" restored hundreds of kilometers of roads, reconnecting areas of the country long isolated from one another by the war, enabling trade to resume, and facilitating humanitarian relief efforts. Drawing on the resources and expertise of different agencies in the political, security, and development fields, the project delivered results in the short term, while facilitating reform in the transport sector in the medium term. Going beyond the confines of infrastructure development, it offered short-term employment opportunities for many ex-combatants and non-combatants.

Liberia's recovery trajectory also shows how regional organizations can help. The ECOWAS worked with donors on confidence building tailored to the Liberian milieu. The Governance and Economic Management Assistance Program (GEMAP, see box 4.2), introduced in the run-up to the 2005 elections, provides "dual key" authority in the areas of revenue earning and expenditure. Jointly managed by the government and the international community, it was designed specifically to reassure a skeptical population and donors that years of official looting and corruption were over and that services would be reliably delivered. Economic governance has improved under GEMAP and, with consistent international commitment and willingness to share risk, it has helped reinforce confidence in state institutions. While noting these positives, critics point out that the slow transfer of knowledge and capacity to local authorities and stakeholders may have created dependency—highlighting the importance of integrated and sustained external engagement with national institutions.

Seven years after signing the CPA, Liberia qualified for the World Bank/IMF Heavily Indebted Poor Countries initiative, setting in motion the largest per-capita debt write-off in history. The peace process has since been consolidated, driven by determined, output-oriented national leadership and pragmatic international support. Today, Liberia has initiated a process of stabilization that few dared imagine a few years earlier. The challenge now is to ensure that this extraordinary and successful episode in international support is not ended prematurely, that emerging stresses continue to be clearly identified, and that legitimate, accountable institutions receive sustained support.

In contrast to the coordinated international support for Liberia, no comparable international effort was made in nearby Guinea-Bissau. This in part reflects a lack of international confidence in national governance and country leadership—but similar conditions existed in Liberia before the 2005 elections.

Guinea-Bissau: Weak national processes, uneven international support

Types of violence: Civil conflict, political violence, organized crime and trafficking, transnational crime	
Transition opportunity: Repeated and brief opportunities for change: multiparty elections, peace agreements after civil war, National Stability Pact	**Key stakeholders:** Federal and local government, military, citizens, regional institutions, international partners, international drug cartels
Key stresses: Legacies of violence and trauma, ethnic competition, external support for domestic rebels, international criminal networks, low incomes, youth unemployment, corruption	**Institutional challenge:** Severe accountability and capacity constraints in public administration, security, judicial, and political institutions; lack of access to services; lack of inclusion of different groups
Dual accountability dilemma: International community that viewed preventive action as too risky; national actors that needed early and sustained support to combat domestic violence and the influence of international trafficking	

Over the past 15 years, there have been sporadic windows of opportunity, but with leadership commitment to overcoming the rifts in society largely found wanting, they received scant support from the international community. Today Guinea-Bissau remains one of the world's most impoverished nations and an "aid orphan," with a human development index rank of 164 among 169 countries in 2010.

Since independence in the 1960s, Guinea-Bissau has been ruled mainly as a one-party regime interrupted by coups and a civil war (1998–99). International pressures for democracy as a condition for aid led to a tentative move toward a multiparty political system in 1991. A moment of opportunity came in 1994 with the first multiparty elections. But aside from proclaiming the elections to be "transparent, free, and fair," the international community remained largely absent. Similarly, during the civil war, the international community kept its distance, while regional institutions such as ECOWAS and the African Union attempted to mediate and enforce peacekeeping.

Peace and elections in 1999–2000 gave rise to new hopes, and the UN set up its Peacebuilding Support Office in Guinea-Bissau (UNOGBIS). A donor conference was organized to support post-war recovery and reconstruction, and the IMF and World Bank provided emergency assistance. Hopes were undermined by continued poor governance—without the supporting mechanisms in place in Liberia.

The response of the international community: further isolation. In what looked like an increasingly risky environment, the IMF suspended assistance while the African Development Bank and the World Bank cut back their programs. Without budgetary support, civil servant salaries went unpaid. Real GDP contracted by 4.1 percent in 2002 and 0.6 percent in 2003. A *coup d'état* soon followed.

Elections were held in 2005, a new government was formed, and the international community slowly reengaged. The UN strengthened UNOBGIS' mandate to include supporting political dialogue and national reconciliation and upholding the rule of law and human rights. There was agreement between the new government and the few donors present in the country on strategic priorities—reforming the security sector, paying salaries to the military and civil service, and restoring some electrical service to the capital.

The IMF resumed assistance and a donor meeting was held in Lisbon in February 2005. But only €1.5 million was pledged. A donors' roundtable in 2006 was more successful—amid growing concerns about the influence of the drug trade and criminal networks, some US$280 million was pledged, though continuing political instability remained an obstacle to delivering funds.

In 2007, in reaction to the president's unconstitutional dismissal of the prime minister, parliamentarians formed a majority coalition. They committed the three largest parties in the assembly to a national stability pact and, after months of negotiations, passed a vote of no confidence that forced the president to appoint a new prime minister. Hopes were dashed when the pact collapsed, triggering a new political crisis and the fall of the government. In 2008, another round of elections, which received some limited international assistance to ensure the electoral staff was paid, produced another new government.

Guinea-Bissau remains deeply fragile and insecure. In 2009, it was thrown into further turmoil with the assassination of the president, a top general, and two ministers. Drug trafficking has become a major concern. Security sector reforms remain integral in addressing this rising violence, but so far have received limited backing from international actors. The EU and ECOWAS have helped settle some salary arrears, and Angola and South Africa have modest programs in place. But the international community is largely absent—without responsible national leadership, it is unwilling or unable to take the risk and provide the kind of sustained support that could have helped Guinea-Bissau back on its feet.

Sources: AllAfrica 2009; Andersen 2010; Atkinson 2008; Bøås 2009; Dwan and Bailey 2006; Jahr 2010; Government of the Republic of Liberia Executive Mansion 2009; Giovine and others 2010; UNDP 2010b; International Crisis Group 2008a, 2009b; Gberie 2003b; Economist Intelligence Unit 2008b; IRIN 2005; Vulliamy 2008.

REFLECTIONS FROM ADVISORY COUNCIL MEMBERS: *2011 WORLD DEVELOPMENT REPORT*

BOX 6.10 *Uneven international support to violence prevention and recovery in West Africa*

Mohamed Ibn Chambas, Secretary-General of the African, Caribbean, and Pacific Group of States (ACP), Former President of the Economic Community of West African States; *WDR Advisory Council Member*

We assumed the successes chalked up in Liberia would be enough justification to see similar quick and strong responses from the international community in Guinea-Bissau to avoid recurrence of violence and conflict. That was not to be. Consequently, the country still totters on the brink of instability, violence, conflict, or state disintegration, given the real threat posed by drug trafficking.

The neglect of the international community made it difficult for a number of regional initiatives to put the country on a path of steady recovery and eventual takeoff. A donor conference in Geneva in 2006 to raise funds for a security sector and national reconstruction plan was poorly attended; ECOWAS ended up pledging the most funding. Nor was the national strategy for combating drug trafficking adequately funded, even though its destabilizing impact on the country and the region was and still is evident.

Above all, the failure to provide funding for the much needed security sector reform has been particularly disappointing and baffling. The impunity and persistent incursion into the political domain by the military can only be tackled through a comprehensive security sector reform that addresses the legal, institutional, and capacity weaknesses of various security agencies (military, police, immigration, prisons, customs) and the judicial system. ECOWAS did not succeed in obtaining for Guinea-Bissau the requisite resources to embark on the urgently needed reforms in this strategic sector.

The contrast in international support to Liberia as compared to Guinea or Guinea-Bissau was quite noticeable and a source of great frustration to us at ECOWAS.

Notes

1. In 1990, Freedom House gave civil liberties in Mozambique the worst possible score and political rights the second-worst on a scale of 1 to 7, whereas the scores had both improved to 3 in 2009. Freedom House uses a 1 to 7 scale, where 7 indicates the lowest level of freedom, with few or no political rights because of severe government oppression, sometimes in combination with civil war. At the other end of the scale, countries and territories with a rating of 1 enjoy a wide range of political rights, including free and fair elections.
2. The megaprojects include the Mozal aluminum smelter, the Cahora Bassa hydroelectric plant, and Sasol gas project. See Cadeado and Hamela 2009; World Bank 2005b.
3. UNDPKO 2010b, 2010c.
4. WDR team calculations based on OECD 2010d.
5. Davies and others 2008; Meidan 2006.
6. South-South bilateral aid increased by some 68 percent, from 2004 to 2008, to an estimated US$626 million. Data for several major non-DAC development partners, such as China and India, are not included in this estimate (see OECD-DAC 2010b).
7. The following multilateral organizations and governments had special envoys or representatives to Afghanistan or Afghanistan and Pakistan in 2009–10: United Kingdom, United States, United Nations, European Union, Netherlands, Sweden, Norway, France, Australia, Belgium, China, Germany, Japan, Denmark.
8. New York University Center on International Cooperation 2009.
9. Harvey and others 2010.
10. This interdependence has been recognized explicitly in, for instance, in the World Bank's framework for rapid response to crisis and emergencies, which enables it to participate in integrated international support efforts for programs that include important linkages to areas outside the Bank's core competencies, while maintaining its engagement in areas of core competencies (World Bank 2007d, 2008b; Stewart and Brown 2007).
11. UN integrated missions are an instrument through which the UN seeks to help countries in the transition from war to lasting peace, or address a similarly complex situation that requires a system-

wide UN response, through subsuming various actors and approaches within an overall political-strategic crisis management framework. See Eide and others 2005; Campbell, Kaspersen, and Weir 2007.

12. "Whole-of-government approaches" refers to how agencies and ministries within a government administration can work coherently together in order to develop a comprehensive response to fragile states in crisis. See DFID 2010, Stewart and Brown 2007; OECD-DAC 2006.
13. "Whole-of-system approaches" specifically refers to how regional and international organizations and the international architecture in general can best develop policy coherence and a comprehensive response to fragile states in crisis. See DFID 2010.
14. These include the U.K. Stabilization Unit (created in 2004 as the Post-Conflict Reconstruction Unit), U.S. Office of the Coordinator for Reconstruction and Stabilization, Canada's Stabilization and Reconstruction Task Force, the UN Peacebuilding Committee and Peacebuilding Support Office; and the AusAID Fragile States Unit (created in 2005).
15. OECD-DAC 2006.
16. Wainwright 2005; Dinnen, Porter, and Sage 2010.
17. Stewart and Brown 2007.
18. OECD-DAC 2007b.
19. Harborne and others 2010.
20. Chalmers 2007.
21. Peixoto, Andrade, and Azevedo 2008.
22. Annual budget costs compiled for UN political missions, Organization for Security and Cooperation in Europe (OSCE) mission, and EU representatives by New York University's Center on International Cooperation.
23. Light mediation start-up budget (LMSB) covers the cost of a small mediation team that is required to address a limited conflict. Such conflicts are typically clearly between two states or coherent parties within a state (without a regional dimension) that are amenable to resolution within a short period of time (possibly within a year). The LMSB will allow UNDPA to establish a mediation effort quickly and sustain it for up to three months, while the full costing for the initiative is being developed and resourced. Heavy mediation start-up budget (HMSB) covers the initial costs of addressing a complex conflict situation. Complex conflicts typically have local and regional dimensions, and the mediation team is likely to be deployed in multiple locations. Complex conflicts are likely to require a heavier presence in the capital and a presence in the regions and neighboring countries. In this regard, the HMSB is intended to facilitate the rapid establishment of the initial UN presence on the ground for a period of one year, while the costing of the full mediation team for the first and subsequent years is developed and resourced.
24. An early, and still relevant, critique of this problem is found in de Soto and del Castillo 1994.
25. World Bank 2008b.
26. For discussion of the interaction between human rights and mediation communities, and the progressively greater incorporation of human rights provisions into peace agreements, see Stedman 1996.
27. Stedman 1996.
28. UN 2000, 2011.
29. For instance, the Guatemalan peace accords incorporated significant commitments for gender equity aimed at the elimination of discrimination against women, including the promotion of women's political participation and their access to education, health, housing, and other resources—a success attributed to the only female member in the peace negotiations. See Potter 2005.
30. UNIFEM, UN Action Against Sexual Violence in Conflict, and UNDPKO 2010.
31. International Alert and Women Waging Peace 2004.
32. A 2010 meeting of anglophone and francophone delegates in Kenya, convened by UNDP, coined the phrase "collaborative capacities" and further refined the institutions relevant to prevention and recovery from violence as "dynamic networks of interdependent structures, mechanisms, resources, values, and skills which, through dialogue and consultation, contribute to conflict prevention and peace-building in a society" (UN Interagency Framework for Coordination on Preventive Action 2010, 1).
33. Commonwealth Secretariat 2006; The Carter Center 2007; UNDPA 2010b.
34. Wolpe and McDonald 2006.
35. The WDR's glossary defines commitment mechanisms as ways to persuade stakeholders that intentions to break with past policies will not be reversed, including creating independent functions

for implementing or monitoring agreements. This follows the common economic definition of commitment mechanisms or commitment devices (e.g., see Dixit 1980, Schelling 1960, and Spence 1977). Doyle and Sambanis (2006, 111) find that treaties and UN missions work in concert and note "a positive (though not large) correlation between UN mandates and the signing of a peace treaty, since treaties are necessary for certain UN operations." The UN can facilitate peace treaties among parties, and enforce peace when agreements become unstuck as "without a treaty and transformational UN mission, the likelihood of success drops substantially from an initial value of about 80 per cent to less than 5 per cent at extreme values of hostility" (Doyle and Sambanis 2006, 130). See also Human Security Centre 2005; Fortna 2008; Walter and Kydd 2002.

36. Hartzell, Hoddie, and Rothchild 2001.
37. Walter and Kydd 2002.
38. The Extractive Industries Transparency Initiative (EITI) is a coalition of governments, companies, civil society groups, investors and international organizations. It aims to strengthen governance by improving transparency and accountability in the extractives sector through the establishment of a global standard for transparency in oil, gas, and mining. See EITI 2009.
39. The Natural Resource Charter is a set of economic principles for governments and societies on how to best manage the opportunities created by natural resources for development. The charter comprises 12 precepts, or principles, that encapsulate the choices and suggested strategies that governments might pursue to increase the prospects of sustained economic development from natural resource exploitation. See Natural Resource Charter 2010.
40. Additional information regarding Liberia's Governance and Economic Management Assistance Program can be found in chapter 4, box 4.3.
41. A comprehensive study of 204 cases of sanctions imposed between 1914 and 2006, half of which took place after 1990, found about one-third to be successful (Hufbauer and others 2007).
42. Nossal 1999; Wallensteen and others 2007.
43. Van Genugten and de Groot 1999; Bessler, Garfield, and McHugh 2004.
44. Cortright, Lopez, and Gerber 2002.
45. UN 2006a, 3.
46. CICIG has presented two legal reform packages to the Guatemalan Congress that seek to improve the legal and institutional framework of the criminal prosecution of crimes that fall under CICIG's jurisdiction. To date, the Congress has approved four essential laws: Law on Arms and Ammunition, Law to Strengthen Criminal Prosecutions, Law on Jurisdiction in High-Risk Criminal Proceedings, and Reforms to the Law Against Organized Crime and Incidents. See CICIG 2009.
47. See, for example, the Lomé Declaration on the Framework for an OAU Response to Unconstitutional Change of Government (Organization of African Unity 2000) and the Inter-American Democratic Charter (OAS 2001).
48. Both the UN and the international financial institutions consider regional stances in their approaches to governments, but no structured mechanisms exist to discuss this with the regional institutions.
49. A major focus of humanitarian assistance in past years has been four deadly disease clusters—acute respiratory infections, diarrheal diseases, malaria, and measles—all of which are major killers in wartime. All are preventable and treatable at very low cost. Worldwide increases in immunization coverage over the past 30-plus years have played a large part in reducing mortality from these diseases. Between 1974 and 2006, coverage for the six major vaccine-preventable diseases rose from less than 5 percent to more than 75 percent of the world's population. In addition to preventing and treating disease, a significant share of humanitarian aid budgets is devoted to treating severe malnutrition. Fatality rates for severely malnourished children have decreased because of this and better treatment protocols. Peacetime immunization drives, together with the life-saving impact of humanitarian assistance, have all contributed to reducing wartime mortality from disease and malnutrition. See Human Security Report Project, forthcoming; Guha-Sapir and D'Aoust 2010.
50. These exceptions include where branding would "compromise the intrinsic independence or neutrality of a program or materials where independence or neutrality is an inherent aspect of the program and material." USAID 2009a, 16; 2010.
51. Stoddard, Harmer, and Haver 2006.
52. The "Brookings Process" brought together Office of the UNHCR, UNDP, and the World Bank in 2000 to more effectively address the "gaps" that occur in relief-to-development programs, funding, and strategies.

53. See section on education and health reforms as crucial medium-term challenges in chapter 5. Also see World Bank 2002a, 2008g.
54. Jones, Gowan, and Sherman 2009.
55. U.S. Government Accountability Office 2010b.
56. Garassi 2010.
57. Government of Nepal, UNDP, and UNDG 2010.
58. World Bank and UN 2007.
59. International conflict and fragility assessment frameworks include: United States: Interagency Conflict Assessment Framework, 2009; United Kingdom: Strategic Conflict Assessment; DFID: Conducting Conflict Assessments: Guidance Notes, 2002; SIDA: Manual for Conflict Analysis, 2006; UNDP: Conflict-Related Development Analysis, 2003; USAID: Conducing a Conflict Assessment, 2005; World Bank, Conflict Analysis Framework, 2002.
60. Chandran, Slotin, and Sorensen 2010.
61. U.S. Department of State 2009; DFID 2002.
62. World Bank and UN 2008.
63. OECD-DAC 2010a.
64. World Bank and UN 2007; see also International Dialogue on Peacebuilding and Statebuilding 2010.
65. Strategies produced by Africa Development Bank (Country Strategy Paper 2008–2011); EC (Country Strategy Paper and Indicative Programme, 2008–2013); UN (UN Development Assistance Framework 2010–2014); World Bank (Poverty Reduction Strategy Paper, 2006–2009; 2008 Country Assistance Strategy); Austria (Three Year Program on Austrian Development Policy, 2006–2008); Belgium (Indicative Cooperation Program, 2007–2009, Indicative Cooperation Program, 2010–2013); France (Framework Partnership Agreement, 2006–2010); Sweden (Strategy to Great Lakes Region, including Burundi, 2004–2008); and United States (Strategic Statement 2006–2008). See AfDB 2008; European Commission and Republic of Burundi 2007; Government of Burundi and UN 2009; Republic of Burundi 2006; World Bank 2008e; Austrian Federal Ministry for European and International Affairs 2006; Belgium Development Agency 2006, 2009; French Ministry of Foreign Affairs 2006; SIDA 2005; Government of Burundi 2005.
66. A notable exception to the fragmentation of donor assistance strategies is the preparation of a country assistance framework in the Democratic Republic of Congo. Following the 2006 elections, donors confronted the need to begin planning for the post-election period in a fragile and uncertain political landscape. A joint strategy framework, building on the five pillars identified in the Poverty Reduction Strategy Program, appealed to the Democratic Republic of Congo's partners as a way of mitigating risk while preparing the way for partners to engage in substantive dialogue with the new government on pre-identified and pre-agreed issues as soon as it was formed. Under an initiative by the UN Integrated Office in the UN Democratic Republic of Congo peacekeeping mission and the World Bank, a Country Assistance Framework was developed as a common strategic approach to recovery and development assistance, and was agreed to by 17 international partners. A challenge with such joint donor planning, however, is to keep it flexible enough to respond to new challenges, as subsequently emerged in the Democratic Republic of Congo. See also Rohland and Cliffe 2002; Republic of Liberia and UN 2007.
67. Ashraf Ghani and Clare Lockhart, in *Fixing Failed States,* analyze the issue of establishing legitimacy and closing the sovereignty gap in fragile and conflict-affected states through the lens of "double compact." The double compact focuses on the "network of rights and obligations underpinning the state's claim to sovereignty . . ." and refers first to the "compact . . . between a state and its citizens . . . embedded in a coherent set of rules," and second, "between a state and the international community to ensure adherence to international norms and standards of accountability and transparency" (Ghani and Lockhart 2008, 8).
68. Cox and Thornton 2010.
69. Aga Khan Development Network 2003.
70. Fully consistent with the findings of the many development assessments and studies conducted in recent years, including Agence Française de Développement and others 2005 and Commission on Growth and Development 2008.
71. Gowan 2007.
72. These points were made forcefully by ministers of finance from 12 African conflict-affected countries at two post-conflict learning events in 2002 and 2003 (World Bank 2002b, 2003).

73. Kharas 2008.
74. Volatility has costs in all economic activity with expectations, reflected by risk premiums. Losses associated with volatility can come in the form of additional costs of financial management; the opportunity costs of idle funds (windfalls) or missed investment opportunities (shortfalls); the costs associated with over borrowing and debt buildup when there is uncertainty about amount needed and concessional credits are used; and the costs associated with volatility in fiscal spending and the real exchange rate that can follow from volatility in aid (Kharas 2008). These costs can be further amplified by donor "herding" behavior, which is often more responsive to political instability and violence. Additionally, the costs of shortfalls may be higher in fragile and conflict-affected states. While an aid shortfall in a typical developing country may lead to the costs above, in a fragile or conflict-affected state, such a shortfall may completely derail transition moments, interrupting reform and possibly leading to political crises.
75. Birdsall and others 2010.
76. Council for the Development of Cambodia 2010.
77. Killick, Castel-Branco, and Gerster 2005.
78. Some forms do travel well, however. For instance, secret ballots and the separation of women and children from men in jails support principled outcomes in most situations.
79. Special Inspector General for Iraq Reconstruction 2009, 326. However, the international community has supported many best-fit measures in complex conflict settings (see chapter 5). As further examples, in 2003–04, while conditions for comprehensive disarmament in Haiti were not in place, UNDP undertook an innovative project that linked disarmament to a community approach involving information campaigns, support to community conflict-resolution mechanisms, and microprojects benefiting community groups as well as former members of armed gangs. In the West Bank and Gaza since 2002, the World Bank and several donors have been financing non-salary recurrent expenditures of the ministries of Health, Education and Higher Education, and Social Affairs through the Emergency Services Support Program MDTF in response to a deepening fiscal and economic crisis.
80. See Collier 2007.
81. These attributes include, for example, the quality and experience of the experts (governments should expect and receive highly competent and committed professionals able to work in difficult environments); a simple and well thought out program that can be implemented quickly; effective coordination among donors to ensure consistent policy advice; the participation of national champions to move the process along; and links to specific programs (so that advice and training reinforces new initiatives) (World Bank 2000).
82. Waldman 2008, 10; Michailof 2007.
83. Institute for State Effectiveness 2007.
84. OECD 2008.
85. National Academy of Public Administration 2006.
86. Civilian surge capacity is typically classified as *standing capacity* (can be in-country within 72 hours of need, and remain deployed for a minimum of 60 days); *standby capacity* (can be in-country within 60 days, and remain deployed for a minimum of 180 days); and *rostered capacity* (can be in-country within 180 days, deployment term subject to contract) (see Chandran and others 2009; Sisk 2010; Korski and Gowan 2009). Australia's International Deployment Group (IDG), for example, is a standing corps of more than 500 Australian federal police officers trained and ready to deploy on peacekeeping missions (see Peake and Brown 2010). The U.S. Office of the Coordinator for Reconstruction and Stabilization is building up a civilian standby capacity of interagency personnel.
87. For example, the United States, the United Kingdom, EU, and Australia.
88. UN, forthcoming.
89. See Baird 2010.
90. Of the different forms that South-South cooperation has taken, technical assistance has been the most common. Although many technical assistance projects focus on economic and social development, countries in the Global South have also developed specialized capacities in post-conflict peacebuilding. Examples include South Africa's support to build structural capacities for public service through peer learning among public sector schools (Management Development Institutes) at the Ministries for Public Administration in Burundi, Rwanda, and Southern Sudan. Cooperation among 45 municipalities in El Salvador, Guatemala, and Honduras helps to manage regional public goods, such as water, in the Trifinio region. See OECD 2010f.

91. In 2008, the African Development Bank Group (AfDB) established the Fragile States Facility (FSF) to "effectively assist eligible fragile states to consolidate peace, stabilize economies and lay foundations for sustainable poverty-reduction and long-term economic growth" (AfDB 2011, 1). The FSF has three grant pillars: Pillar I, the supplemental support window for funding infrastructure, state capacity building, and accountability; Pillar II, the arrears clearance window; and Pillar III, the technical assistance and capacity-building window. Eligible states are those that have a harmonized AfDB/World Bank CPIA rating of less than 3.2, or countries that have had UN or regional peacebuilding, peacekeeping, or mediation operations over the last three years. Pillar III provides technical assistance and capacities aimed at filling critical gaps in carefully selected public sector domains through secondment of seasoned professional staff from neighboring countries and on-the-job training opportunities with the objective of building a sustainable cadre of senior civil servants—fragile states that have the capacity in management and implementation of reforms. The program is usually implemented as integrated components of comprehensive capacity-building plans. By March 2010, this South-South cooperation facility had received resources in the amount of UA (Units of Accounts) 85.39 million, equivalent to13.2 percent of the total FSF resources (AfDB 2010, 5).
92. Viva Rio negotiated a peace accord among 14 rival groups, and the homicide rate in Bel Air fell from 26 per 100,000 in 2006–07 to 17 in 2008–09, lower than in any other major Latin American city (OECD 2010f).
93. See UNPBSO 2010.
94. OECD 2010f.
95. UN, forthcoming.
96. For instance, nearly a third of the "peace and development advisers" who are jointly deployed by UNDP and UNDPA to build such capacities in violence-affected countries are either former internal mediators or facilitators from the "Mont Fleur" visioning exercise in South Africa, which was implemented with discrete UN assistance, or have been trained by them. See UNDP 2010a.
97. Funding provided through the Office of the Transition Initiatives at USAID is one example. This transition funding is not subject to the same policies and procedures as other financing provided by USAID. DFID's Middle East and North Africa Department has created a Program Risk Assessment Matrix that assesses risk factors in conflict programming. The EU is currently developing a framework for analyzing the risks associated with budget support to fragile states.
98. For Cambodia, see Jones 2009. For Liberia, see World Bank 2010k.
99. International Dialogue on Peacebuilding and Statebuilding 2010, 9.
100. Colletta and Tesfamichael 2003.
101. Colletta and Tesfamichael 2003.
102. World Bank 2007a.
103. World Bank analysis prepared for the 2009 workshop in Kinshasa on aid effectiveness.
104. OECD-DAC 2008.
105. Azam, Devarajan, and O'Connell 2002; Bräutigam 2000.
106. UN, forthcoming.
107. Etzioni 1999. The United States, for example, uses several layers of police agencies, most of them under local government control, while many European countries favor national police forces with specialized divisions. The principles underlying security provision can also be quite different in otherwise similar societies: the ubiquitous use of street cameras to track civilians in a number of European cities would be considered invasive in the United States, where history and tradition privilege individual privacy.
108. Lemay-Hébert 2009; Graydon 2005; Greenfell 2006; Wisler 2005; Vetschera and Damian 2006.
109. UNPOL 2011.
110. For a review of the characteristics of the post-conflict private sector and the ways in which the development community can engage with it, see Mac Sweeney 2008.
111. For instance, the International Finance Corporation (IFC) has worked with Nestlé and ECOM, a soft commodity trading company, to support small-scale farmers in the coffee sector around the world (with a mix of investment and advisory interventions) and partnered with Standard Chartered Bank to strengthen practical business skills of small and medium entrepreneurs in Pakistan. IFC also partnered with the BBC in Afghanistan on a series of radio "edutainment" programs that combine education with entertainment on issues such as unemployment, lack of infrastructure, and inadequate service provision and aimed to raise awareness of the benefits of small business enterprises and provide practical information on small-business-related issues. A recent audience

feedback survey found that listeners are learning, through storylines and the experiences of others, how to start small businesses and generate income, and that many have acted upon information in the programs to improve their own financial situation (BBC World Service Trust 2010).

112. OECD and WTO 2008; Kawai and Takagi 2004; Davies and others 2008; Meidan 2006.
113. Battle 2008; World Bank 2011b.
114. OECD-DAC 2007b.
115. World Bank and AfDB 2010.
116. Precisely because the budget is a tool for political bargaining, when the government has few resources available to it within a budget, its scope for negotiating inclusive-enough pacts is diminished. Diminished also is its ability to balance the process of building more inclusive institutions, for which social service delivery is an important tool (see also Ghani, Lockhart, and Carnahan 2005).
117. See Boyce and Forman 2010; Porter, Andrews, and Wescott 2010.
118. For a description of the Holst Fund in West Bank and Gaza, see Schiavo-Campo 2003.
119. Mondo 1995; Colletta, Kostner, and Wiederhofer 1996.
120. For Angola, please see World Bank 2009c. For Guinea-Bissau, see Arzeni, Cesanelli, and Pes 2004.
121. Scanteam 2010; Garrasi 2010.
122. OECD 2010i; Scanteam 2010; Garrasi 2010.
123. Boyce and Forman 2010.
124. OECD 2010i; Scanteam 2010; Garrasi 2010.
125. OECD 2010i.
126. Garrasi 2010.
127. See Harbom and Wallensteen 2010.
128. See Roberts 2010 for a discussion of the Iraq estimates and Butty 2010 for a similar discussion with Andrew Mack of Human Security Report Project on estimates for the Democratic Republic of Congo, 1996 to present.
129. See Conflict and Development Programs in Indonesia website (http://www.conflictanddevelopment.org) for up-to-date information on conflict and violence in Aceh.
130. One example is monthly monitoring of Palestinian perceptions on political, economic, and social conditions by Near East Consulting, http://www.neareastconsulting.com.
131. Scheye and Chigas 2009; Agoglia, Dziedzic, and Sotirin 2008.
132. *DRC Speaks!* is a geo-polling project utilizing cell phone technology to conduct surveys. It was created by Mobile Accord in conjunction with the WDR, and with generous donations of SMS by Vodacom Congo. Using SMS through cell phones, the project allowed more than 140,000 Congolese to share, without any filters, their thoughts, feelings, and concerns.

Chapter 7 extends the analysis of this Report to international efforts to deal with the regional and global stresses associated with the risks of violence. Here we encounter a different lacuna: agencies dealing with country-level support have neglected global stresses, and international agencies tackling global stresses have paid modest attention to the special characteristics of countries affected by violence. Rectifying this requires a two-pronged approach: take more decisive steps to tackle global stresses in their own right, and build into those efforts a conscious effort to reinforce the capacity of states with weak institutions to build up buffers against global shocks. This approach may often need to be initiated at the regional level, where states can pool capacities and share efforts to manage the impacts of global systems. No state or society is impermeable, and most states' economies are deeply interwoven with regional and global economic systems.

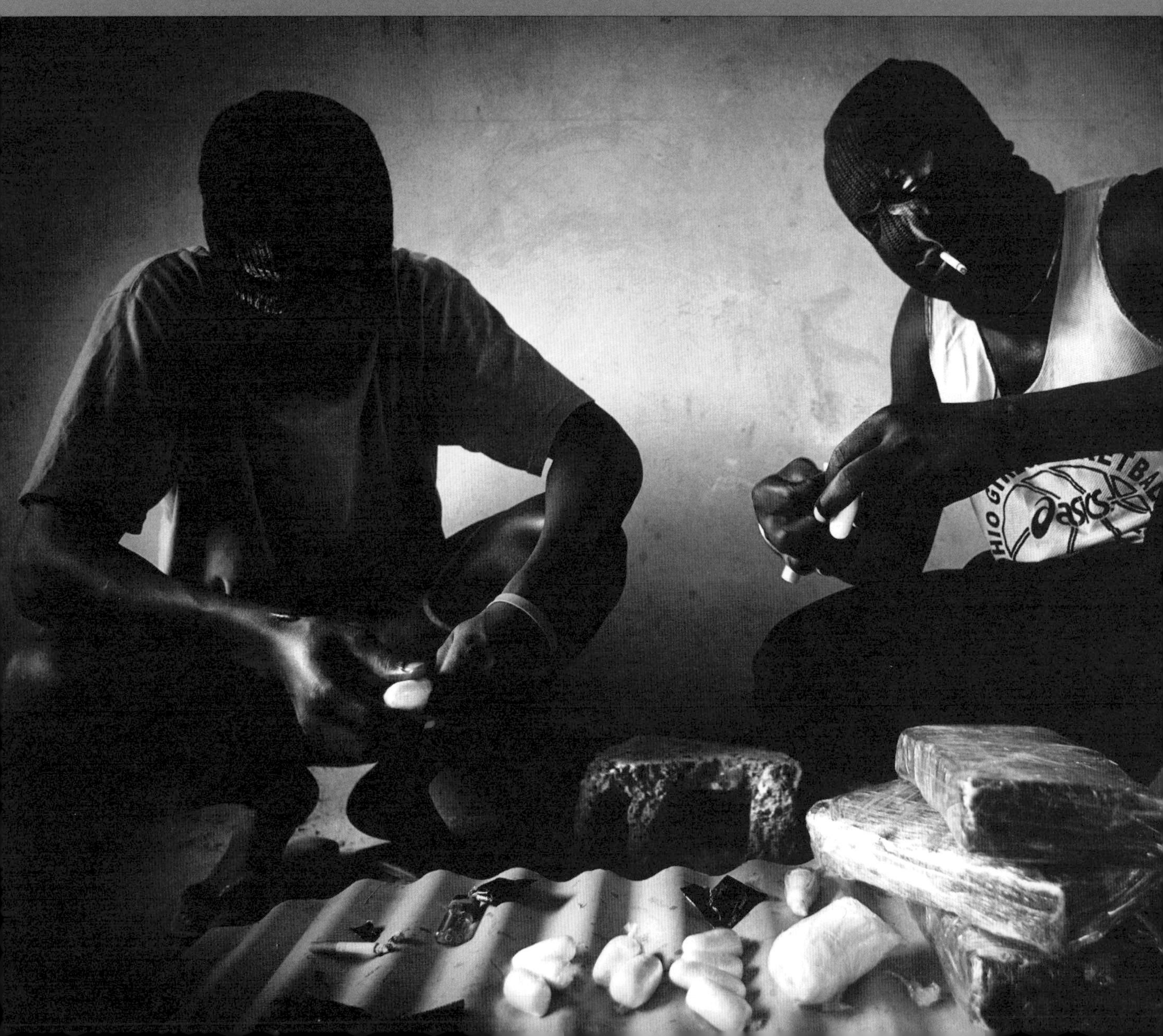

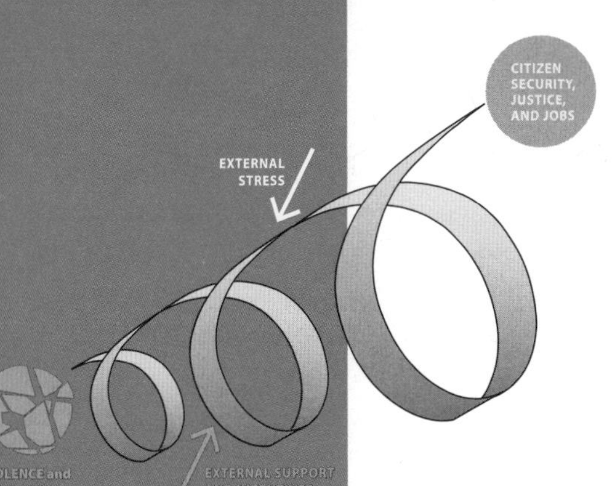

CHAPTER 7

International action to mitigate external stresses

Economic globalization exposes states to external economic stresses ranging from international corruption to resource shortages. States with weak political institutions are also routinely exposed to a variety of forms of external interference in their internal negotiations. Social groups within states often have links to external populations that can be an important source of support—but also of both political and security interference. Increasingly, transnational groups with ideological motivations are forging relationships with internal groups to pressure the state or introduce violence into state-society relations.

As with internal stresses, external security and economic stresses are interlinked. Consider trafficking. Arms traffickers often move drugs and commodities as well,[1] using similar techniques of fraud, corruption, and money laundering.[2] Trafficking has deeply damaging effects on national security and economic systems.

Where buffering institutions are weak, external stresses can overwhelm internal governance. Even states with resilient institutions are exposed to international pressures—think of the impact of drug trafficking on cities in Europe and the United States. These pressures, though serious, have not undermined the legitimacy or resilience of domestic institutions or triggered large-scale violence. But for states with weaker institutions, large changes in the price of oil or food can increase social tensions, which internal mechanisms are ill-equipped to deal with.

Because many fragile states have small populations and small economies, their impact on global markets and systems is slight. International mechanisms that focus on global or transnational issues like drug trafficking have tended to neglect impacts on fragile states. Aid and peacekeeping responses to fragile states are normally country-specific, overlooking both the regional dimension of countries' economic and security arrangements and the impact of transnational or global forces. Where transnational or global mechanisms do interact with fragile states, the policies often are suitable only for the larger, more capable states that contribute the greater part of the global gross domestic product (GDP), in the process overlooking the capacity constraints of fragile states.

Furthermore, international systems designed to address transnational issues are often fragmented and overlapping. For states with substantial administrative capacities, fragmentation in international systems is a nuisance; for states with weak administrative capacities, responding to demands from a fragmented international system can absorb all available capacity in dealing with a single issue area.

Regional cooperation can help national actors navigate internal pressures and build buffers against external ones. For most states, on most issues, the region rather than the world bears the greatest brunt of spillovers from violence. Regional cooperation thus offers large potential rewards on issues like the illegal transit of commodities and the expansion of legal, productive opportunities for trade.

External security stresses

Cross-border insecurity and trafficking, particularly in small arms and drugs, can have highly corrosive impacts on governance and the development of stable, legitimate institutions. Nor are the more fragile states and regions able to counter these challenges without significant amounts of international help: the resources and manpower available to them can be simply overwhelmed by these nonstate actors.

Cross-border insecurity

For many fragile states, the regional dimension of insecurity is central. Chapter 2 shows how external security stresses can amplify internal tensions and undermine initial settlements to end conflict. Invasion, the presence of foreign troops, or occupation can overwhelm the state. Such cases—which include Afghanistan, Iraq, and the West Bank and Gaza in recent years—consume much of the debate around fragile states, though their number today is small.

More commonly, as chapter 1 illustrates, violence in fragile states now involves nonstate organizations that operate across borders. Porous borders can provide rebels or organized criminal gangs with escape routes from national armed forces. In many parts of the world—South Asia, Southeast Asia, West Africa, Central Africa, the Horn of Africa, the Middle East, Central America, the Andean region—states face cross-border attacks by nonstate groups, neighboring state support for internal rebels, or traffickers and transnational terrorists.[3] Many zones of insecurity and violence are concentrated in border areas. With many borders drawn in the colonial era for reasons that had little to do with settlement patterns, populations on either side of an insecure border may share ethnic identities, common cultural norms, and family and trading links.

Chapter 1 describes how many internal conflicts are generated or fueled by cross-border or global dynamics. Where the actors are responsive to a neighboring government, steps by those neighbors may be vital to a successful transition. Relative stability returned to eastern Democratic Republic of Congo (DRC) only after a Rwanda–DRC agreement was concluded in 2007.[4] The Central American "Esquipulas Process," which ended the Nicaraguan war in 1987, involved an accord signed by five Central American presidents and a change in U.S. policy toward the Sandinista regime.[5] Groups of Friends and similar mechanisms have managed to bring together neighbors seeking stable internal pacts that tackle cross-border stresses.[6]

Even so, international security responses are typically organized on a national rather than a subregional level. As chapter 6 points out, international peacekeeping operations are rarely organized to deal with transborder security threats, even when the major source of insecurity is a group that operates subregionally. For example, the United Nations (UN) has three separate peacekeeping operations deployed in areas of Africa infiltrated by the Lord's Resistance Army—but each is mandated and managed at a national level, and none can share resources or move across another's area of operation. The logic that drives this is that Security Council and UN member states are sensitive to national sovereignty; the irony is that the policy hands a tactical advantage to groups that ignore sovereign borders. This vulnerability makes clear the need for enhanced regional roles and capabilities, a point discussed further in chapter 9. The Multi-Country Demobilization and Reintegration Program in central Africa is an exception (box 7.1).

Development programs are also typically organized at a national level, even though borders often divide regions with close socioeconomic ties. As one example, development programming in Pashtun tribal areas that straddle the Afghanistan-Pakistan border requires the two governments to address similar issues of insecurity, weak local administrations, and strong ethnic and social identities—but there is relatively little exchange between national institutions to discuss lessons learned.[7] Of course, international security and development operations are—correctly—designed to reinforce, not abrogate, national sovereignty. Where neighbors have tense relations, orchestrating cross-border programs can be politically complicated.

Some innovative cross-border programs do exist. Recognizing that insecure borders have been recurrent hosts to conflict, the African Union (AU) established the African Union Border Program in 2007 to demarcate sensitive border areas and promote cross-border cooperation and trade as a conflict prevention tool. The program has four components. First, it pursues both land and maritime border demarcation since less than a quarter of Africa's borders have been formally marked and agreed upon, and disputes are likely to continue with future discoveries of oil. Second, it promotes cross-border cooperation to deal with itinerant criminal activities. Third, it supports cross-border peacebuilding programs. Fourth, it consolidates gains in economic integration through the creation of regional economic networks. An initial pilot project was launched in the Sikasso region of Mali and in Bobo Dioualasso in Burkina Faso—bringing together local, private, and public actors to strengthen economic cooperation, but the program has lacked resources.[8]

Another example of cross-border programming is a UN interagency initiative that from 2004 to 2009 supported national efforts to stabilize Ecuador's northern border region with Colombia. Already facing internal social conflict, Ecuador was confronted with spillovers from the activities of armed groups in Colombia, with communities along the border overwhelmed by refugees, gang violence, and drug trafficking. But by 2009, following cross-border programming, crime and violence were reduced, services improved, and dialogue established to resolve local conflicts. More important, despite upswings and downturns in diplomatic relations between the two countries, lasting bilateral collaboration has been established with respect to these issues.[9]

Regional organizations also play a key role in addressing cross-border violence. As the AU example suggests, and as the post–World War II history of European cooperation demonstrates, regional organizations can help countries address mobile populations and

BOX 7.1 *The Multi-Country Demobilization and Reintegration Program: Addressing regional violence*

The Multi-Country Demobilization and Reintegration Program (MDRP) was a World Bank–led regional initiative in which, between 2002 and 2009, over 40 partners collaborated to disarm, demobilize, and reintegrate close to 300,000 combatants in the Great Lakes Region of Africa. Seven neighboring countries embroiled in the regional war fought out in the Democratic Republic of Congo (DRC) participated in the MDRP: Angola, Burundi, Central African Republic, DRC, Republic of Congo, Rwanda, and Uganda.

This regional program was the best response to a regional conflict that transcended borders. Although demobilization, disarmament, and reintegration (DDR) programs were implemented at the national level, the MDRP's regional framework helped build confidence for mutual disarmament by increasing transparency across programs and supporting joint learning and collaborative activities. The regional approach also enabled the pooling of financing for DDR, which in turn promoted efficient resource allocation across participating countries. As a regional program, the MDRP could support cross-border activities, including the DDR of irregular forces that needed to be repatriated to their home countries.

For programs like the MDRP that have both national and regional elements, attention should be paid to regional aspects up front, including putting in place a dedicated team and resources. Generating collective action for regional activities and establishing incentives for actors to think beyond their country borders was not easy, particularly since countries faced problems on their home fronts. Undertaking a large regional multistakeholder initiative like the MDRP was also inherently a high risk, high reward enterprise.

The World Bank, the donors, and the broader development community must be prepared to accept the risks, difficulties, and uncertainties associated with implementing such programs in a post-conflict setting—especially when national peace processes and elections dictate the speed of DDR operations.

Source: Correia 2010.

the seepage of violence across national borders. They can also spur regional adoption of global principles. Many of them, however, need support to operationalize these roles. Euro region cross-border cooperation and integration can offer inspiration in tackling some border area challenges in other regions (see box 7.1 and the later discussion of regional economic integration).

Trafficking

Internal security—and economic—arrangements can also be undermined by external trafficking. In February 2010, the UN Security Council noted "the serious threat posed in some cases by drug trafficking and transnational organized crime to international security in different regions of the world."[10] Chapter 1 discusses the role trafficking plays in generating violence in fragile states, particularly when illicit revenues provide nonstate groups the wherewithal to outbid national police and armed services.

Over the past 15 years, regional and global initiatives have been launched to address illegal trafficking. They typically use one of two types of mechanism to stem activities and bring perpetrators to justice: either they try to identify and intercept smuggled *commodities* at points of production,[11] transit, processing, or consumption; or they attempt to identify and disrupt the *financial* flows that both fund and result from illicit trafficking. Other initiatives, such as the recently released due diligence guidance on "Responsible Supply Chains of Minerals from Conflict Affected and High-Risk Areas," have objectives that focus not just on tracking flows, but also on human rights protection and loss of livelihoods.[12] Efforts to tackle physical trafficking in commodities are discussed here; those dealing with the financial dimensions of trafficking are dealt with in the following section on external economic stresses.

Approaches to tackling the trafficking of commodities is shaped by their physical and market characteristics; these determine the ease of physical tracking and interdiction. Trafficking in commodities with concentrated production, processing, or wholesaling is easier to control (table 7.1). This helps explain some of the initial success of the Kimberley Process in dealing with "conflict diamonds" (box 7.2). Timber, unlike gemstones or point-source resources, has a big footprint, with many upstream production and processing points, and is easily mixed with legal wood—requiring detailed systems for verifying the legality of origin, and permits and expertise to identify restricted species.

In contrast to diamonds, weapons (particularly small arms) are very portable, are manufactured by many enterprises, are sold everywhere—and are cheap. Despite a steady decline in the total dollar value of the arms trade since the end of the Cold War, there is no apparent corresponding decline in the in-

TABLE 7.1 *To defeat trafficking in commodities, pay attention to physical and market characteristics of the products*

Commodity	Estimated annual value of trafficking flows	Value-to-weight ratio/portability	Concentration of production	Concentration of processing or wholesale markets	Ease of tracing origin of product	Ease of consumer identification
Diamonds	US$127 million[13]	High	High	High	Depends[14]	High
Oil	US$1 billion[15]	Medium	Medium	High	Yes	Medium
Timber	US$6 billion[16]	Low	Low	Low	Yes[17]	Low
Arms	US$170 million–US$320 million[18]	Medium	Low[19]	Low	Limited[20]	Low
Drugs (cocaine, heroin)	US$143 billion[21]	High	Medium	Low	No	Low

Sources: UNODC 2009a, 2010a; Lawson and MacFaul 2010; Small Arms Survey Project 2001; Greene 2001.

ternational transfer of small arms and light weapons (SALW). The total annual value of SALW is estimated at between US$4 billion and US$6 billion, of which approximately 10–20 percent constitutes illicit transactions.[22] There are over 900 million small arms in circulation worldwide, produced by more than 1,000 companies dispersed in more than 100 countries.[23] SALWs are responsible for almost 500,000 deaths a year, of which 50,000 to 300,000 occur in armed conflicts, most particularly in poor countries.[24] While SALWs do not *cause* internal conflict, they do multiply its effects. Beyond massive civilian casualties, the misuse of SALWs also impacts negatively on development. The illegal use of SALWs contributes to human insecurity, crippling burdens on health care systems, rising criminality, and violation of human rights.[25]

The focus on arms trafficking in fragile states has shifted from the international to the subregional arena.[26] The UN Department of Disarmament Affairs has increased its efforts, in collaboration with major donors, to pursue subregional trafficking in arms—including opening regional offices, as in West Africa. But the country-specific nature of the UN's peacekeeping presence restricts the interdiction of weapons flowing across borders. Similarly, the UN's peacekeeping operation in southern Lebanon faces mandates and political restrictions to investigating claims of illegal small and heavy weapons shipments to non-state armed forces across regional borders.[27]

Drug trafficking is also increasingly important in fragile states. Heroin, cocaine, and a variety of recreational drugs are illegal in almost all countries. Increases in demand in recent years have driven up prices and created huge profits for the illegal networks that traffic in them (see box 7.3). Heroin and cocaine networks—organized on paramilitary lines, to protect themselves from competitors and law enforcement agencies—are responsible for high levels of death and mayhem.

Tracking and interdiction of drug traders are fragmented. International efforts to track and seize illegal drugs are intense, but given the high value of even small volumes, these efforts have failed to stop global flows. Instead, concentrating efforts in one area has more often simply displaced the trafficking route. Since transshipment costs, including the bribery and intimidation of officials en route, are only a small fraction of what is earned from trafficking, criminal networks have overcome or adapted to even the most sophisticated interdiction systems. Com-

BOX 7.2 *The Kimberley Process for "conflict diamonds"*

The Kimberley Process, a certification scheme to ensure that the origins of rough diamonds are sources free of conflict, was initiated to stem the flow of "conflict diamonds" used to fuel rebellions in countries like the DRC, and has been jointly undertaken by civil society groups, industry, and governments. It evolved from recommendations by a UN Security Council sanctions committee that investigated the relationship between commodity trafficking and violence in the DRC. The Kimberly Process diamond certification scheme imposes extensive requirements on its 49 members (representing 75 countries) to ensure that the rough diamonds shipped have not funded violence.

Although diamonds have high value-to-weight ratios and are very portable, diamond wholesale markets and processing facilities are concentrated in specific locations, with the former primarily in Antwerp and the latter primarily in Mumbai. Some 80 percent of rough diamonds and more than 50 percent of polished stones pass through Antwerp. Only high-value stones are now polished in New York; most small low-value stones are polished in and around Mumbai, whose workshops accounted for an estimated 90 percent of the global polished diamond output in 2009. The number of licit diamond producers is also small. All these factors make it hard to trade conflict diamonds without attracting attention.

Sources: Goreaux 2001; Montgomery 2010; Kimberley Process Certification Scheme 2009, 2010.

BOX 7.3 *The economics of cocaine trafficking*

In 2008, the average kilo of cocaine entered the Mesoamerican transit corridor at a price of about US$1,000.[28] The same kilo could then be sold on the U.S. side of the border for about US$33,500. These numbers, point estimates based on average market values, can vary widely depending on market conditions, purity, organization, and vertical integration in cocaine production and trafficking. Still, taking these rough estimates as a starting point, the average potential profit for moving a kilo of cocaine through the Mesoamerican transit corridor into the United States is over US$30,000 before other costs of trafficking are deducted.

If 10 to 20 percent of the cost is used in transportation, security, and labor, and 20 to 30 percent of cocaine in transit is seized, this would reduce the potential profits from trafficking an individual kilo to between US$15,000 and US$21,000. Even taking these deductions into account, this profit range is far higher than the annual 2008 GDP per capita of any country in the region. But in economic terms, the prospective drug trafficker must consider two other potential costs: the opportunity cost of other gainful employment forgone and the risk premium associated with the dangerous and illegal occupation of drug trafficking. Recent increases in interdictions and arrests would also increase these costs.

Source: WDR staff calculations based on Demombynes 2010; UNODC 2010a

pounding this inherent difficulty is the fragmentation of efforts to halt the flow of drugs (box 7.4).

The majority of efforts against trafficking in drugs have focused on supply—or on actions by producing and transit countries. Because drug consumption is illegal in most countries, only fairly limited mechanisms are available to reduce the links with violence through demand-side measures. The poor record of global attempts to stop the trade in illegal drugs, and the extreme violence associated with these attempts, have spurred debates on legalization and some tentative steps to test the proposition (mainly with marijuana, but more broadly with several drugs in Portugal). Opinions are divided (box 7.5).

Insecurity and injustice: Transnational ideological threats

Violent transnational ideological movements[29] can flourish in violence-affected and fragile states, making common cause with local movements and drawing resources from transnational trafficking routes. The insertion of transnational ideological movements into otherwise localized violence adds resources, expertise, and ideological fuel that can significantly alter the balance of force and severely pressure the domestic capability to respond.[30]

This Report is not the place to engage in a full discussion of the performance of global or regional approaches to counter-terrorism. The adoption by the UN General Assembly last year of a comprehensive strategy for counter-terrorism provides a starting point for engagement on the multilateral front, and governments (through both bilateral and regional mechanisms) are increasing their cooperation on counter-terrorism activities.[31]

However, global terrorist movements can feed on the absence of what the Report has highlighted as critical to building resilience to violence: institutional accountability, legitimacy, and capability. Ideologically motivated groups may have a particular ability to penetrate where the presence and reach of legitimate government are limited (as in the Sahel and Afghanistan). These global movements often cast their cause in terms of injustice and exclusion[32]—a message that can resonate with local perceptions of elite-driven and exclusionary politics and policies. This raises questions about the balance between global and local approaches to reducing the threat from terrorism.

BOX 7.4 *Multiple interdiction efforts: Cocaine in the Americas*

In the Americas, the cocaine trail begins with on-farm production in only three South American countries (in 2008, Colombia accounted for 51 percent of global production, Peru 36 percent, and Bolivia 13 percent);[33] transits through Central America, Mexico, and the Caribbean; and is sold wholesale and retail in the United States. A proliferation of initiatives is trying to stem this flow: 10 bilateral or regional programs, with many countries belonging to more than one program (see map).

This situation raises questions about the coherence of the international response, especially since increased enforcement in one area often leads to diversion to another. The creation of one Caribbean initiative was justified in part because "recent efforts to enhance drug enforcement efforts along the [U.S.] southwest border seem to be having a consequent effect of moving transit routes back into the Caribbean."[34]

The current (fragmented) state of international cooperation against drugs in the Americas

The map illustrates the fragmented regional focus and overlapping mandates of 10 initiatives related to drug trafficking in the Americas. Each colored line indicates a separate initiative and connects the member countries involved in the initiative.

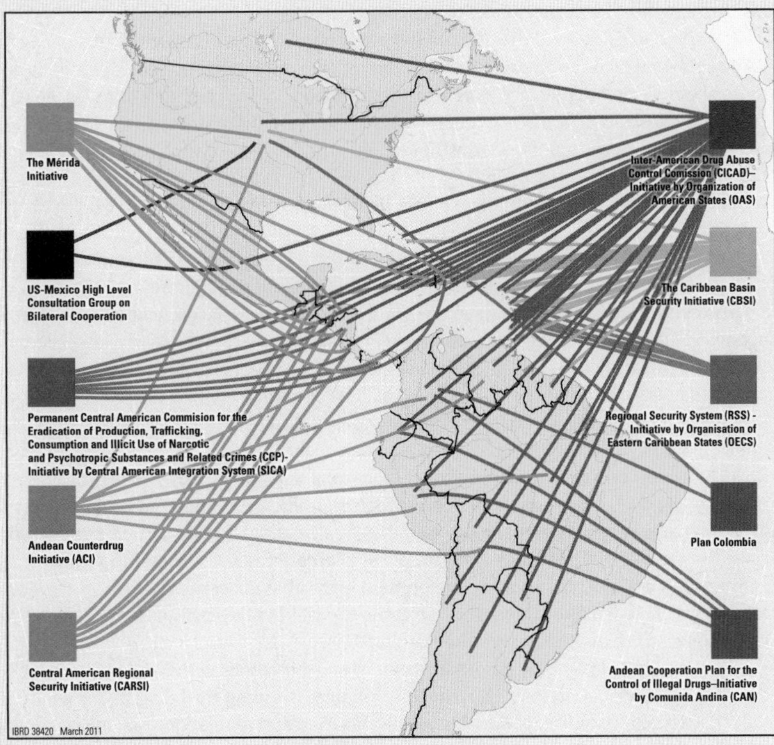

Sources: UNODC 2009b; U.S. Office of National Drug Control Policy 1999; Seelke, Sun Wyler, and Beittel 2011; Central American Integration System 2009; Inter-American Drug Abuse Control Commission 2010; Andean Council of Foreign Ministers 2001; Embassy of the United States in Mexico 2010.

Research into the interactions between the local and the international dimensions of terrorist recruitment and mobilization is too limited to allow for definitive statements about the relationship between violence, development, institutional transformation, and terrorism. What we do know, however, suggests that international development prac-

BOX 7.5 *Expert viewpoints: For and against regulated drug legalization to reduce violence*

The WDR team asked two well-known authorities on the subject to offer their opinions.

Against

Mark A. R. Kleiman, UCLA School of Public Affairs

If the avoidance of failed states were the sole policy goal, the legalization of all drugs would be transparently desirable: failed states and civil conflicts create congenial conditions for illicit drug-dealing, while illicit drug production weakens states and fuels civil conflict, with drug revenues supporting insurgents and other armed nonstate actors and corrupting officials. However, drug abuse creates problems for drug abusers and for their families, neighbors, and co-workers. Prohibition is not a perfect answer: it can exacerbate those problems, create violence and corruption around illicit markets (in producer, transit, and consumer countries), and contribute to the problem of mass incarceration. Yet prohibition also tends to reduce drug consumption. Alcohol abuse is far more common, and generates far more intoxicated violence, than the abuse of any illicit drug. So there is tension between security and governance and the control of drug abuse: blanket drug legalization would be a blow against terrorism, but would also increase the prevalence of substance-abuse disorders.

It is sometimes claimed that the full benefits of prohibition in reducing substance abuse could be achieved through some combination of taxes and regulations, without incurring the costs of prohibition in terms of violence. But that claim rests on two fallacious beliefs: that taxes and regulations would not be profitably defied, and that the economic and political muscle of the newly legalized drug industries would not succeed in eating away at the controls that limit their marketing scope.

Effective taxation and regulation might be technically feasible, with bans on marketing, restriction of commerce to cooperatives, or delegation of authority to physicians and pharmacists operating under professional strictures. But there is no reason to be confident that such systems of effective control would be established or would remain stable.

The current international drug-abuse control regime too rests on twin fallacies: first, that actions in producer countries can greatly restrict drug abuse "downstream," and, second, that, since drug production creates security-and-governance problems, any sort of counter–drug activity naturally helps solve those problems. "Source control" efforts are largely futile, and source-country counter-narcotics efforts—not only enforcement but also alternative development—naturally exacerbate, rather than ameliorate, security and governance problems. They do so by raising prices (and thus revenues, since final demand is highly inelastic to farm gate price) and by conferring competitive advantage on traffickers with the most guns and the most influence: terrorists, insurgents, warlords, armed transnational crime groups, and corrupt officials. The same is true of "crop substitution" or "alternative development." In Afghanistan, a combination of enforcement and development efforts has concentrated poppy growing in areas under Taliban control, and thus increased the yield to the Taliban from whatever "taxes" it can collect from poppy farmers and heroin refiners.

It is possible to imagine a drug-enforcement effort focused on the intersection between drug dealing and security-and-governance problems, pursuing traffickers and growing regions that contribute most to instability. But as with taxation and regulation, imagining a better policy is not the same as implementing it.

Reduced source-country enforcement would have minimal impact on the drug problem in rich consumer countries. Soil in which illicit drug crops can be grown is not a scarce resource, and shrinking the supply from one producer generally means a corresponding increase in production elsewhere.

Successful demand-reduction efforts both reduce substance abuse and shrink the revenues of illicit enterprises, including those that threaten the stability of producer-country governments. Forcing drug abusers under criminal-justice supervision for other crimes has much greater potential to shrink total volumes. We should try to optimize the policies that implement prohibition, developing a drug-control regime that serves the goal of reducing the extent of substance-abuse disorders and the damage they cause at the minimum cost in terms of security and governance.

For

Jeffrey A. Miron, Department of Economics, Harvard University

Worldwide prohibition of drugs is roughly 100 years old. During that time span, national and subnational governments have expended enormous sums on police, prosecutors, and prisons in attempts to enforce it. Advocates of prohibition believe that, despite these costs, the world has benefited by avoiding a far greater incidence of drug use, addiction, and other negatives. Thus, according to this perspective, the benefits of prohibition exceed the costs.

In fact, prohibition causes far more deleterious consequences than it prevents. To see why, consider the consequences of prohibition.

First, prohibition generates violence because it drives markets underground. In legal markets, participants resolve their disputes with advertising and lawsuits, but in underground markets these nonviolent mechanisms are not available, so participants use violence instead. Traffickers engage in turf battles with rival traffickers and shoot employees who steal, customers who do not pay, and suppliers who renege on contracts. Traffickers also employ violence against law enforcement attempts to arrest them, against politicians who support extradition to the United States, and against civilians who cooperate with the police.

Violence soared in the United States, for example, in response to federal alcohol prohibition in 1920 but then declined rapidly after repeal. Prohibition also generates corruption. Those who run afoul of the law have strong incentives for bribery of police, judges, and politicians.

Prohibition contributes to the spread of HIV, hepatitis, and other blood-borne diseases because it raises drug prices. When drugs are expensive, users face an incentive to inject rather than consume in less risky ways because injection delivers the biggest bang for the buck. The impact is not only on drug users but on the broader population.

Prohibition creates a source of finance for violent groups, including terrorist groups and rebel organizations. Traffickers need protection from law enforcement and the military, so they hire terrorist groups to provide this enforcement. Terrorists benefit by earning income that supports their operations. Without this support, terrorist groups like the Taliban in Afghanistan, the FARC in Colombia, and the Shining Path in Peru would face far greater difficulty in funding their activities. On the flip side, legalization would allow police and the military to devote more resources to fighting terrorist or insurgent groups than fighting traffickers.

All these effects are adverse consequences of prohibition. The only possible justification for prohibition, therefore, is that it might reduce drug use or the harmful side-effects of use.

Yet abundant evidence suggests that prohibition has, at most, a modest impact in reducing drug use. Repeal of alcohol prohibition produced only about a 20 percent increase in use, while Portugal's 2001 decriminalization policy for reasonable personal consumption of drugs did not cause a measurable increase (indeed, use was lower afterwards). Across countries, use rates bear little connection to the strictness of the prohibition regime. The Netherlands has a tolerant policy towards use of marijuana, for example, yet use rates differ little from those in the United States.

This evidence does not rule out the possibility that use might increase by measurable amounts under legalization, but assertions that use or addiction would skyrocket are inconsistent with evidence. Societies have the option of legalizing the good but targeting misuse—as is done for alcohol and other goods that can be used irresponsibly but that most people use responsibly. Consistency therefore requires the same approach to drugs.

In sum, prohibition has a broad range of harmful effects and, at best, a modest and speculative benefit. Legalization means the harms from drugs fall mainly on those who choose these risks, many of whom were already doing so under prohibition, rather than on innocent bystanders and law enforcement institutions. The choice between prohibition and legalization is therefore clear. Legalization is not a panacea, but it is unquestionably the lesser of the evils.

titioners and diplomats working to support national coalitions and institutional transformation should pay attention to the potential for excluded groups and neglected regions to become fertile ground for ideologically driven recruitment into violence—while international actors working on global counter-terrorism policy should pay attention to the way local violence and weak institutions can help fuel global movements.

External economic stresses

Fragile states and areas can be exposed to externally generated stresses of an economic nature. Prominent among these are corruption driven by outside corporate interests, illicit financial flows associated with corruption, tax evasion, and trafficking—and both the price shocks associated with rising global demands for food and fuel and the pressure to acquire access to or ownership of essential natural resources (land, water, and energy). Again, states with relatively weak governance systems and bargaining power cannot be expected to address such external stresses without global and regional assistance.

Transnational corruption

As chapter 5 highlights, efforts to counter corruption are an important and politically challenging part of national reform processes. Corruption is often not just a local challenge; international malefactors are significant in corruption dynamics and can pose a substantial obstacle to national efforts at transformation. Progress will depend at least in part on international efforts to address the external dimension of corruption. The principle that states should criminalize acts by their own nationals who corrupt officials of other states is now firmly entrenched in international law, although there is much room for improvement in its implementation.

As recently as 2000, many developed nations actually fostered corruption across national boundaries by allowing their citizens or companies to take a tax deduction for bribes paid to officials of other governments.[35] Ten years on, the situation has changed dramatically. The OECD (Organisation for Economic Co-operation and Development) Anti-Bribery Convention (Convention on Combating Bribery of Foreign Public Officials) and the UN Convention Against Corruption require that state parties prescribe criminal sanctions for bribing a foreign public official. This extraordinary turnaround is particularly important for states with fragile governance. The bribes paid to officials of these countries to win mineral concessions, arms contracts, or other lucrative business opportunities almost always originate outside their borders—so shutting down transnational bribery is crucial to curbing corruption in these states.

Sanctioning those who corrupt foreign public officials, however, is still a work in progress. Transparency International's 2010 evaluation of the OECD Anti-Bribery Convention found that only seven of the 38 countries party to the convention are actively enforcing the provisions of their domestic laws to criminalize the bribery of foreign public officials. Another nine are making some effort to enforce the ban. The remaining 20 are making little or no effort to do so. Although this is an improvement from the group's first report in 2005, when only four parties had prosecuted more than one case, Transparency International concludes that "current levels of enforcement are too low to enable the convention to succeed."[36]

The international community is developing innovative measures to prosecute officials involved in transnational corruption. Yet even when there is evidence that a public official in a fragile state has accepted a bribe, proving the case presents legal, technical, and logistical challenges that are often beyond the capacity of investigators and prosecutors in fragile situations. Where capacity or political constraints prevent prosecution, authorities in weaker jurisdictions have exploited the

BOX 7.6 *Partnering with client countries to curb corruption in World Bank–funded projects*

The World Bank's Integrity Vice Presidency investigates allegations of corruption, fraud, coercion, collusion, and attempts to conceal this conduct in World Bank–funded projects. If a complaint is substantiated, a process is begun and can result in barring firms or individuals from bidding on Bank-financed contracts, with referrals to the appropriate law enforcement authorities for possible criminal prosecution under national law.

Over the past six years, 67 individuals and firms have been barred from bidding on World Bank contracts from two years up to indefinitely. The list includes very small firms and nongovernmental organizations in developing countries to U.K. publisher Macmillan Limited and the China Road and Bridge Corporation, a large state-owned enterprise. During this period, the Bank also concluded a settlement agreement with Siemens AG whereby the Siemens Group agreed to voluntarily refrain from bidding on Bank-financed contracts for two years. As part of its settlement with the Bank, Siemens will commit US$100 million over the next 15 years to global efforts to fight fraud and corruption. Macmillan and others have agreed to cooperate with the Bank's ongoing efforts to combat fraud and corruption in its projects and to implement an anti-corruption compliance program.

The World Bank, the African Development Bank, the Asian Development Bank, the European Bank for Reconstruction and Development, and the Inter-American Development Bank have agreed to honor each other's debarments so that in the future, a firm debarred by one bank will be ineligible to bid on contracts funded by the other banks.

Since it was established in 2001, the Bank's Integrity Vice Presidency has referred 112 cases to national law enforcement agencies. Referrals in 2001–06 resulted in convictions in national courts in Bolivia, Guinea, Norway, and the United States for receiving a bribe, embezzlement, or other corruption offenses. More recently, a referral led the Kenyan Anticorruption Commission to open 38 criminal investigations, two of which are being prosecuted. Acting on information from the World Bank, the Norwegian government indicted three former employees of Norconsult for bribery, and the Palestinian Attorney General's office opened an investigation of a contractor on a World Bank–funded project for fraud.

Source: World Bank 2010h.

laws in other countries to overcome these hurdles. Under U.K. law, for example, using the proceeds of corruption to invest in the U.K. constitutes an offense under anti-money laundering laws—Nigeria's Economic and Financial Crimes Commission has supplied U.K. authorities with information that enabled prosecutions in the U.K. related to stolen Nigerian state assets. Haitian and U.S. officials worked together to convict a senior official of Haiti's telecom authority in a U.S. court for taking bribes from American companies. Three U.S. nationals have also pled guilty to offenses in connection with the payments to the Haitian company.[37]

As ties between law enforcement authorities in developed and developing states have grown, authorities have also begun joint investigations with the evidence available for use in proceedings in both countries. The investigations provide invaluable training opportunities when experienced investigators from developed countries pair up with counterparts from developing states. Indeed, the World Bank's Department of Institutional Integrity plans to follow this model when it refers evidence of corruption in a Bank project to national authorities (box 7.6).

Illicit international financial flows

Prosecuting corruption in commodities is complemented by efforts to interdict the financing flows from these and other corrupt activities, including drug trafficking. Many international initiatives are under way in this area. A large number of laws and programs aim to identify and stem the laundering of illicit funds—whether generated by corruption, tax evasion, or drug trafficking—through the legitimate financial system. This is important for violence prevention: many armed movements in civil and political conflict are financed from these sources. The Financial Action Task Force, established in 1990 to control the flows of drug profits, now has rules for controlling laundering of illicit funds, and financial intelligence units combat money laundering at the national level.[38] Such units, in place in 116 countries, work together under the Egmont Group initiative.[39] This expansion in financial intelligence has been paralleled by greater attention from banks and other financial institutions to monitor and report on customer transactions—and by increased interest in law enforcement agencies in following the "money trail."[40]

Together, these steps in intelligence-gathering, monitoring, and the amassing of evidence increase the ability of the international community to build strong cases against organized and transnational crime. Using the same principle applied in the prosecution of Al Capone for income tax evasion in 1931, evidence of illicit financial dealings provides a way to prosecute violent criminals for "proxy offenses" without having to rely on witnesses to violence—who can be bribed or threatened. In August 2009, 70 countries and dependencies agreed to create a Global Forum on Transparency and Exchange of Information for Tax Purposes to reduce tax evasion through trusts, corporations, and other devices outside the country levying the tax. Modeled on the Financial Action Task Force, the forum will conduct peer reviews of members and selected nonmembers to determine whether they have entered at least 12 tax information exchange agreements, enacted legislation allowing them to comply with requests for information from their treaty partners, and are in fact providing information when requested.

However, the sheer number of initiatives poses a challenge. More than 74 global, regional, and multicountry exercises now collect and use information on money laundering, international corruption, trafficking of specific commodities, and terrorism. Of these, 30 are focused on money laundering or corruption, while another 37 deal with specific commodities (drugs, arms, illicit minerals, and natural resources).[41] In addition, there are numerous national offices: just four OECD countries have at least 22 offices between them dealing with these issues.[42]

The system for identifying money laundering or terrorist financing establishes links between persons and transactions. The more detailed the data, the more likely they are to reveal malfeasance. But tracking and investigating "criteria-based" activities (foreign exchange transactions, international wire transfers) multiplies the flow of data to a financial intelligence unit. To operate well, these initiatives require sophisticated capacity. The analysis of transnational financial flows can uncover information for use in several different jurisdictions, and analysis in higher capacity environments can thus be of great use to developing countries (box 7.7). While analytical capability is high in a few wealthier countries, this is not the case in most low- and middle-income states.[43]

Pulling out information to uncover sophisticated networks requires resources and analytical capacity not found in many units. Nor are the necessary prosecution and judicial system capabilities always in place. Effective international action depends on strong networks and information exchanges between jurisdictions. Even in the medium term, it is unlikely that developing states can build the capacity to operate financial intelligence units at the level required to produce results. Resources may be better devoted to stopping the flow of funds to secrecy jurisdictions[44] than to controlling the flow out of fragile states.

Cooperation across borders is not always smooth. To prosecute cases of cross-border money laundering and trafficking, jurisdictions must share data that may not affect their own nationals or institutions,

BOX 7.7 *The Australian Crime Commission's high-risk money movement strategy*

Under its financial crimes program, the Australian Crime Commission is piloting a risk-based approach to identifying funds linked to organized crime. This approach to money laundering, developed with the Australian Transaction Reports and Analysis Center (AUSTRAC), analyzes bulk financial transaction data to identify and monitor "high-risk" money movements (those most likely to involve illicit funds). To identify these flows and the associated criminal enterprise structures and entities, the commission has developed a methodology to identify unusual and unexpected amounts of money flowing through AUSTRAC and the SWIFT (Society for Worldwide Interbank Financial Telecommunication) banking system.

This highly selective approach allows investigators to target their resources efficiently. Individuals and groups identified this way are cross-checked for police records and, if found suspicious, are further investigated using surveillance, interviews, and, where necessary, coercive powers. The intelligence enables investigators to follow high-risk transactions into and from Australia and to identify potential criminal actors at each end of the money chain.

This approach helped identify one Southeast Asian crime syndicate that imported A$129 million of narcotics over five weeks in 2001. The group is likely to have conducted similar imports throughout the preceding 12 months, or more than A$1 billion in illicit funds for this syndicate alone. Another Southeast Asian crime syndicate of four small shops transferred A$300 million in drug profits overseas over 12 months in 2001.

Sources: Australian Crime Commission 2010; Government of Australia 2010.

and must trust the other jurisdiction not to leak the data to those implicated. NORAD (Norwegian Agency for Development Cooperation) sponsors an informal network that brings prosecutors and anti-corruption agency officials from developed and developing countries together twice a year to share information and collaborate on cases. Under the auspices of the Asian Development Bank and the OECD, anti-corruption officials in East Asia and the Pacific meet regularly to discuss common problems. The World Bank supports the International Corruption Hunters Alliance and, with the UNODC, the Stolen Asset Recovery Initiative.

Getting the most from today's systems will take perseverance. Despite progress to date, three problems need attention. The first is the varying capacity across jurisdictions, with a disproportionate weight in developed country organizations. The second is a misalignment of incentives among countries, and even among institutions within a country. A third is the imperfect harmonization of various international initiatives. In principle, a more unified global system capable of analyzing financial flows and strengthening country financial systems would benefit all countries, particularly if reinforced by stronger justice systems in conflict-affected countries. A global commitment of this complexity and magnitude would require significant additional resources and political will at many levels. Nor should the challenge be underestimated—even though the number of global jurisdictions that account for the bulk of global transactions is fairly small (see chapter 9).[45]

Resource stresses

Fragile states are disproportionately susceptible to globally driven resource shocks. Unlike other low-income countries, fragile states depend heavily on food imports and are vulnerable to globally driven increases in commodity prices and scarcities in essential resources. The pressures are mounting as economic growth

BOX 7.8 *Growing regional and global approaches to food insecurity*

Effective early warning systems. Multi-agency food security early warning systems that use satellite data to anticipate crop failures and food shortages include the Global Information and Early Warning System, which aims to improve food security response planning in 22 drought-prone African countries—and the Famine Early Warning System Network, which monitors food supply and demand in all countries, with special emphasis on 80 low-income, food-deficit nations.

Regional expertise. The Southern African Development Community's (SADC) Remote Sense Unit in Harare, Zimbabwe, and the AGRHYMET Regional Center in Niamey, Niger, are two specialized institutes that provide national and local food security assessments and help build local capacity in agricultural policy and program development. Recent regional efforts include the creation in 2002 of the ASEAN (Association of Southeast Asian Nations) Food Security Information System (AFSIS) by member states plus China, Japan, and the Republic of Korea. AFSIS aims to improve food security in the region through the systematic collection, analysis, and dissemination of food security–related information.

Regional price stability mechanisms. AFSIS is closely linked to the East Asia Emergency Rice Reserve Pilot Project, which is building a mutual assistance mechanism to share rice stocks among the 13 ASEAN and AFSIS countries, addressing shortages, and helping stabilize prices in the region.

Financial mechanisms. Insurance for agricultural communities may prove effective in countries where conflicts over access to and control of natural resources are heightened in periods of drought, flood, or other climate-driven scarcity. Index-based insurance relies on objective measurements such as rainfall (too little, too much), and acts to share risk between farmers and insurance markets. The schemes have been piloted in instances of crop loss (in Ethiopia) or livestock mortality (in Mongolia). Although index-based insurance has been implemented in more than 15 countries, it has yet to be scaled up or become sustainable, especially in low-income countries.

Sources: Bora and others 2010; Brinkman and Hendrix 2010.

in middle-income countries produces new middle classes, which are adopting OECD consumption patterns in food and energy. Climate change—and the search for adaptive measures—is likely to amplify them.

As chapter 1 notes, climate change can multiply natural resource–related pressures due to its potential effects on food production, water availability, energy demand, and land-use patterns (such as carbon sinks and biofuel production). Climate change is already affecting water systems and, in some areas, the supply of arable land. Climate change and economic pressures are not separate: wealthier countries also face declining water supplies and are searching for new sources of food, water, and land overseas, often in fragile states.

Food vulnerabilities need priority attention. The share of agriculture in official development assistance declined from a high of 17 percent in the 1980s to 5 percent in 2006–08, with only 18 percent of this spending (some US$1.2 billion) going to fragile and conflict-affected states.[46] Some regional and global efforts to address food insecurity and agricultural productivity are under way (box 7.8), but much more needs to be done at the country level to develop agriculture in those countries.

By contrast, international water treaties have shown signs of success in reducing the risks of violence. A shared water resource has more often stimulated a search for compromise than conflict, with cooperative interactions between riparian states over the last 50 years outnumbering conflicts by more than two to one.[47] The international community has also helped resolve riparian issues such as water use. But there are qualifiers. Although many shared water systems have cooperative frameworks, some 150 do not. Many feature both high water stress (low per capita water availability) and fragility in one or more riparian state. And climate change may affect regimes based on specific quantities (as opposed to proportions) of a defined water flow (map 7.1). Based on these circumstances, there are instances where it may be appropriate to update and refine certain elements of existing water treaty systems (see chapter 8).

The global search for energy and food supplies is amplifying pressure on arable land in developing countries, especially where institutions are weak. Land-based conflict is typically treated as a purely national issue, or at best a subregional issue, but land use is increasingly subject to external competitive pressures. Commercial leases or purchases by foreign governments or foreign government–backed enterprises can overlap with communal land claims and lead to tensions—famously so in Madagascar, where such an arrangement over a large land leasing deal

MAP 7.1 ***Water availability, fragility, and the potential for riparian conflict in Africa***

Fragile states are not necessarily water stressed. Most have signed international treaties. Still, some vulnerabilities remain. (Red areas on the map indicate riparian areas that have water stress and few or no treaty components. Those in blue have low or mitigated water stress).

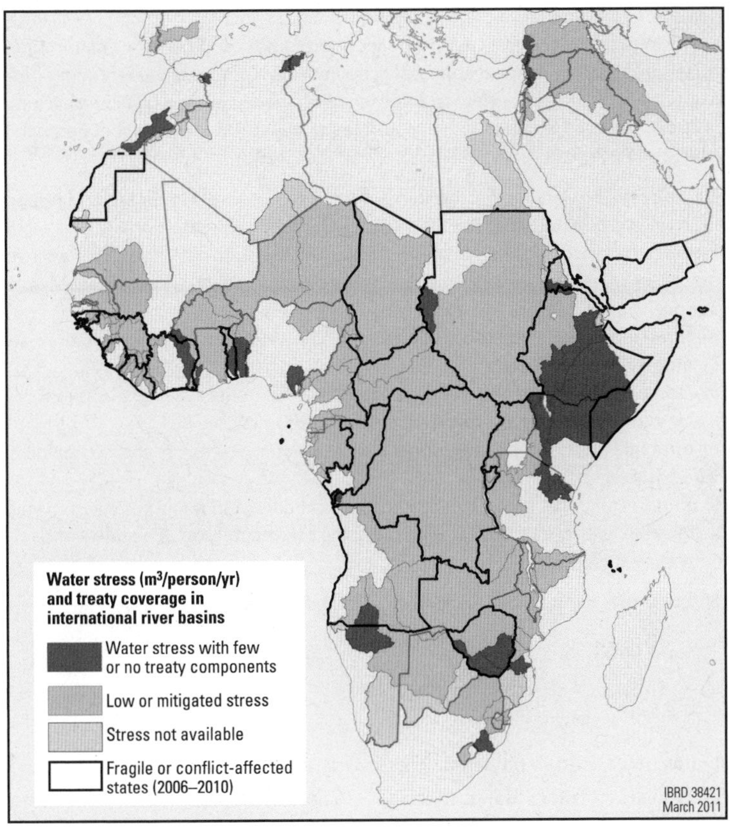

Source: De Stefano and others 2010.

generated popular resentment that, combined with other long-standing tensions, contributed to unrest and the eventual toppling of the government in early 2009.[48]

A recent World Bank research effort suggests that foreign investment in land does not increase with good governance, unlike other types of foreign investment. On the contrary, foreign investment in land tends to be greatest in countries with a combination of weak land governance, abundant land, and low mechanization. This finding lends support to growing concerns about the ability of local and national institutions to provide adequate protection to vulnerable groups against land acquisition.

Contributing to weak governance in areas of increasing land demand are project approvals issued without due diligence, rivalries among institutions with overlapping responsibilities, and insufficient capacity. All these problems are exacerbated by lack of transparency. Official records on land acquisition are often incomplete; poor data on land transfers reduce tenure security and investment, increase the likelihood of conflict, and make it difficult to collect land taxes and monitor project progress.[49]

International attention to land pressures is fragmented. The UN's Food and Agriculture Organization (FAO) examines the impact of changing food production and consumption

BOX 7.9 *Global approaches to land*

In response to a sharp increase in investment involving significant use of agricultural land, water, grassland, and forested areas in developing and emerging countries, the FAO, International Fund for Agricultural Development (IFAD), United Nations Conference on Trade and Development (UNCTAD), and the World Bank launched a consultative process involving governments, civil society, international organizations, and the private sector to develop voluntary guidelines for responsible large-scale acquisition of land rights.

The principles are intended to assist in "alleviating hunger and poverty, enhancing the environment, supporting national and local economic development, and reforming public administration" by setting priorities for domestic food, shelter, and sustainable development needs. The draft set of "Principles for Responsible Agricultural Investment that Respects Rights, Livelihoods and Resources" is as follows:

1. Existing rights to land and associated natural resources are recognized and respected.
2. Investments do not jeopardize food security but rather strengthen it.
3. Processes for accessing land and other resources and then making associated investments are transparent, monitored, and ensure accountability by all stakeholders, within a proper business, legal, and regulatory environment.
4. All those materially affected are consulted, and agreements from consultations are recorded and enforced.
5. Investors ensure that projects respect the rule of law, reflect industry best practice, are viable economically, and result in durable shared value.
6. Investments generate desirable social and distributional impacts and do not increase vulnerability.
7. Environmental impacts due to a project are quantified and measures taken to encourage sustainable resource use while minimizing the risk/magnitude of negative impacts and mitigating them.

The draft guidelines will be available for review by the same parties in 2011.

Source: FAO and others 2010.

patterns on land use; the International Organization for Migration tracks the impact of changing land patterns on migration; the International Commission on Property Rights for the Poor has analyzed the implications for the poorest people of arbitrary or unregulated transfers of land rights. The World Bank has provided a comprehensive view of how international pressures affect domestic land availability and use, and an international working group has presented draft guidelines to improve the governance of land and other natural resources (box 7.9). This exercise needs to be deepened to ensure that land investment does not deprive local populations of the means of sustaining themselves.

In international dialogues on food, energy, and climate, fragile states have weak voices despite bearing substantial impacts. As with international dialogues on counter-terrorism, the impact on fragile areas is often neglected, and the least developed countries have modest capacities to contribute. An important exception is the way African states pooled their diplomatic energies, under Ethiopia's leadership, in the 2010 Cancún climate change negotiations, contributing to agreement on adaptation funding of US$100 billion a year—a model worth replicating in other fora.[50] Moving forward, international negotiations on climate, energy, and food scarcity issues need to keep a careful eye on impacts on fragile states.

International donors can also help fragile states weather volatile external pressures by investing in social protection programs. That assistance can take several forms (see chapters 8 and 9). While the systems are global, many of the buffer mechanisms that warrant most attention are regional—true not just for issues related to resources, but more generally for buffering national authorities and societies against external stresses.

Between the global and the national: Regional stresses, regional support

Like all states, fragile states exist in a regional and global space. The region matters for several reasons. Personal relationships within subregions are often deep, allowing regional actors and institutions to exercise moral suasion and create incentives for responsible leadership. Neighbors are a source of trade, cooperation, and even of potential shared administrative capacity. On the negative side, neighbors can be a source of insecurity and political interference.

Regional organizations provide an increasingly strong platform for action.[51] Since the end of the Cold War, regional organizations have become more prominent, in conformity with the principle of "regional subsidiarity" articulated in chapter 8 of the UN Charter.[52] Chapter 1 of this Report discussed the impressive progress made in combating coups d'état and abusive military rule in Africa and Latin America. The African Union's African Peer Review Mechanism and the mediatory efforts of the Economic Community of West African States (ECOWAS) show that support in the neighborhood has advantages.[53] Member states of the African Peer Review Mechanism participate on a voluntary basis and use this forum to work toward the aims set out in the New Partnership for Africa's Development. The mechanism assesses and reviews progress toward a set of ambitious governance indicators, economic growth, and regional integration.[54] The degree of capacity for action does vary between regions: regional security, political, and economic arrangements are only as strong as the interests they share.

Regional organizations are also combining their comparative advantage in political leadership with global technical capacity. In Southeast Asia, for example, ASEAN has provided political leadership in a number of international engagements with technical support from other organizations. In Timor-Leste, it provided much of the lead diplomatic and peacekeeping capacity within the UN peacekeeping mission. In Aceh, Indonesia, ASEAN led a joint monitoring mission with the European Union, at the Indonesian Government's request, to support the peace agreement. In Myanmar after Cyclone Nargis, the organization helped open access to humanitarian workers, with support from the UN, the Asian Development Bank, and the World Bank.

Regions that have experienced conflict face a dilemma. Organized criminal groups and cross-border support to rebels undermine the potential for cross-border collaboration. But collaboration and shared administrative services could create precisely the net gains in capacity that would allow all participating states to better handle organized violence. In Central America, the peace processes explicitly linked neighbors into monitoring and implementation arrangements, including implementation within their own borders. This not only helped reduce violence—it laid the foundation for greater subregional economic integration. Even states that have had tense relations, or have suffered from disruption inflicted by groups based in each other's territory, can find common interests in tackling transnational threats and protecting shared resources like water. In the Middle East, cross-border initiatives to manage water resources have survived turbulence in political and security relations;[55] Thailand and Myanmar have had successful cooperation on health issues and on trafficking.

The physical, demographic, and economic characteristics of many fragile states increase the potential returns to regional cooperation. Of the 38 states classified by the World Bank as fragile today, 24 have populations under 10 million, and 13 are either landlocked or island nations off the main sea lanes. The economies of many fragile states share structural disadvantages: physical isolation of the whole or part of the country, combined with high transport costs to export destination markets, limited internal demand (and limited economies of scale), weak national institutions, and scarce trained personnel. This lack of competitiveness and consequent

REFLECTIONS FROM ADVISORY COUNCIL MEMBERS: *2011 WORLD DEVELOPMENT REPORT*

BOX 7.10 *The role of regional institutions and initiatives in norm-setting and violence prevention*

ASEAN's experience in crisis prevention and recovery

Surin Pitsuwan, Secretary-General ASEAN; *WDR Advisory Council Member*

There are many conflicts simmering in the ASEAN landscape. But the region is not totally without its own experiences in mediation and conflict resolution. ASEAN has played an important role in endeavors. The ASEAN Troika in the Cambodian conflict of 1997–99, the Timor-Leste peacekeeping operation of 1999 onward, the Aceh Reconciliation of 2005, and the Myanmar Cyclone Nargis catastrophe of May 2008 were cases of mediation and eventual resolution where the regions and some ASEAN member states have made valuable contributions and learned lessons from the process. It has always been like putting pieces of a diplomatic jigsaw together, weaving tapestry of peace, improvising the best modality and pattern from the available and suitable materials at hand.

One important lesson for us is that our ASEAN structures can play an important political convening role when there are sensitivities with member states. There was a higher level of mutual confidence between Indonesia and the ASEAN states participating in the Timor-Leste operation. We got around the rigid principle of "non-interference" by offering troops under a joint command with an "ASEAN" military leader taking an active leadership role. And Indonesia made it easier for all ASEAN partners by issuing an invitation to come and assist. In Myanmar, ASEAN played a central role in the dialogue with the Government after Cyclone Nargis, helping to open up the affected areas, where over 130,000 men, women, and children had died and many more faced traumatic conditions, to international aid.

A second lesson is that we can find useful combinations of capacity between our local knowledge and political convening role, and the technical capacities of other partners. Our work in support of recovery after Cyclone Narghis was supported by technical teams from the World Bank, and performed in conjunction with the United Nations. In the Aceh Monitoring Mission, we worked jointly with colleagues from the European Union who brought valuable technical knowledge.

The third is that the more operations of this type that we undertake, the more our capacity builds. In Timor-Leste, long years of joint military training and exercises between the Philippines, Republic of Korea, and Thailand, supported by partners outside the region such as the United States, paid off. The troops on the ground could communicate, cooperate, and conduct joint operations without any delay—but their experiences in Timor-Leste also added to their capacity. In Myanmar, ASEAN's role meant drawing on personnel from many of our member states, such as Indonesia, Thailand, and Singapore, who have extensive experience of managing post-disaster recovery, and also building capacity within our Secretariat. Linked to long-term programs of capacity-building with some of our donor partners, these experiences make us more ready to face new challenges in the future. The cumulative results of these efforts in managing political conflicts and natural disaster relief have helped ASEAN in enhancing its capacity to coordinate our development cooperation strategies. We have learned to contain sporadic violence and tension in the region and would not allow them to derail our community development efforts aiming at common security and sustainable prosperity for our people.

low national income is often offset only by foreign assistance and rents from natural resource extraction. These factors can create an unhealthy mix of what has been called "enclaved development plus dependency."[56]

Remote and insecure areas have little infrastructure—and need more.[57] Areas that are mountainous or have few roads are difficult for governments to provide basic services or to police. Isolation tends to result both in divided identity groups and in marginalization. And there are few economic opportunities: the average GDP per capita of all landlocked developing countries is three-fifths that of their maritime neighbors.[58] The 2009 *World Development Report* on economic geography underscored the challenge of distance and division for development in Sub-Saharan Africa, and called for spatially blind institutions as the bedrock of integration efforts.[59] In many parts of the world, roads and other infrastructure are absent from the more remote and insecure areas (map 7.2). In the Pacific, the high transport costs associated with small-capacity freighters play the same isolating role as the lack of roads in the Saharan and Sahelian areas of northern Africa and the mountainous drug-producing regions of Myanmar.

A lack of economic incentives for infrastructure explains much of the shortage. The reason for low infrastructure penetration in remote areas is a combination of low economic activity and insecure transit, which lessen the demand from business interests and result in low projected returns to such investments. The returns can be improved if such investments are part of regional networks. But governments can be reluctant, on sovereignty grounds, to allow international or regional investment in troublesome border areas.

Where issues of mistrust can be overcome—say, by involving a neutral third party or joint organization—shared regional services have a good track record. The provision of some government services by regional institutions can result in higher quality of services than countries could otherwise afford—and can build a high-quality cadre of civil servants. For fragile and conflict-affected states, the regional pooling of services can reinforce rather than undermine national sovereignty and citizen confidence in government (box 7.11). This is exemplified in the Caribbean and in Sub-Saharan Africa, where regional solutions have improved the quality of various public services. The Eastern Caribbean Supreme Court is a regional superior court of record for six independent states[60] and three British Overseas Territories.[61] Countries under the court rank high on the World Bank Institute's 2008 Rule of Law rating, derived from enterprise, citizen, and expert surveys. The Pacific Islands Forum's Pacific Plan for Regional Integration and Cooperation includes a provision for regional pooling of national services (customs, health, education, sports).[62]

Shared administration also has significant potential. Small and fragile states can benefit from pooling administrative functions. As chapter 4 discussed, the poor quality of public services is a serious obstacle to economic growth and degrades citizen confidence in government.[63] Most countries spend around 12 percent of GDP on government goods and services, but nonfragile states spend about twice as much as fragile states do in per capita terms[64] (the average low-income fragile or conflict-affected state spends US$38 per capita on government goods and services, while the average low-income non-fragile state spends US$80) (table 7.2). The poor quality of public services is a serious obstacle to economic growth, eroding citizen confidence in governments.[65]

Forging shared regional arrangements often benefits from support by third-party mediation perceived to be neutral. For example, the evolving institutions of the European Union sponsored many arrangements that fostered cross-regional cooperation at the national and local level (see box 7.12). Suspicion between neighbors can be ameliorated by a trusted third party—a role that

MAP 7.2 *Sub-Saharan Africa's regional infrastructure challenge in fragile states*

Regional infrastructure is extremely limited in many of the fragile states in Africa. This map shows the presence of power plants, power lines, and regional roads in Sub-Saharan Africa (fragile states shaded pink). Some areas lacking infrastructure have very low populations to support, but others—such as the border area between the Central African Republic, Chad, and Sudan—are isolated primarily due to insecurity. This reduces trade across borders and access to electricity, locking insecure areas out of economic connectivity.

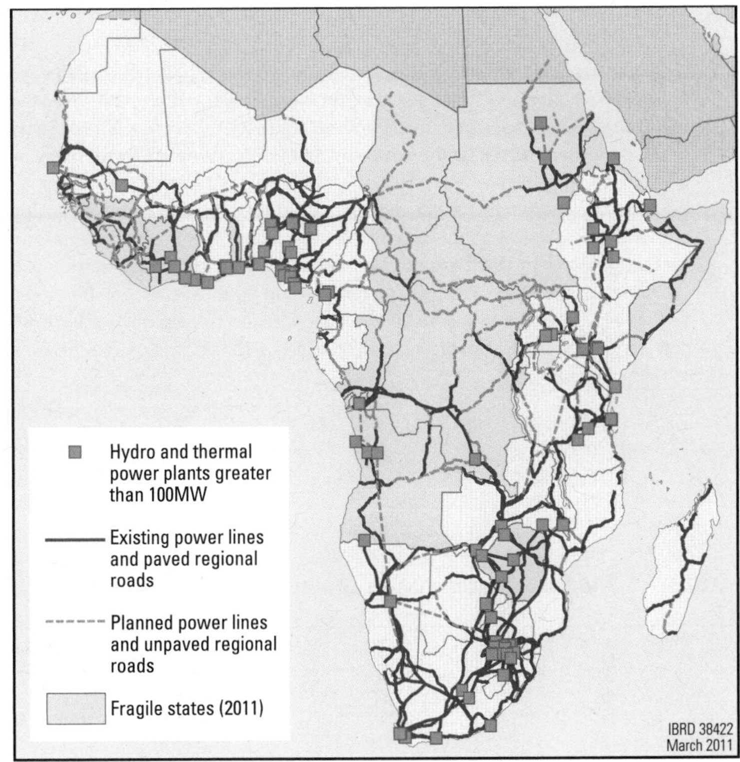

Source: Briceño-Garmendia and Foster 2010.

BOX 7.11 *Pooling services regionally*

In the past three decades, the role of regional organizations as providers of public services has increased in Sub-Saharan Africa and the eastern Caribbean. Political independence brought self-determination but also meant that services formerly provided through colonial institutions had to be supplied by fledgling national institutions. Several countries responded by pooling resources regionally and contracting out some public service provision to the newly created regional organizations.

In most cases, the services contracted out were advisory rather than executive. For instance, countries relied on regional organizations for advisory aspects of banking supervision (as with the Eastern Caribbean Central Bank or the Banque des Etats de l'Afrique Centrale,[66] and the Banque Centrale des Etats de l'Afrique de l'Ouest),[67] while retaining the role of each country's sovereign government in enforcing recommendations. In hindsight, this model worked well when there was a tradition of cooperation in central banking that predated independence.

By pooling resources, countries have produced higher quality services and better civil servants than would have been possible had the countries acted separately. The success of this model has encouraged other experiments. The Eastern Caribbean Central Bank, Civil Aviation Authority, and Supreme Court, regional entities under the Revised Organisation of Eastern Caribbean States Treaty, have been followed by a joint telecommunications regulator, the Eastern Caribbean Telecommunications Authority, and a joint natural disaster risk pooling mechanism, the Caribbean Catastrophic Risk Insurance Fund. These organizations have also raised the bar on what the public and politicians expect for the quality of public services. Similarly, the regional central banks were followed in 1993 by the Organisation pour l'Harmonisation en Afrique du Droit des Affaires in Central and West Africa, founded to harmonize business law among member countries and serve as a supranational appeals court on aspects of business law. The West Africa Telecommunications Regulatory Agreement, established in 2002, has pursued the harmonization and integration of the telecommunications market in West Africa.

Although the role of regional organizations as public service providers has not developed to the same extent in the Pacific, due in part to vast distances and more diverse historical and cultural backgrounds, the University of the South Pacific is an initiative that others can learn from. Opened in 1968 and supported by 12 Pacific Island countries, it is acknowledged internationally as a credible institution of higher learning.

Source: Favaro 2008, 2010.

TABLE 7.2 *Shared administration can help fragile and conflict-affected states provide better quality public services*

	Government expenditure on goods and services		
	Government consumption, % of GDP	US$ per capita	US$ purchasing power parity per capita
Low income			
Fragile and conflict-affected states	11	38	131
Non-fragile states	15	80	267
Lower middle income			
Fragile and conflict-affected states	13	247	858
Non-fragile states	13	470	1,296

Sources: Favaro 2010.
Note: Averages of most recent data available (2001 to 2008) for 88 low- and lower-middle-income countries (data are missing for 11 fragile and conflict-affected countries).

the Asian Development Bank has played with good effect in the Greater Mekong Subregion.[68] Regional organizations have been encouraging national leaders to explore such arrangements—and seek third-party help in managing violence and shepherding transition.

External assistance can help regional initiatives and regional institutions to realize their full potential in addressing security and development links. As with Europe's early integration (see box 7.12), where regions have the political appetite to explore sharing administrative capacity or pooling

BOX 7.12 *Early European measures to create shared economic interests in peace*

The creation of the European Coal and Steel Community (ECSC)—the forerunner to the European Union—shows how economic integration can underpin peace and security. The ECSC was formed to create a common market and jointly monitor the production and use of coal and steel—strategically important goods. The ECSC Treaty was signed in Paris in 1951 and led to the free movement of coal and steel and free access to sources of production. A common High Authority supervised the market, respect for competition rules, and price transparency.

The ECSC enabled the lifting of ceilings on coal and steel production in key German industries in the postwar period without seeming to threaten the security of the country's neighbors. Lifting these ceilings and generating regional confidence in coal and steel markets were important, not just for Germany's economic growth, but also for European economic recovery as a whole. The notion of cross-border cooperation to spur investment, regulate production, open markets, and build confidence and trust are applicable in other regions prone to political instability or recovering from conflict.

Other forms of European cooperation have also managed to develop productive exchanges across borders and individual regions. The "Euro region" began as an innovative form of transborder cooperation (between two or more states that share a common bordering region) in the late 1950s. With the purpose of stimulating cross-border economic, sociocultural, and leisure cooperation, the Euroregion model grew, and was boosted through the creation of the European common market and recent democratic transitions. There are currently more than 100 Euroregions spread across Europe, and the model has in recent times been replicated in eastern and central European territories. Cooperation has not been without problems in areas previously affected by conflict, but there are good examples of cross-border developmental, social, and security programs that involve areas where ethnic minorities reside across several states or in areas that have suffered the trauma of interstate and civil war in the past.

Sources: Lockhart 2010; Eichengreen 2010; Kelley 2004; Kubicek 2003; Schimmelfennig and Sedelmeier 2002; European Union 1951; Greta and Lewandowski 2010; Otocan 2010; Council of Europe 1995; Council of Europe and Institute of International Sociology of Gorizia 2003; Bilcik and others 2000.

functions or services, external assistance to that process can be invaluable. So far, international aid has tended to support national rather than regional efforts. Support to regional organizations has grown in recent years, but it is generally directed as technical assistance to the organization, rather than to larger-scale regional delivery programs (European assistance to African peacekeeping is a significant exception). The potential for regional arrangements to create buffers against external threats and to provide a cost-effective way to enhance institutional capacity warrants much more attention in international assistance—an issue discussed in chapter 9.

FEATURE 7 *Central Asia: External pressures and external assistance*

Types of violence: Political violence, local intergroup conflict, local conflicts with transnational ideological connections	
Transition moment: Moderate space for change	**Key stakeholders:** Governments, opposition parties, regional partners
Key stresses: Legacies of colonial past, transboundary natural resource management, human rights abuses, real or perceived discrimination, corruption	**Institutional challenges:** Lack of political accountability and inclusion, limited capacity of regional forums and institutions

Regional cooperation is widely accepted as a process and instrument for preventing conflict, promoting economic growth, and facilitating country integration within the region and with the international community. The most successful model is the European Union, which evolved over half a century from the original six-nation European Coal and Steel Community. The Association of Southeast Asian Nations (ASEAN) and other subregional groups are also often cited as models to follow for conflict prevention and economic cooperation in Central Asia. But almost 20 years after Kazakhstan, the Kyrgyz Republic, Tajikistan, Turkmenistan, and Uzbekistan emerged as independent states from the former Soviet Union, there has been little progress in regional cooperation in Central Asia, and the risk of conflict may be increasing.

Despite their cultural links and shared development experience as part of a large centrally planned economy for most of the 20th century, the five Central Asian countries have pursued different paths and rates of economic and political transition—partly the outcome of policy choices and partly from their Soviet legacy. Their different approaches and uneven natural resource endowments have resulted in increasingly differentiated outcomes in growth, poverty, and, ultimately, stability. Moreover, their sometimes conflicting interests—in transboundary water use and management, for example—influence their attitudes toward, and thus the prospects for, enhanced regional cooperation.

Is regional cooperation important?

Central Asia's geography, history, and people—as well as its landlocked position and the integrated energy, transport, and water infrastructure it inherited from the Soviet Union—together make the five countries unusually interdependent. In reality, a modicum of day-to-day coordination of transboundary oil and gas pipelines, electricity transmission, and water distribution is a practical necessity.

Given their economies' small size, relative isolation, and reliance on exports of primary products, these countries' regional integration and market development could in principle help develop clusters of suppliers and complementary public services, improving all five countries' access to world markets. Local community associations and networks developed during Soviet times, based on the contours of economic subregions such as the Fergana Valley—now partitioned by the borders of three countries—could be revived as the basis for increased intraregional trade, thus reducing the risk of cross-border conflict.

If regional approaches were adopted and strengthened, several negative externalities could be tackled more effectively and efficiently. These include environmental deterioration, of which the dying Aral Sea is only the most visible example; land degradation and desertification, which have reduced crop yields and the availability of arable land; drug transit and trade; and eventually the impacts of climate change.

Two international studies have estimated that improved regional cooperation could increase Central Asia's regional GDP by between 50 and 100 percent—and regional per capita incomes by up to 100 percent—in about 10 years. Lower transport costs would increase trade with large neighbors such as China, the Islamic Republic of Iran, the Russian Federation, and, indirectly, South Asia. Managing and exploiting transboundary water, irrigated agriculture, and related hydro and other energy resources would be more cost-effective. And collaborative approaches to regional public goods, such as biodiversity, the environment, and public health, would benefit from economies of scale—as would enhancing security, managing natural disasters, and curbing the drug trade.

If so, why is cooperation receding?

The explanation for cooperation not developing, and even receding—less than 20 years after independence—is that each country's interest in regional cooperation is different, and individual nation-building is still under way. Other factors include

- Diverging approaches to, and different rates of, economic transition—exemplified most obviously by the contrast between Kazakhstan's relatively open economy and Uzbekistan's relatively closed one
- Differing views between the two upstream (the Kyrgyz Republic and Tajikistan) and three downstream countries (Kazakhstan, Turkmenistan, and Uzbekistan) over the management of the region's two key transboundary water resources (the Amu Darya and Syr Darya rivers and their tributaries) for hydroelectric power generation and irrigation, respectively
- Rival searches for the same extraregional and global markets, often complicated by the competing interests and motivations of the subregion's principal external actors
- Rekindled cultural, ethnic, and religious identities of the five titular nationalities—following 70 years of suppression during the Soviet era—coupled with the stresses and strains of modern nation-building.

Less tangible but still significant are contending claims to regional leadership by the two largest countries (Kazakhstan and Uzbekistan) and growing instability in the two smallest, most fragile countries (Tajikistan and the Kyrgyz Republic)—particularly in the Kyrgyz Republic where recent political turmoil and interethnic violence could destabilize its neighbors. An outcome of these divergent interests is the dwindling efficacy and influence of the regional forums and institutions, whose managerial and decision-making capacity remains limited.

Institutional constraints

The only regional institution involving all five countries is the International Fund for Saving the Aral Sea—a single-purpose body established in the early 1990s to mobilize financial resources to mitigate the environmental, humanitarian, and social impact of the Aral Sea's drying up. In addition, the UN has sponsored three regional groups. The Special Program for the Economies of Central Asia—a framework for periodic dialogue inspired originally by Kazakhstan—has only very limited resources. The UN Regional Center for Conflict Resolution, based in Ashgabat, promotes regional dialogue, security, and understanding. And the recently established Central Asia Regional Information and Coordination Center, based in Almaty, Kazakhstan, exchanges intelligence to identify and disrupt drug trafficking networks and strengthens regional criminal justice capacity. The Central Asia Regional Economic Cooperation program, initiated and funded mainly by the Asian Development Bank, is a partnership of eight countries and six multilateral institutions to promote and facilitate regional cooperation in transport, trade facilitation, trade policy, and energy.

What lessons can be learned?

A 2008 survey of regional cooperation institutions worldwide suggested five key lessons relevant to Central Asia:

- Effective regional cooperation takes time and effort to develop, requiring incremental, gradual, flexible implementation with visible payoffs.
- It also requires sustained leadership—at the country, institutional, and individual levels.
- The size and membership of regional institutions should be kept manageable.
- Financial resources and instruments are needed to support regional investments and cooperation.
- External actors should assist wherever possible.

In addition to these findings, a 2007 World Bank Independent Evaluation Group analysis of regional programs—including two in Central Asia—listed five design features of successful programs consistent with these principles: strong country commitment to regional cooperation; objectives that match national and regional capacities; clear definition and coordination of the roles of national and regional institutions; accountable governance arrangements; and plans for the sustainability of program outcomes.

Central Asia satisfies few, if any, of these criteria. In particular, there is little or no country commitment to regional cooperation—for the reasons noted earlier—beyond the minimal bureaucratic and technical coordination needed to ensure effective functioning of the countries' integrated infrastructure. Indeed, relations have deteriorated in the last two years, particularly with tensions strained among some countries over plans to complete two Soviet-era hydropower projects. Some of the countries have agreed to accept the conclusions of externally financed, independent assessments of one of the project's economic, environmental, and technical

FEATURE 7 *Central Asia: External pressures and external assistance (continued)*

feasibility—apparently signaling their interest in a mutually acceptable bilateral solution.

From conflict to cooperation

Experience appears to confirm the analysis of at least one Central Asian scholar, Matveeva (2007), who concludes that regional cooperation, however desirable in theory, cannot be prescribed from outside. The mediation of conflicts inherited by the five countries, if not their resolution, is a prerequisite for more broadly based regional cooperation. And regional cooperation is more likely to evolve in limited well-defined areas of obvious mutual interest or concern.

Another couple of scholars, Linn and Pidufala (2008), view relations between the five countries as driven mainly by competition and rivalry—for influence, leadership, markets, and resources—warning, in addition, that this may not be a temporary phenomenon related to nation-building. According to this view, Central Asia's regional problems are unlikely to be resolved in the near term, and the main priority for external actors should be to reduce the risk that they may worsen and cause real conflict.

The need for closer cooperation in Central Asia—to prevent conflict and to maintain and reinforce regional stability—may be greater and more urgent than ever, especially in energy and water, and trade and transport, which have so far proven intractable. While the outlook for enhanced cooperation may have worsened, this makes renewed focus and coordinated effort by external actors all the more important. In this context, the Central Asia Regional Economic Cooperation program's pragmatic emphasis on coordinated country-specific investments in energy and transport infrastructure benefiting two or more countries may be a model for other partners to follow.

If cooperation is indeed more likely to be ad hoc and in narrowly defined areas of common interest or concern—not involving all five countries—a flexible operational framework, rather than an elaborate regional plan or strategy, is the right way to shape external actors' actions. External actors can do much in convening, mediating, and resolving issues, but without mutual interest and political will in the countries, their role will be limited.

Sources: Houdart and Pearce 2010; and others described in endnote.[69]

Notes

1. For a discussion of these linkages, see for example Naim 2006.
2. See Baker 2005.
3. Rubin 2002; Small Arms Survey Project 2005, 2009.
4. Gambino 2010; U.S. Department of State 2010.
5. Oliver 1999.
6. UN "Groups of Friends" began in the post–Cold War period as a mediation tool for countries attempting to prevent or exit conflict. Friends groups have been operating over the past two decades, providing a core group of interested states that apply diplomatic persuasion—carrots and sticks—in promoting peace settlements. Most often these are informal groupings, with a negotiated and varied rather than rigid mandate based on the country context. See Whitfield 2007.
7. Patel and Ross 2007; O'Loughlin, Witmer, and Linke 2010.
8. See African Union 2007a.
9. UNDP 2010a.
10. UN Security Council 2010b.
11. In the case of heroin and cocaine, which are illegal in almost all countries.
12. See OECD 2010h.
13. Estimated value of conflict and illicit diamonds. In 2008, conflict diamonds were estimated to account for 0.1 percent of the total global production of rough diamonds, which stood at US$12.7 billion. See Kimberley Process Certification Scheme 2009, 2010.

14. Gemologists are generally able to identify the origin of diamonds if they receive several parcels of gems coming from the same area. They have great difficulties in identifying origin once stones from different areas have been mixed, and they are completely unable to identify the origins of a polished stone (see Goreaux 2001).
15. This is an estimate for oil trafficked only from Nigeria, where this problem is concentrated, and is based on an estimated 150,000 barrels per day at a price of US$20 per barrel—a significant discount over world oil prices to attract large buyers (see UNODC 2009a).
16. Estimated 2008 value of illegally imported wood products (see Lawson and MacFaul 2010, 125).
17. While it is technically feasible to trace the origins of timber (and this indeed has been the focus of a number of "responsible forestry" initiatives), doing so depends either on tagging at the country of origin and a secure chain of custody, or on a more complicated DNA analysis.
18. UNODC 2010a, 129.
19. The number of legal manufacturers of small arms is estimated to have increased from fewer than 200 companies in 1980 to more than 600 by 2001. As of 2001, at least 95 countries had the capacity to undertake the legal production of small arms. See Small Arms Survey Project 2001.
20. Most, but not all, small arms and light weapons are marked at the point of manufacture, for example, with a serial number and manufacturer's mark that is stamped, etched, or engraved into metallic parts of the weapon. However, where they exist, the marks often contain insufficient information for unique identification and reliable tracing, and there is no centralized record-keeping. See Greene 2001.
21. UNODC 2010a, 82, 111.
22. Illicit trade in small arms and light weapons takes place in both the black and the gray markets. For a definition of both markets, see Stohl and Grillot 2009. For information on the SALW, see Small Arms Survey Project 2006. The estimate of the elicit portion is reported in Marsh 2002.
23. Small Arms Survey Project 2011.
24. See Cukier 2002 and Markowski and others 2009.
25. On the developmental impact of SALW, see Bourne 2007.
26. See Small Arms Survey Project 2009.
27. Ben-Ari 2010; Worsnip 2009; UN Security Council 2009.
28. Demombynes 2010.
29. Although the definition of terrorism is fraught, and the question of which groups should be referred to as terrorist organizations is contested, 12 UN Conventions that have been adopted by the General Assembly specify tactics that are classified as terrorism.
30. An example of this today is the presence of transnational terrorist organizations affiliated with Al-Qaeda in the subnational conflicts in Indonesia and the Philippines (see Putzel 2003; Kilcullen 2009; Acharya and Acharya 2007).
31. UN General Assembly 2006.
32. Berman and others 2009; Berman 2009; Berman and Iannaccone 2006.
33. UNODC 2009b, 65.
34. U.S. Office of National Drug Control Policy, 1999, 26.
35. OECD 1996, 2009; Greenberger 1995; Gantz 1998; Hines 1995.
36. Transparency International 2010, 8.
37. Messick 2011. Also see box 8.4 in chapter 8.
38. The Financial Action Task Force (FATF) was established in 1990 by the finance ministers of G-7 countries to combat the problem of illegal narcotics trafficking and money laundering through strengthened international cooperation. The FATF's initial mission was to focus on preventing the use of the banking system and other financial institutions for the purpose of money laundering. As an initial step and based on an analysis of the existing situation, the FATF developed a series of recommendations on specific measures, including the adaptation of national legal and regulatory systems, that would help detect, prevent, and punish misuse of the financial system for money laundering. Following the terrorist attacks of 9/11, the FATF issued additional guidelines to counter the terrorist financing. The FATF relies on a unique cooperation network involving more than 180 jurisdictions around the world, including multilateral organizations such as the G-20, UN, World Bank, and IMF. Additionally, eight FATF-style regional bodies have been created over the years as part of this network. See Financial Action Task Force 2010.
39. The Egmont Group of Financial Intelligence Units is an informal international gathering of financial intelligence units (FIUs) formed in 1995. FIUs are national centers to collect information on suspicious or unusual financial activity from the financial industry and other entities or professions required to report transactions suspected of being money laundering or terrorism financing. FIUs

are normally not law enforcement agencies; their mission is to analyze the information received. If sufficient evidence of unlawful activity is found, the matter is passed to the public prosecution. The goal of the Egmont Group is to provide a forum for FIUs around the world to improve cooperation in the fight against money laundering and financing of terrorism and to foster the implementation of domestic programs in this field. Intscher 2010.

40. Intscher 2010.
41. WDR team calculations.
42. Such as the U.S. Financial Crimes Enforcement Network (FINCEN), the U.K. Serious Organized Crime Agency (SOCA), the Australian Transaction Reports and Analysis Center (AUSTRAC), and the Canadian Financial Transactions and Reports Analysis Center (FINTRAC).
43. A large proportion of FIUs (about 60–65 percent) receive only Suspicious Transaction Reports, which meet some test of suspicion, and are by and large domestic transactions, usually of a relatively modest amount. This is the mandatory minimum reporting requirement of the FATF Recommendations. A substantial minority of FIUs (about 25–30 percent) also receive, or have access to, Large Cash Transaction Reports, reported solely on the basis of the transaction exceeding a threshold value specified in law or regulation. A small proportion of FIUs (perhaps 10–15 percent) receive some Foreign Exchange Transaction Reports, usually those above a specified value threshold. A quite small proportion of FIUs (maybe 5–8 percent) receive, or have access to, Electronic Funds Transfer Reports ("wire transfers"), usually above a threshold, mostly for international, but in some instances also domestic transfers. See Intscher 2010.
44. Secrecy jurisdictions refer to jurisdictions that facilitate illicit financial flows stemming from three overlapping sources: bribery, criminal activity, and cross-border trade mispricing. Secrecy jurisdictions undermine development for the poorest countries as individuals taking advantage of these jurisdictions can commit a wide range of crimes such as tax evasion, nonpayment of alimonies, money laundering, terrorist financing, drug trafficking, human trafficking, illegal arms trading, counterfeiting, insider dealing, embezzlement, fleeing of bankruptcy orders, fraud, and others.
45. One barrier relates to privacy: access to information on wire transfers, for example, means infringing the privacy of the many millions of customers using wire transfers for entirely legal means.
46. OECD 2010b; Willman 2010.
47. De Stefano and others 2010.
48. Cooke and Brown 2010.
49. World Bank 2010f.
50. The Green Climate Fund will support projects, programs, policies, and other activities in developing country parties using thematic funding windows. The fund will be governed by the Green Climate Board comprising 24 members, as well as alternate members, with equal number of members from developing and developed country parties. The assets of the Green Climate Fund shall be administered by a trustee, and the World Bank was invited to serve as the interim trustee, subject to a review three years after operationalization of the fund. The Cancún negotiations also decided that an independent secretariat shall support the operations of the fund. It was also decided that the Green Climate Fund shall be designed by a Transitional Committee of 40 members, with 15 members from developed country parties and 25 members from developing country parties.
51. The preeminent example of regional cooperation in the cause of conflict prevention is captured in the emergence of today's Europe, after centuries of interstate violence had culminated in the most destructive war in history. From the Marshall Plan and the Organisation for European Cooperation through the creation of the European Union and its absorption of former Soviet bloc countries, this evolving social compact has so far managed to navigate a range of volatile political and social developments and to bring a degree of political and economic unity that few would have foreseen 65 years ago. The current accession process provides very strong incentives for candidate states to attain specified governance, security, and human rights standards. Lockhart 2010; Eichengreen 2010; Grimm 2010.
52. See Wulf and Debiel 2009.
53. See Shiawl-Kidanekal 2004.
54. For further information, see NEPAD 2010.
55. World Bank 2007b; Kramer 2008.
56. "The cost 'wedges' associated with small size, undeveloped human capital and institutions, and market distance mean there is little scope for exports of manufactured goods or services; national economic viability in the Pacific is instead vested largely in three external income streams: i) rents

from natural resource extraction; ii) aid and fiscal flows; and iii) remittances from labor exports." See World Bank 2009b.

57. See, for example, Fearon and Laitin 1999, 2003.
58. Faye and others 2004.
59. World Bank 2008h.
60. Antigua and Barbuda, Dominica, Grenada, St. Kitts and Nevis, St. Lucia, and St. Vincent and the Grenadines.
61. Anguilla, British Virgin Islands, and Montserrat. See Byron and Dakolias 2008.
62. See Pacific Island Forum Secretariat 2005.
63. See also La Porta and others 1999; Acemoglu, Johnson, and Robinson 2001; Hall and Jones 1999.
63. The result holds for both lower- and lower-middle-income countries, both nominally and in purchasing power parity adjusted.
65. Favaro 2010.
66. The Banque des États de l'Afrique Centrale (BEAC) serves six countries: Cameroon, Central African Republic, Chad, Equatorial Guinea, Gabon, and Republic of Congo.
67. The Banque Centrale des États de l'Afrique de l'Ouest (BCEAO) serves eight states: Benin, Burkina Faso, Côte d'Ivoire, Guinea-Bissau, Mali, Niger, Senegal, and Togo.
68. The Greater Mekong Subregion (GMS) countries (Cambodia, China, Lao People's Democratic Republic, Myanmar, Thailand, and Vietnam) have implemented a wide-ranging series of regional projects covering transport, power, telecommunications, environmental management, human resource development, tourism, trade, private sector investment, and agriculture. These projects were carried out with the assistance of the Asian Development Bank, which had a track record of working with each of these countries on a bilateral basis, and was able to offer a platform for dialogue as well as contribute technical knowledge and expertise that helped set consistent standards acceptable to all. The GMS is recognized as having enhanced cross-border trade while reducing poverty levels and creating shared interests in economic stability and peace. See World Bank 2006d.
69. UNDP 2005a; Asian Development Bank 2006; Linn and Pidufala 2008; World Bank 2007c; Matveeva 2007; Olcott 2010.

PART 3

Practical Options and Recommendations

This chapter draws together practical country lessons and options to prevent organized criminal and political violence and recover from their effects. The audience is strategic decision makers in countries grappling with violence or attempting to prevent it—national reformers in government and civil society, as well as international representatives in the field. As this Report has emphasized throughout, efforts to build confidence and transform institutions for citizen security, justice, and jobs need to be adapted to the local political context in each country, at each transition moment—and there is a need for humility, since lessons in how to combat changing patterns of repeated violence are being refined and expanded on the ground all the time. This chapter, therefore, lays out basic principles and a toolkit of options emerging from country lessons and illustrates how these can be adapted to different contexts.

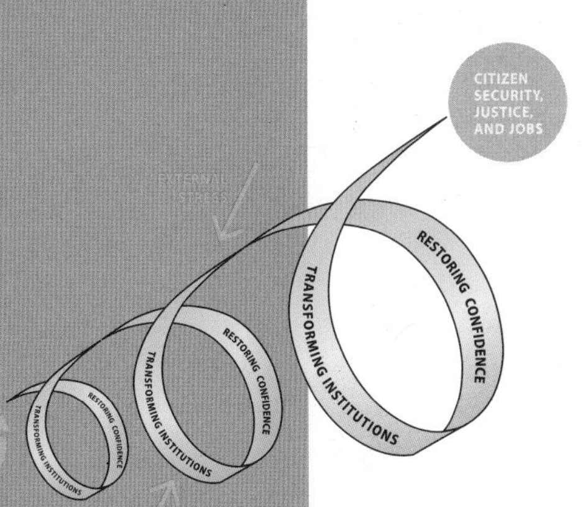

CHAPTER 8

Practical country directions and options

Principles and options, not recipes

This Report lays out a different way of thinking about approaches to violence prevention and recovery in fragile situations. It does not aim to be a "cookbook" that prescribes recipes—every country's history and political context differ, and there are no one-size-fits-all solutions. As described earlier, recovering from fragile situations is not a short, linear process. Countries go through multiple transitions over a period of at least a generation before achieving institutional resilience. Because trust is low in high-risk environments, building confidence and political support among stakeholders in each round of change is a prelude to institutional transformation. Managing these complex dynamics and multiple transitions is the basis of statecraft, and this chapter draws heavily on lessons from national reformers and country experiences in chapters 4 and 5. There is no substitute for the judicious blend of political judgment, deep knowledge of actors, innovation, and tactical calculus that only national reformers can wield.

The first section presents basic principles emerging from many different settings where societies have been able to prevent and recover from episodes of violence and develop institutional resilience, as well as a framework for differentiating these principles in country strategies. The second section summarizes practical tools for confidence-building and gives examples of how these have been adapted to different country circumstances. The third section considers insights from program design to link early results with longer-term institution-building, again illustrating how common tools have been tailored to country contexts. The last section considers, more briefly, lessons on addressing external stresses and marshaling external resources. Some of the challenges in relation to external assistance and regional and global stresses are beyond the capacity of individual states and donor field representatives to resolve. So this chapter should be read with chapter 9, which considers directions for global policy.

Basic principles and country-specific frameworks for sustained violence prevention and recovery

Basic principles

The Report's analysis underlines that institutions and governance, which are important for development in general, work differently in fragile situations. Restoring confidence through inclusion and early, visible results at the local level is important before undertaking wider institutional reforms. The principal tactic national reformers and their partners have used to restore confidence in the face of recent or rising violence and fragility is to build "inclusive-enough" coalitions. Coalition-building efforts will sustain success only if they can address the underlying weaknesses that increase the risks of repeated cycles of violence—deficits in security, justice, and job creation. Cycles of confidence-building and institutional transformation repeat over time. To galvanize and sustain this "virtuous circle" in the face of deep challenges of repeated violence and weak institutional capacity, four key principles emerge.

- ***Inclusion is important to restore confidence, but coalitions need not be "all-inclusive."*** Inclusive-enough coalitions work in two ways. At a broad level, they build national support for change and by bringing in the relevant international stakeholders whose support is needed. At a local level, they work with community leaders and structures to identify priorities and deliver programs. Inclusive-enough coalitions apply just as much to criminal violence as to political violence, through collaboration with community leaders, business, parliaments, civil society—and with regional neighbors, donors, and investors.
- ***Some early results are needed to build citizen confidence and create momentum for longer-term institutional transformation.*** When trust is low, people do not believe grand plans for reform will work. Some early results that demonstrate the potential for success can generate trust, restore confidence in the prospects of collective action, and build momentum for deeper institutional transformation. Transforming institutions takes a generation, but political cycles are short—early results can both meet political imperatives and generate the incentives for the longer-term project of institution-building.
- ***It makes sense to first establish the basic institutional functions that provide citizen security, justice, and jobs*** (and associated services)—and that ensure that new initiatives do not lose credibility due to corruption. Progress in these areas, and coordination among them, are the foundation for broader change. Other reforms that require the accrual of greater social consensus and capacities—political reform, decentralization, deeper economic reform, shifts in social attitudes toward marginalized groups—are best addressed systematically over time once these foundational reforms have made some progress.
- ***Don't let perfection be the enemy of progress—embrace pragmatic, best-fit options to address immediate challenges.*** In insecure situations, it is generally impossible to achieve technical perfection in approaches to security, justice, or development. There is a need to be pragmatic, to address immediate challenges within political realities, with approaches that can improve over time. Sometimes these approaches will have temporary second-best aspects associated with them. For example, jobs generated may not immediately meet long-term goals for high skills and wages. Community and traditional structures may have drawbacks in their representation of women or youth groups. Anti-corruption initiatives may have to focus on major corruption while tolerating financial weaknesses in other areas.

A framework for tailoring country-specific strategies

Within these general principles, each country needs to assess its particular circumstances and find its own path. National reformers will face different types of violence, different combinations of international and external stresses, different institutional challenges, different stakeholders who need to be involved to make a difference, and different transition opportunities. Throughout, this Report has covered some of the most important variations in country circumstances through a simple assessment (table

TABLE 8.1 *Situation-specific challenge and opportunities*

Types of violence: Civil, criminal, cross-border, subnational, and/or ideological	
Transition opportunity: Opportunities can be gradual and limited, or can present more immediate or major space for change.	**Key stakeholders:** Stakeholder balances include internal versus external stakeholders, state versus nonstate stakeholders, low-income versus middle-high-income stakeholders.
Key stresses: Situations pose different mixtures of internal versus external stresses; high versus low levels of division between ethnic, social, regional or religious identity groups.	**Institutional challenges:** Degrees and mixtures of capacity, accountability, and inclusion constraints in state and nonstate institutions affect strategy.

8.1). There are five factors to be considered in applying a tailored strategy—each, of course, tempered by political judgment.

First is the transition moment and opportunity for change. Some situations, because of political, economic, or security factors, offer greater space for change and a major break from the past—a peace agreement, a leadership or electoral succession, or even a crisis that spurs an opportunity for change. Other situations present more limited space for change—a sense of mounting problems that spurs debate, pressure for reform by groups outside government, or a new governmental reform plan. The type of strategy advocated needs to take account of this opening. Is this a moment to put forward a long-term transformational vision or to make incremental advances?

Second is the type of stress. In situations where the internal divisions between ethnic, religious, social, or geographical groups are a major factor in the mobilization for violence, strategies need components that address political, economic, or social inclusion. External stresses such as incursions from drug trafficking networks or global economic shocks clearly require working with regional or global partners.

Third is the type of violent threat. Successful approaches to address political, communal, or criminal violence have commonalities in the underlying institutional deficits that permit repeated cycles of violence—and common priorities to develop the institutions to provide citizen security, justice, and jobs. But the particular mix of different types of violence does make some difference. Capacity for formal investigations and prosecutions in the police and civilian justice institutions is more important, for example, in situations of organized criminal violence than in civil war or communal conflicts—although it is important in both. Ideologically motivated violence may require more emphasis on security, justice, and social inclusion, since this form of violence appears to be less motivated by employment or economic considerations.

Fourth is the type of institutional challenges. Where states have fairly strong capacity but inclusion is weak, reform actions need to draw marginalized groups into decision making and ensure they benefit from national growth, service delivery, and welfare improvements. Where lack of accountability has been a source of tension, strategies need to focus on responsiveness to citizens and to act against abuses. Where both capacity and accountability are weak, it makes sense to make greater use of state-community, state–civil society, state–private sector, and state-international mechanisms in delivering and monitoring early reform efforts.

Fifth is the set of stakeholders. National or subnational political and economic leaders and current combatants or ex-combatants—while not among the poorest groups—can be crucial stakeholders in achieving security and early results, and they may need to see benefits from initial reforms if they are to support them. Where neighboring countries, international donors, and investors affect the success of a reform, they need to be brought into the debates on strategy and the delivery of early results.

For deeper analysis of each country context, national leaders and their international partners need tools to assess risks, develop priorities, and formulate plans for action. National governments can often draw expertise from their own line ministries or political parties, as South Africa did in developing its reconstruction and development program in 1993 and 1994, or as Colombia did in reviewing the strengths and weaknesses of previous efforts to address violence in the early 2000s.[1]

Where external actors play critical roles, national leaders can initiate a joint national-international assessment with help from regional institutions, the United Nations (UN), international financial institutions, or bilateral partners, as in Liberia following the Comprehensive Peace Agreement of 2003 and in the post-crisis needs assessment in Pakistan in 2009–10. Many good international assessment tools exist for these purposes, such as the post-conflict/post-crisis needs assessments developed by the World Bank, UN, and European Commission. More formal national-international processes have the advantage of generating buy-in, as well as possible financial assistance, from international partners, though they may also set high expectations for immediate financial assistance that need careful management.

One key lesson on assessments and planning processes is that they have often been lengthy exercises that have difficulty in later adapting to new challenges. Recognizing the analysis of this Report on the repeated nature of violent threats and the succession of multiple transitions that countries go through to address them, lighter and more regular assessments of risks and opportunities make sense. Assessments can also be strengthened by

- considering where the society stands on the spectra of transition opportunities, stresses, institutional challenges, and stakeholders.
- explicitly considering the history of past efforts and the legacy of earlier episodes of violence.
- identifying both the early results needed for stakeholder confidence-building and the path toward long-term institutional transformation.
- keeping strategies simple, and being realistic about the number of priorities identified and the timelines, as with the changes recommended to the joint UN–World Bank–European Union (EU) post-crisis needs assessment.
- ensuring that political, security, and development actors at national and international levels have joint ownership of assessments and strategy exercises. Where assessments and plans are led by only one ministry, for example, other ministries may resist implementation. Equally, for strategies to bring to bear a range of diplomatic, security, and development assis tance from external partners, all need to be consulted in their preparation.

Practical approaches to confidence-building

Basic tools

When confronted with a rising crisis or transition opportunity, national reformers and their international partners have a variety of tools available for confidence-building and the development of "inclusive-enough" coalitions, based on lessons from a range of country experiences (table 8.2). Key stakeholder groups whose support has often been sought in coalition-building (in different combinations according to country circumstances) include the leaders and populations affected and targeted by violence; security actors, both governmental and nongovernmental, combatants; political leaders with influence, both in ruling and opposition parties; business, and civil society, whose support may be needed to undertake reforms; and neighbors and international partners. Including women leaders and women's groups has a good track record in creating continued pressure for change.

TABLE 8.2 *Core tools for restoring confidence*

Signals: Future policy and priorities	Signals: Immediate actions	Commitment mechanisms	Supporting actions
• Citizen security goals • Key principles and realistic timelines for addressing political reform, decentralization, corruption, basic justice services, and transitional justice • Utilize state, community, NGO, and international capacities	• Participatory processes • Local security, justice, and development results • Credible government appointments • Transparency of expenditures • Redeployment of security forces • Removal of discriminatory policies	• Independence of key executing agencies • Independent third-party monitoring • Dual-key systems • International execution of functions	• Risk and priority assessments • Communicating of costs of inaction • Simple plans and progress measures on 2–3 early results • Strategic communication

Source: WDR team.
Note: NGO = nongovernmental organization.

To build national and local-level support, political and policy signals that demonstrate a break with the past are important. Signals that help to build political support among stakeholder groups are particularly effective when they are based on immediate actions rather than only on announcements of intent.

Signaling through immediate action can include credible government appointments (national and local) who can command the confidence of stakeholder groups. Redeployment of security forces can restore confidence by signaling an increase in civilian protection—as when Colombia redeployed military contingents to protect civilian road transit in 2002–03.[2] Similar effects can be achieved by removing units that have a history of abuse or mistrust with communities. In some cases, the quick removal of legal regimes seen as discriminatory or abusive—apartheid laws, collective punishments, government restrictions on hiring from specific identity groups—can help restore confidence. Transparency in budgets and expenditures can be an important signal of improved governance, as with Timor-Leste's public budget debates and reporting systems to parliament after the renewed violence and instability of 2006–07.[3] Most successful signals require a mix of security, political, and economic content—with credible resource allocations and transparency measures, for example, backing up political and security plans.

Some options for signaling a break with the past will necessarily constitute announcements of future action rather than immediate action. For example, clear signals on approaches and timelines for political- and security-sector reform, decentralization, and transitional justice have often been part of confidence-building—drawing lessons, however, on the generational timelines often required to complete the comprehensive institutional reforms described in chapter 3.

Signals on political reform may include rapid action toward elections or laying out of a series of preparatory steps—as with the transitional executive bodies and constitutional reform processes in South Africa, supported by civic education and national and local action to maintain security during the political process through the National Peace Accords. Where elections will take place quickly, indicating that these are not an end but a step toward transformation of institutions and democratic practices (as described in the inputs by Lakhdar Brahimi and Nitin Desai in chapter 5, box 5.11), is important. Particular attention is also merited on local participatory processes—such as a commitment to involve violence-affected communities in identifying priorities and delivering programs in their areas.[4]

To generate support of stakeholders in low-trust environments, special commitment mechanisms to persuade key political and economic stakeholder groups and citizens that announcements will be carried through have proved useful. These include the creation of special independent agencies to implement programs, as with Indonesia's reconstruction agency in Aceh,[5] and independent third-party monitoring of commitments. Third parties can be national—as with independent agencies or local civil society monitoring—or involve joint national and international cooperation, as with the Governance and Economic Management Action Plan in Liberia[6] and the Commission against Impunity in Guatemala.[7] They also can simply be international and provide either monitoring or direct execution for a transitional period, as with United Nations or regional peacekeeping missions' electoral monitoring, or the ASEAN-European Union Aceh Monitoring Mission, which supported implementation of the Aceh peace agreement.[8]

Several supporting actions can help in confidence-building and in persuading stakeholders whose support is sought of the benefits of collaboration. In some situations, there may be great unwillingness in the national discourse to recognize the potential for an escalation of violence and the depth of challenges. Where the risks of crisis escalation are not fully recognized by all national leadership, providing an accurate and compelling message on the consequences of inaction can help galvanize momentum for progress.[9] For example, technical analysis can be produced on the costs of violence and the benefits of restored security—as for the regional benefits of peace in Afghanistan and for the costs of crime to business in several countries.[10] Economic and social analyses can also show how rising violence and failing institutions are causing national or subnational areas to lag far behind their neighbors in development progress, or how other countries that have failed to address rising threats have faced severe and long-lasting development consequences.

This Report's analysis also provides some clear messages from global experience to underpin efforts to persuade stakeholders of the urgency of action:

- No country or region can afford to ignore areas where repeated cycles of violence flourish or citizens are disengaged from the state.
- Unemployment, corruption, and exclusion increase the risks of violence—and legitimate institutions and governance that give everyone a stake in national prosperity are the immune system that protects from different types of violence.
- Citizen security is a preeminent goal, underpinned by justice and jobs.
- Leaders need to seize opportunities before violence escalates or recurs.

Strategic communication on the need for change and for a positive vision for the future is crucial—no one can be persuaded to support new initiatives if they do not know they exist, or if their intent and content have been distorted in reporting. Common lessons on strategic communications include ensuring that different parts of government communicate consistently on the vision for change and specific plans; fostering supportive messages from civil society and international partners; and directing communications to assuage concerns while avoiding promises that cannot be kept. Traditional consultation mechanisms and new technologies also offer the potential to mobilize broader citizen input into debates, as with the use of traditional community meetings in West Africa[11] or youth activists using social networking tools to mobilize popular support and oppose violent actions by the FARC (Revolutionary Armed Forces of Colombia) in Colombia.[12]

It helps to produce clear plans and budgets that identify early results as well as the approach toward longer-term institution-building early on, informed by a sense of realism in timelines and availability of resources. The key lesson from country experiences is that it is not necessary to generate early results in every area. Two or three early results are sufficient in each period of confidence-building. Once the pursuit of these results is properly resourced and achieved, other available capacities (leadership and managerial, technical, and financial) can be targeted at institutional transformation. Of course, results have to be repeated at regular intervals and help rather than hinder longer-term institution-building.[13]

Early results can take the form of progress on political and justice, security, or development outcomes and often involve successful combinations of all three. In South Africa, transitional mechanisms that ensured broad participation in political, security, and economic decision-making during the transition played a key role. In Kosovo, highway security was a crucial early result to support increased trade, and hence employment.[14] In Liberia, basic improvements in security, electricity, and action against corruption were crucial in restoring confidence.[15] In Afghanistan[16] and in the Democratic Republic of Congo,[17] reopening key transit routes for imports and exports through linked security and development efforts increased supplies in the capitals and lowered producer prices. In Chile and Argentina, responsible macroeconomic management, social protection, and initiation of transitional justice measures helped restore confidence following transitions from military rule.

The choice of early results and how they are delivered is important because it sets incentives for later institution-building. For example, if services and public works are delivered only through national, top-down programs and social protection only through international humanitarian aid, communities have few incentives to take responsibility for violence prevention; neither do national institutions have incentives to take on the responsibility for protecting all vulnerable citizens. Using partnerships in delivering early results with civil society, communities, faith-based organizations or the private sector has two benefits: it expands the range of capacity available to states, and it creates a sense of broader stakeholder and citizen engagement in crisis prevention and recovery. For these reasons, short-term confidence-building and longer-term efforts to transform institutions need to be linked.

Differentiating confidence-building tools to match country circumstances

The particular mix of transition opportunities, stresses, stakeholders, and institutional challenges makes a difference in selecting types of confidence-building approaches. Where political power is contested and opposition groups have the potential to derail progress, developing collaborative capacities among political parties is crucial. Where political leadership is uncontested, more focused approaches to building coalitions between the ruling party and key stakeholders whose support is needed, such as subnational leaders, civil society, the military, and business interests, can be inclusive-enough to create momentum for change. Where the engagement of external partners—investors, donors, diplomatic partners, neighboring countries—can provide additional support or help manage external stresses, signals that build their confidence become more important. (Box 8.1 contrasts the experiences of Colombia and South Africa in initial confidence-building and constructing of inclusive-enough coalitions.)

Two trade-offs to be decided within each country context with regard to using inclusion strategies to build confidence are inclusion versus justice for perpetrators of past abuses and inclusion versus efficiency. With regard to inclusiveness and justice for groups, country experiences indicate that groups may be legitimately excluded from political dialogue where there is an evolving belief among the population that they have sacrificed their right to participate due to past abuses, as the FARC were excluded from political talks in Colombia. But that exclusion can pose dangers when it is driven by international opposition to engagement by groups that have

BOX 8.1 *Confidence-building in South Africa, 1990–94, and Colombia, 2002 onward*

Types of violence: Both countries had faced long-standing civil conflict and high levels of criminal violence.	
Transition opportunity: South Africa faced a more fundamental transition in the run-up 1994 election and the end of apartheid. Before its 2002 election, Colombia faced a sense of rising crisis due to failed peace talks and growing violence, but initially had less space for major institutional change.	**Key stakeholders:** In South Africa, key stakeholders for the two main protagonists, the ruling National Party (NP) and the African National Congress (ANC), were their own members and allied constituencies, Inkatha and other smaller parties, security forces, domestic and international businesses, and neighboring states. In Colombia, before and during the presidential election, key stakeholders in setting a new direction were the ruling party, businesses, the military, and some civil society groups.
Key stresses: South Africa's stresses were primarily internal: huge inequities between black and white citizens; ethnic tensions; high unemployment. Colombia faced high internal social inequity, but also external stresses from organized crime networks.	**Institutional challenges:** Both countries had relatively high capacity, but low accountability in state institutions, as well as low social cohesion.

South Africa

In South Africa, inclusive-enough coalition-building in the run-up to the 1994 election meant involving all political parties and civil society in discussions over the country's future, although the ANC maintained a hierarchy in which it led decision making among other ANC Alliance and United Democratic Front members. In Colombia, an inclusive-enough coalition to implement the new government's Democratic Security Policy did not include all parties: FARC rebels were automatically excluded since they were not recognized by the Colombian government as a political organization. The ruling party instead galvanized support from the military; most business organizations; and some civil society groups, who were also instrumental in leading popular protests demanding action on security; as well as community leaders in violence-affected areas. Business groups were important in supporting the new government's wealth tax, which provided an important source of finance for the Democratic Security Policy.

In both countries, the main protagonists sent signals to demonstrate a break with the past. In South Africa, this involved a move within the ANC to adopt an inclusive approach to other parties and interests and a move by the National Party from discourse over group rights to discourse over individual rights—immediate actions such as the ANC's unilateral suspension of armed struggle and the National Party's decision to release Nelson Mandela and unban the ANC, Communist Party, Pan Africanist Congress (PAC), and Azanian People's Organisation (AZAPO); and announcements on future policy, such as the creation of provincial governments to provide opportunities for power for the smaller parties, job security for white civil servants, and free maternal and child health care for the broader population.

Colombia

In Colombia, the use of the word "democratic" in describing security approaches was intended to show that future policy would not involve the human rights abuses that had been common in the past in Colombia and other Latin American countries. Redeployment of military forces to protect civilian road transit and budget increases to the military were designed to foster business, military, and popular support. In South Africa, however, announcements about future policy went much further than Colombia in the commitments of the Reconstruction and Development Program to social and institutional transformation, reflecting the political background of the ANC Alliance as well as the greater space for change at the time of the transition. In both countries, the degree to which these initial signals have been maintained in the longer term is still a subject of debate, but they were undoubtedly important in mobilizing support.

Leaders in each country used different types of commitment mechanisms to provide guarantees that policy announcements would not be reversed: broad mechanisms for transitional decision making, constitutional and legal change, and electoral monitoring in South Africa, reflecting more inclusive coalition-building; and narrower mechanisms in Colombia to ensure cooperation between the military and civilian agencies, such as the creation of a new coordination framework, Centro de Coordinación de Acción Integral (CCAI), reporting to the President.

Sources: South Africa: WDR consultation with former key negotiators from the ANC Alliance and the National Party in South Africa, 2010; Eades 1999; Piron and Curran 2005; Roque and others 2010. Colombia: Arboleda 2010; Guerrero 1999; Centro de Coordinación de Acción Integral 2010; WDR team consultations with government officials, civil society representatives, and security personnel in Colombia, 2010; WDR interview with former president Álvaro Uribe, 2010.

strong local support. Transitional justice processes can and often should form part of a dialogue on new directions, but inclusion strategies can change over time as it becomes possible to marginalize consistently abusive groups, as with the Revolutionary United Front (RUF) in Sierra Leone.[18]

With regard to the trade-off between inclusion and efficiency, the main question is how far to go. Exclusion of groups or regions from core coalitions has the risk of fostering resentment and generating pent-up pressure for later rounds of contestation and violence. But including everyone risks stretching collaborative decision-making capacity too far. This tension often takes specific form for political leaders in broadening appointments to power through the creation of new senior posts and expanded participation in decision making, when these actions may also slow the delivery of results. For national policy, political parties and governments have been clear that there is a hierarchy of decision making—with many present at the table presenting views and engaged in action to implement strategy, but with one body taking final decisions. For local participatory decision making, the mere fact of engaging communities is often seen as a positive signal, which merits taking the time necessary to gain local buy-in.

Program approaches to link early results to transforming institutions

Basic tools

The way programs are designed must vary according to country circumstances, but experience suggests a core set of basic program tools, delivered at scale either nationally or subnationally, that can be adapted to different country contexts—from low to high income and with different mixes of criminal and political violence (table 8.3). These are programs based on the concept of building a rhythm of repeated successes, linking regular early results for confidence-building with longer-term institutional transformation. They are deliberately kept small in number to reflect country lessons on the priority areas of citizen security, justice, and jobs. These basic program tools are designed to be delivered in combination. Action on security alone has not had a good track record in delivering long-term results on the ground. Nor are economic programs sufficient on their own to address problems of violence. Five common insights for program design can link rapid confidence-building to longer-term institutional transformation.

Insight 1: **Multisectoral community empowerment programs are important to build state-society relations from the bottom up, as well as to deliver development improvements.** Top-down programming through the state can help build technical capacity, but may be misaligned with the process of forging and reforging trust in state institutions and in state-society relations. Bottom-up program design works with community structures to identify and deliver priorities for violence prevention. The clearest signal is to entrust community structures with their own funds to identify and deliver local activities, as with the Afghanistan National Solidarity Program. A second model, which can be combined with community block grants, is for state agencies and NGOs working in concert to consult with community councils on their activities. Examples are the Latin American multisectoral violence prevention programs, which combine community policing with access to local justice and dispute resolution services, creating a safe physical environment (such as public trading spaces, transit); employment and vocational training; civic education; and social and cultural activities. Activities that "recognize" community membership can be an important part of this, through programs as simple as registering births and life events.

Insight 2: **Prioritization of basic security and justice reform programs has been part of the core tools countries use to develop resilience to violence.** Community-based

TABLE 8.3 *Core tools for transforming institutions*

Citizen security	Justice	Jobs and associated services
Foundational reforms and "best-fit" approaches		
Security sector reform: • Designed to deliver citizen security benefits • Capacity increases linked to repeated realistic performance outcomes and justice functions • Dismantling of criminal networks through civilian oversight, vetting, and budget expenditure transparency • Use of low-capital systems for rural and community policing	**Justice sector reform:** • Independence and links to security reforms • Strengthening of basic caseload processing • Extending of justice services, drawing on traditional/community mechanisms **Phasing anti-corruption measures:** • Demonstration that national resources can be used for public good before dismantling rent systems • Control of capture of rents • Use of social accountability mechanisms	**Multisectoral community empowerment programs:** Combining citizen security, employment, justice, education, and infrastructure. **Employment programs:** • Regulatory simplification and infrastructure recovery for private sector job creation • Long-term public programs • Asset expansion • Value-chain programs • Informal sector support • Labor migration • Women's economic empowerment **Humanitarian delivery and social protection:** With planned transition from international provision **Macroeconomic policy:** Focus on consumer price volatility and employment
Gradual, systematic programs		
• Phased capacity and accountability in specialized security functions	• Political and electoral reform • Decentralization • Transitional justice • Comprehensive anti-corruption reforms	• Structural economic reforms such as privatization • Education and health reforms • Inclusion of marginalized groups

Source: WDR team.

programs are important, but they cannot on their own deliver wider institutional change. The lessons from security and justice reform programs are to focus on basic functions that build trust and performance, such as the following:

- Crucial early actions can include strengthening of civilian oversight of the security forces alongside capacity increases; criminal caseload processing in the courts; adequate basic investigation and arrest procedures in policing; and vetting of budget and expenditure transparency to dismantle covert or criminal networks across the security and criminal justice functions. Budget and expenditure analysis and strengthening of public finance processes in these areas form a part of early reforms. In some situations, tolerating an oversize security wage bill (as in South Africa's early reforms) is necessary until opportunities exist to reintegrate former security force members into civilian life. Country experiences that can provide insights include Argentina, Bosnia and Herzegovina, Chile, El Salvador, Indonesia, Mozambique, Nicaragua, and Sierra Leone.
- Linking security and justice reform is important. One of the most common weaknesses in country experiences has been increasing actions to reform security systems without complementary action to reform justice systems. This causes several problems. First, increases in arrests by the security forces not processed by the courts result in either grievances over prolonged detention without due process or the release of offenders back into the community, as in the relatively successful police reforms in Haiti in the 1990s and the 2000s.[19] Second, where civilian justice systems are absent in insecure areas, the mili-

tary and police will end up performing justice and correction functions beyond their mandate and capacity—and perhaps result in abuses.

- Security and justice reforms should go beyond paper reforms, and reach into local communities. Extending access to the formal justice system in underserved areas can help, as with mobile courts. The capacity of formal justice systems to deal with local dispute resolution is often limited, however. Blending of formal and informal systems, such as Timor-Leste's incorporating traditional justice measures into the formal system;[20] community paralegals; and the use of nongovernmental organization (NGO) capacity to support access to justice for the poor, as in Nicaragua and Sierra Leone, can help bridge this divide.[21]

Insight 3: **Shifting back to basics on job creation goes beyond material benefits by providing a productive role and occupation for youth.** There is still debate over what works in generating jobs and widening economic stakes in prosperity—not only in fragile areas but worldwide in the wake of the global financial crisis. Because there is no consensus on the exact set of policies that can generate employment—and even less so in environments where insecurity is a constraint to trade and investment—program design needs to draw from what is known about pragmatic interventions that have worked. The lessons here, drawing from the experiences in chapter 5, include the following:

- The role of jobs in violence prevention argues for judicious public financing of employment programs, as in India or Indonesia. To ensure that these are compatible with long-term job creation and strengthening of social cohesion, it makes sense to deliver employment programs through community institutions, ensure that wages are set to avoid distorting private sector activities and programs, keep the design simple to match administrative capacity, and complement programs with vocational training and life skills.[22]
- Easing the infrastructure constraints to private sector activity is important for early results and longer-term labor-intensive growth. Trade and transit infrastructure such as roads and ports can be crucial for private sector activity, but the number one constraint cited by businesses in World Bank enterprise surveys in violent areas is electricity.[23] Approaches to restitute electricity capacity may involve programs that are fast, even while these are technically suboptimal in the early period, as in the experience of Lebanon and Liberia after the civil war.[24]
- Regulatory simplification, as in Bosnia and Herzegovina's removal of the bureaucratic constraints to business activity, can gain business confidence.[25] Simplification, rather than the addition of complexity in business regulation, is crucial to demonstrating fast results and adapting to institutional capacity constraints.
- Investment in the value chain for labor-intensive sectors—bringing together producers, traders, and consumers—can support job creation and address links between different regional, social, or ethnic groups affected by violence, as in Rwanda's investments in coffee and Kosovo's in dairy.[26]
- Agriculture and informal sector jobs are often viewed as second best in relation to the formal sector—but they often offer the only realistic prospect for large-scale job creation. Support can include access to finance and training, sympathetic regulation, and basic market and transit infrastructure.
- Asset expansion programs have helped in some successful transitions from violence—such as land reform in the Republic of Korea and Japan and housing programs in Singapore.[27] But they require the political capital to succeed in redistribution (in the Republic of Korea and Japan

the power of landowning classes had been considerably weakened) as well as considerable public resources, access to private finance, and institutional capacity. Smaller programs that provide transfers to victims of violence, such as Timor-Leste's transfers to displaced people, provide a simpler model of asset expansion.[28]

- Labor migration agreements also provide an example of best-fit policies in some circumstances: all countries would prefer to generate jobs at home, but where massive youth unemployment exists, managed migration agreements that inform and protect workers are a good "best-fit" alternative.[29]

Insight 4: **Involving women in security, justice, and economic empowerment programs can deliver results and support longer-term institutional change.** While the pacing of involvement of women in reforms will vary by local context, experience across regions and forms of violence shows the value of accelerating the involvement of women. Given the large number of female-headed households in violence-affected communities, women often engage in economic activities out of necessity. Targeting women's economic empowerment can be a core part of job creation programs, as in Nepal,[30] and may have more lasting effects on women's status than national gender action plans. Reforms to increase female staffing and gender-specific services in the security forces and justice systems, as in Nicaragua, Liberia, and Sierra Leone, and a number of high-income police forces facing urban violence have delivered good results.[31] Involving women leaders in decision making in community-driven programs can also shift attitudes toward gender—but as the Afghanistan example in chapter 5 shows, this takes time.

Insight 5: **Focused anti-corruption initiatives demonstrating that new programs can be well governed are crucial for credibility.** This does not mean addressing all corruption at once—it is as impossible for developing countries with high levels of corruption to eliminate it overnight, as it was for OECD (Organisation for Economic Co-operation and Development) societies to do so at earlier stages of their development. Moreover, deep-rooted patronage systems are a way of holding together potentially violent situations, however imperfect, so dismantling them before other, more transparent institutions are embedded to take their place can increase risk. However, high levels of corruption increase the risks of violence, making action on corruption important. Two main mechanisms emerge as realistic early measures to improve controls over corruption in highly fragile situations:

- The first is to prevent serious corruption in major new concessions and contracts, including those for natural resources, by making processes more transparent and drawing on private sector audit and inspection capacity.
- The second is to use social accountability mechanisms to monitor the use of funds—making budgets transparent and using community and civil society capacity to monitor them, as with the use of local budget transparency in community-driven programs.

Managing trade-offs: Toward more systematic reform

The key trade-off in best-fit approaches that link rapid confidence-building with longer-term institutional transformation is balancing their positive effects with their possible negative and distortionary effects. An oversized security sector draws resources away from other productive activities. Services provided by nongovernment groups or the private sector can be costly. Publicly funded employment, if badly designed, can draw people away from private sector work.

Where best-fit approaches can have some costs that will exceed benefits once security, state institutional capacity, and competitive markets return to normal, it helps to design a clear but flexible exit strategy. This can involve the move from nongovernment to state systems, or from informal to formal systems.

Next, mitigate the negative consequences. For example, labor migration agreements can be accompanied by information and protection for workers. And public action to support employment can be designed to avoid pressure on private sector recruitment by keeping wages at self-selecting levels and using controls on incremental job creation by employers.

Similar lessons apply to systematic but more gradual reform (see table 8.3). Marking these areas as "systematic and gradual" does not mean they are unimportant—they have played a big role in successful transitions, from devolution in Northern Ireland to transitional justice and education reform in South Africa and Germany.[32] What they have in common, however, is that they involve a complex web of institutions and social norms. So, in most situations, systematic and gradual action appears to work best.

Monitoring results

National reformers and their international partners in-country need efficient ways to monitor results from these programs, both to demonstrate successes and to create a feedback loop on areas that are lagging. The Millennium Development Goals (MDGs) have been crucial for shifting attention to poverty and social issues, and remain important long-term goals even in the most fragile situations. But they move too slowly to act as a feedback loop for policy-makers—and they do not focus on citizen security, justice, or jobs.

Table 8.4 shows sample indicators for measuring early results of programmatic interventions. These outcome-oriented measures will vary by country context, but could include, for example, freedom of movement along transit routes, electricity coverage, number of businesses registered, and employment days created. These will not, however, provide a more systematic picture of risk and progress. Useful complementary indicators would cover the areas most directly related to citizen security, justice, and jobs over the short and longer terms—actual levels of insecurity; employment; access to justice; and differences in welfare and perceived welfare between ethnic, religious, geographical, and social groups, as shown in table 8.4. They would also cover developments in trust, state society relations, and institutional legitimacy. Governance indicators take time to shift—a useful short-term measure is polling citizen perceptions of institutions, as Haiti did to measure early shifts in the performance of its police.[33] Such polling data are a regular part of government policy information in high-income and many middle-income countries, but much less so in the lowest income fragile states, where, arguably, they would be of most use to policy-makers.

As with the discussion of early results, it is important that progress indicators set the right incentives for later institution-building. For example, if security forces have targets set based on the number of rebel combatants killed or captured or criminals arrested, they may rely primarily on coercive approaches, and there would be no incentive to build longer-term trust with communities. Targets based on citizen security (freedom of movement and so on), by contrast, create longer-term incentives for the role of the security forces in underpinning effective state-society relations. Similarly, if progress on security, justice, and jobs is monitored only through indicators of access, there are fewer incentives for state institutions to work with communities in violence prevention and pay attention to citizen confidence that institutions are responsive to their needs. A mix of indicators that measure citizen perceptions and security, justice, and employment outcomes to monitor progress can help address both areas.

Fitting program design to context

The idea of best-fit approaches has been used throughout the WDR: rather than copying programs that have been used elsewhere, adapting their design to local context can ensure that they will deliver results within local political dynamics. For example, while

TABLE 8.4 *Feasible indicators for results measurement*

Indicators	Citizen security	Justice	Jobs and associated services
Sample program indicators: Outcome-oriented results *(sample associated program in parentheses)*	• Freedom of movement along transit routes (redeployment of security forces, focus on citizen security) • Decline in crime rate statistics	• Number of additional people with access to justice services (e.g., mobile courts, community paralegals, traditional justice systems) • Number of cases prosecuted/backlog (processing of judicial caseloads) • Transparency of decision making and meeting of targets (publication of budgets, expenditures, and audits)	• Coverage and representation in state and community decision-making mechanisms (multisectoral community programs) • Number of employment days and small infrastructure or income-generating projects produced (employment programs) • Number of businesses registered and operating, including large, labor-intensive businesses resuming operations in insecure areas (security, regulatory simplification, infrastructure bottlenecks) • Percentage of vulnerable groups reached with services and transfers through national institutions (community social protection, humanitarian aid, vaccination) • Electricity coverage/number of hours of blackouts • Reduction in level/volatility of consumer prices (macropolicy and/or infrastructure bottlenecks)
Short-term systematic monitoring of confidence in institutions	• Number of violent deaths • Perception survey data on trends in security and trust in security forces	• Perception surveys by groups (ethnic, geographical, religious, class) regarding whether their welfare is increasing over time and in relation to others • Perception survey data regarding trust in national institutions, justice sector; and on corruption, nationally and by region and group	• Perceptions of whether employment opportunities are increasing • Business confidence surveys
Long-term systematic monitoring of institutional transformation	• Victim surveys	• Household survey data on vertical and horizontal inequalities and access to justice services • Governance indicators refocused on degree of progress within historically realistic time frames	• Household data on employment and labor force participation

Source: WDR team.

multisectoral community approaches can be effective in contexts as different as Côte d'Ivoire, Guatemala, and Northern Ireland, specific stresses in Côte d'Ivoire and Northern Ireland linked to geographical or religious divides makes it imperative for program designs to ensure that activities are seen not as targeted to one ethnic or religious group and instead build bonds between groups. Box 8.2 shows how the core tool of multisectoral state-community programs has been adapted to different contexts.

Different types of stresses and institutional challenges make a difference. Box 8.3 shows an example of anti-corruption approaches in Liberia and Mozambique, which both drew on nongovernmental capacities to monitor key functions. In Liberia, a history of funds corrupted from natural resource extraction sources, as well as concern over the risk of diversion of public funds following the Comprehensive Peace Agreement in 2003, argued for the use of intensive state–private sector and state-international partnerships to prevent a recurrence of corruption-fueled violence. In Mozambique, corruption had been less of a divisive issue during the conflict, but increases in trade linked to reconstruction programs created new risks, for example, in customs functions.

BOX 8.2 *Adapting community-level program design to country context: Afghanistan, Burundi, Cambodia, Colombia, Indonesia, Nepal, and Rwanda*

The basic elements of community-based programs for violence prevention and recovery are simple and can be adapted to a broad range of country contexts. All community programs under state auspices consist, essentially, of a community decision-making mechanism to decide on priorities and the provision of funds and technical help to implement them. Within this model there is a great deal of variance that can be adapted to different types of stresses and institutional capacities, as well as to different opportunities for transition. Three important sources of variance are in how community decision-making is done, who controls the funds, and where programs sit within government.

Different stresses and institutional capacities and accountability affect community decision-making. In many violent areas, preexisting community councils are either destroyed or were already discredited. A critical first step is to reestablish credible participatory forms of representation. In Burundi, for example, a local NGO organized elections for representative community development committees in the participating communes that cut across ethnic divides. Similarly, Afghanistan's National Solidarity Program began with village-wide elections for a community development council. But Indonesia's programs for the conflict-affected areas of Aceh, Kalimantan, Maluku, and Sulawesi did not include holding new community elections. Community councils were largely intact, and national laws already provided for local, democratic village elections. Indonesia also experimented with separating grants to Muslim and Christian villages to minimize intercommunal tensions, but eventually used common funds and councils to bridge divides between these communities.

Different institutional challenges also affect who manages the funds. Programs must weigh the trade-offs between a first objective of building trust with the risks of money going missing and the elite capture of resources. Different approaches to program design to fit context include the following:

- In Indonesia, where local capacity was fairly strong, subdistrict councils established financial management units that are routinely audited but have full responsibility for all aspects of financial performance.
- In Burundi, lack of progress in overall decentralization and difficulties in monitoring funds through community structures meant that responsibility for managing the funds remained with the NGO partners. In Rwanda, by contrast, greater space for change after the genocide meant the councils could from the start be integrated into the government's decentralization plans.
- In Afghanistan's National Solidarity Program, NGOs also took on the initial responsibility for managing the funds while councils were trained in bookkeeping, but within a year, block grants were being transferred directly to the councils.
- In Colombia, where the primary institutional challenges were to bring the state closer to communities and overcome distrust between security and civilian government agencies, funds are held by individual government ministries, but approvals for activities are made by multisectoral teams in consultation with communities.
- In Nepal, community programs show the full range of design options, with some programs giving primary responsibility for fund oversight to partner NGOs, to their large-scale village school program, where community school committees are the legal owners of school facilities and can use government funds to hire and train their staff.
- In Cambodia's Seila program, councils were launched under UNDP (United Nations Development Programme) auspices and then moved into the government's newly formed commune structure.

The type of transition moment and governance environment also affects how community decision-making structures align with the formal government administration. Many countries emerging from conflict will also be undergoing major constitutional and administrative reforms, just as the early-response community programs are being launched. There may be tensions between national and local governance and power-holders at the center and the community. In Afghanistan, where center-periphery issues are a key driver of conflict, and where warlords are a continuing threat to stability, community-driven development (CDD) programs must be sensitive to national-local dynamics. Afghanistan's Community Development Councils, though constituted under a 2007 vice presidential bylaw, are still under review for formal integration into the national administrative structure.

In other settings of either prolonged crisis or in authoritarian systems, CDD programs can be designed to sustain human capital and offer an avenue for local-level debate in the absence of national-level progress. CDD programs designed in environments with more limited space for change may rely more heavily on nongovernmental delivery of services, employing local workers for skill building and focusing on "neutral," nonpolitical issues in community debates.

Source: Guggenheim 2011.

BOX 8.3 *Anti-corruption approaches in Liberia and Mozambique*

Types of violence: Both countries had faced long-standing civil war.	
Transition opportunity: Both countries went through major transitions: peace agreements followed by electoral transitions.	**Key stakeholders:** Government, opposition parties, civil society, and donors were important stakeholders relating to corruption issues in both countries: regional institutions played a higher-stake role in Liberia than in Mozambique on corruption-related issues.
Key stresses: Corruption under the transitional government in Liberia between 2002 and 2004 reached extremely high proportions, threatening progress in the peace agreement by denuding the country's large natural resources and potentially financing renewed electoral violence. Increasing trade in Mozambique created the potential for increased customs revenue—but also increased vulnerability to corruption. High unemployment and a legacy of regional and ethnic tensions were issues in both countries—with a commensurate need to attract investors and donor funds to supplement public finances.	**Institutional challenges:** Both countries had low-capacity state institutions and low state revenues, with accountability problems greater in Liberia than in Mozambique.

Both countries outsourced some key functions to the private sector and undertook additional monitoring to guard against corruption and increase revenues. The functions chosen and the nature of external monitoring were different, however. Liberia focused on forestry inspections and natural resource concessions, reflecting the role of natural resource revenues in financing violence, while Mozambique focused on customs as a source of additional revenue that was vulnerable to corruption.

Liberia undertook, through the Governance and Economic Management Assistance Program, "dual key" oversight by regional and international experts of major contracts and concessions. The African Union and ECOWAS (Economic Community of West African States) were instrumental in reaching agreement on this arrangement, along with the international financial institutions, the UN, the United States, and the European Union, in recognition of the potential regional spillover effects of rising corruption. In its initial stages, this arrangement focused more on accountability than capacity transfer, reflecting the severe nature of corruption challenges at the time. More recently, the program has emphasized capacity transfer more strongly. Following the elections, the new government also contracted a private inspection company to build and operate a system to track all timber from the point of harvest through transport to sale. The system ensures the government collects all revenue because it will not issue an export permit until the Central Bank confirms that all taxes have been paid. In Mozambique, the government contracted a private company to run customs inspection functions and collect customs revenues. Both strategies delivered results, with domestic revenues rising and increased donor funds.

Sources: Giovine and others 2010; Dwan and Bailey 2006; Jahr 2010; Government of the Republic of Liberia Executive Mansion 2009; Hubbard 2005; Mosse 2007; De Wulf and Sokol 2004; Crown Agents 2007.

External factors: Reducing external stresses and mobilizing external support

Societies do not have the luxury of transforming their institutions in isolation—they need at the same time to mobilize external support for change and to manage external pressures, whether from economic shocks or from trafficking and international corruption. Many of these constraints on external assistance and the management of external stresses are beyond the control of each nation-state to address. Chapter 9 considers possible directions for international policy in these issues. National leaders and their international partners at a country level can, however, help to mobilize external support and galvanize cooperation programs to address shared stresses with external partners.

Factoring in external stresses

National development strategies rarely involve an assessment of potential external stresses or collaborative action with others to address them—yet action on external stresses may be key to effective violence prevention. Regular assessment of risks and opportunities, as described earlier should also include considering and planning for possible external stresses. One example is the potential security impacts of economic stresses, such as volatile food prices. Another is increased insecurity of neighbors—how to mitigate, for example, the economic spillover of Somalia piracy on the neighboring economies and fishing industries.[34] Still others include, ironically, considering the impact of a successful action against trafficking or rebel groups on neighboring countries—for example, whether these actions will push insecurity over borders, as Colombia's dismantling of drug cartels did for Central America and Mexico.

Actions to address external stresses can be taken in security, justice, and developmental areas (table 8.5). Some of the actions to address potential external stresses and opportunities fall in the purely diplomatic and security sphere. (This Report does not attempt to address these in detail, but it is clear that they can be crucial for confidence-building with external stakeholders.) Border cooperation, redeployment of troops to signal non-interference or engagement in shared security approaches, or simple diplomatic signals, such as the visit of Sheikh Sharif of Somalia to the Government of Ethiopia in March 2010 immediately after his nomination as president or Timor-Leste's outreach to the Government of Indonesia, can all form an important part of the basic tools for restoration of confidence.

Cross-border programs to link security and development approaches can be initiated by national governments. An openness to discussing both security and development cooperation across insecure border regions, based on shared goals of citizen security, justice, and jobs, has the potential to deliver results. Cooperation between China's southeastern provinces and neighboring ASEAN states under the Greater Mekong Subregion initiative, while still with potential for expansion, has addressed some of these issues.[35] EU member states have a range of models to address cross-border cooperation: while some may be appropriate only for advanced economic and institutional environments, many involve subregions that were historically underdeveloped and driven by conflict, either after World War II or more recently after the Balkan War.[36] Lessons from cross-border cooperation in Europe appear to include the need to start with economic and social issues (including pooled administrative capacity in universities), as well as shared actions on border security and trafficking—while avoiding actions that can cause political or cultural tensions, particularly those involving ethnic groups residing across borders.

A promising form of bilateral cooperation to address external stresses further afield is to address the complex web of corruption

TABLE 8.5 *Core tools—National action to address external stresses*

Citizen security	Justice	Jobs and associated services
• Border cooperation • Military, police, and financial intelligence	• Coordination of supply and demand-side responses • Joint investigations and prosecutions across jurisdictions • Building of links between formal and informal systems	• Pooled supplementary administrative capacity • Cross-border development programming • Social protection to mitigate global economic stresses

BOX 8.4 *Bilateral cooperation against corruption and money laundering in Haiti and Nigeria*

Key stresses: In both countries, corruption with international money-laundering links has undermined the capacity of national institutions to combat violence.
Key stakeholders: Government, opposition parties, civil society, and donors were important stakeholders relating to corruption issues in Haiti, with the Unites States playing a particularly important role. Donors were less important in Nigeria, but civil society was much stronger than in Haiti.
Institutional challenges: Political obstacles to prosecuting grand corruption were high in both countries. Capacity in the criminal justice system to prosecute complex corruption cases was present in Nigeria but absent in Haiti.

Both countries developed links with the law enforcement institutions of other nations. Haiti's government drew on capacity from the United States not only during the investigative phase but in the prosecution as well. In Nigeria, by contrast, local officials mainly drew on the investigative capacity of the United Kingdom to gather evidence to be used for convictions in Nigerian courts.

Since former Haitian President Jean-Bertrand Aristide fled into exile in 2004, successive Haitian governments have sought to recoup funds lost from a corrupt agreement with American telecommunications companies. According to the government, Haiti Teleco, Haiti's state-owned telecom firm, had provided services at cut-rate prices to American providers in return for kickbacks to senior government officials and key Teleco staff. The case involved a complex scheme of favorable tariffs with kickbacks channeled through an intermediary's offshore bank account. Proving it in a Haitian court would have been a challenge, given the absence of police and prosecutors with experience handling cases of sophisticated financial crime, and once the earthquake hit in January 2010 it would have been nigh impossible. In December 2009, the U.S. Department of Justice charged two former employees of Teleco who allegedly received kickbacks with money laundering offenses. In June 2010, one of the two was convicted and sentenced to four years in prison and ordered to pay US$1.8 million in restitution to the government of Haiti and forfeit another US$1.6 million. The second employee awaits trial.

In Nigeria, the Economic and Financial Crimes Commission (EFCC) worked closely with the U.K. Crown Prosecution Service and Scotland Yard to develop evidence against the corrupt governors of three Nigerian states. The EFCC alerted British authorities to the possibility that the governors were hiding the proceeds of corruption in London banks or real estate investments. In one of the cases, the governor was prosecuted in the U.K. for money laundering; in the others, the evidence was used to prosecute them in Nigeria. Under the Nigerian constitution, state governors enjoy immunity while in office. In one instance, evidence developed by the U.K. criminal justice agencies was presented by a U.K. law enforcement official to a committee of the state's legislature, which voted to remove the governor from office, thus lifting his immunity and allowing him to be charged in Nigeria. During these investigations, the EFCC worked closely with U.K. officials and received on-the-job training.

Source: Messick 2011.

and money laundering through joint investigations or prosecutions. Where stronger jurisdictions pair with those with weaker institutions, these initiatives have the potential to build capacity as well as deliver practical results in diminishing impunity. Investigations and prosecutions involving trafficking can increase this type of cooperation, which can be differentiated for different environments, as in Haiti and Nigeria (box 8.4).

Mobilizing international support

Some constraints on international support come from policies and systems in the headquarters of multilaterals and donor countries (chapter 9). National leaders and their partners on the ground cannot individually determine these broader changes to the international system, but they can act to maximize the benefits of existing support.

It helps when national leaders and their international partners in the field lay out clear, program-level priorities across the security, justice, and development domains. Where national actors are divided in their priorities (for example, with different ministries putting forth different requests, or donor field representatives disagreeing on overall priorities), international capitals and the governing structures of multilaterals will not receive a clear message to focus efforts. Priorities are better laid out in a very limited number of clear programs, as in Liberia after the civil war or Colombia in the face of rising criminal violence after 2002.[37] Using the national budget process to decide on priority programs creates leverage to coordinate messages and implementation between the security and development ministries.

Being alert to the needs of international partners to show results and manage risks can also improve results from international aid. International partners have their own domestic pressures—such as demonstrating that aid funds are not misused and being able to attribute results to their endeavors. A frank exchange on risks and results helps to find ways to bridge differences. In Indonesia in the aftermath of the tsunami and Aceh peace agreement, the government agreed with donors that incoming assistance would be "jointly branded" from the Indonesian Reconstruction Agency and donors, with special transparency measures in place. This enabled both sides to show visible results and manage risks, while bolstering state-society relations in the aftermath of crisis. In donor coordination arrangements for highly aid-dependent countries, "double compacts," described in chapter 6, can be a useful tool. These agreements lay out the results governments aim to provide to their own citizens as well as clarify mutual commitments between governments and donors.

An important trade-off for national reformers and their international partners is to ensure that international delivery capacity can help deliver fast results while also supporting increases in the legitimacy of national institutions. International humanitarian assistance, for example, not only can save lives but also can help greatly in delivering quick confidence-building results. But humanitarian delivery of food imports can also distort production in local markets, and long-term international humanitarian provision of health, education, and water and sanitation services can undermine efforts to increase the credibility of local institutions. Much of this can be avoided through phased transitions from humanitarian capacity to local institutions (box 8.5). Similar approaches can be used in other sectors: the International Commission against Impunity in Guatemala, for example, combines local judicial capacity-building with the use of international staff to assist in investigations and prosecutions.[38] The Governance and Economic Management Program in Liberia has shifted from an initial focus on international executive support for accountability over public resources to capacity-building in national systems.[39]

National reformers and their international partners in-country have a rich set of experiences to draw on—both in evaluating efforts in the past in their countries and in adapting experiences from around the world. The tools in this chapter offer options for this adaptation. Confidence-building through collaborative approaches and early results and the foundational reforms that can deliver citizen security, justice, and jobs have some elements in common. But they need to be well adapted to the local political context. The task of national reformers and international representatives in the field is made easier—or harder—by the supporting environments in global policy and in the headquarters of bilateral actors and the global institutions. Chapter 9 turns to directions for global policy to support countries struggling to prevent and recover from violence on the ground.

BOX 8.5 ***Phasing the transition from international humanitarian aid to local institutions: Afghanistan and Timor-Leste***

Types of violence: Both countries have a history of external and civil conflict, with significant ongoing violence in Afghanistan and, in Timor, a more limited wave of renewed political and communal conflict and gang-based violence in 2005–06.	
Transition opportunities: Significant transitions occurred in both countries: particularly significant was space for change under the UN transitional authority in Timor in 1999–2002.	**Key stakeholders:** Government, civil society, and humanitarian and development donors were key stakeholders.
Institutional challenges: Limited service delivery, severe capacity constraints, many donor players were the major challenges.	

Timor-Leste

Following the UN supervised referendum on independence of August 1999, Timor-Leste suffered widespread violence and destruction of its infrastructure and collapse of state services. In the transition period before and after independence in 2002, Timor-Leste managed, however, to provide both rapid results and long-term institution-building in the health sector in four phases.

In the first phase international and national NGOs occupied a central role in providing emergency health services throughout Timor, independently funded through humanitarian assistance. In the second phase, the interim health authority established in 2000 developed a health plan and performance indicators and signed memoranda of understanding with NGOs to standardize the service packages provided in different parts of the territory still under independent humanitarian funding. In the third phase, NGOs were contracted directly by the transitional authority to perform both local management and service delivery functions. In the fourth phase, the Interim Health Authority was replaced by a new ministry of health, which assumed district management of the system and facilities, with NGOs important in specialized service delivery and a capacity-building role, but decreased local personnel over time. All the major international agencies in the health sector worked together within this framework.

By 2004 this gradual phasing of responsibility and capacity-building had led to 90 percent of the population having access to health facilities within a two-hour walking distance. Between 2000 and 2004, the use of these facilities rose from 0.75 outpatient visits per capita to 2.13. The health ministry and district operations were among the few state functions resilient to renewed violence in 2005–06, continuing to operate and, indeed, to provide assistance to the displaced population.

Afghanistan

In the wake of the fall of the Taliban in 2002, Afghanistan's basic health services were in a dismal condition, with maternal mortality estimated at 1,600 per 100,000 live births. The Afghan ministry of public health outlined a package of priority health services in response (costing about US$4 per capita per year) and contracted NGOs to deliver them, while also establishing rigorous monitoring and evaluation. The NGOs were selected competitively and sanctioned for poor performance.

Early results have been optimistic, with a 136 percent increase in the number of functioning primary health care facilities between 2002 and 2007. Despite a worsening security situation, the number of outpatient visits between 2004 and 2007 also increased by nearly 400 percent. These outcomes have relied not only on political support but also on a commitment by the ministry of public health not to micromanage the process.

By contracting autonomously operating NGOs while ensuring accountability, the Afghan government both earned and sustained policy leadership in the health sector. It allowed the ministry of public health to address scarce human resources, a lack of physical facilities, and logistical hurdles. The depth of ongoing violence in Afghanistan has not permitted national institutions to assume the role played by NGOs over time, as in Timor-Leste, but the Afghan government and ministry of public health have still managed to achieve much needed health outcomes in an uncertain environment dominated by insecurity and institutional challenges.

Sources: Baird 2010; Rohland and Cliffe 2002; Tulloch and others 2003.

Notes

1. WDR Consultation with former key negotiators from the ANC Alliance and the National Party in South Africa, 2010; WDR team interview with former president Álvaro Uribe, 2010; WDR team consultation with government officials, representatives from civil society organizations, and security personnel in Colombia, 2010.
2. Arboleda 2010; WDR team consultation with government officials, representatives from civil society organizations, and security personnel in Colombia, 2010.
3. Porter and Rab 2010.
4. For more in-depth discussion, see the section on delivering early results in chapter 4.

5. Barron and Burke 2008; World Bank 2010a.
6. Dwan and Bailey 2006; Jahr 2010; Government of the Republic of Liberia Executive Mansion 2009. Also see box 4.3 in chapter 4.
7. CICIG 2009; Férnandez 2010; Donovan 2008; UN 2006a; Hudson 2010. Also see box 6.4 in chapter 6.
8. Braud and Grevi 2005; Schulze 2007. Also see feature 4 in chapter 4.
9. See section on support to building inclusive-enough coalitions in chapter 6.
10. See UNODC 2010a; Duffield 2000; Kohlmann 2004. Also see the section on spillover effects of violence and feature 1 in chapter 1.
11. Robinson 1994; Kingah and Kingah 2010.
12. Salazar 2007; Murphy 2008; Bronstein 2007.
13. For more information, see the section on delivering early results in chapter 4.
14. Cousens and Harland 2006; Statistical Office of Kosovo 2010; Chesterman 2004. Also see box 4.7 in chapter 4.
15. Dwan and Bailey 2006; Jahr 2010; Government of the Republic of Liberia Executive Mansion 2009; Baily and Hoskins 2007. Also see box 4.3 and box 4.6 in chapter 4.
16. BBC News 2010.
17. World Bank 2011a.
18. Dupuy and Binningsbø 2008. Also see discussion on inclusive-enough coalitions in chapter 4.
19. UNDPKO 2010a. Also see box 4.5 in chapter 4.
20. Graydon 2005; Greenfell 2006; Timor-Leste Independent Comprehensive Need Assessment Team 2009.
21. For Nicaragua, see Scheye 2009. For Sierra Leone, see Dale 2009. Also see the section on justice in chapter 5 for more in-depth discussion.
22. Lamb and Dye 2009; Tajima 2009; see section on public finance for employment in chapter 5 for in-depth discussion.
23. World Bank 2010d.
24. For Lebanon, see World Bank 2008f, 2009d; Republic of Lebanon Ministry of Environment 1999, box 5.9 in chapter 5. For Liberia, see Bailey and Hoskins 2007; McCandless 2008, box 4.6 in chapter 4; box 6.5 in chapter 6.
25. Herzberg 2004. Also see section on jobs in chapter 5.
26. USAID Rwanda 2006; Grygiel 2007; Parker 2008; Chohan-Pole 2010; Boudreaux 2010. Also see box 5.8 in chapter 5.
27. For Japanese land reforms, see Kawagoe 1999; For broader statebuilding experience in Japan, see Tsunekawa and Yoshida 2010; For Korean land reforms, see Shin 2006. For Singapore, see box 5.2 in chapter 5.
28. Lopes 2009.
29. World Bank 2006b; Kireyev 2006; *Economic Times* 2008. Also see section on public finance for employment in chapter 5.
30. Ashe and Parrott 2001. Also see box 5.10 in chapter 5.
31. Mobekk 2010; Bastick, Grimm, and Kunz 2007. Also see section on security in chapter 5 for more information.
32. For Northern Ireland, see Barron and others 2010. Also see the section on decentralization and devolution in chapter 5. For South Africa, see Hayner 2010; UNOHCHR 2006. For Germany, see Grimm 2010. Also see the section titled "Transitional justice to recognize past crimes" in chapter 5.
33. UNDPKO 2010a. Also see box 5.5 in chapter 5.
34. Bowden 2010; Gilpin 2009. Also see section on spillover effects of violence in chapter 1.
35. World Bank 2006d. See section titled "Between the global and the national: Regional stresses, regional support" in chapter 7.
36. Greta and Lewandowski 2010; Otocan 2010; Council of Europe 1995; Council of Europe and Institute of International Sociology of Gorizia 2003; Bilcik and others 2000. Also see box 7.11 in chapter 7.
37. Liberia: Giovine and others 2010; box 4.6 in chapter 4. Colombia: WDR team interview with former president Álvaro Uribe, 2010; WDR team consultation with government officials, representatives from civil society organizations, and security personnel in Colombia, 2010.
38. CICIG 2009; Férnandez 2010; Donovan 2008; UN 2006a; Hudson 2010. Also see box 6.4 in chapter 6.
39. Dwan and Bailey 2006; Jahr 2010; Government of the Republic of Liberia Executive Mansion 2009. Also see box 4.3 in chapter 4.

Chapter 9 sets out new directions for international policy. International assistance to strengthen the national institutions and governance that provide citizen security, justice, and jobs, and to alleviate the factors that undermine them, is crucial to break the repeated cycles of violence described in this Report. But it requires an international system better adapted to address 21st-century risks of violence. This means refocusing assistance on preventing criminal and political violence through greater, and more integrated, support for security, justice, and jobs; reforming the procedures of international agencies; responding at a regional level; and renewing cooperative efforts among lower-, middle-, and higher-income countries.

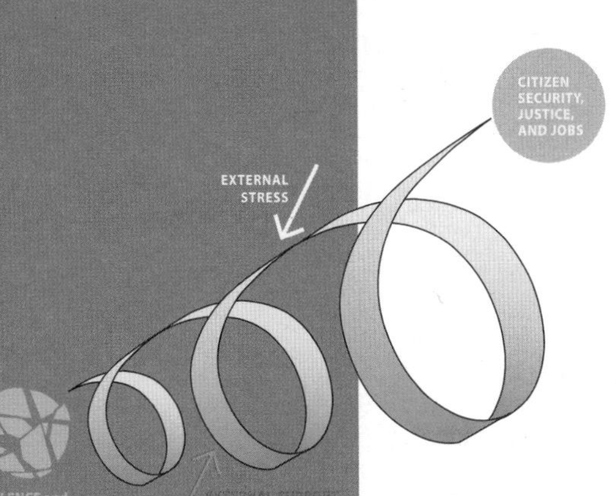

CHAPTER 9

New directions for international support

The international system achieved remarkable progress in reducing 20th-century violence. The overall decrease in interstate war owes a great deal to the establishment and growth of an international architecture after World War II that viewed peace and prosperity as linked and embodied shared global standards and new methods of collective action to address threats. The adaptation of that system at the end of the Cold War provided new tools that contributed to a subsequent reduction in the number and severity of civil wars. This Report stresses that progress in overcoming violence and reducing risk is above all a national process and that national actors need to own their institutional transformation. Yet many of the national responses analyzed in part 2 of this Report, "Lessons from National and International Responses," were achieved with international support. It is difficult to imagine how committed leaders in post–World War II Europe, Indonesia, the Republic of Korea, Liberia, Mozambique, Northern Ireland, Singapore, or Timor-Leste would have stabilized their countries or regions without help from abroad.

The international system is hampered, however, by structures and processes that are not sufficiently adapted to the current challenge as described in chapters 6 and 7. There is relatively little capacity internationally to support the core institutional challenges for violence prevention—citizen security, justice, and jobs. Internal agency processes are often too slow to support confidence-building and too quick to exit, inadequately engaged with building national institutions, and preoccupied with technical "best practice" rather than functionality adapted to the local political context. Divisions between diplomatic, security, and development agencies, and between those initiatives dealing with political conflict and criminal violence, persist, despite the practical links on the ground between these issues. Efforts are targeted more at the national than the regional level, and global initiatives on corruption and trafficking lack robust tools to "follow the money" across fragile jurisdictions. A focus on smarter assistance tools is particularly urgent given the current environment of constraints on aid budgets.

The changing international balance of power is also widening the circle of influential actors. With the rising economic and diplomatic influence of lower- and middle-income countries, the focus of influence on national action is shifting. Middle-income countries, many with a history of solidarity support and increasing aid programs, are taking on greater responsibilities for shaping outcomes beyond their borders. And regional institutions are playing a larger role. In fragile situations, the different domestic pressures faced by OECD (Organisation for Economic Co-operation and Development) donors, recipient countries, and middle-income countries—the "dual accountability dilemma" of accountability pressures both to domestic constituencies and shareholders and to the leaders and citizens of recipient states described in chapter 6—often means that their view on priorities and what is reasonable to expect of national actors are divided.

Taken together, these constraints mean that international assistance is not yet marshaling the resources needed to address the 21st-century challenges of repeated and interlinked violence and weak governance. To achieve real change in approaches, this Report considers four tracks to improve global responses for security and development.

- **Track 1:** Preventing repeated cycles of violence by investing in citizen security, justice, and jobs
- **Track 2:** Reforming internal agency systems to support rapid action to restore confidence and long-term institution-building
- **Track 3:** Acting regionally and globally on external stresses
- **Track 4:** Marshaling experience and support from lower-, middle-, and higher-income countries and global and regional institutions to reflect the changing landscape of international policy and assistance.

Track 1: Preventing repeated cycles of violence by investing in citizen security, justice, and jobs

The demand for international support that can help areas struggling to prevent large-scale political or criminal violence is high. Prevention does not mean only the prevention of new violence in hitherto peaceful areas, but reducing the risk of recurring violence in countries that have already experienced past cycles, for example, Guatemala or Yemen. Repeated cycles of political and criminal violence require thinking outside the box, beyond the traditional development paradigm. Issues of citizen security are not peripheral to "mainstream" development. They are in varying forms a problem for subnational areas of larger and more prosperous countries, for countries emerging from conflict that need to prevent recurrence, and for areas facing new or resurgent threats. More effective international support to risk reduction requires (1) combined tools that link citizen security, justice, jobs, and associated services, and (2) structural investments in justice and employment capacity.

Operational gaps in capacity—New tools for combined action

International actors increasingly recognize that development and security march hand in hand. But most international instruments do not. The basic tools presented in chapter 8 to prevent repeated cycles of violence require linked action from political, security, development, and humanitarian actors. Yet these actors generally assess priorities and develop their programs separately, with efforts to help national reformers build unified programs being the exception rather than the rule. United Nations (UN) "integrated missions" and various bilateral and regional "whole-of-government" initiatives have emerged to address the challenge of merging development, diplomatic, and security strategies and operations. But these models still struggle with the reality that different disciplines bring with them different goals, business models, planning time frames, decision-making processes, funding streams, and risk calculus. Action has often stopped at the level of light "coordination" rather than moving toward programs that combine efforts on the ground.[1]

The range of practical experience available in the international system in supporting integrated approaches to prevent repeated cycles of violence has improved. There has been an increase in global and regional mediation, a greater focus on security-sector reform, an increase in police capacity-building, and strengthening of links between peacekeeping and civilian assistance. Some innovative programs have been developed, such as the "peace infrastructure" supported by the UN Development Programme (UNDP) and Department of Political Affairs (UNDPA),[2] the Inter-American Development Bank's (IADB) community projects for citizen security, and collaboration on safe transit between the World Bank and UN peacekeeping missions. Such initiatives often support combined action relating to citizen security, justice, and jobs, but they are not yet in the mainstream of diplomatic, security, or development implementation on the ground.

A different way of doing business is needed. There is a need to move away from simply tweaking current practices toward a fundamentally new practical set of tools to link development and security, development and mediation, and development and humanitarian assistance. New tools should aim to have a catalytic effect in supporting confidence-building and longer-term institutional transformation.

The key lessons from country experiences of international assistance are that four types of programs requiring combined efforts by development, security, political, and humanitarian actors are needed in insecure situations (table 9.1). These would be the top priority operational tools for international partners to target combined action on the ground. The development of a specialized suite of catalytic products deliverable at scale nationally or subnationally would enhance the ability of international agencies to respond effectively to government requests for assistance in preventing repeated cycles of violence. Amongst the member states of the multilateral organizations, greater coherence and consistency in the positions they take in multilateral governance bodies would help foster such combined operations.

Principles for combined operations

Shared principles for the management of combined operations are also necessary—again moving beyond mere "coordination." For in-country management, much international action remains stuck, aptly characterized by the adage, "everyone wants to coordinate but no one wants to be coordinated." In this case, the Report suggests using the principle of subsidiarity: the closer to violence, the better the understanding of the local priorities and the more effectively the combined management can operate. In general, this would mean empowering national leadership in the coordination of assistance and ensuring that they have the support to do this. In others, thinking about subsidiarity may mean empowering regional institutions to supplement national governments' coordinating role.

Where national coordinating mechanisms lack sufficient authority or capacity to influence the more powerful international actors, joint global-local or global-regional-local leadership could improve confidence and traction. The Association of Southeast Asian Nations (ASEAN), the UN, and the Myanmar Government Tripartite Core Group after Cyclone Nargis in Myanmar is one example, and the Bosnia Board of Principals[3] structure involving international partners and senior government officials is a second. Where regional or UN special representatives are given the task of coordination, the World Bank could consider coordinating the work of its field representatives more closely behind their leadership—with a clear lead on resource mobilization supporting the political convening role of the UN or regional organizations.

Structural gaps in capacity—justice and jobs

As argued throughout this Report, the institutions that provide citizen security, justice, and jobs are crucial in creating resilience to repeated cycles of violence. Unfortunately, these priority areas are underresourced and lack ownership in the current international architecture. In each area, there are structural gaps in knowledge and operational capacity. Economic policy assistance still tends to be focused more on growth than employ-

TABLE 9.1 *International tools to link confidence-building and institutional transformation across the political, security, development, and humanitarian spheres*

Risk and opportunity assessments	***A shift from early warning to contingency planning for repeated cycles of violence.*** While agency and academic models of early warning continue to make useful progress, no such model can ever predict the exact timing of the onset of violence or capture all local variations. More useful is a mode of planning that accepts as a starting point that states and subnational areas with weak institutions continually risk being overwhelmed by a range of stresses. ***Changes to planning and assessment tools as a basis for combined action.*** To adapt to the reality of repeated cycles of violence and multiple transitions, assessment processes would become lighter and more flexible to provide regular, repeated assessments of risks and opportunities. The assessments would benefit from more realism in priorities and timelines; stronger political economy analysis; and a tighter focus on the goals of citizen security, justice, and jobs.
Security, justice, and jobs	***Technical assistance and financing for multisectoral community programs that involve policing and justice as well as development activities.*** These efforts can build on initiatives in Latin America and Africa to provide local dispute resolution and justice services, community policing, employment and training, safe public and trading spaces, and social and cultural programs that promote tolerance. ***Combined technical teams and financing to support the strategic, technical, and public financing aspects of institutional reforms in the security and justice sectors***—with economic, governance, and public finance specialists complementing the efforts of security, police, and judicial personnel. These efforts would build on the insights presented in this Report, focusing on basic functions to build trust and performance (including budget and expenditure functions); connections between the police, civilian justice, and corrections systems; and access to justice services at a local level, including through the blending of formal and informal systems.
Links to sustained mediation	***Supporting of national and local capacities for mediation and coalition-building.*** Countries facing rapid transitions and cycles of violence will need to negotiate new internal pacts, and build consensus, around effective policies to address their many challenges. These negotiations will in turn require that the parties have access to internal mediators, and to their own skills and autonomous platforms, for dialogue and for the resolution of conflicts. By helping build and apply such capacities, development assistance has already contributed to peaceful elections, for instance, in several cases since 2004, and most recently during the constitutional referendum in Kenya in 2010. Further development of national and local capacities for managing cyclical conflict, cascading change, and rapid transitions is therefore not only essential, but also feasible. ***Supporting of expertise for international mediation.*** For these efforts to deliver sustained results, they should be linked to the developmental assistance that can provide confidence-building and institutional transformation and should be available to governments for the longer term. Seconding increased expertise from bilateral agencies and international financial institutions (IFIs) to UN regional and civil society special envoys and mediators would help bridge gaps in political, security, and economic support. ***Developmental help during mounting crises.*** Countries struggling to prevent escalation of criminal and political violence often need timely financial help, although this can be met in part by improving the predictability of funding for mediation, initiating planned development support, and focusing security or development activities on localities with rising threats. Where exceptional additional financial support is needed (for example, in situations of high external stress and weak institutions), the responsible leadership of national reformers can be gauged by the signals they are prepared to give—for example, they might welcome international access to violence-affected areas and transparent reporting of budget and expenditure data under the auspices of an accepted regional prevention plan (see box 9.1 on investment in prevention).
Humanitarian support to national institution-building	***Guidelines on phasing humanitarian assistance to build national institutional capacity over time.*** Where national institutional capacity and governance are improving, guidelines build on good practice by the UNDP, UNICEF (UN Children's Fund), WHO (World Health Organization), WFP (World Food Programme), and many nongovernmental organization (NGO) partners in combining humanitarian services delivery with capacity-building. Timelines for phasing the transition from international humanitarian assistance to national institutional capacity will vary by country. ***A strengthened framework under which international humanitarian assistance can be "jointly branded" with local institutions, or in-kind assistance of humanitarian materials and staff provided to support state social protection operations, with appropriate monitoring.*** Where this is not possible, increased *use of community-driven mechanisms* and local staff to deliver humanitarian aid would help to build resilient local capacities.

REFLECTIONS FROM ADVISORY COUNCIL MEMBERS: *2011 WORLD DEVELOPMENT REPORT*

BOX 9.1 *Preventing violence: Prioritizing investment in citizen security and justice reforms*

Investment in prevention

Kenzo Oshima, Senior Vice President, Japan International Cooperation Agency (JICA), Former Permanent Representative of Japan to the United Nations; *WDR Advisory Council Member*

The vital importance of conflict prevention has been understood for many years, and advocates have argued passionately for it. When Article 1 of the United Nations Charter was written, however, enshrining a mandate "to take effective collective measures for the prevention and removal of threats to the peace," the main focus of concern was interstate war. Since then, the nature of armed conflict has changed. Although for many years we were unaware of the magnitude, there has been a significant shift from interstate to intrastate conflict and then from "classic" civil war to mixed problems of criminal and political violence, demanding a concomitant shift in our prevention focus.

The case of Afghanistan exemplifies the consequences of this unawareness. After the Soviet withdrawal, the international community was largely oblivious to ongoing internal struggles. Then, in the early 2000s, that "forgotten conflict" became a serious global security threat. Our capacity internationally to foresee the risk that a particular country might fall into conflict and to mitigate that risk in a timely manner has been weak and that weakness has contributed to our failure to prevent conflicts from happening.

It is important that the international community find a better way to coordinate, through mechanisms that include not only UN agencies, but also international financial institutions and regional/sub-regional organizations such as African Union (AU), ASEAN, and Economic Community of West African States (ECOWAS). My profound hope is that WDR 2011 will convince these stakeholders that collaboration on investment in conflict prevention is urgently needed.

While the UN Security Council retains the primary authority under international law for the prevention of armed conflict, others can play vital roles. This includes, vitally, national governments themselves, who ultimately have the primary responsibility to manage violence. These actors are all present in the country-specific meetings of the UN Peacebuilding Commission (PBC), which was established in 2005 following on the recommendations of the Secretary-General's High-Level Panel on Threats, Challenges and Change. However, while the two tasks were suggested for it by the High-Level Panel, one focusing on response to the soaring risk of fresh conflicts—"to help states avoid collapse and the slide to war"—was omitted from its core functions. In the face of this limitation, the 2010 review of UN peacebuilding architecture, while recognizing the narrowness of the mandate, recommends that the Commission utilize to the fullest the potential given by its existing mandate to expand its prevention role. Whether through this route or otherwise, the fact remains that linking political, security and economic actors is a critical part of how the international system can better help countries prevent new threats of conflict and other forms of violence.

Security and justice as foundational reforms: Addressing violence and criminality

Zeid Ra'ad Al-Hussein, Ambassador of the Hashemite Kingdom of Jordan to the United Nations; *WDR Advisory Council Member*

War creates crime; and I do not mean the atrocity crimes we commonly associate with war; rather, I refer to the appearance of its oldest companion and practitioner: the war profiteer. The smuggler of weapons, of fuel, of vehicles and narcotics, in war, will often bind with others to create networks of black market activity so efficient that, by the time a peace is struck, their potency means they not only survive the war intact, supremely well-organized, but also they do so with momentum.

A newly formed government in the affected country could only hope to match them, indeed overcome or defeat them in the long term, if two early conditions are fulfilled—with vital action by the international community itself.

The target country must first be provided with security assistance, and then must be in a position to deliver an effective judicial system to its people, including police and corrections. If the nascent government cannot do the latter, and in many cases it would be too weak to do so, the international community must then do it with them. It must supply doctrine for international policing and criminal justice support operations, as well as fast and flexible executive assistance to help Governments carry out police and judicial functions as well as the corrections facilities. And that is all. Nothing more need be done.

With security and a functioning judicial system in place, a country recovering from war could hope to maintain the lowest levels of public corruption, indeed, extinguish organized crime altogether, and be ready to embrace the in-flow of foreign direct investment (FDI) and other forms of financial assistance. Should we fail to grasp just how fundamental security and justice are to the whole enterprise of peacebuilding, the sole beneficiaries of our inattentiveness, and much to their delight—will continue to be organized crime—the very offspring of war itself.

ment, despite rising demands for assistance on employment policy from countries facing fragile situations due to unemployed and disengaged youth populations. Assistance to countries struggling to develop well-governed police forces, civilian justice, and corrections systems in the face of fluid violent threats is much more limited than assistance available to build military capacity, and there is a disconnect between the policing and civilian justice areas. The section below provides recommendations to address gaps in support for employment and the rule of law.

Employment

As described in chapters 5 and 8, there is little consensus on the exact set of policies that can generate sustained labor-intensive growth in the face of high unemployment, and even less so in violent environments. What we have available is a series of "good fit" examples of policies and programs that appear to have delivered results in creating employment in different country circumstances. At the international level, better evaluation of these program interventions and the macroeconomic environment in which they can deliver is an important priority.

At the national level, leaders cannot wait for a more comprehensive international consensus on employment policies to evolve—they need to address the challenges of youth unemployment in insecure areas now, based on the tools they have available. A sensible approach would be to support the types of programs described in chapter 8, combined with evaluations and feedback loops that provide information to refine policies and program design.

Priority programs for job creation to which this approach should be applied include investments in supporting infrastructure, in particular, electricity and transit. A second program cluster is those that invest in skills; develop links among producers, traders, and consumers; and expand access to finance and assets. Last, recognizing that private sector–led growth sufficient to absorb young entrants to the labor market may take a generation in many fragile situations, there is a need to simultaneously support and evaluate transitional employment measures.

Efforts to strengthen international support to employment should draw on joint security, justice, and economic tools. Unemployment is traditionally viewed as simply a function of economic conditions. But in highly insecure areas, international security assistance can help ensure safe trade and transit, enabling productive investment from within and outside the country. For violence prevention, there are also links between employment, justice, and identity issues. Programs that reinforce the role of disengaged youth as community members and support job creation with social and cultural activities merit investment and further evaluation.

These approaches would help. But there is likely to be continued pressure from large unemployed youth populations unless a more significant international effort is launched. A bolder approach could draw together capacities from development agencies, the private sector, foundations, and nongovernmental organizations (NGOs) to support a new global partnership to galvanize investments in countries and communities where high unemployment and social disengagement contribute to the risks of conflict. Focusing primarily on job creation through project finance, advisory support to small and medium businesses, training, and guarantees, the initiative would also support social and cultural initiatives that promote collaborative capacities in communities, social tolerance, and recognition of young people's social and economic roles. Private sector capacities to draw on include large companies that trade and invest in insecure areas (creating links with local entrepreneurs), as well as technology companies that can assist with connectivity and training in remote insecure areas.

Police and justice

To fill the rising demand for assistance with criminal justice issues, systems to provide support for police and justice should be flexible. This, in three senses. First, some states have adequate police capacity but face gaps in other aspects of their civilian justice systems—or the gaps are in police capacity, not in justice systems. Others have gaps across the board. Second, some will need assistance as part of a broader package of conflict management support, often under UN Security Council or regional institution auspices. Others will need specialized assistance to strengthen their police and civilian justice sectors without broader political engagement. Third, some will prefer assistance from within the region, while others will prefer to look to global mechanisms. Any effort to deepen international capacity to provide assistance should build in this flexibility of response. That assistance should also be available to help national authorities deal with specialized transboundary challenges—from financial crimes to trafficking issues. These specialized challenges will be covered in the next section.

The starting point for improving the international response to criminal justice capacity-building is increasing the supply of personnel. National governments, both high and middle income, could usefully invest (or continue to invest) in increasing the pool of police and other criminal justice personnel available for overseas deployment, whether through bilateral or multilateral programs. There are three main options available to increase this supply, all desirable: drawing on retired officers as advisers; secondment of active service members; and provision of formed police units. Formed police units are requested by a relatively small number of countries under UN peacekeeping missions, but demand has clearly grown in recent years in relation to military deployments. Secondment of active service members can be assisted by career and promotion systems that recognize and reward international experience. In all three areas, deployment of women police officers has proved valuable.

For other functions of the civilian justice system, current capacity to supply personnel is weaker than for police. Within ongoing efforts to develop rosters of civilian expertise, the availability of justice professionals and administrators should continue to receive particular attention—but with a focus on capacity from the South that can provide experience of reform of weak systems in difficult environments of political contest.

Police and justice personnel must also be deployed with appropriate training. In both policing and broader civilian justice, national systems differ greatly in their organizational structures, legal frameworks, and practices, far more so than for military capacity. As described in chapter 6, the UN's Standing Police Capacity and its Office of Rule of Law and Security Institutions have begun to make headway on standardized doctrine and training for police units willing to deploy into UN operations. But there is no similar mechanism for joint training of national judicial personnel to expose them to different systems and practices, and less of a body of knowledge on approaching institution-building in fragile settings. Extending training in both areas through global and regional centers would improve the impact of additional personnel capacity. Within bilateral assistance programs, long-term institutional partnerships between agencies providing technical assistance and national counterpart agencies may be another mechanism to strengthen the sensitivity of assistance to the local context.

As with employment, combined security and developmental approaches will be needed to support justice issues. There are areas where, at the request of government, the Bank and other international financial institutions (IFIs) could consider playing a greater role in supporting the developmental underpinnings of violence prevention within their mandates—such as the links between public financial management and security sector reform and institution-building, legal administration, justice systems development and multisectoral approaches at the community level that combine community policing and justice services with social cohesion, developmental, and employment creation programs.

But the IFIs are not well placed to support the core operational aspects of a criminal justice system. A clear lead within the UN system would help. Softer options for change in this area include the "global service provider" model currently under discussion, with one agency leading on police and another on other aspects of the civilian justice system, or one leading on deployments for executive functions and the other on institutional transformation. Since a consistent theme throughout this Report has been the need to link support to police and civilian justice systems, the division of labor in the international system would ideally facilitate this linkage rather than further separate capacities. Bolder options for change could involve breaking down barriers between police and justice assistance, either at a country level by facilitating an integration of the financing and program management of police and justice support, or by identifying a single organizational responsibility.[4]

Track 2: Reforming internal agency procedures

New international commitment to programs that combine citizen security, justice, and employment linkages and an increase in structural capacities to support justice, and employment challenges will be effective only to the extent that international agencies can provide assistance fast, and take the risks necessary to support national institutional development. Without these actions, an increased emphasis on prevention will not be reflected in improved performance on the ground. To address this, internal agency reforms, new tools to manage risks and results, and mechanisms to end the stop-go pattern of international assistance are needed.

Principles for internal agency reforms

To support countries with rapid confidence-building assistance and longer-term institutional transformation, internal reform is needed for international agencies to improve responsiveness. Many individuals working on fragile and conflict-affected states are dedicated professionals attempting to support national efforts. But they are held back by structures, tools, and processes designed for different contexts and purposes. Best-fit approaches designed to fit the local context are as important for international approaches as for national reforms. Budgeting, staffing, results measurement, and fiduciary systems require significant changes to achieve a best fit in fragile situations in almost all the multilateral agencies—and in many bilaterals. Existing systems that implicitly avoid risk—insisting on sophisticated controls initially developed for more stable and higher-capacity countries, and often choosing to delay assistance when risks are high—have not delivered consistent results. For the g7+ group of leaders of fragile states[5] who have begun to meet regularly as part of the International Dialogue on Peacebuilding and Statebuilding, reforming internal agency procedures, particularly procurement procedures, was the number-one suggestion for international reform. Principles to bridge the different perspectives of donors and recipient countries on risks and guide internal agency reforms that emerge from this Report's analysis are as follows.

- First, accept the links between security and development outcomes. Few internal systems in the multilateral agencies are designed to support the links between security and development outcomes. Program objectives tend to be narrowly set. Economic and social interventions in situations of insecurity can justifiably be designed to contribute to citizen security and justice outcomes (a decrease in homicides, for example). Security programs can also be designed to contribute to development outcomes (an increase in trade, for example). This would require agencies to use outcome measures outside their traditional "technical" domains, and work together within the combined program frameworks described above. Rewarding staff for partnership would also help facilitate cooperation.

- Second, adapt to the reality of the absence of security, institutional capacity, and fully competitive markets in fragile situations. When insecurity is high, both the costs and benefits of interventions may change dramatically over a short period. This argues for greater flexibility in administrative budget and staff planning. In program budgets, it implies careful sequencing where some programs will be more beneficial at a later date, but also placing more weight on speed (over some cost-efficiency and quality concerns) in contracting of personnel, goods, works, and services where benefits to fast action are high. Where competitive markets are very thin and not transparent, different procurement controls—such as pre-tendering internationally under variable quantity contracts, or contracting processes that allow direct negotiations with knowledge of regional markets—can be appropriate. Where institutional capacity is insufficient, procedures need to be distilled to the simplest level of due process, together with flexible mechanisms to execute some activities on behalf of recipient institutions.
- Third, balance the risk of action with the risk of inaction. The first implication of this principle is that countries in need of assistance and their international partners have to accept each other's concerns on risk. The prime minister of a country in a fragile situation is not wrong to seek immediate help to pay salaries and provide equipment for the security forces; a minister of development cooperation is not wrong to worry about risks of corruption or human rights abuses. To align their interests, they must understand each other's constraints. The second implication is that solutions will require that these needs are balanced, rather than risk aversion dominating. Decentralizing greater responsibility and accountability to international staff on the ground can increase responsiveness to the risks of inaction. Transparent publication of achievements against target timelines for donor funds release and activities—and reasons for delays—would also help to shift international incentives in favor of action. Donors, though, will need to have different ways to manage the risks of their engagement, which will be covered in the next section.
- Fourth, accept that some programs will fail, and adapt rapidly in response. Rates of success in assistance programs should be lower in fragile situations than in stable development situations, since the contextual risk is by definition higher. This is justified because returns are also far greater when programs work—in peace and security terms, but also in development terms because these countries start from such a low baseline on the Millennium Development Goals (MDGs). The political problem for donors in accepting a certain degree of failure is the perception that international actors are naive about risks and slow to act when problems arise. Having a menu of options to shift modalities rapidly when failures occur is crucial in managing donor risks without abandoning support to national institutions. To avoid disrupting program continuity, embedding contingencies into program design from the beginning is crucial, as will be discussed in the next section.

Adopting these principles would help bilateral and multilateral agencies reform internal systems in an appropriate way, to both manage risks and deliver better results. These principles could be incorporated into agency procedures in several ways: (1) increasing the use of adequate contingency funds under appropriate oversight; (2) adapting models, such as community procurement, already geared to thin markets and low institutional capacity in national procurement processes; (3) putting in place effective best-fit measures to increase transparency and control costs, such as staff able to monitor reasonable regional prices in noncompetitive procurement processes; (4) simplifying processes, delegating authority, and accelerating turnaround times; and (5) changing incentives and performance monitoring mechanisms for staff to ensure that those who learn from failure and adapt quickly are rewarded. Responses will and should vary by agency—but common principles would help improve the complementarity of international agency support.

Risk and results management

Current donor risk management relies on two primary mechanisms: postponing or suspending assistance when risks are too high, and using headquarters controls rather than best-fit delivery mechanisms adapted to local conditions. Both are driven in large part to meet the dual-accountability pressure from domestic constituencies to avoid risks of corruption, wastage, or abuse. This may manage donor risk, but it constrains real progress in institution-building on the ground. Where continuity in aid is needed, risks do exist, and innovation is needed in national strategy to fit the political context (see figure 9.1). An alternative is to embrace faster and more consistent engagement through national institutions but to vary the ways aid is delivered to manage risks and results. Some donors have a higher risk-tolerance and will be able to choose modes that go more directly through national budgets and institutions; others will need greater oversight or nonstate involvement in delivery. Various options exist for managing risk, including the following:

- **Increasing the contingencies in budgets, under transparent planning assumptions.** Where governance is volatile, development program budgets, as well as the budgets for political and peacekeeping missions, would benefit from greater contingency measures so that activities and delivery mechanisms could be adjusted when new risks and opportunities emerge without disrupting overall support. The planning assumptions for such contingencies—for example, that additional oversight mechanisms will be adopted if certain agreed-on measures of governance deteriorate—should be transparent to both recipient governments and the governing bodies of international agencies.
- **Varying the oversight mechanisms when engaging through national budget and institutions.** Oversight mechanisms to

FIGURE 9.1 *Adapting the modality of assistance to risk*

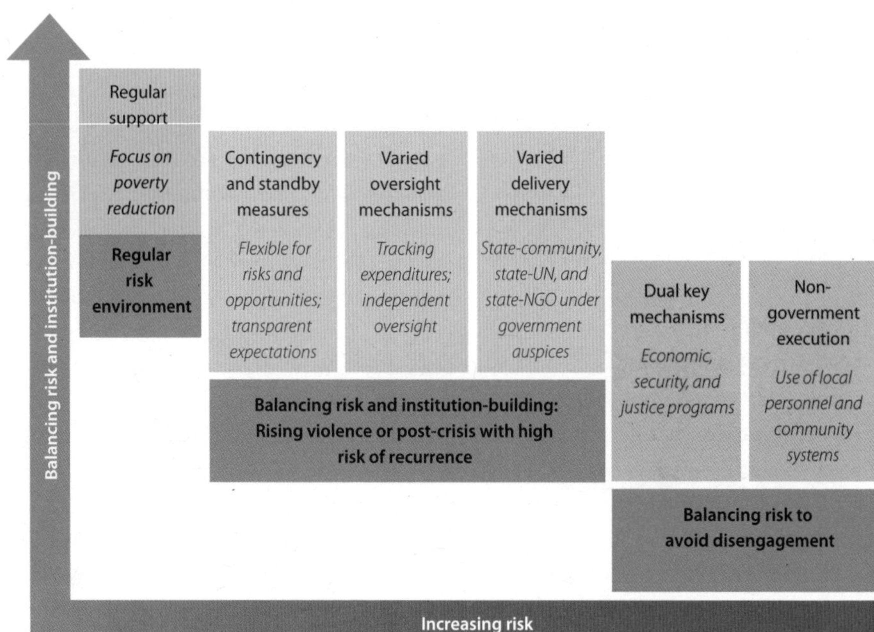

Source: WDR team.

adapt to risk include shifting from budget support to "tracked" expenditure through government systems,[6] and from regular reporting and internal control mechanisms to independent financial monitoring agents, independent monitoring of complaints, and independent technical agents.

- **Varying the delivery mechanisms when engaging through national institutions.** Variations in delivery mechanisms include community structures, civil society, the private sector, and the UN and other international executing agencies in delivering programs jointly with state institutions.

In situations of more extreme risk where donors would normally disengage, the following options could be considered:

- **Consider executive capacity to supplement national control systems,** as with "dual key" mechanisms, where international line management capacity works alongside national actors, and agency processes are governed by joint national and international boards.
- **Use local personnel and community structures** for delivering humanitarian, economic, and social programs, which still maintains some focus on local institutional capacity, mitigating the brain drain of local skills overseas.

Risk can also be shared by pooling funds. To achieve results at scale, pooling funds can provide recipient governments with larger single programs and international partners with a way to support programs that greatly exceed their own national contribution. Pooling funds can also be an effective way to pool risks, shifting the burden of responsibility for risks of waste, abuse, or corruption from the shoulders of each individual donor to the multilateral system. Multidonor trust funds (MDTFs) have delivered excellent results in some situations. But the performance of these funds is mixed, with criticisms ranging from slowness and cumbersome procedures and governance arrangements to a lack of robust monitoring and evaluation of results and limited support through national systems. A small fraction of international assistance in violence-affected countries flows through MDTFs, undermining their overall impact. The combined security-justice-development programs and internal agency reforms described above would help mitigate some of these challenges.

Measuring transitional progress—as discussed in chapter 8 from the perspective of national reformers—can also give international actors help in responding to risks. National reformers and donors need to show results to their parliaments, media, taxpayers, and citizens. Standard development measures, such as economic growth and the MDGs, are excellent long-term goals and indicators, but they are not always helpful in fragile situations in the short term. These indicators move too slowly to give feedback to governments and

TABLE 9.2 *Compelling and feasible short-term indicators*

		Current data coverage: Most recent 5 years		
		Violence		Trust in national institutions
		Battle deaths	Homicide rates	
Low-income countries	Fragile	100% coverage, low precision	24% coverage	Many every 3 to 4 years, some more infrequently
	Non-fragile	100% coverage, low precision	48% coverage	Biennially
Middle-income countries		100% coverage, medium precision	64% coverage	Annually, some more frequently
High-income countries		100% coverage, high precision (low incidence)	78% coverage	Monthly/weekly

Source: WDR team calculations.

their international partners on the speed and direction of progress, and they do not directly measure security, or citizen concerns over issues such as inequality, unemployment, or trust in national institutions.

The development of indicators that can show short-term progress is not just a technical issue—it is important at a political level for both national governments and donors to show short-term improvements and to maintain support for continued investments—and at times for the occasional risky and difficult institutional reforms. The indicators presented in chapter 8 on security, trust in national institutions, and progress in governance in relation to the historic record of how long transformations have taken in other countries can help donors as well as national reformers—by showing that progress is being made even when some setbacks occur.

International actors could also play a role in helping countries develop the capacity to measure these indicators (see table 9.2). WDR estimates indicate that information on deaths in civil conflict is available for all developing countries, although only 24 percent of fragile countries have homicide data and the precision of battle-death information is likely lower. A partnership of member states, the UN Office on Drugs and Crime (UNODC), the IFIs, and the universities and NGOs that collect conflict data could take this forward. A similar effort could develop another useful indicator: measuring confidence in institutions through polling. With regard to trust in institutions, regular information on security and citizen perceptions of the state is available in most high-income and some middle-income countries, but is rarely available in the fragile states, which need it most. Polling surveys are cheap and can be administered frequently—and new technologies are emerging to conduct surveys by cell phone, which this Report did as part of its background research in the Democratic Republic of Congo.[7] The Report estimates indicate that most countries have some polling data—but in fragile states the data are collected very infrequently. A partnership of the regional barometers, Statistics 40, and the IFIs could support poorer and more fragile countries in using the polling tools that richer countries draw upon.

Ending the stop-go pattern of assistance

International agencies will also need to think carefully about how to lengthen the duration of assistance to meet the realities of institutional transformation over a generation without raising costs. As suggested by Commissioner for Peace and Security, Ambassador Ramtane Lamamra and Under-Secretary-General for Peacekeeping Operations Alain Le Roy (box 9.2), the flexible use of alternative modalities for peacekeeping can aid substantially in this regard, including over-the-horizon capacities. Building on growing cooperation, the multilateral security agencies—the African Union Peace and Security Council, UN Department of Peacekeeping Operations, the European Union (EU), and North Atlantic Treaty Organization (NATO)—could work with the IFIs to conduct a thorough examination of the costs and benefits of over-the-horizon deployments and other forms of flexible peacekeeping to provide long-term assistance in fragile situations at reasonable cost.

Better resourcing for mediation and diplomatic facilitation is also an easy win, since it is always low cost and can reduce risks of violence escalation. This could be linked to efforts to foster a norm that mediation or facilitation support should be on call for states longer than is currently the pattern, so that it is available to facilitate ongoing confidence-building beyond the immediate resolution of a crisis.

For development agencies, ending the stop-go pattern of assistance to programs delivering results in citizen security, justice, or jobs—or simply preserving social cohesion and human and institutional capacity—can increase impact without increasing overall cost. As described earlier, volatility greatly reduces aid effectiveness and is twice as high for fragile and conflict-affected countries as for other developing countries, despite the

REFLECTIONS FROM ADVISORY COUNCIL MEMBERS: *2011 WORLD DEVELOPMENT REPORT*

BOX 9.2 *Flexible peacekeeping arrangements*

Ramtane Lamamra, Commissioner for Peace and Security, African Union; *WDR Advisory Council Member;* with **Alain Le Roy,** United Nations Under-Secretary-General for Peacekeeping Operations

Societies trying to move away from violence face acute problems of mistrust, uncertainty, and lack of confidence in the basic institutions of the state. The use of mediation and peacekeeping as "commitment mechanisms," as this Report describes them, can help overcome these obstacles to settlement. It can also extend the authority of the state and contribute to the establishment of the rule of law.

In this context, we welcome the messages in this Report about the role that peacekeeping can play in helping states move away from violence, which broadly accord with our experience. The Report's finding that the deployment of international peacekeepers extends the duration of a political settlement accords with our experience. The conclusion that it also contributes to positive economic growth reinforces the argument that development and security go hand in hand. We also share the Report's emphasis on the importance of transforming national institutions into guarantors of security and prosperity in the long term.

In order to achieve these goals, peacekeeping needs to be given the right capabilities. Although the African Union and the United Nations have different mandates and face different demands, we share the challenge of managing peacekeeping operations deployed to difficult areas, without the full range of capabilities needed to succeed. The international community learned the hard way in the mid-1990s the human and political costs of failing to equip peacekeepers with the necessary resources to fulfill their mandates. In some cases, this is a question of scale; in others, quality or flexibility. Far from the Cold War days of static peacekeeping in buffer zones or alongside contested borders, contemporary operations are dynamic, operate in politically complex environments, and often cover enormous areas.

The UN and the African Union (AU) operate together in Sudan and Somalia to try to meet such challenges. The important partnership between the two organizations is not without complexity and controversy, but represents the shared determination to meet the immediate challenges we confront.

The WDR points to the fact that uncertainty and weak institutions that enable violence can endure in a society for several decades, long after the traditional period of intensive peacekeeping. In too many cases, peacekeepers had to be recalled when a brief period of recovery was followed by a relapse into a new cycle of violence.

The dilemma here is that national authorities and international mandating bodies are often reluctant to contemplate longer term peacekeeping engagements. More creative solutions must be found. These could include combinations of long-term programs for security sector development and reform, light monitoring, and over-the-horizon reinforcements. Over-the-horizon arrangements have been used to good effect in the intensive phase of peacekeeping, for example, with the European Union's Operation Artemis in the Democratic Republic of Congo. If development and security indeed march hand in hand, so too should peacekeeping and economic support to the process of transforming national institutions—including through joint programs, for example, on security sector reform and in the management of natural resources. We welcome the Report's call for a deeper examination of the costs, benefits, and possible arrangements for longer term security and political support to national actors seeking a more permanent shift away from the risk of violence.

fragile countries' greater need for persistence in building social and state institutions. There are options for reducing volatility (see box 9.3), including providing threshold amounts of aid based on appropriate modalities, topping up aid allocations to the most fragile states when specific types of programs have demonstrated the ability to deliver effectively and at scale (as proposed in a recent working paper by the Centre for Global Development),[8] and dedicating a target percentage of assistance to larger and longer-term programs in fragile and conflict-affected states under the OECD-DAC (Development Assistance Committee) framework. As outlined in chapter 6, a 30 percent decrease in volatility could deliver value of around US$30 million per annum to each fragile and conflict-affected state.

Track 3: Reducing external stresses: New regional and global action

Direct assistance to states needs to be complemented by action at a regional and global level to reduce external stresses. The analysis in this Report has consistently emphasized

REFLECTIONS FROM ADVISORY COUNCIL MEMBERS: *2011 WORLD DEVELOPMENT REPORT*

BOX 9.3 *Preventing violence: Prioritizing investment in citizen security and justice reforms*

Resolving the donor risk and results dilemma: Learning from the Tinbergen rule

Paul Collier, Professor of Economics and Director for the Centre for the Study of African Economies, Oxford University; *WDR Advisory Council Member*

In allocating aid, donors currently consider two fundamental objectives: aid should follow need and aid should be well-used. Unfortunately, in fragile states, these two objectives are commonly in conflict: needs are far greater than elsewhere, but governments lack the capacity to spend aid well. The result has often been that aid volumes oscillate around an inadequate average as donors shift between concern for need and concern for effectiveness.

Jan Tinbergen, one of the most revered Nobel laureates, formulated a simple principle which illuminates the donor dilemma and points to a resolution. He showed that a given number of objectives can be achieved only if there are at least as many independent policy instruments. Donors have been attempting to achieve two objectives, meeting need and assuring effectiveness, with a single instrument—the volume of aid. Such an approach is doomed to failure: either one of the objectives must be sacrificed or a second instrument must be introduced. Since clearly neither objective can be abandoned, the implication is that donors must develop another instrument.

That instrument is the modality for aid delivery: modalities should vary according to the capacity of government. While unconditional and unmonitored budget support or unhurried project investments are appropriate for secure and well-governed states, it is essential to develop alternative mechanisms for channeling aid inflows in fragile situations. New types of instruments are needed and should recognise the spectrum of risk, from governments who are well-intentioned but face insecurity and weak institutions, to those who are more abusive. Recurrent expenditures can be supported, and indeed often need to be, if governments are to regain legitimacy in the eyes of their citizens, but should support actions linked to stabilization and be provided only with additional oversight mechanisms which track expenditures. Funds through government can be channeled directly to the local level and monitored through community reporting. Social service provision could be scaled up if aid were channeled through public agencies outside the conventional civil service, co-supervised by government and third parties such as civil society, and donors. The agencies could fund clinics, schools, and public works run by churches, NGOs, and local communities, in return for public accountability and agreed standards of quality.

Tinbergen's rule also says how objectives should be linked to instruments. The donor dilemma can be resolved by linking the objective of meeting needs to the volume of aid, and the objective of using aid well to the choice of delivery modalities. Fragile states need large volumes of aid, but aid delivery should look very different from contexts in which government ministries are effective. Spending money effectively in fragile states is not complicated: for example, community-driven approaches, mission schools, and clinics have been operating successfully in the most difficult environments for many years. The needs are manifestly greater than other environments and so returns on aid can be commensurately higher. But to establish that those needs can indeed be met cost-effectively and build long-term institutional resilience, delivery modalities that encourage experimentation, are evaluated for results, and are adapted to respond quickly to experiences of success and failure are required.

WDR Note: Additional approaches for reducing volatility

The Centre for Global Development proposes the scaling up of successful projects in fragile and conflict-affected states. As outlined in Gelb 2010, this would involve timely monitoring, full transparency, and independent evaluation of projects. Projects that demonstrate early results could then draw upon additional financing through a special multi-donor trust fund designated as a tranche for scaling up. By reducing the length of the feedback loop in project monitoring and evaluation, this approach would align incentives for those delivering aid and those receiving aid and reward successes early in the project cycle, making this approach wholly compatible with output-based aid.

OECD–DAC commitments. A further possibility is to explore a commitment under the OECD-DAC framework for a percentage of aid programs to go into long-term, larger scale support. There is a value to small, rapid interventions in fragile situations, and it would not be desirable to lose the flexibility to provide this type of assistance. But the percentage of aid currently in small, fragmented, and short-term assistance appears to be too high (see chapter 6) to benefit long-term institution-building. The Accra Agenda commits donors to developing long-term modalities to support the building of "capable, accountable, and responsive states."

the role of external stresses in increasing the risks of violence, and it is therefore important that the recommendations for action do not ignore this important area. Firm, practical, and coordinated action can diminish the external stresses that hinder stability in the short and long term. And support can be increased to develop regional and international "buffers" to absorb and mitigate these stresses. Analysis for this Report suggests three areas for such action: cross-border cooperation, strengthening action against the trafficking and illicit financial flows that can fuel violence, and protecting fragile states from food and resource shocks.

Cross-border goods: Development, security, and administrative pooling

Support for regional goods is underresourced. In recognition of the importance of external stresses for violence, donors could increase the proportion of their financial and technical support going to cross-border development programming and regional infrastructure, as well as for various forms of regional administrative and economic cooperation—giving priority to violence-affected regions. Such support could take the following forms:

- **Trade and transit infrastructure.** Numerous conflict and violence-affected regions face obvious gaps in the infrastructure for trade between producer and consumer areas and for ports and airports. They include large regions, such as Central Africa and Central Asia, but also smaller subnational areas that have little access to trade, such as the northeastern states of India. Where infrastructure is constructed in violence-affected areas, care should be taken to use labor-intensive technologies and provide for local labor to avoid tensions over the benefits. In some regions, discussions about shared economic infrastructure with joint benefits could also create an opening for later political or security discussions. In most cases, some simple policy reforms need to be undertaken in parallel as these can be as great a constraint to cross-border trade as lack of infrastructure.
- **Cross-border development programming.** Many insecure border areas share similar social and economic structures, in which a shared terrain, ethnicity, or history creates natural bonds. Yet very few countries take advantage of this to share lessons for development programming on both sides of insecure border areas. Community-driven development programs, for example, are likely to face similar strengths and weaknesses in community organization, as is the private sector. Development sectors like health, which has regional and international public-good aspects, can be a noncontentious form of cross-border cooperation. Cross-border development programming could simply involve special arrangements to share lessons, or it could in some cases move toward formal joint arrangements to design and monitor programs.
- **Regional security support.** Although violence frequently crosses borders, international responses remain largely within them. Two approaches that have been piloted warrant further consideration: regional political missions—including UN offices in Africa and Central Asia, the latter of which has a mandate for preventive diplomacy linked to border and customs management and counter-trafficking initiatives. A second is regional initiatives for counter-trafficking, such as the joint UN/ECOWAS (Economic Community of West African States) West African Coast Initiative on organized crime.
- **Shared regional technical and administrative capacity.** As chapter 7 noted, pooling subregional administrative capacities can allow states to develop institutional capabilities they could not manage on their own. There are a range of initiatives that could be undertaken in this area, depending on regional needs—from programs that deliver the specialized assistance for reform of security and justice

sectors and multisectoral community programs at a regional level, to pooled administrative capacity to address skills and training for youth, as with shared university facilities.

Rather than these somewhat incremental approaches to specific cross-border initiatives, international donors could take a larger step to finance regional approaches. The principle of such an initiative would be to build on the local political knowledge and legitimacy of regional institutions, in combination with the technical and financial capacity of global agencies. Delivered through regional institutions in collaboration with global agencies, this approach could adapt lessons from initiatives that have already successfully pooled developed shared regional capacity, such as justice in the Caribbean.[9] It could also draw lessons from existing cross-border cooperation, such as the Greater Mekong Subregion, West Africa's initiatives on trafficking and economic integration, and the European Union's programs for previously conflict-affected border regions.[10] It would support political initiatives of regional institutions (such as the African Union Border Programme[11] and ASEAN's subregional initiatives) with financial and technical expertise from global partners. Well designed, the expansion of such regional initiatives would also have the advantage of protecting activities from some of the aid volatility caused by fluctuations in national governance.

Stemming the trafficking and illicit financial flows that can fuel violence

Follow the money: at the heart of action against the illegal trafficking of drugs and natural resources is tracking illicit financial flows. For areas seriously affected by illegal trafficking and corruption, such as Central America or West Africa, most countries have nothing approaching the national capacity needed to gather and process information on financial transactions or to investigate and prosecute offenders. Along with initiatives that help to support a global community to address corruption issues, such as the International Corruption Hunter's Alliance and the Stolen Asset Recovery Initiative (STAR), three measures would help in this effort to reduce violence and the illicit financial flows that support it:

- **Strengthening the capacity to conduct strategic analysis of these flows in key countries with the majority of global financial transfers.** About a dozen financial intelligence units in major financial markets or hubs have the integrity, independence, and technical capacity to conduct such analysis. Concerted efforts to analyze suspicious flows and exchange information could greatly increase their ability to detect illicit financial flows.
- **Global financial centers could increase the openness of information provision and their cooperation with stolen asset recovery processes.** As part of this effort, global financial institutions could perform strategic analysis and make it available to countries affected. To respect privacy, this analysis could be based on shifts in aggregate flows rather than individual account information. The analytical tools exist, as chapter 7 describes for Australia's analysis of illicit flows generated by corruption or money-laundering. But these approaches have not yet been applied globally.
- **Developed states and financial centers could commit to ensuring that investing the proceeds from corruption in their countries is a violation of their anti-money-laundering laws.** As part of this commitment, they could also step up their cooperation with law enforcement authorities in fragile states. This would build on recent precedents for joint and parallel investigations, such as those between the United Kingdom and Nigeria, and the United States and Haiti, described in chapter 8.[12]

Mechanisms to coordinate the international spillovers of domestic policies are crucial. Spillovers from successful action against illegal trafficking in one country can affect another—Colombia's actions against drug cartels have had ripple effects across Central America, Mexico, and even West Africa.[13] Similar effects can pertain to other commodities: a ban or restraints on logging in one country, for example, will increase demand in other countries that do not have similar policies. Without limiting sovereign decisions, a platform for dialogue between countries would help governments identify potential impacts in advance, debate costs and benefits at a regional level, and consider options to coordinate policy or take action to mitigate impacts in countries affected by the decisions of others. Regional institutions could lead such a dialogue, as could a global agency such as UNODC.

Joint efforts on trafficking in natural resources can also produce more effective action. The new Natural Resource Charter is an effective way to build on earlier initiatives, such as the Kimberley Process and the Extractive Industries Transparency Initiative, by focusing on widespread communications and citizen pressure.[14] International market regulatory requirements are another form of consumer country action to combat trafficking. In timber, these schemes include certification requirements in the United States under the Lacey Act, European procurement policies that require government agencies to purchase only verifiably legal timber, and forthcoming EU due diligence regulations involving bilateral cooperation with select producer countries. Such market requirement systems could be strengthened by information-sharing arrangements between enforcement in producer and consumer countries to assist consumer countries in acting against suspect shipments. Consumer nations and international actors should also provide additional assistance to build capacity within producer nations to implement effective chain-of-custody systems that keep illegally sourced commodities out of the supply chain.

Forging a new sense of co-responsibility for countering trafficking would also produce better analysis of options. For example, there would be value in joint efforts between producing and consuming countries to understand the implications of current debates on combining demand-side options on drugs, including legalization, with supply-side enforcement. This would require in-depth analysis of the health, social, and economic implications of legalized drug use under different regulatory regimes, as well as trends in consumption patterns. It would also require analysis of the systems to regulate and control drugs that become legal and to ensure enforcement where drugs remain illegal.

New action to protect fragile states from food insecurity and resource shocks

Knowledge about the impacts of food, energy, and resource shocks is limited. Rising global demand for food and energy may impact fragile and violence-affected states severely. New analytical efforts are an important first step in understanding this phenomenon. One forward step would be for the relevant agencies—the World Bank, UN Energy Programme, International Energy Agency, and others—to work together on a World Resources Outlook, bringing together the multiple reports and analysis already undertaken by these agencies independently.[15] Such a report could give policy makers the valuable integrated analysis they currently lack. It could examine the state of scientific knowledge about the availability of key resources, including oil, food, water, and potentially land, together with how climate change will affect each of them; the economic dimensions of resource availability, including the risk of price spikes, inflationary trends, and how resource prices interact with wider trends in the international economy; and vulnerability to scarcity trends among poor people and regions affected by violence. Without such analysis, the risk of unintended consequences from policy may remain unaddressed—as with biofuels, where the possible food security implications of measures to promote energy security were inadequately considered.

For fragile states unable to support comprehensive food security initiatives, best-fit options may be desirable. A reliable global food stock system would be ideal, but a smaller independent emergency reserve—managed regionally—could bridge the lags in food aid response. Held in existing national storage facilities at strategic locations, such a reserve could allow for rapid response. An example is the East Asia Emergency Rice Reserve program established by the 10 ASEAN Member States, China, Japan, and the Republic of Korea, to provide food assistance and strengthen food security in emergencies and for poverty alleviation.[16]

Effective early warning schemes can also be a second-best approach to addressing food insecurity. While reducing the likelihood and impact of food price shocks would be a first best option, effective early warning systems on food and agriculture can be put in place to identify, assess, and monitor the evolution of conflict risks and food security levels, especially in fragile countries. Examples of early warning systems that use satellite data to anticipate crop failure and food shortages are the UN-sponsored Global Information and Early Warning System,[17] which aims at improving food-security response planning in 22 drought-prone African countries, and the United States Agency for International Development (USAID)–sponsored Famine Early Warning System Network,[18] which monitors food supply and demand in all countries with emphasis on 80 low-income food deficit nations.

International trading systems should protect fragile states from the pressure of international resource competition in the search for land or energy. Initiatives addressing these issues, such as the Extractive Industry Transparency Initiative (EITI), the Equator Principles,[19] and the Santiago Principles,[20] have formulated standards to guide engagement in certain sectors, and many institutions and large enterprises have produced guidelines of their own. But broader efforts to build on such ongoing private initiatives are needed. In large-scale agro-investing, where no industry agreement has been reached on self-regulation, the World Bank and the UN Food and Agriculture Organization (FAO), the International Fund for Agricultural Development (IFAD), the UN Conference on Trade and Development (UNCTAD), and other partners have recently formulated a set of principles for responsible agro-investment that stress respect for land and resource rights; food security; transparency; good governance; a proper enabling environment; consultation and participation; and social and environmental sustainability (see box 7.9).[21]

Ahead of potential new impacts from climate change, international support could be provided to subregions where fragile countries share river boundaries. Depending on the circumstances, this effort could encompass a shift from agreements based on precise volume to agreements based on percentages, to account for the potential impact of reduced flow, and to agreements based on sharing the benefits from expanded development of river basins that benefit all riparians, as well as new agreements where none exist. Efforts to foster cross-border or subregional water management arrangements can ease regional tensions even if climate impacts do not end up affecting flow rates.

Track 4: Marshaling support from lower-, middle-, and higher-income countries and from global and regional institutions

The landscape of international assistance in fragile and violence-affected countries has changed in the last 20 years, with more aid and policy input from middle-income countries with a history of solidarity support. Several regional institutions are also playing a greater role in security and development issues. Yet discussions of global conflict and violence, the norms of responsible leadership to respond to them, and the shape of international assistance have been driven more by northern than southern actors. The International Dialogue on Peacebuilding and Statebuilding has been created to help address this deficit. The WDR process has also conducted wide-ranging consultations with violence-affected lower- and middle-income countries, regional policy makers, and regional institutions, as well as with traditional donor partners. It found many areas of agreement—the focus on institution-building and governance and on citizen security, justice, and jobs—but also some areas of difference.

WDR consultations frequently revealed divided views among national actors, regional bodies, middle-income countries, and OECD actors over what is realistic to expect from national leadership in improving governance, over what time period, and over the "forms" versus the "functions" of good governance (for example, elections versus broader democratic practices and processes, and minimizing corruption in practice versus establishing procurement laws and anti-corruption commissions).

Perceived double standards were also criticized by WDR interlocutors, who reflected a sentiment that donor countries and organizations that have faced their own internal governance challenges could approach shortcomings in fragile developing states with more humility. Developed countries are not immune to corruption, bribery, human rights abuses, or failures to account adequately for public finances. Thus, effective implementation of standards of good governance is also a challenge in advanced countries, even more so when the international community has played an executive government or security role in violence-affected areas.

Lack of concerted support for the norms of responsible leadership is a concern, because progress in global norms is crucial for reducing the risk of violence. Regional and global standards, as well as recognition and sanction mechanisms in constitutionality, human rights, and corruption, have provided support and incentives for national leadership, particularly where the capacity of the domestic system to provide rewards and accountability is weak. Human rights standards, for example, have been important reference points for reformers that led efforts to transform authoritarian military regimes in many regions toward more accountable systems, with benefits for citizen security and broader development. The Lomé Declaration in 2000, establishing African standards and a regional response mechanism to unconstitutional changes in government, has, as described earlier, underpinned a significant decrease in coups since the 1990s and strong continental action to uphold constitutional government.[22]

Modest actions that could strengthen collaboration among higher-, middle-, and lower-income countries on shared problems of violence and development, both global and local, are as follows:

- **Increase both South-South and South-North exchanges on violence prevention.** South-South exchanges have enormous potential to provide relevant capacity and lessons in current fragile and violence-affected situations.[23] Lower- and middle-income countries that have gone through their own recent experiences of transition have much to offer to their counterparts—as demonstrated in this Report, where Latin American countries offered perspectives on urban violence prevention and security and justice reforms, China on job creation, India on local public works and democratic practices, Southeast Asian and African countries on community-driven development in conflict areas. Yet, South-North exchanges are also important. While institutional capacities differ, many Northern and Southern countries, provinces, and cities face some similar stresses. Program approaches—such as addressing trafficking, reintegrating ex-gang members and disengaged young people, and fostering tolerance and social bonds among communities that are ethnically or religiously divided—will have lessons relevant for others. Such exchanges would increase understanding that the challenges of violence are not unique to developing countries and that developing countries are not alone in struggling to find solutions.

- **Better align international assistance behind regional governance efforts.** When regional institutions take the initiative, as with the African Union (AU) on constitutionality, they have great comparative advantage in traction with their member states. The potential convening role of regional institutions was also widely recognized in WDR consultations by higher-, middle-, and lower-income country interlocutors alike (see box 9.4). Supporting regional platforms to discuss the application of governance norms is an effective way to increase ownership. Adopting clearer structures to discuss responses to major improvements or deteriorations in governance (such as coups d'états) among bilateral and multilateral actors would also improve information-sharing and the potential for coordinated responses without creating unacceptable binding obligations on international actors.[24]
- **Expand initiatives to recognize responsible leadership.** While there is always a role for frank and transparent criticism, approaches from the North that are seen as disproportionately focused on criticism in fragile situations can be divisive. Initiatives, such as the Ibrahim Prize for African leadership, could be emulated to recognize leaders in different roles (for example, ministers who have a lasting impact on corruption or military leaders who implement successful security-sector reform). Multistakeholder initiatives, such as the Extractive Industries Transparency Initiative, could consider provisions to recognize individual leaders or leadership teams who have improved the transparency of resource revenues and expenditures, whether in governments, civil society, or companies.

More focused and realistic expectations built into the timetables for governance improvements would also help bridge gaps in perspectives among countries receiving international assistance, their middle- and higher-income international partners, and global and regional institutions. This is particularly crucial in the light of recent social protests that demonstrate strong grievances and expectations over governance change—that were not picked up by standard analyses of security and of development progress. The indicators described in chapter 8 aim to address this deficit through a focus on whether countries are on track to make institutional and governance improvements within the realistic generational time frames that the faster reformers have achieved, and how citizens perceive trends in the legitimacy and performance of national institutions across the political security and development domains.

These would be a simple way, as Louise Arbour suggests in box 9.4, to compare progress, stagnation, or deterioration. Ensuring that such indicators measure outcomes rather than just the form of institutions (laws passed, anti-corruption commissions formed) is also important to ensure that they encourage rather than suppress innovative national action and that they foster learning among low-, middle-, and high-income country institutions. The UN Peacebuilding Commission—which brings together fragile states, donors, troop-contributing countries, and regional bodies—has unexploited potential to advise on realistic timelines.

A continuing global learning platform

This Report draws together many rich strands of existing research on security and development, adding to them through new quantitative and qualitative work. But its preparation has made clear the gaps in knowledge—from evolving issues such as the links between organized crime and political violence, glaringly underresearched, to the lack of firm conceptual models and testing of the processes of institutional transformation, and to the absence of evaluation data on key policy

REFLECTIONS FROM ADVISORY COUNCIL MEMBERS: *2011 WORLD DEVELOPMENT REPORT*

BOX 9.4 *The role of regional institutions and initiatives in norm-setting and violence prevention*

Reaffirming consensus on international norms and standards—The role of regional organizations

Louise Arbour, President, International Crisis Group; former UN High Commissioner for Human Rights; *WDR Advisory Council Member*

Whether based on universal values, such as the sanctity of human life, or on international legal rules, there are some universally accepted norms—reflected in the Charter of the United Nations and other international instruments.

These norms are not self-implementing, and because they include the right to cultural diversity, their interpretation must reflect local, national, and regional diversity. The resistance to the exportation of "Western values" might be no more than the rejection of a foreign way of expressing a particular norm, rather than a rejection of the norm itself.

Regional institutions can bridge the distance between universal norms and local customs. Those customs or practices must conform, in substance, to the core international principles from which the international community derives its cohesion. Otherwise, cultural diversity can simply override, and undermine, the international framework.

In the justice sector, for instance, uniformity of institutional models and procedures may obscure radical differences in the actual delivery of justice. But the adjudication of disputes based on principles of fairness, impartiality, transparency, integrity, compassion, and ultimately accountability can take many forms.

In their assistance to development, international actors must resist the exportation of form over substance, and accept the regionalization of norms that enhance, rather than impede, their true universal character. In the same spirit, regional actors must translate, in a culturally relevant way, international norms and repudiate nonconforming practices.

And all must concede that the standards set by universal norms are aspirations. Measures of performance should reflect either progress, stagnation, or regression in a given country, toward a common, universal ideal.

and program options, such as justice and employment interventions. Priorities for future research and policy work are as follows:

- **Filling gaps in data.** There are gaps in the data on violence (particularly criminal violence) and on citizen trust in national institutions. Other variables to fully test conceptual models and evaluate policy options are also missing. Priorities for following up on the WDR's work would be spending on criminal justice systems, institutional performance indicators of capacity and accountability in security and criminal justice systems, and employment data.
- **Testing conceptual models.** The WDR has put forward hypotheses drawn from regional and country consultations that are consistent with available cross-country data or qualitative case analysis. All would benefit from further testing and research to identify detailed pathways of successful reform and reasons for failure. They include the importance of national institutional transformation and governance outcomes for sustained violence prevention; confidence-building as a prelude to wider institutional transformation; the characteristics of inclusive-enough coalitions for reform in fragile situations; how these are adapted or consolidated over multiple transitions; and the design and benefits of early institutional action on citizen security, justice, and jobs. As discussed in chapter 2 (box 2.5), more research is needed on the link between employment and violence prevention.
- **Evaluating policy and program options.** There is also a dearth of impact evaluations on the relationship between specific policy and program interventions and security outcomes. At a macropolicy level, the costs and benefits of second-best reforms in situations of insecurity and weak institutions merit further attention—as do the sequence of reforms to increase revenues and expand government expenditures and the

costs and benefits of regional integration. At the program level, evaluating the importance of rapid development results and of integrated security-development approaches would greatly assist policy makers. A focused evaluation agenda to analyze the impact of programmatic interventions to address unemployment in situations of conflict or rising violence would also contribute to a more proactive international approach to job creation, including the role of private sector development. Analysis of the economic costs and benefits of flexible peacekeeping options, as suggested by Commissioner Lamamra and Under-Secretary-General Le Roy, can inform future policy developments.[25]

- **Tracking the evolving impacts of new phenomena,** including rapidly increasing demand for energy and scarce resource supplies, as well as climate change, on areas at risk of violence.

The future research agenda is rich indeed,[26] and a strong network of public agencies, think tanks, universities, and NGOs could productively collaborate in tackling it. A shared collaborative platform for knowledge on violence, fragility, and development would also have the advantage of drawing together work led by the political and social sciences, including economics, and by the political, security, humanitarian, and development agencies in this most interdisciplinary of areas. Such a platform could foster research by institutes in fragile and conflict-affected states and in middle-income countries that have experienced violence, thus helping to produce the kind of lessons and learning highlighted here, as well as informing a new consensus on critical norms and their adaptation to national contexts. This platform can also draw from a new research initiative, "Democratizing Development Economics," from the research group at the World Bank, which promotes "Open Data, Open Knowledge, and Open Solutions" to support South-South learning and collaborative research on common challenges and solutions.[27]

A compelling agenda for action

Can the international community help build resilience in countries facing repeated or new threats? Significant areas—North Africa and the Middle East; Central Africa, the Horn of Africa, and West Africa; Southwest and Central Asia; and Central America—currently face risks of new or repeated cycles of violence. Will the international community be able to help, not just to halt one acute episode, but reduce the risk of continuing cycles? Business as usual is unlikely to deliver sustained results. What is needed is a renewed consensus among international actors in their dialogue with national leaders, based on expectations that are both principled and realistic. Supporting this consensus at a practical level will require focused and timely assistance to institutions that can help prevent an escalation of violence. It will also require a willingness to try new ways of doing business in humanitarian, development, security, and mediation assistance in order to help build national institutional legitimacy. And it will require decisive action to prevent stresses outside these countries from overwhelming fragile progress.

All the recommendations of this Report have at their heart the concept of shared global risk. Risks are evolving, with new threats to stability arising from international organized crime and global economic instability. The landscape of international power relations is also changing, as lower- and middle-income countries increase their share of global economic influence and their contributions to global policy thinking. A fundamental rethink is needed on the approaches of international actors to manage global risks collectively—and as equal partners.

The recommendations are not easy to implement. They require clear political leadership from both developed and developing countries and sustained attention to change in bilateral development agencies and multilateral institutions. Real change will require a strong rationale for political leadership. But a dual rationale exists: fragility and violence are major obstacles to development, and are no longer confined to poor and remote areas or cityscapes. This decade has seen the increasing penetration of instability in global life—in terrorism, an expanding drug trade, and the rising numbers of internationally mobile refugees. Breaking cycles of repeated violence is thus a shared challenge demanding urgent action.

Notes

1. Stewart and Brown 2007.
2. Ojielo 2007; Odendaal 2010; UNDPA 2010a.
3. Following an extensive study carried out by the Office of the High Representative (the chief civilian peace implementation agency in Bosnia and Herzegovina) at the request of the Peace Implementation Council, the coordinating structure of the International Community in Bosnia and Herzegovina was "streamlined" in 2002 to eliminate overlapping effort and responsibilities and increase effectiveness. As part of this process a Board of Principals was established under the chairmanship of the High Representative to serve as the main coordinating body for international community activity in Bosnia and Herzegovina. The Board of Principals meets once a week in Sarajevo and is attended by Office of the High Representative, NATO-led military Stabilisation Force (SFOR), Office of Security and Cooperation in Europe (OSCE), European Union Police Mission, UN High Commissioner for Refugees (UNHCR), European Commission, the World Bank, the International Monetary Fund (IMF), and the UN Development Programme (UNDP). See Office of the High Representative and European Union Special Representative 2011.
4. Recognizing the public-good benefits of some types of security assistance, as the OECD-DAC is considering by providing a separate channel for reporting assistance in these areas, could also help.
5. g7+ is an open grouping of low-income countries experiencing conflict and fragility. It was established in 2008 and comprises the following countries: Afghanistan, Burundi, the Central African Republic, Chad, Côte d'Ivoire, the Democratic Republic of Congo, Haiti, Liberia, Nepal, the Solomon Islands, Sierra Leone, South Sudan, and Timor-Leste.
6. A practical example of this type of shift is Ethiopia in 2005, when government and donors agreed to move from regular budget support to a program of transfers to local and municipal governments. The program included measures to ensure that all regions of the country, irrespective of how they had voted in elections, received continuing central government support.
7. The WDR team, in conjunction with Mobile Accord and with generous donations of SMS (short message service) by Vodacom Congo, carried out a geo-polling project known as *DRC Speaks!* The project utilized cell phone technology to conduct the survey. Using SMS through cell phones, the project allowed more than 140,000 Congolese to share, without any filters, their thoughts, feelings, and concerns. See section on monitoring progress out of fragility in chapter 6 for more information.
8. Gelb 2010.
9. See Favaro 2010.
10. For the Greater Mekong Subregion, see World Bank 2006d; the section on regional stresses and support in chapter 7. For West Africa, see Favaro 2008, 2010; box 7.10 in chapter 7. For the European border region, see Greta and Lewandowski 2010; Otocan 2010; Council of Europe 1995; Council of Europe and Institute of International Sociology of Gorizia 2003; Bilcik and others 2000; box 7.11 in chapter 7.
11. For the African Union Border Programme Cooperation, see African Union 2007a.
12. See Messick 2011; box 8.4 in chapter 8.
13. See Arboleda 2010; UNODC 2010a; WDR team consultations with government officials, civil society representatives, and security personnel in Colombia, 2010; feature, chapter 3.
14. The Natural Resource Charter is a set of common principles and a practical step-by-step guide for escaping the "resource curse." It has no political heritage or sponsorships and was prepared by an independent group of global experts on economically sustainable resource extraction, assembled by Paul Collier, Director of the Centre for the Study of African Economies at Oxford University. The charter aims to foster coordination, both along the decision chain from exploration to expenditure, and among the international actors and stakeholders, by providing a unifying and overarching

framework for action. It provides the tools and knowledge base necessary to avoid the mismanagement of these diminishing riches and ensure they bring lasting benefit. The charter consists of 12 precepts, detailing the broad princi-ples, specific recommendations, and practical guidance. It is also an information toolkit to guide governments and societies in their use of natural resources so that the opportunities they provide are seized in a way that results in maximum and sustained benefits for citizens. The charter provides a clearinghouse for the collation and dissemination of information and best practice in the governance and management of resource-rich economies. More information on the charter can be found at their website: http://www.naturalresourcecharter.org/.

15. Evans 2010.
16. Brinkman and Hendrix 2010; Bora and others 2010.
17. FAO 2010.
18. USAID Famine Early Warning Systems Network 2010.
19. The Equator Principles (EPs) are a voluntary set of standards for determining, assessing, and managing social and environmental risk in project financing. The EPs are considered the financial industry "gold standard" for sustainable project finance and are based on the International Finance Corporation (IFC) performance standards on social and environmental sustainability and on the World Bank's Environmental, Health and Safety General Guidelines. The principles are intended to serve as a common baseline and framework for the implementation by each adopting institution of its own internal social and environmental policies, procedures, and standards related to its project financing activities. These principles do not create any rights in, or liability to, any person, public or private, and institutions adopt and implement the EPs without reliance on or recourse to IFC or the World Bank. The Equator Principles can be found in full at http://www.equator-principles.com/documents/Equator_Principles.pdf.
20. The Santiago Principles were developed in 2008 by the International Working Group of Sovereign Wealth Funds (SWFs) and represent a collaborative effort by advanced, emerging, and developing country economies to set out a comprehensive framework of 24 voluntary "best practices" guidelines, aiming to provide a clearer understanding of the operations of SWFs. Their adoption on a voluntary basis signals strong commitment to the principles, and their implementation should further enhance the stabilizing role played by SWFs in the financial markets, and help maintain the free flow of cross-border investment. To date, 23 countries are members. For more information, visit the International Working Group of Sovereign Wealth Funds website: http://www.iwg-swf.org.
21. FAO and others 2010.
22. See Organization of African Unity 2000. Also see the section titled "Interstate and civil wars have declined since peaking in the early1990s" in chapter 1.
23. Of the different forms that South-South cooperation has taken, technical assistance has been the most common. Although many technical assistance projects focus on economic and social development, countries in the Global South have also developed specialized capacities in post-conflict peacebuilding. Examples include South Africa's support to build structural capacities for public service through peer learning among public sector schools (Management Development Institutes) at the Ministries for Public Administration in Burundi, Rwanda, and Southern Sudan, all countries that have emerged from violent conflict. Cooperation among 45 municipalities in El Salvador, Guatemala, and Honduras helps to manage regional public goods such as water in the Trifinio region. In Trifinio, regional South-South cooperation has transformed a zone of tensions (no-man's armed borders) into a zone of integration and development. See OECD 2010f.
24. The view of the African Union with respect to West African countries that have recently experienced coups d'états was that donor support to social programs and poverty reduction programs should continue in these countries, but that larger scale support should be paced to support the return to a "constitutional path." In practice, donors were divided between those that suspended assistance completely and those that continued assistance with no change (WDR team consultation with officials in African Union in Addis Ababa, 2010).
25. An example of recent advances in evaluation in fragile states includes the new Development Impact Evaluation (DIME) Initiative, which focuses on questions of legitimacy and utilization of public institutions, public service delivery, local collective action, social capital, and trust in elected officials in projects in Aceh (Indonesia), Afghanistan, Angola, Central African Republic, Cambodia, and Guinea.

26. This report complements research forthcoming in 2011, including a second issue of the *Global Burden of Armed Violence* from the Geneva Declaration, the next volume of the *Human Security Report* published as this report went to press, and the forthcoming *Oxford Handbook of the Economics of Peace and Conflict.*
27. Zoellick 2010a.

Bibliographical Note

This report draws on a wide range of World Bank documents and on numerous outside sources. Background analysis was contributed by: Beatriz Abizanda, Aga Khan Development Network, Nathalie Alvarado, Sanam Naraghi-Anderlini, Matthew Andrews, Jairo Arboleda, Paul Arthur, Claus Astrup, Alexandra Avdeenko, Kathryn Bach, Mark Baird, Patrick Barron, Peter Bartu, Christina Biebesheimer, Arthur G. Blundell, Morten Bøås, Saswati Bora, James Boyce, Henk-Jan Brinkman, Tilman Brück, Rex Brynen, Iride Ceccacci, Brian Center, Pinki Chaudhuri, Asger Christensen, James Cockayne, Tara Cooper, Maria C. Correia, David Craig, Christopher Cramer, Martha Crenshaw, Olivia D'Aoust, Victor A.B. Davies, Pablo de Greiff, Alex de Waal, Dimitri F. De Pues, Frauke de Weijer, Christopher Delgado, Gabriel Demombynes, Deval Desai, Peter Dewees, Sinclair Dinnen, Le Dang Doanh, Barry Eichengreen, Gregory Ellis, Sundstøl Eriksen, FAFO, Alexander Evans, Doug Farah, Edgardo Favaro, James D. Fearon, Ministry of Foreign Affairs of Finland, Hedda Flatø, Shepard Forman, Paul Francis, Anthony Gambino, Esther Garcia, Scott Gates, Alan Gelb, Luigi Giovine, Blair Glencorse, Jack A. Goldstone, Margarita Puerto Gomez, Sonja Grimm, Jean-Marie Guehenno, Scott Guggenheim, Debarati Guha-Sapir, Paul-Simon Handy, Bernard Harborne, Niels Harild, Emily Harwell, Håvard Hegre, Cullen S. Hendrix, Anke Hoeffler, Karla Hoff, Richard Horsey, Fabrice Houdart, Yasheng Huang, Elisabeth Huybens, Inter-American Development Bank, Syeda S. Ijaz, Horst Intscher, Kremena Ionkova, Michael Jacobson, Prashant Jha, Japan International Cooperation Agency (JICA), Michael Johnston, Patricia Justino, Tarcisius Kabutaulaka, Gilbert Khadaglia, Anne Kielland, Robert Krech, Christof P. Kurz, Sarah Laughton, Constantino Lluch, Norman V. Loayza, Clare Lockhart, Megumi Makisaka, Alexandre Marc, Keith Martin, Omar McDoom, Mike McGovern, John-Andrew McNeish, Pratap Bhanu Mehta, Kenneth Menkhaus, Richard Messick, Ministry of Rural Development of India, Nadir Mohammed, Hannah Nielsen, Håvard Mokleiv Nygård, OECD International Network on Conflict and Fragility (OECD/INCAF), David Pearce, Mary Porter Peschka, Nicola Pontara, Douglas Porter, Ministry of Foreign Affairs of Portugal, Monroe Price, Habib Rab, Clionadh Raleigh, Martha Ramirez, Anne Sofie Roald, Esther Rojas-Garcia, Paula Roque, Narve Rotwitt, Caroline Sage, Yezid Sayigh, Mark Schneider, Richard Scobey, Jake Sherman, Sylvana Q. Sinha, Judy Smith-Höhn, Joanna Spear, Anna Spenceley, Radhika Srinivasan, Frances Stewart, Håvard Strand, Scott Straus, Nicole Stremlau, Naotaka Sugawara, Deepak Thapa, Åge Tiltnes, Monica Toft, Robert Townsend, Bakary Fouraba Traore, Keiichi Tsunekawa, the United Nations Development Programme (UNDP), the United Nations Department of Peacekeeping Operations (UNDPKO), the United Nations Department of Political Affairs (UNDPA), Bernice van Bronkhorst, Philip Verwimp, Joaquin Villalobos, Sarah von Billerbeck, Henriette von Kaltenborn-Stachau, Barbara F. Walter, Jusuf Wanandi, Xueli Wang, Clay Wescott, Teresa Whitfield, Alys Willman, Michael Woolcock, Michael Wyganowski, Kohei Yoshida.

Background papers for the Report are available either on the World Wide Web at www.worldbank.org/wdr2011 or through the World Development Report office. The views expressed in these papers are not necessarily those of the World Bank or of this Report.

Many people inside and outside the World Bank gave comments to the team. Valuable comments, guidance, and contributions were provided by Patricio Abinales, Ségolène Adam, James W. Adams, Douglas Addison, Ozong Agborsangaya-Fiteu, Sanjeev S. Ahluwalia, Ahmad Ahsan, Bryant Allen, Noro Andriamihaja, Edward Aspinall, Laura Bailey, Bill Battaile, Ferid Belhaj, Eric Bell, Christina Biebesheimer, Anna Bjerde, Brian Blankespoor, Chris Blattman, Edith H. Bowles, Mike Bourke, Sean Bradley, Cynthia Brady, Anne Brown, Gillie Brown, Colin Bruce, Paola Buendia, Roisín de Burca, William Byrd, Charles Call, Otaviano Canuto, Michael Carnahan, Francis Carneiro, Paloma Anos Casero, Mukesh Chawla, Judy Cheng-Hopkins, Fantu Cheru, Punam Chuhan-Pole, Laurence Clarke, Kevin Clements, Cybèle Cochran, Colombia's Departamento Nacional de Planeación (DNP), Daniele Conversi, Louise Cord, Pamela Cox, Jeff Crisp, Geoffrey Dabelko, Beth Daponte, Monica Das Gupta, Elisabeth David, Martin David, John Davidson, Scott Dawson, Shanta Devarajan, James Dobbins, Joost Draaisma, Gregory Keith Ellis, Ibrahim Elbadawi, Obiageli Kathryn Ezekweli, Kene Ezemenari, Judith Fagalasuu, Oscar Fernandez-Taranco, Ezzedine Choukri Fishere, Cyprian F. Fisiy, Ariel Fiszbein, Robert L. Floyd, Verena Fritz, Francis Fukuyama, Ivor Fung, Varun Gauri, Madhur Gautam, Germany's Deutscher Gesellschaft für Technische Zusammenarbeit (GTZ), Coralie Gevers, Indermit S. Gill, Chiara Giorgetti, Giorgia Giovannetti, Edward Girardet, Jack Goldstone, Kelly Greenhill, Pablo de Greiff, Scott E. Guggenheim, Tobias Haque, Bernard Harborne, David Harland, Jenny Hedman, Joel Hellman, Bert Hofman, Virginia Horscroft, Elisabeth Huybens, Elena Ianchovichina, Patchamuthu Illangovan, Sana Jaffrey, Martin Jelsma, Emmanuel E. Jimenez, Hilde Johnson, Mary Judd, Sima Kanaan, Alma Kanani, Phil Keefer, Caroline M. Kende-Robb, Homi Kharas, Young Chul Kim, Mark Kleiman, Steve Knack, Sahr Kpundeh, Aart Kraay, Keith Krause, Aurélien Kruse, Arvo Kuddo, Sibel Kulaksiz, Julien Labonne, Tuan Le, Theodore Leggett, René Lemarchand, Anne-Marie Leroy, Brian Levy, Esther Loening, Ana Paula Fialho Lopes, Chris Lovelace, Andrew Mack, Charles Maier, Sajjad Malik, David Mansfield, Alexandre Marc, Roland Marchal, Ernesto May, Alastair McKechnie, Dave McRae, Pratap Mehta, Piers Merrick, Jeffrey Miron, Peter Moll, Mick Moore, Adrian Morel, Edward Mountfield, Robert Muggah, Izumi Nakamitsu, Eric Nelson, Carmen Nonay, Antonio Nucifora, Liam O'Dowd, the OECD/International Network on Conflict and Fragility (OECD/INCAF), Adyline Waafas Ofusu-Amaah, Patti O'Neill, Robert Orr, Marina Ottaway, Phil Oxhorn, Kiran Pandey, Andrew Parker, Martin Parry, Borany Penh, Nadia Piffaretti, Nicola Pontara, Rae Porter, Ben Powis, Giovanna Prennushi, Gérard Prunier, Vikram Raghavan, Bassam Ramadan, Peter Reuter, Joey Reyes, Dena Ringold, David Robalino, Michael Ross, Mustapha Rouis, Jordan Ryan, Joseph Saba, Abdi Samatar, Nicholas Sambanis, Kirsti Samuels, Jane Sansbury, Mark Schneider, Colin Scott, John Sender, Yasmine Sherif, Janmejay Singh, David Sislen, Eduardo Somensatto, Radhika Srinivasan, Scott Straus, Camilla Sudgen, Vivek Suri, the Swiss Agency for Development and Cooperation (SDC), Almamy Sylla, Stefanie Teggemann, Thomas John Thomsen, Martin Tisné, Alexandra Trzeciak-Duval, Anne Tully, Carolyn Turk, Oliver Ulich, the United Kingdom's Department for International Development (DFID), the United States Agency for International Development (USAID), Peter Uvin, Manuel Vargas, Antonius Verheijen, Thierry Vircoulon, M. Willem van Eeghen, Axel van Trotsenburg, Juergen Voegele, Femke Vos, Tjip Walker, John Wallis, El Ghassim Wane, Dewen Wang, Achim Wennmann, Alys Willman, Andreas Wimmer, Susan Wong, Rob Wrobel, Tevfik Yaprak, and Philip Zelikow.

We are grateful to persons in locations across the world who participated and provided comments. In addition, we thank guest bloggers and members of the public who committed on our blog: http://blogs.worldbank.org/conflict/.

Despite efforts to compile a comprehensive list, some who contributed may have been inadvertently omitted. The team apologizes for any oversights and reiterates its gratitude to all who contributed to this Report.

References

The word processed describes informally reproduced works that may not be commonly available through libraries.

Abadie, Alberto. 2006. "Poverty, Political Freedom, and the Roots of Terrorism." *American Economic Review* 96 (2): 50–56.

Abbas, Hassan. 2008. "From FATA to the NWFP: The Taliban Spread Their Grip in Pakistan." *CTC Sentinel* 1 (10): 3–5.

———. 2010. "Inside Pakistan's North-West Frontier Province: The Political Landscape of the Insurgency." Counterterrorism Strategy Initiative Policy Paper, New America Foundation, Washington, DC.

Abbink, Klaus, and Benedikt Herrmann. 2009. "Pointless Vendettas." Center for Research in Experimental Economics and Political Decision-Making, University of Amsterdam, Amsterdam.

Acemoglu, Daron, Simon Johnson, and James A. Robinson. 2001. "The Colonial Origins of Comparative Development: An Empirical Investigation." *American Economic Review* 91 (5): 1369–401.

———. 2005. "Institutions as the Fundamental Cause of Long-Run Growth." In *Handbook of Economic Growth,* ed. Philippe Aghion and Stephen N. Durlauf. Amsterdam: Elsevier.

Acemoglu, Daron, and James A. Robinson. 2006. *Economic Origins of Dictatorship and Democracy.* New York: Cambridge University Press.

Acharya, Amitav, and Arabinda Acharya. 2007. "The Myth of the Second Front: Localizing the 'War on Terror' in Southeast Asia." *The Washington Quarterly* 30 (4): 75–90.

Addison, Tony. 2009. "The Political Economy of the Transition from Authoritarianism." In *Transitional Justice and Development: Making Connections,* ed. Pablo de Greiff and Roger Duthie. New York: International Center for Transitional Justice.

Advancement Project. 2009. "Advancement Project." Advancement Project, Washington, DC. http://www.advancementproject.org.

African Development Bank. 2008. "Burundi: 2008–2011 Country Strategy Paper." African Development Bank, Tunis.

———. 2010. "The Fragile States Facility (FSF) Guidelines on Administration of the Technical Assistance and Capacity Building (TCB) Program of Pillar III Operations." African Development Bank, Tunis.

———. 2011. "Accompanying States Towards Sustainable Development." African Development Bank, Tunis. http://www.afdb.org.

African Union. 2006. "Draft Policy Framework for Post-conflict Reconstruction and Development (PCRD)." African Union, Addis Ababa.

———. 2007a. "Declaration on the African Union Border Programme and its Implementation Modalities as Adopted by the Conference of African Ministers in Charge of Border Issues Held in Addis Ababa." African Union, Addis Ababa.

———. 2007b. "Framework for Post-conflict Reconstruction and Technical and Vocational Education and Training (TVET)." African Union, Addis Ababa.

Afrobarometer. 2009. "Afrobarometer." Afrobarometer, Accra.

Afshari, Ali, and H. Graham Underwood. 2009. "The Green Wave." *Journal of Democracy* 20 (4): 6–10.

Aga Khan Development Network. 2003. "Speech by His Highness the Aga Khan." Annual Meeting of The European Bank for Reconstruction and Development. Tashkent, May 5.

———. 2010. "The Aga Khan Development Network: A Long-Term Approach to Development in Conflict-prone Areas." Background note for the WDR 2011.

Agarwal, Sanjay, Rasmus Heltberg, and Myrtle Diachok. 2009. "Scaling up Social Accountability in World Bank Operations." Social Development Department, World Bank, Washington, DC.

Agence Française de Développement, Bundesministerium für Wirtschaftliche Zusammenarbeit und Entwicklung, DFID (U.K. Department for International Development), and World Bank. 2005. "Pro-poor Growth in the 1990s: Lessons and Insights from 14 Countries." World Bank, Washington, DC.

Agence France-Presse. 1999. "East Timorese Rebels Vow to Confine Troops to Barracks: UN." *Agence France-Presse*, July 28.

Agoglia, John, Michael Dziedzic, and Barbara Sotirin, eds. 2008. *Measuring Progress in Conflict Environments (MPICE): A Metrics Framework.* Washington, DC: United States Institute of Peace.

Alda, Erik, and José Cuesta. 2010. "A Comprehensive Estimation of Costs of Crime in South Africa and Its Implications for Effective Policy Making." *Journal of International Development (Online Edition).*

Alden, Christopher. 2001. *Mozambique and the Construction of the New African State: From Negotiations to Nation Building.* London: Palgrave Macmillan.

AllAfrica. 2009. "Liberia: GEMAP Has Succeeded." *AllAfrica.com*, October 30.

Altbeker, Antony. 2005. "Paying for Crime: South African Spending on Criminal Justice." ISS Working Paper 115, Institute for Security Studies, Pretoria.

Alvarado, Nathalie, and Beatriz Abizanda. 2010. "Some Lessons Learnt in Citizen Security by the IADB." Background note for the WDR 2011.

American Psychological Association. 1996. "Violence and the Family: Report of the American Psychological Association Presidential Task Force on Violence and the Family." American Psychological Association, Washington, DC.

Amnesty International. 2005. "Israel and the Occupied Territories: Conflict, Occupation and Patriarchy: Women Carry the Burden." Amnesty International, London.

Anastasijevic, Dejan. 2006. "Organized Crime in the Western Balkans." Paper presented at the First Annual Conference on Human Security, Terrorism and Organized Crime in the Western Balkan Region, Ljubljana, November 23.

Andean Council of Foreign Ministers. 2001. "Andean Cooperation Plan for the Control of Illegal Drugs and Related Offenses." Andean Community General Secretariat, Cartagena, Colombia.

Anderlini, Sanam. 2000. "Women at the Peace Table: Making a Difference." UN Development Fund for Women, New York.

———. 2010a. "Gender Background Paper." Background paper for the WDR 2011.

———. 2010b. "What the Women Say: Participation and UNSCR 1325." International Civil Society Action Network, Washington, DC; Center for International Studies, Massachusetts Institute of Technology, Cambridge, MA.

Andersen, Louise. 2010. "Outsiders Inside the State. Post-conflict Liberia between Trusteeship and Partnership." *Journal of Intervention and Statebuilding* 4 (2): 129–52.

Andeweg, Rudy B. 2000. "Consociational Democracy." *Annual Review of Political Science* 3: 509–36.

Andreas, Peter. 2004. "The Clandestine Political Economy of War and Peace in Bosnia." *International Studies Quarterly* 48 (1): 29–52.

Andrews, Matthew. 2010. "Good Government Means Different Things in Different Countries." *Governance* 23 (1): 7–35.

Anyanwu, John C. 2004. "Economic and Political Causes of Civil Wars in Africa: Some Econometric Results." *Peace, Conflict, and Development* 4: 1–15.

Arai, Yukiko, Ata Cissé, and Madjiguene Sock. 2010. "Promoting Job Creation for Young People in Multinational Enterprises and Their Supply Chains: Liberia." Employment Sector Report 7, International Labour Organization, Geneva.

Arboleda, Jairo. 2010. "Security and Development in Colombia." Background note for the WDR 2011.

Argandoña, Antonio. 2003. "The Social Dimensions of Labour Market Institutions." In *The Social Dimensions of Employment: Institutional Reforms in Labor Markets*, ed. Antonio Argandoña and Jordi Gual. Cheltenham, U.K.: Edward Elgar Publishing.

Arias, Patricia. 2009. "Seguridad Privada en América Latina: El Lucro y los Dilemas de una Regulación Deficitaria." Facultad Latinoamericana de Ciencias Sociales, Santiago.

Arnson, Cynthia J., and I. William Zartman, eds. 2005. *Rethinking the Economics of War: The Intersection of Need, Creed and Greed.* Washington, DC: Woodrow Wilson International Center for Scholars.

Arzeni, Simone, Enrico Cesanelli, and Stefano Pes. 2004. "Programme de Démobilisation, Réinsertion et Réintégration des Ex-combatants (PDRRI): Rapport Final." International Organization for Migration, Bissau.

Ashe, Jeffrey, and Lisa Parrott. 2001. "Impact Evaluation: PACT's Women's Empowerment Program in Nepal: A Savings and Literacy Led Alternative to Financial Institution Building." Brandeis University; Freedom from Hunger, Waltham, MA.

Ashforth, Adam. 2009. "Ethnic Violence and the Prospects for Democracy in the Aftermath of the 2007 Kenyan Elections." *Public Culture* 21 (1): 9–19.

Asian Development Bank. 2006. "Central Asia: Increasing Gains from Trade through Regional Cooperation in Trade Policy, Transport, and Customs Transit." Asian Development Bank, Mandaluyong City, Philippines.

Aspinall, Edward. 2005. *The Helsinki Agreement: A More Promising Basis for Peace in Aceh?* Washington, DC: East-West Center.

Atkinson, Philippa. 2008. "Liberal Interventionism in Liberia: Towards a Tentatively Just Approach?" *Conflict, Security and Development* 8 (1): 15–45.

Atos Consulting. 2009. "Evaluation of the Law and Order Trust Fund for Afghanistan (LOTFA) Phase IV: Report." Atos Consulting, Paris.

Atran, Scott. 2003. "Genesis of Suicide Terrorism." *Science* 299 (5612): 1534–39.

AusAID. 2009. "Australian Aid to Water Supply and Sanitation Service Delivery in East Timor and Indonesia: Evaluation Report." AusAID, Canberra.

Australian Crime Commission. 2010. "Australian Crime Commission: Unite the Fight Against Nationally Significant Crime." Australian Crime Commission, Sydney.

Austrian Federal Ministry for European and International Affairs. 2006. "Three Year Programme on Austrian Development Policy 2006–2008." Austrian Federal Ministry for European and International Affairs, Vienna.

Axelrod, Robert. 1984. *The Evolution of Cooperation.* New York: Basic Books.

Azam, Jean-Paul, Shantayanan Devarajan, and Stephen A. O'Connell. 2002. "Equilibrium Aid Dependence." University of Toulouse, Toulouse, France. Processed.

Azam, Jean-Paul, and Alice Mesnard. 2003. "Civil War and the Social Contract." *Public Choice* 115 (3–4): 455–75.

Bagwitz, Daniel, Reinhold Elges, Helmut Grossmann, and Gabriele Kruk. 2008. "Private Sector Development in (Post-) Conflict Situations: Guidebook." Deutsche Gesellschaft für Technische Zusammenarbeit, Eschborn, Germany.

Baily, Virginia, and Veronica Hoskins. 2007. "Liberia: Peacebuilding Fund." *Africa Research Bulletin: Economic, Financial and Technical Series* 44 (9): 17550B.

Baird, Mark. 2010. "Service Delivery in Fragile and Conflict-Affected States." Background paper for the WDR 2011.

Baker, Paul, Friedrich von Kirchbach, Mondher Mimouni, and Jean-Michel Pasteels. 2002. "Analytical Tools for Enhancing the Participation of Developing Countries in the Multilateral Trading System in the Context of the Doha Development Agenda." *Aussenwirtschaft* 57 (3): 343–69.

Baker, Raymond W. 2005. *Capitalism's Achilles Heel: Dirty Money and How to Renew the Free-Market System.* Hoboken, NJ: John Wiley & Sons.

Ball, Nicole, and Malcolm Holmes. 2002. "Integrating Defense into Public Expenditure Work." U.K. Department for International Development, London.

Ballentine, Karen, and Heiko Nitzschke. 2006. "Beyond Greed and Grievance: Policy Lessons from Studies in the Political Economy of Armed Conflict." In *Security and Development: Investing in Peace and Prosperity*, ed. Robert Picciotto and Rachel Weaving. Oxfordshire, U.K.: Routledge.

Banerjee, Abhijit V., and Esther Duflo. 2009. "The Experimental Approach to Development Economics." *Annual Review of Economics* 1: 151–78.

Bannon, Ian, and Paul Collier. 2003. *Natural Resources and Violent Conflict: Options and Actions.* Washington, DC: World Bank.

Barakat, Sultan. 2006. "Mid-term Evaluation Report of the National Solidarity Programme." Post-war Reconstruction and Development Unit, University of York, York, U.K.; Ministry of Rural Rehabilitation and Development, Islamic Republic of Afghanistan, Kabul.

Barron, Patrick. 2010. "Community-Driven Development in Post-conflict and Conflict-Affected Areas." Background paper for the WDR 2011.

Barron, Patrick, Paul Arthur, Peter Bartu, and Teresa Whitfield. 2010. "Sub-national Violence in Middle- and Higher-Income Countries." Background paper for the WDR 2011.

Barron, Patrick, and Adam Burke. 2008. "Supporting Peace in Aceh: Development Agencies and International Involvement." Policy Studies 47, East-West Center, Washington, DC.

Barron, Patrick, Macartan Humphreys, Laura Paler, and Jeremy Weinstein. 2009. "Community-Based Reintegration in Aceh: Assessing the Impacts of BRA-KDP." Indonesian Social Development Paper 12, World Bank, Washington, DC.

Bartoli, Andrea. 2005. "Learning from the Mozambique Peace Process: The Role of the Community of Sant'Egidio." In *Analyzing Successful Transfer Effects in Interactive Conflict Resolution*, ed. Ron Fisher. Lanham, MD: Lexington Books.

Bastick, Megan, Karin Grimm, and Rahel Kunz. 2007. *Sexual Violence in Armed Conflict: Global Overview and Implications for the Security Sector.* Geneva: Geneva Centre for the Democratic Control of Armed Forces.

Batchelor, Peter, and Paul Dunne. 1998. "The Restructuring of South Africa's Defence Industry." *Africa Security Review* 7 (6): 27–43.

Bateson, Regina. 2010. "Summary of Recent Research: Public Security in Post War Guatemala." PhD thesis, Yale University, New Haven, CT.

Battle, Clare. 2008. "'Fighting Talk': The DCED Expert Meeting on Private Sector Development in Post-conflict Situations." The Donor Committee for Enterprise Development, Cambridge, U.K.

Bayer, Resat, and Matthew C. Rupert. 2004. "Effects of Civil Wars on International Trade, 1950–92." *Journal of Peace Research* 41 (6): 699–713.

BBC News. 2002. "What is Loya Jirga?" *BBC News*, July 1.

———. 2010. "The Salang Tunnel: Afghanistan's Lifeline." *BBC News*, February 10.

BBC World Service Trust. 2010. "Afghan Education Projects." BBC World Service Trust, London. http://www.bbc.co.uk.

Beasley, Kenneth W. 2006. "Job Creation in Postconflict Societies." Issue Paper 9, Center for Development Information and Evaluation, U.S. Agency for International Development, Washington, DC.

Beath, Andrew, Christia Fotini, Ruben Enikolopov, and Shahim Ahmad Kabuli. 2010. "Randomized Impact Evaluation of Phase-II of Afghanistan's National Solidarity Program: Estimates of Interim Program Impact from First Follow-up Survey." World Bank, Washington, DC. http://www.nsp-ie.org/reportsimpacts.html.

Beato, Claudio C. 2005. "Case Study 'Fico Vivo' Homicide Control Project in Belo Horizonte." World Bank, Washington, DC.

Becker, Gary S. 1968. "Crime and Punishment: An Economic Approach." *Journal of Political Economy* 76 (2): 169–217.

Bedeski, Robert. 1994. *The Transformation of South Korea: Reform and Reconstitution in the Sixth Republic Under Roh Tae Woo, 1987–1992.* London: Routledge.

Beijing Declaration and Platform for Action. 1995. "Chapter IV. E. Women and Armed Conflict." Fourth World Conference on Women, United Nations, Beijing.

Belgium Development Agency. 2006. "Indicative Cooperation Programme (2007–2009)." Belgium Development Agency, Brussels.

———. 2009. "Indicative Cooperation Programme (2010–2013)." Belgium Development Agency, Brussels.

Bellina, Séverine, Dominique Darbon, Stein S. Eriksen, and Ole J. Sending. 2009. "The Legitimacy of the State in Fragile Situations." Report 20/2009 Discussion, Norwegian Agency for Development Cooperation, Oslo; The French Ministry of Foreign and European Affairs, Paris.

Ben-Ari, Benyamin. 2010. "An International Band-Aid: UNIFIL II and the Endeavor into Southern Lebanon." Publications in Contemporary Affairs, Provo, UT.

Berger, Rachel. 2003. "Conflict over Natural Resources Among Pastoralists in Northern Kenya: A Look at Recent Initiatives in Conflict Resolution." *Journal of International Development* 15 (2): 245–57.

Berman, Eli. 2009. *Radical, Religious and Violent: The New Economics of Terrorism.* Cambridge, MA: Massachusetts Institute of Technology.

Berman, Eli, Joseph Felter, Jacob N. Shapiro, and Michael Callen. 2009. "Do Working Men Rebel? Insurgency and Unemployment in Iraq and the Philippines." Working Paper 15547, National Bureau of Economic Research, Cambridge, MA.

Berman, Eli, and Laurence R. Iannaccone. 2006. "Religious Extremism: The Good, the Bad, and the Deadly." *Public Choice* 128 (1): 109–29.

Berrebi, Claude. 2007. "Evidence About the Link Between Education, Poverty, and Terrorism among Palestinians." *Peace Economics, Peace Science, and Public Policy* 13 (1): 1–38.

Besley, Timothy, and Torsten Persson. 2009. "Repression or Civil War?" *American Economic Review* 99 (2): 292–97.

———. 2010. "State Capacity, Conflict and Development." *Econometrica* 78 (1): 1–34.

Bessler, Manuel, Richard Garfield, and Gerard Mc Hugh. 2004. "Sanctions Assessment Handbook: Assessing the Humanitarian Implications of Sanctions." UN Office for the Coordination of Humanitarian Affairs; Inter-Agency Standing Committee, New York.

Betancourt, Theresa S., and Timothy Williams. 2008. "Building an Evidence Base on Mental Health Interventions for Children Affected by Armed Conflict." *Intervention* 6 (1): 39–56.

Bhavnani, Ravi, and Dan Miodownik. 2009. "Ethnic Polarization, Ethnic Salience, and Civil War." *Journal of Conflict Resolution* 53 (1): 30–49.

Bijleveld, Catrien, Aafke Morssinkhof, and Alette Smeulers. 2009. "Counting the Countless: Rape Victimization during the Rwandan Genocide." *International Criminal Justice Review* 19 (2): 208–24.

Bilcik, Vladimir, Alexander Duleba, Michal Klyap, and Svitlana Mitryayeva. 2000. "Role of the Carpathian Euroregion in Strengthening Security and Stability in Central and Eastern Europe." Paper presented at the Carpathain Euroregion: Prospects and Challenges workshop, Truskavets, Ukraine, November 23–25.

Birdsall, Nancy, Homi Kharas, Ayah Mahgoub, and Rita Perakis. 2010. "Quality of Official Development Assistance Assessment." Brookings Institution; The Center for Global Development, Washington, DC.

BizCLIR (Business Climate Legal and Institutional Reform). 2007. "Overhauling Contract Enforcement: Lessons from Rwanda." BizCLIR Issues Paper 17, U.S. Agency for International Development, Washington, DC.

Blattman, Christopher. Forthcoming. "Post-conflict Recovery in Africa: The Micro Level." In *Oxford Companion to the Economics of Africa*, ed. Shantayanan Devarajan, Ernest Aryeetey, Ravi Kanbur, and Louis Kasekende. Oxford, U.K.: Oxford University Press.

Blattman, Christopher, and Edward Miguel. 2010. "Civil War." *Journal of Economic Literature* 48 (1): 3–57.

Blum, Rachel, and Jerome LeBleu. 2010. "Employment Generation in Post-conflict Environments: Linking Short- and Long-Term Initiatives." In *Civil Power in Irregular Conflicts*, ed. Franklin D. Kramer, Thomas Dempsey, Joseph Gregoire, and Susan Merrill. Alexandria, VA: CNA Analysis & Solutions; Carlisle, PA: U.S. Army Peacekeeping and Stability Operations Institute; Arlington, VA: Association of the U.S. Army.

Blundell, Arthur G. 2010. "Forests and Conflict: The Financial Flows That Fuel War." Background paper for the WDR 2011.

Bøås, Morten. 2009. "Making Plans for Liberia: A Trusteeship Approach to Good Governance." *Third World Quarterly* 30 (7): 1329–41.

Bøås, Morten, Åage Tiltnes, and Hedda Flatø. 2010. "Comparing the Cases." Background paper for the WDR 2011.

Boko, Sylvain H. 2008. "Social Accountability in Post-conflict and Fragile States." Paper presented at the Affiliated Network for Social Accountability: Africa Annual Stakeholder Conference, Addis Ababa, May 19–20.

Bora, Saswati, Robert Townsend, Iride Ceccacci, and Christopher Delgado. 2010. "Food Security and Conflict." Background paper for the WDR 2011.

Bott, Sarah, Andrew Morrison, and Mary Ellsberg. 2005. "Preventing and Responding to Gender-Based Violence in Middle- and Low-Income Countries: A Global Review and Analysis." Policy Research Working Paper 3618, World Bank, Washington, DC.

Boudreaux, Karol C. 2010. "A Better Brew for Success: Economic Liberalization in Rwanda's Coffee Sector." World Bank, Washington, DC.

Boudreaux, Karol C., and Jutta Tobias. 2009. "The Role of Entrepreneurship in Conflict Reduction in the Post-genocide Rwandan Coffee Industry: Quantitative Evidence from a Field Study." Working Paper 09-24, Mercatus Center, George Mason University, Arlington, VA.

Bourne, Mike. 2007. *Arming Conflict: The Proliferation of Small Arms*. New York: Palgrave Macmillan.

Bowden, Anna. 2010. "The Economic Cost of Maritime Piracy." One Earth Future Foundation, Louisville, CO.

Bowman, Brett, Richard Matzopoulos, Alexander Butchart, and James A. Mercy. 2008. "The Impact of Violence on Development in Low- to Middle-Income Countries." *International Journal of Injury Control and Safety Promotion* 15 (4): 209–19.

Boyce, James, and Shepard Forman. 2010. "Financing Peace: International and National Resources for Post-conflict Countries and Fragile States." Background paper for the WDR 2011.

Bradbury, Mark. 2008. *Becoming Somaliland.* Bloomington, IN: Indiana University Press.

Braithwaite, Valerie, and Margaret Levi, eds. 1998. *Trust and Governance.* New York: Russell Sage Foundation.

Brancati, Dawn. 2006. "Decentralization: Fueling the Fire or Dampening the Flames of Ethnic Conflict and Secessionism?" *International Organization* 60 (3): 651–85.

Brands, Hal. 2009. "Los Zetas and Mexico's Transnational Drug War." *World Politics Review (Online Edition).*

Braud, Pierre-Antoine, and Giovanni Grevi. 2005. "The EU Mission in Aceh: Implementing Peace." Occasional Paper 61, European Union Institute for Security Studies, Paris.

Bräutigam, Deborah. 2000. *Aid Dependence and Governance.* Stockholm: Almqvist & Wiksell International.

Briceño-Garmendia, Cecilia, and Vivien Foster, eds. 2010. *Africa's Infrastructure: A Time for Transformation.* Washington, DC: World Bank.

Brick, Jennifer. 2008. "The Political Economy of Customary Village Organizations in Rural Afghanistan." Paper presented at the Annual Meeting of the Central Eurasian Studies Society, Washington, DC, September 18–21.

Brinkman, Henk-Jan, and Cullen S. Hendrix. 2010. "Food Insecurity and Conflict: Applying the WDR Framework." Background paper for the WDR 2011.

Bronstein, Hugh. 2007. "Outraged Colombians March Against Rebel Kidnappers." *Reuters,* July 5.

Brown, Michael E. 1996. "Introduction." In *The International Dimensions of Internal Conflict,* ed. Michael E. Brown. Cambridge, MA: Center for Science and International Affairs, John F. Kennedy School of Government, Harvard University.

Brück, Tilman, Valpy Fitzgerald, and Arturo Grigsby. 2000. "Enhancing the Private Sector Contribution to Post-War Recovery in Poor Countries." Queen Elizabeth House Working Paper 45, University of Oxford, Oxford, U.K.

Brück, Tilman, and Kati Schindler. 2008. "The Impact of Conflict and Fragility on Households: A Conceptual Framework with Reference to Widows." Research Paper 2008/83, United Nations University–World Institute for Development Economic Research Paper, Helsinki.

Brückner, Markus, and Antonio Ciccone. 2010. "International Commodity Prices, Growth and the Outbreak of Civil War in Sub-Saharan Africa." *The Economic Journal* 120 (544): 519–34.

Buhaug, Halvard, and Kristian S. Gleditsch. 2008. "Contagion or Confusion? Why Conflicts Cluster in Space." *International Studies Quarterly* 52 (2): 215–33.

Buhaug, Halvard, and Henrik Urdal. 2010. "An Urbanization Bomb? Population Growth and Social Disorder in Cities." Paper presented at the Urban Affairs Association Annual Conference, Honolulu, HI, March 10.

Butchart, Alexander, David Brown, Alexis Khanh-Huynh, Phaedra Corso, Nicolas Florquin, and Robert Muggah. 2008. "Manual for Estimating the Economic Costs of Injuries Due to Interpersonal and Self-Directed Violence." World Health Organization, Geneva; Department of Health and Human Services, Washington, DC; Centers for Disease Control and Prevention, Atlanta, GA.

Butty, James. 2010. "A New Study Finds Death Toll in Congo War Too High." *Voice of America,* January 21.

Byron, Dennis, and Maria Dakolias. 2008. "The Regional Court Systems in the Organization of Eastern Caribbean States and the Caribbean." In *Small States, Smart Solutions: Improving Connectivity and Increasing the Effectiveness of Public Services,* ed. Edgardo Favaro. Washington, DC: World Bank.

Cadeado, Calton, and Hipolito Hamela. 2009. "A Suis Generis Case of Power-Sharing in Mozambique." Peace and Development Research, World Bank, Washington, DC.

Campbell, Susanna P., Anja T. Kaspersen, and Erin Weir. 2007. "Integrated Mission Revisited: Synthesis of Findings." Norwegian Ministry of Foreign Affairs, Oslo.

Carl, Andy, and Lorraine Garasu. 2002. "Weaving Consensus: The Papua New Guinea–Bougainville Peace Process." Conciliation Resources, London.

Carpenter, R. Charli. 2006. "Recognizing Gender-Based Violence against Civilian Men and Boys in Conflict Situations." *Security Dialogue* 37 (1): 83–103.

Carter, Stephen, and Kate Clark. 2010. "No Shortcut to Stability: Justice, Politics and Insurgency in Afghanistan." Chatham House, London.

Cederman, Lars-Erik, Andreas Wimmer, and Brian Min. 2010. "Why Do Ethnic Groups Rebel?: New Data and Analysis." *World Politics* 62 (1): 87–119.

Central American Integration System. 2009. "Central American Integration System." General Secretariat of Central American Integration System, Antiguo Cuscatlán, El Salvador. http://www.sica.int.

Centre for Good Governance. 2009. "Social Audit of NREGS (AP) in Andhra Pradesh." Centre for Good Governance, Hyderabad, India.

Centro de Coordinación de Acción Integral. 2010. "Reporte Ejecutivo Plan Nacional de Consolidación." Centro de Coordinación de Acción Integral, Bogotá.

Cerra, Valerie, and Sweta C. Saxena. 2008. "Growth Dynamics: The Myth of Economic Recovery." *American Economic Review* 98 (1): 439–57.

Chalk, Peter. 2008. "The Maritime Dimensions of International Security: Terrorism, Piracy and Challenges for the United States." RAND Corporation, Santa Monica, CA.

Chalmers, Malcolm. 2007. "Spending to Save? An Analysis of the Cost Effectiveness of Conflict Prevention." *Defense and Peace Economics* 18 (1): 1–23.

Chamarbagwala, Rubiana, and Hilcías E. Morán. 2011. "The Human Capital Consequences of Civil War: Evidence from Guatemala." *Journal of Development Economics* 94 (1): 41–61.

Chandran, Rahul, Jake Sherman, Bruce Jones, Shepard Forman, Anne le More, Andrew Hart, and Yochino Funaki. 2009. "Rapid Deployment of Civilians for Peace Operations: Status, Gaps and Options." Center on International Cooperation, New York University, New York.

Chandran, Rahul, Jenna Slotin, and Gigja Sorensen. 2010. "Strategic Planning, Peacebuilding and Statebuilding: Background Paper for the International Dialogue." Center on International Cooperation, New York University, New York.

Chang, Yun-Shik, and Steven H. Lee. 2006. *Transformations in Twentieth Century Korea.* New York: Routledge.

Chauveau, Jean-Pierre, and Paul Richards. 2008. "West African Insurgencies in Agrarian Perspective: Côte d'Ivoire and Sierra Leone Compared." *Journal of Agrarian Change* 8 (4): 515–52.

Cheeseman, Nic, and Blessing-Miles Tendi. 2010. "Power-Sharing in Comparative Perspective: The Dynamics of 'Unity Government' in Kenya and Zimbabwe." *Journal of Modern African Studies* 48 (2): 203–29.

Chen, Shaohua, Martin Ravallion, and Prem Sangraula. 2008. "Dollar a Day Revisited." *World Bank Economic Review* 23 (2): 163–84.

Chesterman, Simon. 2004. *You, the People: The United Nations, Transitional Administration, and State-Building.* New York: Oxford University Press.

Christensen, Clayton M. 2003. *The Innovator's Dilemma: The Revolutionary Book that Will Change the Way You Do Business.* New York: HarperCollins.

Chuhan-Pole, Punam. 2010. "Yes Africa Can: Success Stories from a Dynamic Continent." Office of the Chief Economist, Africa Region, World Bank, Washington, DC.

Chun, Suk, and Inger Skjelsbæk. 2010. "Sexual Violence in Armed Conflicts." Policy Brief I/2010, International Peace Research Institute of Oslo, Oslo.

CICIG (Comisión Internacional Contra la Impunidad en Guatemala). 2009. "Two Years of Work: A Commitment to Justice." CICIG, Guatemala City.

———. 2010. "Mensaje a los Jóvenes de Guatemala Acerca de la Elección de Fiscal General de la Nación." CICIG, Guatemala City.

Cincotta, Richard, Robert Engelman, and Daniele Anastasion. 2003. "The Security Demographic: Population and Civil Conflict after the Cold War." Population Action International, Washington, DC.

Cingranelli, David L., and David L. Richards. 1999. "Measuring the Level, Pattern, and Sequence of Government Respect for Physical Integrity Rights." *International Studies Quarterly* 43 (2): 407–17.

———. 2010. "CIRI Human Rights Data Project." Cingranelli-Richards (CIRI) Human Rights Data Project, Binghamton, NY. http://ciri.binghamton.edu/.

Clark, John F. 1994. "The National Conference as an Instrument of Democratization in Francophone Africa." *Journal of Third World Studies* 11 (1): 304–35.

Clark, Phil, and Zachary A. Kaufman. 2011. "Rwanda: Recent History." In *Africa South of the Sahara 2012,* ed. Iain Frame. London: Routledge.

Clements, Kevin P. 2010. *Traditional, Charismatic and Grounded Legitimacy.* Eschborn, Germany: Deutsche Gesellschaft für Technische Zusammenarbeit.

Cliffe, Sarah, Scott Guggenheim, and Markus Kostner. 2003. "Community-Driven Reconstruction as an Instrument in War-to-Peace Transitions." Conflict Prevention and Reconstruction Series Working Paper 7, Social Development Department, World Bank, Washington, DC.

Coalition for International Justice. 2005. "Following Taylor's Money: A Path of War and Destruction." Coalition for International Justice, Washington, DC.

CODEH (Comité de Defensa para los Derechos Humanos en Honduras). 2008. "Crimen, Delincuencia e Impunidad: Manifestaciones de Violencia y Conflictividad Social." CODEH, Tegucigalpa.

Coldham, Simon. 1984. "The Settlement of Land Disputes in Kenya: An Historical Perspective." *The Journal of Modern African Studies* 22 (1): 59–71.

Colletta, Nat J., and Michelle L. Cullen. 2000. *Violent Conflict and the Transformation of Social Capital: Lessons from Cambodia, Rwanda, Guatemala, and Somalia.* Washington, DC: World Bank.

Colletta, Nat J., Markus Kostner, and Ingo Wiederhofer. 1996. "Case Studies in War-to-Peace Transition: The Demobilization and Reintegration of Ex-combatants in Ethiopia, Namibia and Uganda." Discussion Paper 331, Africa Technical Department Series, World Bank, Washington, DC.

Colletta, Nat J., and Gebreselassie Tesfamichael. 2003. "Bank Engagement after Conflict: A Client Perspective." World Bank, Washington, DC.

Collier, Paul. 2007. *The Bottom Billion: Why the Poorest Countries Are Failing and What Can Be Done about It.* New York: Oxford University Press.

Collier, Paul, Lisa Chauvet, and Håvard Hegre. 2007. "The Security Challenge in Conflict-prone Countries." Challenge Paper, Copenhagen Consensus 2008, Copenhagen.

Collier, Paul, Lani Elliott, Håvard Hegre, Anke Hoeffler, Marta Reynal-Querol, and Nicholas Sambanis. 2003. *Breaking the Conflict Trap: Civil War and Development Policy.* Washington, DC: World Bank.

Collier, Paul, and Anke Hoeffler. 1998. "On Economic Causes of Civil War." *Oxford Economic Papers* 50 (4): 563–73.

———. 2002. "On the Incidence of Civil War in Africa." *Journal of Conflict Resolution* 46 (1): 13–28.

———. 2004. "Greed and Grievance in Civil War." *Oxford Economic Papers* 56 (4): 563–95.

Collier, Paul, Anke Hoeffler, and Mans Söderbom. 2008. "Post Conflict Risks." *Journal of Peace Research* 45 (4): 461–78.

Collier, Paul, and Nicholas Sambanis, eds. 2005. *Understanding Civil War: Evidence and Analysis.* Washington, DC: World Bank.

Commission on Growth and Development. 2008. "The Growth Commission Report: Strategies for Sustained Growth and Inclusive Development." Commission on Growth and Development, Washington, DC.

Commission on Human Security. 2003. "Human Security Now: Protecting and Empowering People." Commission on Human Security, New York.

Commonwealth Secretariat. 2006. "Guyana General and Regional Elections: Report of the Commonwealth Observer Group." Commonwealth Secretariat, London.

Comunità di Sant'Egidio. 2010. "The BRAVO! (Birth Registration for All Versus Oblivion) Programme." Comunità di Sant'Egidio, Rome.

Cooke, Julian, and Mervyn Brown. 2011. "Recent History: Madagascar." Europa World Online, London. http://www.europaworld.com.

Correia, Maria C. 2010. "MDRP and Regionality." Background note for the WDR 2011.

Cortright, David, George Lopez, and Linda Gerber. 2002. "Sanctions Sans Commitment: An Assessment of UN Arms Embargoes." In *Sanctions and the Search for Security Challenges to UN Action*, ed. David Cortright, George Lopez, and Linda Gerber. Boulder, CO: Lynne Reinner.

Council for the Development of Cambodia. 2010. "The Cambodia ODA Database." Cambodian Rehabilitation and Development Board, Government of Cambodia, Phnom Penh. http://cdc.khmer.biz.

Council of Europe. 1995. "Examples of Good Practice of Transfrontier Co-operation Concerning Members of Ethnic Groups Residing on the Territory of Several States." Council of Europe, Strasbourg, France.

Council of Europe and Institute of International Sociology of Gorizia. 2003. "Cross-Border Cooperation in the Balkan/Danube Area: An Analysis of Strengths, Weaknesses, Opportunities and

Threats." Council of Europe, Strasbourg, France; Institute of International Sociology of Gorizia, Gorizia, Italy.

Cousens, Elizabeth, and David Harland. 2006. "Post-Dayton Bosnia and Herzegovina." In *Twenty-First Century Peace Operations*, ed. William J. Durch. Washington, DC: United States Institute of Peace.

Cox, Marcus, and Nigel Thornton. 2010. "Applied Knowledge: Managing Results in Conflict-Affected and Fragile States: A Stock-Take of Lessons, Experience, and Practice." U.K. Department for International Development, London.

Cramer, Christopher. 2002. "Homo Economicus Goes to War: Methodological Individualism, Rational Choice and the Political Economy of War." *World Development* 30 (11): 1845–64.

———. 2006. *Violence in Developing Countries: War, Memory, Progress.* Bloomington, IN: Indiana University Press.

———. 2010. "Unemployment and Participation in Violence." Background paper for the WDR 2011.

Crawford, Adam. 1999. *The Local Governance of Crime: Appeals to Community and Partnerships.* New York: Oxford University Press.

Crisis Management Initiative. 2011. "Aceh." Crisis Management Initiative, Helsinki. http://www.cmi.fi/.

Crook, Richard C., and James Manor. 1998. *Democracy and Decentralisation in South Asia and West Africa: Participation, Accountability and Performance.* Cambridge, U.K.: Cambridge University Press.

Cross, Tim. 2010. "Youth Violence Prevention around the World: The Youth Build Case Study." In *Beyond Suppression: Global Perspectives on Youth Violence*, ed. Robert Cohen, Joan S. Hoffman, and Lyndee Knox. Santa Barbara, CA: ABC-CLIO.

Crown Agents. 2007. "Customs Reform Programme 1997–2006: The Modernisation of Alfândegas de Moçambique." Crown Agents, Sutton, U.K.

Cukier, Wendy. 2002. "Small Arms and Light Weapons: A Public Health Approach." *Brown Journal of World Affairs* 9 (1): 261–80.

Cumings, Bruce. 2005. "State Building in Korea: Continuity and Crisis." In *States and Development: Historical Antecedents of Stagnation and Advance*, ed. Matthew Lange and Dietrich Rueschemeyer. New York: Palgrave Macmillan.

Cunningham, Wendy, Lorena M. Cohen, Sophie Naudeau, and Linda McGinnis. 2008. "Supporting Youth at Risk: A Policy Toolkit for Middle-Income Countries." World Bank, Washington, DC.

Curtis, Glenn. E., and Tara Karacan. 2002. "The Nexus among Terrorists, Narcotics Traffickers, Weapons Proliferators, and Organized Crime Networks in Western Europe." Federal Research Division, Library of Congress, Washington, DC.

D'Anieri, Paul. 2006. "Explaining the Success and Failure of Post Communist Revolutions." *Communist and Post-Communist Studies* 39 (3): 331–50.

Dahlberg, Linda L. 1998. "Youth Violence in the United States: Major Trends, Risk Factors, and Prevention Approaches." *American Journal of Preventive Medicine* 14 (4): 259–72.

Dahlberg, Linda L., and Etienne G. Krug. 2002. "Violence: A Global Public Health Problem." In *World Report on Violence and Health*, Etienne G. Krug, Linda L. Dahlberg, James A. Mercy, Anthony B. Zwi, and Rafael Lozano. Geneva: World Health Organization.

Dale, Pamela. 2009. "Delivering Justice to Sierra Leone's Poor: An Analysis of the Work of Timap for Justice." World Bank, Washington, DC.

Davies, Martyn, Hannah Edinger, Nastasya Tay, and Sanusha Naidu. 2008. "How China Delivers Development Assistance to Africa." Centre for Chinese Studies, University of Stellenbosch, Matieland, South Africa.

Davies, Stephen, Dimieari von Kemedi, and Mark Drennan. 2005. "Illegal Oil Bunkering in the Niger Delta." Niger Delta Peace and Security Strategy Working Group, Port Harcourt, Nigeria.

de Figueiredo, Rui J. P. Jr., and Barry R. Weingast. 1999. "The Rationality of Fear: Political Opportunism and Ethnic Conflict." In *Civil Wars, Insecurity and Interventions*, ed. Jack Snyder and Barbara F. Walter. New York: Columbia University Press.

de Greiff, Pablo. 2006. *The Handbook of Reparations.* New York: Oxford University Press.

———. 2010. "Transitional Justice, Security, and Development." Background paper for the WDR 2011.

De Groot, Olaf J. 2010. "The Spillover Effects of Conflict on Economic Growth in Neighbouring Countries in Africa." *Defence and Peace Economics* 21 (2): 149–64.

De Silva, K. M. 2005.*A History of Sri Lanka.* New York: Penguin Books.

de Soto, Alvaro, and Graciana del Castillo. 1994. "Obstacles to Peacebuilding." *Foreign Policy* 94: 69–83.

de Soysa, Indra. 2002. "Paradise Is a Bazaar? Greed, Creed, and Governance in Civil War, 1989–99." *Journal of Peace Research* 39 (4): 395–416.

De Stefano, Lucia, James Duncan, Shlomi Dinar, Kerstin Stahl, Kenneth Strzepek, and Aaron T. Wolf. 2010. "Mapping the Resilience of International River Basins to Future Climate Change: Induced Water Variability." Water Sector Board Discussion Paper 15, World Bank, Washington, DC.

de Waal, Alex, and Julie Flint. 2008. *Darfur: A New History of a Long War.* London: Zed Books; London: International African Institute.

De Wulf, Luc, and José B. Sokol, eds. 2004. *Customs Modernization Initiatives: Case Studies.* Washington, DC: World Bank.

de Zwart, Frank. 2000. "The Logic of Affirmative Action: Caste, Class and Quotas in India." *Acta Sociologica* 43 (3): 235–49.

del Ninno, Carlo, Kalanidhi Subbarao, and Annamaria Milazzo. 2009. "How to Make Public Works Work: A Review of Experiences." Social Protection Discussion Paper 905, World Bank, Washington, DC.

Demirgüc-Kunt, Asli, Leora F. Klapper, and Georgios A. Panos. 2011. "Entrepreneurship in Post-conflict Transition: The Role of Informality and Access to Finance." *Economics of Transition* 19 (1): 27–78.

Demombynes, Gabriel. 2010. "Drug Trafficking and Violence in Central America and Beyond." Background paper for the WDR 2011.

Demombynes, Gabriel, and Michael Clemens. 2010. "When Does Rigorous Impact Evaluation Make a Difference? The Case of the Millennium Villages." Working Paper 225, Center for Global Development, Washington, DC.

Development Alternatives Incorporated. 2010. "Facility for New Market Development (FNMD)." Development Alternatives Incorporated, Bethesda, MD.

DFID (U.K. Department for International Development). 2002. "Conducting Conflict Assessments: Guidance Notes." DFID, Center for Conflict Analysis and Prevention, London.

———. 2009. "Building the State and Securing the Peace." DFID, London.

———. 2010. "Working Effectively in Conflict-Affected and Fragile Situations." DFID, London.

Di John, Jonathon, and James Putzel. 2009. "Political Settlements." Governance and Social Development Resource Centre, International Development Department, University of Birmingham, Birmingham, U.K.

Dinnen, Sinclair, Douglas Porter, and Caroline Sage. 2010. "Conflict in Melanesia: Common Themes, Different Lessons." Background paper for the WDR 2011.

Dixit, Avinash. 1980. "The Role of Investment in Entry Deterrence." *Economic Journal* 90 (357): 95–106.

Dobbins, James, Seth G. Jones, Keith Crane, and Beth C. DeGrasse. 2007. *The Beginner's Guide to Nation-Building.* Santa Monica, CA: RAND Corporation.

Dobbins, James, Seth G. Jones, Keith Crane, Andrew Rathmell, Brett Steele, Richard Teltschik, and Anga Timilsina. 2005. *The UN's Role in Nation-Building: From the Congo to Iraq.* Santa Monica, CA: RAND Corporation.

Donovan, Megan K. 2008. "The International Commission against Impunity in Guatemala: Will Accountability Prevail?" *Arizona Journal of International and Comparative Law* 25 (3): 779–824.

Doyle, Michael W., and Nicholas Sambanis. 2006. *Making War and Building Peace: United Nations Peace Operations.* Princeton, NJ: Princeton University Press.

Duailibi, Sergio, William Ponicki, Joel Grube, Ilana Pinsky, Ronaldo Laranjeira, and Martin Raw. 2007. "The Effect of Restricting Opening Hours on Alcohol-Related Violence." *American Journal of Public Health* 97 (12): 2276–80.

Dudley, Steven S. 2010. "Drug Trafficking Organizations in Central America: Transportistas, Mexican Cartels and Maras." In *Shared Responsibility: U.S.-Mexico Policy Options for Confronting Organized Crime,* ed. Erik L. Olson, David A. Shirk, and Andrew Selee. Washington, DC: Woodrow Wilson International Center for Scholars; San Diego, CA: Trans-Border Institute, University of San Diego.

Duffield, Mark. 2000. "Globalization, Transborder Trade, and War Economies." In *Greed and Grievance: Economic Agendas in Civil Wars,* Mats R. Berdal and David M. Malone. Boulder, CO: Lynne Rienner.

Dupuy, Kendra, and Helga M. Binningsbø. 2008. "Buying Peace with Diamonds? Power-sharing Agreements in Sierra Leone." CSCW Policy Brief 7, Center for the Study of Civil War, Peace Research Institute of Oslo, Oslo.

Dwan, Renata, and Laura Bailey. 2006. "Liberia's Governance and Economic Management Assistance Program (GEMAP): A Joint Review by the Department of Peacekeeping Operations' Peacekeeping

Best Practices Section and the World Bank's Fragile States Group." Fragile States Group, World Bank, Washington, DC; Best Practices Section, Department of Peacekeeping Operations, United Nations, New York.

Eades, Lindsay M. 1999. *The End of Apartheid in South Africa.* Westport, CT: Greenwood Press.

Easterly, William, Jozef Ritzen, and Michael Woolcock. 2006. "Social Cohesion, Institutions, and Growth." *Economics and Politics* 18 (2): 103–20.

Economic Times. 2008. "Australia Announces Pacific Guest Worker Scheme." *Economic Times,* August 17.

Economist Intelligence Unit. 2008a. "Country Profile: Burundi." Economist Intelligence Unit, London. http://www.eiu.com.

———. 2008b. "Country Profile: Guinea-Bissau." Economic Intelligence Unit, London. http://www.eiu.com.

———. 2010. "Country Profiles." Economist Intelligence Unit, London. http://www.eiu.com.

Edis, Richard. 1995. "Mozambique's Successful Peace Process: An Insider's View." *Cambridge Review of International Affairs* 9 (2): 5–21.

Eichengreen, Barry. 2010. "Lessons from the Marshall Plan." Background paper for the WDR 2011.

Eide, Espen B., Anja T. Kaspersen, Randolph Kent, and Karen von Hippel. 2005. "Report on Integrated Missions: Practical Perspectives and Recommendations." UN Executive Committee on Humanitarian Affairs, New York.

EITI (Extractive Industries Transparency Initiative). 2009. "What is the EITI?" EITI, Oslo.

Ekeh, Peter. 2002. "A Review of HRW's and CLEEN's Report *The Bakassi Boys: The Legitimization of Murder and Torture* on State Sponsored Vigilante Groups in Nigeria." Dawodu.com, May 27.

El Jack, Amani. 2003. "Gender and Armed Conflict Overview Report." Institute of Development Studies, University of Sussex, Brighton, U.K.

Elbadawi, Ibrahim, Håvard Hegre, and Gary J. Milante. 2008. "The Aftermath of Civil War." *Journal of Peace Research* 45 (4): 451–59.

Embassy of the United States in Mexico. 2010. "Borders and Law Enforcement. A Border Community United: The U.S.-Mexico Border." U.S. Department of State, Mexico City. http://mexico.usembassy.gov/.

Encyclopedia of the Nations. 2010. "Benin-History." Encyclopedia of the Nations. http://www.nationsencyclopedia.com/.

Epstein, David L., Robert H. Bates, Jack A. Goldstone, Ida Kristensen, and Sharyn O'Halloran. 2006. "Democratic Transitions." *American Journal of Political Science* 50 (3): 551–69.

Esteban, Joan, and Debraj Ray. 2008. "Polarization, Fractionalization and Conflict." *Journal of Peace Research* 45 (2): 163–82.

Estrada, Daniela. 2010. "Unfinished Business." *Inter Press Service News Agency* July 30.

Etzioni, Amitai. 1999. *The Limits of Privacy.* New York: Basic Books.

Europa Publications. 2001. "Europa World Online." Europa Publications. http://www.europaworld.com.

European Affairs. 2010. "Led by the EU and NATO, International Efforts to Stem Maritime Piracy Begin to Pay Off." European Affairs, European Institute, Washington, DC.

European Commission and Republic of Burundi. 2007. "République du Burundi: Communauté Européenne: Document de Stratégie Pays et Programme Indicatif National 2008–2013." European Commission, Lisbon.

European Union. 1951. "Treaty Establishing the European Coal and Steel Community, ECSC Treaty." European Union, Brussels. http://europa.eu.

Europol. 2007. "EU Terrorism Situation and Trend Report 2007." Europol, The Hague, Netherlands.

Evans, Alex. 2010. "Resource Scarcity, Climate Change and the Risk of Violent Conflict." Background paper for the WDR 2011.

Even-Zohar, Chaim. 2003. "Sierra Leone Diamond Sector Financial Policy Constraint." Management Systems International, Washington, DC; Peace Diamond Alliance, Freetown, Sierra Leone.

Everett, Silas. 2009. "Law and Justice in East Timor: A Survey of Citizen Awareness and Attitudes regarding Law and Justice." The Asia Foundation, San Francisco, CA.

Fabio, Sanchez. 2007. *Las Cuentas de la Violencia.* Bogotá: Grupo Editorial Norma.

Falch, Åshild. 2010. "Women's Political Participation and Influence in Post-conflict Burundi and Nepal." Peace Research Institute of Oslo, Oslo.

FAO (Food and Agriculture Organization of the United Nations). 2010. "Global Information Early Warning System on Food and Agriculture." FAO, Rome.

FAO (Food and Agriculture Organization of the United Nations), IFAD (International Fund for Agricultural Development), UNCTAD (UN Conference on Trade and Development), and World Bank. 2010. "Principles for Responsible Agricultural Investment That Respects Rights, Livelihoods and Resources." Discussion Note, FAO, Rome; IFAD, Rome; UNCTAD, Geneva; World Bank, Washington, DC.

Farrell, Graham, and Ken Clark. 2004. "What Does the World Spend on Criminal Justice?" HEUNI Paper 20, European Institute for Crime Prevention and Control, Helsinki.

Favaro, Edgardo, ed. 2008. *Small States, Smart Solutions: Improving Connectivity and Increasing the Effectiveness of Public Services.* Washington, DC: World Bank.

———. 2010. "Using Regional Institutions to Improve the Quality of Public Services." Background paper for the WDR 2011.

Faye, Michael L., John W. McArthur, Jeffrey D. Sachs, and Thomas Snow. 2004. "The Challenges Facing Landlocked Developing Countries." *Journal of Human Development and Capabilities* 5 (1): 31–68.

Fearon, James D. 1995. "Rationalist Explanations for War." *International Organization* 49 (3): 379–414.

———. 2004. "Why Do Some Civil Wars Last So Much Longer than Others?" *Journal of Peace Research* 41 (3): 275–301.

———. 2005. "Primary Commodity Exports and Civil War." *Journal of Conflict Resolution* 49 (4): 483–507.

———. 2006. "Ethnic Mobilization and Ethnic Violence." In *Oxford Handbook of Political Economy*, ed. Barry R. Weingast and Donald A. Wittman. New York: Oxford University Press.

———. 2010a. "Governance and Civil War Onset." Background paper for the WDR 2011.

———. 2010b. "Homicide Data." Background note for the WDR 2011.

Fearon, James D., and David D. Laitin. 1999. "Weak States, Rough Terrain, and Large-Scale Ethnic Violence Since 1945." Paper presented at the 1999 Annual Meetings of the American Political Science Association, Atlanta, GA, September 2.

———. 2003. "Ethnicity, Insurgency, and Civil War." *American Political Science Review* 97 (1): 75–90.

Fearon, James D., Macartan Humphreys, and Jeremy Weinstein. 2009. "Can Development Aid Contribute to Social Cohesion after Civil War? Evidence from a Field Experiment in Post-conflict Liberia." *American Economic Review* 99 (2): 287–91.

Fenton, Wendy, and Melissa Phillips. 2009. "Funding Mechanisms in Southern Sudan: NGO Perspectives." *Humanitarian Exchange Magazine* 42: 25–7.

Férnandez, Carlos Castresana. 2010. "CICIG Review: A Report on CICIG's Activities." Paper presented at the Central American Regional Workshop on the World Development Report 2011: Conflict, Security, and Development, Mexico City, June 21.

Filippini, Leonardo. 2009. "Criminal Prosecutions for Human Rights Violations in Argentina." International Center for Transitional Justice, Buenos Aires.

Financial Action Task Force. 2010. "20 Years of the FATF Recommendations: 1990–2010." Financial Action Task Force, Paris; Organisation for Economic Co-operation and Development, Paris.

Finegan, T. Aldrich, and Robert A. Margo. 1994. "Added and Discouraged Workers in the Late 1930s: A Re-examination." *Journal of Economic History* 54: 64–84.

Formisano, Michel. 2002. "Econometría Espacial: Características de la Violencia Homicida en Bogotá." El Centro de Estudios sobre Desarrollo Económico, Bogotá.

Fortna, Virginia P. 2008. *Does Peacekeeping Work? Shaping Belligerents' Choices after Civil War.* Princeton, NJ: Princeton University Press.

Foxnews.com. 2001. "The Oklahoma City Bombing: Fast Facts." *FoxNews.com*, September 5. http://www.foxnews.com/.

French Ministry of Foreign Affairs. 2006. "Framework Partnership Document: France; Republic of Burundi (2006–2010)." French Ministry of Foreign Affairs, Paris.

Friends Committee on National Legislation. 2009. "Kenya: Temporary Ceasefire or Lasting Peace?" Policy Brief, Friends Committee on National Legislation, Washington, DC.

Frühling, Hugo, Joseph S. Tulchin, and Heather A. Golding, eds. 2003. *Crime and Violence in Latin America: Citizen Security, Democracy, and the State.* Washington, DC: Woodrow Wilson International Center for Scholars.

Fukuyama, Francis. 2004. *State-Building: Governance and World Order in the 21st Century.* Ithaca, NY: Cornell University Press.

Gadir, Ali A., Ibrahim A. Elbadawi, and Atta El-Batahani. 2005. "Sudan's Civil War: Why Has It Prevailed for So Long?" In *Understanding Civil War: Evidence and Analysis*, ed. Paul Collier and Nicholas Sambanis. Washington, DC: World Bank.

Gaibulloev, Khusrav, and Todd Sandler. 2008. "Growth Consequences of Terrorism in Western Europe." *Kyklos* 61 (3): 411–24.
Gambino, Anthony W. 2010. "Democratic Republic of Congo." Background paper for the WDR 2011.
Gantz, David. 1998. "Globalizing Sanctions Against Foreign Bribery: The Emergence of a New International Legal Consensus." *Northwestern Journal of International Law and Business* 18 (2): 457–97.
Garang, John. 1987. *John Garang Speaks.* London: Kegan Paul International.
Garrasi, Donata. 2010. "Funding Peacebuilding and Recovery: A Comparative Review of System-wide Multi-donor Trust Funds and Other Funding Instruments for Peacebuilding and Post-conflict Recovery." U.K. Department for International Development, London.
Garrett, Laurie. 2005. "HIV and National Security: Where Are the Links?" Council on Foreign Relations, Washington, DC.
Garzón, Juan C. 2008. "Mafia and Co.: The Criminal Networks in Brazil, Mexico, and Colombia." Woodrow Wilson International Center for Scholars, Washington, DC.
Gates, Scott, Håvard Hegre, Håvard M. Nygård, and Håvard Strand. 2010. "Human, Economic, and Social Consequences of Fragility and Conflict." Background paper for the WDR 2011.
Gates, Scott, and Kaare Strøm. 2008."Power Sharing and Civil Conflict." CSCW Policy Brief I/2008, Center for the Study of Civil War, Peace Research Institute of Oslo, Oslo.
Gberie, Lansana. 2003a. "L'Afrique de l'Ouest: Entre Pierres et Étincelles. L'Économie Politique des Diamants et la Déstablisation Régionale." Partenariat Afrique Canada, Ottawa.
———. 2003b. "ECOMOG: The Story of an Heroic Failure." *African Affairs* 102 (406): 147–54.
Gelb, Alan. 2010. "How Can Donors Create Incentives for Results and Flexibility for Fragile States? A Proposal for IDA." Working Paper 227, Center for Global Development, Washington, DC.
Gellner, Ernest. 1983. *Nations and Nationalism.* Ithaca, NY: Cornell University Press.
Geneva Conventions. 1949. "Geneva Conventions Relative to the Protection of Civilian Persons in Time of War." Diplomatic Conference of Geneva of 1949, Geneva.
Geneva Declaration. 2008. "Global Burden of Armed Violence." Geneva Declaration on Armed Violence and Development, Geneva.
———. 2010. "More Violence, Less Development: Examining the Relationship between Armed Violence and MDG Achievement." Geneva Declaration on Armed Violence and Development, Geneva.
Gerson, Allan, and Nat J. Colletta. 2002. *Privatizing Peace: From Conflict to Security.* Ardsley, NY: Transnational Publishers.
Gettleman, Jeffrey. 2009. "Radical Islamists Slip Easily Into Kenya." *New York Times,* July 21.
GhanaWeb. 2006. "Workshop on Conflict Resolution Ends at Dodowa." *GhanaWeb,* April 1. http://ghanaweb.net.
Ghani, Ashraf C., and Clare Lockhart. 2008. *Fixing Failed States: A Framework for Rebuilding a Fractured World.* New York: Oxford University Press.
Ghani, Ashraf C., Clare Lockhart, and Michael Carnahan. 2005. "Closing the Sovereignty Gap: An Approach to State-Building." Working Paper 253, Overseas Development Institute, London.
Gilpin, Raymond. 2009. "Counting the Costs of Somali Piracy." Center for Sustainable Economics Working Paper, United States Institute for Peace, Washington, DC.
Giovine, Luigi, Robert Krech, Kremena Ionkova, and Kathryn Bach. 2010. "Holding on to Monrovia: Protecting a Fragile Peace through Economic Governance and Short-Term Employment." Background paper for the WDR 2011.
Gleditsch, Kristian S. 2007."Transnational Dimensions of Civil War." *Journal of Peace Research* 44 (3): 293–309.
Gleditsch, Kristian S., and Michael D. Ward. 1999. "Interstate System Membership: A Revised List of the Independent States since 1816." *International Interactions* 25 (4): 393–413.
———. 2000. "War and Peace in Space and Time: The Role of Democratization." *International Studies Quarterly* 44 (1): 1–29.
Gleditsch, Nils P., Peter Wallensteen, Mikael Eriksson, Margareta Sollenberg, and Håvard Strand. 2002. "Armed Conflict 1946–2001: A New Dataset." *Journal of Peace Research* 39 (5): 615–37.
Glenny, Misha. 2008. *McMafia: A Journey through the Global Criminal Underworld.* New York: Alfred A. Knopf.
Glick, Reuven, and Alan M. Taylor. 2005. "Collateral Damage: Trade Disruption and the Economic Impact of War." NBER Working Paper 11565, National Bureau of Economic Research, Cambridge, MA.

Global Terrorism Database. 2010. "Global Terrorism Database." National Consortium for the Study of Terrorism and Responses to Terrorism, University of Maryland, College Park, MD. http://www.start.umd.edu/gtd/.

Goldstein, Joshua, and Juliana Rotich. 2008. "Digitally Networked Technology in Kenya's 2007–2008 Post-Election Crisis." Research Publication No. 2008–09, Berkman Center for Internet and Society, Harvard University, Cambridge, MA.

Goldstone, Jack A. 2010. "Representational Models and Democratic Transitions in Fragile and Post-conflict States." Background paper for the WDR 2011.

Goldstone, Jack A., Robert H. Bates, David L. Epstein, Ted R. Gurr, Michael B. Lustik, Monty G. Marshall, Jay Ulfelder, and Mark Woodward. 2010. "A Global Model for Forecasting Political Instability." *American Journal of Political Science* 54 (1): 190–208.

Goldstone, Jack A., and Jay Ulfelder. 2004. "How to Construct Stable Democracies." *Washington Quarterly* 28 (1): 9–20.

Gómez, Armando C. 2008. "Diagnóstico de la Seguridad Pública y Privada en Guatemala, Honduras y El Salvador." Organization of American States, Washington, DC.

Gomez, Margarita P., and Asger Christensen. 2010. "The Impacts of Refugees on Neighboring Countries: A Development Challenge." Background paper for the WDR 2011.

Gonçalve, Danyelle N. 2008. "Os Processos de Anistia Política No Brasil: Do Perdão à 'Reparação.'" *Revista Ciencia Sociais* 39 (1): 38–48.

Goreaux, Louis. 2001. "Conflict Diamonds." Africa Region Working Paper Series 13, World Bank, Washington, DC.

Government of Aceh, Syiah Kuala University, and World Bank. 2008. "Managing Resources for Better Outcomes in a Special Autonomy Region: Aceh Public Expenditure Analysis Update 2008." Government of Aceh; Syiah Kuala University; World Bank, Jakarta.

Government of Afghanistan and UNDP (UN Development Programme). 2010. "ARTF Administrator's Report on Financial Status: As of December 21, 2010." Government of Afghanistan; UNDP, Kabul.

Government of Australia. 2010. "Australian Transaction Reports and Analysis Centre." Government of Australia, West Chatswood, Australia.

Government of Burundi, and UN (United Nations). 2009. "Strategie Integree D'Appui des Nations Unies au Burundi 2010-2014: Consolidation de las Paix et Relévement Communautaire." Government of Burundi; UN, Bujumbura.

Government of Nepal, UNDP (UN Development Programme), and UNDG (UN Development Group). 2010. "Third Consolidated Annual Report on Activities Implemented Under the United Nations Peace Fund for Nepal: Report of the Administrative Agent of the United Nations Peace Fund for Nepal for the Period 1 January to 31 December 2009." Government of Nepal; UNDP; UNDG, Kathmandu.

Government of the Republic of Indonesia and Free Aceh Movement. 2005. "Helsinki Memorandum of Understanding." Government of Republic of Indoesia; Free Aceh Movement, Helsinki.

Government of the Republic of Liberia Executive Mansion. 2009. "Liberia Makes Progress on Corruption, Transparency International Index Shows." Government of the Republic of Liberia Executive Mansion, Monrovia. http://www.emansion.gov.lr.

Gowan, Richard. 2007. "EUFOR RD Congo, UNIFIL and Future European Support to the UN." Paper presented at the Security and Defence Agenda: The EU's Africa Strategy: What are the Lessons of the Congo Mission? Brussels, March 7.

Graydon, Carolyn. 2005. "Local Justice Systems in Timor-Leste: Washed Up, or Watch this Space?" *Development Bulletin* 68: 66–70.

Greenberger, Robert S. 1995."Foreigners Use Bribes to Beat U.S. Rivals in Many Deals, New Report Concludes." *Wall Street Journal*, October 12.

Greene, Owen. 2001. "Enhancing Traceability of Small Arms and Light Weapons Flows: Developing an International Marking and Tracing Regime." Biting the Bullet Briefing Paper 5, British American Security Information Council; International Alert; Saferworld, London.

Greenfell, Laura. 2006. "Legal Pluralism and the Rule of Law in Timor Leste." *Leiden Journal of International Law* 19: 305–37.

Greta, Maria, and Krzysztof Lewandowski. 2010. "Euroregion's 'Mission' and the Success of the Lisbon Strategy." *Business and Economic Horizons* 1 (1): 14–20.

Grimm, Sonja. 2010. "Germany's Post-1945 and Post-1989 Education Systems." Background note for the WDR 2011.

Grindle, Merilee S. 2010."Good Governance: The Inflation of an Idea." Faculty Research Working Papers RWP10-023, John F. Kennedy School of Government, Harvard University, Cambridge, MA.

Grossman, Herschel I. 1991. "A General Equilibrium Model of Insurrections." *American Economic Review* 81 (4): 912–21.

Grygiel, Julie. 2007. "Kosovo Dairy Value Chain Case Study: Guided Case Studies in Value Chain Development for Conflict-Affected Environments." Micro Report 95, U.S. Agency for International Development, Washington, DC.

Guehenno, Jean-Marie. 2010. "Public Security, Criminal Justice, and Reforming the Security Sector." Background paper for the WDR 2011.

Guerrero, Rodrigo. 1999. "Programa Desarrollo, Seguridad y Paz DESEPAZ de la Ciudad de Cali." Paper presented at the Banco Interamericano de Desarrollo Programas Municipales para la Prevención y Atención de la Violencia, Rio de Janeiro, July 29–30.

———. 2006. "Violence Prevention Through Multi-sectoral Partnerships: The Cases of Cali and Bogotá." *African Safety Promotion: A Journal of Injury and Violence Prevention* 4 (2): 88–98.

Guerrero-Serdán, Gabriela. 2009. "The Effects of the War in Iraq on Nutrition and Health: An Analysis Using Anthropometric Outcomes of Children." Households in Conflict Network Working Papers 55, Institute of Development Studies, University of Sussex, Brighton, U.K.

Guggenheim, Scott. 2011. "Community-Driven Development versus Flexible Funding to Communities in Conflict and Post-conflict Environments." Background note for the WDR 2011.

Guha-Sapir, Debarati, and Olivia D'Aoust. 2010. "Demographic and Health Consequences of Civil Conflict." Background paper for the WDR 2011.

Gupta, Jyotirindra D. 1970. *Language Conflict and National Development: Group Politics and National Language Policy in India.* Berkeley, CA: University of California Press.

Gurr, Ted R. 1968. "A Causal Model of Civil Strife: A Comparative Analysis Using New Indices." *American Political Science Review* 62 (4): 1104–24.

———. 1970. *Why Men Rebel.* Princeton, NJ: Princeton University Press.

Gutiérrez Sanín, Francisco. 2008. "Telling the Difference: Guerrillas and Paramilitaries in the Colombia War." *Politics and Society* 36 (1): 3–34.

Hall, Robert E., and Charles I. Jones. 1999. "Why Do Some Countries Produce So Much More Output per Worker Than Others?" *Quarterly Journal of Economics* 114 (1): 83–116.

Hanson, Stephanie. 2010. "Combating Maritime Piracy." Council on Foreign Relations, Washington, DC.

Harbom, Lotta, and Peter Wallensteen. 2010. "Armed Conflicts, 1946–2009." *Journal of Peace Research* 47 (4): 501–09.

Harborne, Bernard, and Caroline Sage. 2010. "Security and Justice Overview." Background paper for the WDR 2011.

Harborne, Bernard, Mike McGovern, Gilbert Khadaglia, and Paul Francis. 2010. "Avoidance or Prevention." Background paper for the WDR 2011.

Harild, Niels, and Asger Christensen. 2010. "The Development Challenge of Finding Durable Solutions for Refugees and Internally Displaced People." Background note for the WDR 2011.

Harriott, Anthony, ed. 2004. *Understanding Crime in Jamaica: New Challenges for Public Policy.* Kingston, Jamaica: University of West Indies Press.

———. 2008. *Organized Crime and Politics in Jamaica: Breaking the Nexus.* Kingston, Jamaica: Canoe Press, University of West Indies.

Hartzell, Caroline, Mathew Hoddie, and Donald Rothchild. 2001. "Stabilizing the Peace after Civil War: An Investigation of Some Key Variables." *International Organization* 55 (1): 183–208.

Hartzell, Caroline A. 2006."Structuring the Peace: Negotiated Settlements and the Construction of Conflict Management Institutions." In *Conflict Prevention and Peacebuilding in Post-War Societies: Sustaining the Peace,* ed. T. David Mason and James D. Meernik. New York: Routledge.

Harvey, Paul, Abby Stoddard, Adele Harmer, Glyn Taylor, with Victoria DiDomenico, and Lauren Brander. 2010. "The State of the Humanitarian System: Assessing Performance and Progress." Active Learning Network for Accountability and Performance in Humanitarian Action, London.

Harwell, Emily. 2010. "Forests in Fragile and Conflict-Affected States." Background paper for the WDR 2011.

Hassan, Nasra. 2001. "An Arsenal of Believers: Talking to the 'Human Bombs.'" *The New Yorker* November 19, 2001.

Hayner, Priscilla. 2010. *Unspeakable Truths: Transitional Justice and the Challenge of Truth Commissions.* New York: Routledge.

Hegre, Håvard, and Nicholas Sambanis. 2006. "Sensitivity Analysis of Empirical Results on Civil War Onset." *Journal of Conflict Resolution* 50 (4): 508–35.

Heimann, Fritz, and Gillian Dell. 2010. "Progress Report: Enforcement of the OECD Anti-Bribery Convention 2010." Transparency International, Berlin.

Heinemann-Grüder, Andreas, Tobias Pietz, and Shay Duffy. 2003. "Turning Soldiers into a Work Force: Demobilization and Reintegration in Post-Dayton Bosnia and Herzegovina." Brief 27, Bonn International Center for Conversion, Bonn, Germany.

Henrich, Joseph, Jean Ensminger, Richard McElreath, Abigail Barr, Clark Barrett, Alexander Bolyanatz, Juan C. Cardenas, Michael Gurven, Edwins Gwako, Natalie Henrich, Carolyn Lesorogol, Frank Marlowe, David Tracer, and John Ziker. 2010. "Markets, Religion, Community Size, and the Evolution of Fairness and Punishment." *Science* 327 (5972): 1480–84.

Heraclides, Alexis. 1990. "Secessionist Minorities and External Involvement." *International Organization* 44 (3): 341–78.

Herbst, Jeffrey. 2000. *States and Power in Africa: Comparative Lessons in Authority and Control.* Princeton, NJ: Princeton University Press.

Herz, John. 1950. "Idealist Internationalism and the Security Dilemma." *World Politics* 2 (2): 157–80.

Herzberg, Benjamin. 2004. "Investment Climate Reform: Going the Last Mile: The Bulldozer Initiative in Bosnia and Herzegovina." Policy Research Working Paper 3390, World Bank, Washington, DC.

Heuveline, Patrick, and Bunnak Poch. 2007. "The Phoenix Population: Demographic Crisis and Rebound in Cambodia." *Demography* 44 (2): 405–26.

Hewitt, J. Joseph, Jonathan Wilkenfeld, and Ted R. Gurr. 2010. *Peace and Conflict 2010.* Boulder, CO: Paradigm Publishers.

Hines, James R. 1995. "Forbidden Payment: Foreign Bribery and American Business After 1977." NBER Working Paper 5266, National Bureau of Economic Research, Cambridge, MA.

Hirshleifer, Jack. 1995. "Anarchy and Its Breakdown." *Journal of Political Economy* 103 (1): 26–52.

Hobbes, Thomas. 1651. "Leviathan or The Matter, Forme and Power of a Common Wealth Ecclesiasticall and Civil." Andrew Crooke, London.

Hoeffler, Anke, Sarah von Billerbeck, and Syeda S. Ijaz. 2010. "Post-conflict Recovery and Peace Building." Background paper for the WDR 2011.

Hoff, Karla. 2010. "Experiments and the Study of Conflict." Background note for the WDR 2011.

Hoff, Karla, and Joseph E. Stiglitz. 2004a. "After the Big Bang? Obstacles to the Emergence of the Rule of Law in Post-Communist Societies." *American Economic Review* 94 (3): 753–63.

———. 2004b. "The Transition Process in Postcommunist Societies: Toward a Political Economy of Property Rights." In *Toward Pro-Poor Policies: Aid, Institutions and Globalization*, Bertil Tungodden, Nicholas Stern, and Ivar Kolstad. Washington, DC: World Bank; New York: Oxford University Press.

———. 2008. "Exiting a Lawless State." *Economic Journal* 118 (531): 1474–97.

Horowitz, Donald L. 2000. *Ethnic Groups in Conflict.* Berkeley, CA: University of California Press.

Horsey, Richard, and Nikolas Win Myint. 2010. "Engaging with Countries in Situations of Political Impasse." Background paper for the WDR 2011.

Houdart, Fabrice, and David Pearce. 2011. "World Bank Staff Analysis for the WDR 2011." Background note for the WDR 2011.

Huang, Yasheng, and Xueli Wang. 2010. "Employment and Social Capital Formation in China: Evidence from Rural Migrant Worker Surveys." Background paper for the WDR 2011.

Hubbard, Michael. 2005. "Changing Customs: Lessons from Mozambique." International Development Department, University of Birmingham, Birmingham, U.K.

Hudson, Andrew and Alexandra W. Taylor. 2010. "The International Commission against Impunity in Guatemala: A New Model for International Criminal Justice Mechanisms." *Journal of International Criminal Justice* 8 (1): 53–74.

Hufbauer, Gary C., Jeffrey J. Schott, Kimberly A. Elliott, and Barbara Oegg. 2007. *Economic Sanctions Reconsidered.* Washington, DC: Peterson Institute for International Economics.

Hughes, Richard L., Robert C. Ginnett, and Gordon J. Curphy. 2005. *Leadership: Enhancing the Lessons of Experience.* New York: McGraw-Hill Irwin.

Human Rights Watch. 2009. "Soldiers Who Rape, Commanders Who Condone: Sexual Violence and Military Reform in the Democratic Republic of Congo." Human Rights Watch, New York.

Human Security Report Project. 2005. *Human Security Report 2005: War and Peace in the 21st Century.* New York: Oxford University Press.

———. eds. forthcoming. "*Human Security Report 2009/2010: The Causes of Peace and the Shrinking Costs of War.*" Vancouver: Human Security Report Project.

Hume, Cameron R. 1994. *Ending Mozambique's War: The Role of Mediation and Good Offices.* Washington, DC: United States Institute of Peace.

Hunt, Swanee, and Cristina Posa. 2001. "Women Waging Peace." *Foreign Policy* 124: 38–47.

Huntington, Samuel P. 1968. *Political Order in Changing Societies.* New Haven, CT: Yale University Press.

Huyse, Luc, and Mark Salter, eds. 2008. *Traditional Justice and Reconciliation after Violent Conflict: Learning from African Experiences.* Stockholm: International Institute for Democracy and Electoral Assistance.

Ibáñez, Ana María, and Andrés Moya. 2006. "The Impact of Intra-state Conflict on Economic Welfare and Consumption Smoothing: Empirical Evidence for the Displaced Population in Colombia." Household in Conflict Network Working Paper 23, Institute of Development Studies, University of Sussex, Brighton, U.K.

ICRC (International Committee of the Red Cross). 2001. "Women Facing War." ICRC, Geneva.

IFC (International Finance Corporation). 2008. "IFC Smart Lessons: Creating Opportunities for Women Entrepreneurs in Conflict-Affected Countries." IFC, Washington, DC.

Igreja, Victor, and Beatrice Dias-Lambranca. 2008. "Restorative Justice and the Role of Magamba Spirits in Post-Civil War Gorongosa, Central Mozambique." In *Traditional Justice and Reconciliation After Violent Conflict: Learning from African Experiences*, ed. Luc Huyse and Mark Salter. Stockholm: International Institute for Democracy and Electoral Assistance.

ILO (International Labour Organization). 2009. "Socio-Economic Reintegration of Ex-combatants: Guidelines." ILO, Geneva.

———. 2010. "Local Economic Recovery in Post-conflict: Guidelines." ILO, Geneva.

Imai, Kosuke, and Jeremy Weinstein. 2000. "Measuring the Economic Impact of Civil War." Working Paper 51, Center for International Development, Harvard University, Cambridge, MA.

Indian Ministry of Rural Development. 2005. "The Mahatma Gandhi National Rural Employment Guarantee Act." Government of India, New Delhi. http://www.nrega.nic.in/netnrega/home.aspx.

———. 2010. "Background Material for the World Development Report on Conflict, Security and Development." Background note for the WDR 2011.

INEE (Inter-Agency Network for Education in Emergencies). 2010. "Multiple Faces of Education in Conflict-Affected and Fragile Contexts." INEE, New York, Paris, and Geneva.

Institute for State Effectiveness. 2007. "Kosovo: Developing a Strategy for the Future." Institute for State Effectiveness, Washington, DC.

Instituto Universitario en Democracia Paz y Seguridad. 2010. "Observatorio de la Violencia en Honduras, Muertes Violentas y No Intencionales." Instituto Universitario en Democracia Paz y Seguridad Observatorio Nacional de la Violencia Edición, Tegucigalpa.

Inter-American Drug Abuse Control Commission. 2010. "Statute of the Inter-American Drug Abuse Control Commission (CICAD)." Organization of American States, Washington, DC.

Internal Displacement Monitoring Centre. 2007. "International Displacement: Global Overview of Trends and Developments in 2006." Internal Displacement Monitoring Centre of the Norwegian Refugee Council, Geneva.

———. 2008. "Internal Displacement: Global Overview of Trends and Developments in 2007." International Displacement Monitoring Centre of the Norwegian Refugee Council, Geneva.

———. 2010. "International Displacement: Global Overview of Trends and Developments in 2009." International Displacement Monitoring Centre of the Norwegian Refugee Council, Geneva.

International Alert and Eastern Africa Sub-Regional Support Initiative for the Advancement of Women. 2007. "Women's Political Participation in Countries Emerging from Conflict in the Great Lakes Region of Africa: Report of the Consultation Workshop." International Alert; Eastern Africa Sub-Regional Support Initiative for the Advancement of Women, London.

International Alert and Women Waging Peace. 2004. "Inclusive Security, Sustainable Peace: A Toolkit for Advocacy and Action." International Alert, London.

International Center for Research on Women. 2002. "Women-Initiated Community Level Responses to Domestic Violence: Summary Report of Three Studies." International Center for Research on Women, Washington, DC.

International Center for Transitional Justice. 2010. "Truth Seeking." International Center for Transitional Justice, New York. http://www.ictj.org.

International Centre for the Prevention of Crime. 2005. "Urban Crime Prevention and Youth at Risk: Compendium of Promising Strategies and Programmes from Around the World." Paper presented at the 11th United Nations Congress on Crime and Criminal Justice, Bangkok, April 18–25.

———. 2008. "Crime Prevention and Community Safety: Trends and Perspectives." International Centre for the Prevention of Crime, Montreal.

International Crisis Group. 1999. "Macedonia: Towards Destabilization?" Europe Report 67, International Crisis Group, Brussels.

———. 2003. "Serbia After Djindjic." Europe Briefing 46, International Crisis Group, Brussels.

———. 2005. "Aceh: So Far So Good." Asia Briefing 44, International Crisis Group, Brussels.

———. 2007. "Burundi: Finalizing Peace with the FNL." Africa Report 131, International Crisis Group, Brussels.

———. 2008a. "Guinea-Bissau: In Need of a State." Africa Report 142, International Crisis Group, Brussels.

———. 2008b. "Kenya in Crisis." Africa Report 137, International Crisis Group, Brussels.

———. 2009a. "Congo: Five Priorities for a Peacebuilding Strategy." Africa Report 150, International Crisis Group, Brussels.

———. 2009b. "Guinea-Bissau: Building a Real Stability Pact." Africa Briefing 57, International Crisis Group, Brussels.

———. 2009c. "Yemen: Defusing the Saada Time Bomb." Middle East Report 86, International Crisis Group, Brussels.

———. 2009d. "Zimbabwe: Engaging the Inclusive Government." Africa Briefing 59, International Crisis Group, Brussels.

International Dialogue on Peacebuilding and Statebuilding. 2010. "Dili Declaration and Annex: Statement by the g7+." International Dialogue on Peacebuilding and Statebuilding, Dili.

Intscher, Horst. 2010. "Financial Intelligence Unit Capabilities." Background note for the WDR 2011.

IRIN (UN Integrated Regional Information Networks). 2005. "Guinea-Bissau: Donors to Firm up Aid Pledges after 2005 Presidential Election." UN Office for the Coordination of Humanitarian Affairs, Bissau.

———. 2009. "South Africa 2009: Land Reform: Same Problem, Different Approach." UN Office for the Coordination of Humanitarian Affairs, Johannesburg.

———. 2010. "Kenya-Somalia: Insecurity without Borders." UN Office for the Coordination of Humanitarian Affairs, Garissa/Mandera.

Jahr, Nicholas. 2010. "Can Liberia's Anti-corruption Program Serve as New Model?" *World Politics Review*, May 14.

Jayaraman, Anuja, Tesfayi Gebreselassie, and S. Chandrasekhar. 2009. "Effect of Conflict on Age at Marriage and Age at First Birth in Rwanda." *Population Research and Policy Review* 28 (5): 551–67.

Jeffries, Richard, and Clare Thomas. 1993. "The Ghanaian Elections of 1992." *African Affairs* 92 (368): 331–66.

Jervis, Robert. 1978. "Cooperation under the Security Dilemma." *World Politics* 30 (2): 167–214.

Jeyaseelan, L., Shuba Kumar, Nithya Neelakantan, Abraham Peedicayil, Rajamohanam Pillai, and Nata Duvvury. 2007. "Physical Spousal Violence against Women in India: Some Risk Factors." *Journal of Biosocial Science* 39 (5): 657–70.

Jha, Prashant. 2010. "Politics and Violence in the Tarai." Background note for the WDR 2011.

Johnston, Michael. 2010. "Anti-Corruption Strategies in Fragile States." Background paper for the WDR 2011.

Jones, Bruce D. 1999. "Military Intervention in Rwanda's Two Wars: Partisanship and Indifference." In *Civil Wars, Insecurity, and Intervention*, ed. Barbara F. Walter and Jack Snyder. New York: Columbia University Press.

Jones, Bruce D., Richard Gowan, and Jake Sherman. 2009. "Building on Brahimi: Peacekeeping in an Era of Strategic Uncertainty." Center on International Cooperation, New York University, New York.

Jones, David S. 2009."Public Procurement in Cambodia." In *International Handbook of Public Procurement*, ed. Khi V. Thai. Boca Raton, FL: Auerbach Publications.

Jones, Sam. 2008. "Sustaining Growth in the Long Term." In *Post-stabilization Economics in Sub-Saharan Africa: Lessons from Mozambique*, ed. Jean A. P Clément and Shanaka J. Peiris. Washington, DC: International Monetary Fund.

Jordan, David C. 1999. *Drug Politics: Dirty Money and Democracies.* Norman, OK: University of Oklahoma Press.

Jornal O Globo. 2010. "Cálculo Mostra ser Viável Beneficiar com UPPs Moradores de Todas as Favelas do Rio." *Jornal O Globo*, December 14.

Justino, Patricia, and Philip Verwimp. 2008. "Poverty Dynamics, Violent Conflict and Convergence in Rwanda." Research Working Paper 4, MICROCON, Brighton, U.K.

Kalyvas, Stathis. 2006. *The Logic of Violence in Civil War.* New York: Cambridge University Press.

Kambuwa, Marvin, and Malcolm Wallis. 2002. "Performance Management and Integrated Development Planning in South Africa." Paper presented at the Twenty-Fourth Round Table Conference of the African Association for Public Administration and Management (AAPAM). Maseru, November 25–29.

Kang, David. 2002. *Crony Capitalism: Corruption and Development in South Korea and the Philippines.* Cambridge, U.K.: Cambridge University Press.

Kanungo, Prameeta. 2004. "Public Expenditure Tracking Surveys: Application in Uganda, Tanzania, Ghana, and Honduras." Working Paper 51468, World Bank, Washington, DC.

Kaplan, Seth D. 2008. *Fixing Fragile States: A New Paradigm for Development.* Westport, CT: Praeger Security International.

Kaufmann, Daniel, Aart Kraay, and Massimo Mastruzzi. 2010a. "Governance Matters 2009: Worldwide Governance Indicators 1996–2008." World Bank, Washington, DC.

———. 2010b. "The Worldwide Governance Indicators: Methodology and Analytical Issues." Policy Research Working Paper 5430, World Bank, Washington, DC.

Kawagoe, Toshihiko. 1999. "Agricultural Land Reform in Postwar Japan: Experiences and Issues." Policy Research Working Paper 2111, World Bank, Washington, DC.

Kawai, Masahiro, and Shinji Takagi. 2004. "Japan's Official Development Assistance: Recent Issues and Future Directions." *Journal of International Development* 16 (2): 255–80.

Keefer, Philip. 2008. "Insurgency and Credible Commitment in Autocracies and Democracies." *The World Bank Economic Review* 22 (1): 33–61.

———. Forthcoming. "Why Follow the Leader? Action, Credible Commitment and Conflict." In *Oxford Handbook of the Economics of Peace and Conflict*, ed. Michelle Garfinkel and Stergios Skaperdas. Oxford, U.K.: Oxford University Press.

Keefer, Philip, Eric Neumayer, and Thomas Plümper. 2010. "Earthquake Propensity and the Politics of Mortality Prevention." Policy Research Working Paper 5182, World Bank, Washington, DC.

Keita, Kalifa. 1998. "Conflict and Conflict Resolution in the Sahel: The Tuareg Insurgency in Mali." Strategic Studies Institute, U.S. Army War College, Carlisle, PA.

Kelley, Judith G. 2004. *Ethnic Politics in Europe: The Power of Norms and Incentives.* Princeton, NJ: Princeton University Press.

Kelly, Jocelyn. 2010. "Rape in War: Motives for Militia in DRC." USIP Special Report 243, United States Institute of Peace, Washington, DC.

Kenya Ministry of Public Health and Sanitation. 2007. "An Estimate of the Economic Costs of Injuries Due to Interpersonal and Self-Directed Violence in Kenya, 2007." Government of Kenya. Nairobi. Processed.

Kharas, Homi. 2008. "Measuring the Cost of Aid Volatility." Wolfensohn Centre for Development Working Paper 3, Brookings Institution, Washington, DC.

Kilcullen, David. 2009. *The Accidental Guerrilla: Fighting Small Wars in the Midst of a Big One.* New York: Oxford University Press.

Killick, Tony, Carlos N. Castel-Branco, and Richard Gerster. 2005. "Perfect Partners? The Performance of Programme Aid Partners in Mozambique, 2004." Programme Aid Partners; U.K. Department for International Development, Maputo.

Kimani, Mwaura. 2008. "Kenya: MPs Push for Cut in Cabinet Size." *Norweigian Council of Africa: Africa News Update*, May 15.

Kimberley Process Certification Scheme. 2009. "Kimberley Process Rough Diamond Statistics." Kimberley Process Certification Scheme, Kinshasa.

———. 2010. "The Kimberley Process." Kimberley Process Certification Scheme, Kinshasa. http://www.kimberleyprocess.com.

Kimhi, Shaul, and Shemuel Even. 2004. "Who Are the Palestinian Suicide Bombers?" *Terrorism and Political Violence* 16 (4): 815–40.

Kingah, Petronilla K., and Stephen S. Kingah. 2010. "African Traditions and the Modern Human Rights Mechanisms: The Case for Women in Cameroon and Africa." *Cameroon Journal on Democracy and Human Rights* 4 (2): 81–105.

Kingma, Kees. 1997. "Post-War Demobilization and the Reintegration of Ex-combatants into Civilian Life." Paper presented at the USAID Conference: Promoting Democracy, Human Rights, and Reintegration in Post-conflict Societies, Washington, DC, October 30–31.

Kireyev, Alexei. 2006. "The Macroeconomics of Remittances: The Case of Tajikistan." IMF Working Paper 06/2, International Monetary Fund, Washington, DC.

Knox, Colin. 1996. "Emergence of Power Sharing in Northern Ireland: Lessons from Local Government." *Journal of Conflict Studies* 16 (1): 7–29.

Kohlmann, Evan F. 2004. *Al-Qaida's Jihad in Europe: The Afghan-Bosnian Network.* Oxford, U.K.: Berg.

Korski, Daniel, and Richard Gowan. 2009. "Can the EU Rebuild Failing States? A Review of Europe's Civilian Capacities." European Council on Foreign Relations, London.

Kramer, Annika. 2008. "Regional Water Cooperation and Peacebuilding in the Middle East." Initiative for Peacebuilding; Adelphi Research, Brussels.

Kreimer, Alcira, John Eriksson, Robert Muscat, Margaret Arnold, and Colin Scott. 1998. "The World Bank's Experience with Post-conflict Reconstruction." World Bank, Washington, DC.

Krishnan, Suneeta, Corinne H. Rocca, Allan E. Hubbard, Kalyani Subbiah, Jeffrey Edmeades, and Nancy S. Padian. 2010. "Do Changes in Spousal Employment Status Lead to Domestic Violence? Insights from a Prospective Study in Bangalore, India." *Social Science and Medicine* 70 (1): 136–43.

Krueger, Alan B., and David L. Laitin. 2008. "Kto-Kogo?: A Cross-Country Study of the Origins and Targets of Terrorism." In *Terrorism, Economic Development, and Political Openness,* ed. Philip Keefer and Norman Loayza. New York: Cambridge University Press.

Krueger, Alan B., and Jitka Maleckova. 2003. "Education, Poverty, and Terrorism: Is There a Causal Connection?" *Journal of Economic Perspectives* 17 (4): 119–44.

Kubicek, Paul J., ed. 2003. *The European Union and Democratization.* London: Routledge.

Kumar, Vimal, and Stergios Skaperdas. 2009. "On the Economics of Organized Crime." In *Criminal Law and Economics,* ed. Nuno Garoupa. Northampton, MA: Edward Elgar Publishing.

Kuzio, Taras. 2006. "Civil Society, Youth and Societal Mobilization in Democratic Revolutions." *Communist and Post Communist Studies* 39 (3): 365–86.

La Porta, Rafael, Florencio Lopez-de-Silanes, Andrei Shleifer, and Robert Vishny. 1999. "The Quality of Government." *Journal of Law, Economics, and Organization* 15 (1): 222–79.

Lacina, Bethany, and Nils P. Gleditsch. 2005. "Monitoring Trends in Global Combat: A New Dataset of Battle Deaths 2005." *European Journal of Population* 21 (2–3): 145–66.

Lacina, Bethany, Nils P. Gleditsch, and Bruce Russett. 2006. "The Declining Risk of Death in Battle." *International Studies Quarterly* 50 (3): 673–80.

Laitin, David D. 1998. *Identity in Formation: The Russian-Speaking Populations in the Near Abroad.* Ithaca, NY: Cornell University Press.

———. 2000. "What Is a Language Community?" *American Journal of Political Science* 44 (1): 142–55.

———. 2007. *Nations, States, and Violence.* New York: Oxford University Press.

Lamb, Guy, and Dominique Dye. 2009. "Security Promotion and DDR: Linkages between ISM, DDR, and SSR within a Broader Peacebuilding Framework." Congeso Internacional de Desarme, Demovilización y Reintegración, Cartagena, Colombia; Republic of Colombia, Cartagena, Colombia.

Langer, Arnim. 2005. "Horizontal Inequalities and Violent Group Mobilization in Côte d'Ivoire." *Oxford Development Studies* 33 (1): 25–45.

Latinobarómetro. 2009. "Latinobarómetro: Opinion Pública Latinoamericana." Latinobarómetro, Santiago. http://www.latinobarometro.org.

Lawson, Sam, and Larry MacFaul. 2010. "Illegal Logging and Related Trade: Indicators of the Global Response." Chatham House, London.

Lemay-Hébert, Nicolas. 2009. "UNPOL and Police Reform in Timor-Leste: Accomplishments and Setbacks." *International Peacekeeping* 16 (3): 393–406.

Leslie, Glaister. 2010. "Confronting the Don: The Political Economy of Gang Violence in Jamaica." Occasional Paper 26, Small Arms Survey, Graduate Institute of International and Development Studies, Geneva.

Lewis, Dustin A. 2009. "Unrecognized Victims: Sexual Violence against Men in Conflict Settings under International Law." *Wisconsin International Law Journal* 27 (1): 1–49.

Li, Quan, and Ming Wen. 2005. "The Immediate and Lingering Effects of Armed Conflict on Adult Mortality: A Time-Series Cross-National Analysis." *Journal of Peace Research* 42 (4): 471–92.

Lijphart, Arend. 1969. "Consociational Democracy." *World Politics* 21 (2): 207–25.

———. 1977. *Democracy in Plural Societies: A Comparative Exploration.* New Haven, CT: Yale University Press.

Linn, Johannes, and Oksana Pidufala. 2008. "The Experience with Regional Economic Cooperation Organizations: Lessons for Central Asia." Wolfensohn Center for Development Working Paper 4, Brookings Institution, Washington, DC.

Lipman, Janna. 2009. "Charles Taylor's Criminal Network, Exploiting Diamonds and Children." Graduate Student Research, Terrorism, Transnational Crime and Corruption Center, George Mason University. Fairfax, VA. Processed.

Lipton, Michael. 2009. *Land Reform in Developing Countries: Property Rights and Property Wrongs.* New York: Routledge.

Llorente, Maria V., and Angela Rivas. 2005. "Case Study of Reduction of Crime in Bogotá: A Decade of Citizen's Security Policies." Policy Research Working Paper, World Bank, Washington, DC.

Loayza, Norman, Pablo Fajnzylber, and Daniel Lederman. 2002a. "Inequality and Violent Crime." *Journal of Law and Economics* 45 (1): 1–40.

———. 2002b. "What Causes Violent Crime?" *European Economic Review* 46 (7): 1323–57.

Lockhart, Clare. 2010. "EU Accession: Norms and Incentives." Background note for the WDR 2011.

Lockhart, Clare, and Blair Glencorse. 2010. "Afghanistan and Its Neighbors: State-Building and State Failure in the Post-Taliban Period." Background paper for the WDR 2011.

Lopes, Ibere. 2009. "Land and Displacement in Timor-Leste." *Humanitarian Exchange Magazine* 43: 12–4.

Lund, Michael. 2010. *Engaging Fragile States: An International Policy Primer.* Washington, DC: Woodrow Wilson International Center for Scholars.

Lupsha, Peter A. 1991. "Drug Lords and Narco-Corruption: The Players Change but the Game Continues." *Crime, Law, and Social Change* 16 (1): 41–58.

Lustick, Ian S., Dan Miodownik, and Roy J. Eidelson. 2004. "Secessionism in Multicultural States: Does Sharing Power Prevent or Encourage It?" *American Political Science Review* 98 (2): 209–29.

Lutz, Ellen L., and Caitlin Reiger, eds. 2009. *Prosecuting Heads of State.* New York: Cambridge University Press.

Mac Sweeney, Naoise. 2008. "Private Sector Development in Post-conflict Countries: A Review of Current Literature and Practice." The Donor Committee for Enterprise Development, Cambridge, U.K.

Mack, Andrew. 2003. "Re-building Business: The World Bank and Private Sector Development in Post-conflict Nations." World Bank, Washington, DC.

Macmillan, Ross, and Rosemary Gartner. 1999. "When She Brings Home the Bacon: Labor-Force Participation and the Risk of Spousal Violence against Women." *Journal of Marriage and Family* 61 (4): 947–58.

Manning, Carrie, and Monica Malbrough. 2009. "Learning the Right Lessons from Mozambique's Transition to Peace." *Taiwan Journal of Democracy* 5 (1): 77–91.

Mansfield, Edward D., and Jack Snyder, eds. 2005. *Electing to Fight: Why Emerging Democracies Go to War.* Cambridge, MA: MIT Press.

Markowski, Stefan, Stephanie Koorey, Peter Hall, and Jurgen Brauer. 2009. "Multi-channel Supply Chain for Illicit Small Arms." *Defence and Peace Economics* 20 (3): 171–91.

Marsh, Nicholas. 2002. "Two Sides of the Same Coin: The Legal and Illegal Trade in Small Arms." *Brown Journal of World Affairs* 9 (1): 217–28.

Martin, Philippe, Thierry Mayer, and Mathias Thoenig. 2008. "Civil Wars and International Trade." *Journal of the European Economic Association* 6: 541–55.

Mas, Ignacio, and Dan Radcliffe. 2010. "Mobile Payments Go Viral: M-PESA in Kenya." Bill and Melinda Gates Foundation, Seattle, WA.

Mason, Ann. 2003. "Colombia's Democratic Security Agenda: Public Order in the Security Tripod." *Security Dialogue* 34 (4): 391–409.

Mata, Javier F., and Sebastian Ziaja. 2009. "Users' Guide on Measuring Fragility." Deutches Institut für Entwicklungspolitik, Oslo; UN Development Programme, New York.

Mattero, Minna, and Charmagne Campbell-Patton. 2008. "Measuring the Impact of Youth Voluntary Service Programs: Summary and Conclusions of the International Experts' Meeting." World Bank, Washington, DC; Innovations in Civic Participation, Washington, DC.

Matveeva, Anna. 2007. "The Regionalist Project in Central Asia: Unwilling Playmates." CSRC Series 2, Working Paper 13, Crisis States Research Centre, London School of Economics and Political Science, London.

Mayer-Rieckh, Alexander, and Pablo de Greiff, eds. 2007. *Justice as Prevention: Vetting Public Employees in Transitional Societies.* New York: Social Sciences Research Council: International Center for Transitional Justice.

Maynard, Kimberly A. 1997. "Rebuilding Community: Psychosocial Healing, Reintegration, and Reconciliation at the Grassroots Level." In *Rebuilding Societies After Civil War: Critical Roles for International Assistance*, ed. Krishna Kumar. Boulder, CO: Lynne Rienner.

McCall, John C. 2004. "Juju and Justice at the Movies: Vigilantes in Nigerian Popular Videos." *African Studies Review* 47 (3): 51–67.

McCandless, Erin. 2008. "Lessons from Liberia Integrated Approaches to Peacebuilding in Transitional Settings." ISS Occasional Paper 160, Institute for Security Studies, Pretoria.

McCauley, Cynthia D., and Ellen Van Velsor, eds. 2004. *The Center for Creative Leadership Handbook of Leadership Development.* San Francisco, CA: Jossey-Bass.

McLeod, Darryl, and Maria E. Dávalos. 2008. "Post-conflict Employment Creation for Stabilization and Poverty Reduction." UN Development Programme, New York.

McNeish, John-Andrew. 2010. "Natural Resource Management: Rethinking Resource Conflict." Background paper for the WDR 2011.

MDRP (Multi-Country Demobilization and Reintegration Program). 2006. "Reinsertion: Bridging the Gap between Demobilization and Reintegration." MDRP, Washington, DC.

Mehta, Pratap B. 2010. "Some Notes on Conflicts and Decentralisation in India." Background note for the WDR 2011.

Meidan, Michal. 2006. "China's Africa Policy: Business Now, Politics Later." *Asian Perspective* 30 (4): 69–93.

Mejia, Daniel, and Daniel M. Rico. 2010. "La Microeconomía de la Producción y Tráfico de Cocaína en Colombia." Universidad de los Andes, Bogotá; El Centro de Estudios sobre Desarrollo Económico, Bogotá.

Meléndez, Quiñónez. 2007. "Una Visión sobre la Situación de la Seguridad en Nicaragua, Costa Rica y Panamá." Instituto de Estudios Estrategicos y Politicas Públicas. Managua. Processed.

Melville, Amanda. 2003. "Psychosocial Interventions: Evaluations of UNICEF Supported Projects (1999–2001)." UN Children's Fund Indonesia, Jakarta.

Menkhaus, Ken. 2006. "Governance without Government in Somalia: Spoilers, State Building, and the Politics of Coping." *International Security* 31 (3): 74–106.

———. 2010. "Somalia and the Horn of Africa." Background paper for the WDR 2011.

Menon, Nidhiya, and Yana van der Meulen Rodgers. 2010. "War and Women's Work: Evidence from the Conflict in Nepal." Working Paper Series 19, Department of Economics and International Businesss School, Brandeis University, Waltham, MA.

Messick, Richard. 2011. "Anti-Corruption Approaches in Nigeria and Haiti." Background note for the WDR 2011.

Messner, Steven F., Lawrence E. Raffalovich, and Peter Shrock. 2002. "Reassessing the Cross-National Relationship between Income Inequality and Homicide Rates: Implications of Data Quality Control in the Measurement of Income Distribution." *Journal of Quantitative Criminology* 18 (4): 377–95.

Michailof, Serge. 2007. "Review of Technical Assistance and Capacity Building in Afghanistan: Discussion Paper for the Afghanistan Development Forum." World Bank, Kabul.

Michalcik, Vladislav, and Ceara Riggs. 2007. "People Power: Country Studies and Lessons Learned from National Non-Violent Movements 2003–2005." Occasional Paper 18, Institute for Multi-Track Diplomacy, Washington, DC.

Mills, Rob, and Qimiao Fan. 2006. "The Investment Climate in Post-conflict Situations." Policy Research Working Paper 4055, World Bank, Washington, DC.

Mobekk, Eirin. 2010. "Gender, Women and Security Sector Reform." *International Peacekeeping* 17 (2): 278–91.

Mondo, Emilio. 1995. "Uganda's Experience in National Management of Demobilisation and Reintegration." Paper presented at the Workshop on Demobilisation in South Africa, Institute for Defence

Policy; The Hanns Seidel Foundation; and the German Agency for Technical Cooperation (GTZ), Pretoria, May 17–18.

Montalvo, José G., and Marta Reynal-Querol. 2005. "Ethnic Polarization, Potential Conflict, and Civil Wars." *American Economic Review* 95 (3): 796–816.

Montgomery, Michael. 2010. "India's Diamond Industry Strengthening." *Diamond Investing News*, March 15.

Moran, Mary H., and M. Anne Pitcher. 2004. "The 'Basket Case' and the 'Poster Child': Explaining the End of Civil Conflicts in Liberia and Mozambique." *Third World Quarterly* 25 (3): 501–19.

Morel, Adrian, Makiko Watanabe, and Rob Wrobel. 2009. "Delivering Assistance to Conflict-Affected Communities: The BRA-KDP Program in Aceh." Indonesian Social Development Paper 13, World Bank, Jakarta.

Morfit, Michael. 2007. "The Road to Helsinki: The Aceh Agreement and Indonesia's Democratic Development." *International Negotiation* 12 (1): 111–43.

Morozzo Della Rocca, Roberto. 2003. *Mozambique: Achieving Peace in Africa.* Washington, DC: Georgetown University Press.

Morozzo Della Rocca, Roberto, and Luca Riccardi. 2003. "The Peace Process in Mozambique." In *Community and the State in Lusophone Africa*, ed. Malyn Newitt, Patrick Chabal, and Norrie Macqueen. London: King's College.

Moser, Caroline O. N. 2009.*Ordinary Families, Extraordinary Lives: Assets and Poverty Reduction in Guayaquil, 1978–2004.* Washington, DC: Brookings Institution.

Mosse, Marcelo. 2007. "Corruption and Reform in the Customs in Mozambique." Centro de Integridade Publica, Maputo.

MSR (Multi-Stakeholder Review). 2009. "Multi-Stakeholder Review of Post-conflict Programming in Aceh: Identifying the Foundations for Sustainable Peace and Development in Aceh." MSR, Jakarta.

Mufson, Steven. 2009. "Nigerian Rebels Drive Up Oil Prices." *Washington Post*, June 30.

Mungiu-Pippidi, Alina, and Igor Munteanu. 2009. "Moldova's 'Twitter Revolution.'" *Journal of Democracy* 20 (3): 136–42.

Muñoz, Mercedes G. 2010. "Las Jornadas de Trabajo en Las Empresas de Seguridad Privada: Flexibilidad Laboral o un Sistema de Explotación del Sudor?" *Diálogos Revista Electrónica de Historia* 11 (2): 233–63.

Murdoch, James C., and Todd Sandler. 2002. "Economic Growth, Civil Wars, and Spatial Spillovers." *Journal of Conflict Resolution* 46 (1): 91–110.

———. 2004. "Civil Wars and Economic Growth: Spatial Dispersion." *American Journal of Political Science* 48 (1): 138–51.

Murphy, Helen. 2008. "Colombians Stage 'Million Voices' March Against FARC: Update 3." *Bloomberg*, February 4.

Murray, Christopher J. L., Gary King, Alan D. Lopez, Niels Tomijima, and Etienne G. Krug. 2002. "Armed Conflict as a Public Health Problem." *British Medical Journal* 324 (7333): 346–49.

Murshed, S. Mansoob, and Scott Gates. 2006. "Spatial-Horizontal Inequality and the Maoist Insurgency in Nepal." In *Spatial Disparities in Human Development*, ed. Ravi Kanbur, Anthony Venables, and Guanghua Wan . Tokyo: UN University Press.

Murshed, S. Mansoob, and Mohammad Z. Tadjoeddin. 2007. "Reappraising the Greed and Grievance Explanations for Violent Internal Conflict." Research Working Paper 2, MICROCON, Brighton, U.K.

Naim, Moises. 2006. *Illicit: How Smugglers, Traffickers, and Copycats Are Hijacking the Global Economy.* New York: Anchor.

Narayan, Deepa, and Patti Petesch, eds. 2010. *Moving Out of Poverty: Rising from the Ashes of Conflict.* Washington, DC: World Bank.

Nathan, Laurie. 2005. "The Frightful Inadequacy of Most of the Statistics: A Critique of Collier and Hoeffler on Causes of Civil War." Discussion Paper 11, Crisis States Research Centre, London School of Economics and Political Science, London.

National Academy of Public Administration. 2006. "Why Foreign Aid to Haiti Failed: A Summary Report of the National Academy of Public Administration." Academy International Affairs Working Paper 06-04, National Academy of Public Administration, Washington, DC.

National Counterterrorism Center. 2010. "Worldwide Incidents Tracking System." National Counterterrorism Center, McLean, VA. http://wits.nctc.gov.

National Intelligence Council. 2000. "National Intelligence Estimate: Global Infectious Disease Threat and Its Implications for the United States." National Intelligence Council, Washington, DC.

Natural Resource Charter. 2010. "The Twelve Precepts." Natural Resource Charter, London. http://www.naturalresourcecharter.org.

Navarro, Marysa. 2001. "The Personal Is Political: Las Madres de Plaza de Mayo." In *Power and Popular Protest: Latin American Social Movements*, ed. Susan Eckstein. Berkeley, CA: University of California Press.

Ndegwa, Stephen, and Brian Levy. 2004. "The Politics of Decentralization in Africa: A Comparative Analysis." In *Building State Capacity in Africa: New Approaches, Emerging Lessons*, ed. Brian Levy and Sahr Kpundeh. Washington, DC: World Bank.

Ndulo, Muna B. 2009. "The United Nations Responses to the Sexual Abuse and Exploitation of Women and Girls by Peacekeepers during Peacekeeping Missions." *Berkeley Journal of International Law* 27: 127–61.

NEPAD (The New Partnership for Africa's Development). 2010. "African Peer Review Mechanism (APRM)." NEPAD, Midrand. http://www.nepad.org.

Neumayer, Eric. 2003. "Good Policy Can Lower Violent Crime: Evidence from a Cross-National Panel on Homicide Rates, 1980–97." *Journal of Peace Research* 40 (6): 619–40.

New York University Center on International Cooperation. 2009. *Annual Review of Global Peace Operations 2009.* Boulder, CO: Lynne Rienner.

Nilsson, Desirée. 2008. "Partial Peace: Rebel Groups Inside and Outside of Civil War Settlements." *Journal of Peace Research* 45 (4): 479–95.

Nilsson, Desirée, and Anna K. Jarstad. 2008. "From Words to Deeds: The Implementation of Power-Sharing Pacts in Peace Accords." *Conflict Management and Peace Science* 25 (3): 206–23.

Nitsch, Volker, and Dieter Schumacher. 2004. "Terrorism and International Trade: An Empirical Investigation." *European Journal of Political Economy* 20 (2): 423–33.

North, Douglass C. 1989. "Institutions and Economic Growth: An Historical Introduction." *World Development* 17 (9): 1319–32.

———. 1990. *Institutions, Institutional Change and Economic Performance.* New York: Cambridge University Press.

———. 1995. "The New Institutional Economics and Third World Development." In *The New Institutional Economics and Third World Development*, ed. John Harris, Janet Hunter, and Colin M. Lewis. London: Routledge.

North, Douglass C., John J. Wallis, and Barry R. Weingast. 2009. *Violence and Social Orders: A Conceptual Framework for Interpreting Recorded Human History.* New York: Cambridge University Press.

Northouse, Peter G. 2008. *Introduction to Leadership: Concepts and Practice.* Thousand Oaks, CA: Sage Publications, Inc.

Nossal, Kim R. 1999. "Liberal-Democratic Regimes, International Sanctions, and Global Governance." In *Globalization and Global Governance*, ed. Raimo Väyrynen. Lanham, MD: Rowman and Littlefield Publishers.

Nunn, Nathan. 2008. "The Long-Term Effects of Africa's Slave Trades." *Quarterly Journal of Economics* 123 (1): 139–76.

Nunn, Nathan, and Leonard Wantchekon. Forthcoming. "The Slave Trade and the Origins of Mistrust in Africa." *American Economic Review.*

Nwana, Harry. 2000. "Who Are the Bakassi Boys?" *Vanguard*, December 28.

O Dia Online. 2010. "Rio Assina Convênio para Investimentos Privados nas UPPs." *O Dia Online*, August 24.

O'Loughlin, John, Frank D. W. Witmer, and Andrew M. Linke. 2010. "The Afghanistan-Pakistan Wars, 2008–2009: Micro-geographies, Conflict Diffusion, and Clusters of Violence." *Eurasian Geography and Economics* 51 (4): 437–71.

OAS (Organization of American States). 2001. "Inter-American Democratic Charter." OAS, Lima.

Odendaal, Andries. 2010. "Local Peacebuilding in Ghana." Paper presented at the Experience-sharing Seminar on Building Infrastructures for Peace, Naivasha, Kenya, February 2–4.

OECD (Organisation for Economic Co-operation and Development). 1996. "Recommendation of the Council on the Tax Deductibility of Bribes to Foreign Public Officials." OECD, Paris.

———. 2004. "Lessons Learned on Donor Support to Decentralisation and Local Governance." OECD, Paris.
———. 2007. "Enhancing the Delivery of Justice and Security." OECD, Paris.
———. 2008. "Sierra Leone." In *2008 Survey on Monitoring the Paris Declaration: Making Aid More Effective by 2010*, ed. OECD. Accra: OECD.
———. 2009. "Recommendation of the Council on Tax Measures for Further Combating Bribery of Foreign Public Officials in International Business Transactions." OECD, Paris.
———. 2010a. "Do No Harm: International Support for Statebuilding." OECD, Paris.
———. 2010b. "Focus on Aid to Agriculture." OECD, Paris. http://www.oecd.org/dac/stats/agriculture.
———. 2010c. "Monitoring the Principles for Good International Engagement in Fragile States and Situations: Fragile States Principles Monitoring Survey Global Report." OECD, Paris.
———. 2010d. "OECD Stat Extracts." OECD, Paris. http://stats.oecd.org.
———. 2010e. "Second Round of Monitoring: Georgia Monitoring Report." Anti-Corruption Network for Eastern Europe and Central Asia, Istanbul Anti-Corruption Action Plan, OECD, Paris.
———. 2010f. "South-South Cooperation in the Context of Aid Effectiveness: Telling the Story of Partners Involved in More Than 110 Cases of South-South and Triangular Cooperation." OECD, Paris.
———. 2010g. "The State's Legitimacy in Fragile Situations: Unpacking Complexity." OECD, Paris.
———. 2010h. "Towards Clean Minerals from Conflict Zones." OECD, Paris.
———. 2010i. "Transition Financing: Building a Better Response." OECD, Paris.
———. 2011. "Supporting Statebuilding in Situations of Conflict and Fragility: Policy Guidance." OECD, Paris.
OECD (Organisation for Economic Co-operation and Development), and WTO (World Trade Organization). 2008. "Japan." In *Aid for Trade at a Glance 2007: Country and Agency Chapters*, ed. OECD and WTO. Paris: OECD; Geneva: WTO.
OECD-DAC (Organisation for Economic Co-operation and Development–Develompent Assistance Committee). 2006. "Whole of Government Approaches to Fragile States." OECD-DAC, Paris.
———. 2007a. "OECD-DAC Handbook on Security System Reform: Supporting Security and Justice." OECD-DAC, Paris.
———. 2007b. "Principles for Good International Engagement in Fragile States and Situations." OECD-DAC, Paris.
———. 2008. "Scaling Up: Aid Fragmentation, Aid Allocation, and Aid Predictability: Report of 2008 Survey of Aid Allocation Policies and Indicative Forward Spending Plans." OECD-DAC, Paris.
———. 2010a. "Aid Risks in Fragile and Transitional Contexts: Key Messages from the Forthcoming Publication Aid Risks in Fragile and Transitional Contexts." International Network on Conflict and Fragility, OECD-DAC, Paris.
———. 2010b. "Resource Flows to Fragile and Conflict-Affected States: Annual Report 2008." International Network on Conflict and Fragility, OECD-DAC, Paris.
Office of the High Representative and European Union Special Representative. 2011. "Basic Information." Office of the High Representative; European Union Special Representative, Sarajevo. http://www.ohr.int.
Ojielo, Ozonnia. 2007. "Designing an Architecture for Peace: A Framework of Conflict Transformation in Ghana." Paper presented at the First Biennial Conference and General Assembly of the Society for Peace Studies and Practice, Abuja, January 22–25.
Olcott, Martha B. 2010. "Rivalry and Competition in Central Asia: Bringing People Together to Accelerate Growth and Well-Being in Emerging Markets." Paper presented at the Eurasia Emerging Markets Forum, Thun, Switzerland, January 23–25.
Oliver, Johanna. 1999. "The Esquipulas Process: A Central American Paradigm for Resolving Regional Conflict." *Ethnic Studies Report* 17 (2): 149–79.
Orentlicher, Diane. 2004. "Independent Study on Best Practices, Including Recommendations, to Assist States in Strengthening Their Domestic Capacity to Combat All Aspects of Impunity." UN Economic and Social Council, New York.
———. 2005. "Report of the Independent Expert to Update the Set of Principles to Combat Impunity." UN Economic and Social Council, New York.
Organization of African Unity. 2000. "Lomé Declaration on the Framework for an OAU Response to Unconstitutional Change of Government." Organization of African Unity, Lomé.

Østby, Gudrun. 2008. "Inequalities, the Political Environment and Civil Conflict: Evidence from 55 Developing Countries." In *Horizontal Inequalities and Conflict: Understanding Group Violence in Multiethnic Societies*, ed. Frances Stewart. Basingstoke, U.K.: Palgrave Macmillan.

Otocan, Mariano. 2010. "Euroregion as a Mechanism for Strengthening Transfrontier and Interregional Co-operation: Opportunities and Challenges." Paper presented at the European Commission for Democracy Through Law (Venice Commission) and Council of Europe's Interregional and Transfrontier Co-operation: Promoting Democratic Stability and Development Seminar, Trieste, Italy, February 22–25.

Oxford Reference Online. 2001. "The Oxford Companion to the Politics of the World." Oxford University Press. http://www.oxfordreference.com.

Pacific Island Forum Secretariat. 2005. "The Pacific Plan for Strengthening Regional Cooperation and Integration." Pacific Island Forum Secretariat, Fiji.

Padilla, Felix M. 1992. *The Gang as an American Enterprise.* Piscataway, NJ: Rutgers University Press.

Pakistan Ministry of Information and Broadcasting. 2010. "Promise, Policy, Performance: Two Years of People's Government 2008–2010." Government of Pakistan, Islamabad, Pakistan.

Pan, Esther. 2005. "Middle East: Reorganizing the Palestinian Security Forces." Council on Foreign Relations, Washington, DC.

Panda, Pradeep, and Bina Agarwal. 2005. "Marital Violence, Human Development and Women's Property Status in India." *World Development* 33 (5): 823–50.

Papagianni, Katia. 2009. "Political Transitions after Peace Agreements: The Importance of Consultative and Inclusive Political Processes." *Journal of Intervention and Statebuilding* 3 (1): 47–63.

Pape, Robert R. 2003. "The Strategic Logic of Suicide Terrorism." *American Political Science Review* 97 (3): 343–61.

Paris, Roland. 2004. *At War's End: Building Peace after Civil Conflict.* New York: Cambridge University Press.

Parker, Joan C. 2008."A Synthesis of Practical Lessons from Value Chain Projects in Conflict-Affected Environments." Micro Report 105, U.S. Agency for International Development, Washington, DC.

Parson, Devin. 2010. "In the Wrong Hands: Los Zetas and the Gun Laws that Help Them Thrive." Council on Hemispheric Affairs, Washington, DC.

Patel, Ana C., Pablo de Greiff, and Lars Waldorf, eds. 2009. *Disarming the Past: Transitional Justice and Ex-combatants.* New York: Social Science Research Council.

Patel, Seema, and Steven Ross. 2007. "Breaking Point: Measuring Progress in Afghanistan." Center for Strategic and International Studies, Washington, DC.

Patrick, Stewart. 2006. "Weak States and Global Threats: Assessing Evidence of Spillovers." Working Paper 73, Center for Global Development, Washington, DC.

Pavanello, Sara, and Timothy Othieno. 2008. "Improving the Provision of Basic Services for the Poor in Fragile Environments." Overseas Development Institute, London.

Peake, Gordon, and Kaysie Studdard Brown. 2010. "Policebuilding: The International Deployment Group in the Solomon Islands." *International Peacekeeping* 12 (4): 520–32.

Peixoto, Betânia Totino, Mônica Viegas Andrade, and João Pedro Azevedo. 2007. "Avaliação Do Programa Fica Vivo No Município De Belo Horizonte."Associação Nacional dos Centros de Pós-Graduação em Economia, Rio de Janeiro.

———. 2008. "Avaliação Econômica do Programa Fica Vivo: O Caso Piloto." Textos para Discussão Cedeplar, UFMG td336, Cedeplar, Universidade Federal de Minas Gerais, Belo Horizonte.

Peltz, Amelia T. 2006."Gender Based Violence in Palestine." MIFTAH (The Palestinian Initiative for the Promotion of Global Dialogue and Democracy), Jerusalem.

Perry, Alex. 2008. "Congo: The Forgotten Conflict." *Time.com*, June 18.

Peruvian Truth and Reconciliation Commission. 2003. "Peruvian Truth and Reconciliation Commission Report." Peruvian Truth and Reconciliation Commission, Lima.

Peschka, Mary. 2010. "The Role of the Private Sector in Fragile and Conflict-Affected States." Background paper for the WDR 2011.

Peterson, Roger, and Sarah Zuckerman. 2010. "Revenge or Reconciliation: Theory and Method of Emotions in the Context of Colombia's Peace Process." In *Law in Peace Negotiations*, ed. Morten Bergsmo and Pablo Kalmanovitz. Oslo: Forum for International Criminal and Humanitarian Law.

Piron, Laure-Hélène, and Zaza Curran. 2005. "Public Policy Responses to Exclusion: Evidence from Brazil, South Africa, and India." Overseas Development Institute, London.

Plümper, Thomas, and Eric Neumayer. 2006. "The Unequal Burden of War: The Effect of Armed Conflict on the Gender Gap in Life Expectancy." *International Organization* 60 (3): 723–54.

Popkin, Margaret. 2000. *Peace Without Justice: Obstacles to Building the Rule of Law in El Salvador.* University Park, PA: Pennsylvania State University Press.

Porter, Douglas, Matt Andrews, and Clay Wescott. 2010. "Public Finance Management in Fragile and Conflicted Settings." Background paper for the WDR 2011.

Porter, Douglas, and Habib Rab. 2010. "Timor-Leste's Recovery from the 2006 Crisis: Some Lessons." Background note for the WDR 2011.

Posen, Barry. 1993. "The Security Dilemma and Ethnic Conflict." *Survival* 35 (1): 27–47.

Posner, Daniel N. 2004. "Measuring Ethnic Fractionalization in Africa." *American Journal of Political Science* 48 (4): 849–63.

Potter, Antonia. 2005. "We the Women: Why Conflict Mediation is Not Just a Job for Men." Centre for Humanitarian Dialogue, Geneva.

Powell, Jonathan M., and Clayton L. Thyne. 2011. "Global Instances of Coups from 1950 to Present: A New Dataset." *Journal of Peace Research* 48 (2): 249–59.

Presidencia República de Colombia. 1993. "Decreto Numero 2707 de 1993." Presidencia República de Colombia, Bogotá.

———. 2010. "La Agencia Presidencial para la Acción Social y la Cooperation Internacional." Presidencia República de Colombia, Bogotá. http://www.accionsocial.gov.co.

Prieto-Rodríguez, Juan, and Cesar Rodríguez-Gutiérrez. 2003. "Participation of Married Women in the European Labor Markets and the 'Added Worker Effect' in Europe." *Journal of Socio-Economics* 32 (4): 429–46.

Pritchett, Lant, and Frauke de Weijer. 2010. "Fragile States: Stuck in a Capability Trap?" Background paper for the WDR 2011.

Putzel, James. 2003. "The Philippine-US Alliance in Post September 11 Southeast Asia." In *Global Response to Terrorism: 9/11, Afghanistan and Beyond,* ed. Mary Buckley and Rick Fawn. London: Routledge.

Quinn, Michael J. 2007. "Mozambique 1975–1992." In *Civil Wars of the World: Major Conflicts since World War II, Volume 1,* ed. Karl DeRouen Jr. and Uk Heo. Santa Barbara, CA: ABC-CLIO.

Raleigh, Clionadh. 2010. "Conflict Contagion Patterns." Background paper for the WDR 2011.

Raleigh, Clionadh, Andrew Linke, Håvard Hegre, and Joachim Carlsen. 2010. "Introducing ACLED: An Armed Conflict Location and Event Dataset." *Journal of Peace Research* 47 (5): 651–60.

RAND Corporation. 2009. "National Socioeconomic Survey (SUSENAS)." RAND Corporation, Santa Monica, CA.

Randel, Judith. 2010. "Experience with Humanitarian Funds." Paper presented at the OECD-INCAF/EU Risk Management Conference, Brussels, June 15.

Randel, Judith, and Tasneem Mowjee. 2006. "Review of Trust Fund Mechanisms for Transition Financing." Development Initiatives, Somerset, U.K.

Rehn, Elisabeth, and Ellen Johnson Sirleaf. 2002. "Violence Against Women." In *Women, War and Peace: The Independent Experts' Assessment on the Impact of Armed Conflict on Women and Women's Role in Peace Building,* ed. Elizabeth Rehn and Ellen Johnson Sirleaf. NewYork: UN Development Fund for Women.

Republic of Burundi. 2006. "Poverty Reduction Strategy Paper (PRSP)." Republic of Burundi, Bujumbura.

Republic of Lebanon Ministry of Environment. 1999. "Lebanon's First National Communication Report." Government of Lebanon, Beirut.

Republic of Liberia and UN (United Nations). 2007. "United Nations Development Assistance Framework Liberia 2008–2012: Consolidating Peace and National Recovery for Sustainable Development." Republic of Liberia; UN, Monrovia.

Reyntjens, Filip. 2007. "Briefing: Democratic Republic of Congo: Political Transition and Beyond." *African Affairs* 106 (423): 307–17.

Riascos, Alvaro J., and Juan Vargas. 2004. "Violence and Growth in Colombia: What Do We Know After 10 Years of Quantitative Research?" Webpondo.org: Recursos para Economistas & Colombia. http://www.webpondo.org/files_ene_mar04/rgc.pdf.

Rich, Patricia. 2010. "Politician's Assassination Raises Doubts over Mexico Drug Policy." Open Security: Contemporary Conflict. http://www.opendemocracy.net/opensecurity/security_briefings/290610.

Richards, Paul. 1996. *Fighting For the Rainforest: War, Youth and Resources in Sierra Leone.* Oxford, U.K.: Heinemann Educational Books.

Roberts, Adam. 2010. "Lives and Statistics: Are 90% of War Victims Civilians?" *Survival* 52 (3): 115–36.

Robinson, Pearl T. 1994."The National Conference Phenomenon in Francophone Africa." *Comparative Studies in Society and History* 36 (3): 575–610.

Rodgers, Dennis, Robert Muggah, and Chris Stevenson. 2009. "Gangs of Central America: Causes, Costs, and Interventions." Occasional Paper 23, Small Arms Survey, Graduate Institute of International and Development Studies, Geneva.

Rodrik, Dani. 2000. "Institutions for High-Quality Growth: What They Are And How to Acquire Them." NBER Working Paper 7540, National Bureau of Economic Research, Cambridge, MA.

———. 2008. *One Economics, Many Recipes: Globalization, Institutions, and Economic Growth.* Princeton, NJ: Princeton University Press.

Rodrik, Dani, Arvind Subramanian, and Francesco Trebbi. 2004. "Institutions Rule: The Primacy of Institutions over Geography and Integration in Economic Development." *Journal of Economic Growth* 9 (2): 131–65.

Rohland, Klaus, and Sarah Cliffe. 2002. "The East Timor Reconstruction Programme: Successes, Problems and Tradeoffs." CPR Working Paper 26361, World Bank, Washington, DC.

Roque, Paula, Judy Smith-Höhn, Paul-Simon Handy, Le Dang Doanh, David Craig, and Omar McDoom. 2010. "Exit Pathways: South Africa, Mozambique, Vietnam, Cambodia, Rwanda." Background paper for the WDR 2011.

Ross, Michael. 2003. "The Natural Resource Curse: How Wealth Can Make You Poor." In *Natural Resources and Violent Conflict,* ed. Ian Bannon and Paul Collier. Washington, DC: World Bank.

Rosset, Peter, Raj Patel, and Michael Courville, eds. 2006. *Promised Land: Competing Visions of Agrarian Reform.* Oakland, CA: Food First: Institute for Food and Development Policy.

Rozema, Ralph. 2008. "Urban DDR Processes: Paramilitaries and Criminal Networks in Medellín, Colombia." *Journal of Latin American Studies* 40 (3): 423–52.

Rubin, Barnett R. 2002. *Blood on the Doorstep: The Politics of Preventive Action.* Washington, DC: Century Foundation: Council on Foreign Relations.

Sage, Caroline, and Deval Desai. 2010. "Public Security, Criminal Justice, and Reforming the Security Sector." Background paper for the WDR 2011.

Salazar, Hernando. 2007. "Colombians Against Kidnapping." *BBC News,* July 15.

Salehyan, Idean. 2007. "Transnational Rebels: Neighboring States as Sanctuary for Rebel Groups." *World Politics* 59 (2): 217–42.

Salehyan, Idean., and Kristian S. Gleditsch. 2006. "Refugees and the Spread of Civil War." *International Organization* 60 (2): 335–66.

Sambanis, Nicholas. 2001. "Do Ethnic and Nonethnic Civil Wars Have the Same Causes? A Theoretical and Empirical Inquiry (Part I)." *Journal of Conflict Resolution* 45 (3): 259–82.

———. 2004. "What Is Civil War? Conceptual and Empirical Complexities of an Operational Definition." *Journal of Conflict Resolution* 48 (6): 814–58.

Samity, Sharmajibee M. 2003."'Shalishi' in West Bengal A Community-Based Response to Domestic Violence." *Economic and Political Weekly* 38 (17): 1665–73.

Sapelli, Claudio. 2000. "The Political Economy of the Chilean Transition to Democracy." *Cuadernos de Economía* 37 (112): 537–56.

Satyanath, Shanker, Edward Miguel, and Ernest Sergenti. 2004. "Economic Shocks and Civil Conflict: An Instrumental Variables Approach." *Journal of Political Economy* 112 (4): 725–53.

Sawyer, Amos. 2004. "Violent Conflicts and Governance Challenges in West Africa: The Case of the Mano River Basin Area." *Journal of Modern African Studies* 42 (3): 437–63.

Sayigh, Yezid. 2010. "The West Bank and Gaza Strip." Background paper for the WDR 2011.

Scanteam. 2007. "Review of Post-crisis Multi-Donor Trust Funds: Final Report." Scanteam, Oslo.

———. 2010. "Flexibility in the Face of Fragility: Programmatic Multi-Donor Trust Funds in Fragile and Conflict-Affected Situations." World Bank, Washington, DC.

Schelling, Thomas C. 1960. *Strategy of Conflict.* Cambridge, MA: Harvard University Press.

———. 1971. "Dynamic Models of Segregation." *Journal of Mathematical Sociology* 1 (2): 143–86.

———. 1978. *Micromotives and Macrobehavior.* New York: W. W. Norton & Company.

Schelnberger, Anna K. 2005. "Decentralisation as a Means of Conflict Management: A Case Study of Kibaale District, Uganda." IEE Working Papers 181, Institute of Development Research and Development Policy, Ruhr University, Bochum, Germany.

Scheye, Eric. 2009. "State-Provided Service, Contracting Out, and Non-State Networks: Justice and Security as Public and Private Goods and Services." The International Network of Conflict and Fragility, Development Assistant Committee, Organisation for Economic Co-operation and Development, Paris.

Scheye, Eric, and Diana Chigas. 2009. "Development of a Basket of Conflict, Security, and Justice Indicators." Online Publication. http://www.scribd.com/doc/23391272/Conflict-Security-Justice-Global-Indicators-Final-Report.

Schiavo-Campo, Salvatore. 2003. "Financing and Aid Management Arrangements in Post-conflict Situations." CPR Working Papers 6, World Bank, Washington, DC.

Schimmelfennig, Frank, and Ulrich Sedelmeier. 2002. "Theorizing EU Enlargement: Research Focus, Hypotheses, and the State of Research." *Journal of European Public Policy* 9 (4): 500–28.

Schneider, Friedrich, Andreas Buehn, and Claudio E. Montenegro. 2010. "New Estimates for the Shadow Economies all over the World." *International Economic Journal* 24 (4): 443–61.

Schulze, Kirsten E. 2007. "Mission Not So Impossible: The Aceh Monitoring Mission and Lessons Learned for the EU." Internaitonal Policy Analysis, Friedrich Ebert Stiftung, Berlin.

Secretaría de Gobierno de Medellín. 2010. "Informe de Indicadores Objetivos sobre Seguridad Ciudadana." Medellín Como Vamos, Medellín. http://www.medellincomovamos.org.

Seelke, Clare R., Liana Sun Wyler, and June S. Beittel. 2011. "Latin America and the Caribbean: Illicit Drug Trafficking and U.S. Counterdrug Programs." Congressional Research Service, Washington, DC.

Seely, Jennifer. 2001. "A Political Analysis of Decentralisation: Co-opting the Tuareg Threat in Mali." *Journal of Modern African Studies* 39 (3): 499–524.

Selvarajan, S. 2008. "Ex-post Economic Analysis of the National Solidarity Programme (NSP)." World Bank, Washington, DC.

Shanty, Frank, and Patit P. Mishra, eds. 2008. *Organized Crime: From Trafficking to Terrorism.* Santa Barbara, CA: ABC-CLIO.

Sharma, Gopal. 2008. "Nepalis Face 16 Hour Daily Power Cuts by February." *Reuters*, August 24.

Sharp, Kay, Taylor Brown, and Amdissa Teshome. 2006. "Targeting Ethiopia's Productive Safety Net Programme (PSNP)." Overseas Development Institute, London.

Shemyakina, Olga. 2006. "The Effect of Armed Conflict on Accumulation of Schooling: Results from Tajikistan." HiCN Working Papers 12, Institute of Development Studies, University of Sussex, Brighton, U.K.

Sherman, Jake. 2010. "Criminal Justice." Background paper for the WDR 2011.

Shiawl-Kidanekal, Teferra. 2004. "Conflict Prevention and Management in Africa." In *Conflict Prevention: From Rhetoric to Reality*, ed. Albrecht Schnabel and David Carment. Lanham, MD: Lexington Books.

Shin, Gi-Wook. 2006. "Agrarian Roots of Korean Capitalism." In *Transformations in Twentieth Century Korea*, ed. Chang Yun-Shik and Steven H. Lee. New York: Routledge.

SIDA (Swedish International Development Cooperation Agency). 2005. "Strategy for Swedish Support to the African Great Lakes Region Including Country Strategies for Rwanda, the Democratic Republic of the Congo and Burundi: November 2004–December 2008." SIDA, Stockholm.

Siddiqui, Niloufer. 2011. "Broken Justice." *Foreign Policy*, February 1.

Silberschmidt, Margrethe. 1999. *Women Forget that Men are the Masters: Gender Antagonism and Socio-Economic Change in Kisii District, Kenya.* Uppsala, Norway: Nordiska Afrikainstitutet.

———. 2001. "Disempowerment of Men in Rural and Urban East Africa: Implications for Male Identity and Sexual Behavior." *World Development* 29 (4): 657–71.

Sirivi, Josie T., and Marilyn T. Havini. 2004. *As Mothers of the Land: The Birth of The Bougainville Women For Peace And Freedom.* Canberra: Pandanus Books, Research School of Pacific and Asian Studies.

Sirleaf, Ellen Johnson. 2007a. "Challenges for New Leadership Teams in Fragile States." Capacity Development Briefs 21, World Bank Institute, World Bank, Washington, DC.

———. 2007b. "Key Note Address by Her Excellency Ellen Johnson Sirleaf, President of the Republic of Liberia." UN Institute for Training and Research, Torino Retreat, Turin, Italy, August 31.

Sisk, Timothy D. 2010. "Cooperating for Peace: The Challenge and Promise of Partnerships in Peace Operations." Geneva Centre for Security Policy, Geneva.

Skaperdas, Stergios. 1996. "Contest Success Functions." *Economic Theory* 7 (2): 283–90.

Skaperdas, Stergios, Rodrigo Soares, Alys Willman, and Stephen C. Miller. 2009. "The Costs of Violence." World Bank, Washington, DC.

Small Arms Survey Project. 2001. *Small Arms Survey 2001: Profiling the Problem.* Oxford, U.K.: Oxford University Press.

———. 2005. *Small Arms Survey 2005: Weapons at War.* Oxford, U.K.: Oxford University Press.

———. 2006. *Small Arms Survey 2006: Unfinished Business.* Oxford, U.K.: Oxford University Press.

———. 2009. *Small Arms Survey 2009: Shadows of War.* Cambridge, U.K.: Cambridge University Press.

———. 2011. "Small Arms Survey: Weapons and Markets." Small Arms Survey, Geneva. http://www.smallarmssurvey.org/weapons-and-markets.html.

Smith, Anthony L. 2004. "Trouble in Thailand's Muslim South: Separatism, not Global Terrorism." *Asia-Pacific Security Studies* 3 (10): 1–4.

Snyder, Jack. 2000. *From Voting to Violence: Democratization and Nationalist Conflict.* New York: W.W. Norton & Company.

Snyder, Jack, and Robert Jervis. 1999. "Civil War and the Security Dilemma." In *Civil Wars, Insecurity, and Intervention*, ed. Barbara F. Walter and Jack Snyder. New York: Columbia University Press.

Solow, Robert M. 1990. *The Labor Market as a Social Institution.* Malden, MA: Blackwell Publishing.

South Africa Ministry of Defence. 1996. "White Paper on National Defence for the Republic of South Africa." Government of South Africa, Pretoria. http://www.info.gov.za/whitepapers/1996/defencwp.htm.

Spear, Joanna, and Bernard Harborne. 2010. "Improving Security in Violent Conflict Settings." Background paper for the WDR 2011.

Spears, Ian S. 2002. "Africa: The Limits of Power-Sharing." *Journal of Democracy* 13 (3): 123–36.

Special Court for Sierra Leone Office of the Prosecutor. 2007. "The Prosecutor vs. Charles Ghankay Taylor–Indictment." Special Court for Sierra Leone, Freetown, Sierra Leone. http://www.sc-sl.org/CASES/ProsecutorvsCharlesTaylor/tabid/107/Default.aspx.

Special Inspector General for Iraq Reconstruction. 2009. "Hard Lessons: The Iraq Reconstruction Experience." U.S. Independent Agencies and Commissions, Washington, DC.

Spence, A. Michael. 1977. "Entry, Investment, and Oligopolistic Pricing." *Bell Journal of Economics* 8 (2): 534–44.

Stanley, William, and David Holiday. 2002. "Broad Participation, Diffuse Responsibility: Peace Implementation in Guatemala." In *Ending Civil Wars: The Implementation of Peace Agreements*, ed. Stephen Stedman, Elizabeth Cousens, and Donald Rothchild. Boulder, CO: Lynne Reinner.

Statistical Office of Kosovo. 2010. "Export-Import." Kosovo Ministry of Public Administration, Pristina, Kosovo. http://esk.rks-gov.net/eng/index.php?option=com_content&view=article&id=46&Itemid=36.

Stedman, Stephen. 1996. "Negotiation and Mediation in Internal Conflict." In *The International Dimensions of Internal Conflict*, ed. Michael E. Brown. Cambridge, MA: Center for Science and International Affairs, John F. Kennedy School of Government, Harvard University.

Stern, Jessica. 2003. *Terror in the Name of God: Why Religious Militants Kill.* New York: Harper Collins.

Stewart, Frances. 2005. "Horizontal Inequalities: A Neglected Dimension of Development." In *Wider Perspectives on Global Development*, ed. UNU-WIDER (United Nations University–World Institute for Development Economics Research). Helsinki: UNU-WIDER.

———. 2010. "Horizontal Inequalities as a Cause of Conflict: A Review of CRISE Findings." Background paper for the WDR 2011.

Stewart, Frances, Cindy Huang, and Michael Wang. 2001. "Internal Wars: An Empirical Overview of Economic and Social Consequences." In *War and Underdevelopment*, ed. Frances Stewart and Valpy Fitzgerald. Oxford, U.K.: Oxford University Press.

Stewart, Patrick, and Kaysie Brown. 2007. *Greater than the Sum of its Parts?: Assessing 'Whole of Government' Approaches to Fragile States.* New York: International Peace Academy.

Stoddard, Abby, Adele Harmer, and Katherine Haver. 2006. "Providing Aid in Insecure Environments: Trends in Policy and Operations." HPG Briefing Paper 23, Overseas Development Institute, London.

Stohl, Rachel, and Suzette Grillot. 2009. *The International Arms Trade.* Cambridge, U.K.: Polity Press.

Stramm, Andreas, Christoph Jost, Konstanze Kreiss, Katharina Meier, Mike Pfister, Philipp Schukat, and Henning A. Speck. 2006. "Strengthening Value Chains in Sri Lanka's Agribusiness: A Way to Reconcile Competitiveness with Socially Inclusive Growth?" Deutsches Institut für Entwicklungspolitik, Bonn, Germany.

Strassler, Robert, ed. 1996. *The Landmark Thucydides: A Comprehensive Guide to the Peloponnesian War.* New York: Free Press.

STRATFOR. 2009. "Central America: An Emerging Role in the Drug Trade." STRATFOR, Austin, TX.

Straus, Scott. 2010. "Mali and Its Sahelian Neighbors." Background paper for the WDR 2011.

Strom, Kevin J., and John M. MacDonald. 2007. "The Influence of Social and Economic Disadvantage on Racial Patterns in Youth Homicide Over Time." *Homicide Studies* 11 (1): 50–69.

SUCOFINDO (Superintending Company of Indonesia). 2002. "Sucofindo International Certification Services." SUCOFINDO, Jakarta. http://222.124.12.244/sics.htm.

Suhrke, Astri, Torunn Wimpelmann, and Marcia Dawes. 2007. "Peace Processes and State Building: Economic and Institutional Provisions of Peace Agreements." Chr. Michelsen Institute, Bergen, Norway.

Sundberg, Ralph. 2008. "Collective Violence 2002–2007: Global and Regional Trends." In *States in Armed Conflict 2007*, ed. Lotta Harbom and Ralph Sundberg. Uppsala, Sweden: Universitetstryckeriet.

Sutton, Adam, Adrian Cherney, and Rob White. 2008. *Crime Prevention: Principles, Perspectives and Practices.* New York: Cambridge University Press.

Svensson, Jakob. 2000. "The Cost of Doing Business: Firms' Experience with Corruption in Uganda." Africa Region Working Paper 6, World Bank, Washington, DC.

Tajima, Yuhki. 2009. "Background Paper on Economic Reintegration." Congeso Internacional de Desarme, Demovilización y Reintegración, Cartagena; Republic of Colombia, Cartagena, Colombia.

Thapa, Deepak. 2010. "Nepal." Background paper for the WDR 2011.

The Carter Center. 2007. "Final Report to the Guyana Elections Commission on the 2006 General and Regional Elections." The Carter Center, Atlanta, GA.

The Economist. 2010. "Crime and Punishment in Guatemala: Kamikaze Mission: The UN's Prosecutor Resigns, Taking an Enemy with Him." *The Economist,* June 17.

The PRS Group. 2010. "International Country Risk Guide." The PRS Group, East Syracuse, NY. http://www.prsgroup.com.

The SEEP Network. 2009. "Minimum Standards for Economic Recovery after Crisis." The SEEP Network, Washington, DC.

Thornton, Gary, Ray Yannone, Larry Martinez, and Vanessa Trevino. 2011. "Los Angeles Almanac." Los Angeles Almanac, Los Angeles, CA. http://www.laalmanac.com.

Timor-Leste Independent Comprehensive Need Assessment Team. 2009. "The Justice System of Timor-Leste: An Independent Comprehensive Need Assessment." UN Integrated Mission in East Timor, Dili.

Timor-Leste Ministry of Finance. 2010. "Timor-Leste Development Partners Meeting: Background Paper." Government of Timor-Leste, Dili.

Toft, Monica D. 2003. *The Geography of Ethnic Violence: Identity, Interests, and the Indivisibility of Territory.* Princeton, NJ: Princeton University Press.

Torres, Anastasia B. 2002. "Gender and Forced Migration." Forced Migration Online, Oxford, U.K.

Transparency International. 2011. "Building Integrity and Countering Corruption in Defence and Security: 20 Practical Reforms." Defence and Security Programme, Transparency International, London.

Tsunekawa, Keiichi, and Kohei Yoshida. 2010. "State Building, Economic Development, and Democracy: The Japanese Experience." Background note for the WDR 2011.

Tukahebwa, Geoffrey B. 2000. "The Role of District Councils in Decentralisation." In *Decentralisation and Civil Society in Uganda: The Quest for Good Governance,* ed. Apolo Nsibambe. Kampala: Fountain Publishers.

Tulloch, Jim, Fadia Saadah, Rui M. de Araujo, Rui P. de Jesus, Sergio Lobo, Isabel Hemming, Jane Nassim, and Ian Morris. 2003. *Initial Steps in Rebuilding the Health Sector in East Timor.* Washington, DC: National Academies Press.

U.S. Committee for Refugees and Immigrants. 2009. "World Refugee Survey 2009." U.S. Committee for Refugees and Immigrants, Arlington, VA.

U.S. Department of State. 2008. "Interagency Conflict Assessment Framework." Office of the Coordinator for Reconstruction and Stabilization, U.S. Department of State, Washington, DC.

———. 2010. "Background Note: Democratic Republic of the Congo." U.S. Department of State, Washington, DC.

U.S. Energy Information Administration. 2011. "Petroleum & Other Liquids." Independent Statistics and Analysis, U.S. Energy Information Administration, Washington, DC.

U.S. Government Accountability Office. 2007. "Stabilizing and Rebuilding Iraq: U.S. Ministry Capacity Development Efforts Need an Overall Integrated Strategy to Guide Efforts and Manage Risk." Report to Congressional Committees, U.S. Government Accountability Office, Washington, DC.

———. 2010a. "Maritime Security: Actions Needed to Assess and Update Plan and Enhance Collaboration among Partners Involved in Countering Piracy off the Horn of Africa." U.S. Government Accountability Office, Washington, DC.

———. 2010b. "Mérida Initiative: The United States Has Provided Counternarcotics and Anticrime Support but Needs Better Performance Measures." U.S. Government Accountability Office, Washington, DC.

U.S. Office of National Drug Control Policy. 1999. "FY1999 Drug Budget Program Highlights." U.S. Office of National Drug Control Policy, Rockville, MD. http://www.ncjrs.gov/ondcppubs/publications/policy/budget99/spending.html.

UN (United Nations). 1998. "Rome Statute of the International Criminal Court." UN, Rome.

———. 2000. "UN Security Council Resolution 1325." UN, New York.

———. 2002. "Women, Peace and Security." UN, New York.

———. 2004a. "A More Secure World: Our Shared Responsibility: Report of the Secretary General's High-Level Panel on Threats, Challenges and Change." UN, New York.

———. 2004b. "The Rule of Law and Transitional Justice in Conflict and Post-conflict Societies: Report of the Secretary General." UN, New York.

———. 2006a. "Agreement between the United Nations and the State of Guatemala on the Establishment of an International Commission Against Impunity in Guatemala." UN, New York.

———. 2006b. "Integrated Disarmament, Demobilization and Reintegration Standards." UN, New York.

———. 2007. "MDG Monitor: Tracking the Millennium Development Goals." UN, New York. http://www.mdgmonitor.org/.

———. 2011. "UN Security Council Resolution 1960." UN, New York.

———. Forthcoming. "United Nations Review of International Civilian Capacities." UN, New York.

UN Assistance Mission in Afghanistan and UNOHCHR (UN Office of the High Commissioner on Human Rights). 2010. "Harmful Traditional Practices and Implementation of the Law on Elimination of Violence against Women in Afghanistan." UN Assistance Mission in Afghanistan; UNOHCHR, Kabul.

UN General Assembly. 2005a. "Basic Principles and Guidelines on the Right to a Remedy and Reparation for Victims of Gross Violations of International Human Rights Law and Serious Violations of the International Humanitarian Law." UN, New York.

———. 2005b. "Resolution Adopted by the General Assembly: 2005 World Summit Outcome." UN, New York.

———. 2006. "Resolution Adopted by the General Assembly: The United Nations Global Counter-Terrorism Strategy." UN, New York.

———. 2009a. "Activities of the International Commission Against Impunity in Guatemala: Report of the Secretary General." UN, New York.

———. 2009b. "Human Security: Report of the Secretary General." UN, New York.

———. 2010. "Resolution Adopted by the General Assembly: Follow-up to Paragraph 143 on Human Security of the 2005 World Summit Outcome." UN, New York.

UN Inter-Agency Information and Analysis Unit. 2010. "Electricity in Iraq Factsheet." UN Inter-Agency Information and Analysis Unit, New York.

UN Inter-Agency Framework for Coordination on Preventive Action. 2010. "The United Nations Inter-agency Framework Team for Preventive Action." UN Interagency Framework Team for Preventive Action, New York.

UN Security Council. 2006. "Report of the Secretary-General on Timor-Leste pursuant to Security Council resolution 1690." UN, New York.

———. 2009. "Ninth Semi-annual Report of the Secretary-General on the Implementation of Security Council Resolution 1559 (2004)." UN, New York.

———. 2010a. "Haiti Can Return to 'Path of Stability' in Two Years, Given Necessary Support in Weathering Risks of Next 18 Months, Security Council Told." UN, New York.

———. 2010b. "Statement by the President of the Security Council." UN, New York.

UN Verification Mission in Guatemala. 2003. "Fourteenth Report on Human Rights of the United Nations Verification Mission in Guatemala." UN Verification Mission in Guatemala, Guatemala City.

———. 2004. "Informe de Verificación: El Estado de Cumplimiento de las Recomendaciones de la Comisión para el Esclarecimiento Histórico." UN Verification Mission in Guatemala, Guatemala City.

UNDP (UN Development Programme). 2005a. "Central Asia Human Development Report: Bringing Down Barriers: Regional Cooperation for Human Development and Human Security." Regional Bureau for Europe and the Commonwealth of Independent States, UNDP, Bratislava.

———. 2005b. "International Cooperation at a Crossroads: Aid, Trade and Security in an Unequal World." Human Development Report Office, UNDP, New York.

———. 2005c. "¿Cuánto Cuesta la Violencia a El Salvador?" UNDP, San Salvador.

———. 2006. "El Costo Económico de la Violencia en Guatemala." UNDP, Guatemala City.

———. 2008a. "Informe Estadístico de la Violencia en Guatemala: Programa de Seguridad Ciudadana y Prevención de la Violencia del PNUD en Guatemala." UNDP, Guatemala City.

———. 2008b. "Post-conflict 'Economic Recovery: Enabling Local Ingenuity." Bureau for Crisis Prevention and Recovery, UNDP, New York.

———. 2010a. "Building 'Collaborative Capacity': UN Development Assistance for Conflict Prevention through Internally Negotiated Solutions to Crises." Background note for the WDR 2011.

———. 2010b. "The Real Wealth of Nations: Pathways to Human Development." Human Development Report Offices, UNDP, New York.

UNDPA (UN Department of Political Affairs). 2010a. "Input to World Development Report on the Theme of Fragility and Conflict: Conflict Prevention Efforts in West Africa." Background note for the WDR 2011.

———. 2010b. "Lessons Learned from Guatemala and Guyana." Background note for the WDR 2011.

UNDPKO (UN Department of Peacekeeping Operations). 2010a. "Haiti Police Reform." Background note for the WDR 2011.

———. 2010b. "List of Operations." UNDPKO, New York.

———. 2010c. "United Nations Peacekeeping Fact Sheet." UNDPKO, New York. http://www.un.org/en/peacekeeping/resources/statistics/factsheet.shtml.

UNFPA (UN Population Fund). 2002. "The Impact of Conflict on Women and Girls: A UNFPA Strategy for Gender Mainstreaming in Areas of Conflict and Reconstruction." Paper presented at the Impact of Conflict on Women and Girls: A Consultative Meeting on Mainstreaming Gender in Areas of Conflict and Reconstruction, Bratislava, November 13–15.

UNHCR (UN High Commissioner for Refugees). 2009. "2008 Global Trends: Refugees, Asylum-Seekers, Returnees, Internally Displaced and Stateless Persons." UNHCR, Geneva.

———. 2010. "Global Appeal 2010–2011: Real People, Real Needs." UNHCR, Geneva.

UNICEF (UN Children's Fund). 2004. "The Situation of Women and Girls: Facts and Figures." UNICEF, New York. http://www.unicef.org/gender/index_factsandfigures.html.

———. 2007. "Birth Registration and Armed Conflict." Innocenti Research Centre, UNICEF, Florence, Italy.

UNIFEM (UN Development Fund for Women), UN Action Against Sexual Violence in Conflict, and UNDPKO (UN Department of Peacekeeping Operations). 2010. "Addressing Conflict-Related Sexual Violence: An Analytical Inventory of Peacekeeping Practice." UNIFEM; UN Action Against Sexual Violence in Conflict; UNDPKO, New York.

UNODC (UN Office on Drugs and Crime). 2007. "Crime and Development in Central America: Caught in the Crossfire." UNODC, Vienna.

———. 2008. "Crime and its Impact on the Balkans and Affected Countries." UNODC, Vienna.

———. 2009a. "Transnational Trafficking and the Rule of Law in West Africa: A Threat Assessment." UNODC, Vienna.

———. 2009b. "World Drug Report 2009." UNODC, Vienna.

———. 2010a. "The Globalization of Crime: The Threat of Transnational Organized Crime." UNODC, Vienna.

———. 2010b. "World Drug Report 2010." UNODC, Vienna.

UNODC (UN Office on Drugs and Crime) and World Bank. 2007. "Crime, Violence, and Development: Trends, Costs, and Policy Options in the Caribbean." UNODC, Geneva; Latin America and the Caribbean Region, World Bank, Washington, DC.

UNOHCHR (UN Office of the High Commissioner for Human Rights). 2006. "Rule of Law Tools for Post-conflict States: Truth Commissions." UNOHCHR, Geneva.

———. 2010. "Voice of Victims: Transitional Justice in Nepal." UNOHCHR, Geneva.

UNOPS (UN Office for Project Services). 2009. "Rural Roads Connect Villages to the World." UNOPS, New York.

UNPBSO (UN Peacebuilding Support Office). 2010. "Background Note: The Role of the PBC in Marshalling Resources for Countries on Its Agenda." UNPBSO, New York.

UNPOL (UN Police Division). 2011. "Office of Rule of Law and Security Institutions." UNPOL, New York. http://www.un.org/en/peacekeeping/sites/police/orolsi.shtml.

UNSTAT (UN Statistics Division). 2010. "United Nations Statistics Division." UNSTAT, New York. http://unstats.un.org/unsd/default.htm.

Uppsala University. 2009. "Uppsala Conflict Data Program Database." Uppsala University, Uppsala, Sweden. http://www.ucdp.uu.se/gpdatabase.

Urdal, Henrik. 2004. "The Devil in the Demographics: The Effect of Youth Bulges on Domestic Armed Conflict, 1950–2000." Social Development Papers 14, World Bank, Washington, DC.

USAID (U.S. Agency for International Development). 2009a. "ADS Chapter 320: Branding and Marking." USAID, Washington, DC.

———. 2009b. "Bringing Justice to Rural Colombia." USAID, Washington, DC.

———. 2010. "USAID Branding." USAID, Washington, DC. http://www.usaid.gov/branding/.

USAID Burundi. 2005. "Burundi Strategy Statement 2006–2008." USAID, Bujumbura.

USAID Famine Early Warning Systems Network. 2010. "USAID Famine Early Warning Systems Network." USAID, Washington, DC. http://www.fews.net.

USAID Guatemala. 2008. "Fact Sheet: 24-Hour Courts Rule of Law Program." USAID, Pinula, Guatemala.

USAID Rwanda. 2006. "Restoring Hope through Economic Opportunity: Final Report of the Agribusiness Development Assistance to Rwanda (ADAR) Project." USAID, Kisali.

van de Walle, Nicolas, and Michael Bratton, eds. 1997. *Democratic Experiment in Africa: Regime Transformations in Comparative Perspectives.* Cambridge, U.K.: Cambridge University Press.

Van der Elst, Kristel, and Nicholas Davis, eds. 2011. *Global Risks 2011: An Initiative of the Risk Response Network.* Geneva: World Economic Forum, 6th ed.

Van der Graaf, General Henny. 2001. "Flames of Peace: Disarmament and post-Conflict Peacebuilding in Mali." In *Managing the Remnants of War: Micro-disarmament as an Element of Peacebuilding,* ed. Sami Faltas and Joseph Di Chiaro III. Bonn, Germany: Bonn International Center for Conversion.

Van Genugten, Willem J. M., and Gerard A. de Groot, eds. 1999. *United Nations Sanctions: Effectiveness and Effects, Especially in the Field of Human Rights.* Antwerp, Belgium: Intersentia.

Verdú, Rodrigo G., Wendy Cunningham, Linda McGinnis, Cornelia Tesliuc, and Dorte Verner. 2008. *Youth at Risk in Latin America and the Caribbean. Understanding the Causes, Realizing the Potential.* Washington, DC: World Bank.

Verhey, Beth. 2001. "Child Soldiers: Preventing, Demobilizing and Reintegrating." Africa Region Working Paper 23, World Bank, Washington, DC.

Verpoorten, Marijke. 2003. "The Determinants of Income Mobility in Rwanda, 1990–2002." Katholieke Universiteit, Leuven, Belgium. Processed.

Verwimp, Philip, and Jan Van Bavel. 2005. "Child Survival and Fertility of Refugees in Rwanda after the Genocide: Special Issue of the Demography of Violent Conflict." *European Journal of Population* 21 (2–3): 271–90.

Vetschera, Heinz, and Matthieu Damian. 2006. "Security Sector Reform in Bosnia and Herzegovina: The Role of the International Community." *International Peacekeeping* 13 (1): 28–42.

Villaveces, Andrés, Peter Cummings, Victoria E. Espitia, Thomas D. Koepsell, Barbara McKnight, and Arthur L. Kellermann. 2000. "Effect of a Ban on Carrying Firearms on Homicide Rates in Two Colombian Cities." *Journal of the American Medical Association* 283 (9): 1205–09.

Von Kaltenborn-Stachau, Henriette. 2008. "The Missing Link: Fostering Positive Citizen-State Relations in Post-conflict Environments." Brief for Policy Makers, Communications for Governance and Accountability Program, World Bank, Washington, DC.

Vulliamy, Ed. 2008. "How a Tiny West African Country Became the World's First Narco State." *The Observer,* March 9.

Wainwright, Elsina. 2005. "How is RAMSI Faring? Progress, Challenges, and Lessons Learned." Australian Strategic Policy Institute, Canberra.

Walby, Sylvia. 2004. "The Cost of Domestic Violence." Women and Equality Unit, Department of Trade and Industry, London.

Waldman, Matt. 2008. "Falling Short: Aid Effectiveness in Afghanistan." Agency Coordinating Body for Afghan Relief, Kabul.

Wallensteen, Peter, Damien Fruchart, Paul Holtom, Siemon Wezeman, and Daniel Strandow. 2007. "United Nations Arms Embargoes: Their Impact on Arms Flows and Target Behaviour." Stockholm International Peace Research Institute, Stockholm; Uppsala University, Uppsala, Sweden.

Walter, Barbara, and Andrew H. Kydd. 2002. "Sabotaging the Peace: Politics of Extremist Violence." *International Organization* 56 (2): 263–96.

Walter, Barbara F. 1997."The Critical Barrier to Civil War Settlement." *International Organization* 51 (3): 335–64.

———. 1999. "Designing Transitions from Civil War." In *Civil Wars, Insecurity, and Intervention*, ed. Barbara F. Walter and Jack Snyder. New York: Columbia University Press.

———. 2004. "Does Conflict Beget Conflict? Explaining Recurring Civil War." *Journal of Peace Research* 41 (3): 371–88.

———. 2010. "Conflict Relapse and the Sustainability of Post-conflict Peace." Background paper for the WDR 2011.

Ward, Jeanne, and Mendy Marsh. 2006. "Sexual Violence Against Women and Girls in War and Its Aftermath: Realities, Responses, and Required Resources." Paper presented at the Symposium on Sexual Violence in Conflict and Beyond, Brussels, June 21–23.

Weingast, Barry. 1997. "The Political Foundations of Democracy and the Rule of Law." *American Political Science Review* 91 (2): 245–63.

Wennmann, Achim. 2009. "Getting Armed Groups to the Table: Peace Processes, the Political Economy of Conflict and the Mediated State." *Third World Quarterly* 30 (6): 1123–38.

Whitfield, Teresa. 2007. *Friends Indeed? the United Nations, Groups of Friends, and the Resolution of Conflict.* Washington, DC: United States Institute of Peace.

Wilkinson, Steven I. 2000. "India, Consociational Theory and Ethnic Violence." *Asian Survey* 40 (5): 767–91.

Williams, Rocky. 2005. "Demobilisation and Reintegration: The South African Experience." *Journal of Security Sector Management*, Rocky Williams Tribute Issue. http://www.ssronline.org/jofssm/issues/jofssm_sp_04_rocky_ddr.pdf?CFID=2695055&CFTOKEN=53045118.

Williamson, Oliver E. 1985. *The Economic Institutions of Capitalism: Firms, Markets, Relational Contracting.* New York: Free Press.

Willman, Alys. 2010. "Preventing and Reducing Armed Violence in Urban Areas: OECD Programming Note." Organisation for Economic Co-operation and Development, Paris.

Willman, Alys, and Megumi Makisaka. 2010. "Interpersonal Violence Prevention: A Review of the Evidence and Emerging Lessons." Background paper for the WDR 2011.

Wilson, Scott. 2002. "Re-opening Mozambique: Lessons Learned from the Feeder Road Programme." International Labour Organization, Geneva; UN Development Programme, Maputo; Swedish International Development Cooperation Agency, Stockholm; and Administraçao Nacional de Estradas, Maputo.

Wisler, Dominique. 2005. "The Police Reform in Bosnia and Herzegovina." In *After Intervention: Public Security Management in Post-Conflict Societies: From Intervention to Sustainable Local Ownership*, ed. Anja Ebnother and Philipp Fluri. Vienna: Bureau for Security Policy, Austrian Ministry of Defence; Geneva: Geneva Centre for the Democratic Control of Armed Forces; and Partnership for Peace Consortium of Defense Academies and Security Studies, Garmisch-Partenkirchen, Germany.

Wolpe, Howard, and Steve McDonald. 2006. "Burundi's Transition: Training Leaders for Peace." *Journal of Democracy* 17 (1): 126–32.

Women's Refugee Commission. 2008. *Disabilities Among Refugees and Conflict-Affected Populations.* New York: Women's Refugee Commission.

Women's Refugee Commission. 2009. *Refugee Girls: The Invisible Faces of War.* New York: Women's Refugee Commission.

Wood, Elisabeth J. 2003. *Insurgent Collective Action and Civil War in El Salvador.* Cambridge, U.K.: Cambridge University Press.

———. 2008. "The Social Processes of Civil War: The Wartime Transformation of Social Networks." *American Review of Political Science* 11: 539–61.

World Bank. 1999a. "Aid Coordination and Post-conflict Reconstruction: The West Bank and Gaza Experience." Precís 185, Operations Evaluation Department, World Bank, Washington, DC.

———. 1999b. *Violence in Colombia: Building Sustainable Peace and Social Capital.* Washington, DC: World Bank.

———. 2000. "The Economics of War-to-Peace Transition." Post-conflict Unit Discussion Note 4, World Bank, Washington, DC.

———. 2002a. "East Timor SP: Third Community Empowerment Project." World Bank, Washington, DC.

———. 2002b. "Post-conflict Learning Event." World Bank, Dar Es Salaam, Tanzania.

———. 2003. "Post-conflict Workshop." World Bank, Maputo.

———. 2004. "West Bank and Gaza: Country Financial Accountability Assessment." West Bank and Gaza Operational Core Services Unit, Middle East and North Africa Region, World Bank, Washington, DC.

———. 2005a. "Memorandum of the President of the International Bank for Reconstruction and Development to the Executive Directors on a Proposal for the World Bank to Administer Two Multi-Donor Trust Funds for Sudan." World Bank, Washington, DC.

———. 2005b. "Mozambique Country Economic Memorandum: Sustaining Growth and Reducing Poverty." Poverty Reduction and Economic Management, Africa Region, World Bank, Washington, DC.

———. 2006a. "Anti-Corruption in Transition 3: Who is Succeeding and Why?" World Bank, Washington, DC.

———. 2006b. "At Home and Away: Expanding Job Opportunities for Pacific Islanders Through Labor Mobility." World Bank, Washington, DC.

———. 2006c. "Engaging with Fragile States: An IEG Review of World Bank Support to Low-Income Countries Under Stress." World Bank, Washington, DC.

———. 2006d. "Labor Migration in the Greater Mekong Sub-Region Synthesis Report: Phase I." World Bank, Washington, DC.

———. 2006e. "Project Appraisal Document for a Proposed Loan in the Amount of US$29.3 Million to Jamaica for an Inner City Basic Services for the Poor Project." World Bank, Washington, DC.

———. 2006f. *World Development Report 2007: Development and the Next Generation.* Washington, DC: World Bank.

———. 2007a. "Aid Architecture: An Overview of the Main Trends in Official Development Assistance Flows." World Bank, Washington, DC.

———. 2007b. "Making the Most of Scarcity: Accountability for Better Water Management in the Middle East and North Africa." MENA Development Reports, Office of the Chief Economist, Middle East and North Africa Region. World Bank, Washington, DC.

———. 2007c. "The Development Potential of Regional Programs: An Evaluation of World Bank Support of Multicountry Operations." World Bank, Washington, DC.

———. 2007d. "Toward a New Framework for Rapid Bank Response to Crises and Emergencies." World Bank, Washington, DC.

———. 2008a. "Aceh Poverty Assessment 2008: The Impact of the Conflict, the Tsunami, and Reconstruction on Poverty in Aceh." World Bank, Jakarta.

———. 2008b. "Activities within World Bank Core Competencies in the Context of Crises and Emergencies: A Good Practice and Guidance Note." World Bank, Washington, DC.

———. 2008c. "Burundi: Investing in Leadership Development through the Rapid Results Approach." World Bank, Washington, DC.

———. 2008d. "Cash Transfer Programs in Emergency Situations: A Good Practice and Guidance Note." World Bank, Washington, DC.

———. 2008e. "Country Assistance Strategy for the Republic of Burundi for the Period of FY09–FY12 ." World Bank, Washington, DC.

———. 2008f. "Republic of Lebanon: Electricity Sector Public Expenditure Review." World Bank, Washington, DC.

———. 2008g. "State (Trans-) Formation in Timor-Leste: Building Institutions that Contribute to Peace." OPCFC Occasional Note 3, Fragile and Conflict-Affected Countries Unit, World Bank, Washington, DC.

———. 2008h. *World Development Report 2009: Reshaping Economic Geography*. Washington, DC: World Bank.

———. 2009a. "Afghanistan Reconstruction Trust Fund: Newsletter Issue 01." World Bank, Washington, DC.

———. 2009b. "Blue Water: Towards a World Bank Group Pacific Strategy." World Bank, Washington, DC.

———. 2009c. "Implementation, Completion and Results Report on an IDA Grant in the Amount of SDR 24 Million (US$3 Million Equivalent) and a MDRP Grant in the Amount of US$48.4 Million and a European Commission Grant in the Amount of EUR 13.4 Million (US$16.6 Million Equivalent) to the Republic of Angola for an Emergency Demobilization and Reintegration Project." Sustainable Development Department, Fragile States, Conflict and Social Development Unit, Africa Region, World Bank, Washington, DC.

———. 2009d. "Lebanon: Social Impact Analysis for the Electricity and Water Sectors." World Bank, Washington, DC.

———. 2009e. "Nepal: Bringing the Poorest into Schools." World Bank, Washington, DC. http://web.worldbank.org/WBSITE/EXTERNAL/COUNTRIES/SOUTHASIAEXT/0,,contentMDK:22324235~menuPK:158937~pagePK:2865106~piPK:2865128~theSitePK:223547,00.html

———. 2009f. "Rapport sur l'Évaluation de la Gestion Financière des Forces de Défense et de Sécurité en République Centrafricaine." World Bank, Washington, DC.

———. 2010a. "Background Brief on Aceh." Background note for the WDR 2011.

———. 2010b. "Business Warehouse Data." World Bank, Washington, DC. http://go.worldbank.org/Q8GHD25UA0.

———. 2010c. "Crime and Violence in Central America." World Bank, Washington, DC.

———. 2010d. "Enterprise Surveys." World Bank, Washington, DC. http://www.enterprisesurveys.org.

———. 2010e. *Global Monitoring Report 2010: The MDGs after the Crisis*. Washington, DC: World Bank.

———. 2010f. "Implementation and Completion and Results Report (IDA Grant Nos. H246, H325, H451) to the Republic of Tajikistan." World Bank, Washington, DC.

———. 2010g. "Index of Legislative Instruments Applicable from the Beginning of Afghanistan Interim Administration 2001 until 2009." Background note for the WDR 2011.

———. 2010h. "Integrity Vice Presidency Annual Report: Fiscal 2010." World Bank, Washington, DC.

———. 2010i. "LCSPS Comments to the 2011 WDR on Justice Sector Reform in Latin America." Background note for the WDR 2011.

———. 2010j. "Multi-Donor Trust Fund for Southern Sudan: Taking Stock and a Way Forward." World Bank, Washington, DC.

———. 2010k. "Project Paper on a Proposed Additional Grant in the Amount of SDR 13.6 MIllion (US$29 Million Equivalent) from the Pilot Crisis Response Window Resources (As a Part of a Total of US$47 Million Equivalent, including US$27 from Liberia Reconstruction Trust Fund) to the Republic of Liberia for the Urban and Rural Infrastructure Rehabilitation Project." World Bank, Washington, DC.

———. 2010l. "The Global Land Rush: Can it Yield Sustainable and Equitable Benefits?" World Bank, Washington, DC.

———. 2010m. "Violence in the City: Understanding and Supporting Community Responses to Urban Violence." World Bank, Washington, DC.

———. 2010n. "World Development Indicators 2010." World Bank, Washington, DC.

———. 2011a. "In DR Congo, a Bridge Proves Key to Lower Food Prices." World Bank, Washington, DC.

———. 2011b. "World Investment and Political Risk 2010." World Bank Group Multilateral Investment Guarantee Agency, Washington, DC.

World Bank and ADB (Asian Development Bank). 2010. "Post Crisis Needs Assessment." World Bank, Washington, DC; ADB, Islamabad.

World Bank and AfDB (African Development Bank). 2010. "Providing Budget Aid in Situations of Fragility: A World Bank–African Development Bank Common Approach paper." World Bank, AfDB, Washington, DC.

World Bank and UN (United Nations). 2007. "In Support of Peacebuilding: Strengthening the Post Conflict Needs Assessment." World Bank, Washington, DC; UN, New York.

———. 2008. "Georgia: Joint Needs Assessment." World Bank, Washington, DC; UN, New York.

World Bank, USAID (U.S. Agency for International Development), IFC (International Finance Co-operation), and MIGA (World Bank Multilateral Investment Guarantee Agency). 2009. "A Rough Guide to Investment Climate Reform in Conflict-Affected Countries." World Bank, USAID, IFC, and MIGA, Washington, DC.

WHO (World Health Organization). 2010. "Violence and Injury Prevention and Disability." World Health Organization, Geneva. http://www.who.int/violence_injury_prevention/en/.

Worsnip, Patrick. 2009. "UN Council Extends Lebanon Force with Same Mandate." *Reuters*, August 27.

Wright-Neville, David. 2004. "Dangerous Dynamics: Activists, Militants and Terrorists in Southeast Asia." *Pacific Review* 17 (1): 27–46.

Wulf, Herbert, and Tobias Debiel. 2009. "Conflict Early Warning and Response Mechanisms: Tools For Enhancing the Effectiveness of Regional Organisations? A Comparative Study of the AU, ECOWAS, IGAD, ASEAN/ARF and PIF." Crisis States Research Centre Working Paper 49, Development Studies Institute, London School of Economics and Political Science, London.

Zakaria, Fareed. 2003. *The Future of Freedom: Illiberal Democracy at Home and Abroad.* New York: W.W. Norton & Company.

Zamora, Ruben, and David Holiday. 2007. "The Struggle for Lasting Reform: Vetting Processes in El Salvador." In *Justice as Prevention: Vetting Public Employees in Transitional Societies*, ed. Alexander Mayer-Rieckh and Pablo de Greiff . New York: Social Science Research Council.

Zoellick, Robert. 2010a. "Democratizing Development Economics: An Address by the Honorable Robert Zoellick, President of the World Bank." Georgetown University, Washington, DC, September 29.

———. 2010b. "Keynote Speech at the International Institute for Strategic Studies 6th Global Strategic Review Conference." International Institute for Strategic Studies, Washington, DC, September 12.

Selected Indicators 2011

Selected world development indicators

Table A1 Security

	Battle-related deaths (number)	Intentional homicides per 100,000 people	Refugees: By country of asylum	Refugees: By country of origin	Internally displaced persons (number)	Peacebuilding and peacekeeping: Operation name[a]	Peacebuilding and peacekeeping: Troops, police, and military observers (number)	Military expenditures: % of central government expenditure	Military expenditures: % of GDP	Natural disasters (number)	Deaths from natural disasters (number)	Youth population: % of total population ages 15–34	Youth population: % of male population ages 15–34
	2000–08	2000–09	2009	2009	2008	2010	2009	2009	2009	2000–08[b]	2000–09	2009	2009
Afghanistan	26,589	4.5	37	2,887,123	200,000	UNAMA[c]	18	9.2	*2.1*	..	..	34	18
Angola	3,535	..	14,734	141,021	*61,700*			..	4.6	..	..	34	17
Armenia	0	2.5	3,607	18,000	8,000			16.1	4.0	..	..	37	19
Bangladesh	0	2.6	228,586	10,432	65,000			10.8	1.1	137	13,241	34	15
Belize	0	32.7	230	17	..			..	*1.1*	..	..	36	19
Benin	0	..	7,205	411	..			6.8	*1.0*	..	..	34	17
Bhutan	0	1.4	..	89,070	..			..	..	..	..	40	21
Bolivia	0	12.6	679	573	..			*7.9*	1.6	39	916	36	18
Burkina Faso	0	3.6	543	990	..			12.1	1.3	..	..	34	17
Burundi	4,937	..	24,967	94,239	100,000	BINUB	13	..	*3.8*	36	833	33	17
Cambodia	0	..	135	17,025	..			*12.8*	*1.2*	..	..	39	20
Cameroon	0	5.9	99,957	14,766	..			..	1.6	..	..	36	18
Cape Verde	0	..	..	24	..			2.1	*0.6*	..	..	38	19
Central African Republic	350	..	27,047	159,554	108,000	MINURCAT[d]	1,456	..	1.8	..	..	35	17
Chad	4,328	..	338,495	55,014	186,000	MINURCAT		..	6.5	..	..	32	15
China	0	1.2	300,989	180,558	..			*17.9*	2.0	731	111,029	*32*	17
Comoros	0	..	..	268	..			..	..	14	187	*33*	*17*
Congo, Dem. Rep.	75,118	..	185,809	455,852	1,400,000	MONUSCO	19,008	..	1.1	126	8,164	*34*	*17*
Congo, Rep.	116	..	111,411	20,544	7,800			*5.3*	*1.3*	..	..	*33*	*17*
Côte d'Ivoire	1,265	3.9	24,604	23,153	621,000	UNOCI	9,080	8.8	*1.6*	..	..	*36*	18
Djibouti	0	0.7	12,111	622	..			..	*3.7*	..	..	*38*	*17*
Ecuador	0	18.0	116,557	1,027	..			..	3.3	..	..	*35*	*17*
Egypt, Arab Rep.	0	0.6	94,406	6,990	..			7.6	2.1	98	3,189	*37*	*19*
El Salvador	0	51.8	30	5,051	..			2.9	0.6	28	1,813	*36*	17
Eritrea	57	..	4,751	209,168	32,000			..	..	..	..	*34*	*17*
Ethiopia	3,555	3.3	121,886	62,889	200,000			..	1.3	..	..	*33*	*16*
Gambia, The	0	..	10,118	1,973	..			..	*0.7*	..	..	*33*	*17*
Georgia	648	7.1	870	15,020	300,000			29.3	5.6	..	..	*29*	15
Ghana	0	1.8	13,658	14,893	..			1.9	0.7	..	..	*36*	*18*
Guatemala	0	46.0	131	5,768	..			3.6	0.4	41	2,216	33	16
Guinea	1,174	..	15,325	10,920	*19,000*			..	..	35	1,103	*33*	*17*
Guinea-Bissau	0	..	7,898	1,109	..	UNIOGBIS		..	..	..	..	*35*	17
Guyana	0	20.7		727	..			..	..	..	..	*34*	*18*
Haiti	244	18.6	3	24,116	*6,000*	MINUSTAH	11,797	..	0.0	..	..	*36*	*18*
Honduras	0	58.0	19	1,166	..			3.8	0.8	31	435	*37*	*19*
India	31,599	2.8	185,323	19,514	500,000			16.3	2.8	365	63,679	*35*	18
Indonesia	1,940	1.1	798	18,213	150,000			..	0.9	232	182,209	*34*	*18*
Iraq	124,002	..	35,218	1,785,212	2,842,000	UNAMI	233	..	6.3	..	..	*37*	*19*
Jordan	0	1.8	450,756	2,129	160,000			16.1	6.1	..	..	*36*	*19*
Kenya	0	4.8	358,928	9,620	400,000			8.9	1.8	85	2,075	*37*	*19*
Kiribati	0	5.2	..	33	..			..	..	..	..	*36*	*18*
Korea, Dem. Rep.	0	..	..	..	*30,000*			..	..	..	..	31	16
Kosovo	0	..	423	..	..	UNMIK	16	..	..	..	..	*37*	*19*
Kyrgyz Republic	0	7.8	..	2,612	..			21.4	*3.6*	16	323	*38*	*19*
Lao PDR	0	..	..	8,398	..			*3.7*	*0.4*	..	..	*35*	*18*
Lesotho	0	34.8	..	10	..			3.1	2.6	..	..	40	19
Liberia	2,487	1.3	6,952	71,599	6,000	UNMIL	9,369	..	0.8	10	103	*33*	*16*
Madagascar	0	..	..	274	..			*9.9*	*1.1*	..	..	*34*	*17*
Malawi	0	..	5,443	130	..			..	*1.2*	38	2,390	*35*	*17*
Maldives	0	1.1	..	16	..			..	..	..	..	48	30
Mali	97	..	13,538	2,926	..			14.4	2.0	..	..	*32*	*16*
Marshall Islands	0	..	..	..	..			..	..	..	..	*36*	*18*
Mauritania	0	..	26,795	39,143	..			..	3.8	..	..	*35*	*17*
Micronesia, Fed. Sts.	0	..	1	..	..			..	..	..	..	36	18
Moldova	0	7.7	141	5,925	..			1.9	0.5	..	..	*35*	*18*
Mongolia	0	11.9	11	1,495	..			*5.8*	*1.4*	..	..	*39*	*20*
Morocco	0	0.5	73	2,286	..			11.0	3.4	52	1,545	*36*	*18*
Mozambique	0	..	3,547	136	..			..	0.9	50	2,017	*33*	*17*
Myanmar	2,833	0.2	..	406,669	503,000			..	..	17	138,968	*37*	*19*

Table A1 Security *(continued)*

			Refugees			Peacebuilding and peacekeeping		Military expenditures				Youth population	
	Battle-related deaths (number)	Intentional homicides per 100,000 people	By country of asylum	By country of origin	Internally displaced persons (number)	Operation name[a]	Troops, police, and military observers (number)	% of central government expenditure	% of GDP	Natural disasters (number)	Deaths from natural disasters (number)	% of total population ages 15–34	% of male population ages 15–34
	2000–08	2000–09	2009	2009	2008	2010	2009	2009	2009	2000–08[b]	2000–09	2009	2009
Nepal	11,520	1.8	108,461	5,108	50,000	UNMIN	72	*12.8*	1.6	51	3,120	*36*	*17*
Nicaragua	0	13.0	120	1,478	..			..	0.7	20	335	*39*	*20*
Niger	128	..	325	822	..			*10.6*	..	..	..	33	17
Nigeria	124	1.3	9,127	15,609	100,000			..	0.9	..	..	*35*	*18*
Pakistan	11,107	7.3	1,740,711	35,132	50,000			*21.8*	2.9	123	78,582	*36*	*19*
Papua New Guinea	0	8.8	9,703	70	..			..	0.5	25	397	*35*	*18*
Paraguay	0	12.3	89	77	..			5.0	0.8	..	..	*36*	*18*
Philippines	5,433	3.8	95	993	314,000			4.9	0.8	163	10,331	*36*	*18*
Rwanda	3,800	1.5	54,016	129,109	..			..	1.5	..	..	*36*	*18*
Samoa	0	..	..	..	..			..	..	..	..	*33*	*17*
São Tomé and Príncipe	0	..	..	33	..			..	..	..	..	*34*	*17*
Senegal	184	3.0	22,151	16,305	10,000			..	*1.6*	..	..	*35*	*17*
Sierra Leone	212	2.4	9,051	15,417	*3,000*			..	*2.3*	..	..	*34*	*16*
Solomon Islands	0	..	..	66	*4,000*			..	..	..	..	*37*	*19*
Somalia	3,983	..	1,815	678,309	1,100,000			..	..	53	3,161	*32*	*16*
Sri Lanka	24,807	7.4	251	145,721	500,000			18.5	3.5	25	35,891	*33*	*17*
Sudan	12,363	..	186,292	368,195	6,000,000	UNMIS[e]	10,592	..	*4.2*	68	3,794	*36*	*18*
Swaziland	0	1.0	759	32	..			..	*2.1*	..	..	*38*	*20*
Syrian Arab Republic	0	3.0	1,054,466	17,914	65,000			..	4.2	..	..	*38*	*19*
Tajikistan	0	2.3	2,679	562	..			..	..	31	180	*39*	*20*
Tanzania	0	1.0	118,731	1,204	..			..	1.0	67	1,466	*36*	*18*
Thailand	2,067	7.9	105,297	502	..			8.3	1.8	79	9,929	*32*	*16*
Timor-Leste	0	..	1	7	30,000	UNMIT	1,518	..	11.8	..	..	*36*	*19*
Togo	0	..	8,531	18,378	1,000			13.0	*2.0*	..	..	*37*	*18*
Tonga	0	..	..	5	..			..	..	..	..	*40*	*21*
Tunisia	0	1.2	92	2,260	..			4.4	1.4	..	..	*38*	*19*
Turkmenistan	0	2.9	60	743	..			..	..	..	..	*39*	*19*
Tuvalu	..	..	..	..	..			..	..	..	..	..	..
Uganda	5,432	8.7	127,345	7,554	869,000			17.1	2.2	75	1,817	*34*	*17*
Ukraine	0	6.3	7,334	24,522	..			7.2	2.9	..	..	*30*	*15*
Uzbekistan	247	2.5	555	6,669	3,000			..	..	..	..	*39*	*20*
Vanuatu	0	..	4	..	..			..	..	..	..	*38*	*20*
Vietnam	0	1.9	2,357	339,289	..			..	2.2	..	..	*38*	*19*
West Bank and Gaza	0	3.9	..	95,201[f]	100,000			..	..	..	..	*37*	*19*
Yemen, Rep.	0	4.0	170,854	1,934	..			..	*4.4*	..	..	*37*	*19*
Zambia	0	7.5	56,785	206	..			*5.7*	1.7	..	..	*38*	*19*
Zimbabwe	0	8.4	3,995	22,449	880,000			..	..	..	..	*35*	*15*
Low income	..	..	..	..	..			..	1.5	..	..	..	..
Lower middle income	..	..	..	..	..			*16.1*	2.1	..	..	..	..

a. Data are as of October 2010. UNAMA is the United Nations Assistance Mission in Afghanistan, BINUB is the Bureau Intégré des Nations Unies au Burundi (United Nations Integrated Office in Burundi), MINURCAT is the United Nations Mission in the Central African Republic and Chad, MONUSCO is the United Nations Organization Stabilization Mission in the Democratic Republic of Congo, UNOCI is the United Nations Operation in Côte d'Ivoire, UNIOGBIS is the United Nations Integrated Peacebuilding Office in Guinea-Bissau. MINUSTAH is the United Nations Stabilization Mission in Haiti, UNMOGIP is the United Nations Military Observer Group in India and Pakistan, UNAMI is the United Nations Assistance Mission for Iraq, UNMIK is the Interim Administration Mission in Kosovo, UNMIL is the United Nations Mission in Liberia, UNMIN is the United Nations Mission in Nepal, UNMIS is the United Nations Mission in Sudan, and UNMIT is the United Nations Integrated Mission in Timor-Leste. b. Total over the period. c. Political mission administered by the United Nations Department of Peacekeeping Operations. d. Includes peacekeepers in Chad. e. Does not include 22,061 troops, police, and military observers from the African Union–United Nations Hybrid Operation in Darfur. f. Only includes refugees under the United Nations Refugee Agency mandate.

Technical Notes

Table A1. Security

Battle-related deaths

Best estimates of the sum of battle deaths in civil wars from 2000 to 2008. For countries with multiple civil wars, the best estimate for the total number of battle deaths from all conflicts is taken. Source: PRIO Battle Deaths Dataset Version 3.0. Where best estimates were missing in the PRIO Battle Deaths Dataset Version 3.0, best estimates from the UCDP Battle Deaths dataset (v 5) were taken. Where best estimates were unavailable from both the PRIO Battle Deaths Dataset Version 3.0 as well as the UCDP Battle Deaths dataset (v 5), the weighted average of PRIO Battle Deaths Dataset Version 3.0's low and high estimates was taken as the best estimate.

Intentional homicides

Denotes the homicide rate per 100,000 people for the latest year that data are available from 2000 to 2009. The rates have been reconciled into a single figure from all sources collecting homicide statistics from both the health and the criminal justice sectors. Data from United Nations Office on Drugs and Crime (UNOCDC) Crime Trends Survey (CTS) and from the World Health Organization were used as the two main sources of homicide statistics but preference was given to UNODC's CTS because of its superior coverage. Regression analyses were used to determine the degree of correlation between other criminal justice/police-based and health-based sources and the two main sources of data. Where correlations were high with the other sources, these were used to impute single missing observations in the main sources of data. Once single gaps were filled, both data sources were combined into a single set of homicides based on new regression analyses and later complemented with statistics from national sources. Sources: UNODC-CTS; Eurostat (Health and Criminal Justice); Archer and Gartner Comparative Crime Data (1978); World Health Organization (WHO) and United Nations Children's Fund (UNICEF); Pan American Health Organization; TransMONEE Database; national sources.

Refugees by country of asylum

Denotes the number of refugees hosted by a country as of the end of 2009. Source: United Nations High Commission for Refugees (UNHCR).

Refugees by country of origin

Denotes the number of refugees originating from each country. Source: UNHCR.

Internally displaced persons

Denotes the number of internally displaced people in a country as of the end of 2008. Source: U.S. Committee for Refugees and Immigrants.

UN Peacekeeping Operation or Political Mission

The name of the United Nations Peacekeeping Operation or United Nations Political Mission, if one existed as of October 2010. Source: UN.

UN personnel

The number of United Nations troops, civilian police, and military observers as of October 2010. Source: UN.

Military expenditure as a percentage of central government expenditure

Military expenditure as a percentage of central government expenditure for the year. Military expenditures data from Stockholm International Peace Research Institute (SIPRI) are derived from the North Atlantic Treaty Organization (NATO) definition, which includes all current and capital expenditures on the armed forces, including peacekeeping forces; defense ministries and other government agencies engaged in defense projects; paramilitary forces, if these are judged to be trained and equipped for military operations; and military space activities. Such expenditures include military and civil personnel, including retirement pensions of military personnel and social services for personnel; operation and maintenance; procurement; military research and development; and military aid (in the military expenditures of the donor country). Excluded are civil defense and current expenditures for previous military activities, such as for veterans' benefits, demobilization, conversion, and destruction of weapons. This definition cannot be applied for all countries, however, since that would require much more detailed information than is available about what is included in military budgets and off–budget military expenditure items. (For example, military budgets might or might not cover civil defense, reserves and auxiliary forces, police and paramilitary forces, dual-purpose forces such as military and civilian police, military grants in kind, pensions for military personnel, and social security contributions paid by one part of government to another.) Source: Stockholm International Peace Research Institute (SIPRI), Yearbook: Armaments, Disarmament and International Security. Note: Data for some countries are based on partial or uncertain data or rough estimates.

Military expenditure as a percentage of GDP

Military expenditure as a percentage of GDP. Military expenditures data from SIPRI are derived from the NATO definition, which includes all current and capital expenditures on the armed forces, including peacekeeping forces; defense ministries and other government agencies engaged in defense projects; paramilitary forces, if these are judged to be trained and equipped for military operations; and military space activities. Such expenditures include military and civil personnel, including retirement pensions of military personnel and social services for personnel; operation and maintenance; procurement; military research and development; and military aid (in the military expenditures of the donor country). Excluded are civil defense and current expenditures for previous military activities, such as for veterans' benefits, demobilization, conversion, and destruction of weapons. This definition cannot be applied for all countries, however, since that would require much more detailed information than is available about what is included in military budgets and off-budget military expenditure items. (For example, military budgets might or might not cover civil defense, reserves and auxiliary forces, police and paramilitary forces, dual-purpose forces such as military and civilian police, military grants in kind, pensions for military personnel, and social security contributions paid by one part of government to another.) Source: Stockholm International Peace Research Institute (SIPRI), Yearbook: Armaments, Disarmament and International Security. Note: Data for some countries are based on partial or uncertain data or rough estimates.

Number of natural disasters

The sum of natural disasters in a country from 2000 to 2008. This includes biological, hydrological, meteorological, technological, climatological, and geophysical disasters. Source: Center for Research on the Epidemiology of Disasters (CRED).

Number of deaths from natural disasters

Total number of deaths from all natural disasters in a country from 2000 to 2009. This includes biological, hydrological, meteorological, technological, climatological, and geophysical disasters. Source: CRED.

Total youth population ages 15 to 34 years

Percentage of total youth population ages 15 to 34 years out of total population (both males and females). Source: Calculations based on data from the United States Census International Database.

Total male youth population ages 15 to 34 years

Percentage of male youth population ages 15 to 34 years out of total population. Source: Calculations based on data from the United States Census International Database.

Physical Rights Integrity Index

This indicator measures the extent of human rights abuses in a country. It is a composite indicator made up of four subcomponents: torture, politically motivated disappearances, extrajudicial killings, and politically motivated incarceration. The index ranges from 0 (no government respect for these four rights) to 8 (full government respect for these four rights). Source: CIRI (Cingranelli-Richards) Human Rights Data Project, University of Binghamton, New York.

Number of years each leader has been in power. Calculated from the Archigos Dataset of Political Leaders (H. E. Goemans, Kristian Skrede Gleditsch, and Giacomo Chiozza) and the Central Intelligence Agency World Factbook.

Selected World Development Indicators 2011

In this year's edition, development data are in six tables presenting comparative socioeconomic data for more than 130 economies for the most recent year for which data are available and, for some indicators, for an earlier year. An additional table presents basic indicators for 78 economies with sparse data or with populations of less than 3 million.

The indicators presented here are from more than 800 included in *World Development Indicators 2010.* Published annually, *World Development Indicators* (WDI) reflects a comprehensive view of the development process. WDI's six sections recognize the contribution of a wide range of factors: progress on the Millennium Development Goals (MDGs) and human capital development, environmental sustainability, macroeconomic performance, private sector development and the investment climate, and the global links that influence the external environment for development.

WDI is complemented by a separately published database that gives access to more than 900 time-series indicators for 237 economies and regions. This database is available at the Open Data website (http://data.worldbank.org).

Data sources and methodology

Socioeconomic and environmental data presented here are drawn from several sources: primary data collected by the World Bank, member country statistical publications, research institutes, and international organizations such as the United Nations (UN) and its specialized agencies, the International Monetary Fund (IMF), and the Organisation for Economic Co-operation and Development (OECD). (See the data sources in the technical notes following the tables for a complete listing.) Although international standards of coverage, definition, and classification apply to most statistics reported by countries and international agencies, inevitable differences in timeliness and reliability arise from differences in the capabilities and resources devoted to basic data collection and compilation. For some topics, competing sources of data require review by the World Bank staff to ensure that the most reliable data available are presented. In some instances, where available data are deemed too weak to provide reliable measures of levels and trends or do not adequately adhere to international standards, the data are not shown.

The data presented are generally consistent with those in *World Development Indicators 2010.* However, data have been revised and updated wherever new information has become available. Differences may also reflect revisions to historical series and changes in methodology. Thus data of different vintages may be published in different editions of World Bank publications. Readers are advised not to compile data series from different publications or different editions of the same publication. Consistent time-series data are available on the Open Data website (http://data.worldbank.org).

All dollar figures are in current U.S. dollars unless otherwise stated. The various methods used to convert from national currency figures are described in the technical notes following the tables.

Because the World Bank's primary business is providing lending and policy advice to its low- and middle-income members, the issues covered in these tables focus mainly on those economies. Where available, information on the high-income economies is also provided for comparison. Readers may wish to refer to national statistical publications and publications of the OECD and the European Union (EU) for more information on the high-income economies.

Classification of economies and summary measures

The summary measures at the bottom of most tables include economies classified by income per capita and by region. Gross national income (GNI) per capita is used to determine the following income classifications: low income, US$995 or less in 2009; middle income, US$996 to US$12,195; and high income, US$12,196 and above. A further division at GNI per capita US$3,945 is made between lower-middle-income and upper-middle-income economies. The classification of economies based on per capita income occurs annually, so the country composition of the income groups may change annually. When these changes in classification are made on the basis of the most recent estimates, aggregates based on the new income classifications are recalculated for all past periods to ensure that a consistent time series is maintained. See the classification of economies at the end of this discussion for a list of economies in each group (including those with populations of less than 3 million).

Summary measures are either totals (indicated by a **t** if the aggregates include estimates for missing data and nonreporting countries, or by an **s** for simple sums of the data available), weighted averages (**w**), or median values (**m**) calculated for groups of economies. Data for the countries excluded from the main tables (those presented in table 6) have been included in the summary measures, where data are available; otherwise, it is assumed that they follow the trend of reporting countries. This approach gives a more consistent aggregated measure by standardizing country coverage for each period shown. Where missing information accounts for a third or more of the overall estimate, however, the group measure is reported as not available. The section on statistical methods in the technical notes provides further information on aggregation methods. Weights used to construct the aggregates are listed in the technical notes for each table.

Terminology and country coverage

The term *country* does not imply political independence but may refer to any territory for which authorities report separate social or economic statistics. Data are shown for economies as they were constituted in 2009, and historical data are revised to reflect current political arrangements. Throughout the tables, exceptions are noted. Unless otherwise noted, data for China do not include data for Hong Kong SAR, China; Macao SAR, China; or Taiwan, China. Data for Indonesia include Timor-Leste through 1999 unless otherwise noted. Montenegro declared independence from Serbia and Montenegro on June 3, 2006. When available, data for each country are shown separately. However, some indicators for Serbia continue to include data for Montenegro through 2005; these data are footnoted in the tables. Moreover, data for most indicators from 1999 onward for Serbia exclude data for Kosovo, which in 1999 became a territory under international administration pursuant to UN Security Council Resolution 1244 (1999); any exceptions are noted. Kosovo became a World Bank member on June 29, 2009, and its data are shown in the tables where available.

Technical notes

Because data quality and intercountry comparisons are often problematic, readers are encouraged to consult the technical notes that follow the tables, the list of classification of economies by region and income that follows this discussion, and the footnotes to the tables. For more extensive documentation, see WDI 2010.

Symbols

.. means that data are not available or that aggregates cannot be calculated because of missing data in the years shown.

0 or **0.0** means zero or small enough that the number would round to zero at the displayed number of decimal places.

/ in dates, as in 2003/04, means that the period of time, usually 12 months, straddles two calendar years and refers to a crop year, a survey year, or a fiscal year.

$ means current U.S. dollars unless otherwise noted.

> means more than.

< means less than.

Readers may find more information in WDI 2010, and orders can be made online, by phone, or fax as follows:

For more information and to order online: http://data.worldbank.org/data-catalog/world-development-indicators.

To order by phone: 1-800-645-7247

To order by fax: 1-703-661-1501

To order by mail: The World Bank, P.O. Box 960, Herndon, VA 20172-0960, USA

This page shows the correct data for page 344, WDR 2011, sku 18439 and sku 18700.

Table 1. Key indicators of development

	Population			Population age composition	Gross national income (GNI)[a]		PPP national income (GNI)[b]		Gross domestic product	Life expectancy at birth		Adult literacy rate
	Millions	Average annual % growth	Density people per sq. km	% ages 0–14	$ billions	$ per capita	$ billions	$ per capita	per capita % growth	Male Years	Female Years	% ages 15 and older
	2009	2000–09	2009	2009	2009	2009	2009	2009	2008–09	2008	2008	2008
Afghanistan	30	2.6	44	46	*10.6*	*370*	*32.1*[c]	*1,110*[c]	*–0.4*	44	44	..
Albania	3	0.3	115	24	12.5	3,950	25.8	8,170	1.8	74	80	99
Algeria	35	1.5	14	27	154.2	4,420	283.6[c]	8,130[c]	0.6	71	74	*73*
Angola	18	2.9	14	45	64.5	3,490	91.9	4,970	–2.3	45	49	70
Argentina	40	1.0	15	25	304.7	7,570	568.8	14,120	–0.1	72	79	98
Armenia	3	0.0	109	20	9.5	3,100	16.7	5,420	–14.6	70	77	100
Australia	22	1.5	3	19	957.5	43,770	835.7	38,210	–0.8	79	84	..
Austria	8	0.5	101	15	391.8	46,850	322.5	38,550	–3.8	78	83	..
Azerbaijan	9	1.0	105	24	42.5	4,840	79.3	9,030	8.0	68	73	*100*
Bangladesh	162	1.6	1,229	31	95.4	590	256.2	1,580	4.4	65	67	55
Belarus	10	–0.4	48	15	53.5	5,540	119.6	12,380	0.4	65	77	100
Belgium	11	0.6	354	17	488.8	45,310	394.0	36,520	–3.7	77	83	..
Benin	9	3.3	78	43	6.7	750	13.5	1,510	0.6	60	63	41
Bolivia	10	1.9	9	36	16.0	1,620	42.0	4,260	1.6	64	68	*91*
Bosnia and Herzegovina	4	0.2	74	15	17.7	4,700	32.9	8,740	–3.2	73	78	98
Brazil	194	1.2	23	26	1,557.2	8,040	1,988.1	10,260	–1.1	69	76	*90*
Bulgaria	8	–0.7	70	13	43.7	5,770	93.2	12,290	–4.6	70	77	98
Burkina Faso	16	3.3	56	46	8.0	510	18.4	1,170	0.1	52	54	*29*
Burundi	8	2.8	314	38	1.2	150	3.3	390	0.6	49	52	66
Cambodia	15	1.7	82	33	9.7	650	27.4	1,850	–3.7	59	63	78
Cameroon	20	2.3	40	41	22.8	1,170	43.0	2,200	0.1	51	52	76
Canada	34	1.0	4	17	1,423.0	42,170	1,268.2	37,590	–3.7	79	83	..
Central African Republic	4	1.8	7	41	2.0	450	3.3	750	0.5	45	49	55
Chad	11	3.2	9	46	6.9	610	13.8	1,230	–1.1	47	50	33
Chile	17	1.1	23	23	159.9	9,420	227.9	13,430	–2.5	76	82	99
China	1,331	0.6	142	20	4,778.3	3,590	9,018.8	6,770	8.5	71	75	94
Hong Kong SAR, China	7	0.6	6,696	12	*219.2*	*31,420*	*307.5*	*44,070*	*1.6*	79	86	..
Colombia	46	1.5	41	29	225.2	4,930	388.1	8,500	–0.9	69	77	93
Congo, Dem. Rep.	66	2.9	28	47	10.7	160	19.6	300	0.0	46	49	67
Congo, Rep.	4	2.1	11	40	6.7	1,830	10.8	2,940	5.6	53	55	..
Costa Rica	5	1.7	89	26	28.5	6,230	50.1[c]	10,940[c]	–2.8	77	81	96
Côte d'Ivoire	21	2.2	65	41	22.4	1,060	34.5	1,640	1.4	56	59	55
Croatia	4	0.0	82	15	61.2	13,810	84.9	19,170	–5.8	72	80	99
Czech Republic	10	0.2	135	14	181.5	17,310	247.7	23,610	–4.8	74	81	..
Denmark	6	0.4	129	18	325.8	58,930	208.5	37,720	–5.5	77	81	..
Dominican Republic	10	1.5	206	31	45.5	4,510	81.8[c]	8,100[c]	2.0	70	75	*88*
Ecuador	14	1.1	49	31	53.4	3,920	109.5	8,040	–0.7	72	78	*84*
Egypt, Arab Rep.	83	1.9	82	32	172.0	2,070	471.9	5,690	2.8	68	72	*66*
El Salvador	6	0.4	296	32	20.8	3,370	39.2[c]	6,360[c]	–3.0	67	76	84
Eritrea	5	3.6	49	42	*1.5*	*300*	*3.1*[c]	*640*[c]	*–1.0*	57	62	65
Ethiopia	83	2.6	81	44	27.0	330	77.4	930	5.9	54	57	36
Finland	5	0.3	17	17	243.9	45,680	183.8	34,430	–8.2	76	83	..
France	63[d]	0.7[d]	114[d]	18	2,754.6	42,680	2,192.9	33,980	–3.2	78	85	..
Georgia	4	–1.2	62	17	11.1[e]	2,530[e]	20.6[e]	4,700[e]	–4.1[e]	68	75	100
Germany	82	0.0	235	14	3,484.7	42,560	3,026.7	36,960	–4.7	78	83	..
Ghana	24	2.2	103	38	16.6	700	35.3	1,480	1.4	56	58	66
Greece	11	0.4	87	14	323.1	28,630	320.8	28,440	–2.4	78	82	97
Guatemala	14	2.5	128	42	36.8	2,620	64.4[c]	4,590[c]	–2.1	67	74	74
Guinea	10	2.0	40	43	3.8	370	9.5	940	–2.6	56	60	38
Haiti	10	1.7	358	36	..	..[f]	..	..	1.3	59	63	..
Honduras	7	2.0	65	37	13.6	1,820	27.9[c]	3,730[c]	–3.9	70	75	*84*
Hungary	10	–0.2	112	15	130.1	12,980	186.1	18,570	–6.2	70	78	99
India	1,155	1.4	383	31	1,368.7	1,180	3,768.1	3,260	6.2	62	65	*63*
Indonesia	230	1.3	125	27	513.4	2,230	933.2	4,060	3.4	69	73	*92*
Iran, Islamic Rep.	73	1.5	44	24	330.6	4,530	837.7	11,490	0.5	70	73	*82*
Iraq	31	2.5	70	41	69.7	2,210	105.1	3,340	1.6	64	72	78
Ireland	4	1.7	64	21	197.2	44,310	148.1	33,280	–6.5	78	82	..
Israel	7	1.9	338	28	191.6	25,740	201.2	27,040	–1.1	79	83	..
Italy	60	0.6	203	14	2,112.5	35,080	1,886.6	31,330	–5.7	79	85	99
Japan	128	0.1	350	13	4,830.3	37,870	4,245.7	33,280	–5.1	79	86	..
Jordan	6	2.4	66	34	22.3	3,740	34.8	5,840	0.4	71	75	*92*
Kazakhstan	16	0.7	6	24	107.1	6,740	163.2	10,270	–0.2	61	72	100
Kenya	40	2.6	68	43	30.7	770	62.7	1,570	–0.5	54	55	87
Korea, Rep.	49	0.4	502	17	966.6	19,830	1,331.4	27,310	–0.1	77	83	..
Kyrgyz Republic	5	0.9	28	29	4.6	870	11.7	2,200	1.5	63	72	99
Lao PDR	6	1.7	27	38	5.6	880	13.9	2,210	4.5	64	66	*73*
Lebanon	4	1.3	410	25	33.6	7,970	55.9	13,230	7.2	70	74	*90*
Liberia	4	3.7	39	43	0.6	160	1.2	290	0.3	57	60	58
Libya	6	2.0	4	30	77.2	12,020	105.5[c]	16,430[c]	0.1	72	77	88
Lithuania	3	–0.5	54	15	38.1	11,410	55.9	16,740	–14.6	66	78	100
Madagascar	20	2.8	33	43	*7.9*	*420*	*20.1*	*1,050*	–2.2	59	62	71
Malawi	15	2.8	158	46	4.2	280	11.6	760	4.8	52	54	73
Malaysia	27	1.8	82	29	198.7	7,230	371.8	13,530	–3.3	72	77	92
Mali	13	2.4	10	44	8.9	680	15.4	1,190	1.9	48	49	*26*
Mauritania	3	2.6	3	39	3.2	960	6.5	1,960	–3.4	55	59	57
Mexico	107	1.0	55	28	958.8	8,920	1,515.5	14,110	–7.5	73	78	93

Classification of economies by region and income, FY2011

East Asia and the Pacific	
American Samoa	UMC
Cambodia	LIC
China	LMC
Fiji	UMC
Indonesia	LMC
Kiribati	LMC
Korea, Dem. Rep.	LIC
Lao PDR	LIC
Malaysia	UMC
Marshall Islands	LMC
Micronesia, Fed. Sts.	LMC
Mongolia	LMC
Myanmar	LIC
Palau	UMC
Papua New Guinea	LMC
Philippines	LMC
Samoa	LMC
Solomon Islands	LIC
Thailand	LMC
Timor-Leste	LMC
Tonga	LMC
Tuvalu	LMC
Vanuatu	LMC
Vietnam	LMC

Europe and Central Asia	
Albania	UMC
Armenia	LMC
Azerbaijan	UMC
Belarus	UMC
Bosnia and Herzegovina	UMC
Bulgaria	UMC
Georgia	LMC
Kazakhstan	UMC
Kosovo	LMC
Kyrgyz Republic	LIC
Lithuania	UMC
Macedonia, FYR	UMC
Moldova	LMC
Montenegro	UMC
Romania	UMC
Russian Federation	UMC
Serbia	UMC
Tajikistan	LIC
Turkey	UMC
Turkmenistan	LMC
Ukraine	LMC
Uzbekistan	LMC

Latin America and the Caribbean	
Antigua and Barbuda	UMC
Argentina	UMC
Belize	LMC
Bolivia	LMC
Brazil	UMC
Chile	UMC
Colombia	UMC
Costa Rica	UMC
Cuba	UMC
Dominica	UMC
Dominican Republic	UMC
Ecuador	LMC
El Salvador	LMC
Grenada	UMC
Guatemala	LMC
Guyana	LMC
Haiti	LIC
Honduras	LMC
Jamaica	UMC
Mexico	UMC
Nicaragua	LMC
Panama	UMC
Paraguay	LMC
Peru	UMC
St. Kitts and Nevis	UMC
St. Lucia	UMC
St. Vincent and the Grenadines	UMC
Suriname	UMC
Uruguay	UMC
Venezuela, RB	UMC

Middle East and North Africa	
Algeria	UMC
Djibouti	LMC
Egypt, Arab Rep.	LMC
Iran, Islamic Rep.	UMC
Iraq	LMC
Jordan	LMC
Lebanon	UMC
Libya	UMC
Morocco	LMC
Syrian Arab Republic	LMC
Tunisia	LMC
West Bank and Gaza	LMC
Yemen, Rep.	LMC

South Asia	
Afghanistan	LIC
Bangladesh	LIC
Bhutan	LMC
India	LMC
Maldives	LMC
Nepal	LIC
Pakistan	LMC
Sri Lanka	LMC

Sub-Saharan Africa	
Angola	LMC
Benin	LIC
Botswana	UMC
Burkina Faso	LIC
Burundi	LIC
Cameroon	LMC
Cape Verde	LMC
Central African Republic	LIC
Chad	LIC
Comoros	LIC
Congo, Dem. Rep.	LIC
Congo, Rep.	LMC
Côte d'Ivoire	LMC
Eritrea	LIC
Ethiopia	LIC
Gabon	UMC
Gambia, The	LIC
Ghana	LIC
Guinea	LIC
Guinea-Bissau	LIC
Kenya	LIC
Lesotho	LMC
Liberia	LIC
Madagascar	LIC
Malawi	LIC
Mali	LIC
Mauritania	LIC
Mauritius	UMC
Mayotte	UMC
Mozambique	LIC
Namibia	UMC
Niger	LIC
Nigeria	LMC
Rwanda	LIC
São Tomé and Príncipe	LMC
Senegal	LMC
Seychelles	UMC
Sierra Leone	LIC
Somalia	LIC
South Africa	UMC
Sudan	LMC
Swaziland	LMC
Tanzania	LIC
Togo	LIC
Uganda	LIC
Zambia	LIC
Zimbabwe	LIC

High-income OECD

Australia
Austria
Belgium
Canada
Czech Republic
Denmark
Finland
France
Germany
Greece
Hungary
Iceland
Ireland
Israel
Italy
Japan
Korea, Rep.
Luxembourg
Netherlands
New Zealand
Norway
Poland
Portugal
Slovak Republic
Slovenia
Spain
Sweden
Switzerland
United Kingdom
United States

Other high income

Andorra
Aruba
Bahamas, The
Bahrain
Barbados
Bermuda
Brunei Darussalam
Cayman Islands
Channel Islands
Croatia
Cyprus
Equatorial Guinea
Estonia
Faeroe Islands
French Polynesia
Gibraltar
Greenland
Guam
Hong Kong SAR, China
Isle of Man
Kuwait
Latvia
Liechtenstein
Macao SAR, China
Malta
Monaco
Netherlands Antilles
New Caledonia
Northern Mariana Islands
Oman
Puerto Rico
Qatar
San Marino
Saudi Arabia
Singapore
Taiwan, China
Trinidad and Tobago
Turks and Caicos Islands
United Arab Emirates
Virgin Islands (U.S.)

Source: World Bank data.

This table classifies all World Bank member economies and all other economies with populations of more than 30,000. Economies are divided among income groups according to 2009 GNI per capita, calculated using the World Bank Atlas method. The groups are low income (LIC), US$995 or less; lower middle income (LMC), US$996–3,945; upper middle income (UMC), US$3,946–12,195; and high income, US$12,196 or more.

Table 1. Key indicators of development

	Population			Population age composition	Gross national income (GNI)[a]		PPP national income (GNI)[b]		Gross domestic product	Life expectancy at birth		Adult literacy rate
	Millions	Average annual % growth	Density people per sq. km	% ages 0–14	$ billions	$ per capita	$ billions	$ per capita	per capita % growth	Male Years	Female Years	% ages 15 and older
	2009	2000–09	2009	2009	2009	2009	2009	2009	2008–09	2008	2008	2008
Afghanistan	30	2.6	44	46	*10.6*	*370*	*32.1*[c]	*1,110*[c]	*–0.4*	44	44	..
Albania	3	0.3	115	24	12.5	3,950	25.8	8,170	1.8	74	80	99
Algeria	35	1.5	14	27	154.2	4,420	283.6[c]	8,130[c]	0.6	71	74	*73*
Angola	18	2.9	14	45	64.5	3,490	91.9	4,970	–2.3	45	49	70
Argentina	40	1.0	15	25	304.7	7,570	568.8	14,120	–0.1	72	79	98
Armenia	3	0.0	109	20	9.5	3,100	16.7	5,420	–14.6	70	77	100
Australia	2	1.5	3	19	957.5	43,770	835.7	38,210	–0.8	79	84	..
Austria	8	0.5	101	15	391.8	46,850	322.5	38,550	–3.8	78	83	..
Azerbaijan	9	1.0	105	24	42.5	4,840	79.3	9,030	8.0	68	73	*100*
Bangladesh	2	1.6	1,229	31	95.4	590	256.2	1,580	4.4	65	67	55
Belarus	10	–0.4	48	15	53.5	5,540	119.6	12,380	0.4	65	77	100
Belgium	11	0.6	354	17	488.8	45,310	394.0	36,520	–3.7	77	83	..
Benin	9	3.3	78	43	6.7	750	13.5	1,510	0.6	60	63	41
Bolivia	10	1.9	9	36	16.0	1,620	42.0	4,260	1.6	64	68	*91*
Bosnia and Herzegovina	4	0.2	74	15	17.7	4,700	32.9	8,740	–3.2	73	78	98
Brazil	4	1.2	23	26	1,557.2	8,040	1,988.1	10,260	–1.1	69	76	*90*
Bulgaria	8	–0.7	70	13	43.7	5,770	93.2	12,290	–4.6	70	77	98
Burkina Faso	6	3.3	56	46	8.0	510	18.4	1,170	0.1	52	54	*29*
Burundi	8	2.8	314	38	1.2	150	3.3	390	0.6	49	52	66
Cambodia	5	1.7	82	33	9.7	650	27.4	1,850	–3.7	59	63	78
Cameroon	20	2.3	40	41	22.8	1,170	43.0	2,200	0.1	51	52	76
Canada	34	1.0	4	17	1,423.0	42,170	1,268.2	37,590	–3.7	79	83	..
Central African Republic	4	1.8	7	41	2.0	450	3.3	750	0.5	45	49	55
Chad	11	3.2	9	46	6.9	610	13.8	1,230	–1.1	47	50	33
Chile	17	1.1	23	23	159.9	9,420	227.9	13,430	–2.5	76	82	99
China	1	0.6	142	20	4,778.3	3,590	9,018.8	6,770	8.5	71	75	94
Hong Kong SAR, China	7	0.6	6,696	12	*219.2*	*31,420*	*307.5*	*44,070*	*1.6*	79	86	..
Colombia	6	1.5	41	29	225.2	4,930	388.1	8,500	–0.9	69	77	93
Congo, Dem. Rep.	6	2.9	28	47	10.7	160	19.6	300	0.0	46	49	67
Congo, Rep.	4	2.1	11	40	6.7	1,830	10.8	2,940	5.6	53	55	..
Costa Rica	5	1.7	89	26	28.5	6,230	50.1[c]	10,940[c]	–2.8	77	81	96
Côte d'Ivoire	21	2.2	65	41	22.4	1,060	34.5	1,640	1.4	56	59	55
Croatia	4	0.0	82	15	61.2	13,810	84.9	19,170	–5.8	72	80	99
Czech Republic	10	0.2	135	14	181.5	17,310	247.7	23,610	–4.8	74	81	..
Denmark	6	0.4	129	18	325.8	58,930	208.5	37,720	–5.5	77	81	..
Dominican Republic	0	1.5	206	31	45.5	4,510	81.8[c]	8,100[c]	2.0	70	75	*88*
Ecuador	4	1.1	49	31	53.4	3,920	109.5	8,040	–0.7	72	78	*84*
Egypt, Arab Rep.	3	1.9	82	32	172.0	2,070	471.9	5,690	2.8	68	72	*66*
El Salvador	6	0.4	296	32	20.8	3,370	39.2[c]	6,360[c]	–3.0	67	76	84
Eritrea	5	3.6	49	42	*1.5*	*300*	*3.1*[c]	*640*[c]	*–1.0*	57	62	65
Ethiopia	83	2.6	81	44	27.0	330	77.4	930	5.9	54	57	36
Finland	5	0.3	17	17	243.9	45,680	183.8	34,430	–8.2	76	83	..
France	63[d]	0.7[d]	114[d]	18	2,754.6	42,680	2,192.9	33,980	–3.2	78	85	..
Georgia	4	–1.2	62	17	11.1[e]	2,530[e]	20.6[e]	4,700[e]	–4.1[e]	68	75	100
Germany	82	0.0	235	14	3,484.7	42,560	3,026.7	36,960	–4.7	78	83	..
Ghana	4	2.2	103	38	16.6	700	35.3	1,480	1.4	56	58	66
Greece	1	0.4	87	14	323.1	28,630	320.8	28,440	–2.4	78	82	97
Guatemala	4	2.5	128	42	36.8	2,620	64.4[c]	4,590[c]	–2.1	67	74	74
Guinea	0	2.0	40	43	3.8	370	9.5	940	–2.6	56	60	38
Haiti	0	1.7	358	36	..	..[f]	..	..	1.3	59	63	..
Honduras	7	2.0	65	37	13.6	1,820	27.9[c]	3,730[c]	–3.9	70	75	*84*
Hungary	10	–0.2	112	15	130.1	12,980	186.1	18,570	–6.2	70	78	99
India	1,155	1.4	383	31	1,368.7	1,180	3,768.1	3,260	6.2	62	65	*63*
Indonesia	230	1.3	125	27	513.4	2,230	933.2	4,060	3.4	69	73	*92*
Iran, Islamic Rep.	73	1.5	44	24	330.6	4,530	837.7	11,490	0.5	70	73	*82*
Iraq	1	2.5	70	41	69.7	2,210	105.1	3,340	1.6	64	72	78
Ireland	4	1.7	64	21	197.2	44,310	148.1	33,280	–6.5	78	82	..
Israel	7	1.9	338	28	191.6	25,740	201.2	27,040	–1.1	79	83	..
Italy	0	0.6	203	14	2,112.5	35,080	1,886.6	31,330	–5.7	79	85	99
Japan	8	0.1	350	13	4,830.3	37,870	4,245.7	33,280	–5.1	79	86	..
Jordan	6	2.4	66	34	22.3	3,740	34.8	5,840	0.4	71	75	*92*
Kazakhstan	16	0.7	6	24	107.1	6,740	163.2	10,270	–0.2	61	72	100
Kenya	40	2.6	68	43	30.7	770	62.7	1,570	–0.5	54	55	87
Korea, Rep.	49	0.4	502	17	966.6	19,830	1,331.4	27,310	–0.1	77	83	..
Kyrgyz Republic	5	0.9	28	29	4.6	870	11.7	2,200	1.5	63	72	99
Lao PDR	6	1.7	27	38	5.6	880	13.9	2,210	4.5	64	66	*73*
Lebanon	4	1.3	410	25	33.6	7,970	55.9	13,230	7.2	70	74	*90*
Liberia	4	3.7	39	43	0.6	160	1.2	290	0.3	57	60	58
Libya	6	2.0	4	30	77.2	12,020	105.5[c]	16,430[c]	0.1	72	77	88
Lithuania	3	–0.5	54	15	38.1	11,410	55.9	16,740	–14.6	66	78	100
Madagascar	20	2.8	33	43	*7.9*	*420*	*20.1*	*1,050*	–2.2	59	62	71
Malawi	15	2.8	158	46	4.2	280	11.6	760	4.8	52	54	73
Malaysia	27	1.8	82	29	198.7	7,230	371.8	13,530	–3.3	72	77	92
Mali	13	2.4	10	44	8.9	680	15.4	1,190	1.9	48	49	*26*
Mauritania	3	2.6	3	39	3.2	960	6.5	1,960	–3.4	55	59	57
Mexico	107	1.0	55	28	958.8	8,920	1,515.5	14,110	–7.5	73	78	93

Table 1. Key indicators of development *(continued)*

	Population			Population age composition	Gross national income (GNI)[a]		PPP national income (GNI)[b]		Gross domestic product	Life expectancy at birth		Adult literacy rate
	Millions	Average annual % growth	Density people per sq. km	% ages 0–14	$ billions	$ per capita	$ billions	$ per capita	per capita % growth	Male Years	Female Years	% ages 15 and older
	2009	2000–09	2009	2009	2009	2009	2009	2009	2008–09	2008	2008	2008
Moldova	4	–1.4	110	17	5.7[g]	1,590[g]	10.9[g]	3,060[g]	–6.4[g]	65	72	98
Morocco	32	1.2	71	28	90.7[h]	2,790[h]	144.8[h]	4,450[h]	3.7[h]	69	74	56
Mozambique	23	2.5	28	44	10.0	440	20.1	880	3.9	47	49	54
Myanmar	50	0.8	76	27	..	..[f]	..	..	11.8	59	64	92
Nepal	29	2.0	201	37	13.0	440	34.7	1,180	2.8	66	67	58
Netherlands	17	0.4	487	18	815.8	49,350	669.6	40,510	–4.5	78	82	..
New Zealand	4	1.2	16	20	*114.5*	*26,830*	*112.8*	*26,430*	–1.6	78	82	..
Nicaragua	6	1.3	47	35	5.8	1,000	14.1[c]	2,450[c]	–2.3	70	76	*78*
Niger	15	3.6	12	50	5.2	340	10.1	660	–2.9	51	52	*29*
Nigeria	155	2.4	166	43	175.8	1,140	305.7	1,980	0.6	47	48	60
Norway	5	0.8	16	19	417.3	86,440	270.6	56,050	–2.8	78	83	..
Pakistan	170	2.3	215	37	172.9	1,020	459.4	2,710	1.5	66	67	54
Panama	3	1.7	46	29	23.2	6,710	43.3[c]	12,530[c]	0.8	73	78	94
Papua New Guinea	7	2.5	15	40	7.9	1,180	15.3[c]	2,270[c]	2.1	59	63	60
Paraguay	6	1.9	16	34	14.4	2,270	28.1	4,430	–5.5	70	74	*95*
Peru	29	1.3	23	30	120.9	4,150	237.5	8,140	–0.2	71	76	*90*
Philippines	92	1.9	303	34	164.5	1,790	326.1	3,540	–0.9	70	74	94
Poland	38	–0.1	125	15	467.5	12,260	703.5	18,440	1.6	71	80	100
Portugal	11	0.4	116	15	222.6	20,940	243.1	22,870	–2.8	76	82	95
Romania	21	–0.5	94	15	178.9	8,330	310.6	14,460	–8.4	70	77	98
Russian Federation	142	–0.3	9	15	1,329.7	9,370	2,609.0	18,390	–7.8	62	74	100
Rwanda	10	2.5	394	42	4.6	460	10.6	1,060	2.4	48	52	70
Saudi Arabia	25	2.3	12	32	*439.0*	*17,700*	*595.4*	*24,000*	–2.2	71	75	86
Senegal	13	2.6	63	44	12.9	1,030	22.4	1,790	–1.1	54	57	*42*
Serbia	7	–0.3	83	18	43.8	5,990	83.6	11,420	–2.5	71	76	..
Sierra Leone	6	3.3	78	43	1.9	340	4.5	790	1.5	46	49	40
Singapore	5	2.4	6,943	16	185.7	37,220	248.6	49,850	–4.2	78	83	95
Slovak Republic	5	0.1	112	15	87.4	16,130	117.1	21,600	–6.4	71	79	..
Somalia	9	2.3	14	45	..	..[f]	..	..	..	48	51	..
South Africa	49	1.3	40	31	284.5	5,770	496.4	10,060	–2.8	50	53	89
Spain	46	1.5	91	15	1,464.7	31,870	1,453.6	31,630	–4.5	78	84	98
Sri Lanka	20	0.9	312	24	40.4	1,990	95.9	4,720	2.8	70	78	91
Sudan	42	2.1	17	39	51.6	1,220	84.6	2,000	1.7	57	60	69
Sweden	9	0.5	22	17	455.2	48,930	358.7	38,560	–5.7	79	83	..
Switzerland	8	0.8	191	15	*431.1*	*56,370*	*319.9*	*41,830*	*0.5*	80	85	..
Syrian Arab Republic	21	2.7	112	35	50.9	2,410	97.5	4,620	1.5	72	76	84
Tajikistan	7	1.3	49	37	4.8	700	13.5	1,950	1.7	64	69	100
Tanzania	44	2.8	48	45	21.3[i]	500[i]	57.5[i]	1,350[i]	2.5[i]	55	56	73
Thailand	68	0.9	132	22	254.7	3,760	518.0	7,640	–2.8	66	72	*94*
Togo	7	2.6	119	40	2.9	440	5.6	850	0.0	61	64	65
Tunisia	10	1.0	66	23	38.8	3,720	81.5	7,820	2.1	72	76	78
Turkey	75	1.3	96	27	653.1	8,730	1,027.3	13,730	–5.9	70	74	*89*
Turkmenistan	5	1.4	11	29	17.5	3,420	35.7[c]	6,990[c]	6.6	61	69	100
Uganda	33	3.2	161	49	15.0	460	39.0	1,190	3.6	52	53	75
Ukraine	46	–0.7	80	14	128.8	2,800	284.8	6,190	–14.6	63	74	100
United Arab Emirates	5	3.9	54	19	..	..[j]	..	..	–3.2	77	79	*90*
United Kingdom	62	0.5	254	17	2,567.5	41,520	2,310.5	37,360	–5.6	78	82	..
United States	307	0.9	33	20	14,502.6	47,240	14,345.3	46,730	–3.3	76	81	..
Uruguay	3	0.1	19	23	31.3	9,360	43.2	12,910	2.5	72	80	98
Uzbekistan	28	1.3	64	29	30.5	1,100	80.2[c]	2,890[c]	6.3	65	71	99
Venezuela, RB	28	1.7	32	30	288.1	10,150	351.1	12,370	–4.8	71	77	*95*
Vietnam	87	1.3	278	26	88.0	1,010	249.1	2,850	4.2	72	76	93
West Bank and Gaza	4	3.3	654	45	..	..[k]	..	..	..	72	75	94
Yemen, Rep.	24	2.9	43	44	25.0	1,060	55.1	2,340	0.8	61	65	61
Zambia	13	2.4	17	46	12.6	970	16.5	1,280	3.7	45	46	71
Zimbabwe	13	0.1	32	40	..	..[f]	..	..	..	44	45	91
World	**6,775s**	**1.2w**	**52w**	**27w**	**59,219.0t**	**8,741w**	**72,038.7t**	**10,633w**	**–3.0w**	**67w**	**71w**	**83w**
Low income	846	2.2	48	39	425.7	503	1,014.5	1,199	2.5	56	58	66
Middle income	4,813	1.2	61	27	16,231.0	3,373	30,593.8	6,357	1.4	67	71	83
Lower middle income	3,811	1.2	122	28	8,757.7	2,298	18,130.0	4,758	5.6	66	70	80
Upper middle income	1,002	0.9	21	25	7,483.6	7,471	12,500.6	12,479	–3.4	68	75	93
Low and middle income	5,659	1.3	58	29	16,671.5	2,946	31,607.3	5,586	1.3	65	69	80
East Asia & Pacific	1,944	0.8	122	23	6,109.6	3,143	11,640.7	5,989	6.6	70	74	93
Europe & Central Asia	404	0.1	18	19	2,746.1	6,793	5,104.6	12,628	–6.2	65	74	98
Latin America & the Caribbean	572	1.2	28	28	3,970.9	6,936	5,920.5	10,342	–2.9	70	77	91
Middle East & North Africa	331	1.8	38	31	1,189.2	3,594	2,623.1	7,927	1.6	69	73	74
South Asia	1,568	1.6	324	32	1,704.9	1,088	4,658.6	2,972	5.4	63	65	61
Sub-Saharan Africa	840	2.5	35	43	919.8	1,096	1,675.7	1,996	–1.2	51	53	62
High income	1,117	0.7	33	17	42,583.9	38,139	40,723.8	36,473	–3.9	77	83	98

Note: For data comparability and coverage, see the technical notes. Figures in italics are for years other than those specified.

a. Calculated using the World Bank Atlas method. b. PPP is purchasing power parity; see the technical notes. c. The estimate is based on regression; others are extrapolated from the latest International Comparison Program benchmark estimates. d. Data exclude the French overseas departments of French Guiana, Guadeloupe, Martinique, and Réunion. e. Data exclude Abkhazia and South Ossetia. f. Estimated to be low income (US$995 or less). g. Excludes data for Transnistria. h. Data include Former Spanish Sahara i. Data refer to mainland Tanzania only.
j. Estimated to be high income (US$12,196 or more). k. Estimated to be lower middle income (US$996–3,945).

Table 2 Poverty

	National poverty line				International poverty line							
	Population below national poverty line											
	Survey year	National %	Survey year	National %	Survey year	Population below $1.25 a day %	Poverty gap at $1.25 a day %	Population below $2.00 a day %	Survey year	Population below $1.25 a day %	Poverty gap at $1.25 a day %	Population below $2.00 a day %
Afghanistan	2007	42.0		..		..	..	..		..	..	..
Albania	2002	25.4	2005	18.5	2002[a]	<2	<0.5	8.7	2005[a]	<2	<0.5	7.8
Algeria	1988	12.2	1995	22.6	1988[a]	6.6	1.8	23.8	1995[a]	6.8	1.4	23.6
Angola		..		..	2000[a]	54.3	29.9	70.2		..	..	..
Argentina		..		..	2005[b, c]	4.5	1	11.3	2006[b, c]	3.4	1.2	7.3
Armenia	1998–99	55.1	2001	50.9	2003[a]	10.6	1.9	43.4	2007[a]	3.7	0.7	21
Australia		..		..	2001[a]	6.3	1.1	27.1	2005[a]	<2	<0.5	<2
Austria		..		..		..	..	..		..	..	..
Azerbaijan	1995	68.1	2001	49.6		..	..	..		..	..	..
Bangladesh	2000	48.9	2005	40.0	2000[a]	57.8[d]	17.3[d]	85.4[d]	2005[a]	49.6[d]	13.1[d]	81.3[d]
Belarus	2002	30.5	2004	17.4	2005[a]	<2	<0.5	<2	2007[a]	<2	<0.5	<2
Belgium		..		..		..	..	..		..	..	..
Benin	1999	29.0	2003	39.0	2003[a]	47.3	15.7	75.3		..	..	..
Bolivia	2000	45.2	2007	37.7	2005[c]	19.6	9.7	30.3	2007[c]	11.9	5.6	21.9
Bosnia and Herzegovina	2001–02	19.5		..	2004[a]	<2	<0.5	<2	2007[a]	<2	<0.5	<2
Brazil	1998	22.0	2002–03	21.5	2005[c]	7.8	1.6	18.3	2007[c]	5.2	1.3	12.7
Bulgaria	1997	36.0	2001	12.8	2001[a]	2.6	<0.5	7.8	2003[a]	<2	<0.5	<2
Burkina Faso	1998	54.6	2003	46.4	1998[a]	70	30.2	87.6	2003[a]	56.5	20.3	81.2
Burundi	1998	68.0		..	1998[a]	86.4	47.3	95.4	2006[a]	81.3	36.4	93.4
Cambodia	2004	34.7	2007	30.1	2004[a]	40.2	11.3	68.2	2007[a]	25.8	6.1	57.8
Cameroon	2001	40.2[e]	2007	39.9[e]	1996[a]	51.5	18.9	74.4	2001[a]	32.8	10.2	57.7
Canada		..		..		..	..	..		..	..	..
Central African Republic		..		..	1993[a]	82.8	57	90.7	2003[a]	62.4	28.3	81.9
Chad	1995–96	43.4		..	2002–03[a]	61.9	25.6	83.3		..	..	..
Chile	2003	18.7[e]	2006	13.7[e]	2003[c]	<2	<0.5	5.3	2006[c]	<2	<0.5	2.4
China												
Hong Kong		..		..	2002[a]	28.4[f]	8.7[f]	51.1[f]	2005[a]	15.9[f]	4[f]	36.3[f]
SAR, China		..		..		..	..	..		..	..	..
Colombia	2002	55.7	2006	45.1	2003[c]	15.4	6.1	26.3	2006[c]	16	5.7	27.9
Congo, Dem. Rep.	2004–05	71.3		..	2005–06[a]	59.2	25.3	79.5		..	..	..
Congo, Rep.	2005	42.3		..	2005[a]	54.1	22.8	74.4		..	..	..
Costa Rica	1989	31.7	2004	23.9	2005[c]	2.4	<0.5	8.6	2007[c]	<2	<0.5	4.3
Côte d'Ivoire		..		..	1998[a]	24.1	6.7	49.1	2002	23.3	6.8	46.8
Croatia	2002	11.2	2004	11.1	2001[a]	<2	<0.5	<2	2005[a]	<2	<0.5	<2
Czech Republic		..		..	1993[c]	<2	<0.5	<2	1996[c]	<2	<0.5	<2
Denmark		..		..		..	..	..		..	..	..
Dominican Republic	2000	36.5[e]	2007	48.5[e]	2005[c]	5	0.9	15.1	2007[c]	4.4	1.3	12.3
Ecuador	1999	52.2[e]	2006	38.3[e]	2005[c]	9.8	3.2	20.4	2007[c]	4.7	1.2	12.8
Egypt, Arab Rep.	1995–96	22.9	1999–2000	16.7	1999–00[a]	<2	<0.5	19.3	2004–05[a]	<2	<0.5	18.4
El Salvador	2000	38.8[e, g]	2006	30.7[e, g]	2005[c]	11	4.8	20.5	2007[c]	6.4	2.7	13.2
Eritrea	1993–94	53.0		..		..	..	..		..	..	..
Ethiopia	1995–96	45.5	1999–2000	44.2	1999–00[a]	55.6	16.2	86.4	2005[a]	39	9.6	77.5
Finland		..		..		..	..	..		..	..	..
France		..		..		..	..	..		..	..	..
Georgia	2002	52.1	2003	54.5	2002[a]	15.1	4.7	34.2	2005[a]	13.4	4.4	30.4
Germany		..		..		..	..	..		..	..	..
Ghana	1998–99	39.5	2005–06	28.5	1998–99[a]	39.1	14.4	63.3	2006[a]	30	10.5	53.6
Greece		..		..		..	..	..		..	..	..
Guatemala	2000	56.2	2006	51.0	2002[c]	16.9	6.5	29.8	2006[c]	11.7	3.5	24.3
Guinea	1994	40.0		..	1994[a]	36.8	11.5	63.8	2003[a]	70.1	32.2	87.2
Haiti	1987	65.0	1995	..	2001[c]	54.9	28.2	72.1		..	..	..
Honduras	1998–99	52.5	2004	50.7	2005[c]	22.2	10.2	34.8	2006[c]	18.2	8.2	29.7
Hungary	1993	14.5	1997	17.3	2002[a]	<2	<0.5	<2	2004[a]	<2	<0.5	<2
India	1993–94	36.0	1999–2000	28.6	1993–94[a]	49.4[f]	14.4[f]	81.7[f]	2004–05[a]	41.6[f]	10.8[f]	75.6[f]
Indonesia	1996	17.6	2004	16.7	2005[a]	21.4[f]	4.6[f]	53.8[f]	2007[a]	29.4	7.1	60
Iran, Islamic Rep.		..		..	1998[a]	<2	<0.5	8.3	2005[a]	<2	<0.5	8
Iraq		..		..		..	..	..		..	..	..
Ireland		..		..		..	..	..		..	..	..
Israel		..		..		..	..	..		..	..	..
Italy		..		..		..	..	..		..	..	..
Japan		..		..		..	..	..		..	..	..
Jordan	1997	21.3	2002	14.2	2002–03[a]	<2	<0.5	11	2006[a]	<2	<0.5	3.5
Kazakhstan	2001	17.6	2002	15.4	2003[a]	3.1	<0.5	17.2	2007[a]	<2	<0.5	<2
Kenya	1997	52.0	2005/06	46.6	1997[a]	19.6	4.6	42.7	2005–06[a]	19.7	6.1	39.9
Korea, Rep.		..		..		..	..	..		..	..	..
Kyrgyz Republic	2003	49.9	2005	43.1	2004[a]	21.8	4.4	51.9	2007[a]	3.4	<0.5	27.5
Lao PDR	1997–98	38.6	2002–03	33.5	1997–98[a]	49.3[d]	14.9[d]	79.9[d]	2002–03[a]	44[d]	12.1[d]	76.8[d]
Lebanon		..		..		..	..	..		..	..	..
Liberia		..		..	2007[a]	83.7	40.8	94.8		..	..	..
Libya		..		..		..	..	..		..	..	..

Table 2 Poverty *(continued)*

	National poverty line				International poverty line							
	Population below national poverty line											
	Survey year	National %	Survey year	National %	Survey year	Population below $1.25 a day %	Poverty gap at $1.25 a day %	Population below $2.00 a day %	Survey year	Population below $1.25 a day %	Poverty gap at $1.25 a day %	Population below $2.00 a day %
Lithuania		..		..	2002[a]	<2	<0.5	<2	2004[a]	<2	<0.5	<2
Madagascar	1999	71.3[e]	2005	68.7[e]	2001[a]	76.3	41.4	88.7	2005[a]	67.8	26.5	89.6
Malawi	1997–98	65.3	2004–05	52.4	1997–98[a]	83.1	46	93.5	2004–05[a, h]	73.9	32.3	90.4
Malaysia	1989	15.5		..	1997[c]	<2	<0.5	6.8	2004[c]	<2	<0.5	7.8
Mali	1998	63.8		..	2001[a]	61.2	25.8	82	2006[a]	51.4	18.8	77.1
Mauritania	1996	50.0	2000	46.3	1995–96[a]	23.4	7.1	48.3	2000[a]	21.2	5.7	44.1
Mexico	2002	50.6	2004	47.0	2006[a]	<2	<0.5	4.8	2008[c]	4	1.8	8.2
Moldova	2001	62.4	2002	48.5	2004[a]	8.1	1.7	28.9	2007[a]	2.4	0.5	11.5
Morocco	1990–91	13.1	1998–99	19.0	2000[a]	6.3	0.9	24.3	2007[a]	2.5	0.5	14
Mozambique	1996–97	69.4	2002–03	55.2	1996–97[a]	81.3	42	92.9	2002–03[a]	74.7	35.4	90
Myanmar	2004–05	32.0		..		..	..	..		..	..	..
Nepal	1995–96	41.8	2003–04	30.9	1995–96[a]	68.4	26.7	88.1	2003–04[a]	55.1	19.7	77.6
Netherlands		..		..		..	..	..		..	..	..
New Zealand		..		..		..	..	..		..	..	..
Nicaragua	1998	47.9	2001	45.8	2001[c]	19.4	6.7	37.5	2005[c]	15.8	5.2	31.8
Niger	1989–93	63.0		..	1994[a]	78.2	38.6	91.5	2005[a]	65.9	28.1	85.6
Nigeria	1985	43.0	1992–93	34.1	1996–97[a]	68.5	32.1	86.4	2003–04[a]	64.4	29.6	83.9
Norway		..		..		..	..	..		..	..	..
Pakistan	1993	28.6	1998–99	32.6	2001–02[a]	35.9	7.9	73.9	2004–05[a]	22.6	4.4	60.3
Panama	1997	37.3	2003	36.8	2004[c]	9.2	2.7	18	2006[c]	9.5	3.1	17.8
Papua New Guinea	1996	37.5		..	1996[a]	35.8	12.3	57.4		..	..	..
Paraguay	1990	20.5[i]		..	2005[c]	9.3	3.4	18.4	2007[c]	6.5	2.7	14.2
Peru	2003	52.2	2004	51.6	2005[c]	8.2	2	19.4	2007[c]	7.7	2.3	17.8
Philippines	1994	32.1	1997	25.1	2003[a]	22	5.5	43.8	2006[a]	22.6	5.5	45
Poland	1996	14.6	2001	14.8	2002[a]	<2	<0.5	<2	2005[a]	<2	<0.5	<2
Portugal		..		..		..	..	..		..	..	..
Romania	1995	25.4	2002	28.9	2002[a]	2.9	0.8	13	2007[a]	<2	<0.5	4.1
Russian Federation	1998	31.4	2002	19.6	2002[a]	<2	<0.5	3.7	2007[a]	<2	<0.5	<2
Rwanda	1999–2000	60.3[e]	2005–06	56.9[e]	1984–85[a]	63.3	19.7	88.4	2000[a]	76.6	38.2	90.3
Saudi Arabia		..		..		..	..	..		..	..	..
Senegal	1992	33.4		..	2001[a]	44.2	14.3	71.3	2005[a]	33.5	10.8	60.3
Serbia		..		..	2003[a]	<2	<0.5	<2	2008[a]	<2	<0.5	<2
Sierra Leone	1989	82.8	2003–04	70.2	1989–90[a]	62.8	44.8	75	2003[a]	53.4	20.3	76.1
Singapore		..		..		..	..	..		..	..	..
Slovak Republic	2004	16.8		..	1992[c]	<2	<0.5	<2	1996[c]	<2	<0.5	<2
Somalia		..		..		..	..	..		..	..	..
South Africa	2000	38.0[e]	2008	22.0[e]	1995[a]	21.4	5.2	39.9	2000[a]	26.2	8.2	42.9
Spain		..		..		..	..	..		..	..	..
Sri Lanka	1995–96	25.0	2002	22.7	1995–96[a]	16.3	3	46.7	2002[a]	14	2.6	39.7
Sudan		..		..		..	..	..		..	..	..
Sweden		..		..		..	..	..		..	..	..
Switzerland		..		..		..	..	..		..	..	..
Syrian Arab Republic		..		..		..	..	..		..	..	..
Tajikistan	2003	72.4	2007	53.5	2003[a]	36.3	10.3	68.8	2004[a]	21.5	5.1	50.8
Tanzania	1991	38.6	2000–01	35.7	1991–92[a]	72.6	29.7	91.3	2000–01[a]	88.5	46.8	96.6
Thailand	1994	9.8	1998	13.6	2002[a]	<2	<0.5	15.1	2004[a]	<2	<0.5	11.5
Togo	1987–89	32.3		..	2006[a]	38.7	11.4	69.3		..	..	..
Tunisia	1990	7.4	1995	7.6	1995[a]	6.5	1.3	20.4	2000[a]	2.6	<0.5	12.8
Turkey	1994	28.3	2002	27.0	2002[a]	2	<0.5	9.6	2006[a]	2.6	<0.5	8.2
Turkmenistan		..		..	1993[c]	63.5	25.8	85.7	1998[a]	24.8	7	49.6
Uganda	2002–03	38.8[e]	2005–06	31.1[e]	2002[a]	57.4	22.7	79.8	2005[a]	51.5	19.1	75.6
Ukraine	2000	31.5	2003	19.5	2005[a]	<2	<0.5	<2	2008[a]	<2	<0.5	<2
United Arab Emirates		..		..		..	..	..		..	..	..
United Kingdom		..		..		..	..	..		..	..	..
United States		..		..		..	..	..		..	..	..
Uruguay		..		..	2005[b, c]	<2	<0.5	4.5	2007[c]	<2	<0.5	4.3
Uzbekistan	2000–01	31.5	2003	27.2		..	..	..		..	..	..
Venezuela, RB	1989	31.3	1997–99	52.0	2003[c]	18.4	8.8	31.7	2006[c]	3.5	1.2	10.2
Vietnam	1998	37.4	2002	28.9	2004[a]	24.2	5.1	52.5	2006[a]	21.5	4.6	48.4
West Bank and Gaza		..		..		..	..	..		..	..	..
Yemen, Rep.	1998	41.8		..	1998[a]	12.9	3	36.3	2005[a]	17.5	4.2	46.6
Zambia	1998	72.9	2004	68.0	2002–03[a]	64.6	27.1	85.1	2004–05[a]	64.3	32.8	81.5
Zimbabwe	1990–91	25.8	1995–96	34.9		..	..	..		..	..	..

Note: For data comparability and coverage, see the technical notes.

a. Expenditure base. b. Covers urban area only. c. Income base. d. Adjusted by spatial consumer price index information. e. Due to security concerns, the survey covered only 56 percent of rural villages and 65 percent of the rural population. f. Weighted average of urban and rural estimates. g. Covers rural area only. h. Due to change in survey design, the most recent survey is not strictly comparable with the previous one. i. Survey covers Asunción metropolitan area.

Table 3 Millennium Development Goals: Eradicating poverty and improving lives

	Eradicate extreme poverty and hunger			Achieve universal primary education	Promote gender equality	Reduce child mortality	Improve maternal health	Combat HIV/AIDS and other diseases		Ensure environmental sustainability		Develop a global partnership for development
	Share of poorest quintile in national consumption or income %	Vulnerable employment % of employment	Prevalence of child malnutrition % of children under age 5	Primary completion rate %	Ratio of girls to boys enrollments in primary and secondary school %	Under-five mortality rate per 1,000	Maternal mortality rate per 100,000 live births	HIV prevalence % of population ages 15–49	Incidence of tuberculosis per 100,000 people	Carbon dioxide emissions per capita metric tons	Access to improved sanitation facilities % of population	Internet users per 100 people[a]
	1995–2008[b]	2008	2000–08[b]	2008	2008	2009	2008	2007	2008	2007	2008	2008
Afghanistan	..	..	32.9	..	*58*	199	1,400	..	190	0.0	37	1.7
Albania	7.8[c]	..	6.6	..	..	15	31	..	16	1.4	98	23.9
Algeria	6.9[c]	..	11.1	114	..	32	120	0.1	58	4.1	95	11.9
Angola	2.0[c]	..	27.5	..	..	161	610	2.1	290	1.4	57	3.1
Argentina	3.6[d,e]	19[f]	2.3	*102*	*105*	14	70	0.5	30	4.6	90	28.1
Armenia	8.6[c]	..	4.2	*98*	104	22	29	0.1	73	1.6	90	6.2
Australia	..	*9*	..	..	97	5	8	0.2	7	17.7	100	70.8
Austria	8.6[e]	9	..	99	97	4	5	0.2	0	8.3	100	71.2
Azerbaijan	13.3[c]	*53*	8.4	121	98	34	38	0.2	110	3.7	45	28.2
Bangladesh	9.4[c]	..	41.3	54	*106*	52	340	..	220	0.3	53	0.3
Belarus	8.8[c]	..	1.3	96	*101*	12	15	0.2	43	6.9	93	32.1
Belgium	8.5[e]	10	..	86	98	5	5	0.2	9	9.7	100	68.1
Benin	6.9[c]	..	20.2	65	..	118	410	1.2	92	0.5	12	1.8
Bolivia	2.7[c]	..	5.9	*98*	*99*	51	180	0.2	140	1.4	25	10.8
Bosnia and Herzegovina	6.7[c]	..	1.6	..	102	14	9	<0.1	51	7.7	95	34.7
Brazil	3.0[e]	*27*	2.2	..	103	21	58	0.6	46	1.9	80	37.5
Bulgaria	8.7[c]	9	1.6	90	97	10	13	..	43	6.8	100	34.7
Burkina Faso	7.0[c]	..	37.4	38	85[g]	166	560	1.6	220	0.1	11	0.9
Burundi	9.0[c]	..	38.9	45	91	166	970	2.0	360	0.0	46	0.8
Cambodia	6.5[c]	..	28.8	79	*90*	88	290	0.8	490	0.3	29	0.5
Cameroon	5.6[c]	..	16.6	73	84	154	600	5.1	190	0.3	47	3.8
Canada	7.2[e]	*10*[f]	..	*96*	*99*	6	12	0.4	5	16.9	100	75.3
Central African Republic	5.2[c]	..	21.8	35	69	171	850	6.3	340	0.1	34	0.4
Chad	6.3[c]	..	33.9	*31*	*64*	209	1,200	3.5	290	0.0	9	1.2
Chile	4.1[e]	24	0.5	*95*	*99*	9	26	0.3	11	4.3	96	32.5
China	5.7[e]	..	6.8	96	104	19	38	0.1[h]	97	5.0	55	22.5
Hong Kong SAR, China	5.3[e]	7	..	..	..	..	..	..	91	5.8	..	67.0
Colombia	2.3[e]	46	5.1	110	104	19	85	0.6	36	1.4	74	38.5
Congo, Dem. Rep.	5.5[c]	..	28.2	53	76	199	670	..	380	0.0	23	..
Congo, Rep.	5.0[c]	..	11.8	73	..	128	580	3.5	390	0.4	30	4.3
Costa Rica	4.4[e]	*20*	..	93	102	11	44	0.4	11	1.8	95	32.3
Côte d'Ivoire	5.0[c]	..	16.7	48	..	119	470	3.9	410	0.3	23	3.2
Croatia	8.8[c]	*16*[f]	..	*102*	*102*	5	14	<0.1	25	5.6	99	50.5
Czech Republic	10.2[e]	13	2.1	95	101	4	8	..	9	12.1	98	57.8
Denmark	8.3[e]	5	..	*101*	*102*	4	5	0.2	7	9.1	100	83.3
Dominican Republic	4.4[e]	*42*	3.4	91	103	32	100	1.1	73	2.1	83	21.6
Ecuador	3.4[e]	*34*[f]	6.2	106	100	24	140	0.3	72	2.2	92	28.8
Egypt, Arab Rep.	9.0[c]	*25*	6.8	*95*	..	21	82	..	20	2.3	94	16.6
El Salvador	4.3[e]	*36*	6.1	89	98	17	110	0.8	32	1.1	87	10.6
Eritrea	..	..	34.5	47	77	55	280	1.3	97	0.1	14	4.1
Ethiopia	9.3[c]	*52*[f]	34.6	52	85	104	470	2.1	370	0.1	12	0.4
Finland	9.6[e]	9	..	98	102	3	8	0.1	7	12.1	100	82.5
France	7.2[e]	6	..	..	100	4	8	0.4	6	6.0	100	67.9
Georgia	5.4[c]	*62*	2.3	100	96	29	48	0.1	110	1.4	95	23.8
Germany	8.5[e]	7	1.1	104	98	4	7	0.1	5	9.6	100	75.5
Ghana	5.2[c]	..	13.9	82	96	69	350	1.9	200	0.4	13	4.3
Greece	6.7[e]	27	..	*101*	*97*	3	2	0.2	6	8.8	98	43.1
Guatemala	3.4[e]	..	17.7	80	94	40	110	0.8	63	1.0	81	14.3
Guinea	5.8[c]	..	22.5	55	77	142	680	1.6	300	0.1	19	0.9
Haiti	2.5[e]	..	18.9	..	..	87	300	2.2	250	0.2	17	10.1
Honduras	2.5[e]	..	8.6	90	107	30	110	0.7	64	1.2	71	13.1
Hungary	8.6[c]	7	..	95	98	6	13	0.1	16	5.6	100	58.5
India	8.1[c]	..	43.5	*94*	*92*	66	230	0.3	170	1.4	31	4.5
Indonesia	7.4[c]	*63*	19.6	106	98	39	240	0.2	190	1.8	52	7.9
Iran, Islamic Rep.	6.4[c]	*43*	..	*117*	116	31	30	0.2	20	7.0	..	32.0
Iraq	..	..	7.1	..	..	44	75	..	64	3.3	73	1.0
Ireland	7.4[e]	12	..	99	103	4	3	0.2	9	10.2	99	62.7
Israel	5.7[e]	7	..	99	101	4	7	0.1	6	9.3	100	47.9
Italy	6.5[e]	19	..	*101*	*99*	4	5	0.4	7	7.7	..	41.8
Japan	..	*11*	..	..	100	3	6	..	22	9.8	100	75.2
Jordan	7.2[c]	..	3.6	100	102	25	59	..	6	3.8	98	27.4
Kazakhstan	8.7[c]	..	4.9	105[g]	98[g]	29	45	0.1	180	14.7	97	10.9
Kenya	4.7[c]	..	16.5	..	96	84	530	..	330	0.3	31	8.7
Korea, Rep.	7.9[e]	*25*	..	99	97	5	18	<0.1	88	10.4	100	75.8
Kyrgyz Republic	8.8[c]	*47*	2.7	92	100	37	81	0.1	160	1.2	93	16.1
Lao PDR	8.5[c]	..	31.6	75	87	59	580	0.2	150	0.3	53	8.5
Lebanon	..	..	4.2	87	103	12	26	0.1	14	3.2	..	22.5
Liberia	6.4[c]	..	20.4	58	86	112	990	1.7	280	0.2	17	0.5
Libya	..	..	5.6	..	*105*	19	64	..	17	9.3	97	5.1
Lithuania	6.8[c]	9	..	92	100	6	13	0.1	71	4.5	..	54.4
Madagascar	6.2[c]	..	36.8	71	97	58	440	0.1	260	0.1	11	1.7
Malawi	7.0[c]	..	15.5	*54*	99	110	510	11.9	320	0.1	56	2.1
Malaysia	6.4[e]	*22*	..	*96*	*103*	6	31	0.5	100	7.3	96	55.8
Mali	6.5[c]	..	27.9	57	78	191	830	1.5	320	0.0	36	1.6
Mauritania	6.2[c]	..	23.2	64	*103*	117	550	0.8	320	0.6	26	1.9
Mexico	3.8[c]	*30*	3.4	104	102	17	85	0.3	19	4.5	85	22.2

Table 3 Millennium Development Goals: Eradicating poverty and improving lives *(continued)*

	Eradicate extreme poverty and hunger			Achieve universal primary education	Promote gender equality	Reduce child mortality	Improve maternal health	Combat HIV/AIDS and other diseases		Ensure environmental sustainability		Develop a global partnership for development
	Share of poorest quintile in national consumption or income %	Vulnerable employment % of employment	Prevalence of child malnutrition % of children under age 5	Primary completion rate %	Ratio of girls to boys enrollments in primary and secondary school %	Under-five mortality rate per 1,000	Maternal mortality rate per 100,000 live births	HIV prevalence % of population ages 15–49	Incidence of tuberculosis per 100,000 people	Carbon dioxide emissions per capita metric tons	Access to improved sanitation facilities % of population	Internet users per 100 people[a]
	1995–2008[b]	2008	2000–08[b]	2008	2008	2009	2008	2007	2008	2007	2008	2008
Moldova	6.7[c]	*32*	3.2	91	102	17	32	0.4	170	1.3	79	23.4
Morocco	6.5[c]	*51*	9.9	81	*88*	38	110	0.1	120	1.5	69	33.0
Mozambique	5.4[c]	..	21.2	59	87	142	550	12.5	420	0.1	17	1.6
Myanmar	..	..	29.6	99	*99*	71	240	0.7	400	0.3	81	0.2
Nepal	6.1[c]	..	38.8	..	..	48	380	0.5	160	0.1	31	1.7
Netherlands	7.6[e]	9	..	..	98	4	9	0.2	7	10.6	100	87.0
New Zealand	6.4[e]	*12*	..	..	103	6	14	0.1	8	7.7	..	71.4
Nicaragua	3.8[e]	*45*	4.3	75	102	26	100	0.2	46	0.8	52	3.3
Niger	5.9[c]	..	39.9	40[g]	74	160	820	0.8	180	0.1	9	0.5
Nigeria	5.1[c]	..	27.2	..	*85*	138	840	3.1	300	0.6	32	15.9
Norway	9.6[e]	6	..	98	99	3	7	0.1	6	9.1	100	82.5
Pakistan	9.1[c]	*62*	31.3	60	80	87	260	0.1	230	1.0	45	11.1
Panama	2.5[e]	*28*	..	102	101	23	71	1.0	47	2.2	69	27.5
Papua New Guinea	4.5[c]	..	18.1	..	..	68	250	1.5	250	0.5	45	1.8
Paraguay	3.4[e]	*47*	..	*95*	*99*	23	95	0.6	47	0.7	70	14.3
Peru	3.6[e]	*40*[f]	5.4	101	99	21	98	0.5	120	1.5	68	24.7
Philippines	5.6[c]	*45*	26.2	*92*	102	33	94	..	280	0.8	76	6.2
Poland	7.3[c]	19	..	*96*	*99*	7	6	0.1	25	8.3	90	49.0
Portugal	5.8[e]	19	..	..	*101*	4	7	0.5	30	5.5	100	42.1
Romania	7.9[c]	31	3.5	96	99	12	27	0.1	130	4.4	72	28.8
Russian Federation	5.6[c]	*6*	..	95	98	12	39	1.1	110	10.8	87	31.9
Rwanda	5.4[c]	..	18.0	54	100	111	540	2.8	390	0.1	54	3.1
Saudi Arabia	..	..	5.3	95	91	21	24	..	19	16.6	..	31.3
Senegal	6.2[c]	..	14.5	56	96	93	410	1.0	280	0.5	51	8.4
Serbia	9.1[c, i]	*23*	1.8	100	102	7	8	0.1	18	..[j]	92	44.9
Sierra Leone	6.1[c]	..	28.3	*88*	*84*	192	970	1.7	610	0.2	13	0.3
Singapore	5.0[e]	*10*	3.3	..	..	3	9	0.2	39	11.8	100	69.6
Slovak Republic	8.8[e]	11[f]	..	96	100	7	6	<0.1	12	6.8	100	66.0
Somalia	..	..	32.8	..	*53*	180	1,200	0.5	390	0.1	23	1.1
South Africa	3.1[c]	*3*	..	*86*	*100*	62	410	18.1	960	9.0	77	8.6
Spain	7.0[e]	12	..	107	103	4	6	0.5	17	8.0	100	55.4
Sri Lanka	6.8[c]	*41*[f]	21.1	98	..	15	39	..	66	0.6	91	5.8
Sudan	..	..	31.7	57[g]	89[g]	108	750	1.4	120	0.3	34	10.2
Sweden	9.1[e]	7	..	94	99	3	5	0.1	6	5.4	100	87.7
Switzerland	7.6[e]	*10*	..	94	97	4	10	0.6	5	5.0	100	75.9
Syrian Arab Republic	..	..	10.0	114	97	16	46	..	22	3.5	96	17.3
Tajikistan	7.8[c]	..	14.9	98	91	61	64	0.3	200	1.1	94	8.8
Tanzania	7.3[c]	*88*[f]	16.7	*83*	..	108	790	6.2	190	0.1	24	1.2
Thailand	6.1[c]	*53*	7.0	*87*	103	14	48	1.4	140	4.1	96	23.9
Togo	5.4[c]	..	22.3	*61*	*75*	98	350	3.3	440	0.2	12	5.4
Tunisia	5.9[c]	..	3.3	93	103	21	60	0.1	24	2.3	85	27.1
Turkey	5.4[c]	35	3.5	93	93	20	23	..	30	4.0	90	34.4
Turkmenistan	6.0[c]	..	..	..	..	45	77	<0.1	68	9.2	98	1.5
Uganda	6.1[c]	..	16.4	56	99	128	430	5.4	310	0.1	48	7.9
Ukraine	9.4[c]	..	4.1	99	99	15	26	1.6	100	6.8	95	10.5
United Arab Emirates	..	..	..	*105*	*101*	7	10	..	6	31.0	97	65.2
United Kingdom	6.1[e]	11	..	..	101	6	12	0.2	12	8.8	100	76.0
United States	5.4[e]	..	1.3	95	100	8	24	0.6	5	19.3	100	75.8
Uruguay	4.3[e]	*25*	6.0	*104*	*98*	13	27	0.6	22	1.9	100	40.2
Uzbekistan	7.1[c]	..	4.4	95	98	36	30	0.1	130	4.3	100	9.0
Venezuela, RB	4.9[e]	*30*	..	95	102	18	68	..	33	6.0	..	25.7
Vietnam	7.1[c]	..	20.2	..	..	24	56	0.5	200	1.3	75	24.2
West Bank and Gaza	..	*36*	2.2	82	104	30	..	..	19	0.6	89	9.0
Yemen, Rep.	7.2[c]	..	43.1	61	..	66	210	..	88	1.0	52	1.6
Zambia	3.6[c]	..	14.9	93	95	141	470	15.2	470	0.2	49	5.5
Zimbabwe	4.6[c]	..	14.0	..	*97*	90	790	15.3	760	0.8	44	11.4
World		..w	22.4w	88w	96w	61w	260w	0.8w	140w	4.6w	61w	23.9w
Low income		..	28.1	63	91	118	580	2.3	300	0.3	35	2.3
Middle income		..	22.2	92	97	51	200	0.6	140	3.3	57	17.0
Lower middle income		..	25.0	90	95	57	230	0.4	150	2.8	50	13.7
Upper middle income		26	..	100	101	22	82	1.5	100	5.3	84	29.9
Low and middle income		..	23.5	87	96	66	290	0.9	160	2.9	54	15.0
East Asia & Pacific		..	11.9	*99*	*102*	26	89	0.2	140	4.0	59	19.4
Europe & Central Asia		19	..	96	97	21	32	0.6	94	7.2	89	26.4
Latin America & the Caribbean		32	4.5	101	102	23	86	0.5	47	2.7	79	29.0
Middle East & North Africa		37	12.2	95	96	33	88	0.1	44	3.7	84	18.9
South Asia		..	41.0	*79*	*91*	71	290	0.3	180	1.2	36	4.7
Sub-Saharan Africa		..	25.2	64	88	130	650	5.0	350	0.8	31	6.5
High income		12	..	98	99	7	15	0.3	15	12.5	99	68.3

Note: For data comparability and coverage, see the technical notes. Figures in italics are for years other than those specified.

a. Data are from the International Telecommunication Union's (ITU) World Telecommunication Development Report database. Please cite ITU for third-party use of these data. b. Data are for the most recent year available. c. Refers to expenditure shares by percentiles of population, ranked by per capita expenditure. d. Urban data. e. Refers to income shares by percentiles of population, ranked by per capita income. f. Limited coverage. g. Data are for 2009. h. Includes Hong Kong SAR, China. i. Includes Montenegro. j. Includes Kosovo and Montenegro. k. Includes emissions not allocated to specific countries.

Table 4 Economic activity

	Gross domestic product		Agricultural productivity		Value added as % of GDP			Household final consumption expenditure	General government final consumption expenditure	Gross capital formation	External balance of goods and services	GDP implicit deflator average
		Average annual % growth	Agricultural value added per worker 2000 $		Agriculture	Industry	Services	% of GDP	% of GDP	% of GDP	% of GDP	Annual % growth
	2009	2000–09	1990–92	2005–07	2009	2009	2009	2009	2009	2009	2009	2000–09
Afghanistan	10,624	..	..	..	32	26	42	98	10	28	–36	6.9
Albania	11,834	5.3	837	1,663	21	20	59	84	10	29	–25	3.4
Algeria	140,577	4.0	1,823	2,232	12	55	34	41	14	41	4	8.6
Angola	69,067	13.1	176	222	10	54	36	..	..	17	9	40.5
Argentina	308,741	5.4	6,919	11,192	10	32	58	59	13	23	4	12.9
Armenia	8,714	10.5	1,607[a]	4,510	21	35	45	81	11	31	–24	4.5
Australia	924,843	3.3	20,676	30,830	3	29	68	57	17	28	–2	4.0
Austria	384,908	2.0	13,607	20,744	2	31	67	53	18	23	5	1.7
Azerbaijan	43,019	17.9	1,000[a]	1,198	8	60	32	37	14	22	28	9.9
Bangladesh	89,378	5.9	255	387	19	29	53	80	5	24	–10	5.2
Belarus	48,984	8.3	2,042[a]	4,017	10	45	45	57	15	38	–8	23.3
Belgium	468,552	1.7	..	35,974	1	23	76	54	23	24	–1	2.1
Benin	6,656	4.0	429	661	..	..	..	..	..	25	–14	3.4
Bolivia	17,340	4.1	703	732	12	29	58	74	11	18	–3	6.8
Bosnia and Herzegovina	17,122	5.0	..	10,352	9	27	64	85	20	20	–25	4.0
Brazil	1,571,979	3.6	1,611	3,315	7	27	66	64	20	17	0	8.1
Bulgaria	47,100	5.3	2,686	8,015	6	30	64	73	8	26	–8	5.8
Burkina Faso	8,141	5.4	126	182	33	22	44	75	22	18	–15	2.5
Burundi	1,325	3.0	117	70	..	..	..	91	29	16	–36	10.4
Cambodia	10,028	9.0	..	366	35	24	41	83	3	21	–8	4.8
Cameroon	21,837	3.4	409	703	19	31	50	72	9	18	–6	1.9
Canada	1,336,067	2.5	28,541	46,138	..	..	..	55	19	23	2	2.3
Central African Republic	2,006	0.8	322	404	56	15	30	93	4	11	–8	2.7
Chad	6,680	10.4	209	..	24	36	40	69	7	18	6	5.3
Chile	163,670	4.1	3,618	6,160	4	43	53	60	12	19	7	6.3
China	4,984,731	10.9	269	459	10	46	43	34	11	45	5	4.3
Hong Kong SAR, China	215,355	5.2	..	..	0	8	92	60	8	20	11	–1.7
Colombia	230,844	4.7	3,342	3,001	9	36	55	66	9	23	2	6.7
Congo, Dem. Rep.	10,779	5.2	209	162	43	24	33	74	8	30	–12	27.2
Congo, Rep.	8,695	4.0	..	..	5	68	27	40	14	26	21	6.1
Costa Rica	29,225	5.1	3,158	5,132	7	28	65	80	7	17	–3	10.2
Côte d'Ivoire	23,042	0.8	652	875	25	25	50	72	9	11	8	3.4
Croatia	63,034	3.9	5,545[a]	14,804	7	29	64	58	18	28	–4	3.9
Czech Republic	190,274	4.1	3,256	5,945	2	37	60	51	22	22	6	2.2
Denmark	309,596	1.2	15,190	34,613	1	26	73	49	27	22	2	2.3
Dominican Republic	46,598	5.5	2,055	3,829	6	30	64	94	6	8	–8	13.7
Ecuador	57,249	5.0	1,801	1,879	8	49	43	63	14	27	–4	9.1
Egypt, Arab Rep.	188,334	4.9	1,826	2,758	11	35	53	82	7	19	–8	8.3
El Salvador	22,174	2.6	1,774	2,404	14	27	59	92	11	13	–16	3.8
Eritrea	1,654	1.3	..	118	24	19	56	86	31	11	–28	18.0
Ethiopia	28,537	8.5	..	187	47	14	39	88	10	20	–18	10.8
Finland	237,512	2.5	19,011	35,783	3	33	64	52	22	22	4	1.0
France	2,649,390	1.5	22,126	47,679	2	20	78	57	23	22	–2	2.1
Georgia	10,737	7.4	2,359[a]	1,871	10	21	69	82	15	29	–23	7.0
Germany	3,346,702	0.9	13,863	27,015	1	30	69	56	18	19	6	1.1
Ghana	15,619	5.6	352	388	33	25	42	74	19	30	–25	18.3
Greece	329,924	3.6	7,668	8,383	3	20	77	71	17	21	–9	3.1
Guatemala	36,788	3.8	2,304	2,736	11	29	59	89	6	15	–11	5.2
Guinea	4,103	2.5	156	311	11	33	57	84	5	14	–3	20.1
Haiti	6,693	0.7	..	..	..	..	..	..	..	29	–29	15.2
Honduras	14,632	4.9	1,227	1,842	13	31	55	83	21	34	–30	6.6
Hungary	128,964	2.9	3,943	8,136	4	29	66	67	9	22	1	4.9
India	1,310,171	7.8	359	530	17	28	55	58	12	35	–5	5.3
Indonesia	540,277	5.3	519	657	14	47	39	56	3	28	–10	11.1
Iran, Islamic Rep.	331,015	5.4	2,042	2,931	10	44	45	45	11	33	11	16.4
Iraq	65,837	–0.3	..	..	..	..	..	..	..	..	..	11.6
Ireland	227,193	4.0	..	15,308	2	34	64	47	16	26	11	2.0
Israel	194,790	3.5	..	..	..	..	..	57	24	16	2	1.4
Italy	2,112,780	0.5	11,714	26,800	2	27	71	59	20	21	0	2.5
Japan	5,067,526	1.1	20,350	41,492	1	29	69	56	18	24	2	–1.1
Jordan	22,788	7.1	2,348	2,440	3	34	63	86	17	18	–22	4.8
Kazakhstan	109,155	8.8	1,776[a]	1,730	5	40	54	42	11	39	8	14.6
Kenya	30,200	4.4	379	367	28	20	52	73	17	21	–11	6.3
Korea, Rep.	832,512	4.2	5,804	14,501	3	36	61	55	15	31	–1	2.2
Kyrgyz Republic	4,578	4.6	684[a]	1,018	29	19	51	86	23	22	–31	8.3
Lao PDR	5,939	6.9	382	495	35	28	37	66	8	37	–12	8.9
Lebanon	34,450	4.5	..	31,410	5	18	78	89	15	19	–23	2.6
Liberia	876	0.0	..	..	61	17	22	202	19	20	–142	10.3
Libya	62,360	5.4	..	..	2	78	20	23	9	28	40	17.9
Lithuania	37,206	6.3	..	4,635	4	31	64	65	19	27	0	4.0
Madagascar	9,052	3.9	210	182	24	18	59	85	4	34	–24	11.3
Malawi	4,975	4.9	86	126	36	21	44	68	13	22	–3	17.7
Malaysia	191,601	5.1	398	583	9	55	36	54	13	24	17	3.9
Mali	8,996	5.3	405	515	37	24	39	77	10	22	–9	4.5
Mauritania	3,031	4.7	671	414	13	47	41	61	20	26	–7	10.6

Table 4 Economic activity *(continued)*

	Gross domestic product		Agricultural productivity		Value added as % of GDP			Household final consumption expenditure	General government final consumption expenditure	Gross capital formation	External balance of goods and services	GDP implicit deflator average
		Average annual % growth	Agricultural value added per worker 2000 $		Agriculture	Industry	Services	% of GDP	% of GDP	% of GDP	% of GDP	Annual % growth
	2009	2000–09	1990–92	2005–07	2009	2009	2009	2009	2009	2009	2009	2000–09
Mexico	874,902	2.2	2,274	3,022	4	38	58	65	13	25	−2	7.8
Moldova	5,405	5.6	1,349[a]	1,276	11	10	79	98	20	19	−36	11.0
Morocco	90,859	5.0	1,788	2,306	20	27	53	63	15	36	−14	2.0
Mozambique	9,790	7.9	117	174	29	24	47	86	13	22	−20	7.9
Myanmar	..	..	..	..	..	..	..	..	..	..	..	..
Nepal	12,531	3.7	245	241	34	16	50	81	11	30	−22	6.6
Netherlands	792,128	1.7	24,752	39,634	2	25	73	46	25	21	8	2.1
New Zealand	125,160	2.9	19,148	25,946	..	..	..	58	19	24	−1	2.6
Nicaragua	6,297	3.2	..	2,334	20	30	50	90	13	32	−35	8.3
Niger	5,384	4.4	242	..	..	..	..	..	..	..	..	3.0
Nigeria	168,994	6.4	..	..	33	41	27	..	..	..	4	15.3
Norway	381,766	2.1	19,077	38,445	1	46	53	39	19	23	19	4.6
Pakistan	166,545	5.3	765	890	21	24	55	79	11	20	−10	8.6
Panama	24,711	6.9	2,341	4,011	6	17	77	73	11	26	−10	2.4
Papua New Guinea	7,893	3.4	555	643	36	45	20	71	11	20	1	6.5
Paraguay	15,015	3.4	1,648	2,136	24	19	57	74	9	18	−1	10.5
Peru	126,734	6.0	879	1,390	7	36	56	64	8	25	3	3.4
Philippines	160,476	4.9	905	1,148	15	33	53	83	11	14	−6	5.1
Poland	430,076	4.4	1,605	2,629	5	31	64	64	16	20	−2	2.7
Portugal	227,676	0.7	4,642	6,135	2	24	74	67	21	22	−10	2.8
Romania	161,110	5.6	2,129	6,179	7	26	67	61	15	31	−7	15.9
Russian Federation	1,230,726	5.9	1,917[a]	2,913	5	37	58	49	18	23	11	15.9
Rwanda	5,064	6.8	193	215	39	13	48	86	10	23	−18	10.5
Saudi Arabia	369,179	3.7	8,476	17,419	2	69	28	39	26	25	10	7.5
Senegal	13,059	4.2	251	223	16	21	63	81	10	29	−20	3.0
Serbia	42,594	5.0	..	..	13	29	58	78	21	19	−16	16.4
Sierra Leone	1,942	9.5	..	..	51	22	27	84	14	15	−13	9.5
Singapore	182,232	6.5	22,695	50,828	0	26	74	43	10	29	18	1.2
Slovak Republic	87,642	5.8	..	8,149	3	35	63	47	20	38	−4	3.4
Somalia	..	..	..	..	..	..	..	..	..	..	..	..
South Africa	285,983	4.1	2,149	3,149	3	31	66	61	21	19	−1	7.2
Spain	1,460,250	2.8	9,583	17,939	3	29	68	57	19	30	−6	3.7
Sri Lanka	41,979	5.5	697	823	14	28	58	67	16	25	−8	10.7
Sudan	54,677	7.3	526	844	27	36	37	58	17	25	0	10.0
Sweden	406,072	2.3	22,319	41,905	2	27	71	47	26	19	7	2.0
Switzerland	500,260	2.0	19,369	22,884	1	27	71	59	11	22	9	1.1
Syrian Arab Republic	52,177	4.4	2,778	4,479	21	34	45	72	14	16	−2	8.0
Tajikistan	4,978	8.2	370[a]	501	22	24	54	93	28	22	−43	20.9
Tanzania[b]	21,623	6.8	261	324	45	17	37	73	16	17	−6	9.5
Thailand	263,856	4.6	480	654	12	44	44	56	12	29	3	3.2
Togo	2,855	2.5	345	394	..	..	..	..	9	..	−21	1.4
Tunisia	39,561	4.9	2,975	3,424	8	30	62	63	13	27	−3	3.2
Turkey	617,099	4.9	2,198	3,223	9	28	63	72	15	15	−1	15.3
Turkmenistan	19,947	13.9	1,272[a]	2,087	12	54	34	49	10	11	30	13.0
Uganda	15,736	7.5	175	191	38	30	32	83	12	24	−19	5.7
Ukraine	113,545	5.6	1,232[a]	2,010	10	52	38	65	18	19	−1	16.4
United Arab Emirates	261,348	7.0	10,414	29,465	2	61	38	46	10	20	23	10.2
United Kingdom	2,174,530	1.9	21,236	27,450	1	24	76	64	22	17	−3	2.6
United States	14,256,300	2.1	20,353	45,285	1	21	77	71	16	18	−5	2.9
Uruguay	36,093	4.1	6,278	9,370	10	26	64	68	9	23	0	7.7
Uzbekistan	32,817	6.9	1,427[a]	2,231	21	32	47	56	16	20	7	24.7
Venezuela, RB	326,498	4.9	4,584	7,386	..	..	..	60	14	22	3	25.0
Vietnam	91,854	7.6	229	335	22	39	39	63	6	38	−7	8.2
West Bank and Gaza	..	−0.9	..	..	..	..	..	..	..	..	..	3.4
Yemen, Rep.	26,365	3.9	412	..	..	..	..	..	..	..	..	13.0
Zambia	12,748	5.4	189	227	21	58	21	74	8	20	−1	16.5
Zimbabwe	..	−5.7	271	239	..	..	..	..	..	..	..	232.0
World	58,228,178 t	2.9 w	801 w	1,035 w	3 w	28 w	69 w	61 w	17 w	22 w	0 w	
Low income	419,652	5.5	244	278	27	26	47	81	9	24	−15	
Middle income	16,095,002	6.4	493	743	10	36	54	57	13	28	0	
Lower middle income	8,805,089	8.5	368	569	13	39	47	50	11	36	−1	
Upper middle income	7,280,007	4.3	2,132	3,232	6	33	61	63	16	21	1	
Low and middle income	16,526,605	6.4	463	674	10	36	54	57	13	28	0	
East Asia & Pacific	6,345,309	9.4	307	491	11	46	43	41	11	40	4	
Europe & Central Asia	2,585,329	5.8	2,012	2,806	7	33	59	60	16	21	3	
Latin America & the Caribbean	3,976,530	3.7	2,213	3,274	6	32	62	66	15	20	−1	
Middle East & North Africa	1,059,429	4.7	1,846	2,824	11	43	46	55	13	28	5	
South Asia	1,634,623	7.3	372	534	18	28	55	62	12	32	−6	
Sub-Saharan Africa	926,544	5.1	305	322	13	30	57	66	17	21	−4	
High income	41,718,726	2.0	13,758	23,429	2	26	73	62	18	21	0	

Note: For data comparability and coverage, see the technical notes. Figures in italics are for years other than those specified. a. Data for all three years are not available. b. Data refer to mainland Tanzania only.

Table 5 Trade, aid, and finance

	Merchandise trade		Manufactured exports	High-technology exports	Current account balance	Foreign direct investment net inflows	Net official development assistance[a]	External debt		Domestic credit provided by banking sector	Net migration
	Exports $ millions	Imports $ millions	% of total merchandise exports	% of manufactured exports	$ millions	$ millions	$ per capita	Total $ millions	Present value % of GNI[b]	% of GDP	thousands
	2009	2009	2009	2008	2009	2009	2008	2008	2008	2009	2005–10[c]
Afghanistan	530	4,200	*35*	..	..	185	168	2,200	4	*3*	1,000
Albania	1,088	4,548	70	4	–1,875	978	123	3,188	21	*67*	–75
Algeria	43,689	39,103	2	*1*	..	2,847	9	5,476	3	*–12*	–140
Angola	39,000	17,000	..	..	*6,408*	2,205	20	15,130	24	32	80
Argentina	55,750	38,771	33	9	8,635	4,009	3	128,285	48	27	30
Armenia	698	3,304	33	2	–1,326	777	98	3,418	27	*17*	–75
Australia	154,043	165,471	19	12	*–47,786*	*47,281*	..	..	..	144	500
Austria	137,217	143,527	81	11	8,731	7,287	..	..	..	..	160
Azerbaijan	21,570	6,469	3	1	10,178	473	27	4,309	12	*17*	–50
Bangladesh	15,081	21,833	*88*	*1*	3,345	674	13	23,644	20	*59*	–570
Belarus	21,282	28,564	48	2	–6,402	1,884	11	12,299	24	*31*	0
Belgium	369,760	351,035	77[d]	8	1,298	34,087	..	..	..	..	200
Benin	1,000	1,800	..	*0*	*–535*	93	74	986	10[e]	19	50
Bolivia	4,850	4,410	6	4	*2,015*	423	65	5,537	14[e]	*55*	–100
Bosnia and Herzegovina	3,953	8,811	61	4	*–2,764*	235	128	8,316	44	58	–10
Brazil	152,995	133,609	39	12	–24,302	25,949	2	255,614	19	*118*	–229
Bulgaria	16,435	23,300	53	7	–4,340	4,489	..	38,045	91	*67*	–50
Burkina Faso	800	1,900	..	..	..	171	66	1,681	14[e]	15	–65
Burundi	65	410	*18*	8	*–212*	10	63	1,445	80[e]	*35*	323
Cambodia	4,550	5,390	*96*	..	*–1,051*	530	51	4,215	42	*16*	–5
Cameroon	3,100	3,800	..	*3*	–1,137	340	27	2,794	4[e]	7	–19
Canada	315,552	330,268	50	15	–22,612	19,898	..	..	..	*178*	1,050
Central African Republic	110	300	..	..	..	42	59	949	41[e]	17	5
Chad	2,700	2,100	..	..	..	462	38	1,749	19[e]	8	–75
Chile	53,024	42,378	*12*	6	4,217	12,702	4	64,277	41	*116*	30
China	1,201,534	1,005,688	94	29	*426,107*	78,193	1	378,245	10	145	–1,731[f]
Hong Kong SAR, China	329,739[g]	352,688	79[g]	22	18,278	48,449	..	..	..	*125*	113
Colombia	32,853	32,898	28	4	–5,146	7,260	22	46,887	23	*43*	–120
Congo, Dem. Rep.	3,200	3,300	..	..	..	951	26	12,199	100[e]	*9*	–100
Congo, Rep.	5,700	2,700	..	..	*–2,181*	2,083	129	5,485	74[e]	–18	–50
Costa Rica	8,777	11,395	47	39	*–2,729*	1,347	15	8,812	33	*54*	30
Côte d'Ivoire	9,300	6,500	*12*	16	1,670	381	30	12,561	76[e]	23	–145
Croatia	10,474	21,203	67	9	–3,154	2,906	90	..	..	*75*	10
Czech Republic	113,319	104,982	87	14	–2,147	2,666	..	..	..	*58*	226
Denmark	93,102	82,893	67	16	12,490	7,712	..	..	..	*211*	30
Dominican Republic	5,460	12,230	70	8	*–4,437*	2,067	15	10,484	24	*39*	–140
Ecuador	13,724	15,093	9	5	*1,120*	316	17	16,851	34	*20*	–350
Egypt, Arab Rep.	21,150	44,946	*37*	1	–3,349	6,712	17	32,616	20	*78*	–340
El Salvador	3,797	7,255	72	4	*–1,596*	431	38	10,110	47	*50*	–280
Eritrea	15	515	..	..	..	0	29	962	38[e]	*113*	55
Ethiopia	1,490	7,310	9	6	*–1,806*	94	41	2,882	8[e]	*37*	–300
Finland	62,586	60,037	81	21	3,444	2,570	..	..	..	..	55
France	474,972	551,092	79	20	–51,857	59,989	..	..	..	..	500
Georgia	1,135	4,378	*55*	3	–1,257	764	206	3,380	24	*33*	–250
Germany	1,120,927	931,434	82	14	168,019	35,841	..	..	..	..	550
Ghana	5,530	8,140	*19*	1	–1,198	1,685	55	4,970	20[e]	..	–51
Greece	19,886	59,398	*54*	10	–37,043	3,340	..	..	..	..	150
Guatemala	7,360	11,521	43	4	–217	566	39	15,889	42	*40*	–200
Guinea	980	1,400	*32*	0	*–434*	141	32	3,092	49[e]	..	–300
Haiti	549	2,140	..	..	–232	38	92	1,935	17[e]	*26*	–140
Honduras	5,235	7,830	35	*1*	*–1,977*	500	77	3,430	12[e]	*56*	–100
Hungary	83,965	77,550	*80*	24	409	–5,858	..	..	..	*81*	75
India	155,249	243,636	67	6	*–36,088*	34,577	2	230,611	18	73	–1,000
Indonesia	119,776	91,720	41	11	10,746	4,877	5	150,851	35	*37*	–730
Iran, Islamic Rep.	78,050	51,450	..	*6*	..	3,016	1	13,937	4	*45*	–500
Iraq	39,500	37,000	*0*	*0*	*15,519*	1,070	322	..	..	*–25*	–577
Ireland	114,662	61,871	86	26	–6,499	25,233	..	..	..	..	200
Israel	47,670	49,150	94	16	7,189	3,894	..	..	..	78	85
Italy	404,653	410,385	83	7	–66,199	28,976	..	..	..	..	1,650
Japan	580,845	550,679	*89*	18	142,194	11,834	..	..	..	*379*	150
Jordan	6,366	14,075	73	1	–1,265	2,382	128	6,577	32	109	250
Kazakhstan	43,189	28,374	14	22	–3,405	12,601	21	107,595	106	*34*	–100
Kenya	4,335	9,670	*37*	5	*–1,978*	141	35	7,441	19	*40*	–189
Korea, Rep.	363,534	323,085	*87*	*33*	42,668	1,506	..	..	..	112	–30
Kyrgyz Republic	1,439	3,037	34	*2*	*–631*	189	68	2,464	42[e]	*14*	–75
Lao PDR	1,070	1,430	..	..	*107*	190	80	4,944	83	*10*	–75
Lebanon	4,187	16,574	*71*	*0*	–7,555	4,804	257	24,395	95	165	–13
Liberia	165	640	..	..	*–1,187*	378	330	3,484	340[e]	*145*	248
Libya	35,300	10,150	..	..	*35,702*	2,674	10	..	..	–63	20
Lithuania	16,288	18,193	55	11	1,492	307	..	31,719	78	*64*	–100
Madagascar	1,150	2,900	57	1	..	1,384	44	2,086	20[e]	11	–5
Malawi	960	1,600	*10*	2	..	60	61	963	9[e]	30	–20
Malaysia	157,433	123,832	70	40	*38,914*	1,609	6	66,182	35	*116*	130
Mali	2,100	2,600	*22*	3	*–1,066*	109	76	2,190	11[e]	11	–202
Mauritania	1,360	1,410	*0*	..	..	–38	97	1,960	41[e]	..	10
Mexico	229,707	241,515	76	19	–5,238	11,418	1	203,984	20	*46*	–2,430
Moldova	1,298	3,278	23	4	–439	86	82	3,787	67	*40*	–172

Table 5 Trade, aid, and finance *(continued)*

	Merchandise trade		Manufactured exports	High-technology exports	Current account balance	Foreign direct investment net inflows	Net official development assistance[a]	External debt		Domestic credit provided by banking sector	Net migration
	Exports $ millions	Imports $ millions	% of total merchandise exports	% of manufactured exports	$ millions	$ millions	$ per capita	Total $ millions	Present value % of GNI[b]	% of GDP	thousands
	2009	2009	2009	2008	2009	2009	2008	2008	2008	2009	2005–10[c]
Morocco	13,848	32,804	65	*9*	–4,570	1,333	39	20,825	24	99	–425
Mozambique	1,950	3,750	12	4	–1,171	881	89	3,432	15[e]	*14*	–20
Myanmar	6,620	4,600	..	..	..	323	11	7,210	35	..	–500
Nepal	680	3,550	67	..	–10	38	25	3,685	21	*53*	–100
Netherlands	498,648	445,802	*55*	22	42,819	31,938	..	..	..	..	100
New Zealand	24,936	25,583	22	9	–3,694	470	..	..	..	156	50
Nicaragua	1,391	3,454	*35*	*4*	*–1,513*	434	131	3,558	32[e]	*71*	–200
Niger	900	1,550	*7*	8	*–351*	739	41	966	13[e]	12	–28
Nigeria	52,500	39,000	*5*	0	22,889	5,787	9	11,221	6	*27*	–300
Norway	120,710	68,506	20	20	53,531	6,870	..	..	..	..	135
Pakistan	17,695	31,720	76	2	*–15,663*	2,387	9	49,337	24	*46*	–1,416
Panama	885	7,785	10	0	–4	1,773	8	10,722	54	*85*	11
Papua New Guinea	4,530	3,480	..	..	..	424	46	1,418	21	*26*	0
Paraguay	3,191	6,940	11	9	–196	274	21	4,163	29	*21*	–40
Peru	26,885	21,706	*16*	2	247	4,760	16	28,555	28	19	–625
Philippines	38,335	45,802	86	66	8,552	1,948	1	64,856	37	*46*	–900
Poland	134,452	146,626	*80*	5	–7,207	11,546	..	218,022	46	*60*	–120
Portugal	43,192	69,238	72	8	–23,380	2,808	..	..	..	..	200
Romania	40,500	54,075	79	7	–7,139	6,310	..	104,943	57	*41*	–200
Russian Federation	303,978	191,868	17	7	48,971	37,134	..	402,453	30	*26*	250
Rwanda	205	1,750	*4*	7	–379	119	96	679	8[e]	..	15
Saudi Arabia	188,500	92,200	*9*	*1*	22,765	10,499	*–5*	..	..	1	150
Senegal	2,180	5,210	41	5	*–1,311*	208	87	2,861	16[e]	26	–100
Serbia	8,345	15,582	*66*	..	–2,413	1,921	142	30,918	70	*39*	0
Sierra Leone	205	505	..	..	–193	74	66	389	10[e]	11	60
Singapore	269,832[g]	245,785	*70*[g]	51	*27,181*	16,809	..	..	..	94	500
Slovak Republic	55,933	55,186	*86*	5	–2,810	–31	..	..	..	*54*	20
Somalia	..	..	..	..	..	108	85	2,949	..	..	–250
South Africa	62,627	71,950	47[h]	5	–11,295	5,628	23	41,943	16	*215*	700
Spain	218,027	290,240	*73*	*5*	–78,683	6,451	..	..	..	..	1,750
Sri Lanka	7,360	9,883	*67*	2	–215	404	36	15,154	35	*43*	–300
Sudan	7,800	8,200	*0*	0	*–1,314*	2,923	58	19,633	78[e]	*16*	135
Sweden	130,742	118,758	76	16	30,232	10,708	..	..	..	*133*	150
Switzerland	172,742	155,595	90	23	23,636	24,803	..	..	..	*181*	100
Syrian Arab Republic	10,400	16,300	*35*	*1*	*66*	1,434	7	..	..	*37*	800
Tajikistan	1,010	2,569	..	..	–180	16	43	1,466	23	*28*	–200
Tanzania	2,970	6,347	25	*1*	*–2,307*	645	55	5,938	14[e, i]	*17*	–300
Thailand	152,498	133,801	75	25	20,284	5,956	–9	64,798	31	*146*	300
Togo	780	1,400	*62*	*0*	*–222*	50	51	1,573	51[e]	30	–5
Tunisia	14,449	19,100	75	5	*–1,711*	1,595	46	20,776	58	75	–20
Turkey	102,139	140,869	80	2	–13,961	7,955	27	277,277	40	*53*	–44
Turkmenistan	6,595	6,750	..	..	..	1,355	4	638	5	..	–25
Uganda	3,560	4,410	*27*	1	–875	604	52	2,249	10[e]	*11*	–135
Ukraine	39,782	45,487	*70*	3	–1,801	4,816	13	92,479	63	*82*	–80
United Arab Emirates	175,000	140,000	*4*	3	..	..	..	..	..	115	343
United Kingdom	350,728	479,890	72	19	–28,690	24,799	..	..	..	229	948
United States	1,056,895	1,603,768	67	27	–419,870	134,710	..	..	..	*272*	5,052
Uruguay	5,386	6,907	26	4	259	1,139	10	11,049	40	*34*	–50
Uzbekistan	9,850	7,615	..	..	..	750	7	3,995	15	..	–400
Venezuela, RB	57,595	42,220	67	3	8,561	–3,105	2	50,229	21	*20*	40
Vietnam	56,574	68,936	*55*	*9*	*–10,706*	7,600	30	26,158	29	*95*	–200
West Bank and Gaza	..	..	..	..	*535*	*52*	659	..	..	..	–10
Yemen, Rep.	*9,270*	*9,300*	2	0	*–1,251*	129	13	6,258	18	19	–135
Zambia	4,238	3,791	8	2	*–1,046*	699	86	2,986	6[e]	*19*	–85
Zimbabwe	1,700	2,900	34	*3*	..	60	49	5,199	177	..	–700
World	**12,465,631t**	**12,553,525t**	**70**w	**17w**		**1,116,269s**	**19w**	..s		***185*** w	..[j]s
Low income	76,234	124,812	*50*	*3*		12,033	45	129,218		*32*	–2,737
Middle income	3,708,999	3,509,321	64	17		346,573	11	3,329,192		*78*	–13,203
Lower middle income	2,090,954	2,027,292	78	22		177,941	11	1,342,220		127	–9,231
Upper middle income	1,617,007	1,476,640	53	9		168,632	13	1,986,972		*61*	–3,972
Low and middle income	3,785,241	3,634,105	64	16		358,605	23	3,458,409		*77*	–15,941
East Asia & Pacific	1,747,818	1,492,279	80	28		102,488	5	771,628		145	–3,781
Europe & Central Asia	650,221	624,980	34	6		85,053	20	1,138,859		*38*	–1,671
Latin America & the Caribbean	676,338	669,803	60	12		73,902	16	894,367		*72*	–5,214
Middle East & North Africa	273,042	290,458	..	*4*		28,095	73	131,545		*36*	–1,089
South Asia	197,030	316,340	68	5		38,311	8	326,311		73	–2,376
Sub-Saharan Africa	241,607	248,900	*33*	3		30,756	49	195,699		*78*	–1,810
High income	8,682,510	8,926,538	72	18		757,664	0	..		*245*	15,894

Note: For data comparability and coverage, see the technical notes. Figures in italics are for years other than those specified.

a. The distinction between official aid, for countries on the Part II list of the Organisation for Economic Co-operation and Development (OECD) Development Assistance Committee (DAC), and official development assistance was dropped in 2005. Regional aggregates include data for economies not listed in the table. World and income group totals include aid not allocated by country or region. b. The numerator refers to 2008, whereas the denominator is a three-year average of 2006–08 data. c. Total for the five-year period. d. Includes Luxembourg. e. Data are from debt sustainability analysis for low-income countries. f. Includes Taiwan, China. g. Includes reexports. h. Data on total exports and imports refer to South Africa only. Data on export commodity shares refer to the South African Customs Union (Botswana, Lesotho, Namibia, and South Africa). i. GNI refers to mainland Tanzania only. j. World total computed by the UN sums to zero, but because the aggregates shown here refer to World Bank definitions, regional and income group totals do not equal zero.

Table 6 Key indicators for other economies

	Population			Population age composition	Gross national income (GNI)[a]		PPP gross national income (GNI)[b]		Gross domestic product	Life expectancy at birth		Adult literacy rate
	Thousands	Average annual % growth	Density people per sq. km.	% ages 0–14	$ millions	$ per capita	$ millions	$ per capita	per capita % growth	Male years	Female years	% ages 15 and older
	2009	2000–09	2008	2009	2009	2009	2009	2009	2008–09	2008	2008	2008
American Samoa	67	1.7	331	..	..	..[c]	..	..	..	..	..	..
Andorra	85	3.3[d]	178	..	*3,447*	*41,130*	..	..	*1.6*	..	..	..
Antigua and Barbuda	88	1.4	197	..	1,058	12,070	1,550[e]	17,690[e]	−9.5	..	..	99
Aruba	107	1.8	586	19	..	..[f]	..	..	..	72	77	98
Bahamas, The	342	1.3	34	26	*7,136*	*21,390*	..	..	*1.5*	71	76	..
Bahrain	791	2.2	1,092	26	*19,712*	*25,420*	*25,967*	*33,480*	*4.1*	74	78	91
Barbados	256	0.2	593	17	..	..[f]	..	..	..	74	80	..
Belize	333	3.2	14	35	*1,205*	*3,740*	*1,917*[e]	*5,950*[e]	*0.4*	74	78	..
Bermuda	64	0.4	1,284	..	..	..[f]	..	..	*0.4*	76	82	..
Bhutan	697	2.4	18	31	1,406	2,020	3,697	5,300	5.8	64	68	*53*
Botswana	1,950	1.4	3	33	12,159	6,240	25,065	12,860	−7.4	54	54	83
Brunei Darussalam	400	2.0	74	27	*10,211*	*27,050*	*19,598*	*50,920*	*−1.3*	75	80	95
Cape Verde	506	1.6	124	36	1,520	3,010	1,785	3,530	1.4	68	74	84
Cayman Islands	55	3.5	209	..	..	..[f]	..	..	..	..	..	*99*
Channel Islands	150	0.2	787	16	*10,242*	*68,610*	..	..	*5.7*	77	82	..
Comoros	659	2.2	346	38	571	870	860	1,300	9.6	63	68	74
Cuba	11,204	0.1	102	18	..	..[c]	..	..	..	77	81	100
Cyprus	871	1.1	93	18	*21,366*[g]	*26,940*[g]	*22,248*[g]	*28,050*[g]	*2.4*[g]	77	82	98
Djibouti	864	1.9	37	36	1,106	1,280	2,143	2,480	3.2	54	57	..
Dominica	74	0.3	98	..	359	4,870	624[e]	8,470[e]	−1.3	..	..	..
Equatorial Guinea	676	2.7	24	41	8,398	12,420	13,088	19,350	−7.8	49	51	93
Estonia	1,340	−0.2	32	15	18,846	14,060	25,316	18,890	−14.1	69	80	100
Faeroe Islands	49	0.7	35	..	..	..[f]	..	..	..	*77*	*81*	..
Fiji	849	0.6	46	31	3,356	3,950	3,878	4,570	−3.1	67	71	..
French Polynesia	269	1.5	73	26	..	..[f]	..	..	..	72	77	..
Gabon	1,475	2.0	6	36	10,869	7,370	18,381	12,460	−2.7	59	62	87
Gambia, The	1,705	3.0	166	42	743	440	2,273	1,330	1.8	54	58	45
Gibraltar	31	0.8	3,103	..	..	..[f]	..	..	..	..	..	..
Greenland	56	0.0[h]	0[h]	..	*1,857*	*32,960*	..	..	*0.8*	66	71	..
Grenada	104	0.3	305	28	577	5,550	803[e]	7,720[e]	−7.1	74	77	..
Guam	178	1.5	325	28	..	..[f]	..	..	..	73	78	..
Guinea-Bissau	1,611	2.3	56	43	826	510	1,706	1,060	0.7	46	49	51
Guyana	762	0.1	4	30	*1,109*	*1,450*	*2,313*[e]	*3,030*[e]	*3.1*	64	70	..
Iceland	319	1.4	3	21	13,789	43,220	10,653	33,390	−7.0	80	83	..
Isle of Man	80	0.6	141	..	*3,972*	*49,310*	..	..	*7.4*	..	..	..
Jamaica	2,700	0.5	248	29	13,481	4,990	19,749[e]	7,320[e]	−3.1	69	75	86
Kiribati	98	1.7	119	..	185	1,890	328[e]	3,350[e]	0.0	*59*	*63*	..
Korea, Dem. Rep.	23,906	0.5	198	22	..	..[i]	..	..	..	65	69	100
Kosovo	1,805	0.7	165	..	5,842	3,240	..	..	3.4	67	72	..
Kuwait	2,795	2.7	153	23	*116,984*	*43,930*	*142,710*	*53,590*	*1.9*	76	80	*94*
Latvia	2,255	−0.6	36	14	27,936	12,390	37,236	16,510	−17.6	67	78	100
Lesotho	2,067	1.0	68	39	2,139	1,030	4,027	1,950	1.3	44	46	90
Liechtenstein	36	1.0	223	..	*4,034*	*113,210*	..	..	*1.0*	80	85	..
Luxembourg	498	1.5	189	18	37,056	74,430	28,694	57,640	−5.2	78	83	..
Macao SAR, China	538	2.2	18,659	13	*18,142*	*35,360*	*26,890*	*52,410*	*10.4*	79	83	*93*
Macedonia, FYR	2,042	0.2	80	18	8,983	4,400	21,550	10,550	−0.8	72	77	97
Maldives	309	1.4	1,017	28	1,197	3,870	1,620	5,230	−4.4	70	73	*98*
Malta	415	0.7	1,287	16	*6,826*	*16,690*	*9,259*	*22,640*	*3.1*	77	82	*92*
Marshall Islands	61	1.9	331	..	186	3,060	..	..	−2.2	..	..	..
Mauritius	1,275	0.8	625	23	9,236	7,240	16,924	13,270	1.6	69	76	88
Mayotte	197	2.9[j]	511	39	..	..[c]	..	..	..	72	80	..
Micronesia, Fed. Sts.	111	0.4	158	37	246	2,220	311[e]	2,810[e]	−15.4	68	69	..
Monaco	33	0.3	16,358	..	*6,670*	*203,900*	..	..	*9.7*	..	..	..
Mongolia	2,671	1.2	2	26	4,361	1,630	8,895	3,330	−2.7	63	70	97
Montenegro	624	−0.6	46	19	4,089	6,550	8,194	13,130	−7.3	72	77	..
Namibia	2,171	1.9	3	37	9,323	4,290	13,908	6,410	−0.9	60	62	88
Netherlands Antilles	198	1.0	244	21	..	..[f]	..	..	..	73	79	96
New Caledonia	250	1.8	13	26	..	..[f]	..	..	..	72	81	96
Northern Mariana Islands	87	2.6	186	..	..	..[f]	..	..	..	..	..	..
Oman	2,845	1.9	9	31	*49,833*	*17,890*	*67,892*	*24,370*	*10.4*	74	78	87
Palau	20	0.7	44	..	182	8,940	..	..	−2.6	*66*	*72*	..
Puerto Rico	3,967	0.4	446	20	..	..[f]	..	..	..	75	83	90
Qatar	1,409	9.2	111	16	..	..[f]	..	..	*−0.7*	75	77	*93*
Samoa	179	0.1	63	39	508	2,840	764[e]	4,270[e]	−5.5	69	75	99
San Marino	31	1.3[k]	517	..	*1,572*	*50,670*	..	..	*0.4*	*79*	*85*	..

Table 6 Key indicators for other economies *(continued)*

	Population			Population age composition	Gross national income (GNI)[a]		PPP gross national income (GNI)[b]		Gross domestic product	Life expectancy at birth		Adult literacy rate
	Thousands	Average annual % growth	Density people per sq. km.	% Ages 0–14	$ millions	$ per capita	$ millions	$ per capita	per capita % growth	Male years	Female years	% ages 15 and older
	2009	2000–09	2008	2009	2009	2009	2009	2009	2008–09	2008	2008	2008
São Tomé and Príncipe	163	1.7	167	41	185	1,140	302	1,850	2.4	64	68	88
Seychelles	88	0.9	189	..	746	8,480	1,480[e]	16,820[e]	−8.7	68	79	92
Slovenia	2,043	0.3	100	14	48,063	23,520	53,821	26,340	−8.8	76	83	100
Solomon Islands	523	2.6	18	39	478	910	976[e]	1,860[e]	−4.5	65	67	..
St. Kitts and Nevis	50	1.3	189	..	501	10,100	677[e]	13,660[e]	−8.8	..	..	..
St. Lucia	172	1.1	279	26	890	5,170	1,527[e]	8,880[e]	−4.9	*70*	*76*	..
St. Vincent and the Grenadines	109	0.1	280	27	558	5,110	965[e]	8,840[e]	−2.8	70	74	..
Suriname	520	1.2	3	29	*2,454*	*4,760*	*3,447*[e]	*6,690*[e]	*4.2*	66	73	91
Swaziland	1,185	1.0	68	39	2,787	2,350	5,428	4,580	−1.0	46	45	87
Timor-Leste	1,134	3.7	74	45	*2,706*	*2,460*	*5,162*[e]	*4,700*[e]	−1.3	60	62	..
Tonga	104	0.6	144	37	339	3,260	476[e]	4,580[e]	−0.8	69	75	*99*
Trinidad and Tobago	1,339	0.4	260	21	22,076	16,490	33,599[e]	25,100[e]	−4.8	66	73	99
Turks and Caicos Islands	33	6.1	34	..	..	..[f]	..	..	..	..	..	..
Tuvalu	..	..	*348*	..	..	..[l]	..	..	..	..	..	..
Vanuatu	240	2.6	19	39	628	2,620	1,029[e]	4,290[e]	1.4	68	72	81
Virgin Islands (U.S.)	110	0.1	314	21	..	..[f]	..	..	..	76	82	..

Note: For data comparability and coverage, see the technical notes. Figures in italics are for years other than those specified. a. Calculated using the World Bank Atlas method. b. PPP is purchasing power parity; see the technical notes. c. Estimated to be upper middle income (US$3,946–12,195). d. Data are for 2003–09. e. The estimate is based on regression; others are extrapolated from the latest International Comparison Program benchmark estimates. f. Estimated to be high income (US$12,196 or more). g. Data are for the area controlled by the government of the Republic of Cyprus. h. Less than 0.5. i. Estimated to be low income (US$995 or less) j. Data are for 2002–07. k. Data are for 2004–07. l. Estimated to be lower middle income (US$996–3,945).

Technical notes

These technical notes discuss the sources and methods used to compile the indicators included in this edition of Selected World Development Indicators. The notes follow the order in which the indicators appear in the tables.

Sources

The data published in the Selected World Development Indicators are taken from *World Development Indicators 2010.* Where possible, however, revisions reported since the closing date of that edition have been incorporated. In addition, newly released estimates of population and gross national income (GNI) per capita for 2009 are included in table 1 and table 6.

The World Bank draws on a variety of sources for the statistics published in the *World Development Indicators.* Data on external debt for developing countries are reported directly to the World Bank by developing member countries through the Debtor Reporting System. Other data are drawn mainly from the United Nations and its specialized agencies, from the International Monetary Fund (IMF), and from country reports to the World Bank. Bank staff estimates are also used to improve currentness or consistency. For most countries, national accounts estimates are obtained from member governments through World Bank economic missions. In some instances these are adjusted by staff to ensure conformity with international definitions and concepts. Most social data from national sources are drawn from regular administrative files, special surveys, or periodic censuses.

For more detailed notes about the data, please refer to the World Bank's *World Development Indicators 2010.*

Data consistency and reliability

Considerable effort has been made to standardize the data, but full comparability cannot be ensured, and care must be taken in interpreting the indicators. Many factors affect data availability, comparability, and reliability: statistical systems in many developing economies are still weak; statistical methods, coverage, practices, and definitions differ widely; and cross-country and intertemporal comparisons involve complex technical and conceptual problems that cannot be unequivocally resolved. Data coverage may not be complete because of special circumstances or for economies experiencing problems (such as those stemming from conflicts) affecting the collection and reporting of data. For these reasons, although the data are drawn from the sources thought to be most authoritative, they should be construed only as indicating trends and characterizing major differences among economies rather than offering precise quantitative measures of those differences. Discrepancies in data presented in different editions reflect updates by countries as well as revisions to historical series and changes in methodology. Thus readers are advised not to compare data series between editions or between different editions of World Bank publications. Consistent time series are available from the Open Data website (http://data.worldbank.org).

Ratios and growth rates

For ease of reference, the tables usually show ratios and rates of growth rather than the simple underlying values. Values in their original form are available from the Open Data website (http://data.worldbank.org). Unless otherwise noted, growth rates are computed using the least-squares regression method (see the section on "Statistical methods" later in this dicussion). Because this method takes into account all available observations during a period, the resulting growth rates reflect general trends that are not unduly influenced by exceptional values. Constant price economic indicators are used to exclude the effects of inflation in calculating growth rates. Data in italics are for a year or period other than that specified in the column heading—up to two years before or after for economic indicators and up to three years for social indicators, because the latter tend to be collected less regularly and change less dramatically over short periods.

Constant price series

An economy's growth is measured by the increase in value added produced by the individuals and enterprises operating in that economy. Thus, measuring real growth requires estimates of gross domestic product (GDP) and its components valued in constant prices. The World Bank collects constant price national accounts series in national currencies that are recorded in the country's original base year. To obtain comparable series of constant price data, it rescales GDP and value added by industrial origin to a common reference year, 2000 in the current version of the WDI. This process gives rise to a discrepancy between the rescaled GDP and the sum of the rescaled components. Because allocating the discrepancy would give rise to distortions in the growth rate, it is left unallocated.

Summary measures

The summary measures for regions and income groups, presented at the end of most tables, are calculated by simple addition when they are expressed in levels. Aggregate growth rates and ratios are usually computed as weighted averages. The summary measures for social indicators are weighted by population or by subgroups of population, except for infant mortality, which is weighted by the number of births. See the notes on specific indicators for more information.

For summary measures that cover many years, calculations are based on a uniform group of economies so that the composition of the aggregate does not change over time. Group measures are compiled only if the data available for a given year account for at least two-thirds of the full group, as defined for the 2000 benchmark year. As long as this criterion is met, economies for which data are missing are assumed to behave like those that provide estimates. Readers should keep in mind that the summary measures are estimates of representative aggregates for each topic and that nothing meaningful can be deduced about behavior at the country level by working back from group indicators. In addition, the estimation process may result in discrepancies between subgroup and overall totals.

Table 1. Key indicators of development

Population is based on the de facto definition, which counts all residents, regardless of legal status or citizenship. Except for refugees who are not permanently settled in the country of asylum, such refugees are generally considered part of the population of the country of origin. The values shown are midyear estimates.

Average annual population growth rate is the exponential rate of change for the period (see the section on statistical methods).

Population density is midyear population divided by land area *in square kilometers.* Land area is a country's total area, excluding area under inland water bodies.

Population age composition, ages 0–14 refers to the percentage of the total population that is ages 0–14.

Gross national income (GNI) is the broadest measure of national income. It measures total value added from domestic and foreign sources claimed by residents. GNI comprises gross domestic product plus net receipts of primary income from foreign sources. Data are converted from national currency to current U.S. dollars using the World Bank Atlas method. This approach involves using a three-year average of exchange rates to smooth the effects of transitory exchange rate fluctuations. (See the section on statistical methods for further discussion of the Atlas method.)

GNI per capita is GNI divided by midyear population. It is converted into current U.S. dollars by the Atlas method. The World Bank uses GNI per capita in U.S. dollars to classify economies for analytical purposes and to determine borrowing eligibility.

PPP GNI is GNI converted into international dollars using purchasing power parity (PPP) conversion factors. Because exchange rates do not always reflect differences in price levels between countries, this table converts GNI and GNI per capita estimates into international dollars using PPP rates. PPP rates provide a standard measure allowing comparison of real levels of expenditure between countries, just as conventional price indexes allow comparison of real values over time. The PPP conversion factors used here are derived from the 2005 round of price surveys covering 146 countries conducted by the International Comparison Program. For OECD countries, data come from the most recent round of surveys, completed in 2005. Estimates for countries not included in the surveys are derived from statistical models using available data. For more information on the 2005 International Comparison Program, go to http://www.worldbank.org/data/icp.

PPP GNI per capita is PPP GNI divided by midyear population.

Gross domestic product (GDP) per capita growth is based on GDP measured in constant prices. Growth in GDP is considered a broad measure of the growth of an economy. GDP in constant prices can be estimated by measuring the total quantity of goods and services produced in a period, valuing them at an agreed set of base year prices, and subtracting the cost of intermediate inputs, also in constant prices. See the section on statistical methods for details of the least-squares growth rate.

Life expectancy at birth is the number of years a newborn infant would live if patterns of mortality prevailing at its birth were to stay the same throughout its life. Data are presented for males and females separately.

Adult literacy rate is the percentage of persons ages 15 and older who can, with understanding, read and write a short, simple statement about their everyday life. In practice, literacy is difficult to measure. To estimate literacy using such a definition requires census or survey measurements under controlled conditions. Many countries estimate the number of literate people from self-reported data. Some use educational attainment data as a proxy but apply different lengths of school attendance or level of completion. Because definition and methodologies of data collection differ across countries, data need to be used with caution.

Table 2. Poverty

The World Bank periodically prepares poverty assessments of countries in which it has an active program, in close collaboration with national institutions, other development agencies, and civil society groups, including poor people's organizations. Poverty assessments report the extent and causes of poverty and propose strategies to reduce it. Since 1992 the World Bank has conducted about 200 poverty assessments, which are the main source of the poverty estimates using national poverty lines presented in the table. Countries report similar assessments as part of their Poverty Reduction Strategies.

The World Bank also produces poverty estimates using international poverty lines to monitor progress in poverty reduction globally. The first global poverty estimates for developing countries were produced for *World Development Report 1990: Poverty Using Household Survey Data for 22 Countries* (Ravallion, Datt, and van de Walle 1991). Since then the number of countries that field household income and expenditure surveys has expanded considerably.

National and international poverty lines

National poverty lines are used to make estimates of poverty consistent with the country's specific economic and social circumstances and are not intended for international comparisons of poverty rates. The setting of national poverty lines reflects local perceptions of the level of consumption or income needed not to be poor. The perceived boundary between poor and not poor rises with the average income of a country and so does not provide a uniform measure for comparing poverty rates across countries. Nevertheless, national poverty estimates are clearly the appropriate measure for setting national policies for poverty reduction and for monitoring their results.

International comparisons of poverty estimates entail both conceptual and practical problems. Countries have different definitions of poverty, and consistent comparisons across countries can be difficult. Local poverty lines tend to have higher purchasing power in rich countries, where more generous standards are used, than in poor countries. International poverty lines attempt to hold the real value of the poverty line constant across countries, as is done when making comparisons over time, regardless of average income of countries.

Since the publication of *World Development Report 1990* the World Bank has aimed to apply a common standard in measuring extreme poverty, anchored to what poverty means in the world's poorest countries. The welfare of people living in different countries can be measured on a common scale by adjusting for differences in the purchasing power of currencies. The commonly used $1 a day standard, measured in 1985 international prices and adjusted to local currency using purchasing power parities, was chosen for *World Development Report 1990* because it was typical of the poverty lines in low-income countries at the time. Later this $1-a-day line was revised to $1.08 a day measured in 1993 international prices. More recently, the international poverty lines were revised using the new data on PPPs compiled by the 2005 round of the International Comparison Program, along with data from an expanded set of household income and expenditure surveys. The new extreme poverty line is set at $1.25 a day in 2005 PPP terms, which represents the mean of the poverty lines found in the poorest 15 countries ranked by per capita consumption. The new poverty line maintains the same standard for extreme poverty—the poverty line typical of the poorest countries in the world—but updates it using the latest information on the cost of living in developing countries.

Quality and availability of survey data

Poverty estimates are derived using surveys fielded to collect, among other things, information on income or consumption from a sample of households. To be useful for poverty estimates, surveys must be nationally representative and include sufficient information to compute a comprehensive estimate of total household consumption or income (including consumption or income from own production), from which it is possible to construct a correctly weighted distribution of consumption or income per person. Over the past 20 years the number of countries that field surveys and the frequency of the surveys have expanded considerably. The quality of data has improved greatly as well. The World Bank's poverty monitoring database now includes more than 600 surveys representing 115 developing countries. More than 1.2 million randomly sampled households were interviewed in these surveys, representing 96 percent of the population of developing countries.

Measurement issues using survey data

Besides the frequency and timeliness of survey data, other data issues arise in measuring household living standards. One relates to the choice of income or consumption as a welfare indicator. Income is generally more difficult to measure accurately, and consumption comes closer to the notion of standard of living. Also, income can vary over time even if the standard of living does not. However, consumption data are not always available: the latest estimates reported here use consumption for about two-thirds of countries. Another issue is that even similar surveys may not be strictly comparable because of differences in number of consumer goods they identify, differences in the length of the period over which respondents must recall their expenditures, or differences in the quality and training of enumerators. Selective nonresponses are also a concern in some surveys.

Comparisons of countries at different levels of development also pose a potential problem because of differences in the relative importance of the consumption of nonmarket goods. The local market value of all consumption in kind (including own production, which is particularly important in underdeveloped rural economies) should be included in total consumption expenditure, but may not be. Surveys now routinely include imputed values for consumption in-kind from own-farm production. Imputed profit from the production of nonmarket goods should be included in income, but sometimes it is omitted (such omissions were a bigger problem in surveys before the 1980s). Most survey data now include valuations for consumption or income from own production, but valuation methods vary.

Definitions

Survey year is the year in which the underlying data were collected.

Population below national poverty line, national is the percentage of the population living below the national poverty line. National estimates are based on population-weighted subgroup estimates from household surveys.

Population below $1.25 a day and **population below $2.00 a day** are the percentages of the population living on less than $1.25 a day and $2.00 a day at 2005 international prices. As a result of revisions in PPP exchange rates, poverty rates for individual countries cannot be compared with poverty rates reported in earlier editions.

Poverty gap is the mean shortfall from the poverty line (counting the nonpoor as having zero shortfall), expressed as a percentage of the poverty line. This measure reflects the depth of poverty as well as its incidence.

Table 3. Millennium Development Goals: Eradicating poverty and improving lives

Share of poorest quintile in national consumption or income is the share of the poorest 20 percent of the population in consumption or, in some cases, income. It is a distributional measure. Countries with more unequal distributions of consumption (or income) have a higher rate of poverty for a given average income. Data are from nationally representative household surveys. Because the underlying household surveys differ in method and type of data collected, the distribution data are not strictly comparable across countries. The World Bank staff has made an effort to ensure that the data are as comparable as possible. Wherever possible, consumption has been used rather than income.

Vulnerable employment is the sum of unpaid family workers and own-account workers as a percentage of total employment. The proportion of unpaid family workers and own-account workers in total employment is derived from information on status in employment. Each status group faces different economic risks, and unpaid family workers and own-account workers are the most vulnerable—and therefore the most likely to fall into poverty. They are the least likely to have formal work arrangements, are the least likely to have social protection and safety nets to guard against economic shocks, and often are incapable of generating sufficient savings to offset these shocks.

Prevalence of child malnutrition is the percentage of children under age five whose weight for age is less than minus two standard deviations from the median for the international reference population ages 0–59 months. The table presents data for the new child growth standards released by the World Health Organization (WHO) in 2006. Estimates of child malnutrition are from national survey data. The proportion of children who are underweight is the most common indicator of malnutrition. Being underweight, even mildly, increases the risk of death and inhibits cognitive development in children. Moreover, it perpetuates the problem from one generation to the next, because malnourished women are more likely to have low-birthweight babies.

Primary completion rate is the percentage of students completing the last year of primary school. It is calculated by taking the total number of students in the last grade of primary school, minus the number of repeaters in that grade, divided by the total number of children of official graduation age. The primary completion rate reflects the primary cycle as defined by the International Standard Classification of Education, ranging from three or four years of primary education (in a very small number of countries) to five or six years (in most countries) and seven (in a small number of countries). Because curricula and standards for school completion vary across countries, a high rate of primary completion does not necessarily indicate high levels of student learning.

Ratio of girls to boys enrolled in primary and secondary school is the ratio of the female gross enrollment rate in primary and secondary school to the male gross enrollment rate.

Eliminating gender disparities in education would help to increase the status and capabilities of women. This indicator is an imperfect measure of the relative accessibility of schooling for girls. School enrollment data are reported to the United Nations Educational, Scientific, and Cultural Organization Institute for Statistics by national education authorities. Primary education provides children with basic reading, writing, and mathematics skills along with an elementary understanding of such subjects as history, geography, natural science, social science, art, and music. Secondary education completes the provision of basic education that began at the primary level, and aims at laying foundations for lifelong learning and human development, by offering more subject- or skill-oriented instruction using more specialized teachers.

Under-five mortality rate is the probability per 1,000 children under five years of age that a newborn baby will die before reaching age five, if subject to current age-specific mortality rates. The main sources of mortality data are vital registration systems and direct or indirect estimates based on sample surveys or censuses. To make under-five mortality estimates comparable across countries and over time and to ensure consistency across estimates by different agencies, the United Nations Children's Fund (UNICEF) and the World Bank developed and adopted a statistical method that uses all available information to reconcile differences. The method fits a regression line to the relationship between mortality rates and their reference dates using weighted least squares.

Maternal mortality rate is the number of women who die from pregnancy-related causes during pregnancy and childbirth, per 100,000 live births. The values are modeled estimates. The modeled estimates are based on an exercise by the WHO, UNICEF, the United Nations Population Fund, and the World Bank. For countries with complete vital registration systems with good attribution of cause-of-death information, the data are used as reported. For countries with national data, either (1) from complete vital registration systems with uncertain or poor attribution of cause-of-death information, or (2) from household surveys, reported maternal mortality was adjusted usually by a factor of underenumeration and misclassification. For countries with no empirical national data (about 35 percent of countries), maternal mortality was estimated with a regression model using socioeconomic information, including fertility, birth attendants, and GDP.

Prevalence of HIV is the percentage of people ages 15–49 who are infected with HIV. Adult HIV prevalence rates reflect the rate of HIV infection in each country's population. Low national prevalence rates can be very misleading, however. They often disguise serious epidemics that are initially concentrated in certain localities or among specific population groups and threaten to spill over into the wider population. In many parts of the developing world, most new infections occur in young adults, with young women especially vulnerable. The Joint United Nations Programme on HIV/AIDS and WHO estimate HIV prevalence from sentinel surveillance, population-based surveys, and special studies.

Incidence of tuberculosis is the estimated number of new tuberculosis cases (pulmonary, smear positive, and extrapulmonary). Tuberculosis is one of the main causes of death from a single infectious agent among adults in developing countries. In high-income countries tuberculosis has reemerged largely as a result of cases among immigrants. The estimates of tuberculosis incidence in the table are based on an approach in which reported cases are adjusted using the ratio of case notifications to the estimated share of cases detected by panels of 80 epidemiologists convened by WHO.

Carbon dioxide emissions are those stemming from the burning of fossil fuels and the manufacture of cement and include carbon dioxide produced during consumption of solid, liquid, and gas fuels and gas flaring divided by midyear population (Carbon Dioxide Information Analysis Center, World Bank).

Access to improved sanitation facilities is the percentage of the population with at least adequate access to excreta disposal facilities (private or shared, but not public) that can effectively prevent human, animal, and insect contact with excreta. Facilities do not have to include treatment to render sewage outflows innocuous. Improved facilities range from simple but protected pit latrines to flush toilets with a sewerage connection. To be effective, facilities must be correctly constructed and properly maintained.

Internet users are people with access to the worldwide network.

Table 4. Economic activity

Gross domestic product is gross value added, at purchasers' prices, by all resident producers in the economy plus any taxes and minus any subsidies not included in the value of the products. It is calculated without deduction for the depreciation of fabricated assets or for the depletion or degradation of natural resources. Value added is the net output of an industry after adding up all outputs and subtracting intermediate inputs. The industrial origin of value added is determined by International Standard Industrial Classification (ISIC) revision 3. The World Bank conventionally uses the U.S. dollar and applies the average official exchange rate reported by the IMF for the year shown. An alternative conversion factor is applied if the official exchange rate is judged to diverge by an exceptionally large margin from the rate effectively applied to transactions in foreign currencies and traded products.

Gross domestic product average annual growth rate is calculated from constant price GDP data in local currency.

Agricultural productivity is the ratio of agricultural value added, measured in 2000 U.S. dollars, to the number of workers in agriculture. Agricultural productivity is measured by value added per unit of input. Agricultural value added includes that from forestry and fishing. Thus interpretations of land productivity should be made with caution.

Value added is the net output of an industry after adding up all outputs and subtracting intermediate inputs. The industrial origin of value added is determined by the ISIC revision 3.

Agriculture value added corresponds to ISIC divisions 1–5 and includes forestry and fishing.

Industry value added comprises mining, manufacturing, construction, electricity, water, and gas (ISIC divisions 10–45).

Services value added correspond to ISIC divisions 50–99.

Household final consumption expenditure is the market value of all goods and services, including durable products (such as cars, washing machines, and home computers), purchased by households. It excludes purchases of dwellings but includes imputed rent for owner-occupied dwellings. It also includes payments and fees to governments to obtain permits and licenses. Here, household consumption expenditure includes the expenditures of nonprofit institutions serving households, even when reported separately by the country. In practice, household consumption expenditure may include any statistical discrepancy in the use of resources relative to the supply of resources.

General government final consumption expenditure includes all government current expenditures for purchases of goods and services (including compensation of employees). It also includes most expenditures on national defense and security, but excludes government military expenditures that are part of government capital formation.

Gross capital formation consists of outlays on additions to the fixed assets of the economy plus net changes in the level of inventories and valuables. Fixed assets include land improvements (fences, ditches, drains, and so on); plant, machinery, and equipment purchases; and the construction of buildings, roads, railways, and the like, including commercial and industrial buildings, offices, schools, hospitals, and private dwellings. Inventories are stocks of goods held by firms to meet temporary or unexpected fluctuations in production or sales, and "work in progress." According to the 1993 System of National Accounts, net acquisitions of valuables are also considered capital formation.

External balance of goods and services is exports of goods and services less imports of goods and services. Trade in goods and services comprise all transactions between residents of a country and the rest of the world involving a change in ownership of general merchandise, goods sent for processing and repairs, nonmonetary gold, and services.

GDP implicit deflator reflects changes in prices for all final demand categories, such as government consumption, capital formation, and international trade, as well as the main component, private final consumption. It is derived as the ratio of current to constant price GDP. The GDP deflator may also be calculated explicitly as a Paasche price index in which the weights are the current period quantities of output.

National accounts indicators for most developing countries are collected from national statistical organizations and central banks by visiting and resident World Bank missions. Data for high-income economies come from the OECD.

Table 5. Trade, aid, and finance

Merchandise exports show the free on board (f.o.b.) value of goods provided to the rest of the world valued in U.S. dollars.

Merchandise imports show the c.i.f. value of goods (the cost of the goods including insurance and freight) purchased from the rest of the world valued in U.S. dollars. Data on merchandise trade come from the World Trade Organization in its annual report.

Manufactured exports comprise the commodities in SITC sections 5 (chemicals), 6 (basic manufactures), 7 (machinery and transport equipment), and 8 (miscellaneous manufactured goods), excluding division 68.

High-technology exports are products with high research and development intensity. They include high-technology products such as aerospace products, computers, pharmaceuticals, scientific instruments, and electrical machinery.

Current account balance is the sum of net exports of goods and services, net income, and net current transfers.

Foreign direct investment (FDI) is net inflows of investment to acquire a lasting management interest (10 percent or more of voting stock) in an enterprise operating in an economy other than that of the investor. It is the sum of equity capital, reinvestment of earnings, other long-term capital, and short-term capital, as shown in the balance of payments. Data on FDI are based on balance of payments data reported by the IMF, supplemented by World Bank staff estimates using data reported by the United Nations Conference on Trade and Development and official national sources.

Net official development assistance (ODA) from the high-income members of the OECD is the main source of official external finance for developing countries, but ODA is also disbursed by some important donor countries that are not members of the OECD's Development Assistance Committee (DAC). DAC has three criteria for ODA: it is undertaken by the official sector; it promotes economic development or welfare as a main objective; and it is provided on concessional terms, with a grant element of at least 25 percent on loans (calculated at a 10 percent discount rate).

Official development assistance comprises grants and loans, net of repayments, that meet the DAC definition of ODA and that are made to countries and territories on the DAC list of aid recipients. The new DAC list of recipients is organized on more objective needs-based criteria than its predecessors, and includes all low- and middle-income countries, except those that are members of the Group of 8 or the European Union (including countries with a firm date for EU admission).

Total external debt is debt owed to nonresidents repayable in foreign currency, goods, or services. It is the sum of public, publicly guaranteed, and private non-guaranteed long-term debt, use of IMF credit, and short-term debt. Short-term debt includes all debt having an original maturity of one year or less and interest in arrears on long-term debt.

Present value of debt is the sum of short-term external debt plus the discounted sum of total debt service payments due on public, publicly guaranteed, and private nonguaranteed long-term external debt over the life of existing loans.

Data on external debt are mainly from reports to the World Bank through its Debtor Reporting System from member countries that have received International Bank for Reconstruction and Development loans or International Development Association credits, with additional information from the files of the World Bank, the IMF, the African Development Bank and African Development Fund, the Asian Development Bank and Asian Development Fund, and the Inter-American Development Bank. Summary tables of the external debt of developing countries are published annually in the World Bank's *Global Development Finance.*

Domestic credit provided by banking sector includes all credit to various sectors on a gross basis, with the exception of credit to the central government, which is net. The banking sector includes monetary authorities, deposit money banks, and other banking institutions for which data are available (including institutions that do not accept transferable deposits but do incur such liabilities as time and savings deposits). Examples of other banking institutions include savings and mortgage loan institutions and building and loan associations. Data are from the IMF's *International Finance Statistics.*

Net migration is the net total of migrants during the period. It is the total number of immigrants less the total number of emigrants, including both citizens and noncitizens. Data are five-year estimates. Data are from the United Nations Population Division's *World Population Prospects: The 2008 Revision.*

Table 6. Key indicators for other economies

See the technical notes for Table 1.

Statistical methods

This section describes the calculation of the least-squares growth rate, the exponential (endpoint) growth rate, and the World Bank's Atlas methodology for calculating the conversion factor used to estimate GNI and GNI per capita in U.S. dollars.

Least-squares growth rate

Least-squares growth rates are used wherever there is a sufficiently long time series to permit a reliable calculation. No growth rate is calculated if more than half the observations in a period are missing.

The least-squares growth rate, *r*, is estimated by fitting a linear regression trendline to the logarithmic annual values of the variable in the relevant period. The regression equation takes the form

$$\ln X_t = a + bt,$$

which is equivalent to the logarithmic transformation of the compound growth equation,

$$X_t = X_o\,(1 + r)^t.$$

In this equation, *X* is the variable, *t* is time, and $a = \log X_o$ and $b = \ln\,(1 + r)$ are the parameters to be estimated. If b^* is the least-squares estimate of *b*, the average annual growth rate, *r*, is obtained as $[\exp(b^*)-1]$ and is multiplied by 100 to express it as a percentage.

The calculated growth rate is an average rate that is representative of the available observations over the entire period. It does not necessarily match the actual growth rate between any two periods.

Exponential growth rate

The growth rate between two points in time for certain demographic data, notably labor force and population, is calculated from the equation

$$r = \ln\,(p_n/p_1)/n,$$

where p_n and p_1 are the last and first observations in the period, *n* is the number of years in the period, and ln is the natural logarithm operator. This growth rate is based on a model of continuous, exponential growth between two points in time. It does not take into account the intermediate values of the series. Note also that the exponential growth rate does not correspond to the annual rate of change measured at a one-year interval, which is given by

$$(p_n - p_{n-1})/p_{n-1}.$$

World Bank Atlas method

For certain operational purposes, the World Bank uses the Atlas conversion factor to calculate GNI and GNI per capita in U.S. dollars. The purpose of the Atlas conversion factor is to reduce the impact of exchange rate fluctuations in the cross-country comparison of national incomes. The Atlas conversion factor for any year is the average of a country's exchange rate (or alternative conversion factor) for that year and its exchange rates for the two preceding years, adjusted for the difference between the rate of inflation in the country and that in Japan, the United Kingdom, the United States, and the Euro Area. A country's inflation rate is measured by the change in its GDP deflator. The inflation rate for Japan, the United Kingdom, the United States, and the Euro Area, representing international inflation, is measured by the change in the SDR deflator. (Special drawing rights, or SDRs, are the IMF's unit of account.) The SDR deflator is calculated as a weighted average of these countries' GDP deflators in SDR terms, the weights being the amount of each country's currency in one SDR unit. Weights vary over time because both the composition of the SDR and the relative exchange rates for each currency change. The SDR deflator is calculated in SDR terms first and then converted to U.S. dollars using the SDR to dollar Atlas conversion factor. The Atlas conversion factor is then applied to a country's GNI. The resulting GNI in U.S. dollars is divided by the midyear population to derive GNI per capita.

When official exchange rates are deemed to be unreliable or unrepresentative of the effective exchange rate during a period, an alternative estimate of the exchange rate is used in the Atlas formula.

The following formulas describe the calculation of the Atlas conversion factor for year *t*:

$$e_t^* = \frac{1}{3}\left[e_{t-2}\left(\frac{p_t}{p_{t-2}} \Big/ \frac{p_t^{S\$}}{p_{t-2}^{S\$}}\right) + e_{t-1}\left(\frac{p_t}{p_{t-1}} \Big/ \frac{p_t^{S\$}}{p_{t-1}^{S\$}}\right) + e_t\right]$$

and the calculation of GNI per capita in U.S. dollars for year *t*:

$$Y_t^{\$} = (Y_t/N_t)/e_t^*,$$

where e_t^* is the Atlas conversion factor (national currency to the U.S. dollar) for year *t*, e_t is the average annual exchange rate (national currency to the U.S. dollar) for year *t*, p_t is the GDP deflator for year *t*, $p_t^{S\$}$ is the SDR deflator in U.S. dollar terms for year *t*, $Y_t^{\$}$ is the Atlas GNI per capita in U.S. dollars in year *t*, Y_t is current GNI (local currency) for year *t*, and N_t is the midyear population for year *t*.

Alternative conversion factors

The World Bank systematically assesses the appropriateness of official exchange rates as conversion factors. An alternative conversion factor is used when the official exchange rate is judged to diverge by an exceptionally large margin from the rate effectively applied to domestic transactions of foreign currencies and traded products. This factor applies to only a small number of countries, as shown in the primary data documentation table in *World Development Indicators 2010*. Alternative conversion factors are used in the Atlas methodology and elsewhere in Selected World Development Indicators as single-year conversion factors.

Index

Boxes, figures, notes, and tables are i by b, f, n, and t following page numbers. Features are specially noted.

J

K

S

T

Y

Z

ECO-AUDIT

Environmental Benefits Statement

The World Bank is committed to preserving endangered forests and natural resources. The Office of the Publisher has chosen to print ***World Development Report 2011*** on recycled paper with 50 percent postconsumer fiber in accordance with the recommended standards for paper usage set by the Green Press Initiative, a nonprofit program supporting publishers in using fiber that is not sourced from endangered forests. For more information, visit www.greenpressinitiative.org.

Saved:

- 284 trees
- 10 million Btu of total energy
- 28,900 pounds of net greenhouse gases
- 130,319 gallons of wastewater
- 8,261 pounds of solid waste